Agathangelos

History of the Armenians

AGATHANGELOS
HISTORY OF THE ARMENIANS

Translation and Commentary by

R. W. Thomson

Albany
State University of New York Press
1976

Robert W. Thomson
is Professor of Armenian Studies
at Harvard University

First Edition

Published by State University of New York Press
99 Washington Avenue, Albany, New York 12246

Library of Congress Cataloging in Publication Data

Agat'angeghos.
History of the Armenians.

Armenian text and English translation of Patmowt'iwn.
The chapter entitled
The teaching of Saint Gregory
is omitted.
Bibliography: p.
Includes indexes.
1. Armenia—History—T. 428.
2. Gregorius Illuminator, Saint.
3. Tiridates III, King of Armenia, d. 330.
4. Armenian Church.
I. Thomson, Robert W., 1934-
II. Title.   Jan 25 77
DS181.A6313   939'.55   76-2613
ISBN 0-87395-323-1

CONTENTS

FOREWORD

The conversion of Armenia to Christianity in the early fourth century A.D. not only wrought a momentous change within Armenia itself but was also significant for the general history and culture of the Near East. Christian Armenia produced an original art and architecture as well as a rich native literature. The Armenian church played a major role in the development of Eastern (non-Greek) Christianity. And Armenian culture in general developed a fascinating amalgam of indigenous traditions and foreign influences, sifted and adapted over the centuries.

But despite the importance of this fundamental change in Armenian life and thought, there is no contemporary historical record of the conversion to Christianity. Foreign sources have but few references to the internal affairs of Armenia, while native Armenian writing does not begin until the fifth century. However, there does exist an enigmatic work which purports to tell the story of the conversion of the Armenian king Trdat (Tiridates) and of the missionary activity in Armenia of St. Gregory the Illuminator— this is the *History of the Armenians,* attributed to a certain Agathangelos. The work is enigmatic not only because it is a curious mixture of remembered tradition and invented legend; it also exists in several languages and different recensions, not all of which derive from the text extant in Armenian.

In view of the importance of this work it is rather astonishing that there has only been one complete translation of Agathangelos into any modern language, that published in Italian in 1843 by the Mechitarist Fathers of Venice. The French translation by V.

Langlois in his important *Collection des historiens anciens et modernes de l'Arménie* (vol. I, Paris, 1867) is not only loose and periphrastic (often based on the earlier Italian translation rather than a rereading of the Armenian), but it also omits long passages which Langlois considered to be unworthy of the attention of a nineteenth-century reader because of their boring theological content. In 1909 a scholarly critical edition of the Armenian text was published, so these earlier translations are now outmoded.

The purpose of the present work is thus twofold: to offer the first English translation of this "received" tradition, with elucidation of the literary sources of the Armenian redactor. And secondly, to compare the content of the different versions and to discuss the date and tendentious purpose of the Armenian text as we have it. The work will, I trust, also serve two further purposes: it will present in a critical fashion some of the evidence to be considered in any historical study of the conversion of Armenia; and it will show the literary background of a major fifth-century Armenian author, his affinities with other Armenian writers, and his typically wide knowledge of Greek and Syriac texts.

But in view of the technical nature of the Introduction and Commentary to this translation of Agathangelos, it will no doubt be useful to the non-specialist to have some general comments on the historical and literary background against which Agathangelos' *History* must be set.

———————

Although Armenia emerged onto the historical scene in the sixth century B.C. as part of the Old Persian empire, and although she had her moment of

political power under Tigran the Great before coming
into fatal conflict with Rome, it is difficult to point to
a specifically "Armenian" culture before the conversion to Christianity and the development of a native
literature and artistic tradition. In the pre-Christian
period, Armenian culture had close parallels with that
of other Near Eastern states, now perished, which
flourished after Alexander destroyed the Old Persian
empire and before the Near East was divided between
the Romans and Sasanians. But Armenia was to survive when others disappeared as national states; and
it is in large measure to the centripetal force of the
Armenian church as a national institution that Armenia's longevity is to be ascribed.

The conversion of Armenia was part of a larger
process of Christian expansion into the Caucasus from
the south and the west. Just as pagan Armenia reflects
an amalgam of Iranian and Hellenistic cultures, so too
Christian Armenia reflects the confluence of more
than one Christian tradition. The first missionaries
came to Armenia from Syria. We have little contemporary evidence of their work, but a significant pro-
portion of basic Christian terms in Armenian are direct borrowings from Syriac. On the other hand, the
development of organized Christianity and a regular
hierarchy is associated with Asia Minor. It was at
Caesarea that Gregory the Illuminator was consecrated as bishop of Armenia (probably in A.D. 314),
and this direct link persisted for most of the fourth
century.

Armenia was not converted overnight. We have the
first references to Christians there in the third century,
and there were pagans still in the fifth century. Nonetheless the work of Gregory and the baptism of king

Trdat (Tiridates to the Greeks) have twofold significance: historically they gave the impetus to the transformation of Armenian life and culture, and in retrospect they came to be regarded as the symbols of
Christian Armenia. Gregory and Trdat provide a point
of reference for the national historians, and not un-
naturally the events of a century were later telescoped
into a few years. But the figures behind the tradition
are difficult to grasp and the political history of Armenia at this crucial transition is obscure and contro-
versial.

The treaty of Rhandeia (A.D. 63) had settled the
Armenian question between Rome and Parthia: the
monarchs of Armenia were to be a branch of the royal
Parthian Arsacid line but also vassals of Rome. This
arrangement was formalized in 66 when Nero crowned
Tiridates I in Rome. But the overthrow of the Parthian
dynasty by Artashir the Sasanian in 224 upset this deli-
cate balance. The Arsacid kings of Armenia were
faced by hostile shahs; for the Sasanians were to regard themselves as the heirs to Armenia and other
lands that had belonged to the Old Persian empire.
By the middle of the third century they had made
themselves masters of Armenia, and the Armenian
throne became the prerogative of the Sasanian crown
prince. Rome's military fortunes reached their nadir
in 260 when Shapur I defeated and captured the emperor Valerian.

However, twenty years later Narses, king of Armenia until his accession as shah in 293, made peace. Armenia was divided and in the Western part an Arsacid
line was restored. When Narses later succeeded to
the Sasanian throne he was congratulated by "Tirdat
the king" among others. Tirdat now became the sov-

ereign of a reunited Armenia under Iranian aegis. But Narses had less success than Shapur in his wars with Rome. Defeated by the Caesar Galerius he made peace at Nisibis in 298 and Armenia became an ally of Rome under Tiridates. This Tiridates, the nephew of the pro-Iranian Tirdat, by his conversion to Christianity was to transform Armenia culturally and politically.

But Armenian tradition has compressed these complicated turns of fortune into a simpler and shorter framework. The Christian Tiridates is made the son of the Armenian king who resisted Artashir in the early third century and who was murdered at Artashir's instigation. Tiridates' restoration to Armenia (the division of which is glossed over entirely) is then attributed to Diocletian in the third year of his reign, i.e., 287/8. Since Tiridates did not die until 330, his life-time thus comes to span a complete century.

Gregory who baptised Trdat (to use the latter's proper Armenian name) is an equally shadowy figure. Unanimous Armenian tradition makes him the son of the Parthian who murdered Trdat's father. He was then taken to Caesarea in Cappadocia and brought up as a Christian. Supposedly he accompanied Trdat back to Armenia when he was installed on the throne by Roman arms. Gregory later returned to Caesarea for consecration as bishop, probably in 314, but he had withdrawn from the primacy of Armenia before 325, for his son Aristakes attended the Council of Nicaea as Armenia's representative. Gregory's see was at Ashtishat, west of Lake Van in the province of Tarawn, and from here he began the organized development of a regular Armenian hierarchy.

The greatest puzzle, though, is what to make of his career before 314. Armenian tradition conveniently keeps him in prison for thirteen or more years as punishment for refusal to worship Anahit, the protectress of pagan Armenia. The occasion of his release, which was also the occasion of Trdat's conversion, is associated with the political capital Valarshapat in the northeast, near modern Erivan. For Trdat is credited with martrying numerous holy virgins there. These had supposedly fled from Diocletian in Rome, and since Trdat was Diocletian's protégé he was happy to oblige the emperor. However, divine punishment fell upon Trdat: he was changed into the form of a boar, and only Gregory could guide him to conversion and healing.

The martyrdoms at Valarshapat are a key feature of Armenian tradition. But whether they should be directly linked to the life of Gregory is less certain. Some modern scholars have associated the martyred nuns with Maximin's persecution in Armenia in 311/12, which is briefly mentioned in Eusebius' *Church History,* but there is no corroboration of this association in Armenian or Greek sources. On the other hand, this ancient tradition does point to the existence of Christians in Greater Armenia before Trdat's conversion. Trdat's early anti-Christian policy is linked by the Armenian historians to Diocletian, while the Christian Trdat is associated with Constantine. It can hardly be fortuitous that the religious policy of the Armenian king, an ally and vassal of Rome, fitted with that of his protectors.

The king's support of Gregory and the developing church met with continuing opposition from much of the Armenian nobility. Indeed the history of fourth century Armenia is dominated by this struggle, which reflects the perennial conflict of interests and loyalties between the pro-Iranian and the pro-Roman groups. And when the Roman emperors were Arian, a further complication was to mar the earlier harmonious relations between church and throne.

The spread of Christianity throughout Armenia was a slow process. Enduring success only became possible after the development of a script for Armenian so that religious services and the scriptures could be understood. Until then Greek or Syriac were the languages of the church, though oral preaching was naturally done in the vernacular. The invention of a national script was the work of an indefatigable missionary, Mashtots'—also known as Mesrop by later Armenian writers. As soon as the script had been fashioned, c. 400, groups of young men were set to learning it; they were then sent abroad to make translations of the major church fathers and of other texts important for the dissemination of the Christian message. Returning to Armenia with copies of the scriptures, ecclesiastical canons, service books, biblical commentaries, homilies, lives of saints, historical works and other books of Christian interest in Greek or Syriac, these young men not only gave Armenia a vast mass of translated literature within one generation; they in turn became the first original writers in their native tongue. Before the time of Mashtots' Armenians had written in Greek or Syriac, but nothing of this early Christian or the pre-Christian literature survives. However, within a century of the invention of a script Armenians had developed a rich literature of their own, marked not only by its Christian orientation but by a deep interest in historical writing on the pattern of classical antiquity.

It was with this background that Armenians began to write about their own earlier history. The life of Mashtots' was composed by one of his pupils, Koriun, not very long after the master's death in 440. Although it is invaluable as the only detailed record of Mashtots' missionary work, it is marred as historical writing by a confused, and often absent, chronology. Nor is the style of the easiest: elaborate rhetorical passages alternate with historical passages in tortuous and involved periods. More straightforward in appearance, yet more enigmatic in interpretation, is the *History* of Faustos, which traces the fortunes of Armenia from the death of Trdat in 330 to the division of the country between Rome and Sasanian Iran in 387. Although some have thought that this work was written in Greek before the invention of the Armenian script and then later translated, Faustos' frequent misconceptions of fourth century realities in Armenia and his use of legendary material make such an early date improbable. So he cannot be identified with the Faustos who was contemporary with the patriarch Nerses (murdered in 371) and his identity remains unknown.

Lazar, a monk of difficult personality who had trouble with his colleagues at the patriarchal cathedral, continued the tradition of Armenian historical writing, but in a less episodic and more classical mode than Faustos. His *History,* written at the end of the fifth century, describes the division of Armenia in 387, the final demise of the Armenian Arsacid royal line forty years later, the struggle for religious freedom of the Armenians in the Eastern sector under Sasanian rule, and the emergence to pre-eminence of the Mamikonean family. Lazar begins the long tradition of writing for a specific patron, normally the head of one of the great noble families. This direct patronage, often leading to tendentiousness in the historian, was a common feature of Armenian historiography; there were few writers who described all their compatriots in an equally dispassionate manner.

Enlarging upon the narrower theme of the struggle with Iran that erupted in unsuccessful revolt in 450/51, Ełishē has left us with a very different work. There is still much uncertainty about the date of his *History:* some take it to be the account of an eyewitness, others place it at the end of the sixth century. But the most interesting feature of this work, which has assured it a place among the two or three most influential Armenian writings, is that Ełishē sees in the events he describes the playing of a moral drama. Virtue, religion and patriotism are pitted against vice, apostasy and betrayal. More than any other Armenian historian, Ełishē underlines the Christian lessons that it is the historian's duty to impart to his readers.

Of wider significance than Ełishē's work is the *History* of Moses Khorenats'i, which traces the history of Armenia from the time of the giants down to the death of Mashtots'. Moses collected the unwritten Armenian traditions about their legendary heroes and shaped them into a chronological schema that would fit in with the history of the ancient world as described in Eusebius' *Chronicle.* Although he claims to be a pupil of Mashtots', Moses has used numerous Armenian and foreign sources of later times and his work is primarily aimed at glorifying the Bagratuni family which rose to power in the eighth century. The date of this work still remains for Soviet Armenian scholars a matter of canonical authority rather than dispassionate investigation. However, Moses Khorenats'i's *History* has a pre-eminent place in Armenian historiography as the "received" account of the origins and development of the Armenian nation.

Apart from the more strictly theological literature produced in the fifth century, one further work merits brief notice. This is the treatise on freedom of the will and the problem of evil by Eznik. Eznik was one of the pupils of Mashtots' who was sent abroad to study. He learned Syriac in Edessa and then travelled to Constantinople, where he involved himself in contemporary theological disputes. In later life he composed his masterpiece, which treats his main theme through the refutation of four false sects or religions: the pagans, the Mazdaeans, the Greek philosophers, and the Gnostic Marcion. Eznik had assimilated a great amount of classical and Christian scholarship; but his work is also remarkable for its lean and direct style in contrast to the rhetorical flourishes of the majority of Armenian writers.

Such, very briefly, was the fifth-century literary background in Armenia against which the *History* of Agathangelos must be measured. The identity of "Agathangelos" is unknown. The author of this enigmatic compilation claims to have been an eyewitness of the conversion of king Trdat and to be a learned Roman scribe. But we are not dealing with a contemporary version of events. This Armenian text is an original work composed in the second half of the fifth century and must be interpreted as such.

Even more than Faustos, one of his major sources, Agathangelos evinces serious misconceptions of historical realities in the Armenia of earlier times. He has remodeled the reminiscences of fact and legend current in the later fifth century into a more or less coherent whole for purposes of his own time. And more than any other Armenian historical work the narrative is extensively based on texts that originally had nothing to do with the subject. Some of the texts were original compositions, such as Koriun's biography of Mashtots', which Agathangelos adapted to fit Gregory. Other texts were translations: biblical and apocryphal texts, lives of saints from Syriac and Greek, homilies of the major church fathers. So although the translation that follows may be of interest simply because it presents for the first time in English the standard, "received" tradition concerning the conversion of Armenia to Christianity, the reader must be on his guard. Therefore the Introduction is devoted to a critical analysis of Agathangelos' sources and to an evaluation of his tendentious purposes.

I should stress that it is not my purpose here to write a history of the conversion of Armenia. Indeed I doubt whether the time is ripe for such an undertaking for two basic reasons. First, we have no detailed study of the *History* of Faustos which describes the struggles of the church party during the fourth century. (For by "conversion" I do not mean the single act of an Armenian king but the whole cultural transformation of the country.) And secondly, a proper understanding of the political situation in late third- and early fourth-century Armenia depends on a much greater use of Iranian material than has been made until recently. In the history of the conversion of Armenia this work of Agathangelos in its various recensions will appear as evidence; but such evidence will mostly be corroborative, not primary. On the other hand, the *History* of Agathangelos was to become the standard, "received" version of what happened, and therefore it plays a major role in the outlook of later generations of Armenians down to the present.

Once more I am indebted to Carol Cross for her patient willingness to type preliminary and final versions of the manuscript. And I am grateful to Dr. Krikor Maksoudian for several helpful comments.

Robert W. Thomson
Harvard University
September 1975

Transcription

It is impossible to provide a strictly one-to-one transcription of Armenian in Latin characters without the extensive use of diacritical marks. And in view of the fact that this translation is directed at an English speaking readership unfamiliar with linguistic conventions, the transcription used in the *Revue des Etudes arméniennes* would be positively misleading. (For example, *c, j, x* do not have the same value as they have in English). I have therefore adopted the system used by the Library of Congress (see their *Bulletin 47,* September 1958, p. 1), with two changes and one addition: *ŋ* is rendered by ḷ, making the spelling of proper names more comprehensible, *ռ* by ṙ, since *rh* is unnecessarily ambiguous, and *ու* by *u*. The complete alphabet thus runs as follows:

ա	բ	գ	դ	ե	զ	է	ը	թ	ժ	ի	լ	խ	ծ	կ	հ	ձ	ղ	ճ	մ
a	b	g	d	e	z	ĕ	ē	t'	zh	i	l	kh	ts	k	h	dz	ḷ	ch	m

յ	ն	շ	ո	չ	պ	ջ	ռ	ս	վ	տ	ր	ց	ւ	փ	ք	ու
y	n	sh	o	ch'	p	j	ṙ	s	v	t	r	ts'	w	p'	k'	u

ō is used only for modern Armenian; classical forms are rendered by the classical aw.

For proper names familiar to Western readers I have used the familiar forms: John, Moses, Faustos, etc.

INTRODUCTION

The Texts[1]

The earliest known Armenian witness to the text of the *History* of Agathangelos is that of a palimpsest in the Mechitarist library at Vienna (No. 56); the original writing is earlier than the tenth century but is not precisely dated.[2] Other fragments are known of the tenth and succeeding centuries.[3] The earliest manuscripts with a complete text of the *History* date from the twelfth and thirteenth centuries. The first printed edition appeared in 1709 at Constantinople, and the same text was reprinted four times in the nineteenth century. The only critical edition of the text appeared in 1909 at Tiflis, and the text of this edition, without the apparatus, was reprinted in the *Lukasean Matenadaran* in 1914.[4] The division of the text into 900 paragraphs, as established by the editor of the 1909 edition, has been retained for ease of reference—though these paragraphs are not always the most appropriate subdivisions. The division of the whole *History* into 14 chapters (plus *Prologue* and *Epilogue* which are so marked in the critical edition) is my own division for ease of comparison with the versions in Greek, Arabic, and Karshuni. The text of the Armenian critical edition is referred to throughout as *Aa*.

The Greek version made directly from *Aa* was first published in 1762 in the *Acta Sanctorum* for September, volume 8, at Antwerp. This was based on a poorly made copy of the twelfth-century manuscript in Florence, *Laurentianus* VII 25. The edition of Paul de Lagarde in 1889,[5] based on the Laurentianus with numerous corrections, is far superior. Several earlier

Greek witnesses are known, including a palimpsest of
the seventh/eighth centuries, but the only critical edition of the Greek is that published in 1973 by Lafontaine, which is quoted in the present work under the
siglum *Ag.*[6]

Derived from *Ag* is a later Greek version reworked
by Simeon Metaphrastes in the tenth century; and
from this in turn a Georgian version was made. Also
derived from the version in *Ag* are Latin, Arabic-
Coptic and Ethiopic versions, which are of no direct
relevance to our present study.[7] More interesting are
a ninth- or tenth-century Arabic version of *Ag,* surviving in a manuscript of Mt. Sinai (cited as *Ar*),[8] and
a Georgian version not later than the eighth century
made directly from *Aa.* This Georgian text, however,
only contains the martyrdom of Rhipsimē and her
companions.[9]

All the foregoing texts depend directly, or indi-
rectly, on the Armenian redaction *(Aa)* in a form very
close to the *History* of Agathangelos as we now have
it. But there are several texts which bear witness to
a different Armenian version of the life of Gregory.
These are the two Greek manuscripts, *Escorial gr.*
X III 6 (A.D. 1107)[10] and *Ochrid* no. 4 (10th century),[11]
and Arabic versions dependent on this Greek redaction in *Sinai* 455 of the twelfth/thirteenth centuries
and *Sinai* 460 of the ninth century.[12] These texts are
grouped under the siglum *V* as *Vg, Vo, Var* and *Va*
respectively. Finally, a Karshuni version has recently
been published, which shows knowledge of the two
groups of versions, *A* and *V.*[13]

The significance of these texts in the *V* cycle is
that we now have evidence for traditions about Saint

Gregory and the conversion of Armenia that are independent of the final Armenian redaction *(Aa)*, and which are deliberately aimed at presenting a different interpretation of—or attitude towards—the dominant tradition in Armenian. However, it is with this last, the Armenian redaction represented by *Aa,* that the present study is concerned. The prime emphasis in what follows will be on the literary affinities of the Armenian text rather than with the variants to the story found in the versions, though the major variants will be mentioned in the discussion of each chapter in the *Introduction.*

*Abbreviations used for the various texts and recensions of Agathangelos:**

Aa   the Armenian text of the 1909 Tiflis edition.

Ag   the Greek text published by Lafontaine.

Ar   the Arabic text in *Sinai* 395, as published by Ter-Levondyan.

Vg   the Greek text in *Escorial* gr. X III 6, as published by Garitte.

Vo   the Greek text in *Ochrid* 4, as described by Garitte.

Va   the Arabic text in *Sinai* 460, as published by Marr and translated by Garitte.

Var the Arabic text in *Sinai* 455, as published by Ter-Levondyan.

Vk   the Karshuni version, as published by Van Esbroeck.

---

*Abbreviations for secondary literature and for the manuscripts used in *Aa* will be found at the beginning of the section on *Sources.*

The Story

Prologue (§ 1-17)

The *History* of Aganthangelos *(Aa)* begins with a long and exceedingly tortuous *Prologue* which is well-nigh impossible to translate at all closely. It has been omitted in all the versions except *Ag* (where it is found only in the *Laurentianus,* not the earlier Greek manuscripts). But *Ag* gives only a brief résumé of the first seven paragraphs of the Armenian.[14] And within the Armenian tradition several manuscripts omit the *Prologue* altogether, or give only the first and last paragraphs.[15]

The basic theme of the *Prologue* is the parallel between the merchant who risks his life on the sea in search of pearls and precious stones for princes and the writer who entrusts himself to the "sea of history" for the sake of the pearl of spiritual profit for his readers. Nautical metaphors were extremely popular in antiquity and in the church fathers, and Agathangelos has combined such traditional imagery with biblical motifs drawn from Psalm 106. But he has so over-done the comparison and the imagery is so convoluted that the flow of the argument is often lost. However, Lazar praises the rhetorical skill of Agathangelos; and similar imagery is found in his own *History,* as in the works of Koriun and Ełishē,[16] so we must assume that Agathangelos knew what his readers would appreciate.

In the *Prologue* Agathangelos also introduces himself as a skilled writer and historian summoned from Rome by king Trdat in order to record the great events of his reign. Again in the *Epilogue* Agathangelos speaks for himself and claims to have seen some of these events with his own eyes and to have completed his narrative by gathering information from knowledgeable sources. In the course of the narrative itself, however, there is no mention of the author of this *History,* though there are references to scribes supposedly recording the remarks of Gregory during his interrogation and tortures.

It is most doubtful whether this fictitious character "Agathangelos" (whose name only too appropriately means "bearer of good news" in Greek) was associated with the first traditions concerning the life of Gregory and the conversion of Armenia. The historian Faustos Buzandats'i refers very frequently to Gregory and the conversion of Armenia; he knows of the martyrdom of Rhipsimē and her companions, of the destruction of the pagan temples, of the church built by Gregory, of the presence of Aristakēs at the Council of Nicaea, of the angel who served the emperor Constantine; and he hints that there existed a history of these events (III 1). But he makes no mention of anyone called Agathangelos. Only after the redaction of the Armenian version *Aa* (perhaps around 460)[17] do we find the credit for this given to "Agathangelos." Lazar P'arpets'i, writing at the turn of the fifth and sixth centuries, gives a résumé of this *History* and praises its author whom he calls Agathangelos. The book, however, he entitles "The Book of Gregory *(Girk' Grigorisi).*"[18] This lends credence to the likelihood that the final redaction of the Armenian, with which "Agathangelos" is associated, was based on earlier accounts of the life and acts of Gregory. No previous *written* Armenian "Book of Gregory" is known, but the various recensions of the *V* cycle have preserved details and episodes omitted from *Aa* for a variety of reasons.

Further suspicion is thrown on Agathangelos' claim
to have been an eyewitness by the fact that he has
taken his wording for this statement (§14) directly
from the biography of Masht'ots' written after the latter's death in 440 by his pupil Koriun, who was indeed
an eyewitness. (It was Masht'ots' who invented the
Armenian script at the beginning of the fifth century.)
But there is no hint in "Agathangelos" that his book
was originally written in Greek or Latin, or any suggestion in the Armenian text that it was a translation
from an earlier text written a century before. However, such fraudulent claims to being witnesses of the
events portrayed are so common among writers of
hagiography (into which category the *History* of Agathangelos falls), that it is naive to take them at all
seriously.[19] The description of Agathangelos as Trdat's
chartularius (k'artuḷarn Trdatay) in Moses Khorenats'i
(II 67) is much later; being based on the claims in the
Prologue and *Epilogue,* it has no independent value.

Chapter 1. The wars of Khosrov against Sasanian
  Iran; his murder and the occupation of Armenia.
Aa §18-36
Ag 9b-16[13]
Ar 1-19
Vg begins at *Aa* §48
Vo begins at end of *Aa* §36; the ms. is mutilated
Va begins at *Aa* §104; the ms. is mutilated
Var begins at *Aa* §48
Vk 5-18

Between the *Prologue* and the beginning of the *History* proper as known in the Armenian redaction, the
Greek version *Ag* (only the *Laurentianus* manuscript,

not the earlier witnesses to the Greek recension) has inserted an episode extraneous to the life of Gregory. It is an account of the revolt of Artashir the Sasanian against Artaban, the last king of the Arsacid dynasty in Parthia. This is derived from the Pahlavi *Kārnāmak-i-Artashīr-i-Papākān,* which is a composition of the seventh century. Although this episode was translated first from Pahlavi into Armenian and then into Greek, before some unknown scribe added it to some manuscript of the *Ag* tradition, Armenian writers who refer to Agathangelos evince no knowledge of the story.[20]

The Karshuni version also begins with an episode not found in Agathangelos—the conversion of the Armenian king Sanatruk by the apostle Addai. But these tendentious additions to the story after the redaction of the Armenian are not of relevance to our present study.[21]

The *History* of Agathangelos in its present Armenian form begins with an account of the collapse of the Parthian Arsacid dynasty before Artashir the Sasanian, and the ensuing wars between Khosrov king of Armenia and the Persians.[21a] Unable to resist the successful invasions of the Armenian king, Artashir had recourse to assassination. An Armenian noble of Parthian descent, Anak, himself related to king Khosrov, undertook this act of regicide. Anak was immediately killed in revenge by the Armenian nobles, but one of his sons (Gregory) escaped to Greek territory. The Persian king was now able to take possession of Armenia for himself, at which Khosrov's son, the young Trdat, escaped to the Roman emperor's court.

For this chapter *Ag* offers a close translation; *Ar* is less literal. The witnesses to *V* cycle (except *Vk*) do not include the first chapter: *Vg* begins with the confrontation between Gregory and Trdat (§49 in *Aa*), *Vo* is truncated and starts at the end of §36 of the Armenian, while *Va* is also truncated and begins in the middle of Gregory's tortures (§104 in *Aa*). It is difficult to be certain that this other redaction did originally contain the same introduction as *Aa* and *Ag,* but since the revelation of Gregory's identity before his imprisonment would make little sense unless the reader was already aware of the story of Anak, we may assume that the loss of the beginning in all these texts is accidental. *Vk* offers a shorter account of these events, with a few discrepancies of detail: the murder of Khosrov takes place near Dvin (the later capital) rather than Vaḷarshapat; Gregory is brought by his nurse to Neocaesarea, not Caesarea; Anak is described as the brother of Khosrov. *Vk* also adds details about Gregory's conception which are also found in Moses Khorenats'i.

So far as the life of Gregory himself is concerned, the most significant information given in this section is the account of his ancestry. Gregory was the son of Anak, the Parthian noble who murdered one of his own kin, Trdat's father Khosrov. No Armenian source casts any doubt on Gregory's parentage, although a different tradition concerning the death of Khosrov is reported by Eḷishē.[22] Admittedly in §50 of *Aa* Gregory is called "a stranger and foreigner," but this is natural in the context as his real identity was not revealed until the end of his tortures at §121.[23] *Vg* and *Va,* however, though lacking chapter 1, omit the reference to Gregory's ancestry at the end of his tortures; and furthermore in *Vg* Trdat refers to Gregory as a Cappadocian. This claim was presumably motivated by a Greek Christian who wished to emphasise the connec-

tion between Cappadocia—notably the metropolitan
see of Caesarea—and Armenia.[24]

The Armenian tradition of Gregory's origin under-
went further elaboration in the *History* of Moses Khorenats'i. He claims (II 74ff.) that when Anak arrived
in Armenia, Khosrov sent an escort to bring him to
the province of Artaz where the relics of the apostle
Thaddaeus were preserved. The following tale Moses
claims to have heard from "an old man": while Anak
was there he spent a night at this shrine and here
Gregory's mother conceived the child.[25] Moses then
adds that Gregory later completed the work unfin-
ished by Thaddaeus. This pious invention neatly associates Gregory with the legendary first missionary
in Armenia. The title "throne of Thaddaeus" is found
in Faustos for the patriarchal see of Armenia which
Gregory was considered to have restored.[26] But it is
noteworthy that neither Agathangelos nor other early
Armenian writers mention Thaddaeus.[27] Although the
translation of the Syriac text of the legend of Addai is
usually attributed to the fifth century,[28] and a stage in
its adoption is shown in *Vk,*[29] not until Moses' time
was the story fully integrated into the Armenian tradition. However, Agathangelos is not so much concerned with providing an apostolic origin for the Armenian patriarchate as with enhancing the role of
Gregory as the first bishop of Armenia and the first
to build churches and establish a regular hierarchy.

To return to Anak. Moses reports that he spent two
years in Armenia before murdering Khosrov, and that
he and all his family were put to death with the sole
exception of Gregory. Agathangelos, however, mentions two sons of Anak: Gregory, who escaped to
Greek territory, and another who escaped to Persia

(§34). But nothing further is ever said about this other son. For both Agathangelos and Moses the flight of Trdat did not immediately follow his father's death but was caused by a Persian invasion (§36). But a different tradition was known to Ełishē. He reports in a letter, supposedly sent to the emperor Theodosius by the Armenian patriarch Joseph,[30] that Trdat had fled in his infancy in order to escape from his uncles who had murdered his father, and that he had been brought up in the Greek empire. The letter was intended to remind the emperor of the friendly attitude of his forebears towards the Christian Armenian people, and it goes on to claim that the Armenians had received their faith from the archbishop of Rome. Exactly what Ełishē intended by this latter statement is not clear,[31] but if he knew of the story of Anak's regicide there seems to be no reason why he should ignore it in favor of a story less flattering to the Armenian royal family.[32] More on this below.

Chapter 2. Trdat in exile; his restoration to the throne of Armenia.

Aa §37-47
Ag 16^{13}-21^{11}
Ar 20-30
Vg begins at *Aa* §48
Vo 16-21
Va begins at *Aa* §104; the ms. is mutilated
Var begins at *Aa* §48
Vk 19-48

This chapter gives an account of Trdat's life ·in exile and of the events which led to his return to Armenia as king. There is little variation in this section between the various recensions of Agathangelos. *Ag* and *Ar* follow the Armenian text closely. *Va* is truncated, but *Vo* which contains this section follows *Aa*. However, *Vk* diverges widely from the order of *Aa* and the other versions, first introducing the story of Gregory's marriage and then elaborating on his early relations with Trdat. It then narrates in some detail the story of Trdat's valiant exploits on behalf of Diocletian before his return to Armenia with Roman support.

The traditions found in this chapter of Agathangelos are also found in extended form in Moses Khorenats'i, who elaborates on the information found in the different versions of Agathangelos. First we shall look at his account of Gregory's early life, and then at that of Trdat's exploits in exile.

After telling of Gregory's conception at the shrine of Thaddaeus, Moses (II 80) informs us how Gregory was brought to Caesarea. A Persian of some consequence named Burdar had settled in Caesarea and had married a Christian wife, Sophia, the sister of a wealthy Greek called Euthalius. Burdar set out to return to Persia with his wife, but was dissuaded by Euthalius. The latter, by God's providence, came across Gregory at the time of his birth and took care of him. When Anak and the rest of his family were put to death, Euthalius then brought his sister, her husband, and the child back to Caesarea. Here Gregory was brought up in the Christian faith. On reaching his maturity Gregory married Mariam, the daughter of a Christian named David. But after the birth of two sons they separated. Mariam with the younger child entered a monastery; when this child grew up he became the disciple of a monk called Nicomachus who sent him to the desert. The elder son remained with his tutors and led a secular life, later marrying. But Gregory left them in order to take service with Trdat and to fulfill his destiny. Moses then adds that these even more wonderful children of a wonderful father were not led to boast of their father's high calling; they did not seek fame, "but rather fame followed them, as Agathangelos teaches you."[33]

The two children were Vrt'anēs and Aristakēs, whose careers Agathangelos describes later in his *History* (§859ff). But though Agathangelos refers briefly to Gregory's marriage, this is played down and no details, such as the name of his wife, are given. The recension of Agathangelos represented in *Vg* and *Va* (for *Vk* passes over Gregory's marriage very briefly) not only offers a different account of the later reunion of Gregory and his two sons (for which see chapter 10), but also gives a most interesting story concerning Gregory's wife. This is only found in *Vg*, for *Va* has suppressed the episode, though not without leaving an obvious trace.[34]

The story in *Vg*[35] implies that when Gregory returned to Armenia in Trdat's service he was accompanied by his wife and children. On Gregory's arrest his wife fled with her children to Caesarea and there brought them up as their father would have wished. They all lived from their previous savings and the support of their relations. When Gregory was released from prison, his wife returned to Armenia, leaving the children in school at Caesarea. She told Gregory about their education and about the reports of the martyred nuns and of his torments that had reached Caesarea. But Gregory was unwilling to return to married life, especially as the children were absent, so he proposed to the king that his wife be put in charge of the holy virgins and that with her servants, who were baptised Christians, they lead the praising of God until a priest should arrive to take over the administration of the church. *Vg* then adds at the very end that Gregory's wife was called Julitta.[36]

This episode is entirely unknown to later Armenian tradition, but it is difficult to see what motive the Greek version *Vg,* and its derivative *Va,* would have had in inventing such a story. It may well be that the information about Julitta was deliberately suppressed in the Armenian redaction and consequently was unknown not only to *Ag* and *Ar* but also to later Armenian writers. (When Moses wished to elaborate on the vague hints left in Agathangelos concerning the mother of Vrt'anēs and Aristakēs, he could think of no more suitable name than Mariam, daughter of David.) Garitte has suggested that the suppression of information about Gregory's wife may be due to the influence of ascetic ideals after the early fifth century.[37] But one should also note that the redactor of *Aa* took great pains to model his hero Gregory on the image of Masht'ots' as described in Koriun. Agathangelos' account of Gregory's activities and asceticism in the second part of his *History* are taken directly, and often verbatim, from the biography of the great monk and teacher of the early fifth century.[38] So we may have here nothing but another instance of Gregory being fitted into a monastic and celibate mould that he did not himself fashion.

As with Gregory, so in the case of Trdat, Agathangelos does not report in their appropriate place all the stories he knows about his hero. In this chapter we are told only of his strength (in throwing bales of hay over a wall) and of his single combat with the king of the Goths. Later in the story, when Trdat is worsted by Rhipsimē, the author refers to Trdat's deeds in the Greek empire, once briefly (§181) and once in more detail (§202). There we learn that Trdat excelled in the Olympic games and that once he had swum across the Euphrates with his horse on his back, though gravely wounded.

As usual Moses Khorenats'i has elaborated on this. Following a more strictly chronological approach (in accordance with his famous dictum "without chronology there is no history" II 82), he devotes chapter 79 of Book II of his *History* to the life of Trdat before his restoration. Trdat, according to Moses, was an expert horseman and skilled in the use of arms. He won the prize in the Peloponnesian games dedicated to Hephaistos: in wrestling he beat the Rhodian Clitostratos; he also beat Cerasos the Argive by throwing two bulls with one hand.[39] In the chariot race he was thrown to the ground by a stratagem of his adversary but he seized and stopped the chariot.

Moses only refers in vague terms to Trdat's exploits in the war against the Goths under Probus and does not refer at all to the single combat. But he does give a wealth of circumstantial detail to the episode when Trdat swam across the Euphrates with his horse and arms on his back. Artashir, after an earlier defeat at the hands of the emperor Carus, had gathered reinforcements from Mesopotamia (Tachikistan) and had attacked the Roman forces again on the banks of the Euphrates. Carus was killed, as was his son Carinus who had gone into the desert to attack Kornak, a Persian general. Trdat was with Carinus, and the survivors from this encounter fled. Trdat's horse was wounded, so, unable to flee quickly enough, Trdat picked up his armour, horse and trappings and swam across the Euphrates to safety. (In *Aa* and *Ag* it is Trdat himself who is wounded, not the horse.)[39a]

The restoration of Trdat to the throne of Armenia is attributed by Agathangelos to the direct intervention of the (unnamed) emperor whom Trdat had saved from the Goths by his single combat.[40] Moses elaborates on this by positively identifying the emperor as Diocletian, and saying that Trdat's return took place in the third year of the former's reign. This remark has naturally led to the general supposition that Trdat was restored in A.D. 287. But such a date does not tally with the Greco-Roman evidence or the Iranian inscriptions. And the Armenian tradition as found in Agathangelos and Moses gives an anachronistic and simplistic impression that "Armenia" was a single entity rather than a country divided into two spheres of influence.[41]

Western Armenia was already under Roman aegis by 280 after the peace agreement arranged by Probus and Narses. Narses, son of Shapur I (240-271), was king of Eastern Armenia—Armenshah—before 280 when this peace was concluded; he did not succeed to the throne of Iran until 293. Probus recognised Narses as ruler of Eastern Armenia, while for his part Narses recognised Rome's jurisdiction in Western Armenia. As Toumanoff notes, this was the first partition of Armenia between the rival empires. According to Moses Khorenats'i, this peace was marked by Probus' having ditches dug to mark the frontier. But Agathangelos links the digging of ditches to the expulsion of the Greeks after the murder of Khosrov, an event which he does not date.[42] The important point is that there was no restoration of any Armenian king in 287 because Western Armenia was already under Roman suzerainty, and Narses was Armenshah in Eastern Armenia until his accession to the Sasanian throne in 293.

The Paikuli inscription of this same Narses states that on his accession he was offered congratulations by "Tirdat the king." This cannot be understood by the tradition developed in Agathangelos and Moses, but an explanation is forthcoming if the tradition known to Ełishē about Trdat's regicidal uncles is combined with the dates offered in the second chapter of Sebeos. According to this seventh-century Armenian historian, Khosrov was murdered in 287 and Persian rule lasted for eleven years; according to Ełishē it was his brothers who slew Khosrov, his infant son escaping to the West. So the Trdat who congratulated Narses six years later was the pro-Persian ruler of Western Armenia who had murdered his brother in 287. On Narses' accession as great king in 293 this Trdat became his vassal, and also ruler of Eastern Armenia. The country was thus reunited in 293, but under Iranian rather than Roman suzerainty. This unpleasant episode was later rewritten to make it appear that the murderer of Khosrov was not a member of the Armenian royal family acting for his own ends, but a relative acting under the instigation of the Iranian shah, and the division of the country was passed over completely.

But Narses as shah of Iran soon became engaged in hostilities with the Roman empire. In 297 he was severely defeated in Armenia by the Caesar Galerius; peace followed at Nisibis in 298. The peace terms included the cession of much of Armenia to Rome. Trdat III (the regicide) now disappeared from sight after a reign of eleven years (as Sebeos says) and was replaced by his nephew, who had escaped in 287 and had been brought up in Roman territory. This was Trdat IV, whose subsequent conversion to Christianity gave an entirely new direction to the cultural evolution of his country.

Chapter 3. Gregory's tortures

A. *Dialogue between Gregory and Trdat*

Aa   §48-68
Ag 21^{11}-28
Ar   31-51
Vg   1-11
Vo   22-   [Garitte does not give section numbers for
             Vo 22-58 (= *Aa* 48-136)]
Va   begins at *Aa* §104; the ms. is truncated
Var f. 119b-124b
Vk   49-52

Having briefly mentioned the return of Trdat as king of Armenia, Agathangelos now plunges immediately into the confrontation between Gregory and Trdat which was caused by Gregory's refusal to give offerings to the statue of Anahit in the famous shrine of Erēz. *Ag* reflects more or less faithfully the Armenian text, as does *Ar*. In this section *Vo* and *Var* also follow the same tradition. *Va* is truncated and lacks this episode, while *Vk* offers only the briefest of résumés of the dialogue between Gregory and Trdat before describing the various torments inflicted on Gregory. *Vg* begins at this chapter; there is no attempt to offer any background information, but the text begins: "In those times, when Tiridates was king in Greater Armenia, there was a great persecution of the

Christians . . . ." Then follows the confrontation between Gregory and Trdat, though the story is given in
a much abbreviated form compared to *Aa.*

In the Armenian redaction there are two particularly interesting points which merit some attention:
the references to the worship of Anahit and Aramazd,
and the refutation of idolatry put into Gregory's
mouth.

Anahit is first mentioned in connection with the
famous temple at Erēz—modern Erzinjan—in the prov-
ence of Ekeḷeats' (Acilisene),[43] a site that was already
renowned in classical times. Strabo describes it as
being held in special honor by the Armenians and
mentions the custom whereby the most prominent
men consecrated their daughters to this temple. The
girls were first prostituted in the temple of the goddess
and then given in marriage.[44] Agathangelos, however,
says nothing about the actual cult at Erēz, except that
crowns and thick branches were offered to Anahit.[45]
Her statue *(patker)* was made of gold both at Erēz and
at her shrine in Ashtishat.[46] She also had a temple at
Artashat, but Agathangelos says nothing about it save
that it was built of wood.[47] Faustos speaks of a site
dedicated to her on Lion mountain *(Arewts' learn)*
near Erēz: "the site of the deity that is called the
throne of Anahit."[48]

No other early Armenian writer refers to shrines of
Anahit except Moses Khorenats'i. He calls her by the
name of the Greek goddess with which she was identified in the Greek versions of Agathangelos—'Artemis. According to Moses a gilded bronze statue *(patker)* of Artemis was brought to Armavir from Asia
Minor by king Artashēs; he had also ordered other
statues to be brought from Greece, and after his death

Tigran had that of Artemis set up in Erēz.[49] Moses also mentions a statue of Artemis brought to Artashat from Bagaran.[50] However, Carrière demonstrated long ago that Moses had no independent sources of information but was merely following the story of the destruction of the pagan temples as found later in the *History* of Agathangelos.[51]

Agathangelos also confirms what Strabo had said earlier, that Anahit had a special place in the affections of the Armenian people. She gives Armenia not only life, fertility and protection, but she is the glory of the Armenian race and its protector, to whom special honor is given.[52] She is the benefactor of all human nature and hence is regarded as mother. In more tangible terms, the great wealth showered upon her sanctuaries resulted in the title "golden mother, the golden-born goddess."[53]

Anahit was considered to be the offspring of Aramazd, the father of all the gods.[54] Aramazd himself was known to early Armenian writers in two guises, Aramazd and a later form Ormizd, both of which are derived from the Iranian Ahura-Mazda.[55] Agathangelos first introduces Aramazd as the father of Anahit; he is the creator of heaven and earth; and gives fertility.[56] He is the father of Nanē, of Mihr, and of all the gods, and is identified with Zeus.[57] The Greek versions follow this identification, save that in rendering the Zeus-Aramzad of §785, *Ag* speaks of Cronos, father of Zeus, the supreme deity.

The form Ormizd occurs only once in Agathangelos, in §778, in connection with the god Tir who is called the secretary *(grich')* of Ormizd. This second form of the deity's name was introduced into Armenia in Sasanian times,[58] and it is found frequently in the

works of Eznik and Eḷishē where the myth of Zurvanism is described.[59] Zurvan was considered to be the
father of Ormizd—the creator of good creatures—and
of Ahriman—the creator of evil creatures. Later Armenian writers, when referring to pagan times, sometimes equate Aramazd and Ormizd with no indication
that the variant forms originally had different origins.[60]

We may also note here the question of the seven
altars to which Agathangelos makes a brief reference
in §22. In a clumsy phrase he describes the offerings
that Khosrov made in thanksgiving to "the seven altars
of the temples of the cult of the images of the idols."
This is rendered more simply in *Ag* as "to the seven
temples."[61] The expression "altars of temples" occurs
elsewhere in Armenian[62] and is probably a hendiadys
for "temple" or "shrine." It is not so likely that there
were any temples with seven altars,[63] as that seven
sites of pagan worship are intended. Agathangelos
mentions a total of seven cities where Gregory later
destroyed the images of the pagan gods: Artashat,
T῾ordan, Ani, Erēz, T῾il, Bagayaṙich and Ashtishat.
A problem does arise in that Agathangelos calls the
temple of Vahagn at Ashtishat the "eighth" famous
shrine.[64] But this simply means that it was the eighth
shrine that Gregory destroyed. For there was a total
of ten shrines in the seven main cult centres.[65]

Since the major theme of his *History* is the conversion of Armenia from paganism to Christianity, it is
hardly surprising that Agathangelos should dwell at
length on the folly of idolatry. In general he is content
to reiterate biblical arguments.[66] He presents us with
little precise information about the specific pagan
cults; he knows the names of the principal deities but
speaks only in the vaguest terms about the form of

worship conducted in their temples. Thus, when describing the worship offered to Anahit at Erēz, Agathangelos mentions only "crowns and thick branches." Although some have seen in these branches a reflection of the *barsmunkʻ* (twigs) known to Armenian writers in connection with Zurvanism,[67] they are more likely to be merely another biblical image, for in Maccabees there are several references to "thick branches" used for the honor of the temple. Maccabees was a book well known to Agathangelos and furnished him with many images and parallels.[68] More detailed is Agathangelos' description of the offerings made by Khosrov. Here there are parallels, not to biblical motifs, but to the form of sacrifice attributed by Eḷishē to the Sasanian king Yazdgerd.[69] With these exceptions Agathangelos says nothing precise about the practice of idolatry, but his theories about its origin are not without interest.

Although he frequently discusses idolatry, calling it the result of impiety and lawlessness, only twice does Agathangelos venture upon a theoretical explanation of that aberration. In §59 he offers two explanations, intertwined. The gods were once humans; and they are the invention of demons as a means to deceive men. The first argument is commonly known as euhemeristic, after Euhemerus of Messene. At the turn of the fourth and third centuries B.C., he proposed the rationalistic theory that the gods of popular belief had once been famous mortals whom men had worshipped in gratitude for their benefits. This argument was taken up in the Wisdom literature and by patristic writers.[70] But it did not exclude the possibility that men had also been led astray by demons. Instead of dead men, who may have produced for humanity some

great benefit, evil spirits had tricked men into worshiping them, and thus were able to work their will
among mankind.[71] These motifs were exceedingly
common in patristic writers,[72] and Agathangelos is
repeating a well-worn theme.

The reference in §67 to the sculpted images of
earlier men is a reflection of the famous passage in
Wisdom 14: images were created to preserve the
memory of those who died too soon, or in order to
make the distant authority of the ruler more directly
impressive. The skill of the artists only encouraged
the ignorant to intensify their superstition; admiring
the beauty and exactness of the likeness, they came
to transfer the honor due to the distant king to his
image. Thus they came to ascribe the "incommunica-
ble name" to stones and wood. Again, this theme was
repeated throughout patristic apologetic literature.
Agathangelos offers us neither anything new nor any
special comment on the origins of Armenian paganism.[73]

Chapter 3, *B & C. Gregory's twelve tortures*

Aa   §69-122
Ag   29-55[2]
Ar   52-105
Vg   11-28[3]
Va   1-8 (the ms. is mutilated and begins at *Aa* §104)
Var f. 124b (Levondyan only gives the text as far as
        Aa §103)
Vk   53-71

Agathangelos now proceeds to describe the incredible series of tortures (twelve in all) to which Gregory
was subjected but which failed to break his spirit.

For seven days he was suspended with a block of salt hanging on his back. For seven days he was hung up-side down from one foot and beaten while dung was burnt beneath him; but this did not prevent him from delivering a long and involved prayer replete with elaborate references to scripture and theological commonplaces.[74] Then blocks of wood were tightened around his legs; nails were driven through his feet and he was made to run; he was buffeted on the head. But all this Gregory persisted in calling "happiness." Then salt, borax and vinegar were poured down his nose. For six days a bag of cinders was fixed over his head. Finding Gregory still obdurate, Trday had him held upside down while water was poured into his bottom. Then Gregory was torn with iron scrapers and rolled on iron thistles. The next day he was suspended with iron leggings on his knees and was struck with ham-mers. But three days of this left the martyr as recal-citrant as ever. Molten lead was poured over him, and yet he did not die. Finally, after at least twenty-five days of torment—any one of which would have proved fatal for ordinary mortals—Gregory's identity was re-vealed and he was cast into the deepest dungeon, there to die with the snakes.

Ag and *Ar* follow the Armenian text closely, as does *Vo. Vg* gives but a very abbreviated account, omitting references to the water poured down Gregory's bot-tom and to the iron thistles, as well as to the revela-tion of his ancestry. Nor does *Va* refer to the disclo-sure of Gregory's ancestry; it is truncated and begins at §104 of the Armenian, when Gregory has just had nails put through his feet. In general *Va* follows *Aa* fairly closely, though with certain liberties of ex-pression. *Vk* gives a very brief résumé of nine tortures with very wide divergences from the other versions, but it makes the parallel between Gregory in the pit at Artashat and Daniel in the lions' den explicit.

Although Agathangelos may seem to have let his imagination run riot, the tortures are no more amazing than the products of other hagiographers' minds. There are in fact parallels to many of the details of Gregory's torments in Greek and Syriac hagiography, most notably with those tortures inflicted on the martyrs of Edessa—Shmona and Guria, Habib, and Sharbil.[75] And in other ways also Agathangelos shows that he is acquainted with the general characteristics of hagiography: long prayers recited in public, the accurate recording of all that is said by official secretaries, the insensitivity of the martyr to his pain. But the usual final act of beheading—for martyrs were often too tough to die of their tortures—did not befall Gregory. He was left to die in obscurity in order to rise again from the dead like Lazarus.

The long prayers which Gregory uttered from various uncomfortable positions generally take up themes that were developed at greater length in the *Teaching,* the long sermon supposedly preached by Gregory after his emergence from the bottommost pit. The more important of these themes are discussed below.[76]

Chapter 4. Trdat's prowess; his edicts concerning the gods and against Christians

Aa	§123-126	*Va*	9
Ag	55²-58	*Vk*	72-74
Ar	106-113		
Vg	28⁴-29		
Vo	-58		

In this section Agathangelos speaks of the wars of Trdat and of his anti-Christian policies during the period of Gregory's imprisonment. Trdat's persecution of Christians is hinted at by means of two edicts: the first a general commendation to his subjects that they be assiduous in the worship of the gods lest the latter be offended and bring harm on the state; the second—promulgated at a later, unspecified date—is explicitly aimed at eliminating the Christians, who are a particular menace to the appeasement of the gods. Such edicts were indeed promulgated in the Roman empire; as an example of one contemporary with Trdat we may cite that of Maximin as reported in Eusebius' *Church History,* IX 7. However, similar edicts were part of the stock-in-trade of the pious hagiographer. It is to hagiographical sources rather than historical documents that Agathangelos is indebted. As Delehaye has noted, even in the historical acts of martyrs there is no authentic copy of an imperial edict; and the pastiches of such edicts—taken from inscriptions or authentic rescripts—became a necessary ornament of the epic passions.[77]

Only in *Aa* is the text of both edicts given. *Ag* follows the Armenian except for the text of the first edict; after giving the address (§125 and 127a of the Armenian) *Ag* merely adds "etcetera." *Ar* and *Vo* follow *Ag*. But *Vg* and *Va* are quite divergent in this section. *Vg* has no reference to Trdat's prowess or to his wars; it merely states that Gregory was not troubled by the snakes in the dungeon, that he was given bread and water by a woman of the city, and that Trdat issued a general edict against the Christians in which he mentions Gregory's fate as an example. *Va* is equally brief: Gregory was kept fifteen years in the

pit, preserved with food and water by God's providence (no trace of the widow), and untouched by the
snakes. But *Va* does distinguish two edicts: the first,
of which no direct quotation is given, was aimed at
encouraging the worship of the gods; the second was
directed against the Christians, and *Va* only gives a
brief quotation from its supposed text. *Vk* has no
mention of Trdat's edicts but merely inserts a single
paragraph between Gregory's imprisonment and Diocletian's search for a wife to the effect that Trdat
consolidated his power and that Diocletian instituted
a persecution of the Christians.

Although Agathangelos says that Gregory was tortured and imprisoned in the first year of Trdat's reign,
he does not date precisely the more general persecution in Armenia—if indeed the supposed edicts
refer to an actual historical event. This general persecution took place while Gregory was in prison, before the arrival of Rhipsimē and her companions in
Armenia, and presumably was meant by Agathangelos
to correspond to the imperial persecution of 303. Of
course Agathangelos could not insist on the persecution of Christians in Armenia before Gregory's rescue
since Gregory was supposed to have made the first
conversions! The martyrdom of the Roman Rhipsimē
and her companions at Valarshapat is not considered
to be part of this general persecution, but is linked to
Gregory's emergence from the pit after thirteen, or
fifteen, years.[78] Some have seen in the martyrdoms at
Valarshapat a reflection of the persecution of Maximin Daia in Armenia in 312.[79] But so far as Trdat's
edicts are concerned, their genuineness is most implausible.

Chapter 5. The Martyrdom of Rhipsimē,
Gaianē and their companions

> A. *Diocletian seeks a wife;*
> *prayer of the nuns*

Aa §137-148
Ag 59-64
Ar 114-125
Vg 30-33
Vo 59-   [Garitte does not give section numbers
            for *Vo* 59-75]
Va 10-14
Vk 75-77

The story now jumps several years in time and
many leagues in space. We are abruptly introduced
to a group of nuns, whose eventual martyrdom in
Armenia brings torments on the court as divine retribution and provides the setting for Gregory's reappearance. The story begins with Diocletian's search
for a bride by means of a beauty-contest, a fairy-tale
theme for which there are many parallels in Byzantine
history.[80] But the episode as related in Agathangelos
is presented in phrases taken from the Bible. The rendering in *Ag* and *Ar* follows the Armenian of this
section closely, with only very minor divergences.
Vg, however, is much shorter; it omits all the ver-
bosity of the nuns' long prayer with a single sentence,
and abbreviates the narrative to its essentials. *Vo*
follows *Ag,* while *Va* offers a compromise text. It
gives the long prayer almost in its entirety, but abbreviates the elaborate narrative of *Aa. Vk* narrates the
episode in quite different terms, very succinctly, and
omits the nuns' prayer.

B. The nuns flee to Armenia but are discovered; Rhipsimē's prayer

Aa	§149-177
Ag	65-75
Ar	126-151
Vg	34-44
Vo	-75
Va	15-24
Vk	78-98

We next learn of the nuns' flight to Armenia. Rather implausibly, they take refuge on the outskirts of the capital,[81] in the vineyards for which the plain of Val-arshapat was (and remains) famous. One of the nuns makes glass pearls in order to earn a living for her seventy-odd companions. Diocletian eventually discovers their whereabouts and informs his vassal Trdat about the nuns' flight by means of a letter describing the pernicious sect of the Christians and the bewitching Rhipsimē who had eluded him. At the end of his letter Diocletian suggests that if Trdat finds Rhipsimē and desires her, he may keep her for himself. At this point *Vg* adds a brief reply from Trdat.[82]

This short letter, which reflects the subservient attitude of the vassal Trdat, to his protector and benefactor, is unknown to the other versions. Since *Vg* generally offers an abbreviated rendering of the verbose Agathangelos, since the letter authentically reflects the standing of Trdat with regard to Diocletian in the first decade of the fourth century, and since the unflattering role here attributed to Trdat is more likely to have been omitted by the Armenian redactor than invented by the Greek translator, we may assume that the letter belongs to a stage of the "Book of Gregory"

before the latter was worked up into its present form
by "Agathangelos." But there is no evidence to support directly the opinion that it is "une authentique
pièce de chancellerie."[83]

For this section the texts in *Ag, Ar* and *Vo* follow
the Armenian reasonably closely. *Va* is somewhat
shorter, but only marginally so. *Vg* and *Vk,* on the
other hand, are very much abbreviated and in a few
lines cover the discovery of the nuns, Rhipsimē's long
prayer and the answer from heaven.

C. Rhipsimē is taken to the palace;
she eludes Trdat's clutches

Aa §178-196
Ag 76-82
Ar 152-167
Vg 45-48
Vo 76-   [Garitte does not give section numbers
              for *Vo* 76-88]
Va 25-31
Vk 99-116

There now follows a description of the struggle
between Rhipsimē and Trdat in the palace; the king,
despite his great physical strength, is worsted and the
maiden escapes. As usual, the narrative is filled out
with lengthy prayers which are but strings of biblical
allusions. *Vg* gives only the briefest résumé of this
section. *Va* is also shorter than the Armenian and the
dependent versions in *Ag, Ar* and *Vo,* but it retains
the long exhortation of Gaianē and much of Rhimp-
simē's prayer after her escape. But *Va* does abbreviate her first prayer and is less verbose than *Aa* in its
narrative sections. *Vk* has a number of details of its

own and tells the story in a somewhat different (and briefer) way than *Aa* or *Ag*.

D. The martyrdom of the nuns

Aa	197-210
Ag	83-88
Ar	168-181
Vg	49-50
Vo	-88
Va	32-37
Vk	117-123

The last section of this chapter gives the details of the death of Rhipsimē and of the other nuns. The circumstances of the martyrdoms are as implausible as the rest of the story, and as may be expected *Vg* disposes of the whole episode in a few lines—as does *Vk*.

The significance of this part of the story lies in the precise date given for the martyrdoms, the 26th of Hori for Rhipsimē and the 27th for Gaianē. In *Ag* September is substituted for Hori, and *Ar* follows this equivalence by substituting Eylul for September. The abbreviated version in *Vg* says that all the nuns died on September 26, while *Va* places these events a month later and dates the martyrdom of Rhipsimē to October 26th and that of Gaianē to October 28th— two days later, not one. This is not part of the origi- nal tradition and may be disregarded. *Vk* does not give a date for the martyrdoms.

The precise rendering of these dates in the Greek texts *Ag* and *Vg* and in *Ar* goes back to the first trans- lation of the Armenian into Greek. The 26th of Hori coincided with the 26th of September between 464 and 468, but, as Peeters has noted, this does not prove that the translation can be dated to those years. A general correspondence between Hori and September would have been natural for a translator over the long period when the Armenian movable month ended during the fixed Greek month.[84]

The date that remained in the Armenian popular mind was Hori 26. Gaianē's martyrdom was naturally assimilated with that of Rhipsimē. Hence in §223 Agathangelos says that the bodies of *all* the martyrs had been lying outside the city for nine days. For a further 66 days the Armenians remained repenting before Gregory told them of his vision. The addition of these 75 days to Hori 26 brings us to Kalots' 11, which is the day on which the *Synaxaria* celebrate Gregory's vision—Gregory's major feast day, since the day of his birth or death are unknown to early Armenian tradition. The place and date of the martyrdom of Rhipsimē, Gaianē and their companions are thus the basic stratum in the whole *History* of Agathangelos. For it is around the cathedral and churches at Valar-shapat and the feast-day of Hori 26 that the traditions about Gregory and Trdat have been fitted.[85]

Chapter 6. Punishment falls on Trdat and the
           Armenians; Gregory is rescued

Aa §211-225
Ag 89-93
Ar 182-195
Vg 51-64
Vo 89-   [Garitte does not give section numbers
            for *Vo* 89-103]

Va   38-42
Vk   124-150

As divine retribution for putting the nuns to death, Trdat is changed into the form of a wild boar on the pattern of the fate that befell Nebuchadnezzar after the episode of the fiery furnace.[86] Torments also afflicted the king's household and the whole city. The cure for these misfortunes is revealed to Trdat's sister in a vision that is repeated several times: Gregory must be released from prison. To everyone's astonishment he is still alive after fifteen years. The significance of these fifteen years, thirteen in §122,[87] is not brought out by Agathangelos, but it is perhaps possible to construe the figures as reflections of historical dates. The thirteen years would be the interval between the first years of Trdat's reign (298/299)[88] when Gregory was imprisoned and the time of Maximin's persecution (311/312) from which the traditions concerning Rhipsimē may derive. The fifteen years would be the interval between Gregory's imprisonment and his consecration as bishop for Armenia in 314.[89]

This chapter is recounted in more circumstantial detail in *Vg*, except that the enshrouding of the martyrs is omitted. This latter episode, on the other hand, is elaborated in *Va*: Gregory not only wraps the bodies but prepares coffins and digs graves. These actions are attributed to Gregory, the king and their helpers at a later stage by *Aa* and all the versions;[90] *Va* thus has two different renderings of the preparations for the burial of the nuns. For this chapter *Vk* follows the general development of *Aa* and *Ag,* but adds some details of its own.

Chapter 7. Gregory's sermons

A. *Gregory's preliminary exhortations*

Aa	§226-258
Ag	94-106[10]
Ar	196-222
Vg	64-67
Vo	-103
Va	43-44
Vk	151

B. The "Teaching"

Aa	§259-715
Ag	omits the *Teaching*
Ar	omits the *Teaching*
Vg	68-75
Vo	104-105
Va	45-52
Vk	152-187

C. *Gregory's final exhortation*

Aa	§716-730
Ag	106[10]-111[11]
Ar	223-234[2]
Vg	76
Vo	106-111
Va	72-77
Vk	188-195

By far the longest section in the whole *History* of Agathangelos is the sermon given by Gregory over a period of sixty-five days, which is entitled "The Teaching of Saint Gregory." The *Teaching* can stand by itself as a theological document of some interest and importance; it takes the form of an elaborate catechism, combining exposition of the faith and exhortation to repentance. It is quite extraneous to the *History* as such, though it occasionally refers to the audience of the Armenian court. As it has been studied in detail elsewhere, it is omitted from this translation.[91]

The context of this catechism is identical in *Aa* and all the versions except *Vk*: it follows a preliminary exhortation by Gregory (§226-258 in the Armenian), which is omitted in the Karshuni. For this section *Ag* and *Ar* follow the Armenian closely, but *Vg, Vo* and *Va* present some variations and offer a brief passage from the *Teaching* (which is entirely omitted in *Ag* and *Ar*). *Vg* gives an exceedingly abbreviated version of Gregory's preliminary exhortations; it then says that Gregory cured all the people (which episode comes after the *Teaching* in *Aa* and *Ag*) and offers eight paragraphs of a sermon called the διδασκαλία but which has no parallel in *Aa* or *Ag*.

Va offers a different version. It follows *Aa* to the end of §229, and then introduces a sermon which is explained as an exposition of the scriptures. This sermon is a translation of the διδασκαλία in *Vg*. The other Greek version, *Vo,* follows *Aa* to the end of §251, and then offers a quotation from the original *Teaching,* §652-654 of the Armenian. *Va* also has the first and last of these three paragraphs. These are the only known direct quotations of the *Teaching* in the versions of Agathangelos, although the catechism served as the basis for a Georgian treatise attributed to Hippolytus[92] and it was also quoted briefly in a

Greek florilegium.[93] *Vk* does offer a long résumé of the main arguments in the *Teaching*, but not without elaborations of its own.

The discrepencies between the versions of Agathangelos continue after the *Teaching*. In *Aa, Ag* and *Ar* Gregory gives a final exhortation and dismisses the crowd, though the king and court remain with him. *Vo* and *Va* follow the Armenian closely, but *Vg* abbreviates the whole section to a mere three lines. Following the sixty-five days of instruction and repentance, the king is still in swinish form, and the populace beg for healing. This is omitted in *Vg* and abbreviated in *Vo* and *Va*. In *Vk* the king begs for healing immediately after the long sermon; he is partially cured so that he can join in the building of chapels for the martyrs. But *Vk* omits the whole of the next chapter.

Chapter 8. Gregory's vision

Aa §731-756
Ag 111^{11}-120^{10}
Ar 234^2-256
Vg 77-82
Vo omits the vision
Va 54-62
Vk omits the vision

After the catechism and exhortations Gregory narrates the famous vision in which God revealed where the martyrs were to be buried. This vision plays a very significant role in the *History* of Agathangelos because it provides a divinely ordained foundation for the Armenian cathedral at Valarshapat. And equal in importance to the direct intervention of God is the role of Gregory; it is he who is responsible for the construction of the cathedral and the neighboring churches in honour of the martyrs. So his position as the founder of the national church is enhanced, although his own see was at Ashtishat in the West. It is therefore very surprising that both *Vo* and *Vk* omit the vision entirely, while *Vg* and *Va* give but a very abbreviated rendering. Curiously, *Vg* and *Va* place the vision in Artashat, the site of Gregory's imprisonment, which somewhat spoils the purpose of the vision.

The vision itself, as represented in the extended version found in *Aa, Ag* and *Ar,* does not so much describe any specific monument as give an idealized picture of the heavenly Jerusalem which is mirrored in the Armenian cathedral. Although many of the figures that appear in the vision may have been represented in the decoration of the fifth century cathedral, in the dome, drum and arches, the author of this piece was more concerned with the religious symbolism involved. The features of ecclesiastical architecture are significant insofar as they represent the Christian view of the cosmos.[94] The simile of the sheep and wolves, however, is more directly applicable to a specific historical episode.

There is no doubt that later Armenian writers assumed that the vision referred to a particular occasion, and they used it as a model for similar prophecies after the event in their own histories.[95] The vision refers to a time when many Armenians apostatised: these are the impious ones of §754 who abandoned the covenant *(ukht)*. The covenant is a reference to the solemn oath of the clergy and people to defend their religion which figures so prominently in Ḷazar and Ełishē's accounts of the revolt of 450-451. This is a further indication that the *History* of Agathangelos did not receive its final form before 450.

In view of the vagueness of the terminology in such visions, however, it is not surprising that differing interpretations may be offered. The shortened version in *Va* refers to the wolves who lead others to their own views. This was interpreted by Marr, the editor of the Arabic text, as a reference to the Christological debates over the decrees of Chalcedon. He saw here further confirmation of his opinion that the Arabic version *(Va)* represented a Chalcedonian reworking of the Gregory story.[96] But the phrase in question could as well refer to backsliding—as the Armenian clearly does—as to differing Christological views and cannot bear the precise interpretation that Marr would read into it.

As for the literary motif of such dreams and revelations, it is too common to need special notice here. The Armenian predilection for this genre is well illustrated by the wide diffusion of apocryphal and apocalyptic literature.[97] And Agathangelos himself shows acquaintance with several such documents.[98]

Chapter 9. Chapels are built and the nuns buried; the king and people are cured

Aa   §757-776
Ag   120[10]-127
Ar   257-275
Vg   83-91
Vo   112-113
Va   78-84
Vk   196-206

After Gregory's vision Agathangelos describes the building of the chapels and the healing of the king and people. It is noticeable that in this chapter and in those which follow, not only is the text of the Armenian less certain,[99] but the versions now often diverge and sometimes introduce material not found in *Aa* and its derivatives *Ag* and *Ar*. Furthermore the later history of Gregory and his missionary work in Armenia is modeled on the activity of Mashtʻotsʻ a century later: Agathangelos has borrowed whole paragraphs verbatim from Koriun's biography of Mashtʻotsʻ and has credited his own hero Gregory with these anachronistic achievements.[100] One may reasonably surmise that the earlier part of the story (Anak's regicide, Gregory's confrontation with Trdat, the martyrdom of the nuns, Gregory's rescue and the conversion of the king and people) had at an early date taken the form of a more or less coherent narrative. So the versions may abbreviate or add individual details, but they had no basically different traditions from which to draw. On the other hand, there was no such unified tradition concerning the events in Armenia after Gregory's rescue, so the versions not only relate certain episodes in different ways, but add details and even long passages not found in the Armenian.

In this chapter *Ag* and *Ar* follow the Armenian closely but with minor variants. But the tradition in *Vg, Vo* and *Va* offers wide divergences. In *Vg* the account is greatly abbreviated, but two details are added: the people promise to adorn the martyrs' chapels once Gregory has attained the rank of priest, and Gregory puts the chapels under the care of the guardians of the royal palace. This account is followed faithfully by *Va*. But *Vo* offers an even shorter version, omitting the journey of Trdat to Mount Masis and the setting up of crosses in the chapels built for the martyrs. On the other hand, *Vk* omits the details concerning the building of the chapels and concentrates on Trdat's recovery and his journey to Masis.

Chapter 10. The pagan shrines are overthrown

Aa §777-790
Ag 128-133
Ar 276-288
Vg 92-115
Vo 114-119
Va 85-113
Vk 207-218

It is in this chapter that really important divergences begin to appear. Here the destruction of some of the principal pagan sanctuaries in Armenia is described. Again *Ag* and *Ar* follow closely the Armenian text. *Vo* also follows the Armenian, but in a slightly shorter form which bears no relation to the Greek of *Ag*. *Vg* and *Va*, however, offer an entirely different account. Once Trdat and Gregory had arrived in Vaḷarshapat (where they supposedly were already!), Trdat summons the kings of Georgia and Causasian Albania. At this point *Vg* adds five paragraphs not only giving the story of Gregory's early marriage and of the birth of his sons (which comes later in Agathangelos),[101] but also describing the arrival of Gregory's wife Julitta in Armenia after she had heard of the recent events there. Gregory seems to have been somewhat embarrassed by her appearance and refused to live with his wife; he proposed that she should take care of the

Christian virgins. This episode is unknown to the Armenian text *(Aa)*, which, followed by *Ag* and *Ar*, plays down the role of Gregory's wife, although their sons have places of major importance. But the tradition found only in *Vg* that her name was Julitta may well be authentic.[102]

This episode in *Vg* stops the regular order of the narrative. Now, followed by *Va*, the Greek version describes the gatherings of the kings of the Laz (the Abkhazians in *Va*), the Georgians and the Albanians, plus sixteen Armenian nobles. They all agree to obey Gregory, who proceeds to expound to them from the scriptures the Christian faith. Only then does king Trdat start destroying the pagan temples. The pagan priests he orders to be set to the service of the Christian cult,[102] and the treasures are confiscated—partly for the poor, partly for the royal treasury. *Va* adds in a single sentence that similar measures were taken in Lazica, Georgia and Albania.

Trdat's summoning of the Armenian nobility makes little sense in the position assigned to it in *Vg* and *Va*. It has been taken from the following chapter where the escort that will accompany Gregory to Caesarea is enumerated *(Aa* §795). *Vk* has no mention either of Gregory's wife or of the Caucasian kings and Armenian nobles, but immediately introduces the destruction of the pagan temples. However, the order in which these temples are destroyed is quite different from that of the Armenian and the other versions, and the whole episode is greatly abbreviated.

The particular interest of this chapter lies in the information about the pagan shrines of Armenia that were overthrown. The number and location of these shrines have been noted above in the discussion of the cult of Anahit and of Aramazd.[103] Here we may gather together the sparse details concerning the other dieties to be found in Agathangelos and other early Armenian writers.

In §778 we hear not only of Anahit's altars in Artashat but also of the temple of Tir, the interpreter of dreams. Tir, the planet Mercury in Iranian,[104] has left his imprint in many Armenian names—not least that of Trdat himself, which means "given by Tir."[105] There are also some manuscripts where the name Hermes (the Greek Mercury) of Acts 14.12 is translated by Tir.[106] In *Ag* and Moses Khorenats'i, however, Tir is equated with Apollo. Moses, II 49, describes the erection of a statue *(patker)* of Apollo outside Artashat by Artashēs, but this is merely an elaboration of what Moses read in Agathangelos.[107]

The next diety mentioned (§784) is Barshamin (i.e. Ba'alshamin, the lord of heaven), who had a temple at T'ordan, where according to Faustos (III 2) Gregory himself was later buried.[108] The versions offer differing interpretations of this name. It is merely transliterated in *Ag,* but *Vg* equates him with the female Rhea, and *Va* with Zeus. Moses again offers a history of Barshamin's statue, claiming that it was brought from Mesopotamia to T'ordan by Tigran the Great (II 14).[109]

From T'ordan Gregory moved on to Ani (Kamakh) where an altar of Zeus-Aramazd was destroyed; from here he went to Erēz and destroyed the golden image of Anahit. And nearby in T'il we also hear of the temple of Nanē, "daughter of Aramazd." In *Ag* and *Vg* Nanē is equated with Athena. But this goddess is of Semitic origin; her cult was widely known in Parthia and among the Kushans.[110] This is the only reference to Nanē in early Armenian literature, though as before Moses Khorenats'i has relied on this passage for his remarks about the statue of Athena (II 12, 14).[111]

The next site destroyed by Gregory is the temple of Mihr at Bagayaṙich. Mithra, of which Mihr is the Armenian form, was popular in combination as a personal name,[112] but there are not many references to his cult in early Armenian literature. Ełishē, in his apology for Christianity supposedly sent by the Armenians to Mihr-Nerseh the Sasanian vizier *(hazara-pet)*, refers to Mihr as a deity worshipped by the Persians and to the ridiculous tales about his origin.[113] The shorter version of this apology in Łazar makes no reference to Mithra.[114] In Ełishē there are also two references to Mithra put into the mouth of Persians: in the exchange between the captured priests Łevond and the Persian commander *(anderdzapet)* Movan, the latter defends the worship of Mithra;[115] and later in his *History* Ełishē has the executioner *(dahchapet)* swear by Mithra.[116] Similarly Moses Khorenats'i has the Sasanian king Shapuh swear by Mithra in a letter as does Sebeos Vahram.[117]

The correspondence of Mithra with Hephaistos, made by *Ag,* has parallels in Greek literature.[118] It is also as Hephaistos that Moses Khorenats'i knows of Mithra's cult at Bagayaṙich.[119] The correspondence with Dionysius found in *Vg* and *Va* is presumably arbitrary.[120]

Gregory's final bout of idol smashing took place later, after his return from Caesarea, in Ashtishat[121] which became the site of his first church. Here there were three shrines: one dedicated to Vahagn, the "dragon-handler," one to Anahit and one to Astłik

(Aphrodite in Greek according to Agathangelos) who was called the spouse of Vahagn. It is rather remarkable, in view of the preeminence of Anahit and Vahagn in Armenian paganism, that *Vg* and *Va* omit all reference to these dieties at Ashtishat and only mention Aphrodite's temple.

Vahagn and Astḷik are worthy of further attention.[122] The former is mentioned once elsewhere by Agathangelos: in §127 Trdat invokes the trinity of Aramazd, Anahit and Vahagn, who each bring some special blessing. Aramazd brings fertility, Anahit protection, and Vahagn valour. Vahagn was equated with Hercules by Armenian writers and *Ag.*[123] His cult at Ashtishat is mentioned by Faustos (III 14) and Moses (II 12). Far more interesting is the unique evidence in Moses (I 31), who not only traces the descent of certain Armenian families from this hero,[124] but also gives a fragment of the songs still sung in Moses' own day about the exploits of Vahagn and his victories over the dragons. The most famous of all the fragments of pagan poetry preserved in Armenian literature, it tells of the birth of Vahagn from a reed in the sea: preceded by flame and smoke, the god comes forth as a boy with hair of fire and suns for eyes. This is a precious remnant of the Armenian form of the legend surrounding Vrtrahan—the slayer of the demon Vrtra—known from Indian sources.[125]

The third temple in the complex at Ashtishat was dedicated to Astḷik, little star, or the planet Venus, whom Agathangelos equates with Aphrodite.[126] She is rarely mentioned in early Armenian literature; Moses Khorenats'i repeats the information given by Agathangelos, though he calls her Heracles' "beloved" rather than spouse. He also mentions Astḷik as the sister of the giants Titan, Japheth and Zrvan.[127] Her memory lingered, however, for Thomas Artsruni claims that Satinik (the Alan princess whose marriage to Artashēs was recorded in popular song)[128] was devoted to her cult;[129] and the "History" of Rhipsimē attributed to Moses Khorenats‘i refers to a temple of Aramazd and Astḷik near the Tigris.[130]

This whole chapter has been completely rewritten in *Vk*. All details of the deities whose temples were destroyed have been omitted; only the sites of Bagavan and Erēz are mentioned by name; and at Bagavan *Vk* claims that there existed twelve enormous idols.

Chapter 11. Gregory is consecrated at Caesarea

Aa §791-808
Ag 134-139
Ar 289-304
Vg 116-153
Vo 120-123
Va 104-141
Vk 219-241

The next stage in the establishment of an organised Christian church in Armenia was the consecration of Gregory as the first bishop of that country. To this purpose the king dispatched Gregory with an impressive escort to Caesarea. According to the Armenian (followed by *Ag* and *Ar*) Gregory made an appropriate refusal to accept ordination but was dissuaded by an angel; he was then sent to Caesarea with the leading nobles of Armenia and a letter of introduction from king Trdat to Leontius, metropolitan of Caesarea. There a council of bishops was assembled and they duly consecrated Gregory. The latter then returned home via Sebaste, where he persuaded a great number of monks to accompany him.

The version of Agathangelos represented by *Vg, Vo* and *Va* does have differences from the Armenian (but these are not so divergent as *Vk* which has Gregory go to *Rome* for consecration).[131] The gathering of the nobles who are to escort Gregory to Caesarea is put earlier, before the destruction of the pagan temples. Their journey took them to Caesarea via Sebaste, which they also visited on their return. The assembly of bishops is specifically attributed to Leontius' invitation after Gregory's arrival, and the number of twenty bishops is given in *Vg*. Trdat's letter is then read to the council. Gregory's consecration is described in more liturgical detail, and he is given relics of John the Baptist to take back with him. The reply of Leontius to Trdat's letter is then quoted.[132] On their return journey Gregory and his escort stay for six days in Sebaste, whose bishop Peter is mentioned by name.[133]

But if the circumstantial details differ in the two main recensions of the *History,* the main point of this episode is clear: Gregory was consecrated in Caesarea by the metropolitan Leontius. Is it possible to fix this as an historical event? For the first time the legendary details of Gregory's life and sufferings are tied to a person and an occasion for which outside sources offer corroboration. Leontius was bishop of Caesarea by 325, as he is mentioned among the signatories of the Council of Nicaea, but the date of his consecration is unknown.[134] Peter, who is mentioned by name only in *Vg* and *Va,* is known to have been bishop of Sebaste about 320.[135] Furthermore, the existence of a Council at Caesarea, attended by twenty bishops (the same number as given in *Vg*), is attested soon after the Council of Ancyra in the summer of 314.[136] The likelihood of this being the council mentioned by all the versions of Agathangelos is too great to be a coincidence. And although Agathangelos does not date this council, the *History* does offer a clue. The confrontation between Gregory and Trdat took place soon after the latter gained the Armenian throne, which followed shortly the peace of Nisibis in 298.[137] For fifteen years[138] Gregory remained in prison; his journey to Caesarea took place at some unspecified time after his reappearance, but Agathangelos seems to think that it was soon after the nuns had been buried. The chronology of Agathangelos is too vague, and is based on too much legendary material, to offer a firm base for dead reckoning. But clearly a date of 314 for Gregory's consecration would fit in well with the general story.

If the consecration of Gregory at Caesarea may be an historical event, the circumstantial account in Agathangelos is far from being an accurate picture of it. For many of the details and the terminology of this episode have been lifted directly from Koriun's description of the journey of Masht'ots' to Constantinople—which took place over a century after 314. This, however, is merely another facet of the general tendency in Agathangelos, especially in the latter part of his *History,* not only to borrow expressions from Koriun, but even to attribute to Gregory the deeds and actions of Masht'ots'.[139]

Chapter 12.   Gregory builds the first churches in
                  Armenia; the king and people
                  are baptised

In this chapter Agathangelos describes the activities of Gregory in Armenia after his return from Cappadocia. First he overthrows the three pagan altars at Ashtishat[140] and builds chapels on the same site for the relics of John the Baptist and Athenogenes. It was the first church built in Armenia and Ashtishat became the first see of the Armenian primate—a situation faithfully reflected in Faustos.[141] Then Gregory baptised the princes who had been in his escort and the local inhabitants, a total of 190,000 persons according to *Aa* and *Ag*.

The narrative of this section is not very coherent, as we are next informed that Gregory went to all parts of Armenia building churches and establishing priests. (But as noted above, the description in the Armenian of Gregory's missionary activity is greatly indebted to Koriun; there is much repetition and many vague references to missionary work that interrupt the main story of Gregory's activity.) Then king Trdat and his army came out to greet Gregory. They met on the Euphrates near the mountain Npat,[142] where the Armenian nobles presented Trdat with Leontius' reply to the Armenian king's letter.

Gregory now prepared to baptise the people of Armenia. A month of fasting and prayer was decreed; on its completion the king with his wife and daughter, followed by the army, was baptised in the Euphrates. At the baptism a miracle occurred: the waters of the river turned back and a cross appeared over a pillar of light.[143] That day over 150,000 soldiers were baptised, and during the following week over 4,000,000 people. Finally, the commemoration of the saints John the Baptist and Athenogenes in Bagavan is instituted on New Year's day, in place of the harvest festival.[144]

Although *Ag* and *Ar* follow *Aa* very closely for this chapter, the second recension of Agathangelos shows many variants, both of order and of substance. This indicates that there was not such a fixed tradition concerning Gregory's later activity as there had been for his earlier life. (*Vo* merely gives a very brief account of the destruction of Aphrodite's temple at Ashtishat and of the baptism of the king, his wife and daughter, and 150,000 soldiers.)

In the first place, according to *Vg* and *Va,* Peter of Sebaste accompanied Gregory to Ashtishat. After the baptism of the nobles of Gregory's escort (which is described in more detail in *Va* than in *Vg*), Trdat, with his wife and daughter and the kings of Georgia, Lazica (Abkhazia in *Va*) and Albania, comes to greet the two bishops. Trdat had no difficulty in reading Leontius' reply for himself, as he was well versed in Latin and Greek from the days of his upbringing in the Roman empire. (The text of this letter was given earlier in the narrative by *Vg* and *Va*.) The impression given in these two versions is that Trdat and his entourage meet Gregory at Ashtishat; the mountain Npat and the river Euphrates are not mentioned at this point.

After bidding farewell to Peter of Sebaste, Gregory moved to Bagavan and built a church. He began to

build churches in other sites and sent priests not only
to the rest of Armenia but also to Georgia, Lazica
(Abkhazia in *Va*) and Albania. After thirty days of
fasting, Trdat, the kings of these three countries and
the nobles with their entourages, 370,000 in all, are
baptised. The same miracle occurs as in the Armenian
text on the occasion of the baptism. But *Vg* and *Va*
make no mention of the festival of John the Baptist
and Athenogenes or of the pagan New Year's feast.[145]
As for *Vk* it again has an idiosyncratic version of
these events, with no mention of the foreign princes
or of Leontius' reply to Trdat's letter.

Chapter 13. Gregory's missionary activities;
             his sons are brought to Armenia

Aa §837-866
Ag 149²¹-161
Ar 328⁷-354
Vg 169-173
Vo 128b-129b (end)
Vk 260-274

Agathangelos now turns to the general missionary
activity of Gregory in Armenia. Not only did he supposedly visit every corner of the country in person,
but he instituted several hundred bishoprics. Furthermore he founded many schools where the young—
especially the children of the former pagan priests—
would learn the Christian faith. The children were set
to Greek and Syriac, the languages of the Armenian
church before the invention of a native Armenian
script by Masht'ots'. Monasteries were also established and Gregory himself gave an example of aus-

terity and the eremitic life. In the world he would
take up the defence of those unjustly oppressed and of
prisoners and captives. But more and more Gregory
preferred to withdraw to the desert or the mountains
and concern himself solely with prayer.

All this section in the Armenian (which is followed
by *Ag* and *Ar*) is extremely repetitive and vague. It
is almost entirely based on the descriptions of Mash-
t'ots" activity in Koriun and of Nersēs' work in Faustos. It is therefore hardly surprising that the other
versions give only a brief description of Gregory's
missionary work and omit entirely the verbose description of his eremitic life. *Vg* and *Va* mention briefly
that the pagan priests and their children were set to
the study of the scriptures. But then they add extra
details of the bishoprics established by Gregory, not
merely in Armenia but also in Georgia, Lazica and
Albania. Other regions of Armenia which are not
mentioned in *Aa* also receive bishops, though their
names are not given. Only very briefly do these two
versions mention Gregory's withdrawal to the cave of
Manē; but later in their narrative they do refer again
to Gregory's retirement. *Vk* describes all of Gregory's
missionary work only in the briefest of terms.

According to Agathangelos *(Aa, Ag* and *Ar),* Gregory's unwillingness to act as the primate of Armenia
in favor of life as a hermit worried the king. But then
Trdat heard that Gregory had two sons, and he immediately sent for them to take over the direction of
the Armenian church. A deputation went to Cappadocia and found Vrt'anēs in Caesarea and Aristakēs
living in the desert. The latter was consecrated bishop
by his father, and after Gregory's death he occupied
the throne of the Catholicos. The chapter finishes

with a long description of Trdat's enthusiastic support of the church, his piety and his own preaching activity.

The fact that Gregory had had two sons by an early marriage was brought out much earlier in the other recension of Agathangelos. *Vg* gives the details, and also the name of Gregory's wife, Julitta, in chapter 10, before the destruction of the pagan temples.[146] *Va,* however, follows the order of *Aa* and *Ag,* adding that a letter on this matter was sent by Trdat to Leontius of Caesarea. In *Vk* it is Gregory himself who urges Trdat to summon his sons. The consecration of Aristakēs is described, but *Vk* makes no reference to Trdat's own pious practices. *Vg* and *Va* now resume a common narrative and immediately introduce the episode of Constantine's conversion (chapter 14). The detailed description of Trdat's pious activities are briefly alluded to after the account of Trdat and Gregory's visit to Rome.

Chapter 14. Gregory and Trdat visit Constantine;
 the Council of Nicaea;
 Gregory's last years

Aa 867-891
Ag 162-170
Ar 355-364 (ends at *Aa* §889)
Vg 174-198
Vo — —
Va 167-187
Vk 275-300 (end)

At the end of his *History* Agathangelos launches Gregory and the newly constituted Armenian church onto the stage of world politics. When the news of Constantine's conversion reaches Armenia, Trdat,

Gregory, Aristakēs and an impressive escort of nobles and troops go to present their compliments to the emperor and to confirm an alliance between the two Christian nations. And at a later date, when Constantine summoned the Council of Nicaea, Aristakēs was sent as the Armenian representative. He brought back the Nicene canons (to which Gregory made appropriate additions). The *History* peters out with vague references to Gregory's preaching efforts, but the hero's death is not described. He is, however, credited with the composition of many discourses—another feature taken directly from Koriun's biography of Masht'ots'.

The story of Constantine's conversion and of the visit of Trdat and Gregory to Rome is quite different in *Vg* and *Va*. For them the initiative is taken by Constantine, who having heard of the miracles taking place in Armenia invites Trdat and Gregory to visit him. The episode is described at greater length than in the Armenian, although the list of nobles in the Armenian escort and the details of Constantine's rise to power are omitted. According to *Vg* and *Va,* the Armenian church thereafter celebrated the memory of Constantine and his mother Helen in the liturgy.[147]

It is interesting that the visit to Rome, which in *Aa* (and hence in *Ag* and *Ar*) is often modeled on Masht'ots' visit to Constantinople, is found in such a widely differing form in *Vg* and *Va*. It clearly belongs to a reasonably early stage of the development of the Gregory story into the *History* of Agathangelos and is not the figment of the imagination of the Armenian redactor. This makes even more curious the omission in *Vg* of Aristakēs' participation in the Council of Nicaea (though *Va* follows the Armenian here). For

Aristakēs' signature is found amongst those of the participating bishops at Nicaea,[148] but the visit of Gregory and Trdat to Rome is purely legendary.[149]

The *History* in *Va* ends on a vague tone similar to the ending in the Armenian, though without any reference to Gregory's own compositions. In *Vg,* however, an entirely different episode concludes the book. With Gregory's insistence on withdrawing from active work, Trdat orders his sons to be brought from Caesarea, and Aristakēs is installed on the "apostolic throne" of Armenia. *Vg* has transferred to the end the story of Gregory's sons which the other versions all place before the visit to Constantine.

It is *Vk* that offers the widest divergences from the Armenian at the end of the book. The meeting of Gregory and Trdat with Constantine is set in Constantinople, not Rome. But more significantly, because more tendentiously, *Vk* offers a detailed account of Gregory's retreat in the cave of Manē. Here he remained for thirty years, unknown to the world, and died. At an unspecified later date shepherds found his body, enveloped in the odor of sanctity, but when they informed the citizens of Daranalik' the latter were unable to find the body, which remained hidden like that of Moses. However, in the reign of the emperor Zeno, a pious monk called Amra was told in a vision where Gregory's body lay. He transferred it to T'ordan, buried Gregory next to his children and built above them a fine church. In a final sentence we are told that in the reign of Heraclius, when that emperor took the city he built a splendid church on the site. But *Vk* is a biased compilation of the early seventh century,[150] and the question of what later use was made of Gregory's supposed relics goes beyond our immediate interest in the Armenian recension. Nor in view of the fact that the Armenian recension is already tendentious should we be surprised that the legends surrounding Gregory's relics were later developed in a tendentious fashion by different groups.[151]

Epilogue

Aa	§892-900
Ag	171-172
Ar	——
Vg	199
Vo	——
Va	188
Vk	——

The Armenian text of the *History* closes with an Epilogue in which "Agathangelos" introduces himself once more and claims to be writing from his own personal experience. The wording of this epilogue, however, is almost entirely taken from Koriun's remarks in his biography of Masht'ots'. *Ag* follows *Aa* closely, but there is no epilogue in *Ar* or *Vo* or *Vk*. *Vg* and *Va* both have a brief final paragraph in the first person, but without the name of the author.

The Composition of the Armenian Version

Although the name of Agathangelos was not known to Armenian writers before the time of Lazar (end of the fifth century), there is no dearth of information about Gregory in another Armenian historian writing earlier in that century, Faustos Buzandats'i—whose own identity is something of a mystery.[152] The date of composition of his *History* is not clear, for despite the old view that it was written in Greek during the fourth century and later translated into Armenian,[153] the text shows no incontestable evidence of being a translation,[154] and the book contains legendary material about Basil of Caesarea (died 379) which would imply that several years had passed since that date.[155] Furthermore, the vocabulary of Faustos shows many striking similarities with that of other Armenian compositions of the early fifth century.[156] It seems most plausible to date Faustos' *History* to the first half of the fifth century. It is interesting, therefore, to see what differences, and what extra information, may be found in Faustos as compared to Agathangelos.

The first most obvious feature that emerges from Faustos' various references to Gregory is that although Gregory is called the first Armenian bishop, he is not considered to be the first Christian missionary in Armenia. That honor belongs to Thaddaeus, to whose position Gregory eventually succeeded.[157] The story of Thaddaeus is an Armenian adaptation of the Edessene legend concerning Addai, one of the seventy disciples of Jesus who was sent to convert king Abgar.[158] The details of this legend are not immediately relevant here. We may merely note that although the apostle

Addai was adopted by the Armenians as the founder of their church—to be joined later by Bartholomew as an apostolic founder even closer to Christ, being one of the twelve[159]—such ideas are foreign to Agathangelos. For him Gregory is the first missionary as well as the first patriarch.

This brings us to the next major difference. In Agathangelos particular stress is placed on the connection between Gregory and the martyrs' chapels at Vaḷarshapat. But for Faustos the center of Armenian Christianity is in the West, at Ashtishat where the first church was built and where the patriarchs had their palace.[160] Ashtishat remained the see of the Armenian patriarchs for several generations, and here Gregory's successors were installed after their consecration at Caesarea. This certainly reflects the historical reality more accurately than Agathangelos' emphasis on Vaḷarshapat, the royal capital and holy site.

Although Faustos does not give it a title, he claims that there already existed a written account[161] of the preaching of the Christian gospel in Armenia from the time of Thaddaeus to the death of king Trdat. But no such book is known, and even the fertile imagination of Moses Khorenats'i could not find a role for Christianity in Armenia between the supposed visits of Thaddaeus and Bartholomew and the activity of Gregory. On the other hand, Faustos is acquainted with the main features of the Gregory story as related in Agathangelos: he knows that Gregory is the son of Anak;[162] he refers to the martyrdom of Rhipsimē and Gaianē;[163] to the destruction of the pagan temples,[164] to the building of churches,[165] to the baptism of many Armenians,[166] and to Gregory's withdrawal and death.[167]

But it is remarkable that so many other important features of the *History* of Agathangelos are unknown to Faustos. He does know of Gregory's death and can name some sites connected with Gregory's activity, but he has no reference to Gregory's upbringing, his marriage (though his sons figure prominently in Faustos' *History*), his imprisonment and rescue, his vision, the burial of the martyrs, Gregory's preaching among the Georgians and Albanians (though Faustos does speak of a church built by Gregory on the Armeno-Albanian frontier),[168] or his visit to the emperor Constantine.

Even less mention is made of Gregory's work by other early Armenian writers. Koriun,[169] Ełishē and Eznik have no reference to him at all.[170] Łazar does give a long précis of the "Book of Gregory" by Agathangelos,[171] and interestingly makes no mention of Thaddaeus. In the Armenian ecclesiastical correspondence of the sixth century Gregory figures prominently: by the Catholicos Babgen (writing in 505) he is called the *first* cause of God's mercy to the Armenians;[172] but by the Catholicos John (writing in the second half of the sixth century) he is called the successor to Thaddaeus.[173] In the seventh century the first Armenian catena of patristic quotations contains several attributed to Gregory. These are taken not only from the *History* of Agathangelos, and notably the *Teaching*, but also from a collection of homilies known as the *Yachakhapatum* and traditionally ascribed to Gregory.[174]

As interesting as the references in early Armenian writers to Gregory's activities are the terms which they use to describe them. In Moses Khorenats'i he is called *lusaworich'* (illuminator),[175] a title which has persisted to the present day as the specific epithet that distinguishes this Gregory from the many other Gregories in the roster of Christian saints.[176] Although this title is not found as such in Agathangelos, the verb "to illuminate" is often used of Gregory's missionary efforts. The idea of illumination is not to be taken so much in the metaphorical sense of banishing the darkness of ignorance; rather it refers to baptism.[177] In the fifth-century writers, however, Gregory is not called "Illuminator." They put the emphasis on his status as confessor of the faith and as teacher. Faustos calls him *nakhavastak* (the first laborer), but otherwise uses vague epithets such as *mets* (great), *surb* (holy), *sk'anch'eli* (wonderful), *hogewor* (spiritual). Łazar is more explicit. He calls Gregory *khostovanoḷ* (confessor) and *mets* or *surb nahatak* (great, or holy champion), the term *nahatak* having overtones of a martyr. Łazar also uses several expressions which refer to Gregory's asceticism and piety: *chgnasēr, chgnazgeats'* (ascetic), *ayrn Astutsoy* (the man of God), *barepasht* (pious), *margarēakan* (prophetic). But more significantly Gregory is called "the apostle of the Armenians" and "the teacher of the Armenians";[178] and for the first time in Łazar we hear of prayers directed towards Gregory invoking his assistance.[179]

Of greater interest are the titles given to Gregory's formal position as the first bishop of Armenia. In Agathangelos no one title is applied to Gregory, but he is called "shepherd," "teacher," "leader," "overseer," and more specifically "high-priest," "bishop," and "archbishop."[180] Too much stress should not be placed on the apparent Jewishness of the title "high-priest," as this term was widely used for bishops in both Syrian and Greek Christianity.[181] The title which was to become standard for the leaders of the Armenian church — Catholicos — is used by Agathangelos only for the metropolitan of Caesarea, but he does use the expression "throne of the Catholicosate" *(at'or kat'oḷikosut' ean)* for the supreme dignity to which Gregory's son Aristakēs was appointed.[182] In Faustos the titles of "catholicos" and "patriarch" are frequently found applied to Gregory, and the curiously pleonastic expression "catholiscosate of the patriarchate" is once used for this rank, which remained a prerogative of Gregory's family for several generations.[183]

However, it is quite clear that the dignities ascribed to Gregory by these fifth-century writers are more indicative of the situation in fifth-century Armenia than of that pertaining in the early fourth century. The title of "patriarch" is most inappropriate for the first bishop of the see of Ashtishat, whose successors for the rest of the fourth century remained under the titular authority of the metropolitans of Caesarea.[184]

Such anachronisms are but another reflection of the fact that the *History* of Agathangelos does not offer us an eyewitness account of the conversion of king Trdat, but is rather a tendentious compilation which has expanded and elaborated earlier traditions. Since the major purpose of the present study is the analysis of the literary sources and affinities of Agathangelos, it is in the context of early Armenian literature that our investigation must proceed, and more specifically in the context of ecclesiastical motives and ideology. Our basic question is: given certain traditions about Gregory, Trdat and the martyred nuns, in what terms did Agathangelos express himself? A similar question may be posed of other early Armenian writers, who all had their upbringing in the schools

founded by Masht'ots', Sahak and their circle. But in
Agathangelos the literary sources are more trans-
parent than in other historians who had more "solid"
information on which to base their narratives. Agathangelos' *History* may thus serve as a test-case for
the investigation of the intellectual milieu of early
Armenian ecclesiastical literature.

In view of the basic purpose behind the invention of
the Armenian alphabet—the bringing of the gospel
and the Christian faith to the Armenian people in
their own tongue—it is hardly surprising that the
Bible was the fundamental text studied in the monastic
schools. Koriun tells us that the Book of Proverbs was
the book used by those beginning to learn to read and
write in Armenian.[185] The translation of the Old and
New Testaments, plus the more popular "apocryphal"
books, was the prime consideration of Masht'ots', and
more especially the patriarch Sahak.[186] But not far
behind in importance came the liturgical texts, hagiography and then patristic works on all aspects of theology.[187] Such books, read, studied and translated from
Greek and Syriac by the early Armenian writers, left
a profound impression, not only on their style and
modes of expression, but also on their outlook. Whatever the subject of the narrative, biblical images and
parallels would be foremost in the minds of Armenian
authors.

It is natural in a work of the cast of Agathangelos'
History that biblical quotations should be found on
almost every page, especially in prayers and passages
of theological exposition.[188] But disregarding such
direct quotations, we may note many episodes that are
so based on biblical motifs that it is impossible to
single out separate passages that served as models.

For example, in the confrontation between Gregory and Trdat over idolatry, the well-known passages from *Wisdom* and the Psalms are central, but nearly all of Gregory's remarks are based on biblical allusions. Even more obviously biblically inspired are Gregory's prayers under torture, his sermons, and the various prayers of the nuns. Diocletian's persecution of the church is described only in expressions taken from the Bible, with no precise references to any actual event. Biblical imagery naturally also plays an important role in the correspondence between Trdat and Leontius, metropolitan of Caesarea, as well as in the account of the baptism of the Armenians, the ascetic practices of Gregory, and his preaching and instruction.

The biblical origin of the phraseology in such passages and the direct comparison between Rhipsimē and the heroines of the Old Testament[189] are so natural as to call for no special comment. More interesting is the way in which Agathangelos describes many episodes in his *History* in biblical terms that are not explicitly so identified. Gregory in the pit is nourished by a widow—as was Elijah;[190] Trdat's malady is parallel to that of Nebuchadnezzar;[191] Gregory is called forth from the pit like Lazarus from the grave;[192] when he emerges he resembles Job in the latter's lament;[193] and when the Armenians come to greet him they are described in the same terms as the epileptic in Mark 9. Gregory addresses them in the same way as Peter addressed Cornelius.[194] And when Gregory builds chapels for the martyred nuns there are allusions to the imagery of Ezechiel's vision.[195] This and many other biblical allusions also lie behind the imagery of Gregory's own vision, though since the biblical background had already influenced the architectural symbolism to which Agathangelos is indebted, his reliance on the Bible is here less direct.[196]

Nor is Agathangelos indebted to biblical imagery merely for the style of his narrative. He takes his concept of the historian's role directly from biblical motifs. In the *Prologue,* in words taken from Psalm 106, historians are compared to merchants sailing the deep; historical knowledge is compared to pearls of great price; and the value of historical records is based on the injunction in Deuteronomy 32.7. In the *Epilogue,* Agathangelos elaborates further on the Old Testament parallels: the command to Moses to preserve a record of divine words, the commands to the various prophets and to David that they write down their visions and their teaching so that generations to come would have certain knowledge of God's dispensation. The command of Jesus to his disciples to preach in all parts of the world is also directly relevant to Agathangelos; but it is not without significance that his *History* closes on a theme from the Old Testament: "You are my people."

The special regard that the Armenians had for the race of Israel has often been noted. Although the early Armenian church was greatly influenced by the theory and practice of Christianity in fourth century Jerusalem,[197] it was rather to the Israel of pre-Christian times that the Armenians looked. This is especially noticeable in the popularity of Jewish names and of (fake) Jewish pedigrees. But though one family, the Bagratids, might claim king David as a distant relative,[198] the fortunes of the Maccabees were seen by all Armenians as affording a very close parallel to the fate of the Armenians. Faustos makes a direct comparison between the Maccabees and those Armenians who died for their faith in the war against Persia; Ełishē makes a similar comparison between the Maccabees' struggle against the Seleucid king and that of the Armenians against Sasanian Iran.[199] It therefore comes as no surprise that Agathangelos, though he never mentions the Maccabees by name, was clearly familiar with the Armenian version[200] and frequently used imagery taken from it.

Most of the parallels fall into three distinct categories: expressions of military significance; expressions from royal edicts; and expressions of religious significance. In the first of these categories, the correspondences all occur in the early part of the *History* which describe the military exploits of Khosrov and Trdat: Khosrov's seeking vengeance (§19), his gathering of an army and attacking Persia (§23, 31), and his death (§32); Trdat's advance against the king of the Goths (§45) and his securing of Armenia's borders (§47). There are several similarities in the wording of Trdat's edicts with royal edicts given in Maccabees, notably the promulgation (§125) and the form of greeting (§134).[201]

The parallels between Agathangelos and the Books of Maccabees with regard to religious matters fall into two general groups: verbal and factual. At the least significant end of the scale are expressions describing creation (§95, 169, 226) or rejoicing at salvation (§803); and, not surprisingly, several concerning profanation (§143, 243). But more interesting are the parallels between the description of Hellenistic temples and of pagan Armenian dieties (§809, 836), especially the description of the cult of Anahit (§49), which is based entirely on phrases from the second

Book of Maccabees. Equally significant is the comparison between the massive unhewn stones brought by king Trdat from Mount Masis for the martyrs' tombs (§767) and the whole stones used by Judas to rebuild the altar of the defiled sanctuary. And the insistence in the second half of the *History* that the Armenians could not make offerings to the martyrs' tombs nor Gregory raise altars until there was a properly constituted priesthood in the country depends on Maccabees. For Judas and his priests, having prepared the stones to rebuild the sanctuary, had to wait for a prophet to show what should be done.[202] Lastly, we may note the death of Rhipsimē (§197), when she willingly offered her tongue to be pulled out—like the third brother in II Maccabees 7.

Biblical themes were not the only sources for images and parallels in Agathangelos' *History*. Our author was naturally familiar with the liturgy, whose prayers provided inspiration for Gregory's long public prayer,[203] and with a wide range of hagiographical and theological literature. In the category of hagiographical borrowings we may distinguish between general characteristics and specific details. The former group would include such motifs as the insistence on the authority of an eye-witness; the presence of scribes to record all that was said and done; the insensibility of martyrs to their pain and their long public prayers; the issuing of edicts against Christians; the malady of eating one's own flesh; the miraculous destruction of pagan temples; the disclaimers of worthiness by candidates for ordination; the appearance of a light or the backward flowing of the river when baptism is performed. Nor are the tortures inflicted on martyrs generally entirely the figment of the individual hagiographer's imagination. There are many stock types into which fall some of the sufferings inflicted on Gregory and the nuns: piercing by nails, scraping, the pulling out of the tongue, a final beheading.[204] Among the more specific correspondences with hagiographical literature, there are: the turmoil following the nuns' prayer and the tempest following Mark's martyrdom;[205] the tortures of wooden blocks tied to one's feet,[206] of being bound in leather fetters or iron leggings,[207] and of being doused in molten lead.[208] That these last tortures have closest affinities in the martyrdoms of the Edessene saints is not surprising in view of the close connection between Mashtʻotsʻ and his circle and Edessa,[209] and the early Armenian adoption of the legends surrounding the conversion of the king of Edessa to Christianity.

The theological learning of Agathangelos is most apparent in the long catechism known as the *Teaching*. This has received detailed investigation in a separate work, and we may merely note here that the *Teaching* has a special debt to the biblical commentaries of John Chrysostom, the *Hexaemeron* of Basil of Caesarea and the *Catecheses* of Cyril of Jerusalem.[210] Many of the motifs developed at length in the *Teaching* also emerge in the *History,* mostly in the course of prayers put into the mouth of Gregory or the nuns. But a few points are introduced in the *History* that are not repeated in the *Teaching.* In §149 Agathangelos refers to the future joys of paradise and speaks of "Abraham's banquet." This seems to be a combination of the two common figures for future bliss: the "wedding-feast" with the bridegroom—that is Christ—and Abraham's bosom for the repose of the faithful departed.[211] And in §92 the moon as a figure for the resurrection would seem to be a borrowing from Cyril of Jerusalem,[212] whose influence on the *Teaching* is so important.

The most significant new ideas also come in this long prayer of Gregory's, uttered while he was hanging for seven days from the gibbet. In §79 an elaborate comparison between Eve and the virgin Mary is clearly based on that between the first and second Adam in I Corinthians 15. Pursuing the theme of the comparison between Cain, Eve's son, who brought a curse to the world, and Christ, Mary's son, who brought rest and life, Agathangelos elaborates on Christ as the "image of men." Here the influence of Proclus of Constantinople may be discerned.[213] Proclus was particularly important in early Armenian theology, since his letter to the Armenians was accepted as the authoritive explanation of the decrees of the Council of Ephesus.[214] But more curiously, Agathangelos then says that Christ on the cross became a dead image, similar to the lifeless images worshipped by idolators, so that this familiar image might draw men to God.[215] Agathangelos, however, likens the cross to the hook and Christ's body on the cross to the bait; the metaphor then becomes one of the Eucharist, where Christ's body as food draws men to the divine kingdom. The cross also figures in another comparison, this time with the ark (§169). Just as Noah was saved by the ark, so were men by the cross; it is the common material of wood that provides the link between the ark and the cross. Although the ark was widely used by patristic writers as a figure for the church, the·emphasis on the cross seems to point to an early stage in Christian theology.[217]

The central position of the cross as a cosmic figure in Agathangelos' thought is first introduced in Gregory's prayer (§82): "and instead of carved pieces of

wood he set up his cross in the middle of the universe."
This theme is then taken up and elaborated in the
Teaching, where the four points of the cross point up
to heaven, down to earth, to the joy of the just on the
right and to the torments of sinners on the left.[218] And
in the *Teaching* another theme involving the cross is
introduced: the comparison between the cross and the
tower of Babel. The latter was the cause of scattering,
whereas the former will reunite all men in the worship
of God.[219] This parallelism between the cross and the
tower of Babel is not a feature of the usual early Christian exegesis which seeks typological parallels between the cross and Old Testament references. But
the gathering of the scattered is a significant feature
of exegesis of the cross as a cosmic figure.[220]

It is not necessary to prolong the investigation of
theological motifs. The milieu in which Agathangelos
was writing is already clear enough. It was one dominated by biblical and hagiographical terms; and where
ecclesiastical considerations were paramount. The milieu was that of the first or second generation of the
pupils of Masht'ots' and Sahak—the circle that produced the first translations from Greek and Syriac
into Armenian and then the first original compositions.

Here we must note the many parallels in phraseology found between Agathangelos and some other
early Armenian writers. In the first part of the *History*
there are several similarities with Eḷishē: the description of Khosrov's sacrifice in traditional Arsacid fashion;[221] the description of Diocletian as an enemy of
the church;[222] and Trdat's ravings against the Christians.[223] But although Eḷishē is describing events that
occurred in 450-451, the actual date of his *History* is
still a matter of dispute.[224] These three parallels are

not precise enough to prove that Ełishē was a source for Agathangelos, or vice-versa.

More difficult to dismiss are the many correspondences in the second half of Agathangelos' *History* and in the *History* of Faustos. Although some of these parallels are but short phrases, they are not so commonplace as to be purely coincidental: "worker of all blessings";[225] "fatherly birth";[226] Gregory's institution of bishops in all dioceses under his jurisdiction;[227] the description of the day of death;[228] "the fearsome Ocean sea";[229] the description of Constantine's renown.[230] But these similarities are verbal, and there is no equivalence of events described in the two histories. It is not necessary to posit direct influence of Agathangelos on Faustos or vice-versa;[231] it would be perfectly reasonable to suppose that the first and second generations of Masht'ots'' pupils not only shared a common outlook but often would express themselves in a similar fashion. Certain idioms and turns of phrase would be a reflection of their common education and background.

But when we compare the *History* of Agathangelos with Koriun's biography of Masht'ots', by no stretch of the imagination could the similarities and verbatim parallels be considered to be either fortuitous or the result of a common training in literary expression. Without quoting all the examples in full,[232] we may note here the major points where Koriun and Agathangelos use identical phrasing: the felicity of Armenia on hearing the gospel, and following the invention of the Armenian script by Masht'ots';[233] the instruction given by Gregory and the general characteristics of his preaching and its reception, and the missionary activity of Masht'ots';[234] the reception

given Gregory in Caesarea and that given Masht'ots'
in Edessa, Amida and Samosata;[235] the return of Gregory to Armenia as bishop, and the return of Masht'ots'
with the newly invented script;[236] the reception ac-
corded each by the king of the time;[237] the establishment of schools where the young would be taught
Greek and Syriac by both Gregory and Masht'ots';[238]
the ascetic practices of Gregory, Aristakēs, Albianos
and king Trdat, and those of Masht'ots';[239] the journey
to Rome undertaken by Trdat and Gregory, and that
of Masht'ots' to Constantinople;[240] Gregory's own
original compositions (in an unspecified tongue), and
those of Masht'ots' in Armenian.[241]

It is particularly noticeable and significant that all
of the parallels and similarities between Koriun and
Agathangelos come in the second half of the latter's
History, i.e., after the *Teaching,* where the narrative
is less coherent than in the earlier part and where
doublets abound. Nor can there be any doubt as to
which Armenian author is copying the other. Koriun's
biography is recognized as being generally reliable,[242]
whereas many of the episodes in question in Agathangelos' *History* are of dubious authenticity, if not entirely legendary. Ever since the parallels were recognized, all scholars have agreed in concluding that
Agathangelos was drawing upon Koriun, and that he
was attempting to credit his own hero with the accom-
plishments of the great Armenian saint who lived a
hundred years later.

Before discussing the motivation of "Agathangelos,"
we may here review the arguments for the dating of
the Armenian redaction *Aa.* It cannot predate the invention of the Armenian script, as in its present form
it is clearly the product of an Armenian writer familiar

with many written sources in Armenian. Nor can it postdate the *History* of Ḷazar, who gives a detailed résumé of its contents. Within narrower limits, it must be later than Koriun (whose biography was written after the death of Masht'ots' in 440); and since it refers to the covenant and backsliding that occurred in the revolt of 450-451, *Aa* cannot have received its final form before then. On the other hand, the translation of *Ag* from the Armenian may date to between 464 and 468, although the evidence is not conclusive.[243] But a date of approximately 460 would fit in well with both the scanty literary evidence and the historical situation of Armenia at the time.

Since the division of Armenia in 387 between Theodosius I and Shapur, Greater Armenia had been under Iranian suzerainty.[224] The Arsacid monarchy had been abolished in 427, and Armenian society had no centralizing force, or even symbol, to counteract the centrifugal and self-seeking interests of the noble houses, which had been and were to remain notoriously factious. Their lack of common ground, and even common interest, became painfully obvious in the reign of Yazdgerd II when this Sasanian king made ever greater efforts to bring all the Christian states on the northern borders of his empire under closer control. And conformity implied not merely the payment of taxes and rendering of military service, but also the acceptance of Zoroastrianism, the state religion. As pressure tightened around Greater Armenia, some conformed, some fled to Byzantine Western Armenia, but others decided to resist by force of arms. The party of resistance was able to persuade Vardan Mamikonian, who by hereditary right occupied the position of High Constable *(sparapet),* to lead their forces. But the moral authority behind the whole movement and the only unifying factor was the church in the person of the Armenian patriarch. It is an exaggeration to claim that the Armenian people rallied behind their spiritual leader, but it is true that no other figure in Armenia stood for national considerations over private or family considerations to the same extent as the patriarch.[245]

The leaders of the Armenian church naturally had their own conception of the grounds on which resistance to Sasanian pressure was not only justified but imperative. They saw the struggle as a religious crusade against the forces of impiety. And the Armenian historians—who were all clerics with a religious training—write about these events from the same point of view, none more eloquently than Ełishē, who ends his *History*: "This memorial has been written about him (i.e., the apostate villain Vasak of Siunik') as a reproach for his sins, so that everyone who hears this may know, may cast anathemas on him, and may not become a companion of his deeds."

Agathangelos was writing in the years after this revolt[246]—which though unsuccessful on the field had induced the Sasanian government to soften its hand —and he brought to his work the ideas and purposes of his own time. He wrote about the conversion of Armenia in terms that made it appear as if the entire nation had been converted and baptised within a week. He emphasized the independence and international importance of the monarchy. And he especially stressed the role of Gregory, not only as founder of the first church in Ashtishat, but as the apostle to the entire country, and even to lands beyond the Armenian borders, working hand in hand with the Armenian

king. It was Gregory who established hundreds of
bishoprics, founded schools, and set the standards of
Christian piety and asceticism. There is no hint in
Agathangelos that the conversion of Armenia was not
complete by the end of the fourth century, though he
does admit the existence of backsliders in time of
trouble.[247]

As we have seen, Agathangelos had a ready model
for his description of Gregory's activity, but his ul-
timate purpose was not merely anachronistic glorifi-
cation of his hero. Far more than the monk Masht'ots',
who had no official position, or even the patriarch
Sahak who supported and joined in Masht'ots' efforts,
Gregory was to be depicted as the model of the patriarchs who had come to play the major role in both
ecclesiastical and political affairs. The *History* of
Agathangelos was designed as an authoritive description of the work and teaching of the first Armenian
patriarch, the hero of the Armenian nation, which
would justify and enhance the authority of the fifth-
century patriarchs over *all* Armenians on both sides
of the Byzantine-Sasanian frontier.

This tendentious attitude to historical writing should
not surprise us. It is widely found in Armenian historians, who often wrote to give a glorious and pres-
tigious background to a princely family that had recently risen to prominence and needed a pedigree.
But more basically, this attitude to the past is but
another facet of the general desire for legitimacy found
in ecclesiastical and secular circles alike. Other Armenian writers stressed the antiquity of Christianity
in Armenia and so described the legendary visit to
Armenia of Thaddaeus; and later on, when the claim
to an apostolic foundation had become the hallmark

of a respectable patriarchate, the apostle Bartholomew was introduced as an even closer link to Christ. In the secular field the notorious claims of the Bagratuni family to descent from king David and of the Mamikonian family to an imperial Chinese origin may suffice as examples.[248]

But Agathangelos is not interested in the antiquity of Christianity in Armenia; rather he is concerned with the establishment of an organized hierarchy and with the mutual role of church and state as reflected in the co-operation of Trdat and Gregory. His *History* reflects the preoccupation of the Armenian patriarchs in the middle and later fifth century with the extension of their authority over the whole country, now that the see had moved from Ashtishat to Eastern Armenia, and with the justification of their activity in secular affairs, now that the monarchy was no more and the church was left as the sole focus and instrument of national solidarity.

One final question remains. In view of the existence of various witnesses to traditions not found in *Aa,* i.e. the various Greek, Arabic and Karshuni texts of the V recensions, is there any other evidence for a (lost) Armenian redaction of the Gregory story? That *Vg/o* are translations from an Armenian text has been clearly established;[249] *Var/a* derive from the Greek, and *Vk* is even further removed. The theory of a series of recensions of the History of Gregory was proposed by Marr in 1905; and though his particular arguments have now been discounted, Ter Levondyan with his discovery of *Var* has reopened the question.[250] First we may review the evidence in early Armenian literature.

The only two writers who claim the authority of "Agathangelos" for information not found in *Aa* are Moses Khorenats'i and Zenob of Glak. The latter's *History of Tarawn* is a late and tendentious work, dependent on Moses among other sources, and may be discounted here. But in view of the persistent tendency of scholars in Soviet Armenia to date Moses to the fifth century, a brief review of his references to "Agathangelos" is in order. On six occasions he refers to that author, although he does include in his *History* much information about Gregory not attributed to Agathangelos but to an anonymous source.

II 67. a résumé of *Aa* §18-32.

II 74. "The wonderful old man" is the authority for the story of Gregory's conception at the grave of Thaddaeus. The story is also found in *Vk* 8, but not elsewhere in the *V* recensions.

"Agathangelos informs you of the rest of the story," i.e. of Gregory's escape after the Armenians had put Anak's family to death.

II 79. "Agathangelos informs you of whatever deeds were done in his (Diocletian's) time." This refers to Trdat's relations with Diocletian and the persecution of Rhipsimē and her companions.

II 80. Moses gives details of Gregory's birth, upbringing and marriage that have no reflection in the *V* cycle.

"Honor followed them (the sons of Gregory), as Agathangelos informs you." Cf. *Aa* §859, 862.

II 83. "God removed all the tyrants from before his (Constantine's) face." Cf. *Aa* §868. Silvester appears as the baptizer of Constantine in Moses here and in some MSS of *Aa* §875, following the tradition found in the *Acts of Blessed Silvester* (fifth century); but Moses' mention of Agathangelos does not refer to the whole of this chapter.

II 86.   Nunē sent messengers from Georgia to Gregory and "preached from Klarjk'... to the borders of the Masagetae, as Agathangelos informs you." These are exactly the same confines as were evangelized by Gregory according to *Aa* §842. Moses is here taking liberties with Agathangelos, as the latter took liberties with Koriun.

There are two occasions when Moses does mention episodes unknown to *Aa*; the conception of Gregory at Thaddaeus' grave (II 74) and the summons from Constantine to Trdat (II 89). The former has a parallel in *Vk* [see p. xxviii] and the latter in *Vg/a* [see p. lxxi]. But it is important that in neither case does Moses ascribe these details to "Agathangelos." Moses was writing in the eighth century[251] and was undoubtedly familiar with traditions concerning Gregory that had arisen in preceding centuries. But his *History* offers no support to the supposition that a complete Armenian text differing from the Armenian version as we have it *(Aa)* was circulating in the fifth century.

More difficult to explain are two references in Faustos and Łazar. In his *Letter,* Łazar refers to insults and persecutions inflicted on other churchmen before his own time who are mentioned in the *History of the Martyr Gregory,* namely Nersēs and Sahak. But neither of these Armenian patriarchs, who lived long after Gregory's death, are mentioned in any of the recensions of Agathangelos. Łazar seems to have in mind some history of the Armenian church, a document which may have existed in the archives of Ejmi-

atsin where he was a monk.[252] Faustos, on the other
hand, begins his *History* with a reference to the account, written by others, of the events from the
preaching of the apostle and martyr Thaddaeus to
the death of Gregory and of Trdat, and he frequently
stresses the role of Thaddaeus who brought Christianity to Armenia from Syria.[253]

In can hardly be a coincidence that *Vk,* a translation of a Syriac text, is the only witness to the Gregory cycle (at least, of those so far discovered) that
introduces Thaddaeus. Ter Levondyan is undoubtedly
correct in assuming that Faustos and *Vk* reflect the
Southern strain in Armenian Christianity, the influence from Syria which is reflected in many other
ways.[254] But this is the only evidence to link Thaddaeus with a *Life of Gregory,* a link which may have
been made in a Syriac document (also known to Faustos) rather than an Armenian one.

Ter Levondyan carries his argument a stage further
by supposing that this (lost) Armenian recension was
gradually forgotten as the Greek strain in Armenian
Christianity came to predominate after the Council
of Ephesus (431) and the suppression of "Nestorian"
influences. By the latter expression the followers of
Theodore of Mopsuestia are intended. The circulation
of Theodore's books in Armenia after Ephesus did
indeed elicit protests from the Greeks.[255] But whatever the fate of the "Nestorians," Syrian influences
persisted for many centuries in the history of Armenian Christianity; and one cannot make a clear-cut division between "earlier," that is pro-Syrian, and "later,"
that is, pro-Greek, trends in the Armenian church.
Nor, in fact, was there ever an "official" attitude towards Greeks or Syrians that carried all the Armenian

clergy along with it—witness the numerous schisms when reunion with the Greeks was forced,[256] and the varied fate of Julianist ideas from Syria.[257]

These questions lead us beyond the scope of the present work. Here we have been concerned with the literary motifs of a fifth-century Armenian writer known as "Agathangelos," who was responsible for the only surviving Armenian version of Gregory's life and works and the conversion of Armenia. This redaction is closely associated with the holy site of Ejmiatsin in northeastern Armenia. Another tradition links the origin of Christianity in Armenia to a missionary from Syria. Both traditions reflect different aspects of the historical truth. But the story of the interaction of these traditions and of the later attitude of Armenians to their early Christian past must await another occasion.

Note to the translation

All material in brackets has been added by the translator. Other title headings are translated from the Armenian text (ed. of Tiflis, 1914).

Agathangelos

History of the Armenians

ՅԱՌԱՋԱԲԱՆ

ԱԳԱԹԱՆԳԵՂԵԱՅ ՊԱՏՄՈՒԹԵԱՆ

1 Իղձք բաղձացեալք ցանկալեացն զկամս
նաւելոցն ի նաւահանգիստն հասուցանել՝ խըն-
դութիւն է խաղաղութեամբ. վասն զի ի մէջ ընդոստուցեալ ալեացն որ ընդդէմ դառնան, մրրկա-
ծին օդովքն ի մարտ պատրաստին, ընչաքաղ-
ցիցն և օգտաձարաւեացն ժամ եղեալ բազմաց,
միարան սանձեալ թիակօքն գերիվարս տախտա-
կագործացն բեռնակալ երկաթագործածն՝ գմի-
մեանս քաջալերելով, կասկած երկիւղի սրտիւք
ի կապոյտ դաշտին ձիարձակ լինին, անքայլ գնա-
ցիւք անընթաց ոտիւք թռուցեալ ի վերայ ծովուն մկանանց Ձուրցն ալեացն կուտակելոց. ուր
քարկացայտ ալիքն լեռնաձև կուտակին, մէտ ի
մէտ խոնարհին, լտա աղեգէտն պատմողին մար-
մնաքնար Դաւթեան երգոյն, թէ «Ելանեն լեռ-
նանան, և իջանեն դաշտանան». ուր ուրեմն ապ-
րեալք ի ծփանացն՝ արշաւանս դնեն յիւրաքանչիւր գաւառս. պայս վէպ պատմեն մերձաւոր

THE HISTORY

Prologue

1.   The fervent wish of sailors is the joy of reaching port safely [cf. Ps. 106.30].[1] So in the midst of the surging billows which oppose them with tempestuous winds [cf. Ps. 106.29], the many who are anxious and thirsty for gain join forces and prepare for the struggle; with oars they spur on their steeds that are constructed of wood and iron and held by nails. With mutual encouragement, but anxious fear in their hearts, they race across the azure plain; with motionless step and unmoving feet, they fly over the surface of the sea's piling waves, where the furious billows pile up like a mountain and in turn sink down; as the harpist David sings on the lyre: "They go up and become mountains, and descend and become plains" [Ps. 103.8]. Then finally escaping from troubled water, they race to each one's land. This story they relate to their close

սիրելեաց—զանգս եղելոյ աշխատութեան ուղ-
լոյն ճանապարհաց, զելևէջս տարաբեր անդա-
դարն սահանաց, գրաւական եղեալ զանձինս չա-
հաւորն օգտութեան, և կէտ՝ զմահ մրցանաց յաղթութեան. ընդ մեծանալ վաճառացն փոխանա-
կեն գինքեանս. զի թէպէտ և տեսանիցեն զբբւ-
նութիւն սատակութեան հողմակոծեալ ալեացն
տատանելոյ, որ յերփն երփն զերանգան շրջշըր-
ջեն բատ սատակութեան ծփանացն, դիզադեզ
յեղեղուկ փրփրացեալ գմիմեանց կարգեալ զկնի
տողիցին, և յափնաձիր յալապադիր սահմանա
բարձրացելոցն ընդդէմ՝ հասեալ ի ցամաքակտան
ծիծաղեսցին:

2 Իսկ ի մէջ ընմբռնելոցն խորոցն անդնդոցն
լցեալ խոռոչացեալ խորոջելովն անապետ արաբեալ գործման գուշակեն. զի թէպէտ և գինքեանս
շարժունս տեսանիցեն ի վերայ յաղթ Չուրգն
բազմութեան, սասանելոցն սարսափելոցն, սակայն զկարողեղն առաջի ամեալ ընդ մի՛ս՝ Չանան դիմագրաւեալբ ընդ խռովութիւն անագին
ծովուն, զի թերիս դարձեալբ օգտութեամբ
զգիւտ իւրեանց խնդութեամբ ցուցանիցեն առ
իւրաքանչիւր ընտանիս, և զպարձանս վատա-
կոյն՝ իւրեանց դրացեացն. զի ուր հարկ է զաղ-
քատութեան անուն յանձանց թօթափեալ, և զտա-
ռապեալ ընտանեական թափեալ ի գրաւահարկ
իշխանացն բռնութենէ, և յիւրեանց շահիցն բե-

loved ones: the toilsome course of their journeys, their tossings on the continually agitated waters, the risking of their lives for profit, as they aimed at victory in their struggle against death. To increase their merchandise they risk their lives. For although they may see the great force of the tempestuous and furious waves which in myriad colors are agitated by the ferocious swells and pile up in unstable spray, and which in successive lines rise up against the sandy beaches—yet arriving on dry land they will laugh.[2]

2. Amidst the raging unfathomable depths [cf. Ps. 106.24] that echo with cavernous murmuring, they fearfully await the moment of death. For although they see themselves cast over the vast magnitude of the troubled and terrifying waters, yet looking forward to success they attempt to brave the fearful tumult of the sea, that perchance returning with their gain they may joyfully show to each one's family their profits and to their neighbors the triumphs of their labor. For where necessary they abolish the name of poverty from themselves and relieve their troubled friends from the tyranny of oppressive lords; and from the profits

բելոց հածեալ դպարտս վառանգին՝ ի լծոյ ծառայութեան թագաւորացն ապատացեալ դատար-
կացին։ Եւ լաւութիւն առ ընկերս, և անունն
առատ և բարգաւաճանք առ թշնամիս, և ուրա-
խութիւն առ իւրեանց սիրողս։

3 Վասն այսորիկ ընդ աննահին պատերազմ մարանչին ի մէջ բարձրացելոց Չրեղէն լե-
րանց և ի մէջ խոնարհելոց ծովային ձորոցն,
Չանան գապրուստ անձանց փրկութեան գտանել, գի ի շրջանական շփոթեալ ուռուցիկ փո-
թորկացն բքացելոց դերծանել և յանքոյթ նաւահանգիստն հասանել կարասցեն. գի արդարև
իսկ շատ այնք են, որ ոչ առ ագահութեան
գանձինս ի մահ դնեն, այլ առ չգոյութեան աղ-
քատութեան կարօտութեան յետին տնանկու-
թեան՝ շտապեալք առ վառանգի անկեալք տարակուսանաց վասն գնարկան հածելոյ, թերևս գլխոյ
փրկանս գտանել, ի պարտուց գանձինս թափել
կարասցեն. փոխ իսկ ի պարտուցն ի վերայ առեալ,
թերևս երկկատիկ օգտութեան ելի աղագս գտանել կարասցեն. միանգամայն գպարտառուսն հա-
ձել, և անձանց իսկ միանգամայն օգուտ շահի
աւելագոյն ստանալ։

4 Չի բագումք այն են, որ առ այսպիսի
աղէտս տարակուսանաց ի վաճառականութեան
արուեստս սուայտանօք անկանել յօժարեն։ Իսկ
են բագումք, որ գիւրեանց առատութիւն եղեալ՝

they have brought they settle their onerous debts and free them from the yoke of servitude to kings. And they provide bounty to their friends,[1] a reputation for liberality and prosperity among their enemies, and joy to their loved ones.

3.   Therefore they engage in a terrible struggle amidst the heights of the mountains of water and the deep valleys of the sea; they attempt to find safety and salvation for themselves, in order to escape the surrounding fury of the raging spray of hurricanes and to make harbor safely. For truly many are they who do not put their lives in jeopardy for avarice; but in order to abolish poverty, want and attendant misery they hasten to court danger, to pay their debts or perhaps to find the price of ransom or to free themselves from obligations. In addition to their debts they take additional loans that they may hopefully find a way to double their profit, both satisfying their creditors and gaining for themselves even greater wealth.

4.   For many are they who in similar distress turn to the business of commerce and its attendant afflictions. There are many also who employ their wealth for

աշխարհի օգուտ գործեն, զարդարեալ զԹագա
ւորս ի դիւտ ձանրագին մարգարտին, և զանա
զան ակամբք պատուականօք և կերպասու յե
րանգ երանգս գունոցն։ Նա և զաղքատս մեծա
ցուցանեն՝ զփոքր ինչ ընդ յարգանօք արկեալ,
և զաշխարհ պատկեն նոր և չքնաղ դիւտիւք։ Նո
քա և զկարօտ լցուցանեն մեծամեծ շահիւք
օգտութեամբ։ Նոքա և զփափագելի մարդկան
զպէտսն պատրաստեն։ Նոքա և դարմանեն դան
ձինս բազմաց։ Նոքա և զտունս բժշկաց լցուցա
նեն ազգի ազգի անուշահոտ խնկովք, դեղովք
օգտակարութեան. Նոքա և գանչալի բժշկութեան
արմատող օգտակարութեան բերեալ զպատուրս՝
զպիտողն լցուցանեն։ Նոքա և զարդ քաղաքաց,
նոքա և մեծութիւն գաւառաց։ Նոքա և համա
րակարք երկայն ձանապարհաց։ Նոքա և ուղե
ղնացք աշխարհի։ Նոքա և ձաշակլիչք օտարու
թեան։ Նոքա և դամենեսին խնդացուցանեն։ Նո
քա և ուժ բազմաց, նոքա և կարողութիւն աշ
խարհի։ Նոքա և գմերկս զգեցուցանեն, նոքա և
զքաղցեալս յագեցուցանեն, նոքա և գձարաւիս
արբուցանեն։ Նոքա և մթերեն իսկ զգանձս ըն
չեղաց։

5 Զի Թէպէտ և ի բնութենէ են հարկեալք,
սակայն ուսան առ վշտին հնարաւորութեամբ
գանձինս ապրեցուցանել, և այլոց օգուտ մար
թէն լինել։ Ապա և նոյն իսկ սովորակի իմաս

the profit of their country, adorning kings with valuable pearls, various precious stones, and silks of multifarious hues. Similarly they enrich the poor, selling a little at a good price, and they adorn the land with new and wonderful discoveries. They also fill the needy with their great profits and wealth. They cater for the desires and needs of mankind; they also provide the livelihood of many. They fill the houses of doctors with various sweet-smelling aromas and beneficial herbs, and they also supply the fruits of roots beneficial for healing, filling the needy. They are the adornment of cities and the renown of provinces; they multiply their long journeys as they travel over the world. They are companions abroad and bring merriment to all. They are support to many and strength to the world. They clothe the naked, satisfy the hungry, give drink to the thirsty, and pile up treasures for the rich.

5.   For although they are forced by constraint, yet they learn to save themselves by their acquaintance with distress and they find means to be of help to others. Their habitual wisdom

տութիւնն քաղցրեցաց նոցա. ընդելակի հանա֊
պազորդեալք երթևեկին տարաբերեալ վաճառօքն՝
գվիռքը մասունս յարդել, ի հագարս և ի բիւրս
բազմացուցանելով։ Վասն այսորիկ իսկ ընդ ծագ֊
կացեալ ալիսն բազմութեան համատարած ծո֊
վուն ընդխառնեալք շահատակիցեն, ոչ լրատ ան֊
ձանց կամաց, այլ ըստ վարիչ օդոյն վարելոյ,
քունավարեալք ի վերայ յորձանացն յաճախատա֊
րած լայնացելոցն դանդաչիցեն վասն օգուտն
գոանելոյ. դանձինս ի մէջ մահու և կենաց եղեալ՝
անձամբ դանձինս խորոցն մատնեն, կամ մահու
կամ կենաց, և մի յերկուց գտեալ՝ անձանց հա֊
մարին։

6 Սոյն օրինակ տեսանեմք հարկ վասնդի
հասեալ ստիպեալ գմեզ, առաւել ի հարկէ նա֊
ւեալք ի վերայ իմաստութեան ծովուն. զի ոչ
ոք է ամենևին այն ի մարդկանէ, որ կարող իցէ
գայսպիսի ջան վասատկոց քրոնայից աշխատու֊
թեամբ անձամբ անձին մատուցանել, եթէ ոչ
իշխանութեան հրամանի հասեալ՝ ստիպեալ գայս
առնել տալ տագնապիցէ. և ով այն իցէ կարող,
որ գխորս անդնդոց ծովուն քննել խորոտտիցի.
այլ շահս օգտութեան վաճառացն երկայն ճա֊
նապարհօքն անձանց և եթ կամին մատուցանել։
Սոյն օրինակ և մեք ոչ յանդգնութեամբ տպա֊
յաբար բարուք ինչ ի ներքս անկանել անմտա֊
բար հոսեցաք, այլ ակամայ ընթացեալ ըստ հրա֊

has brought them consolation; they have become accustomed to continuous traveling in their wide-ranging commerce. Valuing even small amounts, they increase them a thousand and myriad-fold. So they venture forth bravely on the wide-spreading expanse of the waves, not following their own inclinations but the direction of the wind, borne along forcibly over the tumultuous expanses in the search for gain. They place themselves between life and death, entrusting themselves to the depths and reckoning to find either death or life, one or the other.

6.   In the same way we see perilous necessity forcing us to set sail over the sea of wisdom.[1] For there is no one among mankind who could approach such labor by the sweat of his own brow, unless the command of some princely power impelled him to undertake it. And who could this be who would presume to scrutinize the unfathomable depths of the sea? Those who undertake long journeys have only the aim of personal profit from commerce. Similarly, we too have not undertaken this rashly or unthinkingly in the manner of youth, but against our will we run

մանացն ի բռնութենէ հարկապահանջ իշխանացն՝
դիմեալ նաւեցաք ի մատենայած ծովուս պատ-
մութեան։

7 Վասն զի ստիպեաց զաղքատիմաստ խա-
նութս մեր հրաման թագաւորաց, և ի մէնջ հարկ
պահանջեալ գանցեալ իրացն եղելոց զիրս մա-
տենանագրել՝ յայտնական պատմութիւնք, որ առ
մեօք գործեցան։ Սակայն մեծ և բազում ջան
եղեալ թողուլ այնոցիկ որ յետ մեր գայցեն՝
զկարգս զրուցաց դարուց ի դարս յիշատակելւ-
զի ոչ եթէ կամօք ինչ յօժարեցաք հաւանել առնել զայս, այլ իբրև ոչ կարի ինչ ընդդէմ մարթացեալ դառնալ արքայատուր հրամանացն, որչափ յուժի կայր՝ մարթացեալ ըստ հրամանացն
պատմեցուք։ Եւ մեր զայս ջան յանձին կալեալ,
անկեալ ի վաճառականութիւն բանից, առեալ
զահ երկիւղի, և տուեալ զզեղեցկագիր յարմա-
րումն պատմութեան։ Վասն զի ի խնդիր եղեալ
և խոյզիւք ի մէջ բերեալ զդարգս դարգս պատ-
մութեան՝ զմարթնալորագն մատենագրութիւն՝
ըստ կարգի պատմութեան, ըստ օրինին, ըստ
ժամանակին, ըստ իրացն եղելոցն, ըստ հրամանացն ի վաճառ մատուցուք։

8 Իսկ գնողորացն առաքինութիւն ա-
տուածատէ սիրողացն մեծութիւն իբրև զմար-
գարիտն պատուական, զբոլորասերն, զլուսա-
լորն, զչքնաղագիւան, որ ոչ ունի զեզութիւն

this course, following the commands and under the pressure of exacting princes.[2] So we have set sail on the sea of history.

7.   For the command of kings has imposed on the poor stores of our intelligence[1] and has demanded tribute from us in the form of historical writing about past events, lucid histories of what has been done in our time. But a great and difficult task has been left to those who will come after us, to recount in order the history of succeeding centuries. For not willingly have we allowed ourselves to be persuaded to do this; but as it is impossible to oppose royal commands, so far as in us lies we shall tell our story according to the command. We have undertaken this task, setting ourselves to the literary trade[2] in fear and trepidation. We offer for sale a well-composed and historical narrative, having submitted the history of men to research and critical investigation, according to the command, in a historical manner, rigorously, chronologically,[3] and accurately.

8.   So we offer (to our patron) the virtue of spiritual events, the glory of the true lovers of God, like the precious pearl, admired by all, shining, incomparable, which has no flaw

բաժանման իւրոյ ճառանչաւոր լուսոյն, այլ լիութեամբ զարդ անձին վայելուչ զթագս թագաւորացն զարդարեցէ։ Եւ կամ ականք պատուականք ի Հնդկային աշխարհէն, որ ի վայելչութիւն զարդու ի խոյր պապկի զարդարիցեն զթա-
գաւորս։ Իսկ արդեօք այս գիմրդ կամ ռրպէս
գտանիցի ումեք վայրապար, եթէ ոչ ի մեծա-
գնաց թանգարացն, որք եւ մեծն աշխատանօք,
երկայնուղոյ ճանապարհաց զթոշակն բաւեցու-
ցին, եւ մեծաջանք եղեալ ի գտանել՝ զթագաւորս
զարդարեցին։ Իսկ սոցա ճաճանչ լուսոյս, գոր
մեր ի վաճառ իջուցեալ, ոչ միայն ի զարդ գէլ-
խոյ թագաւորին բովանդակի առ ի տես այլոցն,
այլ եւ գամենեսեան զարդարէ, գամենեսեան լու-
սաւորէ, գամենեսեան լցուցանէ, ամենեցուն
բաւէ, գամենեսեան մխիթարէ, գամենեսեան
բժշկէ։ Զթագաւորս շեղդագուցանէ ի նմանութիւն արտախոյրն պապկի ի վերջաւորն փողփո-
դելոյ. նա եւ գողքատս լցուցանէ, թօթափէ բարձ-
րացուցանէ յաղբեաց եւ հաւասար իշխանաց կա-
ցուցանէ. նա եւ պակումն աշխարհաց օրհնութեամբ լցուցեալ, պատ բոլորեալ տարւոյ քաղց-
րութեամբ։

9 Նոքա եւ գկարօտս լցուցանեն երկնաւոր
առատութեամբ. Նոքա եւ աշխատութեան կարօ-
տելոցն հանգիստ պատրաստեն. Նոքա դալման
անկարօտ լի ամենայն բարեօք. Նոքա կարեն

to spoil its sparkling light, but perfectly adorns the honorable crowns of kings;—or like precious stones from the land of India, which in splendid array adorn the royal diadems.[1] Indeed, how could anyone find such by chance, save traders in precious goods, who acquire the rewards of their long journeys at great labor, and adorn kings only after extreme efforts at discovery. But their shining light, which we have put on sale, not only suffices for the adornment of the head of a king in the presence of others, but it adorns everyone, gives light to everyone, enriches everyone, pleases everyone, consoles everyone and refreshes everyone; it renders kings majestic like the diadem with interlacing fringes. Similarly it enriches the poor, removing them from their dung-heap and making them equal to princes [cf. I Kings 2.8]. And it also fills nations with blessing, crowning the year with sweetness [cf. Ps. 64.12].

9. They also fill the empty with heavenly plenty; they provide rest for the work-worn and an unfailing remedy full of all blessings. They can give healing without medicines, gums, or roots. They can

տալ բժշկութիւն առանց դեղող ինկից արմատ-
ոտ. նոքա կարեն շինութիւն շնորհել քաղաքաց
մարդասիրութեամբ Տեառն իւրեանց. նոքա կարեն մեծացուցանել գաշխարհ աղօթիւք նաՀատակութեան իւրեանց. նոքա կարեն ցուցանել
զելս երկնաւոր ճանապարհացն առ Աստուած
վերանալոյ. նոքա են ուղղորբ արքայութեանն
ճանապարհացն Աստուծոյ. նոքա են որ շարշա-
րեալք վասն Տեառն իւրեանց մեռան, և ի կենդանութիւն փոխեցան, և դանուն և գոդուտ ալբը-
դող իւրեանց քաջութեան յաշխարհի թողին։ Նոքա կեանք և փրկութիւն այնոցիկ որ մեղօքն
են ապատացեալ. նոքա են մեծութեան գանձ
ծածկեալ յերկրի երկնաւոր արքային. նոքա Հաւատովք իւրեանց ինդացուցանեն և ուրախ առնեն դայնոսիկ, որք յԱստուծոյ մեծացեալ գան-
ձեն. Նոքա գմերկս դգեցուցանեն, և դայնոսիկ,
որք մեղօքն են մերկացեալ ըստ նմանութեանն
Ադամայ՝ լուսաւոր պատմուճանօք դգեցուցանեն. Նոքա և գքաղցեալս յագեցուցանեն, որք
անգիտութեան մեղօքն իցեն սովեալք. Նոքա և
գծարաւիս արբուցանեն առաքինութեան բա-
ժակաւն. Նոքա և գգանձն երկնաւոր յաւելուն
տան այնոցիկ որ առաւելագոյն ունիցին. դի «Որ
ունիցին՝ տացի նմա և յաւելցի»։ և առ ամենեսին բանան դդրունս գՔոյ մարդասիրին Քրիս-
տոսի։ Վասն այսորիկ իսկ սիրեցին գՏէրն իւ-

give prosperity to cities by the benevolence of their Lord. They can enrich the land by the prayers of their endurance. They can show the course of heavenly journeys rising to God: They are the guides of the road to the kingdom of God. They are those who are tortured and die for their God, and gain life, and leave the renown and assistance of the fruits of their bravery to the world. They are life and salvation for those who by sin have become impoverished. They are great hidden treasure of the heavenly ruler's on earth. They by their faith give joy and delight to those whose treasure God has increased. They clothe the naked; and those who through sin have become naked in the likeness of Adam, they dress in garments of light. They satisfy the hungry, who are in want through their sins of ignorance. They give drink to the thirsty from the cup of virtue. They increase heavenly treasure for those who have it in abundance. For "he who has, to him will it be given and increased" [cf. Matt. 13.12; 25.29; Mk. 4.25; Lk. 8.18]. And to everyone they open the gates of the compassion of the loving Christ. Therefore they loved their Lord

բեանց, և սիրեցան ի նմանէ, և բարեխոսու֊
թեամբն լյուցանեն գամենայն կարօտս։

10 Այսպիսի մարգարիտ ոչ միայն ողւոց,
այլ և մարմնոց զարդ և պայծառութիւն է. չի֊
նութիւն աշխարհի՝ յԱստուծոյ նոյա բարեխո֊
սութեամբ է չնորհեալ. զի գութ ատուածու֊
թեանն ի նոսա իջեալ՝ ողորմութիւն և քաւու֊
թիւն չնորհէ աշխարհի. զի վասն այտորիկ իսկ
նաևեալք ընդ մէջ մրրկեալ աշխարճակիր մեղացն
վատանգեցան, պատերազմեալք ճգնութեամբ ընդ֊
դէմ ալեացն, ի վերայ խորոցն սաՀեցան, Հա֊
սանել ի նաւաՀանգիստն խաղաղութեան երկնա֊
ւոր նաւապետօքն։ Մատուցին պասակ պարծանաց
լուսաւոր թագաւորին, գերծեալք ի բքոյ ամբա֊
րըշշտութեան, Հասեալք ի քաղաքն, պատրաս֊
տեալք անանց ուրախութեան և աղցեալք մար֊
գարտովն պատուականաւ, և Հոգևոր լուսոյ ա֊
կամբք պասկեալք. որք և վաճառեցին գկեանս
իւրեանց մատնելեացն ի տաջանս, և մեծացան
յանանցն մեծութիւն, որք և բարձեալ ունին գչի֊
նութիւն աշխարհի կանգուն, անսվթար, անշարժ,
Հաստատեալ ի նաւս Հաւատոց իւրեանց։

11 Իսկ այսպիսի վաճառաց ո՛յր ուրուք ար֊
դեօք գի՞նչ գին բաւիցէ. այո՛ այո՛, և կարի քա՜ջ.
միայն յօժարութիւն կամաց սրտին՝ սիրով մա֊
տուցանել գլսելիս, Հաւատովք ձգտեալ գականչ՛
ամման պատգամաց, և անդէն ի կամս սրտին Հա֊

and were loved by Him, and by their intercession they fill all the needy.

10.   Such a pearl is the adornment and boast not merely of the soul but also of the body. Prosperity has been granted to the world by God through their intercession. For the compassion of the Godhead has descended upon them and grants to the world mercy and propitiation. On this account they set sail through the dangerous storm of the world's sins,[1] battling at great risk the waves and skimming over the deeps to reach the port of the heavenly navigator's[2] peace. They offered a crown of honor to the king of light; when they reached the city they were freed from the spray of impiety and were prepared for unending joy and adorned with the precious pearl and crowned with the gems of spiritual light—they who sold their lives to those who inflicted them with torment. They were elevated to eternal grandeur, they set the prosperity of the world upright, inviolable, immovable, establishing it firmly on the ships of their faith.

11.   For such reward what price would ever suffice? Yes, what indeed? Only a ready willing heart, lovingly offering its attention, in faith extending its ears as a ready receptacle for (God's) words; then, complementing the willing heart,

սեալ դեղեցկագոյն իբրև զպատուական մարգա֊
րիտս ծանրագին ընդ յոճարութեանն զարդ ա֊
կանչաց՝ գինդ եղեալ կախեցի. միայն զզլուխդ
խոնարհեցօ, և անդէն հոգևորական պսակն ի վե֊
րայ զլխոյդ դնի, և առաւել քան զականս պա֊
տուականս գարդարեցց զքեզ։ Միայն յոճարեաց
ի կոչունս արքայականս, և անդէն քաղցրու֊
թեան անուշութիւն խորտկացն ի քիմս քո պա֊
րաբեցի. միայն ծարաւի լեր սիրոյն, և անդէն
ազբիւր կենդանութեան գերաշտութիւն ծարա֊
ւոյն պաքելոյն յագեցուցէ զքեզ. միայն լուա՛
զքեզ յաղոտս, և անդէն անԹառամ և լուսաւոր
զգեստուն առաւելագոյն ես քան դանուշահոտ
շուշան ծաղիկն զքեզ զգեցուցանէ։

12 Արդ Ջան յանձին կալեալ մատնել ի
պատմագիր մատենից խորութիւն, ցուցանել
այնոցիկ, ոյք իմաստութեամբ կամիցին ունկըն֊
դիր լինել օգտակար պատմութեանս։ Արդ՝ հրա֊
ման հասեալ առ իս ոմՌ Ագաթանգեղոս, որ ի
քաղաքէ ի մեծն Հռովմայ, և վարժեալ հայրենի
արուեստիւ, Հոոմայերէն և Յունարէն ուսեալ
դպրութիւն, և ոչ կարի ինչ անտեղեակ լեալ
ծեռնարկութեան նշանագրաց. և ի վերայ այս֊
ցիկ հասեալ ի դուռն Արշակունւոյ, յամա քաջի
և առաքինւոյն, ուժեղ և պատերագմող Տրդա֊
տայ, որ քան դամենայն նախնիան քաջ եղեալ՝
դանցոյց արութեամբք, որ ընպշամարա սկայա֊

it will hang as beautiful earrings like the precious pearl of great price. Only bow your head, and then the spiritual crown will be placed on your head and will adorn you more than would precious gems. Only incline to the royal summons, and then sweet savors will delight your palate. Only be thirsty for love, and then a spring of life will satisfy your arid thirst. Only wash yourself of dirt, and then the immortal and luminous garment will clothe you more splendidly than the sweet-smelling lily.

12.   So I have attempted to penetrate to the core of these historical writings, to reveal their profundity to those who may wish to attend in wisdom to the profitable history. Now a command came to me, one Agathangelos[1] from the great city of Rome, trained in the art of the ancients, proficient in Latin and Greek and not unskilled in literary composition. Thus we came to the Arsacid[2] court in the reign of the brave, virtuous, mighty and heroic Trdat, who has surpassed all his ancestors in valor and who

գոր քաջութիւնս գործեաց ի մարտս պատերազ
մաց։ Ոչ զիւր ինչ քաջութիւն՝ սուտ հրամայեաց
մեզ վիպասանել, և ոչ դքմազարդ բանից ինչ
առասպելս աւելի քան գարժանն ընթանալ. այլ
իբր որ եղեալք վան յեղանակաց յեղափոխ ժա
մանակաց, մարտամբռիս պատերազմաց, սուրա
կոխ բազմահեղ արեանց կոտորածոյ, անհուն գո
րաց շփոթելոց, գերութեան աշխարհաց, աւե
րածոյ գաւառաց, քանդելոյ քաղաքաց, մատնե
լոյ աւանաց, հարկանելոյ բազմութեան մարդ
կան վան քաջութեան քինախնդիր վրիժուց։

13 Արդ՝ հասեալ առ իս հրաման ի մեծ
արքայէն Տրդատայ՝ կարգել ինձ ի ձեռնարկու
թենէ նշանագիր ժամանակագրացն՝ պատմել նախ
գհայրենեցացն գործս քաջութեան քաջին Աոսրո
վու, և որ ինչ գործք գործեալք քաջութեան
մարտից պատերազմացն, ընդ շրշշրշումն ա
ւուրթեանն փոխելոյ ընդ կոյս հարկանելոյ, և
ազգաց խռովելոյ. և կամ վան մածուանն քա
ջին Աոսրովու, թէ ուստի և կամ գիարդ և կամ
որպէս, և կամ գինչ անցք անցին. և կամ վան
հորամոյն քաջութեանն Տրդատայ, և որ ինչ գործ
գործեաց յամս յաւուրս իւրոց ժամանակաց. և
կամ վան սիրելեաց վկայիցն Աստուծոյ, թէ
որպէս և կամ գիարդ եկեալ, իբրև լուսաւորք
ծագեցին, փարատել գմէգ խաւարի ի Հայաս
տան աշխարհէս. կամ որպէս գանձինս իւրեանց

has done deeds in battle worthy of champions and giants. He ordered us to narrate, not a falsified account of his own brave deeds, nor unworthily to elaborate capricious fables, but what really occurred in various times, warlike battles, the slaughter of men with great bloodshed, the clash of vast armies, the subjection of lands, the plundering of provinces, the razing of cities, the capture of towns, the struggle of many men for renown or vindictive revenge.

13. So the order came to me from the great king Trdat to compose a narrative from literary historical sources:[1] first, the valiant deeds of his father the brave Khosrov, and whatever valorous acts were performed in battle when his kingdom was in confusion and flux; and then the death of the valorous Khosrov, whence, why, how and what took place; and then the bravery of Trdat equal to his father's,[2] and whatever deeds he accomplished in his own time; and then about God's beloved martyrs, how and why they came, who arose like luminaries to scatter the mist of darkness from this land of Armenia; then how they gave up their lives

փոխանակեցին ընդ Աստուծոյ ճշմարտութեանն.
և կամ որպէս զԹացեալ Աստուծոյ՝ այդ արաք
Հայոց աշխարհիս, ի ձեռն առ միոջ եցոյց դղքան-
չելիս մեծամեծս, որ համբերութեամբ բազում
և աղդի աղդի փորձութեանց և կապանաւոր վշշ-
տաց մենակրիւ մենամարտիկ երկպատական
բռնութեան յԱրտաշատ քաղաքի վասն Քրիստոսի
յաղթութեամբ տարեալ, որ դվկայ աննւն ժա-
ռանգեալ, որ ի մահ հասեալ մտեալ, և կամօքն
Աստուծոյ այսրէն դարձեալ՝ ի վերակացութիւն
դառնայր յերկիրս Հայոց: Սա մտեալ ի դրունս
մահու՝ դարձեալ անտի կամօքն Աստուծոյ, վարդապետութեանն Քրիստոսի պատգամաւոր գտեալ,
յետ Աստուծոյ աքանչելագործ պատուհասին մար-
դապիրութեան: Իսկ բարեացապարտն Տրդատ
յանկարձակամ՝ կենացն ասպճական ցանկալի
ամենեցուն լինէր, որ աշխարհածնունդ հայրենեացն որդի գտանէր շնորհօքն Աստուծոյ, և յաւիտենական կենացն մերձաւոր լինէր:

14 Եւ արդ՝ քանդի ըստ օրինակի գրելոցս
առ ի մէնջ՝ ոչ եթէ ի նին համբաւուց տեղեկա-
ցեալք մատենագրել դայս կարդաւ, այլ որոց
մեղէն իսկ եղեալ ականատես կերպարանաց և
առընԹերակաց հոգևորական գործոցն, և լւսա-
ւոր շնորհապատում վարդապետութեանն, ըստ
աւետարանական հրամանացն, և կամ որպէս
լուսաւոր վարդապետութիւնն դեր ի վերոյ ամե-

for God's truth; how God had mercy and visited this land of Armenia, and showed great miracles through one man, who endured many and various torments and afflictions in prison, as in his solitary struggle he triumphed for Christ over a double tyranny in the city of Artashat,[3] who acquired the title of martyr, who came as far as death yet by God's will returned from there and was raised up again to life in this land of Armenia. He entered the gates of death [cf. Ps. 106.18] but returned by the will of God; he became the messenger of Christ's teaching, after God's miraculous and merciful punishment. Then how the meritorious Trdat accepted unhoped for salvation and became dear to all, becoming by the grace of God the son of his reborn native land and heir[4] to eternal life.

14. So since we intend to set out this account properly, we have not composed our book by taking our information from ancient reports but after seeing with our own eyes the persons involved and the accompanying spiritual deeds and the illuminating and graceful teaching which followed the precepts of the gospel.[1] (We shall tell) how this illuminating teaching was honored above all else

Նեցուն շնորհօքն Աստուծոյ յարգեցաւ։ Զոր
աւետալ թագաւորին՝ դամենեսեան աստուածակարգ լծոյն հնազանդեցուցանէր. մանաւանդ թէ
ոչ նա, այլ կամք մեծագոյին Քրիստոսի։ Եւ
կամ որպէս գմեհեանան ի ձեռս տուեալ՝ կործանեալ աւերեցին, և սուրբ հիմունք եկեղեցեաց
կանգնէին. կամ որպէս գնոյն ինքն աշխարհի
հովիւ կացուցեալ՝ վայելէին ի նորուն վարդապետութեանն. և կամ որպէս դարձաւ Տրդատ
անդրէն յաշխարհն Յունաց յամս աստուածատէրն
Կոստանդեայ, թագաւորի կացելոյ Յունաց և
Հոռոմայեցլոց աշխարհին, և կամ որպէս ուխտ
եդեալ, հաստատեալ գնա յաստուածապաշտութիւն՝
դարձեալ լինէր անտի մեծաւ պարգևօք և բազում փառօք, և կամ որպէս զբազում տեղիս՝
Աստուծոյ նուիրեալ Տրդատ մատուցանէր։ Զայս
ամենայն մի ըստ միոջէ ոճով պատմեցցուք,
Վարդապետութեամբ սրբոյն, որ արժանի եղև ի
մեծ յեպիսկոպոսական աթոռն հասանել, և գհայ-
րապետական անուն ժառանգեաց, մեծամարան
առաքինութեամբ, թէ ուստի, յորոց կամ ո՞ ոք
էր, կամ յորմէ ազգէ, որ զայս արժանի եղև
գործել աստուածատուր շնորհօքն տուելովք։

15 Արդ՝ ելից ի մտաց երիվարն, և յարմա-
րեցից գասպարէգն հանճարոյ. ուղղեցից գնպա-
տակն խորհրդոյ, և Թափ տաց ուժի բազկօքս և
ձգեցից ի կորովս գրչի մատանցս, և լեգուաւ ս

by the grace of God. This the king accepted, and he subjected everyone to the divine yoke—or rather not he but the will of the all-powerful Christ. And how they undertook the destruction of the pagan temples and the holy foundations of churches were established. How they appointed the same man as shepherd of the land and enjoyed his teaching. And how Trdat went back to the land of the Greeks in the reign of the pious Constantine, the established king of the empire of Greeks and Romans. And how he made a covenant and strengthened him in piety and then returned with great gifts and much honor. And how Trdat dedicated to God many places. All this we shall relate in detailed succession, with the *Teaching*[2] of the saint who was made worthy of ascending the great episcopal throne and who inherited the patriarchal title[3] as the champion of virtue—whence, from what descent, from what family and who was he who became worthy to do this by divine-given grace.

15. So I shall mount the steed of the mind[1] and follow the course of understanding. I shall aim at the goal of thought and spur on by the strength of my arm and draw upon the force of the scribe's finger. With my tongue

գխորհուրդս յուզեցից, և շրթունքս ի շարժել իմաստունս կարասցեն, և կարգել հաստատական, յեղեղուկ ճոլովել գանիւ պատմութեան բանիցս, զի կամակարագոյնս նաւիցեմք գալեօք ժամանակագրական ծովուս. պատմել յազգ յայլ ժողովրդին ստացելոյ, որք օրհնեսցեն գտէր, որք յետ այսր անցեալ ժամանակաց գալոցն իցեն, որք հարցեալ գհայրենական մատեանն՝ պատմեսցի նոցա, և գձրագիր կարգեալ՝ և ատասցի նոցա։

16 Ընթերցեալ գԹորգոմայ ազգիս, գճայաստան աշխարհիս գատուածապարգև աւետեացն աւետարանին քարոզելոյ բանին կենաց, թէ որպէս կամ գիմարդ ընկալման, և որպիսի արամբ, կամ ՛ի ոք ուսաեք, որ գայս նորոգատուր գառաքելաբար շնորհս յանձին ցուցանելով այնպիսի աստուածեղէն շնորհօք երևեցաւ։ Եւ վասն նորին լուսաւոր վարդապետութեանն և հրեշատակրօն վարուցն առաքինութեան և կարգացն, ագնուական համբերութեանգն շնորհալից մեծագօր նախատակին, որ և խոստովանող Քրիստոսի գտեալ և վկայ ճշմարտութեան. և կամ որպէս յայնմ հետէ շինութիւն և խաղաղութիւն, լիութիւն և պողաբերութիւն և բժշկութիւն աղօթիւք նորա շնորհեցաւ յԱստուծոյ։ Եւ թէ գիմարդ նորուն աստուածսիրութեամբ և Քրիստոսի գօրութեամբ նմա տուելով՝ անկան փշրեցան ունայ-

I shall provoke thoughts, and my lips will be able to enunciate wise sayings. I shall keep a steady course and turn the rotating wheel of my historical narrative, so that we may happily navigate the waves of this chronological sea;[2] that it may be told to future generations of this people, who are to come after these times have passed, and who will bless the Lord [cf. Ps. 101.19]. They will inquire in their ancestral books and it will be narrated to them, and (they will inquire) in the ordered accounts and it will be told them [cf. Deut. 32.7].

16.   They will read about the preaching of the divine gospel of the word of life to this race of Tʻorgom,[1] this land of Armenia. How and why they received it, by what man, and who and whence he was who showed in himself this newly-given apostolic grace, and appeared by such divine grace; and concerning his illuminating teaching and the virtue and order of his angelic life, the honorable endurance of this grace-filled and mighty champion, who was a confessor of Christ and a martyr to truth. And how, after this, prosperity and peace, plenty,[2] fruitfulness and healing through his prayers were granted by God. And how by his love for God and the power of Christ given him, the cults of inanity fell and were crushed,

նութեան պաշտամունքն, և ատուածպաշտու֊
թիւն տարածեցաւ ընդ ամենայն երկիրս Հայոց։
Եւ կամ որպէս շինեցան եկեղեցիք ի Հայաս֊
տան աշխարհիս, և քակեցան ունայնութեան
պաշտամունքն, այն որ ի սովորական մոլորու֊
թենէ նախնեացն՝ ընդվայրակոշկոծ, գրթախա֊
դաց քարանցն և փայտից լիմարութիւնքն էին,
և ուրուապաշտ թմբրութիւնքն անզգայութեանց.
իբրև աբբեալք անմտութեամբքն, պակուցեալք
շռայլութեամբն մեղաց, դիւցախելառ մրրովն
գնային ի մէջ ծովացեալ մեղացն չարութեան։
Որ կամօքն Քրիստոսի քարող գտեալ արդարու֊
սոյց՝ ամենեցուն Հայաստան աշխարհիս, չկա֊
պել ընդ գարշապարս մեղաց ի ծովանման յաշ֊
խարհիս յայսմիկ։ Այլ ի հոզմախաղաղ յանքոյթ
նաւահանգիստն հասեալ ատուածաձորն շինու֊
թեան, կենաց մշանջենականաց անդ պատրաս֊
տեաց օթևանս նոցա։

17 Իսկ իմ անցեալ սանեալ շրջեալ ի վե֊
րայ յորձանախոր, լայնանիստ, յարածոծ, ան֊
դընդապլոյո, սարսատեր, անհանգիստ, արշա֊
լասոյր, օդավար, Չրակուռտակ յուզակ ալեացն,
սրավարացն մոլեգնելոյն, ձդտեալ ի կղզիս քա֊
դաքացն և յաշխարհս հեռաքնակս, գտեալ լցեալ
մեծաթեռն խատաքերուՆս, ինչ ինչ պատուական
և արգոյ, ի գարդ և յօգուտ՝ եկեալ հասուցաք
ի կայս հանգստեան ձերոյ օգտութեան. փութա֊

and true piety spread through the whole of this land of Armenia. And how churches were built in Armenia, and the cults of inanity were broken, which through the habitual error of our ancestors had been foolish forms of uselessly worked and beguiling stone and wood, idolatrous fancies of insensibility. They were as if drunk in folly [cf. Prov. 4.17] and stupified by the glamour of sin, and like lees in their demonic frenzy they sank down in the sea of wickedness of sin.[3] But he by the will of Christ became a preacher teaching justice to all in this land of Armenia, lest they be stuck in the footsteps of sin in this world which resembles the sea. But when he entered the calm unruffled harbor of God the Father's tranquility, he there prepared for them lodgings of eternal life.

17. But I have skimmed over the deeply billowing waves, the extensive oceans that are ever swelling, and like a vortex swirl as they are restlessly driven by the wind and piled up to agitated and furious heights. After reaching islands, cities and distant lands, finding heavy argosies filled with treasure, and numerous valuables and wealth for decoration and profit, I have brought them to the sure repose of your profit.

ցեալ բացցուք դթանգարական վաճառս խան-
թից. վաճառեցցուք լսելեաց զգիւտս աշխատութեան մերոյ, առնուլ դունկնդրութիւն և տալ
զպատմութիւն։ Մանաւանդ վասն քոյոյդ նրա-
մանի, քան՛ զ արանց Տրդատ արքայ Հայոց մեծաց, բերեալ դշան վաճառին աշխարհի շինու-
թիւն՛ քեզ ի դանձ յաւելցուք ի մերոյ ծովա-
վատտակ նաւատեացս։

Let us hasten to open the treasures of these stores. Let us sell to the audience the results of our labor, win their attention and offer our story.[1] Especially on account of your command, noblest of men,[2] Trdat, king of Greater Armenia, we shall bring as the gain of our commerce the prosperity of the country, and we shall increase your treasure through the labor of our seagoing voyages.[3]

ԱԳԱԹԱՆԳԵՂԵԱՅ ՊԱՏՄՈՒԹԻՒՆ

ՎԱՐՔ ԵՒ ՊԱՏՄՈՒԹԻՒՆ ՍՐԲՈՅՆ ԳՐԻԳՈՐԻ

18   Ընդ նուագել ժամանակաց Թագա
ւորութեանն Պարթևաց, ի բառնալ տերութեանն
յԱրտաւանայ որդւոյ Վաղարշու, ի սպանանել զնա
Արտաշրի որդւոյ Սասանայ,—որ էր նախարար
ոմն ի Ստահր գաւառէ, որ ելեալ մրքանեաց
զգօրա Պարսից, որք լքին խոտեցին մերժեցին
անարգեցին գտերութիւնն Պարթևաց, և հաճե
ցան հաւանութեամբ ընտրել գտերութիւնն Ար
տաշրի որդւոյ Սասանայ,—արդ իբրև յետ մա
հուն հասանելոյ գուժիս այսորիկ առ Խոսրով
Թագաւորն Հայոց,—որ էր երկրորդ տերութեանն
Պարսից, զի որ Հայոց Թագաւոր էր՝նա էր երկ
լորդ Պարսից տերութեանն,—արդ՝ թէպէտ և
վաղու լուեալ գրոթն՝ ոչ ինչ ժամանեաց հասա
նել յամբովկ գործոյն պատերազմի իրացն պատ
րաստութեան։ Յետ այսորիկ դարձեալ լինէր յի
րացն եղելոց մեծաւ տրտմութեամբ, զի ոչ եհաս
ինչ նմա գործել գործ. ի մեծ ի տրտմութենէն
և յիրացն վճարելոյ դարձեալ անցեալ եկեալ լի
նէր յաշխարհ իւր։

THE LIFE AND HISTORY OF SAINT GREGORY

[Chapter 1. The wars of Khosrov against
              Sasanian Iran; his murder and
              the occupation of Armenia]

18.   The period of the Parthian kingdom came to an
end when sovereignty was taken away from Artavan
son of Vaḷarsh on his murder by Artashir son of Sasan.[1]
The latter was a prince from the province of Stahr[2]
who had come and united the forces of the Persians;
they then abandoned and rejected and disdained the
sovereignty of the Parthians and happily chose the
sovereignty of Artashir son of Sasan. So after the sad
news of his death reached Khosrov king of the Armenians—who was second in the kingdom of the Persians,
for whoever was king of Armenia had second rank in
the Persian kingdom[3]—although he was quickly informed of the sad news, he had no time to complete
preparations for war. Then he returned in great sadness at the course of events, for he had been unable
to accomplish anything. And he returned to his own
country greatly distressed.[4]

19 Արդ՝ ի միւս ևս ի գլուխս տարւոյն սկսանէր Խոսրով Թագաւորն Հայոց գունդ կազմել և զօր բովանդակել, գումարել զզօրս Աղուանից և Վրաց, և բանալ զդրունս Ալանաց և զՃորայ պահակին, հանել զզօրս Հոնաց, ասպատակ դնել ի կողմանս Պարսից, արշաւել ի կողմանս Ասորեստանի, մինչև ի դրունս Տիսբոնի։ Աւար առեալ զերկիրն ամենայն՝ յապականութիւն դարձուցանէր գշինանիստ քաղաքացն և աւանացն ցանկալեաց. զշէն երկիրն ամենայն թափուր և աւերակ թողոյր։ Չնչել ի միջոյ ի բաց կորուսանել, խլել քակել, հիմն ի վեր Ճանայր առնել, համարէր բառնալ զօրէնս տերութեանն Պարսից։ Ուխտ եղեալ մրանգամայն՝ վրէժ խնդրել մե-ծաւ քինութեամբ զանկանեն իւրեանց ի տե-րութենէն. սպառ սպուռ Ճանայր գվրէժ խնդրել, մեծաւ քինու նախանձաբեկ լինելով. մեծամեծ վքայր՝ ի բագմութիւն զօրացն ապաստան եղեալ, և ի քաշութիւն զօրացն յուսացեալ։ Վաղվա-ղակի ի Թիկունս հասանէին մեծաւ բագմու-թեամբ ժիր և քաջ առն և ձիոյ և բուռն կազ-մութեամբ Աղուանք, Լփինք և Ճիղպք, Կասպք և այլ ևս որ ի ամին կողմանց, զի գվրէժ արեանն Արտաւան խնդրեսցեն։

20 Զի Թէպէտ և էր ինքն ի մեծի տերու-թեան վասն բնութեան եղբայրութեան ագ-գատոհմին, զի հնագանդեցան և ի ծառայութիւն

19.   But at the start of the next year Khosrov king of Armenia began to raise forces and assemble an army. He gathered the armies of the Albanians[1] and the Georgians,[2] opened the gates of the Alans[3] and the stronghold of the Chor;[4] he brought through the army of the Huns[5] in order to attack Persian territory and invade Asorestan[6] as far as the gates of Ctesiphon. He ravaged the whole country, ruining the populous cities and properous towns. He left all the inhabited land devasted and plundered. He attempted to eradicate, destroy completely, extirpate, and overthrow the Persian kingdom and aimed at abolishing its civilization. At the same time he made an oath to seek vengeance with great rancor for their (the Parthians')[7] loss of sovereignty; ruthlessly he attempted to exact thorough vengeance [cf. I Macc. 9.42]. He was greatly puffed up [cf. II Macc. 9.4], trusting in the number of his forces and hoping in the valor of his army. There quickly arrived in support great numbers of strong and brave cavalry detachments, Albanians, Lp'ink',[8] Chilpk',[9] Kaspk'[10] and others from those regions, in order to seek vengeance for the blood of Artavan.

20.   For because of[1] his family relationship to that dynasty he was very grieved that they (the Persians) had submitted

մտին համբարձելոյ Թագաւորութեան Սոսանրա֊
ցւոյն, և ընդ նմին միամտեցան. զի Թէպէտ և
էր Խոսրովու և դեսպան արաբեալ, զի իւրեանց
տումայինքն ի Թիկունս եկեացեն և նոցա ընդ֊
դէմ կայցեն ընդ նորա Թագաւորութեանն, ան֊
տի սմա ձեռն տուեալ ի կողմանց Քուշանաց, և
յայնմ մարզէ և յիւրեանց ի բուն աշխարհէն և
ի քաշ ազգաց և ի մարտիկ գօրացն զի ի Թի֊
կունս հասցեն. սակայն տունմքն և ազգապետքն
և նախարարքն և նահապետքն Պարթևաց ոչ լի֊
նէին ունկնդիր. զի միամտեալ և հաւանեալ և
նուաճեալ էին ի տէրութիւնն Արտաշրի, քան
ընդ տէրութիւն իւրեանց ազգատոհմին և եղ֊
բայրութեանն։

21 Սակայն առեալ Խոսրովու զբազմութիւն
գօրաց իւրոց, և որ ուստէք ուստէք եկեալ հա֊
սեալ էին ի Թիկունս օգնականութեան նիզակա֊
կիցք գործոյն պատերազմի։ Իսկ իբրև եկես
Թագաւորն Պարսից պայն ամբոխ բազմութեան
գնդի, զի մեծաւ ուժով դիմեալ եկեալ հասեալ
էին ի վերայ նորա՝ էլ և նա ընդ առաջ նոցա ի
պատրաստութիւն պատերազմի։ Բայց սակայն
ոչ կարաց ունել զդէմ նորա, փախստեայ լինէր
առաջի նոցա. գնետ մտեալ կոտորէին գամենայն
գօրսն Պարսից, և դաշտագն և ճանապարհացն
ցիր դիաթաւալ կացուցանէին և չարախտավատ
վատնէին և աննարին հարուածս ի վերայ հա֊

and accepted the rule of the Stahrian and had united with him. And although Khosrov sent an embassy so that his relatives would support him and with his own kingdom oppose (the Persians), and that there would also come to his aid (contingents) from the regions of the Kushans,[2] brave and valiant armies both from that area and their own land, yet his relatives, the chiefs and princes and leaders of the Parthians paid no heed. For they had attached themselves in obedience and subjection to the rule of Artashir, rather than to the rule of their relative and brother.

21. Nonetheless Khosrov took the vast numbers of his army, plus whatever lancers had arrived to support him in the war. And when the Persian king saw the great size of this force bearing down upon him with enormous strength, he advanced against them in battle array. However, he was unable to resist them, and fled before them. In pursuit they cut down the whole army of the Persians, scattering corpses over the plains and roads, and inflicting cruel and unbearable suffering.

սուցանէին։ Եւ թագաւորն Հայոց դառնայր ի
մեծ կոտորածէն մեծաւ յաղթութեամբ և բա֊
զում աւարաւ և ցնծալից ուրախութեամբ ի կող֊
մանն Հայոց յԱյրարատ գաւառ, ի Վաղարշա֊
պատ քաղաք, մեծաւ ուրախութեամբ և բարի
անուամբ և բազում աւարաւ։

22 Ապա հրամման տայր ընդ կողմանս կող֊
մանս դեսպանս արձակել, հրովարտակս առնել,
յեօթն բագինս մեհենիցն ուխտաւոր լինել պատ֊
կերաց կռոց դիցն պաշտամանն։ Սպիտակ ցլուք
և սպիտակ նոխազօք, սպիտակ ձիովք և սպիտակ
ջորւովք, ոսկեղէն և արծաթեղէն գարդուք, ի
վերջաւորս փողփողեալս, նշանակապ պալարա֊
կապ մետաքսիւքն և ոսկովք պատակօք և արձաթի
գռտարանօք, յանօթս ջանկալիս ակամբք պա֊
տուականօք, ոսկով և արձաթով, ի հանդերձս
պայծառս և ի գարդս գեղեցիկս, զիւր ազգին
Արշակունեաց գհայրենեացն պաշտամանց տե֊
ղիսն մեծարէր։ Նա և հինգերորդ եւս հանէր յա֊
մենայն մեծամեծ աւարացն աձելոց, և մե֊
ծամեծ պարգեւս քրմացն շնորհէր։ Իսկ զորացն
որ զիւրեանն էին՝ եօթն պարգեւս և արձակեաց
յիւրմէ։

23 Իսկ ի գալուստ ամէն միւսոյ գոր
բազում կուտէր յոյժ, գումարտակ առնէր, զնոյն
գոր կոչէր, և եւս բազում քան զնոյն ասպատակ
սփռեալ զկողմամբքն Ասորեստանի. մանաւանդ

After this great slaughter the Armenian king joyfully and victoriously returned with much booty to the land of Armenia, to the province of Ayrarat and the city of Valarshapat,[1] with great rejoicing, with good renown, and with much plunder.

22.   Then he commanded that ambassadors be sent throughout the land, that edicts be composed and vows be made to the seven altars of the temples of the cult of the images of the idols.[1] He honored the sites of the ancestral worship of his Arsacid family[2] with white oxen and white rams, white horses and white mules, gold and silver ornaments, fringed and tasseled silks, gold crowns and silver altars,[3] beautiful vases with precious gems, gold and silver, shining raiment and lovely decoration.[4] Similarly he took a fifth of all the enormous booty he had collected and gave splendid gifts to the priests. And to the soldiers who had followed him he gave gifts before dismissing them.

23.   Then at the beginning of the next year he gathered a great army [cf. I Macc. 4.27-8], summoning the same troops; and with even more than these, because the forces of the Tachiks[1] had come to his support, he spread his invasion over the regions of Asorestan.

գի և զօրք Տաձկաց ի Թիկունս եկեալ էին. աւար
առեալ զերկիրն ամենայն՝ քաշութեամբ դառնային յիւրաքանչիւր տեղիս։ Եւ ամս մետասան
ստէպ ստէպ զայս օրինակ աւար առեալ՝ աւե-
րէին զամենայն երկիր սահմանացն, որ ընդ
Պարսից Թագաւորութեամբն և ընդ իշխանու-
թեամբն էր։

24 Իսկ իբրև զայս ամենայն չարիս ետես
Թագաւորն Պարսից, որ եկին հասին ի վերայ
նորա՝ նեղեցաւ, տառապեցաւ, տագնապեցաւ,
տարակուսեցաւ, վարանէր յանձն իւր. առ ինքն
կոչէր զամենայն Թագաւորս և գիւսակալս և
գնախարարս և զզօրավարս և զպետս և զիշխանս
իւրոյ տերութեանն. ի խորհուրդ մտանէին. ադա-
չէր զամենեսեան՝ հնարս ինչ մարթել խնդրել
գտանել. ադդի ադդի պարդես խոստանայր. Թերևս ոք միայն գացի, ասէ, որ գվրիժուց հա-
տուցումն խնդրել մարթասցէ. յերկրորդական
դահ իւրոյ տերութեանն մատուցանել խոստանայր, Թէ միայն նախանձու մեծի ձեռն արկեալ
հատուսցէ ոք. բայց միայն աթոռովս ես ի վեր
եղեց քան դնա, եԹէ կարի յանարդադ ոք իցէ
կամ ի պատուականաց. ադդի ադդի պատիւս և
պարդես և վարձուց հատուցմունս շնորհել խոս-
տանայր։

25 Արդ՝ ոմն ի միջոյ խորհրդեանն գլխաւոր
նահապետ էր Պարթևաց տերութեանն, որոյ

They plundered the whole land and victoriously returned to their own countries. And for ten[2] years they
made continual incursions in this manner, plundering
all the lands which were under the suzerainty and
authority of the Persians.

24. But when the Persian king saw all these misfortunes which had befallen him, he was oppressed, afflicted, tormented, and plunged into hesitation and
doubt [cf. I Macc. 3.29-31]. He summoned all the kings
and governors and princes and generals and leaders
and nobles of his kingdom[1] and they held council. He
begged them all to seek and find a solution, promising
all sorts of rewards. "If only someone be found," he
said, "who will be able to exact vengeance," he promised to elevate him to second rank in his kingdom, if
only someone would undertake to avenge him. "Only
I and my throne will be above him, be he of very
humble or of honorable origin." He promised to grant
him all sorts of honors and gifts and rewards.

25. Now there was in the council a leading chief-
tain of the Parthian kingdom,

անուն էր Անակ. յուռն կացեալ, ի մէջ անցեալ՝
յիւրմէ ազգէն իբրև ի Թշնամւոյ վերայ խոստանայր վրէժ խնդրել։

26 Ասել սկսաւ ընդ նմա և ասէ. «Եթէ միայն պայդ նախանձ խնդրեսցես միամտութեամբ՝
զքնութիւնն պարթևական, գձեր սեփական Պալհաւն ի ձեզ դարձուցից, և քեզ Թագ եդեալ փա-
ռաւորեցից, և երկելի և փառաւոր ի Թագաւո-
րութեանս իմում արարից, և երկրորդ ինձ կո-
չեցից»։

27 Պատասխանի ետ Պարթևն և ասէ. «Զմ-
ցոլդդ ագգի իմոյ կեցուսցես դու. այլ ես և եդ-
բայր իմ հարազատ այսօր հրաժարիմք ի քէն»։

28 Յայնմ ժամանակի հանդերձեաւ կազ-
մեցաւ Պարթևն եղբարբն իւրով հանդերձ, ըն-
տանեօք կանամբք և որդլովք և ամենայն աղ-
խիւ իւրեանց. չու արարեալ յուղի անկեալ, դէտ
ակն կալեալ ճանապարհացն՝ ելեալ երթայր հա-
տուածի պատճառաւ ի կողմանս Հայոց, իբրև
թէ ապատամբեալ իցէ յարքային Պարսից։ Եկեալ
յանդիման եղև Թագաւորին Խոսրովւլ յՈւտի
գաւառի, ի Խաղխաղ քաղաքի, ի ձմերոցս արքայութեանն Հայոց։

29 Իբրև եւես Թագաւորն Հայոց՝ ընծա-
ցեալ եւ ընդ առաջ նորա և մեծաւ խնդութեամբ
ընկալաւ գնա. մանաւանդ իբրև կեղձաւորու-
թեամբ և դաւով սկսաւ խոսել ընդ նմա և գիւ-

called Anak.[1] He rose, and coming forward promised to exact vengeance from his own king as if from an enemy.

26.   He (the king) began to address him and said: "If only you settle this account loyally, I shall return to you (your) native[1] Parthian (land), your own Pahlav, and I shall honor you with a crown and make you famous and honored in my kingdom and call you second to me."

27.   The Parthian replied and said: "Do you succor the rest of my family, while my brother and I today take our leave from you."

28.   Then the Parthian made his preparations and arrangements, and with his brother, his household, their wives and children, and all his retinue, took his departure; he journeyed, spying out the roads, and came to Armenia on the pretext of emigrating, as if he had revolted against the Persian king. He came before king Khosrov in the province of Uti, at the city of Khalkhal, in the winter quarters of the Armenian king.[1]

29.   When the Armenian king saw him, he gladly went to meet him and welcomed him with great joy— especially when he began to speak deceitfully and fradulently with him and

բոյ գալոյն հաւատարմութիւն ցուցանել։ «Վասն
այնորիկ եկի ես առ քեզ, ասէ, զի հասարակ
գնատարակաց վրէժ խնդրել մարթասցուք։

30 Արդ՝ իբրև եռեա Թագաւորն գայրն, զի
գիմեալ եկեալ էր առ նա ամենայն ընտանեօքն
հանդերձ, և մտերմութեամբ հաւատաց ի նա.
յայնժամ տայր նմա պատիւ ըստ օրինաց Թագաւորաց, և հանէր նստուցանէր զնա յերկրորդ
աթոռ Թագաւորութեանն. և դամենայն ժամանակս ձմերայնոյն ուրախութեամբ զաւուրս ցեր-
տաշունչ հոզմաշունչ սառնամանեացն անցուցա-
նէին։

31 Իսկ իբրև եկին հասին աւուրք Չերոտ
հարաւահողմն գարուն դղանցն բանալոյ՝ համ-
բարձաւ Թագաւորն ի կողմանցն յայնցանէ. եկին
իջին յԱյրարատ գաւառ, ի Վաղարշապատ քաղաք.
և մինչդեռ ուրախութեամբ հանգուցեալ էին, ի
մից արկեալ Թագաւորին՝ գումարտակ առնէր՝
անդրէն արշաւել ի կողմանս Պարսից։

32 Իբրև գայն լսէր Պարթևն՝ գերդուին ու-
խս յիշէր որ ընդ Պարսից արքային ուխտեալ
էր։ Նա և գխոստումնունն յիշէր գպարգևացն, և ի
բուն աշխարհն փափագէր որ Պալհաւն կոչէր, և
վատ խորհուրդ ի մից արկանէր. առնոյր զԹագաւորն մեկուսի նա և եղբայր իւր հարագատ՝
իբրև ի պատճառս ինչ գբօսանաց, իբրև խորհուրդ ինչ խորհել ընդ նմա. և գտւեբան պո-

to show the sincerity of his coming: "I came to you," he said, "in order that we might be able to make common cause in seeking vengeance."

30. Now when the king saw this man arriving with all his household, he sincerely believed in him. Then he honored him in royal fashion and established him in the second rank of his kingdom. And for the whole duration of that winter they passed the days of chilling winds and ice in cheerfulness.

31. But when the warmer days of the southerly winds arrived to open the gates of spring, the king departed from those regions. They descended to the province of Ayrarat, to the city of Vaḷarshapat. And while they happily relaxed there the king decided to gather an army and invade Persian territory [cf. I Macc. 4.35].

32. When the Parthian heard of this he remembered the oath of his compact with the Persian king. He also remembered the promises of rewards, and had a yearning for his own country which was called Pahlav.[1] So he decided on an evil plan. He and his brother took the king aside, as if for recreation and to consult with him [cf. II Macc. 4.46].

դովատիկս թերաքամեալս ունէին. յանկարծ յե-
դակարծումն ժամանակի գէնս վերացուցեալ՝
զթագաւորն դիաթաւալ կացուցեալ յերկիր կոր-
ծանէին։ Անդուստ ուստեռն իրազգած եղեալ
իրացն որ եղեն՝ գոյժ աղաղակի ամբոխին թանձ-
րանայր. մինչ այս մինչ այն՝ նոքա հեծեալ յիւրաքանչիւր երիվարս փախստական լինէին։

33 Իսկ իբրև գայն գիտացին նախարարք
հայակոյտ գօրացն՝ գունդ գունդ հատանէին,
գկնի լինէին. ումանք ընդ ցամաքն աճապարեալ,
հասանէլ ի խելս կամրջացն առ դրունս Արտաշատ քաղաքի։ Զի դեռևս Երասխ յարուցեալ գայր
լի դարիւ և դարիւ, սառնաճալ, Չրակուտակ,
ճիւնասոյգ, ճիւնախադաղ բազմութեամբն յալուրս իւրոյ պղտորութեանն։ Կէսքն անցեալ ընդ
կամուրջն Վաղարշապատ քաղաքի, գօր և կա-
մուրջ Մեծամօրի կոչեն՝ աճապարէին հասանել
յառաջ մի ի խելս կամրջին Արտաշատու. Ի
կիրճս ճանապարհացն արգելին գնոսա, ի մէջ
արարեալ գնոսա՝ ի Տափերական կամրջացն գե-
տավէժ առնէին գնոսա։ Եւ ինքեանք անդրէն
դարձեալ՝ վայլէք, ճչովք և ողբովք, և ամենայն
երկիրն ժողովեալ գթագաւորն աշխարէին։

34 Եւ մինչ դեռ չեռմ ոգիքն ի ծոցոյն չէ
էին թափեալ, և շունչ վախճանին չէ էր հա-
սեալ՝ հրաման տայր գազգատոհին սատակել։
Յայնժամ սկսան սատակել և կոտորել. մինչև ոչ

They had half-drawn their steel swords, and suddenly raised their weapons and struck the king dead to the ground. As soon as the news of this event was divulged, the lamentation of the crowd waxed strong; meanwhile they had mounted their horses and had fled.

33.   But when the princes of the Armenian army learned of this they split into groups and made pursuit. Some hastened by land to reach the head of the bridge at the gate of the city of Artashat. For the river Araxes had risen and was flowing full to both banks [cf. Jos. 3.15] with swollen masses of icy water from melting snow at the time of its flooding. The others passed over the bridge of the city of Valarshapat which is called the bridge of *Metsamawr*[1] and hastened to precede them to the head of the bridge of Valarshapat. In a narrow passage of the road they arrested them and from the bridge of *Tap'er*[2] they cast them into the river. They themselves then returned with cries of woe and lamentation, and the whole land gathered to mourn the king.

34.   Before the warm spirit had left his breast and he had breathed his last [cf. II Macc. 7.14], (the king) ordered the extermination of their family. Then they began to massacre and slaughter them.

Թողին յերիտասարդաց միՆչև յայՆ՝ որ բնաւ
գաշ և գձախ ոչ գիտէր։ Նաև գիզական տանձիս
մաշէին ի սուր սուսերի իւրեանց։ Բայց միայն
երկուս մանկունս փոքրկունս յորդւոցն Պարթև-
լին պրծեալ ոմն ապեցուցանէր ի ձեռն դայե-
կաց ուրումն. գմին ի կողմանս Պարսից, և գմին
ի կողմանս Յունաց առեալ փախչէին։

35   Եւ եղև իբրև լուաւ դայս ամենայն
Թագաւորն Պարսից՝ գուարձանայր, գուարթա-
Նայր, տօն մեծ ուրախութեան առնէր գօրն գայն,
և բազում ուխտ առուշանացն կատարէր։ Զո-
րաժողով լինէր, խաղայր գնայր, ասպատակ սրփ-
ռէր գկողմամբք Հայաստան աշխարհին. գխոսուն
և գանասուն, գձեր և գոդայ, գերիտասարդ և
գմանուկ առ հասարակ խաղացուցանէր ի գե-
րութիւն։

36 ԱՆդ ոմն պրծեալ ապեցուցանէր ի հինէ
անտի որդւոցն Խոսրովու Թագաւորին Հայոց՝
մանկիկ մի փոքրիկ, անուն Տրդատ. առեալ դայեկացն փախուցեալ ի դուռն կայսեր ի կողմանս
Յունաց։ Եւ գերկիրն Հայոց այնուհետև՝ եղեալ
ապքային Պարսից յիւր անուն գտեղդան անուա-
Նէր. և գգօրան Յունաց փախստական արարեալ
հալածական տանէին միՆչև ի սահմանս Յունաց։
Վիճն փոսացուցեալ՝ սահմանս հատատէին, և
տեղլոյն անուն եղեալ Դրունս Փոսից, առ տե-
դեաւն որում Սոյդն կոչէին։ Եւ գայլ մարդիկ

From among the children they left not even those too young to know their right hand from their left [cf. Jonah 4.11]. Likewise they exterminated the female side of the family by the sword. Only two[1] infant sons of the Parthian did someone[2] save and rescue through their nurses, who took them and fled,[3] the one to Persian territory and the other to Greek territory.

35. And it happened that when the Persian king heard of all this he greatly rejoiced, and he made that day a great and joyous festival and carried out many vows to the fire-temples.[1] He assembled an army and hastened to make incursions throughout the regions of Armenia. He brought into captivity men and beasts, old men and infants, youths and children alike.

36. But there escaped from the raid one of the sons of Khosrov king of Armenia, an infant[1] called Trdat; his tutors took him and fled to the emperor's court in Greek territory.[2] Then the Persian king came and imposed his own name on Armenia, and set the Greek army to flight, pursuing it to the borders of Greece. He had ditches dug to fix the frontier, and called the place "the gate of ditches" instead of the earlier title "the Pit."[3]

երկրին խաղացոյց, և դաշխարհն յինքն գրա֊
ւեաց։

37 Արդ՝ երթեալ, անեալ և ուսեալ Տրդա֊
տէս առ կոմսի ումեմն Լիկիանէս անուն կոչե֊
ցելոյ։ Իսկ որդի Պարթևին որ ի կողմանս Յու֊
նաց դաղթեաց՝ անանէր և ուսանէր ի Կեսարիայ
Կապադովկացւոց քաղաքին․ և մերձաւորեալ գնա
անոյց դայեկօք երկիւղիւն Քրիստոսի. և ուսեալ
նա գբրիստոսական դպրութեան հանգամանս, ըն֊
տանի եղեալ գրոց Աստուծոյ, և մերձեալ յեր֊
կիւղ Տեառն, որոյ անուն ճանաչէր Գրիգորիոս։
Իբրև տեղեկացաւ ի դայեկացն հայրենի գոր֊
ծոցն որ եղեալն էին՝ էլ և գնաց առ Տրդատիոս
բատ հեշտ պաշտամանէ։ Եւ Թաքուցանէր գանձն,
և դայն ինչ ի վեր ոչ հանէր, Թէ ո՛յր, կամ ու֊
տի՛, կամ որպէս, կամ գիՃրդ. գանձն ի ծառա֊
յութիւն առւեալ ի Նագանդութեան պաշտէր
առաշի նորա։

38 Ընդ ժամանակս ընդ այնոսիկ իշխանն
Յունաց ի հայածել կայր գեկեղեցի Աստուծոյ։
Իսկ իբրև գգացեալ Տրդատիոս վասն Գրիգորի,
Թէ Քրիստոսական պաշտամանն հաղորդ է՝ սկը֊
սեալ այնուհետև պատուհասակոծ առնէր գնա,
և ազգի ազգի արհաւիրս արկանէր ի վերայ նո֊
րա. բազում անգամ ի բանդա և ի կապանս.տան֊
ջանօք նեղէր գնա՝ Թողուլ ի բաց լինել նմա
յերկրպագութենէն Քրիստոսի, և ի Նագանդու֊

And he deported the other inhabitants of the land[4] and took possession of the country for himself.

[Chapter 2.   Trdat in exile; his restoration
             to the throne of Armenia]

37.   Now Tiridates[1] was raised and educated in the house of a certain count called Licinius.[2] On the other hand, the son of the Parthian who had taken refuge in Greek territory was brought up and educated in Caesarea, the capital of Cappadocia. And he was brought up by his tutors[3] in the fear of Christ; he received a Christian education, became acquainted with the scriptures of God, and drew near to the fear of the Lord. His name was called Gregory. When he had discovered from his tutors the deeds committed by his father, he went to Tiridates and voluntarily entered his service. But he hid his identity and did not reveal whose (son) he was or whence or how or why (he had come). He gave himself over to his employ and served him obediently.

38.   In those times the ruler of the Greeks was engaged in persecuting the church of God.[1] And when Tiridates discovered that Gregory was a member of the Christian cult, he thenceforth began to castigate him and made all sorts of frightening threats to him. Often he imprisoned and bound him and tormented him, that he might abandon the worship of Christ

թիւն դառնալ նմա դիցն մնոտեաց և պղծութեանն պաշտամանէ

39   Յաւուրս ժամանակացն այնոցիկ գո-
րածողով լինէր իշխանն Գթաց, և բազում գունդս
գորաց ժողովեալ՝ գայր տալ մարտ պատերազմի
ընդ իշխանին Յունաց։ Պատգամ յղէր օրինակաւս այսուիկ, եթէ «Ընդէ՞ր բնաւ ելանեմք
խառնամխի ի պատերազմ՝ սպատել զգօրս մեր,
և վառնդ և տագնապ միանգամայն աշխարհի
հասուցանեմք. ես աւասիկ ախոյեան ելանեմ
քեզ ի մերոց գորաց ասաի, և դու ինձ ի յու-
նականաց այտի. հասցուք եկեցցուք ի մարտի
տեղի. եթէ ես զքեզ յաղթահարեցից՝ Յոյնք ինձ
ննագանդեսցին ի ծառայութիւն. և թէ դու ինձ
յաղթեսցես՝ մեր կեանքս քեզ նուաճեսցին և ննագանդեսցին. և առանց արեան և կոտորածոյ լիցի
չինութիւն կողմանցս երկոցունց»:

40   Եւ իբրև գայն ամենայն լուաւ Թագաւորն Յունաց՝ երկեաւ. քանզի օրինօք կագմու-
թեամբ, գունդ առ գունդ ճակատել ոչ առնուին
յանձն, և ըստ պատգամին պաշպանճի ոչ կարէր
ունել յանձին, քանզի տկար էր յոսկերաց գո-
րութեամբ. սրտաթափի եղեալ գարհուրեցաւ,
քանզի ոչ գիտէր, զինչ տացէ քանիցն պատասխանի:

41   Յայնմ ժամանակի հրաման տայր Թագա-
ւորն՝ հրովարտակս և դեսպանս առնել առ իշ-

and turn to comply with the cult of the vain and impure gods.

39.   At about that time the ruler of the Goths raised
an army and assembled many forces and came to wage
war with the ruler of the Greeks.[1] He sent messages
to this effect: "Why do we come to make indiscrimi-
nate battle, to spread abroad our armies and bring
disaster and tribulation on the country? Behold I come
forth as a champion[2] from my army to challenge you,
and do you (come forth) from the Greeks. Let us come
together in a place of battle. If I vanquish you, the
Greeks will submit to my rule. And if you vanquish
me, our lives will be subject to you and in your hands.
And let both our lands be spared blood and slaughter."

40.   And when the Greek king heard all this he was
afraid, because they[1] did not accept battle in fixed
order, army opposing army.[2] And he was unable to
agree to the proposition, because he was weak in
bodily strength. He was disconcerted and terrified,
because he did not know what reply to give.

41.   Then the king gave a command that decrees and
messages should be sent to

խանս և զօրս զօրութեան իւրոյ, զի ուք և իցեն՝ առ նա հասանիցեն վաղվաղակի։ Յայնմ ժամանակի իշխանք և զօրք և նախարարք առ նա հա-
սանէին վաղվաղակի։ Առեալ և Լիկիանէ զբուն
գունդն որ ընդ իւրով ձեռամբն էր՝ փութայր
հասանէր ի տեղի պատերազմին՝ յանդիման լինել Թագաւորին, և Տրդատս ընդ նմա։

42 Եւ մինչ դեռ գային գունդք գօրացն՝
դեպ եղև նոցա գալ մտանել ի նեղագոյն տեղի
մի, յառուամէջս այգեստանւոյն, ի փողոցամէջս
համբարոցացն, առ դրունս քաղաքին. քանզի
զդրունս քաղաքին աղխեալ էր, զի ժամ էր հասարակ գիշերոյ։ Իբրև ոչ գտաւ խար երիվարաց
զօրուն բազմութեան դարման կերակրոյ մինչև
ի մէջգիշերն՝ հայեցեալ տեսանէին ի գուարա-
փակ քաղաքորմի միջոջ, զի խոտահամբար մթե-
րեալ էր. և ոչ ոք կարաց ձգել գձեռն իւր վասն
որմոյն բարձրութեան։ Յայնժամ Տրդատս եղեալ
և իջեալ՝ հոսէր ընկենոյր բարդս բարդս ի մէջ
զօրացն մինչ ի լրութիւն բաւականի։ Նա և գհամ-
բարապանսն իսկ և բազումս ի շանց յայսկոյս
որմոյն ընկենոյր ի մէջ զօրացն, և ինքն անդրէն
եղեալ իջանէր։

43 Զայն ամենայն ույժ անդութեան տեսեալ Լիկիանէս գարմացաւ։ Իսկ իբրև այգն գա-
ռաւօտն մերկացաւ՝ դրունք քաղաքին բացան, և
զօրքն ամենայն առ հասարակ ի ներքս մտանէին.

the nobles and troops of his command,[1] that where-
ever they might be they were to come to him immediately. Then the nobles and troops and princes hastened to his presence. Licinius also took his own force
that was under his command [cf. III Macc. 1.2] and
hastened to the battlefield to meet the king; and Tiridates was with him.

42.   And while the troops of his force were still on
their way, they happened to enter a narrow place in
a sunken pathway through the vineyard and barns
leading to the gate of the city. Now the gates of the
city were locked, it being midnight. Since no forage[1]
could be found for the horses of the vast army in the
middle of the night, they looked around and saw in a
walled pen a great pile of hay. But no one was able
to lay hand on it because of the height of the wall.
Then Tiridates climbed over and threw back heaps
of it to the troops until there was enough. He also
threw the guards and many donkeys[2] over the wall
among the troops, and he himself then climbed back.

43.   When Licinius saw this great feat of strength[1] he
was amazed. So when the morning dawned and the
gates of the city were opened and all the troops had
entered inside,

և Լիկիանէս յանդիման լինէր Թագաւորին, և ամենայն մեծամեծքն և սպարապետքն և գործա- գլուխքն և իշխանքն։

44 Ապա կաց պատմեաց Թագաւորն իշխա- նացն գամենայն պատգամս Թագաւորին Գթաց։ Յայնժամ խոսէլ սկսաւ Լիկիանէս ընդ արքային և ասէ. «Մի՛ ինչ գարհուրեսցի սիրտ տեառն իմոյ. զի գոյ աստ այր մի ի դրան քում, զի իրքդ այդ նովաւ վճարին։ Տրդատէս անուն նո- րա, ի տոհմէ Թագաւորին Հայոց աշխարհին»։ Եւ կաց պատմեաց դերեկորին զգործս քաջու- թեան նորա։ Յայնժամ հրաման ետ, և ածին գՏրդատիոս յանդիման Թագաւորին. և պատմեաց նմա կարգաւ գամենայն։ Յայնժամ ժամ եառն կազմութեան մարտի՝ առ ի ժամ վաղուի գմի- մեանս տեսանել պատերագմաւ։

45 Իսկ ի միւսում աւուրն ընդ այգն ընդ առաւօտն հրամայեաց արկանել ծիրանիս. և գար- դարեցին գՏրդատիոս ի գարդ կայսերականն, ար- կեալ գնովաւ գնշան Թագաւորութեանն. և ոչ ոք գիտէր վասն նորա. հրաման ել ամենեցուն, թէ ինքն իսկ կայսրն իցէ։ Եւ նորա առեալ գգունդն գօրաց բազմութեան՝ ի ձայն փողոյ տագնապաւ յառաջ մատուցանէր մինչև յանդիման թշնա- մեացն։ Իբրև յանդիման եղեն միմեանց կայսե- րակերպն և Թագաւորն՝ մօրակ ի կուշտս. արա- բեալ երիվարացն ի միմեանս հասանէին. անդ

Licinius went to meet the king, with all the magnates and generals and officers and nobles.

44.   When the king told his nobles all the words of the king of the Goths, then Licinius began to speak with the sovereign and said: "Let my lord's heart not be disturbed. There is here in your court a man by whom this affair can be managed. His name is Tiridates and he is from the family of the king of Armenia." And he told of his deeds of strength the previous night. Then he gave a command and they brought Tiridates before the king, and he told him everything in order. Then they agreed to the duel and arranged that they would meet each other in combat the next morning.

45.   At dawn on the next day he ordered him to be clothed in purple, and they robed Tiridates with imperial garb and put on him the royal emblem. And no one recognized him, so the word went out to everyone that it was the emperor himself. So he left the vast mass of the army and with the sound of the trumpet advanced rapidly [cf. I Macc. 9.12] to meet the enemy. When the false emperor and the king came face to face, they whipped the flanks of their horses and charged each other.

յաղթահարէր կայսերակերպն զԹագաւորն. ձեր-
բակալ արարեալ՝ ածեալ յանդիման առաջի կայսերն կացուցանէր։

46 Յայնժամ մեծացոյց յոյժ Թագաւորն
զՏրդատիոս, և մեծամեծ պարգևս հտ նմա.Թագ
կապեաց ի գլուխս նորա և ծիրանեօք գարդա-
րեալ մեծացոյց զնա, և կայսերակերպն գարդու
շքեղացուցեալ մեծարեաց զնա. և գումարեաց ի
ձեռս նորա գօրս բազումս յօգնականութիւն նմա,
և արձակեաց յիւրական աշխարհն Հայոց։

47 Եւ յետ մարտին յաղթութեան քաջու-
Թեանցն գոր արար՝ դարձեալ լինէր ի կողմանցն
Յունաց Տրդատ արքայ Հայոց մեծաց։ Խաղաց
զնաց Թագաւորն ի կողմանս Հայոց, և եկն եգիտ
անդ գօրս բազումս Պարսից, զի գաշխարհն լին-
քեանս գրաւեալ էին ի ծառայութիւն. զբազումս
կոտորէր, և զբազումս փախստականս արարեալ
ի կողմանս Պարսից արկանէր. և գհայրենեացն
տէրութիւն լինքն նուաճեաց, և գօրացաւ ի վերայ սահմանաց նորա։

48 Յառաջին ամին Տրդատայ արքայու-
Թեանն Հայոց մեծաց, խաղացին եկին հասին
լեկեղեաց գաւառ, ի գեւղն Երիզայ, ի մեհեանն
Անահտական, զի անդ գոհս մատուցանեն. և իբրև
կատարեցին զգործն անարժանութեան՝ իջին բա-
նակեցան առ ափն գետոյն գոր Գայլն կոչեն։

49 Իբրև եկն եմուտ ի խորան անդր և յընթ-

Then the false emperor overthrew the king, and seizing him brought him before the emperor.

46. Then the emperor greatly honored Tiridates and bestowed handsome gifts on him. He crowned his head with a diadem, and decorated him with the purple and the imperial insignia. And he entrusted to him a great army for his support, and sent him to his own land of Armenia.[1]

47. So after his victorious show of strength, Trdat, king of Greater Armenia, returned from Greek territory. The king hastened to Armenia; when he arrived he found there a great army of Persians, because they had subdued the country for themselves. Many he slaughtered and many he threw back in flight to Persia. And he brought under his own sway his ancestral kingdom and ruled over its borders [cf. I Macc. 2.46].[1]

[Chapter 3. Gregory's tortures

*A. Dialogue between Gregory
and Trdat*]

48. In the first year of the reign of Trdat in Greater Armenia, they[1] went to the province of *Ekeḷeats'*[2] to the village of *Erēz,*[3] to the temple of Anahit[4] in order to sacrifice there. And when they had completed this unworthy deed, they went down and encamped on the bank of the river called Gayl.[5]

49. When he had entered his tent and sat down to table,

րիս բազմեցաւ, և իբրև ընդ գինիս մտին՝ հրաման ետ Թագաւորն Գրիգորի, զի պատկ և Թաւ
ոստ ծառող Նուէրա տարցի բազնին Անահտական պատկերին։ Այլ նա ոչ առնոյր յանձն պաշ-
տօնատար լինել դիցն երկրպագութեան։

50 Յայնժամ խոսել սկսաւ Թագաւորն ընդ
Գրիգորի և ասէ. «Այր մի օտարական և անաշ-
խարհիկ՝ եկիր յարեցար ի մեզ, և գիւ՞րդ իշխես
պաշտել զԱստուածն դայն, զոր ես ոչ պաշտեմ»։
Եւ առ այն օր պանել հրամայեաց։ Եւ ի վաղիւ
անդր հրաման ետ, և ածին զԳրիգորիոս առաջի
Թագաւորին։

51 Ասել սկսաւ Թագաւորն ընդ Գրիգորի՝
և ասէ. «Այսչափ ամք են, զի տեսի ես զքեզ,
և յամենայն զօրութենէ քումմէ ծառայեցեր դու
ինձ միամտութեամբ. և ես գոհ էի զվաստակոց
քոց և ունէի ի մտի կեցուցանել զքեզ. ընդէ՞ր
ոչ առնես զկամս իմ»։

52 Ետ պատասխանի Գրիգորիոս և ասէ.
«Հրամայեալ է յԱստուծոյ, զի «Ծառայք հնագանդ լիցին մարմնաւոր տերանց», որպէս օրէն
է, որպէս և դուդ իսկ վկայեցեր ինձ, զի ծա-
ռայեցի քեզ յամենայն զօրութենէ իմմէ։ Այլ
զԱստուծոյ պապտին և զպաշտօն ոչ ումէք վայել է տալ. զի նա միայն է արարիչ երկնից և
հրեշտակաց, որ փառաւորիչք են մեծութեան
նորա, և երկրի և մարդկան, որ ի նմանէ են

and when they had drunk well, the king ordered Gregory to present to the altar of Anahit's statue offerings of crowns and thick branches of trees. But he did not agree to serve the worship of the gods.[1]

50. Then the king began to speak with Gregory and said: "You have come and joined us as a stranger and foreigner.[1] How then are you able to worship that God whom I do not worship?" And he ordered him to be imprisoned for that day. The next morning he commanded and they brought Gregory before the king.

51. The king began to speak with Gregory and said: "It is these many years that I have known you, and you have served me faithfully with all your strength. I have been very satisfied with your labors and I intended to reward[1] you. Why then do you not do my will?"

52. Gregory replied and said: "It is commanded by God that 'servants should be obedient to their bodily lords' [Eph. 6.5], as is right and as you have borne witness to me that I have served you with all my strength. But it is not fitting to pay to any one else the honor and worship due to God. For he alone is the creator of heaven and of the angels, who glorify his majesty, and of earth and of men, who have been fashioned by him

ատեղծեալ. որոց պարտ է պաշտել զնա և առնել
զկամս նորա. և այլ ամենայն որ է ի նոսա, որ
ի ծովու և ի ցամաքի»։

53 Արքայ ասէ. «Գիտաստ՛էբ, զի ապախտ
արարեբ զկաստական դոր ինձն վաստակեցեբ,
որում ես եմ վկայ։ Արդ՝ փոխանակ կենացն
դոր պարտ էբ առնել քեզ՝ յաճախեմ քեզ նե-
դուԹիւնս, և փոխանակ պատուին՝ անարգանս.
և փոխանակ բարձ տալոյ և յառաջ ձգելոյ՝ բանդ
և կապանս, և մահ՛ որ հատանէ զյոյս կենաց
մարդկան, եԹէ ոչ առնուցուս յանձն դիցն պաշտօն մատուցանել, մանաւանդ այսմ մեծի Անահ-
տայ տիկնոջա, որ է փառք ազդիս մերոյ և կեցուցիչ, դոր և Թագաւորբ ամենայն պատուեն,
մանաւանդ Թագաւորն Յունաց. որ է մայր ամենայն զգաստուԹեանց, բարերար ամենայն մարդկան բնուԹեան, և ձնունդ է մեծին արին Արամազդայ»։

54 Ասէ Գրիգորիոս. «Ես քեզ միամու-
Թեամբ վաստակեցի. ինձէն երբեք զիմ վաս-
տակս ապախտ ոչ արարից. զի և գրեալ է յԱստուծոյ, եԹէ «Մառայեսցեն մարմնաւոր տերանց». զի այնմ տեր է հատուցանող բարեաց.
զի ոչ ինչ ակն ի քէն ունելի եԹէ հատուցես
ինձ, այլ յՍբարշէն, որոյ են ստացուածք իւր,
երկելի և անեբկոյԹ արարածք ամենայն։

55 «Այլ վասն որոյ ասեան, Թէ նեղուԹիւն

and whose duty it is to worship him and do his will; (as also should) everything else that is in them, in the sea and on land."[1]

53. The king said: "Know that you have made useless the services which you have rendered me and to which I am witness. Now, instead of the rewards which you should have received, I shall increase affliction upon you; and instead of honor, dishonor; and instead of elevation to high rank, prison and bonds and death which removes all hope of life for men—unless you agree to offer worship to the gods, and especially to this great lady Anahit.[1] She is the glory of our race and our savior; her all kings honor, especially the king of the Greeks. She is mother of all virtues, benefactor of all human nature, and the offspring of the great and noble Aramazd."[2]

54. Gregory said: "I have served you loyally. I myself shall never render vain my services. For it is written by God that 'they should serve their bodily masters' [Eph. 6.5]; because such the Lord recompenses[1] with blessings. For I had no expectation that I would receive compensation from you but from God, whose creation are all creatures visible and invisible.

55. "But as for your saying 'I shall increase affliction

յաճախեմ քեզ փոխանակ կենաց՝ հանելով զիա
յայաց կենաց աՀա յաճախես ինձ դպատրաստեալ
ուրախութիւնն Քրիստոսի. այն որոյ տեզրութիւնն
յաւիտենից է, և արքայութիւնն ոչ անցանէ, և
բարիքն ոչ պակասեն։ Եւ փոխանակ պատուին
որ ասես անարգանս՝ շնորհես ինձ դպատուին
հրեշտակաց, փառաւորչաց Արարչին իւրեանց
ցնծութեամբ։

56 «Եւ որ ասեդ, Թէ փոխանակ բարձ տալոյ և յառաշ ձգելոյ ի բանտ և ի կապանս ար-
կանեմ՝ երանի է ինձ, դի աուիգ յանձան դորինակ
կապանաց Տեառն իմոյ. և ընդ նմին ուրախ եղէց
և ցնծացայց յաւուր դալատեան նորա։ Եւ մեր-
ժելով ի քոց բադմականացդ՝ աՀա արկանես ինձ
բադմականս աու Հօրն Հաւատոյ Աբրահամու, և
ընդ արդարսն ամենայն, որ ուրախ լինելոց են
յարքայութեանն Աստուծոյ։

57 «Եւ որ սպառնաս ինձ մաՀու՝ աՀա խաս-
նես դիս ի գունդն Քրիստոսի, ուր են ամենայն
կոչեցեալքն, Հարքն և արդարք, և մարդարէքն
և աոաքեալքն, մարտիրոսքն և ամենայն ընտ-
րեալքն։

58 «Այլ որ ասեդ, եթէ մաՀուամբ դյոյս
Հատանեմ կենաց՝ որպէս քո յոյսդ Հատեալ է,
և ամենայն ատուածապաշտաց և ատուածա-
սիրաց յոյսն դորացեալ է. Իսկ որ միանդամ են
իբրև դբեղդ, որ պաշտէք դկուոս Համերս և ան-

for you rather than rewards,' by removing me from this life you will merely increase for me the joy of Christ that has been prepared for me [cf. Jn. 14.2-3]; his majesty is eternal, his kingdom passes not away [cf. Dan. 7.27], and his blessings do not fail. And instead of the dishonor which you promise in place of honor, you will grant me the honor of the angels, the joyous praisers of their creator.

56.   "And as for your saying 'instead of elevation to high rank I shall cast you into prison and bonds,' I would be blessed to accept the example of my Lord's bonds. And with him I would be happy and rejoice in the day of his coming. And by depriving me of your company at table, you will merely cast me into the company of Abraham,[1] the father of the faith, and of all the just who will rejoice in the kingdom of God [cf. Matt. 8.11].

57.   "And as for your threatening me with death, you will merely join me to the band of Christ, where are all those called, the fathers and the just, the prophets and the apostles, the martyrs and all the elect.

58.   "You say 'by death I shall cut off hope of life,' just as your own hope is cut off, whereas the hope of all who serve and love God is strengthened. But those who are like you, who worship gods that are mute and

շունչս, ձեռագործս մարդկան՝ արդարև իսկ էք
յուսահատք ի ճշմարիտ կենաց անտի Աստուծոյ։

59 «Այլ զոր դուք կոչէս մեծ Անահիտ տիկնին՝ լեալ իցեն արդեօք մարդիկ օք յայնժամ
երբեմն ժամանակի։ Քանզի դիցապաշտ կախարդութեամբ զմարդիկն որ յայնժամն էին, ցնորբիք կերպս ի կերպս լինելով դիւացն՝ հաւանեցուցին մեհեանս շինել և պատկերս կանգնել և
երկիր պագանել։ Որ ոչ իսկ են, ոչ չար և ոչ
բարի ումեք ինչ կարեն առնել. ոչ պատուել կարեն զպաշտօնեայս իւրեանց, և ոչ անարգել
զթշնամանադիրս իւրեանց. զոր դուքն ցնորեալ
պաշտէք յափշութիւն մտաց ձերոց։ Եւ փոխանակ Աստուծոյ, յորոյ ի բարիոզ վայելէք՝ պաշտէք զդայոտեղէնոդ և զքարեղէնոդ և զոսկեղէնոդ
և զարծաթեղէնոդ, զոր Աստուծոյ կարգեալ է
ի սպաս և ի պէտս և ի փառաւորութիւն մարդկան։

60 «Իսկ ինձ լիցի ամենայն հնազանդութեամբ և ամենայն միամտութեամբ և երկիւղիւ
պաշտել զԱստուած արարիչ և զՈրդին հատիչ
և զՀոգին կազմիչ արարածոց, որ արար գամենային, և եղծանել կարէ, և դարձեալ նորոգէ
ողորմութեամբ իւրով։ Այլ մեր կեանքս չեն յուսահատութեամբ. զի պաշտեմք զկենդանին, որ
կարող է կենդանութիւն տալ մեզ, յորժամ և
կամի. զի թէպէտ և մեռանիմք՝ կենդանի եմք։

lifeless, the work of men's hands [cf. Wis. 14.29; Is. 46.6], truly you are without hope of the true life of God.[1]

59. "But as for the one whom you call the great lady Anahit, there may well have been some such person at some time. For the demons by impious magic and by assuming various deceiving forms persuaded the men who lived at that time to build temples and set up images and worship them. But they do not really exist; they can do neither harm nor good to anyone; they can neither honor their worshippers nor dishonor their opponents. Your mind is deranged if you worship them. Instead of God, in whose blessings you rejoice, you are worshiping objects of wood and stone and gold and silver, which God has established for the service and needs and glory of mankind.[1]

60. "But may I in all obedience [cf. I Tim. 2.11] and all sincerity and fear worship God the creator and the Son the establisher[1] and the Spirit the disposer[2] of all creatures,[3] who made everything and can destroy and renew again by his mercy. Our life is not hopeless, for we worship the living one who can give us life when he wishes [cf. Rom. 4.17]. For although we die, yet we live.

Չի որպէս որդին Աստուծոյ մեռաւ և եկեաց՝ և
մեզ եզոյց օրինակ կենդանութեան յարութեամբն
իւրով. զի որ մեռանիմքս վասն նորա՝ լինելոց
եմք կենդանիք, յորժամ յայտնեցցի Թագաւորութիւն Արաքչին առ արարածս իւր, յորժամ
խնդրեցցէ գվրէժ ամբարշտութեան, անաչառ
դատաստանաւ ստուգութեամբ պահանջեալ յամենեցունց առ հասարակ»:

61 Արքայ ասէ. «Որ ասացերդ, թէ ի քէն
ակն ոչ ունէի և ոչ պիտի իսկ՝ ես գիտեմ զի
մահ խնդրես դու և անդէն ի գերեզմանի գնա-
տուցուՁն քեզ, ուր են իսկ առաշինքն որ մե-
ռանն. վաղվաղակի յղեմ գքեզ՝ ուր կամիսն երթալ: Կամ ՞վ այն Քրիստոսն իցէ. ցՕյց ինձ, զի
գլտտացից. ՞է այն ոք իցէ հատուցանող վատա-
կացն քոց, զոր կոչես դու արարիչ. միԹէ ՞նա ոք
իցէ շահապետ գերեզմանաց, որում դուն ցան-
կաս հասանել, կամ բանդակալ կապանաց քոց
՞նա իցէ արձակիչ:

62 «Եւ ՞ուր իցեն արդեօք անպակաս ուրախութիւնքն զոր ասես, և կամ զՕ՞նչ գալուստն
իցէ, ոչ գիտեմ. կամ զՕ՞նչ հրեշտակք իցեն,
զոր ասես, կամ զՕ՞նչ յոյան ճեր իցէ և մեր
յուսանհատութիւնն. աղէ, դու ասա ինձ դայս
ամենայն մեղմով: Այլ ոչ Թողից քեզ գանարգանս
դիցն զոր Թշնամանեցեր գնոսա. զի ասացեր,
բա՛ս, մարդիկ են, և ի մահկանացու բնութիւն

For just as the Son of God died and rose[4] and by his resurrection showed us the model[5] of life, so we who die for his sake will come alive [cf. I Thess. 5.9] when the kingdom of the creator will be revealed to his creatures, when he will seek vengeance for impiety, demanding it with impartial and rigorous judgment from all alike [cf. II Thess. 1.8-9]."

61.   The king said: "As for your statement 'from you I expected nothing, nor have I need,' I know that you are seeking death and recompense for yourself in the tomb, where are the former men who died. I shall quickly send you where you wish to go. But show me who that Christ may be, that I may know who might be that recompenser [cf. Rom. 2.6; II Tim. 4.8] of your labors, he whom you call Creator. Could he be some ruler of the tombs whom you wish to meet, or is he one who would free you from your imprisoning bonds?[1]

62.   "Where then the unfailing joy of which you spoke might be, or what the coming might be, I know not. Or what the angels are of whom you spoke, or what are your hope and our hopelessness. Come then and kindly explain all this to me. But I shall not absolve you from the opprobrium of the gods whom you have insulted. For you yourself said 'they are men' and you brought them down to mortal nature.

իՉուցեր զնոսա. և աննաքին թշնամանս գոր եղեր
դիցն և կամ մեզ իսկ թագաւորացս. զի ասացեր, ե-
թէ խելագարք են թագաւորք որ պաշտեն զնոսա»:

63 Գրիգորիոս ասէ. «Քրիստոս է որդի Աստուծոյ, յորոյ ի ձեռն արար նա դաշխարհս և
կազմեաց. դատիչ կենդանեաց և մեռելոց, տէր
և հատուցանող բարերարացն բարիս և չարա-
րարացն չարիս միանգամայն:

64 «Նա, որպէս ասացեր իսկ դու, արդարև
շահապետ է գերեզմանաց և պանապան. զի իբրև
մեռաւ նա կամօքն իւրովք և եմուտ ի գերեզ-
ման, որ պանէ գոսկերս ամենայն մարդկան, և
յարութեամբն իւրով եցոյց և յայտնի արար
գյարութիւն մեռելոց. զի ինքն իսկ է յարութիւն և կեանք, և յարուցիչ և նորոգիչ ամենայն մարմնոց. և պանէ զգուշս մարդկան կեն-
դանիս։ Վասն զի նա ինքն է կենդանութիւն, զի
նորոգեցէ զգուշս մարդկան` զգեցեալ նովին
մարմնով. և ապա յայտնի արասցէ ըստ իւրաքանչիւր վատտակոցն գիւրաքանչիւր հատուցմունս. զի նա արձակեսցէ զկապեալս ի տանէ
կապանաց կռապաշտութեան, որ կապեալ են ի
մեղս, և խզեսցէ զզղթայս անօրէնութեան` որ
են իբրև զբեզգ։ Իսկ յայդպիսի կապանաց, զոր
դուդ սպառնաս` սովոր է յայտնել զողորմու-
թեան զշնորհս և փրկել գյուսացեալս իւր։

65 «Եւ անպակաս ուրախութիւնքն այն են,

And the terrible insult which you made to the gods (applies)[1] also to us kings, for you said that the kings who worship them are insane."

63.   Gregory said: "Christ is the Son of God, through whom he made this world and fashioned it [cf. Jn. 1.3]; he is the judge of the living and the dead [cf. II Tim. 4.1], Lord and recompenser of bounty to the bountiful and of evil to the evil [cf. Matt. 16.27; Rom. 2.6; II Tim 4.8].

64.   "He, as you indeed said, is truly the lord and guardian of the tombs. For he died willingly and entered a tomb, which guards the bones of all men; and by his resurrection he demonstrated and revealed the resurrection of the dead. For he himself is resurrection and life [cf. Jn. 11.25], the raiser and renewer of all flesh[1] [cf. I Cor. 15.52; Phil. 3.21], and he keeps the breath of men alive[2] [cf. Acts 17.25]. For he himself is life that he may renew the breath of men, having been clothed in the same flesh.[3] And then he will reveal each one's recompense for each one's labors [cf. Col. 3.24]. For he will bring forth the bound from the house of bondage to idolatry, those who are bound in sin; and he will break the chains of lawlessness (for) those who are like you. But from such bonds as you threaten, he is accustomed to reveal the grace of mercy and to save those who hope in him.

65.   "And the unfailing joy is this,

յորժամ զիւր սիրեցեալն և զկոչեցեալն և գնրա-
վիրեալն և զպատուիրանապանան անմահացուցէ
յիւր աստուածութիւնն, և գմեղաւորն անմահացուցէ ի տանջանան յաւիտենից։ Եւ գղլուսան
այն է, յորժամ դայցէ առնել դայս ամենայն։
Եւ հրեշտակքն այն են, որ սպասաւորքն են նորա մեծութեանն և ատտուածութեանն, մշանջենաւոր աբքայութեանն։

66 «Իսկ մեր յոյսն այժմ ակն կալեալ սպա-
սէ. և ձեր յուսանատութիւն այն է, զի ոչ ճա-
նաչէք զԱրարիչն ձեր, որ պանանչէ ի ձեն
վաան այնորիկ, զի ոչ եէք ի խնդիր տեառն
Արարչին ձերոյ, և ոչ ծանեայք գնա։ Արդարև
իսկ իբրև գձիս եղէք կամ իբրև գշորիս, զի ոչ
գոյ ի նոսա իմաստութիւն, և քան գեզն և գեշ
ես պակասամատգոյն գտայք, զի ոչ ծանեայք
գձեր հատիչն. որ ի ժամանակի իւրում ի սանձ
և ի դանդանաւանդա ճմլեացէ զկզակս ձեր, որ
առ նա դուք ոչ մարթայցէք մերձենալ։

67 «Այլ գոր ատացերն, թէ դիցն թշնամանս
եղիր, գի՞նչ ինչ արդեօք իցէ նոցա այն թշնա-
մանք՝ որ երբեք և պատուելոյն ուրուք գնոսա
ոչ գգան. զի ի ձեռաց մարդկան են ստեղծեալք,
և ի խելացնոր կարծեաց յերագոց իջեն հաս-
տեալք և եղեալք։ Քանզի յանդրիագործ պատկերաց առաջին մարդկանն հրապուրեցան գործել դայն, յոր և անդէն իսկ մոլորեցան, կու-

when he will make immortal and raise to his own divinity his beloved and called and invited[1] and those
who kept the commandments; whereas the sinners he
will make immortal in their eternal torments. And
the coming is this, when he will come to do all this.[2]
And the angels are those who are the servants of his
majesty and divinity and of the eternal kingdom.[3]

66. "Our hope expects and awaits this. And your
hopelessness is this, that you do not recognize your
Creator who makes this demand on you, nor do you
seek the Lord your creator nor have you recognized
him. Truly you have become like horses or mules,
since there is no wisdom in you. And you have been
found to be less intelligent than an ox or donkey since
you have not recognized your fashioner, who in his
own time will fit your cheeks into a bridle and bit,
you who will not be able to approach him [cf. Ps. 31.9;
Is. 1.3].

67. "But as for your saying 'you have insulted the
gods,' what could this insult mean to them who have
no sensation even of anyone's honoring them? For
they have been fashioned by the hands of men, and
have been created by aberrant and dreaming thoughts.
For (men) were enticed by the sculpted images of
earlier men to work these, in which indeed they have
gone astray,

րացեալք ի լուսոյ Արարչին։ Իսկ որ գնոսայն
պաշտեն՝ յիրաւի են իբրև զանասունս. զի «Թե-
րան է նոցա, և ոչ խօսին. աչս ունին, և ոչ տե-
սանեն. ականջս ունին, և ոչ լսեն. ունչս ունին,
և ոչ հոտոտին. ձեռս ունին, և ոչ շօշափեն. ոտս
ունին, և ոչ գնան, և ոչ գոյ շունչ ի բերանս
նոցա։ Նման նոցա եղիցին որք արարին զնոսա,
և ամենեքեան որք յուսացեալ են ի նոսա»։

68   Ասել սկաւ Թագաւորն և ասէ. «Քա-
նի՞ցս անգամ տուեալ է քեզ խրատ և պատուէր,
զի մի երկրորդեսցես առաջի իմ գնատուածծ
բանիցդ առասպելեաց, զոր յօդեալ և ունեալդ ես,
զոր ոչդ վայել է քեզ խօսել. վասն որոյ ես
խնայեցի ի քեզ՝ իբրև ի վատակաւոր, զի եկես-
ցես ի կարգ ուղղութեան՝ պաշտել գդիան։ Զորոց
դու առեալ զնոցա պատին՝ ումպէտ կարդաս
արարիչ. և որ են իսկ ճշմարտիւ արարիչ՝ Թշնա-
մանես, և գմեծն Անահիտ, որով կեայ և գկենդա-
նութիւն կրէ երկիրս Հայոց. և ընդ նմին և գմեծ
և գաբին Արամագդ, գարարիչն երկնի և երկրի. ընդ
նմին և գայլ աստուածան կոչեցեր անշունչս և
անմռունչս. և ի մեզ ես ձգտեցար դնել Թշնամանս,
համարձակեցար ասել ձիս և Չորիս. Եւ քանգի
գամենայն Թշնամանս յանձախեցեր, մինչ իշխեցեր իս մեզ ասել անասունս՝ արդ ես արկից
գքեզ ի տանջանս և եղից դանդանաւանդ ի կգակա
քո. զի գիտացես եթէ ի սին բանից քոց, զոր

deprived of the creator's light. But those who worship the same are truly like animals. For 'they have a mouth and do not speak. They have eyes and see not. They have hands and feel not. They have feet and move not. There is no breath in their mouths. Those who made them will become like them, and also all those who hope in them [Ps. 113.13-16; 134.16-18].'"

68.   The king began to speak and said: "How often have I given you warning and commands not to repeat in my presence these compositions of fabulous stories which you have pieced together and learned up and which it is unfitting for you to tell? So I have spared you, because of your services, in order that you might come to the right path and worship the gods, whose honor you have slighted by calling someone else creator. And those who are truly creator you insult, calling lifeless and mute the great Anahit,[1] who gives life and fertility to our land of Armenia, and with her the great and noble Aramazd,[2] the creator of heaven and earth, and with him the other gods. And you have gone so far as to insult us as well, daring to call us horses and mules. Because you have multiplied all these insults—even to calling us animals—now I shall cast you into torments and I shall place a bridle on your cheeks, that you may know that for your futile words, which

յաճախեցեր առաջի իմ ասել՝ վաղվաղակի եղեն
քեզ արդիւնքն։ Եւ այս, ասէ, մեծ է ինձ, որ
խոսեցայս ընդ քեզ և մեծարանս եղի քեզ, և
դու եաուր ինձ պատասխանի իբրև ընկերի»։

69 Եւ եռ կապել գնա ձեռս յետս, և արկանել գայլ ի բերան նորա. և եռ կախել շա-
ռաշեղս ադի ի վերայ ոդին նորա, և տալ գե-
լոցս կրծից նորա, և արկանել առասանս ի կապս
կրծից գելարանացն, կապել և համբառնալ ի
բարձրաւանդակ տանիս ապարանից որմոյն մեն-
քենայիւք։ Եւ կայր պրկեալ կապեալ այնպէս
գաւուրս եօթն։ Եւ յետ եօթն աւուրն եռ հրաման, և լուծին գնա ի չարաչար և ի դառն կա-
պանացն, և ածին կացուցին առաջի նորա։

70 Սկսաւ հարցանել գնա, թէ «Զիարդ կա-
րացեր ժուժալ, տոկալ, տնել, մնալ և հասանել
մինչև ցայսօր։ Եւ կամ առէր դշապ, թէ արդարև իբրև գէշ և իբրև դշորի այնպէս ըստանձ-
նեալ բերքնս պանեցեր և եռեղական կացեր դու
բեռամէն հանդերձ։ Վասն դի իշխեցեր դու Թշ-
նամանել գդիսն թէ անշարժ են՝ վասն այտորիկ
հատուցին քեզ գայսպիսի պատուհաս։ Իսկ արդ՝
եթէ ոչ առցես դու յանձն պաշտօն տանել դիցն,
և յաճախեցես դու ի նոյնպիսի Թշնամանս առ-
տուածոցն՝ և այլ ևս չարբ չարագոյն անցբ ան-
ցանիցեն ընդ քեզ»։

71 Գրիգորիոս ասէ. «Վասն դիցն թէ ասես,

you repeated before me, you immediately received your deserts. This," he said, "was a great courtesy on my part in speaking with you and honoring you, yet you replied to me as an equal."

[B. The first and second tortures;
Gregory's prayer]

69.   So he had his hands bound behind him, and a muzzle put in his mouth; and he had a block of salt hung on his back and a noose placed round his chest, and cords put round and tightened on him; and he had him bound and raised up by machines to the highest part of the palace wall. And he remained thus, tightly bound, for seven days. And after the seventh day he commanded and they released him from this torture and binding, and they brought him before (the king).

70.   He began to question him. "How could you suffer, resist, endure, and last until today? Did you perceive that truly like a donkey or mule[1] you took on and carried such a great load and were stationary under your burden? Because you dared to insult the gods by saying they are immobile, therefore they have repaid you with such punishment. So now, if you will not agree to worship the gods, and if you repeat such insults to the deities, then still worse and crueler sufferings will come upon you."

71.   Gregory replied: "Concerning the gods that you mention,

գոր կոչես դու աստուածՙ ստոյգ իսկ են հա-
տուածք. վասն զի ՙհատեալք են ի մարդկանէ,
և եղեալք պատկերք ի ձեռաց ճարտարի. ոՙմն
վայլեայք են և ոՙմն քարեայք. ոՙմն են պղնձիք
և ոՙմն են արծաթիք և ոՙմն ոսկիք. ոչ խօսեալ
ՙնոցա երբեք և ոչ իմացեալ և ոչ գմտաւ ինչ
աձեալ, ոչ վասն քո և ոչ վասն իմ։ Եւ դու ինքՙ-
ՙնին իսկ քեզէն վկայես ինձ, թէ ոչ երբէք ասացեալ է ՙնոցա ցքեզ գայդ վասն իմոյ տանՋելոյս
ի քէն. և կամ բնաւ արդեօք իմացմՙն քարինք
անմուՙնչք գցաս մարդկան։

72 «Այլ վասն որոյ կապեցեր ինձ աղ, զի
կատեցայց ես կապանօք՝ յուսամ ես ի Տէրն իմ,
որոյ են ստացուածք իւր երկինք և երկիր, և
յՈրդին համագործ և ի Հոգին բարեխօս, զի հա-
մեմեսցեն դանմաՙնութիւնս իմ ստուգութեամբ
աղւն ճշմարտութեան որ ոչ անցանէ։ Եւ ինձ
տացէ գամենաՙհեշա լուծն խոՙնարհութեան թե-
թևութեան պարգևացն, որ ոչ անցանէ յաւիտեանս յաւիտենից. որ քարձրացուցանէ գխո-
նարՙհս իւրով մարդասիրութեամՙէն յայն յան-
րապաւ և յանվախճան հատուցմուՙնան, յանկէտ և
յանժամանակ, յանթիւ յաւուրն ընտրութեան
դարին մտելոյ եօթՙներորդին, իբրև հանգուցանէ
գամեՙնայն վաստակաւորս իւր և պարգևեսցէ
իւրով մեծութեամՙէն»։

73 «Իսկ որ պաշտեն գկուս քարեղէնս՝

whom you call deities, they truly are fabricated, because they have been made by men and set up as
images by the hands of an artisan. Some are of wood
and some of stone, some are of bronze and some of
silver and some of gold. They have never spoken nor
thought nor made any decision—neither for you nor
for me. And you yourself bear me witness that they
have never spoken to you about the torments you are
inflicting on me. Have indeed mute stones ever com-
prehended the sufferings of men?

72.   "But as for your hanging[1] salt on me in order to
torment me with bonds, I hope in my Lord, whose
creation are heaven and earth, and in the co-worker
the Son, and in the Spirit, the intercessor [cf. Rom.
8.26, 34], that they may season[2] my immortality with
the real salt of the truth that passes not away [cf. Matt.
5.13]. And (I hope) that he may give me the very easy
yoke [cf. Matt. 11.30] of the gifts of humility and calm,
which passes not away for ever and ever. He raises the
humble [cf. Lk. 1.52] by his benevolence to that inexhaustible and unending recompense, to the infinite,
timeless, and unending day of election, in the seventh
age to come[3] when he will give rest to all his laborers
and reward them in his majesty.

73.   "But of those who worship stone idols,

ատ մարգարէն վասն նոցա, թէ «Իշխեն որպէս
գվէմա ի չուրս բացումս»։ Իսկ որ գփայտակերա
քանդակեալն պաշտեն՝ այսպէս ատ վասն նոցա, թէ «Հուր վառեցաւ ի վերայ ամենայն փայտի ապարակի, և այրեացէ զմեղաւորս, և մի շիշ-
ցի»։ Իսկ որ պաշտեն գարձաթեղէնս և գոսկե-
ղէնս՝ այսպէս ատ. «Արծաթ նոցա և ոսկի նոցա մի կարացէ փրկել գնոսա յաւուր բարկութեան Տեառն»։ որ կարողն է կախել նոցա բե-
ռինս ձանրութեան և ամենայն դիմադարձաց և
մեղաւորաց, որ իբրև գբեգդ իցեն ամբարիշոք»։

74   Եւ յետ այսորիկ հրամայեաց կախել
գնա գլխիվայր գմիոյ տառնէն. գի մինչ դեռ
կայցէ գլխիվայր՝ ծխեցեն ի ներքոյ նորա աղբ,
և արբցէ գան սաստիկ բրոք դալարուվք։ Եւ տան-
ջեցին գնա տառն այր՝ ըստ հրամանի թագաւորին. և կայր նա կախեալ այնպէս աւուրս եօթն։

75 Արդ՝ մինչ դեռ կայր նա կախեալ՝ սկսաւ
խօսել ի կախադանին այսպէս. «Գոհանամ գբէն,
Տէր, որ արժանի արարեր գանարժանութիւնա
իմ քոյոյ պարգևիդ. գի ի սկգբանէ իսկ սիրեցեր
գատեղծուածս ձեռաց քոց, և հտուր գբտափկու-
թիւն անաշխատ հանգստեան դրախտին վայելչութեան. անմանա, անցաւս, անանց կենաց վի-
ճակացն ուրախութեան պատրաստեցեր՝ եթէ կացեալ էաք ի պատուիրանին, գոր եղեր ի ձա-
ռոյն չճաշակելոյ. գի ասացեր, թէ «Մի ուտի-

the prophet says: 'They will go down like stones in many waters' [Ezra 19.11 = Neh. 9.11; cf. Ex. 15.5]. And of those who worship wooden sculptures he speaks thus: 'Fire burned over all the wooden field, and it will consume sinners, and will not be extinguished' [Jer. 7.20]. As for those who worship (images) of silver and gold, he speaks thus: 'Their silver and their gold will not be able to save them in the day of the Lord's anger' [Ez. 7.19; Zeph. 1.18]. He is able to impose on them heavy loads [cf. Lk. 11.46] and also on all resisters and sinners who may be impious like you."

74. Then he ordered him to be hung upside-down from one foot and that while he was upside-down they should burn dung beneath him and he should be flogged with vicious green rods. Ten men tormented him according to the king's command. And he remained suspended thus for seven days.

75. While he was hanging he began to speak from the gibbet[1] as follows: "I am grateful to you, Lord,[2] for making my unworthiness worthy of your gift. For from the beginning you have loved the creatures of your hands, and you have given (us) the joy of untroubled repose in the garden of delight. You made us immortal and free of pain and prepared for us the joyful destiny of unending life, (which we would have enjoyed) if we had kept the commandment that you placed on us not to eat from the tree.[3] For you said: 'Do not eat

ցէք յայդմ ծառոյ, զոր պատուիրեցի չուտել ի
դմանէ»։ իբրև ոչ թէ ծառն անուանեալ կենաց՝
կարէր տալ կենդանութիւն առանց քրյոյ բանիդ
հրամանի կամացգ բարեբարութեան, որ է կամք
քո և բանդ և բարեբարութիւնդ՝ միածին Որդիդ,
ծնունդդ ատուածութեան քո. և Հոգիդ սուրբ,
որ ի քէն բղխէ ընու դամենային տիեզերս, որ
է ընդ քեզ և ընդ միածնիդ յէութեանդ քում։

76 «Զի եթէ կացեալ էաք ի պատուիրանիդ
քում, Տէր, և պահեալ էր զպատուիրանս, զոր
եդեր վասն լաւութեան հանդիսի փորձութեան
մերոյ՝ շնորհեալ լինէր քո մեզ զկեանս անցաւս,
անաշխատս, անբիծս, անհոգս, անտրտումս, ա-
ռանց ձեռանալոյ։ Եւ յետ սերելոյն և բազմա-
նալոյն, որ պատուիրեցեր կեալ մարմնաւորա-
պէս, անամօթ փառօքն զգեցեալ իբրև հանդեր-
ձիւ ի դրախտին քում, յոր եդեր զմեզ, և յետ
այնորիկ, որպէս յետ սրբութեան ամուսանու-
թեան և որդի ծնանելոյ ենովքայ, վերացուցեր
զնա ի կարգս հրեշտակաց յուրախութեան վի-
ճակն անմահութեան. արդ՝ եթէ կացեալ էաք ի
պատուիրանիդ ի քում հրամանի՝ ցուցեր դու
մեզ օրինակ զենովք, դի և զմեզ յետ ի դրախտին վայելից և յետ երկրաւոր կարգացս՝ յանմահութիւն փոխեալ լինէր քո զմեզ իբրև զենովք
ի կարգս հրեշտակաց. և միահագոյն աձեալ լինէր զարքայութիւն քո, զոր պատրաստեցեր կան-

from that tree from which I have commanded you not to eat' [Gen. 2.17; 3.11]. Not that the tree, called of life, could give life without your command and benevolent will—and your will and word and benevolence are the only-begotten Son, the offspring of your divinity, and the holy Spirit who proceeds from you and fills all the world, who is with you and with your only-begotten in your being.[4]

76. "For if we had observed your commandment, Lord, and had kept the command which you imposed for the sake of testing our virtue, you would have granted us life without pain, free of labor, fault, care, sadness or old age.[1] We sowed and increased, as you commanded us to live in bodily fashion [cf. Gen. 1.28], being clothed in shameless glory for a garment in your garden in which you had placed us. Thereafter, as after the holy marriage and birth of a son to Enoch you raised him to the ranks of the angels, to the destiny of joy and immortality [cf. Gen. 5.22, 24], so, if we had observed your commandment, you would have shown us the example[2] of Enoch. For you would have transferred us from the delightful garden and from our earthly condition to immortality, as (you transferred) Enoch to the ranks of the angels.[3] And you would have brought in your universal kingdom, which you had prepared

խաւ ի փառս մեր՝ մինչ չև էր աշխարհ. զի «Զոր
ակն ոչ ետես և ունկն ոչ լուաւ և ի սիրտ մարդոյ ոչ անկաւ՝ պատրաստեցեր դու սիրելեաց
քոց յառաջագոյն», զոր տացես դու, Տէր, այնոցիկ, որ սիրեցին զօր երևելոյ գալստեան Միածնիդ քո։

77 «Իսկ արդ՝ իբրև ետես թշնամին զմեզ
պատուեալս ի մարդասիրութենէ կամարար կամաց քոց՝ նախանձեալ ընդ պատիւ թագի պարծանաց մերոց, պատուին քո որ տուաւ ի քէն,
զի ասացեր, եթէ «Ի նմանութիւն պատկերի
կերպարանաց իմոց արարի ես զմարդն, և կա-
ցուցի զնա տէր ամենայնի»։ որ առ նախանձ
թշնամւոյն բանսարկուի՝ հրապոյրբ ցոփացու-
ցիչք մտին յաշխարհ, և արկին զմարդիկ ի կենաց և ի հանգստեանց, զոր դու առ քում բարերարութեանդ շնորհեցեր մարդկան, որ կորու-
սին զայն։

78 «Իսկ իբրև գթացաւ ատուածութիւնդ
քո առ մարդկութիւն տկարութեանս մերոյ, վասն
յանձախ ողորմութեանդ քո՝ ոչ թողեր ի ձեռանէ
վասն բարերարութեանդ քո. ի ներբել երկայն-
մտութեանդ քո առաքեցեր զուսրբ զմարգարէան
յերկիր և զսիրելիս քո, որ եղեն լուսաւորք յերկրի, ի խաւարչտական միջոյ ազգացն հեթանոսաց. որ և յանմիտ և յանօրէն մարդկանէն ատե-
ցեալք հալածեցան. որք յայտնեցին զքո խոր-

previously for our glory before the world existed [cf. Jn. 17.5]. For 'what eye has not seen, nor ear heard, nor has fallen into the heart of man, you have prepared for those who earlier loved you' [I Cor. 2.9], which you will give, Lord, to those who have loved the day when your only-begotten will be revealed.

77.   "But when the enemy saw us being honored by the benevolence of your will, he was jealous[1] of the honor of the crown of our boasting, of the honor given by you in that you said 'I have made man in the likeness of the image of our form and I have set him up as lord of all' [Gen. 1.27; Ps. 8.7]. At the jealousy of the slandering enemy the charms of debauchery [cf. II Macc. 6.21][2] entered the world and threw men from life and repose [cf. Wis. 2.24], which you in your mercy had granted mankind who lost them.

78.   "But since your divinity had compassion on the weakness of our humanity, in your perpetual mercy you did not abandon us because of your benevolence. In your long-suffering indulgence you sent the holy prophets, your beloved ones, to earth, who became luminaries on earth in the midst of the benighted heathen races [cf. II Pet. 1.19]. But by these irrational and lawless men they were hated and persecuted; they revealed the mysteries

հուրդս լուսաւորութեանդ, և քարոզեցին զկամս
քո և զզալս Որդւոյդ քո յաշխարհ, որ դալոցն
էր և բառնալոց զկարիս յանցուցելոց պատու-
հասի մեղաց մարդկութեան։

79 «Որք վասն դայ քարոզելոյ յաշխարհի
չարչարանօք մեռան, տանջանօք և պեսպես փորձութեանց խոովութեամբք, դառնութեան ճաշա-
կօքն կեցին յաշխարհի, վասն դքեզ քարոզելոյն
առ նեղիս ուրեանց. և նեղիչք և թշնամիքն՝
նոքա տկարական և անկան։ Վասն որոյ ընդ յարուցեալ ի վերայ իմ պատերագմիս ոչ երկիցէ
սիրտա իմ. և ընդ յարուցեալ ի վերայ իմ ճակա-
տամարտի ի քեզ եմ յուսացեալ. որ ի վախճան
ժամանակացն յայտնեցեր զխորհուրդս կամաց
քոց, դոր յառաջագոյն պատմեցեր ազգացն ա-
ռաջնոց սիրելի Որդւովդ քոյ առ նոսա, ի ճեռն
սրբոց քոց մարգարէից, դոր ի քէն առաքեցեր
դալ ծնանել ի կուսէն սրբոյ։ Զի դոր օրինակ ի
ճեռն կուսին առաջնոյ Եւայի մահ եմուտ յաշ-
խարհ՝ սոյն օրինակ և ի ճեռն այսր կուսի կեանք
մոցեն յաշխարհ։ Զի դոր օրինակ ի ճեռն ծնըն-
դեան Եւայի՝ Կահելի անէծք և քրտունք և աշ-
խատութիւնք և երերմունք և տատանմունք մտին
յաշխարհ՝ սոյն օրինակ և ծնանելով Որդւոյ քոյ
ի կուսէն հանգիստք և կեանք և օրհնութիւնք
մոցեն յաշխարհ։

80 «Որ առաքեցեր դմիածին Որդիդ քո յաշ-

of your illumination, and they preached your will and the coming of your Son to the world, who was to come and remove the burden of the punishment for the sins of erring mankind.[1]

79. "Because they preached this in the world they were put to death with torture, torments and all sorts of trials and tribulations; they led a bitter life in the world for the sake of preaching you to their tormentors. But their tormentors and enemies weakened and fell. Therefore at this encounter which has come upon me my heart will not fear; and in the struggle which faces me I have placed my hope in you [cf. Ps. 26.2-4]. At the end of time you have revealed the mystery of your will, of which you previously informed the first races through your holy prophets [cf. Heb. 1.1-2], by means of your beloved Son, who was sent by you to come and be born of the holy virgin. For as through the first virgin, Eve, death entered the world, so through this virgin life will enter the world.[1] For as through Eve's giving birth, Cain's curse and sweat and toil and agitation and troubles entered the world; so through the birth of your Son from the virgin, rest and life and blessings will enter the world.

80. "You sent your only-begotten Son into the world,

խարհ, լոյս ի լուսոյ, կեանք ի կենաց, որ եկն
զգենուլ զմեր նմանութիւնս մարմնոյ ի կուսէ
անտի, զի զմեզ անդրէն առ աստուածութիւնն
յաբեցցէ իւրով նմանութեամբն, որ իբրև զմեզ
եղև։ Ծնաւ ի կուսէն մարմնով և մարդացաւ և
մարմնացաւ իբրև զմեզ, այլ կայ և մնայ ի փառս
աստուածութեան իւրոյ. և ոչ ընկալաւ փոփո-
խումն յաստուածութենէ իւրմէ. այն նոյն է՝ որ
էրն և է և կայ և մնայ յաւիտեան ընդ Հօր և
ընդ սուրբ Հոգւոյն։ Այլ զի սիրեաց զմարդիկ՝
վասն այնորիկ եղև իբրև զմեզ, զի զմեզ աճցէ
յառաւելութիւն չնորհօք աստուածութեան իւրոյ, որ են կամք ծնողին իւրոյ. և կատարեաց
զկամս նորա. որ զաւրբս իւրով փառաւորեաց
համբերութեամբն, ի կրել իւրում զանարգու-
թիւն վշտաց մահու տանջանաց, մահուամբն և
Թաղմամբն հանդերձ. որ վասն զի սիրեցին մարդիկ պաշտել զպատկերս մարդադէմս փայտա-
գործծ ճարտարապգործ հիւսանց՝ եղև ինքն պատկեր մարդկան, զի զպատկերագործան և զպատկե-
րասէրան և զպատկերապաշտան յիւր պատկեր
աստուածութեանն հնագանդեցուցէ։

81 «Եւ վասն զի սովոր էին մարդիկ երկիր
պագանել անշունչ պատկերաց մեռելոց՝ եղև ինքն
մեռեալ պատկեր ի վերայ խաչին. և մեռաւ և
անշնչացաւ, զի ընդելականաւն գնոստ արաղ
արաղ հնագանդեցուցէ իւրում պատկերին. իբ-

light from light, life from life, who came to put on the likeness of our flesh from the virgin [cf. Phil. 2.7], in order by his own likeness to raise us to the divinity, who became like us. He was born from the virgin in the flesh and became man and was incorporate like us, yet he is and remains in the glory of his divinity. He is the same, who was and is and remains for ever with the Father and with the holy Spirit. But because he loved mankind, therefore he became like us, that he might bring us to abundance by the grace of his divinity, which is the will of his begetter. And he fulfilled his will. He glorified the saints by his own endurance, in enduring himself the indignity of affliction, death and torments, with his death and burial. Because men loved to worship images in human shape, skillfully carved from wood, he himself became the image of men,[2] that he might subject to his own image of his divinity the image-makers and image-lovers and image-worshippers.

81.   "And because men were accustomed to worship lifeless and dead images, he himself became a dead image[1] on the cross. He died and breathed his last, in order that by this (image) familiar to them he might quickly subject them to his own image.

բե զկարթ երեեցուցեալ զխաչն, և գմարմին իւր առնէր կերակուր տիեզերաց. զի այնու որասացէ յարքունական սեղանն, մշանչենաւոր արքայու֊ թեանն ատտուածութեանն իւրոյ:

82 «Եւ փոխանակ դրոշելոց փայտիցն՝ զխաչ իւր կանգնեաց ի մէջ տիեզերաց, զի որ սովորն իցեն երկիր պագանել փայտի՝ սովորականաւ ընդելականան հաւանեսցին երկիր պագանել խա֊ չին փայտի և որ ի վերայ նորա պատկերն և մարդադէմն իցէ: Զի ի վերայ խաչին ասէր այս֊ պէս, զոր նշանակեալ մարգարէին յերեսաց տեա֊ ուրն ասէ, Թէ «Եդէ ես որպէս զխաւլ՝ որ ոչ լսէ, և իբրև զհամր՝ զի ոչ բանայ զբերան իւր»: Զի դու, Տէր, ասէիր մարգարէիւն յառաջ, մինչ չև էր հասեալ ժամ կրելոյ որդւոյ քոյ Յիսուսի զայս ամենայն համբերութիւնս, Թէ «Արաբից զբեզ համր, և կապեցից զլեզու քո ի քիմս քո. և եղիցիր դու իբրև զայր մի, որոյ ոչ գուցեն բանք յանդիմանութեան ի բերան իւրում»:

83 «Քանզի սիրեցին մարդիկ զանխոս կուռս պատկերաց դիցն սնոտեաց՝ վասն այսորիկ և որդին Աստուծոյ մարմնովն պատկեր եղեալ մար֊ դոյ, ի նմանութիւն մարդկան պատկերաց, եղեալ ի բարձրաւանդակ խաչին, իբրև ի վերայ բարձր դիտակի եղեալ՝ ցուցանէր զանբարբառ մեռե֊ լութիւնն առ արարածս. վասն որոյ տեսին զնա ի վերայ բարձուն տիեգերբք, ցնծացան և երկիր

He made the cross appear as a hook,[2] and he made his body food[3] for the universe, that thereby he might catch[4] (men) for the royal altar of the eternal kingdom of his divinity.

82. "And instead of carved pieces of wood he set up his cross in the middle of the universe,[1] that those who were accustomed to worshipping wood, by this familiar and accustomed (object) might be persuaded to worship the cross of wood and the image and bodily form upon it. For on the cross he spoke thus, as the prophet indicated on behalf of the Lord: 'I shall become like a deaf man who does not hear, and like a mute, for he does not open his mouth' [Ps. 37.14]. For you, Lord, previously said through the prophet, before the time had come for your Son Jesus to endure all these sufferings: 'I shall make you mute and shall bind your tongue in your palate [Ez. 3.26]. And you will become like a man in whose mouth there are no words of reproach' [Ps. 37.15].

83. "Because men loved the dumb idols of the images of the vain gods, therefore the Son of God too became in the flesh an image of man, in the likeness of human images, mounting the elevated cross as if climbing a high summit;[1] and he showed (his) speechless lifelessness to creation. So the world saw him on a high place and rejoiced,

պագին և հնազանդեցան։

84 «Եւ վասն զի սովոր էին մարդիկ ուրախ լինել ի մեհեանս կռոցն գոճիւքն, զոր ան-
մբռնչողն մատուցանէին՝ վասն այնորիկ և դու
կոչեցեր ի գենուեն Որդւոյ քոյ գոթեզերս և
ասացեր. «Զպարաբակ իմ գենեալ է, գճաշ իմ
պատրաստեալ է»։ և բազմացուցեր գուլախու-
թիւն ի խաչելոյ Որդւոյ քոյ․ և յագեցուցեր գամենայն տիեզերս ի կենդանարար մարմնոյն, որ
էն կերակուր և կենդանութիւն բաւական ամենայն երկրպագուաց քոց ընդ ամենայն տիե-
զերս։ Իսկ որ ոչն կամեցան գալ ի կոչունս
հարասանեաց հոգևոր սեղանոյն՝ պատրաստեցեր
գնոսա տանջանացն լալիտենից, յանմահ սատա-
կումն յանանց դատաստանացն, և գքաղաքս նոցա չինեցեր պատրաստեցեր ի մէջ հրոյն տանջանացն պատրաստելոց բարկութեան։

85 «Եւ քանզի ուտէին և ըմպէին մարդիկ
գարիւն գոճից անսանог դիցապաշտութեան՝ վասն
այսորիկ եւեղ գարիւնն իւր ի վերայ փայտին․
զի փայտն ընդ դրոշեալ փայտին, և ինքն ընդ
մարդագէմ պատկերացն պղծութեան, և աբիւնն
իւր ընդ նուազացն ուրախութեան արեանցն,
որով և նորոգուեն մարմնոց դալարութեան մարդ-
կան։ Զի եկն գնեցաց գմեզ արեամբն իւրով ի
սարկութենէ ծառայութեան ատուածութեամ-
բըն իւրով, և ագատեաց ի ծառայութենէ չա-

worshiped, and submitted.

84. "And because men were accustomed to rejoice in the temples of the idols with sacrifices which they offered to the speechless (idols), therefore you summoned the world to the sacrifice of your Son and said: 'I have sacrificed the fatted (calf), I have prepared a meal' [cf. Matt. 22.4; Lk. 15.23]. And you increased their joy by the crucifixion of your Son. And you satisfied the whole world from the living flesh, which is sufficient food and life for all your worshippers throughout the whole world.[1] But those who did not wish to come to the invitation to the spiritual marriage of the altar,[2] these you have prepared for eternal torments, for unending destruction by irrevocable judgments; and their cities you have established in the midst of the fire of the torments prepared (by) your anger.[3]

85. "And because men ate and drank the blood of idolatrous animal sacrifices, therefore he shed his own blood on the wood, so that the wood (might replace) the wooden sculptures,[1] and he himself the impure images in human form,[2] and his blood the blood of joyful feasting,[3] whereby (might be effected) the renewal of the flesh for the blossoming of mankind [cf. Phil. 3.21]. For he came and redeemed us [cf. Gal. 3.13] with his blood from bondage to servitude by his divinity, and freed us from slavery

բութեան մեղացն. զի մեք եմք գինք արեան Որդւոյ քոյ, փրկեցաք և ապատեցաք արեամբ և մարմնով նորա. զի ոչ եմք անձանց տեարք՝ եթէ րստ կամա դիւրութեան անձանց մերոց գնասցուք, և կամ րստ կամաց ամենայն մահկանացու մարդկան, թէպէտ և իցեն մեր տեարք մարմնապէս։ Սակայն պարտ է պատուել գնոսա, որչափ ի քէն է հրամայեալ, և ոչ գբեզ ընդ անհ մահկանացու մարդկան փոխանակել. զի սքա գմարմին և եթ կարող են չարչարել, իսկ Որդիդ միածին, տէր մեր Յիսուս Քրիստոս, կարող է արկանել ի տանջանան յաւիտենից հասարակ, ոգւով և մարմնով հանդերձ, ի հուրն անշէջ և յորդնն անմահ։

86 «Այլ, Տէր, տուր ինձ գօրութիւն համբերութեան նեղութեան ցաւոց վառնգիս իմոյ, և ողորմեաց ինձ իբրև ի վերայ աւագակլին, որ ընդ քեզ էր կցորդ չարչարանաց խաչի քոյ. և արա առ իս գգուժ մարդպատէր շնորհաց քոց, որով կեայ ամենայն երկիր առ հասարակ, արդարք և մեղաւորք, վասն ներելոյ քաղցրութեան քոյ. «Զի ծագես գարեգակն քո ի վերայ չարաց և բարեաց, և ածես գանձրև ի վերայ արդարոց և մեղաւորաց»։ զի պանես գբարկութիւն քո, և ցուցանես գողորմութիւն քո առ ամենայն մարդիկ առ հասարակ։

87 «Տուր ինձ, Տէր, շնորհս համբերութեան

to the wickedness of sin [cf. Rom. 8.2]. For we are the price of your Son's blood [cf. I Cor. 6.19; 7.23], who have been saved and freed by his blood and flesh. For we are not masters of ourselves if we follow our own will or the will of mortal men—although they might be our bodily masters. But we must honor them as is commanded by you [cf. Eph. 6.5; Col. 3.22; I Pet. 2.18], yet not exchange you for fear of mortal men. For they are only able to torture the body, whereas your only-begotten Son, our Lord Jesus Christ, can cast everyone into eternal torments, with soul and body into the inextinguishable fire and the undying worm [cf. Matt. 10.28; Mk. 9.43].

86.   "But, Lord, give me power to endure the affliction and pain of my torment, and have mercy on me as on the thief who shared with you the sufferings of your cross [cf. Lk. 23.43]. Bestow on me the compassion of your benevolent grace whereby the whole world lives, the just and the sinners, through your sweet indulgence. 'For you make your sun to rise over the evil and the good, and you bring rain on the just and on sinners' [Matt. 5.45]. For you restrain your anger and demonstrate your mercy to all men alike.

87.   "Give me, Lord, grace to endure

դառն տանջանացս՝ որով կատեն զիս. զի և ես արժանի եղեց պանել զաւանդութիւն լուսաւորութեան հաւատոցս, զոր եառւր ինձ՝ ճանաչել զքեզ և առնել զկամս քո: Զի մի՛ ամաչեսցեն յուսացեալքն ի քեզ, որոց միանգամ պարծեցեալ են ի միածին Որդիդ քո ի տէր մեր Յիսուս Քրիստոս, որ ի քէնդ առաքեցաւ. զոր դու առաքեցեր ի մահ վասն մեղաց մերոց, զի առ ցէ զմեղս մեր յանձն իւր, և վասն յանցանաց մերոց պատժեսցի, և առ ցէ զմեղան յանձն իւր, և ընդ նմին տարցի զպատուհասն յանցանաց մերոց յանձն իւր չարչարանօք խաչին, կատարեսցէ և տացէ շնորհս պարգևաց՝ իւրոց հաւատացելոցն:

88 «Եւ արդ Տէր բարերար, որ ասացեր, եթէ «Ես ընդ ձեզ եմ զամենայն աւուրս մինչ ի վախճան աշխարհիս»՝ մի՛ թողուր զմեզ ի ձեռանէ քումմէ, այլ զօրացո զմեզ ի կամս քո, զի համբերել կարասցուք պատերազմիս՝ վասն մեծի անուանդ քոյ. զի յայտնի լիցի պարծանք հաւատոցս մերոց ծառայից քոց ի տէրութիւն աստուածութեան քոյ. զի և այս յայտնի լիցի, եթէ ոչ կարէ ոք ի թշնամեաց յաղթել յուսացելոց քոց, որք անձանց են թշնամիք:

89 «Այլ, Տէր, խառնեա՛ զմեզ ի թիւ արդարոց քոց վասն մարդասիրութեան քոյ, որ ոչ թողեր զմեզ ընդ վայր ի մեղս հարցն մերոց և

these bitter torments which they are inflicting on me,
that I may become worthy to keep the tradition [cf.
II Tim. 1.12] of this faith of light which you gave me,
to know you and do your will. May those who hoped
in you not be ashamed [cf. Rom. 9.33; I Pet. 2.6], those
who once boasted in your only-begotten Son, our Lord
Jesus Christ, who was sent by you; whom you sent to
death for our sins, that he might take our sins upon
himself and therewith bring upon himself the punishment for our transgressions by his sufferings on the
cross, that he might fulfill and grant the grace of rewards to those who believe in him.

88. "And so, benevolent Lord, who said: 'I am with
you every day until the end of the world' [Matt. 28.20],
do not deprive us of your hand [cf. Eccl. 7.18], but
strengthen us in your will, that we may be able to
endure this struggle on behalf of your great name,
that the boast of us your faithful servants in the majesty of your divinity may be revealed; and that this
too may be revealed—that none of your enemies can
vanquish those who hope in you, who are enemies to
themselves.

89. "But, Lord, join us to the number of your just
because of your benevolence; you did not haphazardly
abandon us in the sins of our fathers and

ի մոխրապաշտութեան նախնեաց մերոց և յա-
նօրէնութիւնս առաջնոցն մերոց։ Եւ խտուր ճանաչել զբնութիւն արաբչութեանդ ատուածութեանդ քոյ, զի մի՛ կորիցուք յունայնութեան
հեթանոսութեան։ Այլ գթացար յարարածս քո,
զի մի՛ եկեացէ ի վերայ մեր ի սպառ բարկութիւն քո, և մի՛ վախճանեցէ զմեզ սրտմտու-
թիւն քո և մի՛ յաղթեցի ցասումն քո առ արարածս քո։

90 «Եւ արդ՝ տուր, Տէր, զօրութիւն պա-
տերազմել ի վերայ ճշմարտութեան անուանդ
քոյ և մեռանել, և դարձեալ նորոգել փառօք
միւսանգամ, յորժամ դարձեալ առաքեսցես առ
մեզ զհատուցմանց գիւրաքանչիւր կշռիչ, զՏէր
մեր Յիսուս Քրիստոս. զի կացցուք և մեք զու-
արթ երեսօք առաջի նորա, և ացցուք զպսակն
յաղթութեան ընդ սիրելիս քո. զի դու միայն
կալոց և մնալոց ես յաւիտեան, և ամենայն տար-
րական անցաւոր արարածք բանիւ քով մաշես-
ցին. բայց դու միայն ես յաւիտեանս, և ամփո-
փես զմարդիկ իբրև զցորեան ի շտեմարանս ի
ժամանակի իւրեանց, և դարձեալ միւսանգամ
նորոգես։ Բուսուցանես յերկրէ զոսկերս մարդկան, դալարացուցանես, նորափետուր գարդա-
րես իբրև զարձուիս գսիրելիս քո։

91 «Տէր տունջեան և հասրիչ խաւարի,
արաբիչ լուսոյ, քո է տիւ և քո է գիշեր, որ

the fire-worship[1] of our ancestors and the lawlessness of our forefathers. And you permitted us to know your nature as creator and God, lest we be lost in the vanity of paganism. But you had mercy on your creatures, lest your anger overwhelm us, lest your indignation destroy us, and lest your wrath be aroused against your creatures.

90.   "So, Lord, give (me) strength to fight for the truth of your name and to die, and once again be renewed in glory [cf. II Cor. 3.18], when you will send again to us the apportioner of each one's deserts [cf. Col. 3.24], our Lord Jesus Christ, that we too may be joyful of face in his presence and receive the crown of victory with your beloved [cf. I Cor. 9.25]. For you only will exist and remain for ever, while every material and transitory creature at your word will pass away. But you alone are eternal,[1] and you gather mankind like grain in barns [cf. Matt. 3.12; 13.30; Lk. 3.17] in their time and again renew them. You make grow from the earth men's bones,[2] you make them blossom and give new wings to your beloved like eagles [cf. Is. 40.31].

91.   "Lord of the day and establisher of darkness, creator of light, yours is the daytime and yours the evening;

կարգեցեր լուսաւորս ի պետոս՝ առաջնորդս արարածոց քոց, որ են յերկրի քում. որ արարեր
զերկուս լուսաւորս առ ի պետոս շրջմանց տարեաց, ամաց, ժամանակաց, առ ի բոյորել գժա-
մանակս չափովք աւուրց՝ որ են յաշխարհի.
գմին՝ իշխանական տունջեան, որ ունի գօրինակ
Միածնիդ քոյ, գանչե՞ լ և գանպակաս, գաննուագ
և գանխապան լուսոյդ, որ յայտնելոց է իւրոց
արդարոց ի հանդերձեալ աշխարհին, ուր ո՛չ
աւուրք և ո՛չ գիշերք, ո՛չ շաբաթք և ո՛չ ամիսք,
և ո՛չ ամք և ո՛չ ժամք և ո՛չ ժամանակք, և ո՛չ
շրջմունք տարեաց և ո՛չ շրջանք ժամանակաց.
բայց միայն Տէր է, և անուն նորա միայն։ Որ
աննես գնատուցութ ուրախութեան քոյոց եր-
կերպագուաց բարեօքն, որոց ո՛չ գոյ փոփոխութ
բարեացն, և ո՛չ հանունտ պարգևացն տուելոց։

92 «Իսկ գնացք իշխանականին գիշերոյ, որ
ունի քոյով կամօք գՄիածնիդ քո գօրինակ՝ գնորոգութ յարութեան յանձին բարձեալ բերէ, ցուցանել նշանակել ամենայն երկրաւորաց գքաջա-
լերութիւն ամենայն մեռելոց յարութեան։ Յա-
րեմոից մինչև յարեելս երթայ ի մանկութին.
դարձեալ յարեմուս կամօք քովք ծերացեալ
հասանէ. պատի, թաղի, գուշակ թաղելոց յարութեան մեռելոց, մխիթարութիւն քաշալերու-
թեան առ արարածս մատուցանէ, գգալուստ
Որդւոյդ նշանակէ յերկնից և գնորոգութ տիե-

you have set luminaries for use as guides to your creatures that are in your earth. You created the two luminaries for the service of the years' seasons, months and periods, to complete the periods by the (appropriate) measures of days (for those) who are in the world [cf. Gen. 1.14].[1] The one is the lord of the daytime, who has the example[2] of your Only-begotten,[3] the unextinguishable, unfailing, inexhaustible and uninterrupted light, who will be revealed to his just in the future world, where there are no days and no evenings, no weeks and no months, no years and no hours and no periods of time, no changing of years and no flowing of time. But he alone is Lord and his name is unique. You make recompense of joy with blessings to your worshippers, whose blessings have no variation and whose rewards have no diminution.

92. "But the course of the lord of the evening, who has by your will your Only-begotten as example, supports and carries (the example of) the renewal of the resurrection, in order to show and indicate to all earthly creatures the encouragement of the resurrection of all the dead.[1] From the West to the East he moves toward youth, and again by your will he reaches the West in his old age. He is shrouded and buried, as a prediction of the resurrection of the buried dead, and he brings the comfort of encouragement to creatures; he indicates the coming of your Son from heaven and alludes to the renewal of the universe;

գերաց ակնարկէ, գհաշուՄն մաշմանն մեղաւորաց ուսուցանէ, գծագել արդարոցն յարքայութեանն ի գալստեան, դարձեալ գպահանջուՄն
հնացելոց ի մեղ՝ ցուցանէ։ Նա և գուշակէ մաշա-
կանն գյաւիտենականէդ, անցականն դանանցէդ,
հնականն գնորոգչէդ իւրմէ. որ կամօք քովք փո-
փոխի ի կերպարանս՝ որպէս կամք քո հրամա-
յեցին լինել. մինչև քարձցին առակք լինելոցն,
գոր եղեր պատրաստեցեր յօր կատարման խոստ-
մանց քող, յորժամ առնիցես ամենեցուն հա-
տուցուՄն ի ձեռն Միածնիդ և Հոգւոյդ սրբոյ.
գի քոյ է, և քեզ վայելեն փառք յաւիտեան և
յաւիտեանս։

93 «Տէր ամենակալ, որ պասէս գյուսացեալս ի քեզ և կատարես գկամս երկիւղածաց
քող, արժանի արա գիս, Տէր, գի պահեցից գյոյն
իմ որ ի քեզ, և գերկիւղն գմեծ՝ գոր աձելոց
ես առ դիմադարձ ամբարշտութեանն ի քէն, և ինձ
տուր համբերութիւն կատարել գրնթացս իմ նե-
դութեամբս՝ յոր կամ։ Բժիշկ ցաւոց մերոց,
ողջացուցիչ բեկելոց, անդորրիչ նեղելոց և արձակիչ կապելոց, մխիթարիչ սգաւորաց, յոյս
անյուսից, խռովելոց հանգիստ, աշխատելոց նաւահանգիստ, որ նայիս սիրով յաբարածս քո և
կերակրես գամենեսեան քաղցրութեամբ քով.
տուր ինձ, Տէր, առնուլ պասկ ընդ այնոսիկ,
գորս արժանիս արարեր մեռանել վասն անուան

he teaches the perdition and decay of sinners and the rising of the just in the kingdom at the coming, and shows again the vengeance made on those grown old in sin. Similarly, that which decays indicates you the eternal, the transitory you the permanent, that worn old you its renewer; by your will it is changed in form as your will commanded to occur, until the parables of the future be abolished, which you established and prepared for the day of fulfillment of your promises,[2] when you will exact retribution on everyone through your Only-begotten and your holy Spirit; for yours is, and to you is fitting, glory for ever and ever [cf. Rom. 16.27; II Tim. 4.18].[3]

93. "Lord omnipotent, who crown those who hope in you and fulfill the will of those who fear you, make me worthy, Lord, to keep my hope [cf. II Tim. 4.7] in you and the great fear which you will bring on the impious who oppose you. And give me, Lord, endurance to complete my course [cf. II Tim. 4.7] in the suffering that I am enduring. Doctor [cf. Matt. 9.12] of our ills, healer of the broken, comforter of the oppressed, liberator of the bound [cf. Ps. 145.7], consoler of the mourning [cf. Is. 61.2; Matt. 5.4], hope of the despairing [cf. Jud. 9.16], rest [cf. II Thess. 1.7] for the troubled, harbor [cf. Ps. 106.20] for the toiling, who lovingly care for your creatures and feed them all with your sweetness [cf. Ps. 103.28; 144.16]—grant me, Lord, to receive the crown with those whom you have made worthy to die for your name,

քոյ, որոց փառաւորեալ են մանք իւրեանց առաջի քո. զի և ես արժանի եղէց վերանալ ընդ առաջ Որդւոյ քոյ սիրելոյ, յորժամ յափշտակեսցէ դանձկացեալսն իւր ի ճառագայթ լուսոյ իւրոյ, դատել ճշմարտութեամբ զամենայն տիեզերս հրով բարկութեամբ իւրով։

94 «Այլ այժմիկ, Տէր, զօրացո գձառայս քո վասն անուան քոյ, զի յաղթեսցուք զօրութեանց թշնամւոյն. և բարձ և փարատեա գմեգ չարութեան կռապաշտութեան հեթանոսութեան քաղցրութեամբ սիրով քով առ արարածս քո. որ եդեր գանձն քո ի վերայ խաշանց քոց, մի թողուր գծօտ քո, զի ածցես յուղղութիւն. որ դու միայն կարող ես թողուլ գմեղս, և քաւել գյանցանս և գանօրէնութիւնս քոյոց արարածոց, զի դքեզ միայն պաշտեսցեն և գկամս քո արասցեն, և լիցին փառաւորիչք աստուածութեանդ քոյ. և ապրեսցին ի դատաստանագդ քոց, և վայելեսցեն յանճառ բարիս քո. զի ամենեքին արժանի լիցին առանց ամօթոյ և պատկառանաց կալ առաջի մեծութեանդ քոյ. զի և գգործ ագիտութեան սոցա անմեղութիւն համարեսցիս։

95 «Եւ զի սովոր ես յարդել յոչնչէ, գանինչան յինչ ածել, և յոչնչէ ի լինելութիւն արարածոց. որ ոչ թողեր գազգ մարդկան ի կամս անձանց գինչպիտութեան իւրեանց. այլ գթացար առաքեցեր գմիածին Որդիդ քո, որ եկն

whose deaths are glorious before you, that I too may become worthy to be raised to the presence of your beloved Son when he will carry off those who long for him to the rays of his light,[1] to judge in truth the whole world by fire and his anger.

94.   "But now, Lord, strengthen your servants for your name's sake, that we may overcome the forces of the enemy. Remove and scatter the fog of evil and heathen idolatry by your sweet love for your creatures. You who laid down your life for your sheep [cf. Jn. 10.11], do not abandon your flock but lead them to the true path. You alone are able to forgive sins and expiate the transgressions and lawlessness of your creatures, that they may worship you alone and do your will, and become glorifiers of your divinity, and be saved from your judgment and rejoice in your ineffable blessings, that all may become worthy to stand in the presence of your majesty without shame or confusion [cf. Ps. 70.13], so that you may reckon their acts of ignorance as innocence.

95.   "For you are accustomed to create from nothing, to bring into existence non-existent things and to bring into being creatures from nothing [cf. II Macc. 7.28; Rom. 4.17],[1] you who did not abandon the races of mankind to their own inane desires, but had mercy and sent your only-begotten Son, who came

դարձոյց զաբարածա յատուածութիւն քո, և
հրամայեաց քարոզել Աւետարանին ընդ ամենայն տիեզերս։ Այն զի քո միայն է փառաւորութիւն, և քեզ իսկ վայել է երկրպագութիւն
յամենայն արաբածող. զի դու միայն ես փառաց և պատուոյ արժանի։ Արդ՝ զԹա յարաբածա
քո, քոյով բաբերաբութեամբ շնորհօքդ և առ
երկիրս Հայոց աշխարհիս, զի և առքա ծանիցեն
զքեզ և զմիածին Որդի քո, զՏէր մեր Յիսուս
Քրիստոս, որ ի քէնդ առաքեցաւ առ մեզ, և
զգեցաւ զմարմին մարդկութեան մերոյ, և նկա-
րեաց և տպաւորեաց զանձն իւր ի ստեղծուածս
ձեռաց իւրոց, զի զգեցցի զմարմին մարդկեղէն,
և ազգականաւն մերձեցուցէ զմարդիկ առ քեզ։
Քանզի ոչ հանդարտէին մարդիկ տեսանել զերեսս քո և ապրել. վասն այնորիկ եղև նա ի
նմանութիւն մարդկան, զի զմարդիկ արժանիս
արասցէ աստուածութեանն իւրում. զի ազգա-
կից մարմնով որ ի մէնջ տեսեալ զաստուածու-
թիւնն Որդւոյն՝ յարգեցուցէ բաբերաբութեամբ
Հօր, և ընդ նմին ընկալցուք զշնորհս բաբերա-
բութեան Հոգւոյդ սրբոյ որ ի քէն. զի և շնոր-
հեսցին պատգամք Աւետարանի քոյ այժմ աշխարհի. զի և առքա ծանիցեն զքեզ և զերախտիս
բաբերաբութեանդ շնորհի քոյ, որ առ ամենեսին է։

96 «Այլ որ առատանաւդ ամենեցուն՝ տուր

and brought back creatures to your divinity, and ordered the Gospel to be preached throughout the
whole world [cf. Matt. 28.19]. For yours alone is glory
and to you is worship from all creatures fitting, as you
alone are worthy of glory and honor [cf. I Tim. 1.17].
Now have pity on your creatures in your benevolence
and grace towards this land of Armenia, that they may
know you and your only-begotten Son, our Lord Jesus
Christ, who was sent by you to us and who put on the
flesh of our humanity,[2] and who depicted and im-
printed himself[3] on the creatures of his own hands,
that he might put on human flesh and by its relation
to theirs bring men close to you. For men could not
endure to see your face and live [cf. Ex. 33.20]. Therefore he became in the likeness of men [cf. Phil. 2.7],
that he might make men worthy of his divinity, that
we, seeing the divinity of the Son through the flesh
related to ours, might honor (the same) in the benevolence of the Father, and in him receive the grace of
the benevolence of the holy Spirit who (proceeds)
from you. Thus the words of your Gospel may be
granted to this world, so that they may know you and
the benefits of your benevolent grace which extends
to all.

96.   "You who are bountiful to all, grant

մեզ, զի լիցուք վկայք աստուածութեանդ քոյ,
չարչարել վասն անուան քոյ, և մեռանել վասն
ճշմարտութեան քոյ, և նորոգել միւսանգամ ի
գալստեան քոյ. զի դու եկիր և մեռար ի վերայ
արարածոց քոց, և խանեցեր զմահկանացու
բնութիւնս մեր յանմահութիւն քո։ Վասն այսորիկ և մեք մինչև ի մահ լիցուք վկայք կենդանութեան քոյ, զի խանեցուք ի թիւ վկայից քոց. զի այլ զի՞նչ ինչ արդեօք կարիցեմք
առնել դարձուածա փոխարէն բարեացն որ ի
քէն՝ եթէ ոչ տացուք զանձինս մեր փոխանակ
պատուիրանաց քոց, ի հաճութիւն կամաց քոց.
զի լիցուք ժառանգորդք արքայութեան քում ընդ
այնոսիկ որ հաճոյ եղեն առաջի քո. զի մա-
տուսցուք զանձինս մեր պատարագ աստուածութեան քում. զի կորուսցուք զանձինս, և դարձեալ գտցուք զնա յաւուր յարութեան. կացցուք
ընդ աշմէ քումմէ զանմեղութիւն զգեցեալ ընդ
գառինս աջակողմեան դասուն, կամարարաց քոց,
յուրախութիւն սրբոց քոց, որ սիրեցին գաս-
տուածութիւն քո և զմիածին Որդիդ, զՏէր մեր
Յիսուս Քրիստոս. որ եղև գառն ճշմարիտ և մատոյց զանձն իւր քեզ պատարագ վասն մեղաց
ամենայն աշխարհի, զի լիցի հաճեցուցիչ և բարեխօս ընդ արարիչդ և ընդ արարած։ Իսկ որ
յայս հաճութիւն ընթացեալ մերձեցան՝ պատ-
րաստեայ նոցա օթևանս յարքայութեան աս-

us to become martyrs for your divinity, to be tortured for your name's sake [cf. Phil. 1.29], to die for your truth [cf. Acts 21.13], and to be renewed again at your coming. For you came and died on behalf of your creatures and joined[1] our mortal nature to your immortality. Therefore let us be martyrs unto death for your life, that we may be joined to the number of your martyrs. For what other return indeed can we make for the blessings (that come) from you, unless we give up our lives for your commandments to the good-will of your desire, that we may become inheritors of your kingdom with those who were pleasing before you and we may offer ourselves as a sacrifice to your divinity;[2] that we may lose our lives and again find them [cf. Matt. 10.39] on the day of resurrection, when we sit on your right hand clothed in innocence among the lambs of the group on the right-hand side [cf. Matt. 25.33], your servants, in the joy of your saints, who have loved your divinity and your only-begotten Son, our Lord Jesus Christ? He was the true lamb [cf. Jn. 1.36] and offered himself to you as a sacrifice for the sins of the whole world, that he might be a reconciler and intercessor between you the creator and the creatures [cf. Gal. 3.19; Heb. 7.27; 9.14-15]. But for those who have hastened to draw near to this good-will, he has prepared dwellings in the kingdom

տուածութեանն իւրոյ։ Իսկ որք ոչն կամեցան
մտանել ի հաճութիւն ննազանդութեան դալրա-
տեան նորա՝ յաւիտենից տանջանս խոստացաւ։

97 «Եւ արդ՝ Տէր բարերար, որ եկիր և
խոնարհեցար և առեր զկերպարանս մարդկան, և
եսուր գանձն քո ամենայն համբերութեան, և
ոչ դարձուցեր գանձն քո յանարգանաց ընդ երեսս
թքանելոյ, և մատուցեր հարկանելեաց գծնոտ
քո, քացախ և լեղի դառնութեան վասն մեր ար-
բեր, քաղցրացո՛ գիքրտ ամենայն մարդկան ի
պաշտօն քո, զի ննազանդեսցին ընդ ամենահեշտ
լծով քով և ապրեսցին ի յաւիտենից տանջանացն. զի լցաւ իսկ երկիր աստուածապաշտու-
թեամբ քով. և որ մնացեալս են՝ զի և սոքա մի՛
վրիպեսցին ի ճշմարտութեան ճանապարհաց քոց,
և հրաւիրեսցին յարքայութեան սեղանդ և վայելեսցեն ի համբերութենէ քումմէ։ Որ վասն
ամենեցուն եկիր ի սպանումն իբրև գգառն, և
ուրախ արարեր ի մարմին քո, դոր եսուր ի
վիրկութիւն ամենեցուն, և դուղխս փափկութեան
քոյ եսուր ըմպել, գաքին քո, վասն կենաց ա-
մենայն աշխարհի, գթա՛, զի յիշեսցեն և դարձ-
ցին և եկեսցեն առ քեզ ամենայն ծագք երկրի,
և երկիր պագցեն առաջի քո ամենեքեան, ոյք
իջանեն ի հող. զի կարող ես միւսանդամ կանգնել, կենդանացուցանել և առնել արժանիս մար-
գասիրութեան քոյ. զի քո իսկ արեամբ են փրր-

of his divinity [cf. Jn. 14.2]. But to those who did not wish to enter into obedience to the good-will of his coming he promised eternal torments [cf. Matt. 25.46].

97. "So, benevolent Lord, who came and was humbled and took the form of mankind [cf. Phil. 2.8] and gave yourself to every endurance, and did not turn yourself from the insults of being spat in the face [cf. Matt. 26.67], and offered your cheek to those striking you [cf. Lam. 3.30; Lk. 6.29] and drank bitter vinegar and gall for us [many refs.]—sweeten the heart of all men for your service, that they may submit to your easy yoke [cf. Matt. 11.30] and be saved from eternal torments; for the earth has been filled with piety towards you. And as for those who remain, let them not miss your paths of truth, and may they be invited to your royal table[1] and may they enjoy your long-suffering. You came for the sake of all to be slaughtered like a lamb [cf. Acts 8.32], and you made (them) rejoice in your flesh which you gave for the salvation of all. And you gave as drink the stream of your gentleness [cf. Ps. 35.9], your blood, for the life of the whole world. Have pity, that all corners of the earth may remember and turn and come to you [cf. Ps. 21.28], and that all may worship before you, who go down to the dust [cf. Ps. 21.30]. For you are able to raise them up again, to revive them and make them worthy of your benevolence. For by your blood they have been saved

կեայք և ապատեայք յիշխանութենէ խաւարի։
Արդ՝ ծանիցեն զքեզ՝ յորոց վերայ մեռար դու.
զի քո իսկ են ծառայք և քեզ լիցին երկրպագուք.
զի մի՛ եկեսցէ ի վերայ մարդկան բարկութիւն
սրամտութեան քո։

98 «Արա գմեզ որդիս լուսոյ և որդիս տուըն-
ջեան, զի փառաւորեսցի անուն քո ի վերայ
ամենայն տիեզերաց. զի դու ես փառաւորեալ
ի մշանջենաւոր արքայութեանդ, որ եսդ յեու-
թեանդ, յիսկութեանդ, յինքնութեանդ։ Որ եաուր
օրինակ չարչարանաց քոյովդ չարչարանօք խո-
նարհութեամբ՝ քոյոց սիրելեաց, և ցուցեր գնա-
լածանս քոյով հալածելովդ, և ցուցեր գտանջանս
քոց սրբոց՝ ի քո մտանել ի տանջանս կոփանա-
րութեանդ։ Իսկ մեք հողեղէնքս բնաւ իսկ զի՞նչ
բերիցեմք ի համար գմեր նեղութիւնս չարչարանաց. զի դու, Տէր, խոնարհեցար և աւեր
յանձն գամենայն, և բարձեր գվիշտս և գշարչարանս ամենայն տիեզերաց։ Արդ՝ գօրացո գիս,
Տէր, ի ժուժկալութիւն անդուութեան նեղու-
թեանն՝ ուր կամ։ զի յերկարեսցի իմս պարծել
ի նեղութիւնս տանջանաց։ զի հաւասարեցացյ և
ես ընդ սիրելիս քո յալուրն, յորում հատուցա-
նիցես գանպատում բարիդ, որ կայ պահի յուսացելոց քոց որ յալիտենից»։

99 Եւ մինչդեռ կայր նա կալսեալ այս-
պէս՝ խօսեցաւ դայս ամենայն. և գրեցին ատե-

and freed from the power of darkness [cf. Col. 1.13-14]. So let them know you who died for them. For they are your servants and will become your worshippers, lest there come upon men the anger of your wrath.

98.   "Make us sons of light and sons of the daytime [cf. I Thess. 5.5], that your name be glorified over all the universe. For you are glorified in your eternal kingdom,[1] you who exist in your essence, in your being, in your individuality.[2] You gave an example of suffering to your loved ones through your own sufferings and humility;[3] you showed torment by being tormented yourself; you showed torture to your saints by enduring the torture of being buffeted yourself [cf. Matt. 26.67]. But we earthly creatures, how at all can we number our tribulations and sufferings? For you, Lord, humbled yourself and accepted everything, and you removed the afflictions and torments of the whole universe. So strengthen me, Lord, to endure the severity of the tribulation in which I find myself, that my boasting in the tribulation of (my) torments [cf. Rom. 5.3] may endure, so that I too may be considered equal with your beloved ones on the day in which you will bestow your ineffable blessings, which are stored up for those who hope in you for ever [cf. I Cor. 2.9; Pet. 1.4]."

99.   All this he said while hanging thus suspended. And the scribes of the tribunal[1] wrote it down.

նակալ դպերքն նշանագրացն. զի առ ոչինչ հա
մարեալ զկախապանն, և ոչ զբրածեծ գանին
գրեաց ինչ զվիշտա. զի ջարդեալ էր գամբնայն
մարմինան յոզորածեծն առնելոյ։ Եւ այլ ևս բա
զում քան զայս խոսեցաւ՝ մինչդեռ կայր կա
խեալ գլխիվայր, և գրեցին և մատուցին դայն
առաջի Թագաւորին. քանզի էր կախեալ դեօթն
օր գմիոյ ոտանէն։ Եւ յետ այսորիկ ետ հրա
ման, և իջուցին զնա անտի։

100 Սկսաւ խոսել ընդ նմա Թագաւորն Հա
յոց Տրդատ և ասէ. «Զի՞նչ ունիս, և կամ զի՞նչ
եղեր ի մոի, լինե՞լ կզորդ կենաց իմոց, որպէս
աշխատեցարն ընդ իս ի մանկութենէ վաստա
կովք, եթէ մեռանել տարապարտուց, ի տարա
պարտ խորհուրդս ընդունայնութեան մոացդ՝
ուր կաղ իսկ»։ Նա պատասխանի ետ և ասէ.
«Փութամ ես եղանել ի մարմնոյս, և առնուլ
զկեանսն յաւիտենից. այլ տուր հրաման վասն
իմ որպէս և կամիս, զի՞նչ մահ և հրամայես ի
վերայ իմ»։

101 Ետ պատասխանի արքայ և ասէ. «Ոչ
տամ զայդ պարգև՝ եթէ լիցի քեզ վախճան մա
հու երագ երագ և հանգչել ի տանջանաց, զոր
կոչես դու կեանս յաւիտենից. այլ կոտել զբեզ
յերկար, զի ոչ լիցի ճնար քեզ երագ մեռանել,
այլ տանջել զբեզ յերկար և պահանչել ի քէն
զանարգանս դիցն և գյամառութիւնդ քո, որ ոչ

For he paid no heed to the gallows and disregarded the blows of the bastinado. For they had broken all his body from the flagellation. And he said many more things while he was hanging upside down, and they wrote them down and brought them before the king, since he was hanging for seven days from one foot. Then he gave a command and they brought him down.

[*C. The other ten tortures;
the revelation of Gregory's
ancestry and his imprisonment*]

100.   Trdat, king of Armenia, began to speak with him, saying: "What is your opinion and what decision have you made? To share in my life just as you have labored with me from a young age; or to die vainly in the inane thoughts of your foolish mind?" He replied and said: "I am anxious to leave this body [cf. II Cor. 5.8] and receive eternal life. But command in my case as you wish, whatever death you impose on me."

101.   The king replied and said: "I shall not give you that reward, for you to receive death quickly and have respite from tortures, which you call eternal life. But I shall cause you to be tormented for a long time to prevent you from dying quickly, and shall rather torture you at length and exact retribution from you for your insults to the gods and your obstinacy

կամեցար պաշտել զնոսա»։

102 Եւ եւս հրաման բերել կոճեղս փայտից, և առնել ըստ ողքի խոռցաց ռտից նորա.
և դնել և պնդել ուժգին առատկոք, մինչև իջանէր
արիւնն ընդ ձայրց ռտից մատանց նորա. և ասէ.
«Գիտիցե՞ս կամ զգայցե՞ս ինչ արդեօք զցաւոդ»։
Նա պատասխանի ետ և ասէ. «Տուաւ ինձ զօրութիւն, քանզի խնդրեցի եւս յԱրարչէն արարածոց, որ է ճարտարապետ և Արարիչ ամե-
նայնի՝ որ երկի և որ ոչն երկիր»։ Եւ հրամայեաց, և լուծին զնա յայնմանէ։

103 Եւ եւս հրաման բերել բևեռս երկաթիս
և վարել ընդ ներբանս ռտից նորա. և առեալ
գձեռանէ նորա աստի և անտի՝ ընթացուցանէին
զնա յայս կոյս և յայն կոյս. և արիւնն հոսէր
իջանէր յոտից անտի, և ռոզանէր զերկիրն սատիկ յոյժ։ Եւ դարձեալ ասէ ցնա. «Ա՛յդ են ա-
ներևոյթ արարածք Աստուծոյն քո, զոր դուն
տեսանես»։

104 Նա ասէ. «Բարիոք ասացեր, եթէ այս
իցեն աներևոյթ արարածք Աստուծոյն իմոյ.
վասն զի «Սերմանի տկարութեամբ՝ և յառնէ
զօրութեամբ. սերմանի անարգութեամբ՝ և յառնէ
փառօք»։ Զի «Լալով լա՛ն՝ որք տանիցին գսերբ-
մանիս իւրեանց», այսինքն են վիշտ և չարչարանք, որ հասանեն մեզ որ վասն աստուած-
պաշտութեանն են. այլ յորժամ որայն ի հունձ

in being unwilling to worship them."

102.   He commanded that blocks of wood be brought and fixed to his shins and feet and tightened with strong cords until the blood ran down to the tips of his toes.[1] And he said: "Do you feel or sense your pain at all?"[2] And he replied and said: "I have been given strength [cf. Acts 1.8], because I asked the Creator of creation, who is the architect and creator of everything visible and invisible [cf. Heb. 11.10]." And he commanded, and they loosed him.

103.   And he commanded iron nails to be brought and driven through the soles of his feet.[1] They took him by the hand and made him run this way and that. And the blood ran out from his feet and watered the earth in great abundance. And again he said to him: "Are these the invisible creations of your God, which you now see?"

104.   He replied: "Rightly have you said that these are the creations of my God, because 'it is sown in weakness and rises up in power; it is sown in dishonor, and rises up in glory' [I Cor. 15.42-3]. For 'they weep indeed, who will take away their seeds' [Ps. 125.6a]—that is toil and torment which come upon us for the sake of piety. But when the germ of wheat comes to harvest

եկեալ մատուսցէ զատոքութեանն բերրի զպը-
տուղ սերմանողացն՝ ընդ նմին և զգնձութիւն
բերկրութեան ուրախութեանց ամենայնի բերէ»։

105 Ասէ Թագաւորն. «Բախեցէ՛ք զաման
լալոյ արտասուացն. Թող եկեացէ դմա ուրա-
խութիւն»։ Եւ հանին նմա կռուիս ի գլուխն,
հարկանելով զնա աննհարին։ Սկսաւ հարցանել
զնա և ասէ. «Ա՞յդ է ուրախութիւնն»։ Եւ նա
ասէ. «Այս այս է. զի թէ ոչ քրանեցցի մշակն
ի տապ խորշակի Ջերմոյն արեգակնակէզ լինե-
լով՝ ոչ ընբռնէ զարդիւնս շայեկանս ուրախութեան պողոզն ձմերայնւոյն հանգստեան»։ Եռ
պատասխանի արքայ և ասէ. «Դու աստէն իսկ
աշխատեաց ի մշակութիւն տանՋանացդ, յորում
կացդ»։

106 Եւ եռ հրամանն բերել աղ և բորակ և
քարկ քացախ, և ընկենուլ զնա յորսայս, և դնել
զգլուխս նորա ի հիւսանց մամուլս և դնել փող
եղեգան ի քիթս նորա, և արկանել գայն ընդ
քիթս նորա։

107 Եւ յետ այսորիկ եռ հրամանն, և բերին պարկս օձենիս մեծամեծս և լցին դայն մոխ-
րով հնոցի. և արաբին Թուլագոյն, զի մի կարի
լի իցէ, վասն տուրևառ չնչոյն, զի հարկանելով
ընդ խելսն վառանգեցցէ զնա։ Եւ ագուցին դայն
ի գլուխս նորա, և կապեցին զբերան պարկին ի
փողս նորա. և կաց նովաւ աւուրս վեց։ Եւ յետ

it will offer to the sowers the ripe fruit of its maturity, and likewise it brings the joy of happy fruitfulness to all [cf. Ps. 125.6b]."

105. The king said: "Break the vessel of these tears of weeping; let joy come to him." They buffeted him on the head, striking him cruelly. He began to question him and said: "Is this happiness?" He replied: "Yes, it is. For unless the laborer sweats in the torrid heat of the shining sun, he will not gain the true reward of joyful fruit, rest in the winter." The king answered and said: "You indeed have labored here at the toil of these torments in which you find yourself."

106. And he ordered salt and borax and rough vinegar to be brought, and for him to be turned on his back, his head to be placed in a carpenter's vice, and a reed tube to be put in his nose, and this liquid to be poured down his nose.

107. After that he commanded and they brought a large sack[1] of sheepskin and filled it with cinders from a furnace. They made it not quite full in order to let him breathe, but so that his brain was affected and he would be thus tormented. They fixed this over his head and tied the mouth of the sack round his neck. And he remained thus for six days.

այսորիկ ետ հրաման, և աժին առաջի թագաւորին, և ի բաց հանին զպարկն ի գլխոյն։

108 Սկսաւ խօսել Թագաւորն և ասէ. «Ու-
մէ՞ դաս. Թերևս յարքայութենէ անտի դայցես
զոր ասէիր»։ Ետ պատասխանի Գրիգորիոս և ասէ.
«Այ՛ն, իսկ յարքայութենէ զոր ասէի՛ անտի զամ.
վասն զի արժանի արար զիս Աստուած զայս
ամենայն կրել յանձին վասն անուան իւրոյ։
Արդարև իսկ կայ մնայ ինձ արքայութիւնն որ
ոչ անցանէ. փոխանակ մոխրոյն՝ անթառամ ծա-
ղիկքն, և փոխանակ քացախոյն՝ անսպառ ուրախութիւնքն»։

109   Եւ սատակացեալ Թագաւորին՝ ետ
պնդել գոտս նորա ի հրապոյրս տկաց, և կախել
զնա գլխիվայր. և ետ դնել ճագար ի նստոյ տեղւոջ նորա, և արկանել ջուր տկաւ յորովայն նորա. Եւ ետ հրաման, և իջուցին յայնմանէ. և
սկսաւ հարցանել զնա և ասէ. «Առնե՞ս զկամս
իմ, թէ ոչ պաշտես զդիան, որ են ամենայն
երկրի կեանք և շինութիւն»։

110 Ետ պատասխանի Գրիգորիոս և ասէ.
«Ես տեառն Աստուծոյ իմոյ երկիր պագանեմ,
զի նա է արարիչ և կեանք և շինութիւն. և զՈրդին հասոիչ և համագոր և համագործ, և զՀոգի
նորին, որ ելից իմատութեամբ զամենայն տիե-
զերս։ Այլ զկուռս կռեալս, կոփեալս, քերեալս և
արարեալս՝ ոչ կալայ երբեք առ աստուածս, և

After that he commanded and they led him before the king and removed the sack from his head.

108.   The king began to speak, and said: "Whence come you? Perhaps you come from the kingdom which you mentioned?" Gregory replied and said: "Yes, I indeed come from the kingdom of which I spoke. For God made me worthy to endure all this for his name's sake. Truly there awaits me the kingdom that passes not away—instead of cinders, unfading [cf. I Pet. 1.4] flowers; instead of the vinegar, inexhaustible joy [cf. Job 36.26; Lam. 3.22]."

109.   The king, even more incensed, ordered his feet to be bound with cords of wineskins[1] and him to be hung upside down. And he had a funnel placed in his bottom and had water poured from a wine-skin into his belly. Then he gave a command and they brought him down. And he began to question him, saying: "Will you do my desire, will you not serve the gods who are the life and prosperity of the whole earth?"

110.   Gregory replied and said: "I worship the Lord my[1] God, for he is creator and life and prosperity; and the Son, fashioner and equal in power and deed; and his Spirit, who filled the whole universe with wisdom.[2] But the hammered idols, sculpted and polished and worked [cf. Wis. 13.11; Is. 41.7], I never held to be gods—and

մի լիցի այլ ունել՝ մինչև իցէ շունչ իմ ի մարմնի իմում»։ Եա պատասխանի Թագաւորն և ասէ.
«Փոխանակ զի իշխեաց ասել կռեալս և քերեալս
դիցն՝ պաճանՉեացի դա ընդ այդորիկ»։

111 Եւ եա հրամա՛ն քերել զկողս նորա երկաԹի քերչօք, մինչև ուռգա՛ն վայրքն ամենայն
յարեն՛է նորա։ Եւ սկսաւ ասել գնա. «Արդ արաս-
ցե՛ս զկամս իմ, Գրիգորիոս, որ յայդպիսի տանջանս մատնեցար»։ Ասէ գնա. «Ինձ լիցի պանել
գուխտ ասաուածպաշտութեան, գոր ուսայ ի
մանկութենէ իմմէ, որ կարողն է վրկել զիս
յամենայն նեղութենէ, և դքեզ արկանել ի տան-
ջանս՝ որ ոչ ճանաչես գնա, և դարձեալ գայլս
ևս դարհուրեցուցանել կամիս և քակել ի պաշտ-
մանէ սիրոյ նորա»։ Եա պատասխանի Թագաւորն և ասէ. «Ո՞ւր է Աստուած քո, որ վրկէն
դքեզ ի ճեռաց իմոց, և կամ դատի, որպէս ասացեր, դատասատանօք իւրովք»։

112 Եւ եա հրամա՛ն, և բերին տատասկ
երկաԹի բագում սակառեօք, և արկին ի վերայ
գեանի Թանձր. և մերկացուցին զԳրիգորիոս, և
արկին ի վերայ տատասկին մերկ. և ծակոտեալ
լինէին մարմինք նորա առ հասարակ. և քարշե-
ցին և Թաղեցին գնա ի տատասկին. և շրՋարՋեին
գնա անդէն, մինչև առ հասարակ ծակոտեցան
մանրիկ մարմինք նորա, մինչ գի ոչ մնաց ի
նմա տեղի ողՋ։

may I never so hold any other so long as my breath is in my body." The king replied and said: "In return for daring to call the gods hammered and polished, let him pay retribution for that."

111.   He ordered his flanks to be torn with iron scrapers[1] until all the ground was running with his blood. And he began to say to him: "So will you do my desire, Gregory, now that you have been given over to such torments?" He replied: "May I keep the covenant of piety which I learned from my youth [cf. II Tim. 3.15]; (God)[2] can save me from every tribulation [cf. I Tim. 4.8], and cast into torment you who do not know him and wish to frighten others still more and separate them from the service of his love." The king replied and said: "Where is your God, who will save you from my hands, or is judged, as you said, by his own judgments?"

112.   He gave a command and they brought iron "thistles"[1] in many baskets and cast them thickly on the ground. They stripped Gregory and threw him naked onto the "thistles." His flesh was pierced all over. They dragged and buried and rolled him in the "thistles" until every part of his body was torn, leaving[2] no place intact.

113 Եւ ի միւսումʼ աւուրն աձին գնա ա-
ռաջի նորա։ Սկսաւ հարցանել գնա և ասէ. «Չար-
մացեալ զարմացեալ եմ, և կարի քաշ. դիւրդ
կեաս դու կենդանի. և ոչ ինչ գրկեցեր դու
զցաւդ, և խոսիս ես. զի արժան էր, թէ վա-
ղուց էիր դու վախճանեալ ի տանջանաց այտի»։

114 Եռ պատասխանի Գրիգորիոս և ասէ.
«Ոչ է իմ ժուժկալութիւն տոկալոյդ՝ իմով գո-
րութեամբ, այլ ուժով շնորհի Տեառն իմոյ, և
իմոյ յօժարութեան կամացս, որ խնդրեցի ի
նմանէ, զի և դու գփորձ առցես գձառայիս Աստուծոյ. զի գիտասցես, թէ ոչ ոք կարէ մեկնել
գյուսացեալս ի նա ի սիրոյ նորա։ Զի նա տայ
ոյժ և գօրութիւն համբերութեան՝ համբերել նեղութեանց և փորձութեանց. զի ամաչեսցեն անո-
րէնք յունայնութեան իւրեանց և յամբարշտութեան և յապատամբութեան իւրեանց, որ իբրև
գբեզդ իցեն, և կացցեն ամօթով յաւուրն այցե-
լութեան և յանդիմանութեան»։

115 Եւ եռ հրաման արկանել կապիճս
երկաթիս ի ծունկս նորա, և վարել ուռունս
ատուասս, և բանալ ի կախաղան՝ մինչև յօշ-
ցին ծունկք նորա անդէն։ Եւ կաց կախեալ այնպէս զերիս աւուրս։

116 Եւ յաւուրն չորրորդի հրաման եռ
Թագաւորն, և իջուցին գնա ի կախաղանէն, և
աձին կացուցին գնա առաջի նորա։ Խօսել սկսաւ

113.   The next day they brought him before (the king).[1] He began to question him, saying: "I am very greatly amazed how you are able to stay[2] alive. You have counted your pains as nothing and you still speak. For long before now you should have died from (such)[3] torments."

114.   Gregory replied and said: "My ability to endure this is not through my own power but through the strength of the grace of my Lord and of my well-disposed will, which I sought from him so that you might test this servant of God, that you might know that no one can separate from his love those who hope in him [cf. Rom. 8.39]. For he gives strength and power to endure and bear afflictions and testings, that the lawless may be ashamed in their inanity and impiety and rebellion [cf. Ps. 24.4]—who will become like you and will stand in shame at the day of visitation and reproach."

115.   And he commanded iron leggings[1] to be put on his knees, and that he be struck with heavy hammers and be suspended on the gibbet until his knees were broken. And he stayed hanging thus for three days.

116.   And on the fourth[1] day the king gave a command, and they brought him down from the gibbet and led him before him. The king began to speak

Թագաւորն և ասէ. «Տեա դու, Գրիգորիոս, զի ոչ
փրկեաց զքեզ սնոտի յոյսն քո, յոր յուսայիր
դու. չեհան զքեզ ի ձեռաց իմոց»։

117 Եռ պատասխանի Գրիգորիոս և ասէ. «Տեա
դու, զի սնոտի են յոյսքն քո, և ոչ կարացին
հաւանեցուցանել և ոչ երկեցուցանել զիս. զի զոր
դուն պաշտես՝ սնոտի է, և ամենայն գործ մոլորու-
թեան քոյ։ Այլ տես դու, զի ոչ ի տանջանաց քոց
երկեայ ինչ ես, և ոչ զատ անի քոյ համարեցայ
ինչ. այլ զօրութեամբ Տեառն իմոյ մարտեալ ընդ
թշնամւոյն՝ որ ի ծածուկն քե պատերագմի ընդ
ճշմարտութեան, և մանեցի զմարմինս իմ ի
կիզումն տանջանաց. զի եթէ վաղ եթէ անագան՝
սակայն քակտի հնացեալ մարմինն. զի եկեսցէ
ճարտարապետն, գտեալ զորդիս մարդկան՝ միւսանգամ զնոյն հնացեալն անդրէն նորոգեսցէ։ Զի
զորոց զոգիսն գտանէ ի պարկեշտութեան, ի
զգաստութեան, ի սրբութեան, ի քաղցրութեան,
ի հեզութեան, յաշտուածպաշտութեան կեցեալ՝
նորոգէ, զարդարէ, կեցուցանէ զնոյն ոգիս նովին մարմնով։ Իսկ զորս գտանէ յանօրէնութեան
և յամբարշտութեան, յաստուածատեցութեան, ի
կռապաշտութեան կեցեալ՝ թէպէտ և թուսանել
թուսանին մարմինք նոցա առ ժամանակ մի՝ այլ
զնոսին նովին ոգւով և նովին մարմնով արկանէ
ի գեհեն, յանշէջ հուրն, յաւիտենից տանջանս,
մանաւանդ զայնոսիկ, որ իբրև զքեզդ են ի կռա-

and said: "See, Gregory, that your futile hope in which you had confidence did not save you or deliver you from my hands."

117. Gregory replied and said: "See, your hopes are vain and they could not persuade me or make me doubt. For that which you serve is vain, as is the whole activity of your error. But see, I was not in the least afraid of your torments and I considered as nothing your fearsome menaces. But through the power of my Lord I fought with the enemy, who in hidden fashion wars through you against the truth, and I submitted my body to the burning torments. For be it sooner or later, nonetheless the body grows old and is dissolved [cf. II Cor. 5.1]. The architect [cf. Heb. 11.10] will come and find the sons of men, and will renew this same that has grown old [cf. Phil. 3.21]. For those whose souls he finds living in decency, in sobriety, in holiness, in sweetness, in gentleness, and in piety [cf. Tit. 2.12]—he will renew, adorn and vivify these same souls with the same body.[1] But those whom he finds living in lawlessness and impiety, hating God and worshipping idols, although their bodies may flourish for a while, yet with that same soul and body he will cast them into hell, into the inextinguishable fire [cf. Mk. 9.43], into eternal torments—and especially those who are like you in idolatry."

պաշտութեան»։

118 Իսկ իբրև լուաւ զայն թագաւորն՝ բար-
կացաւ ընդ բանսն և ասէ. «Ինձ ոչ է փոյթ
զայնմանէ, թէ նորոգեսցէ զքեզ Աստուածն քո
թէ ոչ. ինձ ոչ է պետ զայնմանէ։ Այլ զի ասացեր, եթէ զքեզ յանշէջ հուրն արկանէ՝ ես զքեզ
ասաէն իսկ այրեցից շիջանուտ հրով. տեսցուք,
քո Աստուածն զի՞ արասցէ»։

119 Եւ ետ հրաման երկաթի պուտամբք
հալել կապար, և մինչդեռ ջերմ էր՝ իբրև զշուրբ
հոսել արկանել գմարմնով նորա։ Եւ այրեցին
գմարմինս նորա առ հասարակ, և ոչ մեռաւ.
այլ կայր մեծաւ ուժով, և գինչ հարցանէին՝
վաղվաղակի տայր պատասխանի։

120 Եւ զարմացեալ թագաւորն ընդ ժուժկալութիւն համբերութեանն կարի աննաբին և
ընդ տոկալ նորա՝ և ասէ, թէ «Չիմ՞որդ կայ իքեզ
շունչդ յայդչափի ժամանակաց, և ի չարաչար
տանջանացդ, որով զքեզն կոտեցի»։ Ետ պատասխանի Գրիգորիոս և ասէ. «Ո՞չ վաղ իսկ
ասացի քեզ, եթէ զի առցես դու գփորձ համբերութեան ծառային Աստուծոյ. զի տայ զօրութիւն յամօթ առնել գայնոսիկ, որ առանց նորա իցեն և մարանչիցին ընդդեմ նորա իբրև
զքեզդ։ Զի այապէս ասէ. «Ո՞չ թողից գձեզ, և ոչ
ընդ վայր հարից»։ Արդ՝ այս է պանպանութիւն
նորա առ արարածս իւր և առ սիրելիս իւր,

118.   When the king heard this he was angry at the speech and said: "I have no interest in that; whether your God will renew you or not is not my concern. But because you said 'he will cast you into inextinguishable fire,' I now will burn you with fire that can be extinguished. Let us see what your God will do."

119.   He ordered lead to be melted in iron cauldrons,[1] and while it was still hot to be poured like water over his body. And his flesh was completely burned. Yet he did not die, but withstood it with great fortitude. And to whatever they asked he immediately replied.

120.   And the king was amazed at his incredible fortitude and endurance and at his persistence, and said: "How does there remain breath in you after so long and after these cruel tortures with which I have afflicted you?" Gregory replied and said: "Did I not tell you earlier to test the endurance of this servant of God? For he gives strength in order to confound those who are without him and who fight against him like you. For thus he says: 'I shall neither abandon you nor cast you down' [Ps. 36.28; Jn. 14.18]. So this is his protection towards his creatures and his loved ones,

գի պահեացէ զնոսա ի հալածս իւրեանց որ ի
նա, մինչև հատուցէ նոցա ի գալստեան իւ֊
րում»:

121   Եւ մինչդեռ խորհէր Տրդատիոս
խոսել և այլ ողոքով ընդ նմա, և յղել պատգամ
և խոստանալ կեանս և պատիւս, որում ոչ ինչ
էր լսելոց,—«եթէ այնմ ես ոչ լսից՝ ասէ, և
այլ ես յաւելից, և ի տող կատեցից».—յառաջ
մատուցեալ ոմն ի նախարարացն, որում անուն
էր Տաճատ, փեսայ Արտաւանայ սպարապետի
արքայի՝ սկսաւ խոսել և տալ տեղեկութիւն և
ասել այսպէս վասն նորա, թէ «Վասն գի չէ
պարտ կենաց՝ վասն այնորիկ ոչ կամի կեալ և
զլոյս տեսանել: Զի այսքան ժամանակք են, որ
առ մեզ բնակեալ ·է, և ոչ գիտէաք զսա. այլ
դա է որդի Անակայ մահապարտի, որ սպան գհայր
քո Խոսրով, և արաբ խաւար Հայոց աշխարհիս և
ի կորուստ մատնեաց զայս աշխարհ և ի գերու֊
թիւն. արդ՝ չէ պարտ կեալ դմա, գի որդի վրի֊
ժապարտի է դա»:

122 Եւ յետ այսչափի հարցից և տանջանաց,
գանից և բանտից, գելարանաց և կապարանաց,
դառն նեղութեանց և ամենայն կտտանաց, որով
կտտեցին գնա, բազում համբերութեամբ յանձն
իւր տարեալ վասն անուան Տեառն մերոյ Յի֊
սուսի Քրիստոսի. այդ՝ իբրև այնմ ես հաստանէր
Թագաւորն ի վերայ իրացն, եթէ արդարև որդի

to keep them in their faith in him until he will reward them at his coming."

121.   While Tiridates was planning to speak with him in a gentler fashion and to reply and promise him life and honors, to which he would not have agreed—"If he does not agree to this, he said, then will I increase (the tortures)[1] still more and break his endurance"—there came forward one of the princes, whose name was Tachat, son-in-law of Artavan the High Constable,[2] and he began to speak and give information about him as follows: "Because he is unworthy of life, therefore he does not wish to live and see the light. For it is all this time since he has been living among us and we did not recognize him. But he is the son of the guilty Anak, who killed your father Khosrov and plundered this land of Armenia and brought this country to destruction and captivity. So it is not right for him to live, because he is the son of a guilty man."[3]

122.   After so many interrogations and torments, beatings and imprisonments, bindings and hangings, bitter afflictions and every torture that they had inflicted on him, which he accepted with great patience for the sake of the name of our Lord Jesus Christ, then when the king discovered this further about him that he was in truth the son

Անակայ Պարթևի է, որ սպան զԽոսրով հայր
նորա՝ հրաման տայր կապեալ ոտիւք և կապեալ
ձեռօք և կապեալ պարանոցաւ խաղացուցանել
զնա յԱյրարատ գաւառ, և տալ զնա ի դղեակ
բերդին Արտաշատ քաղաքի, և իՉուցանել ի վիրապն ներբին, որ աննաբին էր խորութեամբ,
մինչև անդէն մեղցի։ Եւ եղև նա յայնմ վիրապի
ամս երեքտասան։ Եւ ինքն իսկ Թագաւորն խա-
պայր զնայր ի ձմերոց յԱյրարատ գաւառ, ի
Վաղարշապատ քաղաք, ի Հայոց աշխարհ յա-
րևելս։

123 Իսկ Թագաւորն Տրդատ գամենայն ժամանակս իւրոյ Թագաւորութեանն ւեբէր քան-
դէր զերկիրն Պարսից Թագաւորութեանն և դաշխարհն Ասորեստանի, ւեբէր և հարկանէր ի
հարուածս աննաբինս։ Վասն այսորիկ պատշա-
ճեցան բանքս այս ի բանս կարգի առակաց, Թէ
«Իբրև գսէցն Տրդատ, որ սիզալովջ ւեբեաց
զԹումբս գետոց, և ցամաքեցոյց իսկ ի սիգան
իւրում գյորձանս ծովուց»։ Վասն գի ասկ իսկ
էր առ հանդերձս և այլ ուժով անդութեան,
հարստութեամբ, բուռն ոսկերօք և յաղթ մարմնով, քաշ և պատերազմող աննաբին, բարձր և
լայն հասակաւ. որ գամենայն ժամանակս կենաց իւրոց պատերազմեալ և առնէր մարտին
յաղթութիւն։ Մեծ անուն պարձանաց քաջութեան անձին ստանայր, և գհոյակապ շքեղութիւն

of Anak the Parthian who had killed his father Khosrov, he ordered him to be bound hand and foot and
neck and to be taken and shut up in a dungeon in the
province of Ayrarat, that he should be taken to the
acropolis[1] of the city of Artashat[2] and let down into
the bottommost pit[3] that was incredibly deep until he
died there. And he was in that pit thirteen[4] years.
But the king himself went to the province of Ayrarat
to his winter-quarters in the city of Vaḷarshapat, in
the East of Armenia.

[Chapter 4. Trdat's prowess; his edicts
                  concerning the gods and
                  against Christians]

123.   King Trdat spent the whole period of his reign
devasting the land of the Persian kingdom and the
land of Asorestan.[1] He plundered and caused terrible
distress. Therefore this saying was adopted among the
proverbial sayings: "Like the haughty Trdat, who in
his pride devastated the dykes of rivers and in his
arrogance dried up the currents of seas."[2] For truly
he was haughty in dress and endowed with great
strength and vigor; he had solid bones and an enormous body, he was incredibly brave and warlike, tall
and broad of stature. He spent his whole life in war
and gained triumphs in combat. He acquired a great
renown for bravery

յաղթութեան ընդ ամենայն աշխարհ կացուցա
նէր. հարկանէր ի հարուածս գթշնամիսն, և խընդ
րէր դքէնա վրիժուց իւրոց հայրենեացն· առնոյր
աւար բազում ի կողմանցն Ասորւոց, և թափէր
կապուտ սատիկ անհնարին ի նոցանէն: Արկա
նէր ի սուր զզօրս Պարսից, և թափէր կողոպուտ
անհնարին. լինէր առաջնորդ առն և ձիոյ զօրացն
Յունաց, և մատնէր նոցա զբանակս նոցա. հա
նէր զզօրս Հոնաց սատիկ յոյժ, և գերէր զկող
մանս Պարսից:

124 Եւ դայն ամա երեքտասան, որ եղև
Գրիգորիս ի բերդին բանդին և ի խոր վիրա
պին, կին ումն այրի, որ էր ի բերդին յայնմիկ,
հրաման առեալ յարհաւրաց՝ զի աւուրն նկանակ
մի արարեալ պատրաստական ընկենու ի ներքս
ի խոր վիրապն. և այնու կերակրեալ լինէր նա
ի հրամանէն Աստուծոյ դայն ամա որ եղև նա
անդ· Իսկ յայն վիրապ, ուր ընկեցին զնա՝ պա
հեալ լինէր նա կենդանի շնորհիւ Տեառն իւրոյ:
Իսկ այլ մարդիկ, որ միանգամ իՉուցեալ էր
անդր՝ ամենեքեան մեռեալ էին վաան դժնդակ
շարաշունչ դառնութեան տեղւոյն, վաան կարա
կում տղմին, օձախառն րնակութեան և խորու
թեանն: Վաան չարագործաց իսկ էր շինեալ դայն
տեղի և ի սպանումն մահապարտացն ամենայն
Հայոց:

125 Եւ յետ այսորիկ հրաման ետ Տէր

and extended throughout the whole world the glorious splendor of his victories. He threw his enemies into disarray and revenged his ancestors. He devasted many of the regions of Syria[3] and took a great amount of booty from them. He put to the sword the armies of the Persians and acquired enormous booty. He became commander[4] of the cavalry of the Greek army, and handed over to them the camps (of the enemy). He expelled the armies of the Huns by force and subjected the regions of Persia.[5]

124.   And during the thirteen[1] years that Gregory was in the dungeon of the fortress, in the deep pit, a widow who lived in that castle received a command in a dream to prepare a loaf[2] a day and to throw it into the deep pit. And thereby Gregory was nourished[3] by God's command for the years he was there, and in that pit where they had thrown him he was kept alive by the grace of his Lord. But other men, once they had been let down there, all perished because of the atrociously bad air of the place, because of the muddy mire, the snakes who lived there and the depth. That place had been constructed for evil-doers and in order to execute those condemned to death in all Armenia.

125.   Then king Trdat ordered an edict to be made

դատ արքայ՝ հրովարտակ առնել ընդ ամենայն
աշխարհն իշխանութեան իւրոյ, հրաման հանեալ
օրինակ պայս.

126 «Տրդատ արքայ Հայոց մեծաց, առ մեծամեծս և առ իշխանս և առ նախարարս և առ
գործակալս և առ այլ մարդիկդ, որ ընդ իմով
իշխանութեամբ էք, յաւանս, ի շէնս, ի գեօղս,
յագարակս, առ ազատս և առ շինականս, միանգամայն իսկ առ ամենեսեան, ողջոյն։

127 «Ողջոյն հասեալ և շինութիւն դիցն
օգնականութեամբ, լիութիւն պարարտութեան
յարոյն Արամագդայ, խնամակալութիւն յԱնահիտ
տիկնոջէ, և քաջութիւն հասցէ ձեզ ի քաջէն
Վահագնէ ամենայն Հայոց աշխարհիս. իմաստութիւն Յունաց հասցէ դաստակերտիդ կայսե-
րաց, և ի մեր դիւցախառն Պարթևաց հասցէ
այցելութիւն, ի փառաց թագաւորաց և ի քաջ
նախնեաց։

128 «Ամենայն որ գիտասցէ ի մերոց հրա-
մանացս որ առ ձեզ, զի վասն ձեր շինութեան
եմք հոգացեալք. զի յորժամ էաք մեք ի Յունաց աշխարհին՝ անդ տեսանէաք գհոգաբարձու-
թիւն թագաւորացն, ի հոգալ ընդ շինութիւն
իւրեանց աշխարհին, ի պատուել դրագինս դիցն
աստուածոց շինուածովք և սպանդիւք գոհիցն,
և երևելի պատարագացն ընծայիւք, և գունակ
գունակ նուիրօքն և ի պաղոցն՝ յամենայնէ պա-

throughout the whole land of his kingdom [cf. III
Macc. 3.7], with a command as follows:

126. "Trdat, king of Greater Armenia, to the magnates, the nobles, the princes, the officials and other
men under my authority [cf. III Macc. 7.2], in the
towns, villages, hamlets, and estates, to the freemen
and the peasants, to everyone together, greeting.

127. "May there be greeting and prosperity by the
help of the gods [cf. III Macc. 3.9], abundant fertility
from noble Aramazd, protection from Lady Anahit,
valor from valiant Vahagn[1] to you and all our land of
Armenia; may[2] there be the wisdom of the Greeks to
the province[3] of the Caesars, protection (to us) from
our heroic Parthians, from the glory[4] of (our) kings
and brave ancestors.[5]

128. "Let everyone know from this command of
ours to you, that we are concerned for your prosperity.
For when we were in the land of the Greeks we saw
there the solicitude of their kings in caring for the
prosperity of their land, in honoring the altars of the
gods with buildings and sacrifices and gifts of notable
offerings, and all kinds of presents and fruits,

մենայն նոցա մատուցանելով, և Ջերմենանդն
եռալ գեռալ պաշտամանն, շքեղացուցանելով և
գարդուքն գարդարելով և գեբևելի գհոյակապ
գանեղծ դլոսն մեծարելով։ Եւ գայն իս տեսանէաք ի նոցանէ՝ ինոցունց դիզ անտի՝ գխապա-
պասէր շինութիւն մարդաշատութեան, հոծ բազմամբոխ լիութեամբ պարապտութեամբ՝ նոցա
գայն փոխագարձ փոխարինացն շինութիւն շնոր
հեալ, ամենալրիւք բարութեամբ մեծացեալք
խաղաղացեալք ի բարիսն վայելէին։

129 «Վասն որոյ պատուէր տուեալ, անա-
բեկ արաբեալ Թագաւորաց աշխարհին՝ գմար-
դիկն գարհուրեցուցանէին վասն պաշտաման դիցն
յոլովելոյ. մի գուցէ թէ խառնազան՞ բազմամբոխ խամամուժ մարդիկ առ ոգխտութեան ինչ
արհամարհիցեն. կամ եթէ ոք յանկարծ առ փո-
խեցուլութեան իշխեցէ արհամարհել գպաշտօն դիցն՝
հրաման ելեալ գոբացեալ ի Թագաւորաց, գի
խլեցեն բրեացեն իշխանքն որ իցեն յիւրաքանչիւր գործակալութեան, գի շինութիւն աշխարհի
ի դիցն բագմասցի։ Չի գուցէ թէ յանկարծ
ոք գդիսն անգոսնեսցէ՝ վնաս մեծ ի ցատմանէ
դիցն յուցեսցի. այնպիսքն դանձինս կորուսանեն, և աշխարհի մեծ ոճիրս վնասուց ի նոցանէն ընդոստուցանեն. վասն այտորիկ իսկ և եռուն
գհրամանս ստապից այնպիսեացն՝ պատուհաս
մահու՝ Թագաւորքն Յունաց յիւրեանց աշխարհին։

offering them a share of everything, being most assiduous in worshiping, embellishing, adorning and mag-
nifying the noble, magnificent and eternal gods. And
this further we saw, how from the same gods in compensation they gained peaceful and populous prosperity, abundant and overflowing fertility, and were
honored with every blessing and enjoyed peace and
happiness.

129.   "Therefore the kings of that land by their commands[1] instilled fear in men to be assiduous in the
cult of the gods. Lest perchance some of the common
masses in ignorance might neglect it, or someone in
a sudden derangement might dare to scorn the cult of
the gods, a strong command was issued by the kings
that the nobles in each one's sphere of office should
extirpate and remove (such people), so that the prosperity of the country might be increased by the gods.
For if perchance someone were suddenly to disdain
the gods, great harm would be occasioned by the gods'
anger. Such people would destroy themselves and
bring upon the country terrible damage from them
(the gods). Therefore the kings of the Greeks ordered
such threats of the death penalty in their land.

130 «Արդ՝ և մեք հրաման շինութեան կամեցեալ ձեզ, հոգացեալ զի և ձեզ ամենալրիւքն
ամենաբարիքն ի դիցն բաղմասցին. զի ի ճէնջ՝
պաշտօն նոցա և փառաւորութիւն, և ի նոցանէ՝
շինութիւն, լրութիւն և խաղաղութիւն. զի որպէս ամենայն տանուտէր ընդ տան իւրոյ և ընդ
ընտանեաց հոգայ՝ սոյնպէս և մեք հոգամք ընդ
մեր Հայոց աշխարհիս շինութեան.

131 «Արդ՝ ամենայն նախարարք մեծամեծք
և ապառք և գործակալք և սիրելիք մեր Թագաւորաց, և շինականք, բնակք և ձերատունկք և
ձերասունք մեր Արշակունեաց, զոր յանձան-
ձեալոդ և մնուցեալոդ է, անխայեալոդ և յառա-
ջեալոդ, վասն մեր օգտի հասարակաց հոգացեալ, զի զդիսն պատուեսջիք։ Արդ՝ եթէ յանկարծ օք թէ գոցի, որ զդիսն անպատուեսցէ, և
գոցեն զայնպիսին՝ կապեալ ոտիւք և կապեալ
ձեռօք և կապեալ պարանոցաւ ի դուռն արքունի
ածցեն. և տուն և կեանք և արաբք և ստացուածք և դանձք՝ այն ամենայն այնոցիկ լիցի,
որ զայնպիսին ի մէջ ածցեն։ Ողջ լերուք ի դիցն
օգնականութենէ դուք ամենեքին և ի մեր Թա-
գաւորաց՝ որ ընդ այս հրաման կամիք, և ի շինութեան բնակեսջիք ամենեքեան, զի մեք գըլ-
խովին իսկ ողջ եմք»։

132 Իսկ զամենայն ամս ժամանակաց իւրոց Թագաւորն Տրդատ զոռացեալ ընդ Պարսից

130. "So, we, desiring prosperity for you and anxious that fruitful blessings be increased by the gods for you, command that on your part you pay them worship and glory, (then) from them (will flow) prosperity, abundance and peace. For as every householder cares for his house and family, so do we care for the prosperity of our land of Armenia.

131. "So, all princes and magnates[1] and freemen and officials and beloved of our majesty, peasants and inhabitants and clients of our Arsacid family, whom we provided for, raised, took care of and promoted in order to care for our common advantage, do you honor the gods. But if unexpectedly someone be found who may dishonor the gods—if such be found let them be bound foot and hand and neck and be brought to the royal court. And let their house and sustinence and goods and property and treasure belong to all those who expose such people. May you all be well by the help of the gods and of our majesty, you who abide by this command; may you all live in prosperity, as we are well."

132. All the years of his reign king Trdat warred against the Persian empire,

տերութեանն՝ խնդրէր զքէնս վրիժուց մարտիք
պատերազմաց։ Իսկ ի ՛նուլ ամացն, որ եղե Գրիգորիոս ի վիրապին, իբրև ամս երեքտասան, և
էր մարտ ստատիկ խստութեան Տրդատայ ընդ
Պարսից Թագաւորին՝ զամենայն աւուրս կենաց
իւրոց։

133 Իսկ միւս ես այլ հրովարտակ հրամայեաց գրել ընդ աշխարհս և ընդ գաւառս իշխանութեանն իւրոյ՝ օրինակաւս այսուիկ.

134 «Տրդատիոս Հայոց մեծաց արքայ. առ
աշխարհս և առ գաւառս, առ նախարարս և առ
գործ և առ շինականս և առ ամենեսին ողջոյն.
ողջ լիջիք, և մեք մեզէն իսկ ողջ եմք։

135 «Դուք ինքնին գիտէք, զիարդ ի բնէ
ի նախնեացն իսկ յաղթութիւն խապաղութեան
բազում էր շնորհեալ մեզ դից օգնականութեամբ, և կամ թէ որպէս զամենայն ազգ նուաճեալ էր, և ի հնազանդութեան ունէաք։ Իսկ
յորժամ զդիան ոչ մարթացաք հաճել պաշտա-
մամբն, զկամս նոցա քաջրացուցանել ընդ մեզ՝
հանին մերժեցին ի ցասմանն իւրեանց զմեզ ի
մեծ տերութենէն։ Մանաւանդ վասն ապանդին
քրիստոնէից պատուիրեալ ձեզ, զի հազար և բիւր
դեկ է եթէ գոցի ոք, զի նոքա աննարին լինին խափան դից պաշտամանն, զայնպիսին թէ
գոցեն և վաղվաղակի ի մէջ ածցեն՝ յարքունուստ պարգեք և պատիւք նոցա լիցին շնոր-

seeking vengeance in battle. And so for all the years that Gregory was in the pit, about thirteen,[1] were continued Trdat's fierce struggle with the Persian king all the days of his life.

133. Then[1] he ordered another edict to be published throughout the lands and provinces of his realm, as follows:

134. "Tiridates, ruler of Greater Armenia, to the lands and provinces, princes and soldiers and peasants, to all, greetings. Be well, as we ourselves are well.[1]

135. "You yourselves know how from the time of our ancestors we were granted many victories and peace by the help of the gods, and how we subjected all races and held them in obedience. But when we were not able to please the gods with worship or favorably incline their will towards us, then in their anger they deprived us of our great authority. So we particularly command you in the matter of the sect of Christians, that if any are found, be they thousands or tens of thousands,[1] because they are an insuperable obstacle to the worship of the gods, that if such people be found and immediately exposed, those who reveal them will be granted gifts and honors from the royal treasury.

հեալ որ գնոսայն յայտնեցեն։ Ապա թէ ոք
չյայտնեցէ դայնպիսին, կամ Թագուսցէ, և գոցի՝
այսպիսին ընդ մահապարտ համարեալ լիցի, և
ի հրապարակ արքունի եկեալ մեղցի, և տուն
նորա յարքունիս երթիցէ։

136 «Արդ՝ գոր օրինակ ես ոչ խնայեցի յիմ
վաստակաւոր Գրիգորիոս, յիմ սիրելին, որ վասն
դորին իսկ իրաց չարաչար և ստտիկ տանջա-
նոք տանջեցի, և յետ այնորիկ եստւ գնա ընկենուլ ի խոր վիրապն յանհնարին, զի անդէն իսկ
միանգամայն օձից լիցի կերակուր. զի և ոչ գմեծ
վաստակն նորա համարեցայ ինչ՝ առ սիրով և
առ անիւ դիցն, զի և ձեզ ան լիցի այս և եր-
կիւղ ի մահուանէն։ այլ զի կեցչիք ընդ հովա-
նեաւ դիցն և ի մէնչ բարիս մարթասչիք գտա-
նել։ Ողչ լերուք, և մեք մեղէն ողչ եմք»։

137   Եւ եղև ընդ ժամանական ընդ այնոսիկ խնդրեաց իւր կին կայսրն Դիոկղետիանոս. և այնուհեան ընդ ամենայն կողմանս տե-
րութեան իւրոյ արձակեալք շրջէին պատկերա-
գործք նմանահանք ճչգրտագործք. դեղատխ-
տակ պայծառակշիր հասակաչափ դղեղ երեսացն
և գմրագարդ յօնիցն ի տախտական համանմանս
դեղովքն պաճուճէին, զի յայտ յանդիման ցուց-
ցեն առաչի ակնահածոյ կամաց Թագաւորին։

138 Ցայնմ ժամանակի եկեալ գտանէին ի
քաղաքին Հռոմայեցւոց արդելւվանս մի կուսա-

But if anyone does not reveal such people but hides them and he be discovered, then let such a one be accounted among those condemned to death, and after being brought to the royal tribunal may he die and his house be confiscated to the court.[2]

136. "Similarly, I did not spare my deserving Gregory, my friend, who for this same cause I tortured with cruel and severe torments, and then had him thrown into the incredibly deep pit that he might be food for the snakes there; for I accounted as nothing his merits in my love and fear of the gods, that you too might have this fear and dread of death. So may you live under the protection of the gods and from us find blessings. Be well, and we ourselves are well."

[Chapter 5. The Martyrdom of Rhipsimē, Gaianē and their companions

A. *Diocletian seeks a wife; prayer of the nuns*]

137. It happened in those times that the emperor Diocletian sought a wife. Then were sent out and circulated throughout his whole empire painters who could produce a true likeness. Rendering naturally on tablets the beauty of the face and the mascaraed eyebrows, with faithful colors they made accurate pictures to show before the king and please his eye.[1]

138. Then they came and found in the city of Rome a convent of nuns,

նաց՝ միանձնական լեռնական, ընդակերս, զգաս-
տացեալս, պարկեշտականս, սրբամատոյց կա-
նայս քրիստոսական հաւատող, որ զգայգ և զգե-
րեկ և յամենայն ժամանակի փառաւորութեամբ
և օրհնութեամբ զկատարեալ աղօթսն իւրեանց
առ Աստուած առաքել ի բարձունս արժանի լի-
նէին։ Որոյ անուն էր գլխաւորին Գայիանէ, և
սան նորին՝ ի դստերաց ուրումն յատտուածա-
պաշտ և ի թագակալ տոհմէ, զի անուն էր նորա
Հռիփսիմէ։

139 Եւ իբրև եկին հասին՝ բռնութեամբ
մտեալ ի սուրբ կայեանս առաքինեացն, տեսեալ
զպարկեշտագեղն Հռիփսիմէ, զարմացեալ սքրաս-
ցեալ ընդ սքանչելատեսիկն տեսլէ՝ ի նկարապա-
ճոյճ ի տախտական յօրինելին, և առ թագաւորն
հասուցանէին։

140 Եւ իբրև ետես թագաւորն զգեղապանծ
վայելչութիւն պատկերակերպ նկարագրին Հռիփսիմեայ, մոլեգնական ցանկութեամբ տոչողաց
գեղեցեալ, զի անկարգ ցանկութիւն յիմարու-
թեանն մոլութեան ստիպէր, ժամ տուեալ ուրախութեան հարսանեաց՝ ձեպով տագնապաւ
փութայր գուբախութիւնս հարսանեացն կատա-
րել։ Յայնմ ժամանակի տագնապափոյթ ստիպով
դեսպանս արձակեալ, պատուիրակս հանեալ ընդ
աշխարհս ամենայն, զի ամենեքեան օժտակեր
ընծայատար լիցին մեծի հարսանեացն, և բա-

living solitary hermetic lives, eating vegetables, sober, modest, and pure women of the Christian faith, who day and night and the whole time by praising and blessing were worthy[1] to raise to God in the heights their perfect prayers. Their abbess was called Gaianē, and her protégée, who was one of the daughters of a pious man and of royal lineage, was called Rhipsimē.[2]

139.   When they arrived, they entered by force into the holy dwelling-place of these virtuous women; and seeing the modest beauty of Rhipsimē they were amazed and charmed at her wonderful appearance. They painted her likeness on their tablets and sent it to the emperor.

140.   And when the emperor saw the graceful beauty of Rhipsimē's portrait, he went mad with licentious desire.[1] The unbridled passion of his folly increased, and he set a time for the marriage, anxiously anticipating the wedding celebration. Then he urged envoys and messengers to be sent throughout the whole empire, so that everyone might bring gifts and presents to the grand wedding,

գում ուրախութեամբ գալ կատարել առ հասարակ ամենեցուն զօրէնս արքայական փեսային՝ ըստ օրինացն Թագաւորաց։

141 Իսկ իբրև տեսին առաքինիքն զգաղտնածիդ նետս Թշնամւոյն, որ ի ծածուկն սովոր էր ձգել ի սուրբսն քրիստոսասէրսն, աման չարի գտեալ զԹագաւորն․ որպէս ի դրախտի անդ զօձն անդրուվար արարեալ, առ ի պատուիրանն մոռանալոյ, մտեալ յանգգամ յունկն կնոջն առաջնոյ․ սոյնպէս և աստ զԹագաւորն անօրէն իբրև զվահանակ երեսաց գտեալ՝ նովաւ մարտուցեալ ընդ աստուածաշէն եկեղեցիս։

142 Իսկ զԹագաւորն նախարատացուցեալ ամբարհաւածեցուցանէր որոգայթադիր Թշնամին՝ ի գրգռել յարուցանել հալածանս ի վերայ եկեղեցեաց Աստուծոյ, խելացնորեցուցեալ զնա առ ի տալ պագանել երկիր ուրուականաց մեռելութեանց, ոսկեղէն և արծաթեղէն, փայտեղէն և քարեղէն պղնձագործ պատկերաց դիցն անտեաց, և պղծութեանն պաշտամանն։ Ուս եղեալ համբառնայր հարկանել ընդ վիմին հաստատնոյ, ընդ հալատոցն եկեղեցւոյ․ վիմին ինչ ոչ տանանել կարացեալ՝ ինքն առ վիմին խորտակեցաւ։ Սակայն յամբարհաւածութիւն մոլեգնութեանն վրատահացեալ՝ բազում և անչափ էր այն, որ ի նմանէ անցանէր ընդ եկեղեցիս Աստուծոյ։

143 Իսկ երանելին պարկեշտասէրն Գա-

and that all might come and joyfully celebrate the emperor's marriage according to royal custom.

141.　But when the pious women saw the hidden arrows of the enemy [cf. Eph. 6.6], who is accustomed to shoot secretly at the saints who love Christ, they found that the emperor (had become) a vessel of evil [cf. Jer. 51.34], and that just as in the garden he had used the snake as a vehicle for causing the forgetting of the commandment, entering into the foolish ear of the first woman [cf. Gen. 3], so here too he had used the lawless emperor as a mask[1] through which he could fight with the church built by God.

142.　The beguiling enemy aroused the king's vanity and arrogance so that he stirred up persecutions against the churches of God; he maddened him so that he worshiped futile corpses[1] [cf. Jer. 16.18], images of vain gods of gold and silver, wood and stone, and their impure cult. He was emboldened to attack the firm rock, the faith of the church [cf. Matt. 16.18]. But unable to harm the rock he was himself broken against the rock. Nonetheless, trusting in the arrogance of his folly, he was the cause of very great harm to the churches of God.

143.　But the blessed and chaste Gaianē,

յիանէ, սրբանելովն Հոգւովմբեաւ հանդերձ և
այլ ընկերօքն իւրեանց, յիշեալ գլխաւն սրբութեան, զօրինաւոր կրօնիցն զգաստութեան սրբ-
բութիւնն յոր մտեալ էին՝ ողբային յանձինս
իւրեանց վասն նկարացոյց հրամանին, առ ի
նկատել զգպատկերս նոցա սիրդ և անօրէն թագաւորին. ճգնութեամբ մատուցեալ յաղօթս՝
խնդրել ի բազումողորմ Տեառնէն օգնականու-
թիւն՝ փրկել զնոսա ի փորձութենէն, որ հասեալ
էր ի վերայ նոցա։ Եւ յաղաչէին իւրեանց այսպէս ասէին.

144 «Տէր տերանց, Աստուած աստուծոց,
Աստուած յաւիտենական, Աստուած երկնից, Աստուած անճառ լուսոյ, որ հաստատեցեր գամենայն բանիւ քով. որ արարեր զերկինս և զերկիր և գամենայն զարդ նոցա. որ ստեղծեր
զմարդն հող յերկրէ և իմաստուն կացուցեր և
բաղմացուցեր գնա ի վերայ երկրի, և օգնական
եղեր նոցա ի դարս իւրաքանչիւր՝ որ յուսացան
ի քեզ։

145 «Արդ՝ օգնեա և մեզ, Տէր, ի պատե-
րազմիս որ նեղեա գմեզ, զի յաղթեացուք որո-
գայթից նենգութեանց սատանայի, և անուն քո,
Տէր, փառաւոր լիցի, և եղջիւր եկեղեցւոյ քոյ
բարձրացեալ լիցի. զի և մեք արժանի լիցուք
հասանել յօթևանս արքայութեան պատուիրա-
նապահաց քող։ Եւ մի՛ լիցի պակասութիւն ձի-

with the saintly Rhipsimē and their other companions, remembered the covenant of holiness, the religious rule [cf. II Macc. 4.11; 6.23] of chastity into which they had entered, and lamented amongst themselves [cf. I Macc. 2.7] over the impure and impious emperor's command to have their portraits painted. They fervently prayed, seeking help from the all-merciful Lord, that he would save them from the trial which had come upon them [cf. Mt. 6.13]. And in their supplication they prayed as follows:

144. "Lord of lords, God of gods, God eternal, God of heaven, God of ineffable light, who established everything by your word, who made heaven and earth and all their order, who fashioned man (as) dust from the earth [cf. Gen. 2.1,7] and rendered him wise and made him increase over the earth [cf. Gen. 1.28], and were helpful to those who hoped in you in each one's age [cf. Ex. 15.2],

145. "now help us too, Lord, in this struggle which oppresses us, that we may overcome the traps and deceits of Satan [cf. II Tim. 2.26]. And let your name, Lord, be glorious, and the horn of your church exalted [cf. Lk. 1.69; Psalms, *passim*], that we too may become worthy to attain the dwelling-places of the kingdom of those who keep your commandments [cf. Jn. 14.2]. And let there be no lack of oil

թոյ ի լապտերաց մերոց. և մի շիշքին ճրագունք
հաւատող ուխտի սրբութեան մերոյ. և մի հացէ
տիրական մթացուցիչն գիշերոյ կորստեան ի
վերայ լուսաւոր ճանապարհաց մերոց. և մի
գայթակղեցին որք մեր ի լուսաքնաց շաւղաց
քոց. և մի կուրասցին բիբք տեսանելեաց մերոց ի դուարթութարար ճառագայթից ճշմարտութեան
քոյ. և մի յափշտակեսցէ թոշունն մահացան
գետերմանիան բուսոյն կենաց, զոր սերմանեաց ի
մեզ միածին Որդիդ քո, տէր մեր Յիսուս Քրիստոս. և մի տարցի գզգատութիւն սուրբ հօտի քոյ
գապաննն ապատամբ. և մի յաղթահարեսցէ գզա-
րինս հօտի քոյ գայլն ապականիչ. և մի վարա-
տեսցէ թշնամին ուխտիս մերոյ գոչխարս առաքելական եկեղեցւոյ քոյ սրբոյ:

146 «Տէր Աստուած մեր, որ առաքեցեր
գմիածին Որդիդ քո, որ եկն և եկից դամենայն
տիեղերս հոգւով իմաստութեամբ քով, զի գամենեսեան յիսրայէլ անուն ասասւածատես
գրեցից: Եւ մեք լուաք գի ասաց, «Թէպէտ և
հայածեցին գձեգ քաղաքէ ի քաղաք՝ ոչ կա-
րասչիք սպառել գքաղաքս Իսրայէլի, մինչի ի
դարձ գալստեան իմոյ այսրէն»:

147 «Արդ խնայեա, Տէր, յանձինս մեր, որ
ապաւինեցաք յանունն քո սուրբ, զի մի խառնա-
կեսցուք ընդ անարգութիւն պղծութեան հեթանոսաց. և մի տար գզգատութիւն սրբութեան մե-

for our lamps [cf. Matt. 25.8], nor let the torches of the faith of our oath of holiness be extinguished [cf. Lk. 12.35]. Let not the sad gloom of the night of destruction overshadow our shining paths. Let not our feet stumble from your luminous ways [cf. Ps. 16.5]. Let not the pupils of our eyes be blinded to the bright rays of your truth [cf. II Cor. 4.4]. Let not the bird of death snatch away the seeds of the plant of life which your only-begotten Son, our Lord Jesus Christ, sowed in us [cf. Matt. 13.4]. Let not the rebellious beast carry off the virtue of your holy flock. Let not the corrupting wolf prevail over the lambs of your flock [cf. Ez. 34]. Let not the enemy of our covenant scatter the sheep of your holy apostolic church [cf. Jn. 10.12].

146. "Lord our God, who sent your only-begotten Son, who came and filled the whole world with your Spirit and wisdom in order to inscribe everyone with the name of Israel, 'seers of god.'[1] And we heard him say 'Although they will persecute you from city to city, you will not be able to exhaust the cities of Israel until my return there' [Matt. 10.23].

147. "Now have mercy, Lord, on us who have taken refuge in your holy name. Let us not be joined to the degredation of pagan filthiness. Permit not the chastity of our holiness

բոյ բոգանոց անօրէն շանագգեաց լկաութեան
նոցա, և մի զկուսութեան մարգարիտ հալատոց
մերոց՝ ի շալիզդ խոզագնայ ամբարշտութեան
նոցա։ Եւ մի շարժեցէ ուղխանյաց Հուրց բագ-
մութեանց մոլորահոդիՍ խաբէութեան գրանե-
դեդն ասատկութեան գՂիմունս սուրբ եկեղեցւոյ
քոյ, որ բագմապատիկ վիմօքն արդարովք շի-
նեցաւ ի վերայ վիմին Հասատանոյ, որոյ գլուխ
անկեանն կատարման եղև Տէր մեր Ցիսուս
Ֆրիստոս ի ձեռն մարՍանալոյն, մահուամբ խա-
շին, Հեդմամբ արեանն, յարութեամբն և յերկինս
վերանալոյն, նստելովն յաՋմէ աստուածութեան
քոյ, ուր էրն յառաՋ։

148 «Արդ նայեաց, Տէր, յերկնից ի սրբ-
բութենէ քումմէ, գի մի լիցուք մեք իբրև գայն
տունն, որ ի վերայ աւազոյն շինեալ էր, գոր
դրդուեցին խոռվութիւնք նեդութեանց պեսպես
փորձութեանց. այլ Հասատատեա գմեզ ճշմարտութեամբ Աւետարանին խաղադութեան, և առաՋ-
նորդեա մեզ ընդ կամաց քոց, և արժանիս արա
գմեզ գիշերոյն լուսոյ Հարսանեաց. յորում գգի-
շերն իբրև գաիբ լուսաւոր առնիցես ի ծագել
ճառագայթից յերեսաց փառաց քոց, և ապրեցն
գմեզ ի ներքոյ թևոց քոց, և մեք Հասցուք ի
նաւահանգիստ կամաց քոց։ Եւ տուր մեզ, գի
արբցուք գբաժակ նահատակութեան, գի աղցուք
գփոխարէն պսակն յալուր արդար դատաստանին

to be a brothel for those obscene dogs; give not the pearl of the virginity of our faith to their impious and swinish ways [cf. Matt. 7.6]. Let not the torrent of the voracious floods of error and deceit [cf. Ps. 17.5] shake the foundations of your holy church, which was built with many true stones on the firm rock [cf. Matt. 7.24; Lk. 6.48], whose chief corner-stone was our Lord Jesus Christ [cf. I Pet. 2.6] through his incarnation and by his death on the cross, the shedding of his blood, his resurrection and ascension into heaven, his sitting on the right hand of your Godhead where he was before.

148. "Now look down, Lord, from heaven from your holiness [cf. Ps. 101.20; Baruch 2.16], lest we become like that house which was built on the sand, and which was toppled by the buffetings of afflictions and various trials [cf. Matt. 7.26]. But confirm us in the truth of the gospel of peace [cf. Eph. 6.15], and lead us according to your will, and make us worthy of the marriage of the evening light, when you will make the evening as bright as the day [cf. Ps. 138.12] at the dawning of the rays from the face of your glory. And preserve us under your wings [cf. Psalms, *passim*], that we may reach the haven of your will [cf. Ps. 106.30]. And give us to drink the cup of martyrdom, that we may receive the crown as reward in the day of the just judgment at the revelation of your glory."

ի յայտնութեան փառաց քոց»։

149 Եւ յետ այսորիկ սուրբն Գայիանէ սա
նականաւն Հռիփսիմեաւ և պարկեշտամօղով ըն
կերօքն հանդերձ՝ դէմ եղեալ տարադէմ գնա
ցեալ փախստեայ լինէին, զի գանձինս իւրեանց
սրբութեամբ պանեցեն յայսմիկ հղաթաւալ,
մեղստութաւ, մեղանչական, անօրէն ի դիւա
կան խառնից մարդկան. զի առաւելութեան յու
սոյն կենդանութեան և լուսոյն յարութեան ար
ժանի լինիցին հասանել, ընդ առաքելական սահ
մանօքն ապրեալ յանվախճան ի հանդերձեալ դա
տաստանաց անտի, և յաշակողմն գահուն մեծալ՝
խոստացելոց բարեացն հասանել, անթառամ
պսակօքն գարդարեալ՝ ընդ ճգեկան կամարարն
կուսանաց, գործովքն բարութեան լուսաւորեալք
ի հանգիստ նորոգական վայելչութեան դրախ
տին, ընդ աստուածական փեսային ի բաղմաժո
ղովս արդարոցն, ի բաղմականս Աբրահամու ան
պակաս ուրախութեանցն լինել ժառանդորդ։ Որ
պէս և Տէրն յԱւետարանի անդ ասաց, եթէ «Որ
թողցէ զընակութիւն իւր վասն անուան իմոյ՝ ի
միւսանգամ գալստեան իմում զկեանս յաւիտե
նականս ժառանգեցուցից նմա»։ Իբրև ոչ ի ժա
մանակեան մահուանէս փախուցեալք, այլ յան
ճարէն մոլեկան անօրէն ցանկութեանցն ճողո
պրեալք։ Իբրև ոչ զի զմարմինս իւրեանց ի տան
ճանաց երկրակրծաց ի զրպարտութենէս ապրե

[*B. The nuns flee to Armenia
but are discovered;
Rhipsimē's prayer*]

149.   Then Gaianē and her protégée Rhipsimē and their group of chaste companions decided to flee to a distant land[1] in order to preserve themselves in purity from those swinish, sin-stained, pernicious, impious and devilish men; so that they might become worthy to attain the abundance of the hope of life and the light of resurrection, saved through the apostolic precepts from the everlasting future judgment and gaining a place on the right-hand side [cf. Matt. 25.33]; to attain the promised blessings, adorned with unfading crowns with the five obedient virgins [cf. Matt. 25.2], shining with deeds of virtue in the peace of the renewed splendor of paradise, with the divine bridegroom among the multitudes of the just, to become heirs of unfailing joys at Abraham's banquet.[2] As the Lord in the gospel said: "Who will leave his dwelling for my name's sake, at my coming again I shall make him heir to eternal life" [cf. Matt. 19.29; Mk. 10.29; Lk. 18.29]. Not as fleeing from this temporal death, but escaping from the terrible passion of impious desires; not to save their bodies from earthly torments and calumny,

ցուցեն, այլ զի զոգիան իւրեանց սրբութեամբ առանց ադտեզութեան պահել մարթասցեն յա֊
նորէն զիձնութեան պղձութեան ադտեզութեան
խառնից մարդկան անօրէն կրօնից. այլ զի դան֊
ձինս իւրեանց բանդից և կապանաց և պատժոց,
մահու և աննարին նեղութեանց վասն անուան
Տեառն պատրաստեալ, զի արդարութեան պա֊
կին արժանի լինիցին հասանել։ Վասն այսորիկ
թողեալ զերկիր ծննդեան իւրեանց, զինչս և
գատացուածս և զմերձաւոր զազգակից և զտոհ֊
մականս վասն առուածական հրամանին, դան֊
ձինս իւրեանց հրեշտակական դուարթական կար֊
գօք լուսաւորեալ վարուցն քաջութեամբք, զի
զԱստուած տեսանել կարացեն։

150 Յայնմ ժամանակի դային հասանէին
յերկիրն Հայոց, յԱյրարատ դաւառ, ի Վաղար֊
շապատ քաղաք, դոր և նորաքաղաքն կոչեն, ի
նիստս թագաւորացն Հայոց։ Այնուհետև եկեալ
մտանէին ի հնձանայարկս այզետստանուոյն, որ կան
չինեալ ի հիւսիսոյ յարևելից կուսէ. և կերակրէին
ընչիւք իւրեանց ի վաձառաց քաղաքին. և ոչ
ինչ այլ ինչ դոյր թոշակ ընդ նոսա դոր ունէին,
բայց մի ումն ի նոցանէ ունէր արուեստ ապա֊
կագործութեան՝ առնել ուլունս ապակեղէնս,
և տալ զինս ընդ կերակրոյ աւուրն պարենի ռոձկի։

151 Յայնմ ժամանակի ոչ սակաւ ինչ
խռովութիւն լինէր ի մէջ Յունաց աշխարհին. ի

but to be able to preserve their souls in purity without stain from the impious ways of impure and filthy men. Because they had prepared their bodies for prison and and bonds and punishment and death and incredible afflictions for the sake of the Lord's name [cf. Acts 9.16], that they might become worthy to attain the crown of righteousness, therefore they left the land of their birth, their possessions and property and close relations and families for the sake of the divine commandment [cf. Matt. 19.29]; they illumined their souls in angelic form by the virtue of their conduct so that they might be able to see God.

150.   Then they arrived in the land of Armenia, in the province of Ayrarat, in the city of Vałarshapat, which is also called Nor Kʻaḷakʻ,[1] the residence of the Armenian kings. Then they entered the vat-stores[2] of the vineyard which were constructed to the North-East. And they lived from what they bought from shops in the city. And they had no other source of income save that one of them possessed the skill of glassmaking and could make glass pearls,[3] which paid for their daily sustenance.

151.   Meanwhile there was no little turmoil in the land of the Greeks.

կողմանս կողմանս յուզախնդիրք եղանէին, դես֊
պանս արձակէին, թերևս ուրեք գտանել կա֊
րասցեն։ Յայնմ ժամանակի գայր հասանէր դես֊
պան առ Տրդատ արքայ Հայոց մեծաց, և յան֊
դիման լինէր Թագաւորին ի Վաղարշապատ քա֊
ղաքի։ Եւ իբրև մատոյց գերովարտակն՝ առ ի
ձեռանէ նորա խնդալով։ Եւ էր պատճէն հրո֊
վարտակին օրինակ գայս.

152 «Ինքնակալ կայսր Դիոկղետիանոս, առ
սիրելի եղբայր աթոռակից մեր Տրդատ ողջոյն։

153 «Գիտութիւն լիցի եղբայրութեանդ
քում նիզակակցի մերում վասն չարեացս, որ ան֊
ցանէնն ընդ մեզ հանապազ ի մոլար ազանդէս
քրիստոնէից. զի յամենայնի զարովեալ լինի աե֊
րութիւնս մեր յուխտէ նոցա, և արհամարհեալ լինի
արքայութիւնս մեր ի նոցանէ. և ինչ համես֊•
տութիւն ոչ գոյ ի նոսա։ Զի ինքեանք գմեռեալ
ումն գխաչեալ պաշտեն, և փայտի երկիր պագա֊
նեն, և դոսկերս սպանելոցն պաշտեն, որ գիւ֊
րեանց մահն, որ վասն Աստուծոյն իւրեանց է՝
փառս և պատիւս համարքին։ Եւ ի մերոց արդար
օրինացս դատապարտեալ լինին. վասն զի և գմեր
գնախնիան, գառաջին հարսն գԹագաւորսն, դառ֊
նացուցեալս ճանձրացուցին. զի մեր սուրբս
բԹեցան, և նոքա ոչ գարհուրեցան ի մեռանե֊
լոյ։ Զի ինքեանք գնետ Հրէի ուրումն խաչելոյ
մոլորեալ են, և գԹագաւորս անպատուել ուսու֊

Searchers went out and messengers were sent to every region, to see if they could find them anywhere. Then an emissary came to Trdat, ruler of Greater Armenia, and met the king in the city of Valarshapat. When he presented the edict,[1] he received it from his hand with joy. And the text of the edict ran as follows:

152.   "The emperor Caesar Diocletian to our beloved brother and colleague Trdat, greeting.[1]

153.   "Let your fraternity, our comrade in arms, know of the evils that continually befall us from this erring sect of the Christians:[1] in everything our majesty is derided by their religion and our rule is despised by them, and there is no respect in them. For they worship some dead and crucified man, and adore a cross, and worship the bones of those put to death, and they consider their own death on behalf of their God to be glory and honor. They have been condemned by our just laws because they embittered and angered our forefathers, our fathers and predecessors. Our swords have been blunted and they have not feared death. They have gone astray after some crucified Jew, and they teach dishonor for kings

ցանեն, և զլխովին իսկ գպատկերս դից՛ն գա-
տուածոց անարգել ուսուցանեն։

154 «Նա և զլուսաւորագղ գործութիւն, գա-
րեգական և զլուսնի աստեղօքդ հանդերձ՛ առ
ոչինչ համարին, նա և արարած առնեն այնր
խաչելոյ։ Եւ զլխովին գպատկերս դից՛ն աստուա-
ծոյն անարգել ուսուցանեն. և գաշխարՀս ամենայն փոխեցին ի պաշտամանէ դից՛ն. մինչև գէ
և զկանայս անգամ յարանց և գարս ի կանանց
կենդանւոյն մեկնեալս Հեռացուցանեն։ Թէպէտ
և ազգի ազգի պատուՀաս տանջանաց ի վերայ
եղաք՛ առաւել իս տոչորեալ յորդագոյնս տարածեցաւ աղանդ նոցա։ Թէպէտ և բիւրապատիկ
ինչ արՀաւիրս ստատից արկաք ի վերայ նոցա՛
ի Հեղումն արեան նոցա առաւել իս բղխեաց
՝յորդեաց աղանդ նոցա։

155 «Իէպ եղև տեսանել ինձ յաղանդոյ
ուսման նոցա օրիորդ մի կոյս և գեղեցիկ, և
կամեցայ առնուլ գնա ինձ կնութեան. սակայն
և գայն իշխեցին խորամանգել յինէն։ Եւ ոչ իբրև ի Թագաւոր ցանկութեամբ փափաքեցին յիս.
և ոչ ի ստատից սպանաւեալ ինոց երկեան ինչ
նոքա. այլ առաւել իս վասն աղանդոյն իւրեանց՛
ազտեղի և պիղծ և գարշ համարեցան գիս, և
սնուցիչ նորին դայեկաւն ի կողմանս ձերոյ տէ-
րութեանդ փախուցեալս յուղարկեցին։

156 «Արդ՛ փոյթ լիցի քեզ, եղբայր մեր,

and complete disrespect for the images of the divine gods.

154. "Similarly they regard as naught the power of the luminaries, the sun, moon and stars, and hold them to be creatures of that crucified one. And they teach complete disrespect for the images of the divine gods,[1] and dissuade the whole world from the worship of the gods. They even separate during their lifetime[2] women from their husbands and men from their wives. Although we have inflicted on them all kinds of cruel punishments, their sect has become inflamed all the more and has spread only wider. Although we have made countless terrible threats against them, at the shedding of their blood their sect has even more flourished and spread.

155. "I chanced to see a young and beautiful girl among the following of their sect, and I wished to take her to wife. But of this too they were able to cheat me. Not only were they not happy with me as king, they did not even fear my severe threats. But because of their sect they regarded me even more as stained, impure and abominable, and with their governess they have fled to the regions of your kingdom.

156. "So, my brother, be quick

գի ուր և իցեն զկողմամբքդ գայդոքիւք՝ դѕետ
նոցա գտանել մարթասցես. և որ ընդ նմայն իցեն
դայեկուԱն ѕանդերձ՝ վրիժուց մաѕու արժանի
արասցես. և գѕրապուրեա՞ն գշքնադագեդն ինձ ի
սոյն այսրէն յուղարկեսցես. ապա թէ ѕաձոյ
թուեսցի քեզ տեսիլ գեդոյ նորա՝ այդրէն առ
քեզ պաѕեսցես, դի ոչ երբէք գտաւ նման նմա
ի մէջ Յունաց աշխարѕիս: Որձ լեր դիցն պաշտամամբ ամենայն պատուով»:

157   Եւ եղև իբրև ընթերցան գթուղթն
ѕրամանաց ѕրովարտակին այնորիկ՝ ѕրաման այր
թագաւորն մեծաւ սատկութեամբ պատուիրա-
նաւ, դի գամենայն տեղիս իշխանութեան իւրոյ
քննայոյզ խուզիւ փութով խնդրեսցեն: Վաղվա-
դակի դեսպանս արձակէր ընդ կողմանս կողմանս,
դի ուր և գտցեն՝ ի մէջ աձցեն վաղվաղակի. և
որ գտցէ գնոսա՝ մեծամեծ պարգևս ѕատուցա-
նել խոստանայր:

158 Մինչդեռ յայն յոյզ քննութեան էին յաշ-
խարѕին սաѕմանացն Հայոց՝ սուրբ վկայքն այնո-
քիկ եկեալ դոդեալ էին յարքայական կայանին,
ի նմին թագաւորականին ի Վաղարշապատ քա-
դաքի: Եւ յետ սակաւ ինչ աւուրցն այնոցիկ վաղվաղակի ի մէջ եկեալ խուզիւք իրքն յայտնէին:

159 Այլ ոչ իսկ եր պարտ թոդչել ձշմարտու-
թեանն և վկայիցն առաքինութեան, և ոչ լուսոյ
ձրագի ընդ գրուանաւ ծածկել, և ոչ ի ներքոյ

to find their traces, wherever they may be in your parts. And take vengeance of death on whoever may be with her and their governess. And send back to me that beautiful charmer. But if her beauty pleases you, then keep her for yourself, for no one like her has ever been found in Greek lands. Be well by the worship[1] of the gods with all honor."[2]

157.   When the letter with this edict was read, the king gave a most strict command that they should quickly search every place in his realm with care and diligence. Immediately he sent messengers through every region, that wherever they might find them they should bring them immediately. And he promised to reward their finder with magnificent gifts.

158.   While this careful search was being conducted within the borders of Armenia, these holy martyrs had hidden themselves in the capital, in the same royal city of Vaḷarshapat. And after a few days of searching their whereabouts were discovered.

159.   It was not right for the truth and virtue of the martyrs to remain hidden, nor for the light of a torch to be hidden under a bushel or under

ստուերաց կաթեղբացն անեբևայթ լինել. այլ վերայ աշտանակացն ոսևոց գարդարելոց, և ոսևովք
ծրագարանօք գիւղև պարաբտութեան անուշու-
թեան, գարդարութեան հաւատոցն՝ վառեալ գլոյան
համապայծառ. որպէս և ինքեանք իսկ յառաջին
աղօթս իւրեանց ապաչէին. որպէս և Տէրն իսկ ատէր
առ իւր սիրելիսն, թէ «Տեսցեն զգործս ձեր բարիս, և փառաւորեսցեն զՀայր ձեր որ յերկինս է»:

160 Տեսանէ՞ս զի վասն գործոցն բարութեան ճշմարիտ Որդին Աստուծոյ ոչ գաբշի տալ
գիւր ժառանգութիւն իւրոց սիրելեացն ծառա-
յիցն. Որ ինքն բնութեամբ Որդի է՝ անվեհեր
մատուցանէ գիւր պատուիրանապաՀան յիւր բնութիւնն. բայց միայն թէ ոք իցէ, որ պաՀիցէ զբանս
նորա՝ իբրև գմարդպարիտ պատուական գտեալ
խնդութեամբ, գևեալ և գգուշացեալ լինի նմա՝
առեալ գնշան պատուին, գպասևն Թագաւորութեան և յարքայականն մատուցանի: Որպէս պա-
տուականութիւն լուսոյ այսորիկ երևեալ առաջի
ՆեԹանոսաց Հայաստան աշխարՀիս ակամայ,
իսկ փառաւորութիւնն առ ատուածութիւնն
Ննչիւք լցին գտիեգերս:

161 Արդ՝ գտեալ լինէին նոքա ի ճնձանս
շինուածոցն: Քանգի իբրև եկին հասին հրամանք
հրովարտակացն ի մեծ Թագաւորէն Յունաց առ
Տրդատ արքայն Հայոց Մեծաց՝ ոչ սակաւ ինչ
խռովութիւն եղև ի մէջ աշխարՀին Հայոց. գի

the shadow of a chair; but on candlesticks ornamented in gold and with golden torches one should (set) the oil[1] of sweet plenty, of the righteous faith, and kindle the glorious light [cf. Matt. 5.15; Mk. 4.21; Lk. 8.16, 11.33]. As they too had asked in their earlier prayer, and as the Lord said to his beloved: "They will see your good works and will glorify your Father in heaven" [Matt. 5.16].

160.   Do you see that for the sake of good deeds the true Son of God does not disdain to give his inheritance to his own beloved servants [cf. Eph. 1.18; Heb. 9.15]. He who is by nature Son,[1] freely brings those who keep his commandments to share his own nature.[2] And if there be anyone who keeps his words, when he finds him he joyfully buys and treasures him like a precious pearl [cf. Matt. 13.46]; then he receives the sign of honor, the royal crown [cf. II Tim. 4.8], and is exalted to royal (rank). Just as the honor of that light shone out before the heathen of this land of Armenia, despite their will, so their glory filled the universe with their divine fame.

161.   So they were found in the vat-stores. For when the order of the edict from the great emperor of the Greeks came to Trdat, king of Greater Armenia, there was no little turmoil in the land of Armenia.

պահէին գամենային անցս ճանապարհաց պոզո-
տայցն և գամենայն գաւառացն. ի կողմանս
կողմանս յուգախնդիրք եղեալ քննէին։ Իսկ ուրումն տեսեալ՝ պատմեաց գնոցանէ։

162 Իսկ իբրև իրքն հոչակեցան գնոցանէն՝
ապա աւուրս երկուս ապարափակ արարեալ՝
տուեալ պահել գնոսա անդէն ուր գտինն լեզէոն
հետևակ գորուն. ապա յետ երկուց աւուրցն
համբաւն հոչակեալ պարկեշտութեան գանագան
գեղեցկութեանն Հռիփսիմեայ ի մէջ բազմամբոխս
հրապարակացն լինէր. ամենային այր առ այր և
մարդ առ մարդ գարմացուֆ յաճախէր։

163 Իսկ ի տես գեղոյ նորա կուտեալ յե-
դեալ գեղեալ խուռն կաճառացն կուտակէր. նա
և նախարարք և մեծամեծք աւագանւոյն ընթացեալք ի տեսանել՝ գմիմիամբք եյանէին. նա
և ագատակոյան, խառնաճաղանճ ամբոխին հանդերձ, գմիմեամբք դիգանէին ի միմեանց վերայ,
առ պակշոտ յիմարութեան ցոփութեան բարո-
յիցն, այլանդակ մտացն գեղխութեան գիճու-
թեանն հեթանոսաբար սովորութեանցն։

164 Իսկ երանեյիքն իբրև գիտացին գանմիա
և գշղուաբարոյ մարդկանն գյռութիւն, կակա-
նաբարձ արտասուելից, գձեռս լի աղօթիւք յերկինս համբառնային, խնդրել դիրկութիւն յամե-
նագոր յամենակալ Տեառնէն, որ յառաշին նուա-
գին ապրեցոյց գնոսա յանօրէն պղծութենէն չա-

They guarded all the roads and paths in all the provinces. Scouts went out to search all parts. And when someone saw them, he informed about them.

162. When their whereabouts became known, then for two days he had a legion of infantry keep armed guard over the spot where they had been found. After those two[1] days the report of the chastity and wonderful[2] beauty of Rhipsimē became known to the public. And astonishment multiplied as word passed from man to man.

163. To see her beauty a great and confused crowd gathered—princes and nobles rushed to view her, competing with each other; freemen and common people together jostled one another in the passion of their dissolute concupiscence and the debauched, polluted and heathen habits of their deranged minds.[1]

164. But the blessed ones, when they realized the evil intentions of these senseless and depraved men, with loud lamentations and tears they raised their hands to heaven in prayer, seeking salvation from the almighty omnipotent Lord, who had rescued them the previous time from the impious, impure,

բութեան զագրութեան հեթանոսացն. զի նոյն
տացէ նոցա գմարտին յաղթութիւն, գհաւատոցն
լուսաւորութիւն. և գերեսս իւրեանց պատեալ՝
անկեալ դնէին յերկիր, յամօթոյ լկտեացն տե-
սողաց, որ ժողովեալն էին ի տեսանել։

165 Եւ ապա յետ այսորիկ գարմացուցեալ
գԹագաւորն բագում տեսողացն, որ մտերիմքն
էին որ եկեալն էին ի տեսիլ գեղոյ նորա, և պատմեալ առաջի Թագաւորին։ Իսկ ի միւսում աւուրն
ընդ այգն ընդ առաւօտն, և ես վաղագոյն, հրաման
ելեալ ի Թագաւորէ անտի, գի գերանելին Հռիփսիմէ տանել յարքունիս, և գուրբն Գայիանէ անդէն պանել պարկեշտամաժողով ընկերօքն հանդերձ։

166 Եւ անդէն յարքունուստ վազվազակի
ոսկիապատ գահաւորակս սպասաւորօք հանդերձ
հասուցանէին առ դուրս հնձանին, ուր էին վանք
նոցա արտաքոյ քաղաքին։ Նա և հանդերձս ագ-
նիւս գեղեցիկս փափուկս պայծառս, և գարդա-
րանս երևելիս մատուցանէին նմա յարքունուստ,
գի գարդարեցից, և շքով և պատուով մացէ ի
քաղաքն և յանդիման լիցի Թագաւորին. քանգի
չէ էր տեսեալ գնա՝ խորհեցաւ կին առնել գնա,
վասն այնորիկ որ պատմեցինն գնմանէ վասն
վայելչութեան գեղոյ նորա։

167 Արդ՝ իբրև եռես սուրբն Գայիանէ՝
խօսէլ սկսաւ առ սանն իւր և ասէ այսպէս. «Յի-
շեա, որդեակ իմ, գի Թողեր լքեր գմեծապատիւ

wicked and licentious heathens; (they begged) that he would give them victory and glorify their faith. And covering their faces, they fell to the ground in shame at the impudent sightseers who had gathered to stare.

165.   After this, many of those who were friends of the king and had come out to see her beauty, informed the king and made him marvel. So on the next day, very early in the morning, a command was issued by the king that blessed Rhipsimē should be brought to court, while saint Gaianē and the group of her chaste companions should be kept where they were.

166.   Then straightway they sent a golden litter with attendants from the palace to the door of the vat-store, where they had been dwelling outside the city. They also brought for her from the palace honorable raiment, beautiful, soft and shining, and fine ornaments for her to adorn herself, so that she might enter the city and meet the king in splendor and honor. For he had not yet seen her, but planned to take her to wife because of what they had told him about her wonderful beauty.

167.   When saint Gaianē saw this she began to speak to her protégée as follows: "Remember, my child, that you have left and abandoned the honor

շքեղաշուք ոսկիակուռ գաթունն քո հայրենի, գծի-
րանեաց թագաւորութեանն, և ցանկացար անանց
ճառագայթարձակ լուսոյ թագաւորութեանն
Քրիստոսի, որ է արարիչ և կեցուցիչ և նորոգիչ,
և խոստացեալ պահէ գանպատում բարբոս իւ-
րոցն յուսացելոց։ Եւ դու, որդեակ, անարգեցեր
գանցաւուրս քոյոյ բնութեանն գծիրանիան. ալդ՝
գիմ՛րդ արդեօք տացես դու գգպաստութիւն սըր-
բութեանդ քոյ կերակուր շանց յայսմիկ ի բար-
բարոս յաշխարհի։ Քա՛ն քեզ, որդեակ, եթէ լինիցի այդ այդպէս. այլ ընկալցի գմեզ քն հանդերձ այն՝ որ առաջնորդեաց մեզ ի մանկութենէ
մերմէ մինչև յօրս յայս և ի ժամս յայս, յորում
այժմիկ հասեալ կամք»։

168 Արդ՝ իբրև եսեա սուրբն Հռիփսիմէ
գայն ամենայն ամբոստ շարաց, և գոր լուաւն ի
դայեկէն իւրմէ՝ վառեցաւ իբրև գինու Հոգւոյն
գօրութեամբ Տեառն իւրոյ. գի գգեցեալ էր գնա-
ւատս մանկութեան տիրոյն իբրև սպառազէն գրա-
հիւք. ճչեաց մեծաձայն ուժով և տարածեաց
գբազուկս իւր ի նմանութիւն խաչին, և սկսաւ
ասել մեծաձայն այսպէս.

169 «Տէր Աստուած ամենակալ, որ հաստատեցեր գբարաձս քո ի ձեռն Որդւոյ քոյ
միածնի և սիրելւոյ, և կազմեցեր յօրինուածս
երկելի և աներկիւթ արարածոց ի ձեռն Հոգւոյդ
սրբոյ. դու ես որ յոչնչէ գամենայն յէութիւն

and splendor of the golden throne of your fathers and the royal purple,[1] and have yearned for the unfading rays of the light of the kingdom of Christ, who is creator, vivifier and renewer, and keeps the promised, ineffable blessings for those who hope in him. And you, my child, have despised the transitory purple of your own nature. So why then will you give your holy chastity as food to dogs in this barbarian land [cf. Matt. 7.6]? Heaven forbid, my child, that this be so. But let us, with you, be received by him who has led us from our youth until today and to this very hour in which we now find ourselves."

168.   Now when saint Rhipsimē saw all this crowd of evil men and heard her governess, she was fortified as with the arms of the Spirit [cf. Rom. 13.12] through the power of her Lord. For she had put on faith from the years of her youth like an armored cuirass [cf. I Thess. 5.8]. She cried out with a loud voice and stretched out her arms in the form of a cross.[1] And in a loud voice she began to speak as follows:

169.   "Lord God almighty, who fashioned your creatures through your only-begotten and beloved Son, and formed the order of the visible and invisible creatures through your holy Spirit; who brought everything from nothing into being [cf. II Macc. 7.28; Rom. 4.17];

յօրինեցեր, և քոյով հրամանաւ վարին ամենայն գործութիւնք երևելիք և աներևոյթք, որ են յեր֊ կինս և յերկրի, ի ծովու և ի ցամաքի։ Քանզի դու ես, տէր, որ եառ յողող Չուրց զանօրէն պղծալից մարդիկ ուՔերորդ դարուն, և փրկե֊ ցեր գսիրելին քո զնոյ, որ պահեաց գՀրաման բանի քո, և ապրեցուցեր խաչանման փայտին ի Չուրցն Հեղեղէ։ Որ յայնժամ օրինակաւ խա֊ չին արարեր գփրկութիւն և այժմ արա ձշմար֊ տութեամբ խաչիդ քոյ, յոր ելեր և Հեղեր գա֊ րին քո ի բժշկութիւն ցաւոց մերոց։

170 «Որ պաՀեցեր գԱբրաՀամ ի մէջ ամբա֊ րիշտ ազգացն Քանանացւոց. որ յամօթոյ նա֊ խատանաց պղծութենէ մաՀու ապրեցուցեր գա֊ դախին քո գԱառա. որ գԹացար յիսանակ ծա֊ ռայ քո, և պաՀեցեր գագախին քո գերեփիկա յանօրէն Փղշտացւոց անտի, մի Թողուր գմեգ ի ձեռաց վասն սրբոյ անուանդ քոյ. որ ուսուցեր, վարդապետեցեր և եառուր գդանս քո ի բերան մեր, գի այնու ապրել մարԹասցուք յորոգայ֊ Թից Թշնամւոյն, և ասես. «Անուն իմ ի վերայ ձեր կոչեցեալ է», և «Դուք ատձար էք ատտուա֊ ծութեան իմոյ». և ասես, եԹէ «Ջանուն իմ սուրբ աոնիշչիք ի սիրտս ձեր». և եղեր բանս ի մաբ՝ խնդրել ի քէն և ասել, «Սուրբ եղիցի ա֊ նուն քո» ի վերայ մեր՝ գոր խնդրեմք ի քէն. և աՀա ժողովեալք չարք բագումք պղծել գանուն

and at your command move all visible and invisible powers which are in heaven and earth, in the sea and on dry land.[1] For you it is, Lord, who drowned in the flooding waters the impious and impure men of the eighth generation,[2] and saved your beloved Noah who had kept the command of your word [cf. Gen. 6.22ff.], and rescued him from the flood through the cross-like wood.[3] You who then worked salvation through the symbol of the cross, now work (the same) through the true cross, on which you hung and shed your blood for the healing of our woes.

170.   "You who saved Abraham in the midst of the impious races of Canaanites and who saved your handmaid Sarah from the stain of shameful outrage and death [cf. Gen. 20]; who had mercy on your servant Isaac and rescued your handmaid Rebecca from the impious Philistines [cf. Gen. 26.7]; do not deprive us of your support for the sake of your holy name. You taught, instructed and gave your words to our mouths, that we might thereby be saved from the snares of the enemy. And you said: 'My name has been called over you' [Gen. 48.16; cf. Acts 15.17] and: 'You are the temple of my divinity' [cf. I Cor. 3.16; 6.19]. And you said: 'Make my name holy in your hearts' [cf. Matt. 6.9; Lk. 1.49, 11.2; I Pet. 3.15]. And you taught us to ask you and say: 'Holy be your name' [Matt. 6.9; Lk. 11.2] over us. This[1] we ask from you. Behold many evil men have gathered to sully

սուրբ քո որ ի վերայ մեր է, և զտառաձար անուանդ քոյ. զի թէպէտ և մեք տկար և անարժան եմք՝ սակայն դու, տէր, պանեա զանձինս մեր յա֊ նարժան խայտառակութացս:

171 «Մարդասէր և քաղցր, որ արկեր զմեզ յայս փորձութիւն, տու՛ր մեզ յաղթել քոյով զո֊ րութեամբդ, զի քո է յաղթութիւն, և յաղթեցցէ քո անունդ՝ պանել զմեզ յուսով զգաստութեամբ. զի այսու մոցուք ի թիւ վիձակաց արդարոց քոց. զի և առցուք զվարձս վաստակոց, գոր տա֊ ցես այնոցիկ, և հատուցես իւրաքանչիւր այ֊ նոցիկ, որ կացեալ իցեն յահի քում և պանեալ իցեն գնրամանս քո:

172 «Որ ապրեցուցեր զնոյ ի Չուրցն նե֊ դեդէ՝ ապրեցո՛ և զմեզ յանօրէնութեանցս նե֊ դեդէ որ շուրջ պատեալ է զմեօք: Զի եթէ զգա֊ զանս և զանասունս ապրեցուցեր ի տապանին, ո՛րչափ ևս խնայեսցես ի քո պատկերս, որ զքեզ փառաւորեմք: Իսկ եթէ ի սողունս և ի թռչունս խնայեցեր, ո՛րչափ ևս խնայեսցես ի մեզ, գոր անուանեցեր տաձար կամաց քոց»:

173   Սրդ՝ իբրև այս այսպէս եղև՝ ժո֊ ղով ամբոխին ի վերայ կուտեր բազմութիւն մարդկան, և էին բազում սպասաւորք արքունի, որ եկեալ էին գնմանէն՝ տանել յարքունիս, և նախարարքն և մեծամեծք աւագանույն, որ եկեալ էին շքաղիրք՝ պատիւ առնել նմա և երթալ ընդ

your holy name which is upon us, and the temple of your name. For although we are weak and unworthy, yet do you, Lord, save our souls from dishonorable scandal.

171. "Benevolent and sweet one, who cast us into this trial, grant us victory through your power; for yours is victory [cf. I Chr. 29.11] and your name will conquer; keep us in hope and chastity, that thereby we may enter the allotted number[1] of your just ones [cf. Col. 1.12], that we may receive the rewards of our labors which you will give in compensation to each one of those who stand in your fear and keep your commandments [cf. I Cor. 3.8].

172. "You who saved Noah from the watery flood, save us from the flood of impieties that surrounds us. For if you saved the beasts and animals in the ark, how much the more will you care for your images[1] that glorify you? While if you cared for the reptiles and birds, how much more will you care for us, whom you have called the temple of your will?"[2]

173. After this the press of the crowd increased, there being many royal servants who had come to bring her to court, and princes and great magnates who had come to pay homage and honor her and escort

նմա յարքունիս. գի տարցին գնա կնութեան թագաւորին Տրդատայ և Հայոց տիկնութեան։

174 Իսկ նոքա արտասուագոչ ողորմ ողորմ գձեռս համբարձեալ յերկինս՝ խնդրէին ի կամարար Տեառնէն՝ ապրեցուցանել գնոսա յանօրէն յանարժան հարսանեացն պղծութենէն։ Զգոչին բարձեալ լալով մեծաձայն ճչէին և ասէին. «Քաւ լիցի մեզ, թէ պատրեացէն գմեզ մեծութիւնք, կամ խողտեացէն գմեզ փափկութիւնք, կամ հրապուրեացէն գմեզ թագաւորութիւնք, կամ նեղեացէն գմեզ հալածանք, կամ վտանգեացէն գմեզ տանջանք հարուածոց, թէպէտ և բիւր ազգի ազգի տանչիցէք գմեզ. կամ երկիցուք մեք արդեօք յահագին մահուանէն, գոր ածելոց էք դուք ի վերայ մեր։ Քաւ լիցի մեզ, թէ փոխանակեսցուք գանցաւոր կեանս ընդ յաւիտենական կենացն որ ոչն անցանէ. քաւ լիցի մեզ, թէ ուրասցուք գէն Աստուած գամենահաստիչն, որոյ տերութիւնն յէութենէ հաստատեալ՝ անփոփոխ են բարիքն ամենայն և ոչ անցանեն։ Այլ ոչ խորութիւնք և ոչ բարձրութիւնք, ոչ վիշտք և ոչ չարչարանք, ոչ կապանք և ոչ տանջանք, ոչ հուր, ոչ Հուր և ոչ սուր, ոչ դբոսանք և ոչ պատրանք, ոչ մեծութիւնք և ոչ աղքատութիւնք, ոչ այն աշխարհ և ոչ այս աշխարհս, ոչ կեանք և ոչ մահ՝ ոչ ոք կարէ մեկնել գմեզ ի սիրոյն Քրիստոսի։ Զի նմա նուիրեցաք գկուսութիւնս մեր, գի նմա

her to court, in order to marry her[1] to king Trdat and make her queen of Armenia.

174.   But (the maidens) raised their hands to heaven with tearful and piteous cries, begging the benevolent Lord to save them from the impurity of this lawless and unworthy marriage. Raising a cry they loudly wept and said: "Heaven forbid that riches should deceive us, or luxury charm us, or kingdoms allure us, or torments oppress us, or torture and persecution imperil us, no matter in how many ways they torment us. Will we really fear the terrible death which you are about to bring upon us? Heaven forbid that we exchange for this transitory life the eternal life that passes not away. Heaven forbid that we deny the God 'who is' [Ex. 3.14], the creator of all, whose authority is established by his essence, whose blessings are all immutable and pass not away. Neither depths nor heights, neither tribulations nor torments, neither bonds nor tortures, not fire nor water nor sword, neither pleasure nor deceit, neither riches nor poverty, neither that world nor this world, neither life nor death—no one can separate us from the love of Christ [cf. Rom. 8.38-39]. For to him we have dedicated our virginity, to him

աւանդեցաք զարբութիւնս մեր, զի նմա միամբ
և սիրոյ նորա ցանկացեալ սպասեմբ, մինչև կացցուք առաջի փառաց գովութեան նորա առանց
ամօթոյ և պատկառանաց»։

175 Եւ արդ՝ եղեալ որոտումն յերկնից սաստիկ անհնարին, զի ատաբեկեալ զամենայն ամբոխն, և ձայն՝ զի ասէր առ նոսա, թէ «Զօրա-
ցարուք, պինդ կացէք, քաջալերեցարուք, զի ես
ընդ ձեզ եմ, և պահեցի զձեզ յամենայն ճանապարհս ձեր, և ամի զձեզ պահեալս անարատութեամբ, և հասուցի զձեզ մինչև ի տեղիս յայս,
զի և ատտ փառաւորեցցի անունն իմ առաջի հեթանոսաց կողմանց հիւսիսականաց։ Մանաւանդ
գուլ, Հռիփսիմէ, ըստ անուանդ քում արդարև
ընկեցկալ եղեր Գայիանեաւդ և քոյովք սիրե-
լեօքդ ի մահուանէ ի կեանս. և մի երկնչիք,
այլ եկեսջիք ի տեղի յայն՝ գոր ես և հայր իմ
պատրաստեցաք ձեզ, զանքնին ուրախութեան
տեղին, ձեզ և որ միանգամ իբրև զձեզդ իցեն»։

176 Եւ այնպէս յերկար որոտացեալ, մինչև
թմբրեալ լինէին մարդիկն յահէ անտի. և բազմաց ընդոստուցեալ, անգուշեալ բազում երի-
վարք հեծելոց յահէ անտի՝ զբազումս ընկեցեալ
և զբազումս առաջուր հարեալ սատակէին։ Եւ
մարդկանն իսկ ընդ միմեանս ամբոխեալ՝ ընդ
կուտակելն բազումք զբազումս կոխեալ սատա-
կէին. և բազմաց լինէր կոտորած, և ձայնադա-

we have commended our purity, for him we wait and his love we await with longing until we stand before his praiseworthy glory without shame or timidity."

175. Then there occurred a fearfully loud thundering from heaven which terrified the whole throng, and a voice which said to them: "Be strong [cf. I Cor. 16.13], stand firm [Gal. 5.1], be of good cheer [Matt. 14.27; Mk. 6.50], because I am with you [Matt. 28.20], and I have preserved you in all your journeys and led you safely in purity and have brought you to this place, that here my name might be glorified before the heathens of the Northern regions.[1] Especially you, Rhipsimē, who according to your name were truly 'thrown'[2] with Gaianē and your friends from death to life. Do not fear; but you will come to that place which my Father and I have prepared for you [cf. Jn. 14.2-3], the place of inscrutable joy, for you and for those who will be like you."

176. And thus it thundered a long time until the people were overcome by fear, and many horses took fright and started, throwing many of their riders and trampling and killing many under foot. And the people rushed about, crushing each other and trampling many to death. Many were killed and there was a great sound

պակի և վայոյ, և աննհարին չարիք և արհաւիրք
ի վերայ մարդկանն հասանէին. և բազումք մեռան, և բազմաց արիւնն հեղեալ գերկիրն ոռո-
գանէր։ Արդ՝ իբրև այս շփոթ ամբոխի եղև ի
նոցանէն ի մէջ կուտակելոցն մարդկան բազմու-
թեանն՝ ումանք ի մեծամեծ սպասաւորացն արքունի անդէն ընթացան պատմել Թագաւորին
գամենայն բանս նոցա. քանդի դիպեցան անդ
նշանագիրք, որ գրեցին գամենայն բանս, և ընթերցան առաջի Թագաւորին։

177 Եւ ասէ Թագաւորն. «Փոխանակ զի ոչ
կամեցաւ գալ պատուով շքեղութեամբ կամօք՝
բռնաբար ածցեն մինչի յապարանսս և մուծցեն
գնա ի սենեակն արքունի»։

178 Արդ՝ առեալ գսուրբն Հռիփսիմէ սպասաւորացն բռնաբար, մերթ վերամբարձ, մերթ
ի քարշ. և նա ազագակէր և ասէր. «Տէր Յիսուս
Քրիստոս, օգնեա ինձ»։ և ամենայն ամբոխն
գկնի նորա փողեալ՝ Թնդէր երկիրն ի բազմութենէ անտի։ Արդ՝ ածին մուծին գնա մինչև յա-
պարանս Թագաւորին, ի սենեակն արքունի։ Իսկ
իբրև արգելին գնա ի սենեակն՝ սկսաւ խնդրել
ի Տեառնէ և ասէ.

179 «Տէր գօրութեանց, դու ես Աստուած
ճշմարիտ։ Դու ես, որ հերձեր գծովն Կարմիր, և
անցուցեր գքո ժողովուրդն։ Դու ես, որ գամուլ
վէմն դարձուցեր ի ծննդականութիւն Ջուրցն

of shouting and crying. And terrible trouble and fear came over the people, and many died, and the blood of many watered the earth.[1] When this confusion occurred in the great press of the crowd, some of the noble servants of the court ran to tell the king all their words, because there were there secretaries[2] who wrote down all that was said, and they read it before the king.[3]

177. And the king said: "Because she did not wish to come willingly in honor and pomp, let them bring her forcibly to my palace and lead her to the royal chamber."

> [*C. Rhipsimē is taken to the palace;*
> *she eludes Trdat's clutches*]

178. So the servants took Rhipsimē by force, now lifting her, now dragging her. And she cried out and said: "Lord Jesus Christ, help me." And the whole crowd followed her, making the earth loudly shake from their great numbers. They brought her to the king's palace and led her to the royal chamber. But when they had shut her in the chamber, she began to beseech the Lord, saying:

179. "Lord of hosts, you are the true God. You it was who parted the Red Sea, and brought your people across [cf. Ex. 14]. You it was who turned the sterile rock into streams of fertile waters

վատկաց, և արբուցեր գժողովուրդն ծարաւեալ։
Դու ես, որ իջուցեր գձառայն քո գԹովեան յան֊
դունդս խորոց ծովուն, և եատւր առնուլ գչափ
քոյոյ գօրութեանդ, և արտաքսեցեր գնա ի դուրս
քան գմարդկային բնութիւնս. և միսանգամ այս֊
րէն առանց ապականութեան աձեր ողջանդամ և
կացուցեր ի կենդանութեան, գի և մազ մի ան֊
գամ ոչ շարժեալ լինէր ի վարսից նորա։ Դու
ես Աստուած ճշմարիտ, որ և գԴանիէլ, կուր
արկեալ գագանաց՝ ապրեցուցեր յանագին ժա֊
նեացն, և կացուցեր գգրպարատեալն առաջի նեզ֊
չացն փառաւորութեամբ։ Դու և գերիս ման֊
կունսն, որ արկեալ յայրեալ վասն գբեզ պաշտե֊
լոյն՝ ողջ և անարատ ի հրոյն պահեցեր. գի փա֊
ռաւորեցգէն գբեզ՝ որք տեսին գպանչելիս քո։
Դու եատւր խոտաճարակ լինել խիստ և անօրէն
Թագաւորին Բաբելացւոց, գի ոչ իմացաւ փա֊
ռաւորել գբեզ ի վերայ սքանչելեացն քոց գոր
գուցեր նմա. փոխեալ գնա ի կերպարանս անաս֊
նոց և ընդ գազանս անապատի եդեր գբնակու֊
թիւն նորա, և ընդ ցիռս վայրի գարօտ նորա։
Դու և գագախին քո Շուշան կրկին ապեցուցեր,
յերկուց մանուց փրկեալ, և խայտառակեցար սա֊
տակեցեր գանօրէն Թշնամիսն, և պսակ պարծա֊
նաց արդարութեան յուսացելոյն քոյ շնորհեցեր
և կանգնեցեր։ «Դու նոյն ինքն ես, և ամբ քո
ոչ անցանեն»։ «Դու, տէր, գփառս քո այլում

and gave drink to your thirsty people [cf. Ex. 17.6].
You it was who brought down your servant Jonah to
the unfathomable depths of the sea and made him
experience your power; you cast him out from our
human state and brought him back again to life whole
and unharmed, for not one hair of his head was
touched [cf. Acts 27.34]. You are the true God who
saved Daniel, thrown as food to wild beasts, from their
fearful teeth, and rendered him who had been de-
famed glorious in the sight of his tormentors [cf. Dan.
6]. You also saved alive and unharmed by fire the
three children who had been thrown into the furnace
because they worshiped you [cf. Dan. 3], for they
glorified you, who had seen your wonders. You made
the fierce and lawless Babylonian king pasture on
grass, because he did not consent to glorify you for
your wonders which you had shown him; you changed
him into the form of animals and made his habitat
with the beasts of the desert and his pasturage with
wild asses [cf. Dan. 5.21]. You twice saved your handmaid Susanna, delivering her from a double death,
and destroyed her lawless enemies with an opprobri-
ous death, and graciously set a glorious crown of righteousness on her who hoped in you. 'You are the same,
and your years do not pass' [Ps. 101.28; Heb. 1.12].
'You, Lord, do not give your glory to another' [Is.
42.8; 48.11].

ոչ տաս». Դու ես որ փառաւորեալդ ես ի վերայ ամենայն տիեզերաց. մի պղծեսցեն գանունն սուրբ քո ճեթանոք։ Դու կարող ես վեր-
կել դիս ի պղծութենէս յայսմանէ. դի վախճա-
նեցայց սրբութեամբ մեռանել վասն անուանդ
քոյ մեծի»։

180   Արդ՝ մինչդեռ սուրբն Հռիփսիմէ
պայս ամենայն աղօթս առ Աստուած մատուցա-
նէր՝ եկն եմուտ Թագաւորն Տրդատ ի ներքս ի
սենեակն՝ ուր էրն գնա արգելեալ։ Արդ՝ իբրև
եկն եմուտ նա ի ներքս՝ առ հաստակ մարդիկն, ոմանք արտաքոյ ապարանից, կէսքն ի
փողոցս ի ներքսագոյնան, առ հաստակ երգս
առեալ բարբառեան կայթիւք վագելով, ցուց
բարձեալ մարդկանն. կէսքն ի բերդամիչին, և
կէսք դպաղաքամէչն լցին խնձոյիւք. առ հասա-
իրակ համարէին հարստանեացն գպարսն պարել և
գկաքաւան յորդորել։ Իսկ տէր Աստուած նայե-
ցաւ յիւր սիրելին Հռիփսիմէ՝ ապրեցուցանել
գնա, դի մի կորիցէ աւանդն որ պահեալ գգուշացեալ էր, և լուաւ աղօթից նորա՝ գօրացու-
ցանել գնա իբրև գՅայէլն և իբրև գԴեբովրայն.
եաա գօրութիւն նմա, դի ապրեցցի ի ստամբակ
բռնութենէ անօրէնութեանն։

181 Արդ՝ մտեալ Թագաւորն՝ բուռն հարկանէր գնմանէն, կատարել գկամս ցանկութեանն։
Իսկ նա գօրացեալ լինէր ի Հոգւոյն սրբոյ. գա-

You are the one glorified over the whole world [cf. Dan. 3.45]; let not the heathen profane your holy name [cf. Ez. 36.20]. You are able to save me from this profanation, that I may in purity die for your great name."

180.   While saint Rhipsimē was offering all these prayers to God, king Trdat entered the chamber where she had been shut up. Now when he came in, all the populace, some outside the palace, others in the streets, and others inside (the city), all together struck up songs [cf. III Macc. 6.23] and dancing.[1] Some filled the citadel, others the center of the town, with merry-making. They all intended to celebrate the wedding with dancing. But the Lord God looked down on his beloved Rhipsimē in order to save her, lest the treasure she had preserved so carefully be lost [cf. II Tim. 1.12], and he heard her prayers and fortified her like Jael and like Deborah [cf. Judges 4]. He strengthened her to be saved from the impious tyrant's grasp.

181.   When the king entered, he seized her in order to work his lustful desires. But she, strengthened by the holy Spirit,

գանաքար ոզորեալ, առնաքար մարանչէր. իբրև
յերեք ժամուց սկսեալ մարանչել մինչև ի տան
ժամն՝ պարտեալ լինէր զԹագաւորն իսկ դայն,
որ անճնարին համարեալ ուժով. որ մինչ ի Յունաց աշխարհին էր՝ բազում ոյժ պնդութեան ու-
կերաց ցուցեալ էր, զարմացուցեալ դամենեսեան. և ի Թագաւորութեանն իսկ, իբրև ի հայրենի բնութիւնն դարձեալ էր՝ բազում գործա
արութեան քաջութեան և անդ ցուցեալ. և որ
այնպէս հաչակեալ էր ամենայնիւ՝ արդ յաղՉր-
կանէ միոջէ պարտեալ վատթարանայր կամօք և
զօրութեամբն Քրիստոսի։

182 Արդ՝ իբրև պարտեցաւ, վատակեցաւ
և լքաւ՝ էլ նա արտաքս, և ետ աձել զերանելին
Գայիանէ, և արկանել խառան ի պարանոց նորա, և աձել ունել զնա առ դուրս սենեկին. և
ինքն անդրէն ի ներքս մտանէր. և եդ բանս ի
բերան սպասաւորացն, զի ստիպեսցեն դանհրա-
պոյրն Գայիանէ՝ ասել ի դրաց անտի ի ներքս ի
սենեակն առ Հռիփսիմէ, Թէ արա զկամս դորա,
և կեաց դու և մեք։

183 Իսկ նա յանձին կալեալ խոսել ընդ
սանուն իւրում, և մատուցեալ ասէ ի դրաց անտի ի ներքս ի սենեակն առ Հռիփսիմէ. «Որդեակ, պանեսցէ զքեզ Քրիստոս ի պղծութենէդ
և լիցի քեզ զօրալիցն. բաւ քեզ, որդեակ, եթէ
լիցի քեզ ելանել ի ժառանգութենէ անտի կե-

struggled like a beast and fought like a man. They fought from the third hour until the tenth and she vanquished the king who was renowned for his incredible strength. While he was in the Greek empire he had shown such bodily strength that everyone had been amazed; and in his own realm, when he had returned[1] to his native land, he had shown there too many deeds of mighty valor.[2] And he, who was so famous in every respect, now was vanquished and worsted by a single girl through the will and power of Christ.

182. When he had been defeated, and was exhausted and discouraged, he went out and had blessed Gaianē brought in and a collar put on her neck, and he had her led to the door of the chamber. He himself then entered, and prompted his servants to force the intractable Gaianē to say through the door into the room to Rhipsimē, "do his will and you and we shall live."

183. She agreed to speak with her protégée, and coming close spoke through the door into the room to Rhipsimē: "My child, may Christ save you from this profanation, and may he be your support. Heaven forbid, my child, that you lose the inheritance

նացն Աստուծոյ, և ժառանգել քեզ գանցաւորս, որ ոչ ինչ իսկ է, այսօր է, և վաղիւն կորնչի»:

184 Իբրև իմացան, Թէ գիր խրատ յաճախեաց մատուցանել՝ բերեալ քարինս՝ հարկանէին զբերանն, մինչև Թափել ատամանցն. և սաիպէին ասել նմա, զի արասցէ զկամս Թագաւորին:

185 Նա ես քան զես պնդէր և ասէր. «Թաչալերեաց, պինդ կաց, և այժմ տեսանես զՔրիստոս, առ որ անձկացեալն ես: Յուշ լիցի քեզ, որդեակ, հոգեխառն մնունդդն, որով զքեզ անուցի: Յուշ լիցի քեզ աստուածեղէն խրատն, որով զքեզ պարարեցի: Յուշ լիցին հալածանքն իմ և քո ի միասին: Յուշ լիցի քեզ և բաժակ մահուն, զոր ի միասին եմք ըմպելոց: Յուշ լիցի քեզ և յարութիւն ամենայն տիեզերաց: Յուշ լիցի քեզ և մեծատանն յանդիմանութիւն: Յուշ լիցի քեզ այրումն յալիտենական գեհենին տանջանաց: Յուշ լիցի քեզ անապական պարգեքն արդարոց, զոր և մեզն է պատրաստեալ: Յուշ լիցի քեզ աստուածեղէն բարբառն երկնաւոր, զոր լուար իսկ դու քեզէն քոյովք ականջօք յայսմ աւուր. որ քաջալերեաց և զօրացոյց զքեզ մեօք հանդերձ՝ նոյն և արժանիս արասցէ պսակին և հանգստեանն զոր խոստացաւ. և զօրացուսցէ զքեզ մեօք հանդերձ, զի լիցուք ընակիցք Աստուծոյ լուսեղէն յարկացն յալիտենականաց ընակութեան:

of the life of God and inherit transitory life, which is nothing today and is lost tomorrow" [cf. Matt. 6.30].[1]

184.   When they realized what advice she was offering, they brought stones and struck her mouth until her teeth were knocked out, and they tried to force her to tell (Rhipsimē) to do the will of the king.

185.   But she persisted all the more and said: "Be of good cheer [cf. Matt. 9.22], stand firm [cf. Gal. 5.1], and now you will see Christ for whom you long. Remember, my child, the spiritual upbringing in which I raised you. Remember the divine instruction with which I nourished you. Remember your and my persecutions together. Remember the cup of death which we have to drink together [cf. Matt. 26.39]. Remember the resurrection of the whole world. Remember the reproach of the rich man[1] [cf. Lk. 6.24]. Remember the fire of the torments of eternal hell [cf. Mk. 10.42]. Remember the incorruptible rewards of the just which he has also prepared for us[2] [cf. Lk. 14.14]. Remember the divine voice from heaven which you yourself heard divine voice from heaven which you yourself heard with your own ears today,[3] which encouraged and strengthened you and us also; the same will also make (us)[4] worthy of the crown and the rest which it promised, and will strengthen you and us, so that we may dwell[5] in God's eternal habitations of light [cf. Lk. 16.9].

185 «Այլ տէր մեր և Թագաւոր մեր և Ա֊
տուած մեր, որ վասն մեր խոնարհեցաւ յա֊
նարգութիւն, մի թողցէ զմեզ անարգս, զի գո֊
րութեանց նորա ցանկացաք. փրկիչն աշխարհաց
օգնեցէ մեզ, որ ոչ եթող ընդ վայր զմեզ գյու֊
սացեալս իւր, և արժանիս համարեցաւ իւրոց
բանիցն՝ քաջալերութիւն տալոյ։ Չի նա անար֊
գամեծար տէր է, և նա ինքնին պանեցէ զմեզ
գաղափնեայս իւր յամենայն մեղաց. որպէս և
այսօր իսկ լուաք, զի էր պանեալ զմեզ ամենա֊
գօր աՇոյն, և պանեցէ զմեզ մինչև յաւիտեան.
բայց միայն ի սիրոյ նորա մի մեկնեցուք։ Այլ
գարթուցէ զզօրութիւնս իւր, և եկեցէ կե֊
ցուցէ զմեզ, և մեք դանուն Տեառն կարդաս֊
ցուք. երևեցուցէ զերեսս իւր ի մեզ, և կեց֊
ցուք. զի նա է Աստուած փրկիչ մեր. վասն նո֊
րա համբերեցցուք գործանապաղ։

187 «Յուշ լիցի քեզ Տէրն, որ վասն զմեզ
բարձրացուցանելոյ խոնարհեցաւ, և հեղ գարիւն
իւր ի վերայ խաչին. վասն կենաց մերոց և
փրկութեան մերոց ի մահ վիրաւորեցաւ։ Դիր
գնա ի մտի քում, և կարգ՚ա սրտիւ քով գնա.
անա հատեալ է քեզ յոգնականութիւն, և գօրա֊
ցուցէ զբազուկս քո, որպէս զմանկանն Դաւ֊
թի ի վերայ արՇոցն և առիւծուցն, որ իբ֊
րև գուլա այծեաց ճեղքեալ բեկանէր։ Նա և որ
գանարի հակայն Չարդեաց ի ճեռն ծառայի իւ֊

186. "But our Lord and King and God, who for our sake was humbled to disgrace [cf. Phil. 2.8], may he not leave us despised [cf. I Cor. 4.10] because we desired his power.[1] May the savior of the world help us, who did not helplessly abandon us who hoped in him but considered us worthy of comfort by his words. For he is the Lord who glorifies the humbled,[2] and may he keep us his handmaidens from all sin, as we heard today. For his almighty right hand has preserved us, and will preserve us for eternity. But only let us not be deprived of his love [cf. Rom. 8.35, 39]. But may he arouse his hosts and come and rescue us [cf. Ps. 79.3-4]; and we shall invoke the name of the Lord [cf. Ps. 79.19]. Let him reveal his face to us and we shall live [cf. Ps. 79.20]. For he is God our savior, and for his sake we shall endure[3] for ever [cf. Ps. 24.5; 43.23].

187. "Remember the Lord who was humbled in order to raise us up, and who shed his own blood on the cross; for our lives and salvation he was wounded[1] to death. Recall him and invoke his name in your heart. Behold, he has come to help you, and will strengthen your arms like those of the young David against bears and lions, who struck and broke (them) like kids [cf. I Kings 17.34]. Similarly, he who destroyed the ignoble giant through his servant

րոյ Դաւթի՝ նոյն խորտակեացէ գչարութիւն անօ-
րէննութեան դորա առաջի քո։

188 «Դուսար մարգարէութեան հաւատոցն
Դաւթի և մնեալ յարդարութեան ի վերայ բազ-
կաց իմոց. առաջի սուրբ և փառաւորեալ սեղանոյն Աստուծոյ մնար դու ապախին Քրիստոս.
այն որ այսօր իսկ յայտնութեամբ՝ գթութեամբ
և մարդասիրութեամբ իւրով յայտնեցաւ մեզ,
որ իմաստութեամբն խնդրեցաք գնա՝ նոյն տացէ
քեզ մեօք հանդերձ առանց ամօթոյ տեսանել գնա
դէմ յանդիման»։

189 Արդ՝ պայս ամենայն խոսեցաւ սուրբն
Գայիանէ ի բարբառ Հռոմայեցւոց ընդ իւրում
սանուն ի դրաց սենեկին, մինչդեռ Թագաւորն
ոգորէր ընդ սրբոյն Հռիփսիմեայ։ Բայց գոյին
անդ ումանք ի սպասաւորացն արքունի, որ լսէին
գայն ամենայն ի բարբառ Հռոմայեցւոց։

190 Եւ արդ՝ իբրև լուան գայն ամենայն,
գոր խոսեցաւն Գայիանէ ընդ սանուն իւրում՝ ի
բաց առին գնա ի դրաց անտի։ Չի Թէպէտ և
բազում անգամ հարին գնա, և ծեծեցին քարամբք
գերեսս նորա, և Թափեցին գատամունս նորա, և
չարդեցին գմուր բերանոյ ընդաց նորա՝ սակայն
ոչ շրջեաց գբանս իւր՝ խոսել ընդ աղշկանն այլ
ինչ. այլ գոր սկիզբն արարեալ էր բանիցն իւրոց
առաջնոց՝ գնոյն յաճախեալ բազմացուցանէր։

191 Իսկ նա մարտեաւ եւս ընդ նմա ի տան

David [cf. I Kings 17.50], the same will break this evil impiety before you.

188. "Daughter of the prophetic faith of David, brought up in justice in my arms, you were raised before the holy and glorious altar of God as a hand-maid[1] of Christ. He who today in his mercy and benevolence appeared in a revelation to us who piously beseeched him, the same will grant you and us to see him face to face[2] [cf. I Cor. 13.12] without shame."

189. Now saint Gaianē said all this in Latin[1] to her protégée through the door of the chamber, while the king was struggling with saint Rhipsimē. But there were there some of the palace servants who heard all this in Latin.

190. And when they heard everything that Gaianē had said to her protégée, they took her away from the door. And although they frequently beat her and struck her face with stones, and knocked out her teeth, and broke her jaws, yet she did not change her speech or say anything different to the maiden. But as she had begun speaking at the beginning, she repeated in the same tenor.

191. But (Rhipsimē) was still fighting with the king from the tenth

ժամէ աւուրն մինչև ի պահ մի գիշերոյն, պար-
տեաց զԹագաւորն։ Եւ գօրացեալ լինէր աղՉիկն
ի Հոգւոյն սրբոյ. Հարեալ վանեալ պարտեալ,
վաստակաբեկ առնելով զԹագաւորն՝ մեղկեալ
ընկենոյր։ Մերկ կողոպուտ ևս ի Հանդերձից
զԹագաւորն կացուցանէր, և զպատմուճանն պա-
տառեալ և զնշան Թագին ցրուեալ կողոպտեալ՝
ամօթալից Թողոյր։ Չի Թէպէտ և զիւր զգեստիկն
քճճեալ պատառատուն ի նմանէն ի դուրս բերէր՝
սակայն յաղթող պանէր գանձն իւր սրբութեամբ։

192 Եւ բացեալ զդուրս տանն բնակարար՝ ի
դուրս ելանէր, Հերձեալ գամբրս մարդկանն. և
ոչ ուրուք կարացեալ յաղթահարել զնա։ Եւ
ընթացեալ ընդ քաղաքամէՉան՝ ելանէր ընդ արե-
ւելս կոյս, ընդ Արեգ դուռն քաղաքին։ Երթեալ
առ Հնձանօքն, ուր էինն իսկ յառաՉ վանք իւ-
րեանց՝ ճայն աւետեաց մատուցանէր ընկերացն.
և ինքն անցանէր Հարուստ մի ի քաղաքէն ի
կողմն մի Հիւսիսոյ, ի տեղի մի յարևելս կոյս,
ի սարաւանդակ ի բարձրաւանդակ յաւագին տեղի
մի, մօտ ի բուն պողոտային, որ երթայր յԱրտաշատ քաղաք․

193 Իբրև եհաս յայն տեղի՝ ծունր եդեալ
կայր յաղօթս և ասէր. «Տէր ամենայնի, ո̄ կարիցէ Հատուցանել քեզ փոխանակ բարեացն, որ
ի քէն շնորՀեցաւ մեզ. զի պաՀեցեր գյույս մեր
Հաստատուն որ ի քեզ էր․ և ապեցուցեր զմեզ

hour of the day until the first evening watch, and she overcame him. The maiden was strengthened by the holy Spirit; she struck him, chased him and overcame him; she wore the king out, weakened him and felled him. She stripped the king naked of his clothes; she tore his robes and threw away his royal diadem, leaving him covered with shame. And although her own clothes had been torn to shreds by him, yet when she went out she still victoriously retained her purity.

192.   Opening the doors by force she went out, cutting through the crowd; and no one was able to hold her. She ran through the city and went out on the eastern side, through the Sun-gate[1] of the city. Coming to the vat-stores where their earlier dwelling had been, she told the story to her companions. She herself went a long way from the city to the North-east, to a high and sandy point near the main road which led to the city of Artashat.

193.   When she arrived there she knelt down in prayer and said: "Lord of all, who could repay you for the blessings which have been granted us by you? For you have kept firm the hope we had in you, and you have saved us

ի պղծալից ժանեաց գազանին որ ապականէին գմեզ։ Այլ գի՞նչ եւ կայցէ ի մեզ կար՝ փոխարէնս հատուցանել քեզ. բայց անձինք մեր լիցին փոխանակ փրկութեան քում. զի դու ինքն արժանիս արարեր գմեզ աբբանելութեան, կրել գանունդ քո, որով ապրեցուցեր գմեզ. զի բայց ի քէն, Տէր, գայլ ոչ ոք գիտեմք, եւ գանունն քո անուանեմք գոր հանապազ։

194 «Այլ մեզ լաւ է մեռանել ի սրբութեան քում, քան թէ ձգիցեմք գեռս մեր յաստուածս օտարս, որ չիցեն իսկ. այլ ոչ ինչ իսկ են ամենայն պաշտամունք հեթանոսաց. զի դու եւս արարիչ, եւ ամենայն ի քէն է եւ Որդւովդ քո միածնաւ, առանց որոյ եղեւ եւ ոչինչ, եւ «Հոգիդ քո բարի առաջնորդեսցէ մեզ յերկիր ուղիղ», որ տանի գմեզ ի բարութիւնն յաւիտենականն յերկրաւորս։

195 «Որոյ յանդիման լինելոց եմք առաջի Միածնիդ քո. զի առանց ամօթոյ կայցեմք ի կողմն աջակողմանն, յորժամ առաքեսցես զդա «ի պատրաստ լուսոյ բնակութենէդ հայել յամենայն բնակիչս երկրի»։ Որ ստեղծ իսկ գսիրտս որդւոց մարդկան, որ ի մխա առնու գամենայն գործս նոցա։ Զի եւ մեք ի ժողովրդենէ քումմէ եմք եւ ի խաշնէ արօտի քոյ. մացուք ի յարկող, զոր պատրաստեցեր սիրելեաց քոց։ Փութամք, Տէր, զի ելցուք ի մարմինոյս, զի խառնեսցուք ի

from the filthy teeth of the wild beast who would have ravaged us. But what more could we offer you in return save our souls in thanks for your salvation. For you have made us worthy of your service, to bear your name wherewith you saved us. For save you, Lord, none other do we know, and we invoke your name all the day [Is. 26.13].

194. "But it is better for us to die in our[1] purity than to stretch out our hands to foreign gods who really do not exist. All the cults of the heathen are but nothing. For you are the creator, and everything is from you and through your only-begotten Son, without whom nothing at all was made [cf. Jn. 1.3]. And 'your good Spirit will lead us in a straight land' [Ps. 142.10], who will bring us to the eternal and heavenly blessings.

195. "We must come before your only-begotten Son, to stand without shame on the right hand side [cf. Matt. 25.33], when you will send him 'from your prepared habitation of light to look on all the inhabitants of the earth' [Ps. 32.14]. He created the hearts of the sons of men,[1] and he considers all their deeds [cf. Ps. 32.15]. For we are from your people and from the flock of your pasture [cf. Ps. 78.13]; let us enter the mansions which you have prepared for your beloved [cf. Jn. 14.2]. Let us hasten, Lord, to leave this body in order to be joined to

գունդ միածնի Որդւոյդ քոյ սիրելւոյ, և ի թիւ
այնոցիկ, որ սիրեցին զօր երևելոյ գալստեան
տեառն մերոյ Յիսուսի Քրիստոսի։ Ի պղծութե֊
նէս և եթ ապրեցուք. այլ եթէ եկեսցեն տան֊
ջանք ի վերայ մեր վասն անուան քոյ՝ պատ֊
րաստ եմք։ Չի ոչ գրկես դու գմեզ. գի դու,
Տէր, ինքնին վկայես ինձ, գի վարուց երկրա֊
կեաց կենացս ես ինչ ոչ ցանկացայ ի մանկու֊
թենէ իմմէ. վասն գի նայեցայ և հաւատացի
բանի քում գոր ասացեր, թէ «Վա՛յ իցէ ձեզ,
յորժամ բարի ասիցեն գձէնջ մարդիկ»։ այլ
«Երանի է ձեզ, յորժամ նախատիցեն գձեզ և
հալածիցեն, և ասիցեն գամենայն բան չար սուտ
գձէնջ վասն իմ. ցնծացէք և ուրախ լերուք»։

196 «Արդարև իսկ, Տէր, ցնծացաք և ու֊
րախ եղաք ընդ այս պատերազմ որ եհաս մեզ,
մարանչել սիրով քով. գի յաղթեաց յաղթող գո֊
րութիւնդ քո, և կտ մեզ յաղթել։ Ուրախ եղաք
ընդ այս փոխանակ աւուրցս, որ խռնարհ արա֊
րին գմեզ, և ամացս, յորս տեսաք գչարչարանս։
Հայեաց, Տէր, ի ժառանգութիւն քո և ի գործս
ձեռաց քոց, և առաջնորդեա՛ մեզ ի վերին քա֊
ղաքդ քո երուսաղէմ որ ի բարձունսդ է, ուր
ժողովեցողդ ես գամենայն արդարս, գսուրբս և
գսիրելիս անուան քոյ. եղիցի լոյս տեառն Աս֊
տուծոյ ի վերայ մեր»։

197   Եւ մինչդեռ երանելին սուրբն

the company[1] of your beloved only-begotten Son and to the number of those who have loved the day of the revelation and coming of our Lord Jesus Christ. Only let us be saved from this profanation. But if there come upon us torments for your name's sake [cf. Matt. 5.11; Jn. 15.20], we are ready. For you will not abandon us; since you, Lord, yourself bear me witness that from my youth I have had no desire at all for earthly life. Because I had regard for and faith in your saying: 'Woe to you when men will say good about you' [Lk. 6.26], but 'Blessed are you when they will insult and persecute you and will make every wicked and false accusation against you for my sake; rejoice and be glad!' [Matt. 5.11; Lk. 6.22-23].

196. "Truly, Lord, we rejoiced and were glad at this struggle, which has overtaken us, to fight by your love. Because your victorious power has won, and given us the victory [cf. I Cor. 15.57]. We were glad for these days that cast us low,[1] and for these months in which we have seen torments [cf. Ps. 89.15]. Look down, Lord, on your inheritance[2] and on the works of your hands, and lead us to your celestial city, Jerusalem, which is in the heights [cf. Gal. 4.26], where you will gather all the just, the saints and those who loved your name. Let the light of the Lord God be over us."

[*D. The martyrdom of the nuns*]

197. While blessed saint

Հովփսիմէ խօսէր դայս ամենայն՝ անդէն ի նմին
գիշերի եկին դասին վաղվաղակի ի տեղի անդր
իշխանք Թագաւորին, և դանճապեան դանճօքն
հանդերձ ընդ նոսա, և ջանք լուցեալք առաջի
նոցա։ Եւ մատեան վաղվաղակի, կապեցին գնա
ձեռս յետս, և խնդրէին զի հացեն գլեգուն։
Իսկ նա իւրովի կամօք բացեալ զբերանն՝ հանեալ մատուցանէր գլեզունէ

198 Եւ անդէն գհանդերձիկն պատառատուն
որ գնով[ա]ն էր՝ ի բաց գերծուին ի նմանէ. և
հարբեալ շուրս յիցս ի գետինն, երկուս ոտիցն և
երկուս ձեռացն՝ և պրկեցին գնա. և մատուցին
գկանթեղունան գմեծ ժամս. այրէին և խորովէին
գմարմինս նորա հրով կանթեղացն։ Եւ քարբնս
վարեցին ընդ գոզս նորա և ի վայր վայթեցին
պապիս նորա. և մինչդեռ կայր կենդանի՝ փորե-
ցին գայս երանելւոյն։ Ապա անդամ անդամ յո-
շէին գնա և ատէին, եթէ «Ամենեքեան որ իշխեսցեն անգոնել և անարգել գհրամանս Թա-
գաւորաց՝ ըստ դմին օրինակի կորիցեն»։

199 Իսկ էին և այլ սուրբք, արք և կանայք, որ ընդ նոսա եկեալ էին, աւելի քան գեո-
Թանասուն մարդ. այլ որ ի ժամուն անդ հասին
ի տեղին յայն ի նոցանէն, որ խնդրէին ամփոփել և Թաղել գմարմինս նոցա, յորոց վերայ
սուր եղեալ կոտորեցին իբրև երեսուն և երկու
ոգիս։

Rhipsimē was saying all this, that same evening the king's nobles, the chief-executioner with the torturers[1] quickly arrived there, with torches lit before them. They quickly approached and bound her hands behind her back, and tried to pull out her tongue. But she willingly opened her mouth and offered her tongue [cf. II Macc. 7.10].[2]

198.   Then they stripped from her the torn clothing which was around her. And they fixed four stakes in the ground, two for her feet and two for her hands, and tied her to them. And they applied the torches to her for a long time, burning and roasting her flesh with their fire. And they thrust stones into her entrails, eviscerating her. And while she was still alive they plucked out the blessed one's eyes. Then limb by limb they dismembered her, saying: "All who dare to despise and insult the king's commands will perish in the same way."

199.   And there were other saints, men and women, who had come with them, more than seventy people. But of those who came there at that time and who sought to wrap and bury their bodies, they put to the sword and killed thirty-two.[1]

200 Որոց ասացեալ եւ նոցա գայս. «Սիրե-
ցաք զբեզ, Տէր, զի լուիցես զձայն աղօթից մերոց. խոնարհեցուցեր գունկն քո բարերար, եւ
մեք կարդացուք առ քեզ։ Քեզ փառք, որ ոչ
գրկեցեր զմեր անարժանութիւնս ի քոց բա-
րեացդ, մարդասէր. որ պանեցեր զմեզ իբրեւ
զքիք ական, եւ ի հովանի թեւոց քոց ապրեցաք
յանօրէնութեանցս բազմութենէ. եւ անա մեռանիմք վասն փառաւորեալ անուանդ քոյ»։ Եւ
զայս միաբան ասացեալ՝ առ հասարակ սպա-
ռեցան։

201 Եւ մի ոմն որ անդէն ի ներքս սպանին
ի հնձանի անդ, ուր էին վանք նոցա. որ այսպէս ասէր ի ժամ հրաժարելոյն իւրոյ. «Գոհանամ
զքէն, Տէր բարերար, զի եւ զիս ոչ գրկեցեր. զի
ես հիւանդ էի, եւ ոչ կարացի ընթանալ՝ եւ գնալ
ընկերացն ժամանել. սակայն դու, Տէր մարդասէր եւ քաղցր. ընկալ եւ խառնեա եւ զիմ ոգիս ի
գունդ քոյ սուրբ վկայիցն, ընկերացն իմոց եւ
քերցն, առ քս ադախինն եւ մայրն մեր եւ գլուխ
Գայիանէ, եւ զքեզ սիրիչ եւ որդեակ մեր Հռիփսիմէ»։ Եւ սա այսու օրինակաւ խոստեալ՝ փոխե-
ցաւ։ Եւ քարշեալ ի բաց ընկեցին զմարմինս նո-
ցա՝ առ ի կեր լինել շանց քաղաքին եւ գազանաց երկրի եւ թռչնոց երկնից։

202   Իսկ Թագաւորին Թողեալ զիւր
ամօթն կորանաց, որ պարտ էր նմա ամաչել,

200.   These said as follows: "We have loved you, Lord, that you might hear the voice of our prayers. You inclined your benign ear and we invoked you [cf. Ps. 114.1]. To you be glory, for you did not deprive our unworthiness of your blessings. You preserved us like the apple of an eye and saved us under the shadow of your wings from the multitude of these iniquities [cf. Deut. 32.10-11; 16.8-9; Ps. 60.5].[1] And behold we die for your glorious name." Saying this with one voice, together they breathed their last.

201.   And there was one[1] killed in the vat-store, which had been their lodging-place, who spoke thus at the moment of her death: "I thank you, benign Lord, for not excluding me. For I was ill and could not run to follow my companions. But do you, benevolent and sweet Lord, receive and join my soul to the company of your holy martyrs, my companions and sisters, with your handmaid and our mother and leader, Gaianē, and Rhipsimē our child who loved you."[2] And speaking thus she died. They dragged out their bodies and threw them as food for the dogs of the city and beasts of the land and birds of the sky.

202.   But the king paid no regard to his shameful humiliation, of which he should have been ashamed,[1]

որ այնչափ անուանի եղեալ՝ քաջութեամբ առա-
ւելոյր ի մարտս պատերազմացն. նաև և յՈղիմ-
պիադսն Յունաց հականագոր երևեալ, բազում
գործս արութեան և անդ ցուցեալ, և ոչ սակաւ
ձղեալ պատերազմունս յայնկոյս Եփրատ գետոյ
ի կողմանս Տաճկաց. ուր և կարևվեր խոցեալ՝
եւանէր երիվարաւն ի պատերազմէն. իսկ նորա
առեալ գերիվարն, և գասպագէն նորին և գիւր
գառնագէնն առեալ կապեալ ի Թիկունսն՝ ի վերայ մկանանցն ի լիւղ անցանէր ընդ գետն Եփրատ. արդ՝ որ այնչափ հզոր գօրաւորն էր և
բուռն ոսկերօք՝ յաղՋկանէ միոջէ յաղթահարեալ
լինէր կամօքն Աստուծոյ։ Եւ գայն ոչ էր եղեալ
ի մի գամօՋն նախատանացն, այլ ի տեսիլ սիրոյ նորա Ջենեալ՝ որոմեալ ընդ մահ աղՋկանն,
տխրացեալ սգայր։

203 «Տեսէք, ասէ, զկախարդասար աղանդ
ապզիդ քրիստոնէից. զիարդ կորուսանեն դանձինս բազումս մարդկան, հանեալ յատուածոյն
պաշտամանէ. յերկրաւոր վայելից կենացս խա-
վանեն, և ի մահուանէ ոչ դողան. մանուանդ
վասն սքանչելոյն հոփիսիմեայ, որոյ ոչ գոյր հա-
մեմատ յերկրի ի ծնունդս կանանց։ Վասն զի
սիրա հատեալ գՆետ անՆնարին և անմռոաց՝ ի
մատս չանկանի, մինչ կենդանի եմ ես, Տրբ-
դատ արքայ։ Զի գՅունաց աշխարհն և գՀոռոմոց
քաշ գիտեմ, և գմեր Պարթևաց կողմանսն, վասն

he who was so renowned for bravery in battle. Not least in the Greek Olympics[2] he had seemed as strong as a giant, showing there many deeds of prowess. He had waged no few battles beyond the river Euphrates in the regions of the Tachiks;[3] where once he was leaving the combat on horseback gravely wounded,[4] he picked up the horse and its armor and his own armor, and fastening them to his back[5] he swam across the Euphrates river. So he, who was such a powerful soldier and strong of body, by the will of God was defeated by a single girl. But he paid no thought to this shameful disgrace, but was rather inflamed at the sight of his love; and saddened at the death of the maiden, he bitterly mourned.

203. "Do you see, he said, that bewitching sect of the race of Christians, how they destroy many men's souls, drawing them away from the worship of the gods? They deprive them of[1] the pleasures of this earthly life and do not tremble at death, (I am speaking) especially about the wonderful Rhipsimē who had no equal among women on earth. For my heart is broken for that amazing and unforgettable girl, who will never pass from my mind so long as I, king Trdat, remain alive. I know well the land of the Greeks and Romans, and our Parthian territory, for that

գի բնութիւն իսկ է մեր, և զԱսորեստան և զՏաճկաստան և զԱտրպատական։ Եւ զի՞ մի ըստ միոջէ թուեմ. գի բազում տեղիք այն են, որ իմ խաղաղութեամբ է հաստեալ, և բազումք այն են, որ մարտիւ պատերազմաւ աւարի ասպատակեալ։ Որ ուրեք տեսեալ է նման նմանութիւն այսր գեղոյ, գոր էր կորուսեալ այս կախարդացն. գի այսպէս գործման կախարդինքն, մինչև ինձ յաղթեցին»։

204 Իսկ ի վաղիւ անդր մատուցեալ՝ առնոյր հրաման դանճապետն վասն սրբոյն Գայիանեայ սպանման։ Իսկ նա իբրև լուաւ՝ առ սէրն յեղեալ գեղեալ յիմարեալ ապշեալ և ոչ յիշեալ վասն մահուան սրբոյն Հռիփսիմեայ՝ համարեցաւ եթէ կենդանի իցէ։ Սեծ աւագութեան, բարձի և պատուոյ պարզիս խոստանայր՝ եթէ յանկարծ օք ճնարեացէ պատրել հանել գմիտս աղջկանն՝ գալ առ նա։ Իսկ նա ասէ, թէ «Այնպէս կորիցեն ամենայն թշնամիք քո, արքայ, և որ գատտուածս անարգենն և գ հրամանս ձեր թագաւորաց. այլ կայ կախարդն այն, որ ապականեալ կորոյս գ ջքնագագեղն, և երկու ես ընկերք նորունն»։

205 Իբրև լուաւ, թէ մեռաւ սուրբն Հռիփսիմէ՝ դարձեալ ի նոյն որտմութիւն ընկլաւ, և իջեալ նստէր ի վերայ գետնոյ, և լայր և ի սուգ տտանէր։ Դարձեալ հրաման տայր վասն առա-

is our homeland, and Asorestan and Tachikistan and Azerbaijan.[2] Why should I enumerate them one by one? For there are many regions to which I have come in peace, and many which I have plundered in war. Yet in none have I seen the like of this beauty, whom these magicians have destroyed; for their sorcery has become so strong as even to overcome me."

204. The next day the chief executioner came forward to receive orders for the execution of saint Gaianē. But (the king) when he heard, was overwhelmed, frenzied and stupified for love, nor did he remember the death of saint Rhipsimē but thought that she was still alive. He promised to bestow great dignities, promotion and honor on anyone who could entice or persuade the maiden to come to him. But (the executioner) said: "So will perish all your enemies, O king, and those who dishonor the gods and the commands of your majesty. But there still lives that witch who corrupted and destroyed the beautiful girl, and two more companions of hers."

205. When he heard that saint Rhipsimē was dead, he was cast down into the same despondency, and fell down and sat on the ground, weeping and mourning. Then he commanded that

քինւոյն Գայիանեայ, թէ նախ գլեգուն ընդ ծոր-
ծորական հանել, և ապա սպանանել. վասն զի
իշխեաց փասակար խրատուն իւրով կորուսանել
գայնպիսին, որ դղիցն գեղեցկութիւն ունէր ի
մէջ մարդկան։ Իսկ դորին խրատոդ անշնորհ առ-
բել դղիան իշխեաց, որոց նմայն գայն շնորհեալ
էր գեղեցկութիւն. վասն այնորիկ գնա կոտա-
մահ սպանցեն։

206 Արդ՝ ելեալ դանձապեան պարծելով՝
չարամած առնել գնա, և ետ հանել գնոսա շրդ-
թայիւք ի քաղաքէն ընդ դուռն հարաւոյ, ընդ
կողմն պողոտային որ հանէր ի Մեծամօրի կամուրջն, ի տեղին յայն, ուր սովոր էին սպանանել գամենայն մահապարտս, ի ճախճախուտ տե-
դի մի, մօտ ի պարկէն փոսին որ շուրջ գայր
գքաղաքւսն։ Եւ վարեցին չորս չորս ցիցս մի-
ւում միում ի նոցանէն։

207 Եւ մինչդեռ կագմէին գայն՝ սկսաւ
ասել սուրբն Գայիանէ ընկերոքն հանդերձ այսպէս. «Գոհանամք գքէն, Տէր, որ արժանի արարեր գմեզ մեռանել վասն մեծի անուանդ քոյ,
և յարդեցեր գշողեղէն բնութիւնս մեր, գի լիցուք արժանի ատուածութեանդ քում. և հա-
դորդեցեր գիս մահուան սրբոց քոց վկայից,
Հռիփսիմեայ և ընկերացն։ Եւ արդ՝ փութամ և
անձկացեալ եմ հասանել նոցա որ գքեզն սիրեցին, և ուրախ եմ, գի ժամանեցից գկնի դրա-

the virtuous Gaianē first have her tongue pulled out and then be put to death, since she had dared[1] to corrupt with her harmful advice her who had the beauty of the gods among mankind. And her advice had displeased the gods, who had given that girl such beauty,[2] therefore they should torture her to death.

206.   So the chief-executioner came out boasting that he would put her to a cruel death. He had them taken in chains out of the city by the South gate,[1] along the road that leads to the *Metsamawr* bridge,[2] to the place where they were accustomed to execute those condemned to death, a marshy place near the moat which ran round the city. And they brought four stakes for each one of them.

207.   And while they were setting these out, saint Gaianē with her companions began to speak as follows: "We thank you, Lord, for making us worthy to die on behalf of your great name, and for honoring our earthly nature so that we might become worthy of your divinity, and for making me share in the death of your holy martyrs, Rhipsimē and her companions. So now I[1] am anxious and impatient to join those who have loved you; and I am happy to follow

տերն իմոյ և որդեկին իմոյ Հրփսիմեայ և
քերցն իմոց և ընկերացն։ Արդ՝ յիշեա՛ զմեզ,
Տէր, որ «վասն անուան քոյ մեռանիմք գործա-
նապադ. համարեցաք իբրև գոչխար ի սպանումն»։
«արի՛ և մի՛ մերժեր զմեզ վասն անուան քոյ»։
և դու տուր մեզ գյաղթութիւնդ քո, և չարն
գործակցօքն հանդերձ նկուն լիցի յանէ փառաց
քոց»։

208 Եւ յետ այսորիկ մատեան և պատա-
ռեցին գհանդերձս նոցա յանդամոց նոցա, և
պրկեցին գնոսա մի մի ի չորս չորս ցիցս։ Եւ
ծակեցին գմորթան ի պճղունս նոցա և եղին
փողս և փչելով այնպէս կենդանւոյն մորթեցին
գաւրբան երեսին, ի ներքուստ ի վեր մինչև ի
ստինան, և ծակեալ գծոբծորական՝ և գլեգունն
ընդ այն հանէին։ Եւ վարեցին հա քարինս ընդ
գոգս նոցա, և ցրուեալ գազիս նոցա յորովայ-
նիցն ընդ գոգս նոցա. և քանզի դեռ հա կային
կենդանի՛ և ապա բարձին գգլուխս նոցա սրով։

209 Արդ՝ որք միանգամ եկեալ էին ընդ
նոսա անտուստ ի Հռոմոց աշխարհէն, որ միանգամ միաբանք եկին հասին յերկիր Հայաստան աշխարհիս՝ աւելի էին քան գեօթանասուն
մարդ։ Իսկ որ սպանան ընդ սուրբ տիկնայան,
ընդ Գայիանեայ և ընդ Հռփսիմեայ, նոքիմբք
հանդերձ որ Թուեցան ի թիւ վկայելոցն՝ ընդ
ամենայն սպանեալն երեսուն և եօթն մարդ։

my daughter and my child Rhipsimē and my sisters
and companions. Now remember us, Lord, who 'for
your name's sake die daily; we have been considered
as a lamb for the slaughter. Arise and do not abandon
us for your name's sake' [Ps. 43.23-24]. Give us your
victory, and the evil one and his co-workers will be
abased from fear of your glory."

208.   Then they came forward and tore the clothes
from their limbs and bound each one to four stakes.
They pierced the skin of their soles and put in tubes,
and by blowing they flayed the three saints alive, from
their feet to their breasts.[1] They pierced their gullets
and pulled out their tongues. They forced stones into
their entrails, eviscerating them. And because they
were still alive they then cut off their heads with a
sword.[2]

209.   Now those who had once come with them from
the land of the Romans and had arrived together in
this land of Armenia[1] were more than seventy people.
But those who were put to death with the saintly ladies
Gaianē and Rhipsimē, with those who were counted
in the number of the martyred, altogether those killed
were thirty-seven.

210 Արդ՝ ի քահն և ի վեց ամսոյն հուրի կատարեցաւ սուրբն Հռիփսիմէ դասուն սրբով, երեսուն և երեք նահատակակից ընկերօքն հանդերձ. և ի քահն և եօթն ամսոյն հուրի՝ սուրբն Գայիանէ երկու իւրովք ընկերօքն, որք ընդ նմա պատերագմեալք պսակեցան և առին գպսակն յաղթութեան.

211 Արդ՝ աւուրս վեց ի խոր տխրութեան և յանննարին որտմութեան կացեալ Թագաւորն առ անձուկ սիրոյ գեղոյն Հռիփսիմեայ. ապա յետ այսորիկ ժամ տուեալ որսոյ՝ ամենայն գօրաց աձել կուտել գպառականն, խուձապական սփռեալ, երագագ տուեալ, Թակարդ ձգեալ, կամեցեալ որս առնել, երթեալ ի դաշտն Փառական Շեմակաց:

212 Այն ինչ ի կառս ելեալ կամէր Թագաւորն բատ քաղաքն ելանել՝ անդէն վաղվաղակի պատուհաս ի Տեառնէ ի վերայ հասանէր. և հարեալ գԹագաւորն այստն պղծութեան՝ ի կառացն ի վայր կործանէր: Եւ անդէն մոլեգնել սկսաւ, և իւրովի ուտել գիւր մարմինն. նա և բատ նմանութեաննն Նաբուգոդոնոսորայ աբքային Բաբելացող, ելեալ բատ մարդկային բնութիւնս արատաք՝ ի նմանութիւն վայրենի խոզաց, իբրև գնոսա ընդ նոսա ի մէջ նոցա երթեալ բնակէր: Եւ այնուհետև մտեալ յեղէգն, խոտաձարակ լեալ անննարին անզգայութեամբ, մերկ գանձն ընդ դաշտան

210. So on the twenty-sixth of the month Hori[1] saint Rhipsimē died with the holy company of thirty-three[2] fellow-martyrs; and on the twenty-seventh of the month of Hori saint Gaianē with her two companions, who with her fought the fight and were crowned and received the palm of victory [cf. II Tim. 4.7-8].

[Chapter 6. Punishment falls on Trdat
and the Armenians;
Gregory is rescued]

211. The king spent six days in profound grief and deep mourning because of his passionate love for the beautiful Rhipsimē. Then afterwards he arranged to go hunting; he had his soldiers gather the pack of hounds, the beaters scattered, the nets fixed, and the traps set;[1] then he went out to hunt in the plain of *P'aṙakan Shemak.*[2]

212. But when the king, having mounted his chariot, was about to leave the city, then suddenly there fell on him punishment from the Lord. An impure demon struck the king and knocked him down from his chariot. Then he began to rave and to eat his own flesh. And in the likeness of Nebuchadnezzar, king of Babylon, he lost his human nature for the likeness of wild pigs and went about like them and dwelt among them [cf. Dan. 4.12-13].[1] Then entering a reedy place, in senseless abandon he pastured on grass,[2] and wallowed[3] naked in the plain.

կոծելով: Զի թէպէտ կամեցան արգելուլ անդէն ի քաղաքին՝ ոչ կարացին. մի՝ վասն բնական ու֊
ժոյն, և մի՝ վասն զի էր և ոյժն դիւաց որ ի նմայն հարեալ էին:

213 Նա և ամենայն մարդիկն որ ի քաղա֊
քին էին՝ նոյն օրինակ դիւաբախք մոլեգնէին. և
աննարին կործանումն ի վերայ աշխարհին հա֊
սանէր: Եւ ամենայն ընտանիք Թագաւորին, ծա֊
ռայք և սպասաւորք առ հասարակ, հարուածովք
հարեալք լինէին. և աննարին սուգ վասն հա֊
րուածոցն լինէր:

214 Յայնմ ժամանակի տեսիլ երևեալ յԱ֊
տուծոյ ի վերայ քեռ Թագաւորին, որոյ անուն
էր Խոսրովիդուխտ: Արդ՝ եկեալ խօսէր ընդ մարդ֊
կանն, պատմէր գտեսիլն և ասէր. «Տեսիլ երև֊
եցաւ ինձ յայսմ գիշերի. այր մի ի նմանութիւն
լուսոյ եկեալ՝ պատմեաց ինձ, եթէ «Ոչ այլ ինչ
գոյ բժշկութիւն հարուածոցդ, որ եկին հասին ի
վերայ ձեր՝ եթէ ոչ յղեսջիք դուք ի քաղաքն
յԱրտաշատ, աձել անտի գկապեալն Գրիգորիոս.
նա. եկեալ ուսուսցէ ձեզ դեղ ցաւոցդ բժշկու֊
թեան»:

215 Արդ՝ իբրև լուան մարդիկն՝ սկսան ձի֊
ծաղել գբանիւքն գոր ասաց. սկսան խօսել ընդ
նմա և ասեն. «Եւ դու ուրեմն մոլեգնեցար. դե
ուրեմն հարաւ ի քեզ: Զիա՞րդ է, գի այս նագե֊
ատասան ամ է, գի ընկեցին գնա յաննարին խոր

For although they wished to restrain him in the city, they were unable to do so, partly because of his natural strength and partly because of the force of the demons who had possessed him.

213. Likewise all the populace in the city went mad through similar demon-possession. And terrible ruin fell upon the country. All the king's household, including slaves and servants, were afflicted with torments. And there was terrible mourning on account of these afflictions.

214. Then there appeared a vision from God to the king's sister, whose name was Khosrovidukht.[1] So she came to speak with the people and related the vision, saying: "A vision appeared to me this night. A man in the likeness of light came and told me 'there is no other cure for these torments that have come upon you, unless you send to the city of Artashat and bring thence the prisoner Gregory. When he comes he will teach you the remedy for your ills.' "

215. When the populace heard this they began to mock at her words. They began to say: "You too then are mad. Some demon has possessed you. How is it, because it is fifteen years[1] since they threw him into the terribly deep

վիրապն, և դուլ ատես եթէ կենդանի է․ արդ և
ոսկերոտքն իսկ ճւբ իցեն․ զի նոյն օրին, իբրև
իՉուցին զնա անդր՝ յօձիցն իսկ տեսլենէն նոյն-
ժամայն ատակեալ իցէ»։

216 Իսկ կրկնեաց դարձեալ իս կնոջն զնոյն
տեսիլ, և ՛նդկնեաց սպառնալեօք, զի եթէ ոչ
պատմեսցէ ստէպ ստէպ՝ մեծամեծ տանջանս
ընկալցի, և հարուածք մարդկան և թագաւորին
իս քան զես սատակասցին մահու և պէսպէս տան-
ջանօք։ Եւ մտեալ անդրէն Խոսրովիդուխտն մեծաւ երկիւղիւ և զգուշութեամբ ասաց զբանսն
հրեշտակին։

217 Իսկ նոքա վաղվաղակի յղէին անդր
նախարար գումն աւագ, որոյ անուն Օտայ կո-
չէր։ Եւ գնաց նա ի քաղաքն Արտաշատ՝ հանել
զնա ի խոր բանդէ վիրապին։ Արդ՝ իբրև եկն
եհաս Օտայն ի քաղաքն յԱրտաշատ՝ ընդ առաջ
ելանէին նմա քաղաքացիքն՝ հարցանէլ գպատ-
ճառս գալոյն։ Եւ նա ասէ ցնոսա, թէ «Վասն
կապելոյն Գրիգորի եկեալ եմ, տանել գնա»։
Իսկ նոքա գարմացեալ առ հասարակ ասէին․ «Ո՞
գիտէ թէ կայցէ․ զի բազում ամք են, զի ընկեցին գնա անդր»։ Իսկ նա պատմեաց զիրս տես-
լեանն և զգործն գինչ եղեն իսկ։

218 Եւ եկին բերին կարս պարանաց երկայնս և ստուարս, և կցեցին իՉուցին ի ներքս։
Աղաղակեաց Օտայ նախարարն ի ճայն մեծ և

pit, that you say he is alive? Where would even his bones be? For on the same day when they put him down there, he would have immediately dropped dead at the very sight of the snakes."

216.   But the princess had the same vision again, five times,[1] with threats that unless she reported it immediately she would suffer great torments and the afflictions of the people and of the king would become even worse, with death and various tortures. So Khosrovidukht came forward again in great fear and hesitation, and told the angel's[2] words.

217.   Then they straightway sent there a noble prince, whose name was Awtay.[1] He went to the city of Artashat in order to bring him out of the dungeon and deep pit. Now when Awtay arrived at the city of Artashat, the citizens came out to meet him to ask the reason for his coming. He told them: "I have come to take away the prisoner Gregory." But they were amazed and all said: "Who knows if he is there? For it is many years since they threw him there." But he related to them the details of the vision and everything that had happened.

218.   So they went and brought long, thick, strong ropes, which they attached and let down inside; Awtay the prince shouted with a loud voice and

աէ. «Գրիգորիոս, եթէ կայցես ուրեք՝ եկ ի
դուրս. զի տէր Աստուածն քո, զոր պաշտէիրն
գու՛ նա հրամայեաց հանել զքեզ այտի»։ Եւ անդէն յոտն կացեալ՝ վազվազակի շարժեաց զգա-
րանն, և բուռն հարեալ ունէր։

219 Իսկ սոցա գիտացեալ՝ ձգեալ հանին
զնա ի վեր, և տեսին զի քիացեալ էր մարմին
նորա իբրե գաձող սեացեալ. և անդէն հանդերձս մատուցեալ զգեցուցին նմա, և ինդու-
թեամբ առին դնացին յԱբրաշատ քաղաք, տանել
ի վաղարշապատ քաղաք։ Յայնմ ժամանակի առ
վտանգի տարակուսի ցաւոցն՝ եղեալ թագաւորն
յերամէ խոգիցն՝ դիւին առեալ աձէր ընդ առաջ
նորա մերկ խայտառակ։ Եւ նախարարքն արտաքոյ քաղաքին սպասէին նոցա։

220 Արդ՝ իբրե տեսանէին գնոսա ի բացէ,
զի դային Գրիգորիոս Օտային հանդերձ, և այլ
բազում մարդիկ, որ դային ընդ նոսա յԱբրաշատ քաղաքէ՝ ընդ առաջ խաղացեալ, մոլեգնե-
լով և ուտելով զմարմինս իւրեանց՝ դիւահարէին
և փրփրէին առաջի նորա։

221 Իսկ նա վազվազակի ձունր եղեալ յաղօթս կայր, և նոքա անդրէն ի զգաստութիւն
դառնային։ Եւ նա անդէն հրամայեաց, զի արկ-
ցեն գանձամբք իւրեանց հանդերձս և ծածկես-
ցեն զամօթ իւրեանց։ Եւ մատուցեալ թագաւորն և նախարարքն՝ բուռն հարեալ ունէին գո-

said: "Gregory, if you are somewhere down there,[1] come out [cf. Jn. 11.43]. For the Lord your God whom you worshiped has commanded that you be brought forth." Then he stood up, and straightway moved the rope and shook it strongly.

219. When they felt this they pulled him up; and they saw that his body was blackened like coal [cf. Job 30.30]. Then they brought clothing and dressed him, and joyfully took him from the city of Artashat and led him to Valarshapat. Then, sorely afflicted, the king left the herd of swine; led by the demon he came to meet them, naked and ignominious. And the princes waited for them outside the city.

220. Now when they saw afar off Gregory coming with Awtay and many other men coming with them from Artashat, they ran to meet them, raving and eating their own flesh, possessed and foaming [cf. Mk. 9.19].

221. Then he immediately knelt in prayer, and they returned to sobriety. He then commanded that they cover their bodies with clothes and hide their shame. The king and the princes approached, took hold of

տից սբբոյն Գրիգորի և ասէին. «Խնդրեմք ի
քէն, թող մեզ գյանցումն մեր, զոր մեք ընդ
քեզ արարաք»:

222. Իսկ նա մատուցեալ կանգնեաց գնոսա ի
գետնոյ անտի և ասէ. «Ես մարդ եմ իբրև զձեզ,
և մարմին ունիմ իբրև զձերդ. բայց դուք ծաներուք զձեր արարիչն, որոյ գերկինս և գերկիր
արարեալ է, զաբեզական և զլուսին և զաստեղս,
զծով և զցամաք. և նա կարող է զձեզ բժշկել»:

223 Իսկ անդէն սկսաւ հարցանել Գրիգորիոս, թէ ո՞ւր եդեալ են մարմինք վկայիցն
Աստուծոյ: Իսկ նոքա ասեն, թէ «Զործց վկայից
ասես»: Եւ նա ասէ. «Որ վասն Աստուծոյն մեռան
ի ձէնչ»: Իսկ նոցա ցուցեալ նմա գտեղիսն: Իսկ
նա ընթացեալ ժողովել և ամփոփել զմարմինս
նոցա ի սպանման տեղեացն, գի կային անդէն:
Եւ տեսին գի գորութեանն Աստուծոյ պաշեալ
էր գմարմինս նոցա. գի այն ինն տիւ էր և ինն
գիշեր, գի արտաքոյ ընկեցեալ կային մարմինք
նոցա, գի ոչ գազանի էր մատուցեալ և ոչ շան,
քանզի անդէն շուրջ գքաղաքաւն էին, մօտ ի
քաղաքն. և ոչ հաւու ճասեալ ես էր նոցա. և
ոչ հոտեալ էին մարմինք նոցա:

224 Իսկ նոքա բերին հանդերձ սուրբս պատանաց. բայց երանելին Գրիգորիոս ոչ արժանի
համարէր զպատանան բերեալս թագաւորին, կամ
գայլոց մարդկանն. այլ իւրաքանչիւր պատառ-

saint Gregory's feet and said: "We beg you, forgive us the crime that we committed against you."

222.   Then he came forward and raised them from the ground and said: "I am a man like you [cf. Acts 10.26], and I have a body like yours. But do you recognize your creator, who made heaven and earth, the sun and moon and stars, the sea and the dry land. He is able to heal you."

223.   Then Gregory began to ask them where the bodies of the martyrs of God had been placed. They said: "Of what martyrs are you speaking?" He replied: "Those who died at your hands for their God." Then they showed him the places. And he hastened to bring together their bodies from the places where they had been killed, for they were still lying there, and to enshroud them. And they saw that the power of God had preserved their bodies; for it was the ninth day and ninth night that their bodies had been lying outside and no animal or dog had approached, although they were around the city near to it; nor had any bird harmed them, nor did their bodies stink [cf. Jn. 11.39].[1]

224.   Then they brought clean clothes for shrouds. But blessed Gregory did not consider the shrouds brought by the king worthy, nor those of other people. But

տուն հանդերձիւն պատեր գաւըրան. «Առ անգամ մի, ասէ, մինչև լիշիք դուք արժանի պա-
տել գմարմինս նոցա»։ Եւ ամփոփեաց, առ գնաց
ի հնձանն, ուր վանքն իսկ լեալ էին նոցա. և իբր
իսկ վանս անդէն կալեալ՝ օթեվանս առներ։ Եւ
երանելին Գրիգորիոս գգայգն ամենայն առ Աստուած աղօթս մատուցանէր վասն նոցա փրկութեան, և ինդրուածս առներ, զի դարձին և
ապաշխարութեան հնարս գտանել մարթասցեն։

225 Եւ ի վաղիւ անդր թագաւորն և նախարարքն և մեծամեծ ուագանին խառնադանձ
ամբոխիւն բագմութեամբ եկեալ ի ծունր իշեալ
առաշի սրբոյն Գրիգորի և առաշի սուրբ ոսկերաց վկայիցն Աստուծոյ՝ ինդրեին և ասէին.
«Թող մեզ գամենայն յանցուֆն չարեացն, գոր
մեք ընդ քեզ արարաք. և ինդրեա դու վասն
մեր յԱստուծոյ քումմէ, զի մի կորիցուք»։

226 Իսկ կապեալն Գրիգորիոս անդէն
խօսել սկսաւ և ասէ. «Որ ասէքդ, թէ «Աստուած
քո»՝ Աստուած է և Արարիչ, ամենագոր կամա-
յական բարերարութեամբն յանուստեք յաննիւ-
թոյ գնիւթական արարածս գոյացոյց. նոյն ինքն
էական գորութեամբն յանտեղեաց, յանվայր յո-
չընչէ իմեքէ հրամայեաց հաստատել երկրի. որ
գամենայն ինչ արար՝ Աստուածն ամենակալ,
ամենաբարն, ամենատէրն։ Չնա ծաներուք, գի
քժշկեսցին ձեր ցաւքդ յանցանաց ի պատուհասէ

he wrapped each saint in her torn clothing. "For a while," he said, "until you are worthy to wrap their bodies." And he enshrouded them and took them to the vat-store, where they had had their lodging, and he made it his own dwelling-place. Then blessed Gregory prayed all night to God for their (the Armenians') salvation, and begged that they might be converted and find a way to repentance.

225. In the morning the king and the princes and the great magnates and the common people came in a great crowd and knelt before saint Gregory and before the holy bones of God's martyrs, and begged: "Forgive us all the evil crimes that we have committed against you. And beg your God on our behalf that we perish not."

[Chapter 7. Gregory's sermons
         A. Gregory's preliminary exhortations]

226. Then the prisoner Gregory began to speak: "The one you call 'your God' is God and creator, who in his almighty benevolence has brought material creatures into being from immaterial nothing [cf. II Macc. 7.28; Rom. 4.17]. The same ordered the earth to be established by his essential power from uncircumscribed, boundless nothing.[1] He who created everything is the almighty, all-creative and all-loving God. Recognize him, in order that your pains from the punishment of your crimes may be healed.

այտի։ Որ վասն խրոյ մարդասէր ողորմութեանն
խրատեաց գձեզ, ըստ քանի աստուածական
Իմաստութեանն, որպէս ասաց իսկ, թէ «Զոր
սիրէ Տէր՝ խրատէ. գանալից առնէ զորդի՝ զոր
յակն առնու»։ Իսկ նա բարերարութեամբ իւրով
կոչէ գձեզ յորդեգրութիւն։

227 «Իսկ ճշմարիտ Որդին Աստուծոյ ոչ
ամօթ համարի գայնոսիկ իւր եղբարս անուա-
նել, որք դաձցին յերկրպագութիւն Հօր։ Եւ Հոգին սուրբ շնորհեացէ ձեզ գառհաւատչեայ սիրոյն իւրոյ, գուարձացուցանել գսիրոս ձեր յուրախութիւն որ ոչն անցանէ. բայց միայն եթէ
դարձջիք և ըստ կամաց նորա գնաջիք, տացէ
ձեզ գանմահութիւն կենաց։

228 «Այլ գի կոչեցէքզդ «Աստուած քո»՝ բարիոք ասացէք. քանզի որք ճանաչեն գնա՝ նա
նոցա Աստուած է։ Իսկ որք ոչն ճանաչեն, թէպէտ և են նորա արարածք՝ օտար են ի խնամոց
և ի սիրոյ մարդասիրութենէ անտի նորա. իսկ
երկիւղածք նորա մերձ են առ նա, և այյելու-
թիւն նորա շուրջ է գնոքօք, և պահէ գնոսա։

229 «Իսկ թերևս ասիցես դու, թէ ո՞ւր պահէ գերկիւղածս իւր. գի որ ի ձեռս մեր անկան՝
չարչարեցան և մեռան, և մեք ըստ կամաց մերոց դատեցաք գնոսա։ Տես գի կամեցաւ Աստուած գհանդիստ մահու մարդկան, և ի միւսանգամ գալստեան փառացն երկեցուցանէ՝ տալ

He warned you in his benevolent mercy according to the saying of the divine Wisdom: 'Whom God loves he warns; he castigates the son for whom he cares' [Prov. 3.12; 13.24; Heb. 12.6]. Now in his benevolence he summons you to adoption [cf. Eph. 1.5].

227. "The true Son of God considers it no shame to call his brothers [cf. Heb. 2.11] those who will turn to the worship of the Father. And the holy Spirit will grant you the pledge of his love [cf. II Cor. 1.22], and awaken your hearts to the joy which passes not away. But only if you turn and walk according to his desires will he give you eternal life.

228. "But in saying 'your God' you spoke well, because for those who recognize him he is their God [cf. Heb. 11.16]. But for those who do not recognize him, even though they are his creatures, they are estranged from his care and from his benevolent love. But those who fear him are near to him [cf. Ps. 84.10], and his providence surrounds them and guards them [cf. Ps. 33.8].

229. "But perhaps you[1] will say: 'Where does he guard his worshippers? For those who fell into our hands were tortured and killed, and we judged them according to our own desires.' See that God desired the repose of death for men, and at his second and glorious coming he will reveal [cf. Acts 3.20] and give

գբարիան սիրելեաց իւրոց և այնոցիկ որ ճանա
չենն և առնեն զկամս նորա։

230 «Այլ տես դու զայս, թէ զիարդ զո
րութեամբ ատուածութեան իւրոյ պանեաց հաս
տատուն զուրբք վկայան սիրելիան, և ոչ նեզու
թիւնք բազումք երկմտեցուցին զմի ոք ի նո
ցանէն։ Եւ ապրեցոյց զուրբք զերանելին Հռիփ
սիմէ ընկերօքն հանդերձ ի ձերոյ պղծութենէ և
յանօրէնութենէ։

231 «Արդ՝ պատրանք մեքենայից թշնամ
լոյն, որ ի սկզբանէ իսկ խաբեցին պատրեցին
զմարդիկ և կորստական ճանապարհացն ուղենրս
հաստատեցին։ Եւ կամ զիմ իսկ զանարժանու
թիւնս, զի՞ որպէս բարեբարութեամբն իւրով
արժանի արար պատրաստել զիս՝ չարչարել վասն
անուան իւրոյ մեծի, և եւս ի՞նձ համբերել, զի
հասուցէ զիս ի վիճական երկնաւորա, որպէս
ասաց իսկ մեծ առաքեալն Պաւղոս, զոր հանցէ
ձեզ ճանաչել, և ի նմին իսկ և ի նորուն բանս
վայելել մարդասիրութեամբն Քրիստոսի, թէ
«Օրհնեալ է այն, որ արժանիս արար զմեզ՝ հա
սանել ի մասն ժառանգութեան սրբոցն ի լոյս»։
Եւ արդարև հասաք պարծանօք ի խաչն Քրիս
տոսի, զի չարչարանօքն Քրիստոսի վայելիցեմք
ի նորա կամս և ի նորին վարդապետութեանն։

232 «Արդ՝ դնա ծանիջիք, որ զձեզ ի խա
լարէն կոչեաց յիւր սքանչելի լոյս փառաց. մա

blessings to his beloved and to those who recognize him and do his will.

230.   "But see this, how by the power of his divinity he kept firm his beloved holy martyrs; nor did many tribulations make a single one of them lose heart. And he saved the holy and blessed Rhipsimē and her companions from your impurity and impiety.

231.   "Now (see how) the deceit of the enemy's machinations, which from the beginning beguiled and deceived men [cf. Eph. 4.14], made them travelers on the path to destruction. Or (see) my unworthiness, and how by his benevolence he made me worthy and prepared me to suffer for his great name's sake. And he gave me endurance, to bring me to the heavenly inheritance, as the great apostle Paul said [cf. Acts 26.18; Col. 1.12] —whom you could recognize and at whose words you could rejoice through the benevolence of Christ: 'Blessed is he who made us worthy to attain the portion of the inheritance[1] of the saints in light [cf. Acts 20.32; Eph. 1.18; Col. 1.12; Heb. 11.8]. And truly we have attained gloriously the cross of Christ, that by the passion of Christ we may enjoy his will and his teaching.

232.   "Now recognize him who called you from darkness to the wonderful light of his glory [cf. I Pet. 2.9].

տիջիք առաջի աթոռոյ շնորհաց նորա, և գտջիք
զողորմութիւն ի նմանէ. և ի բաց թօթափեսջիք
գամենայն ադա չարեաց անօրէնութեան. լուաս-
ջիք զանձինս ձեր կենդանի Քրոֆէ, և գփառաց
լուսոյ զպատմուճանն արժանի լինիջիք զգենուլ
յանձինս ձեր:

233 «Այլ վասն սրբոյն Հռիփսիմեայ դուք
իսկ ինքնին գիտէք, թէ որպէս պանեաց գնա
Տէր և ապրեցոյց ի ձեռաց ձերոց, ի պղծութենէ անօրէնութեան: Եւ դու ինքնին գի-
տես գչափ քաջութեան ուժոյ պնդութեան ոսկերաց քոց. գիմրդ եղեր տկարացեալ առաջի
աղջկան միոջ. գի պանեաց գնա գօրութիւն ամենատեան Քրիստոս: Իսկ վասն իմ դու իսկ գի-
տես, գի Հնգետասան ամ է իմ՛ գի կայի ես ի
խաւարչուտ ի խոր յանՀնարին վիրապին. ի մէջ
օձից էր բնակութիւն իմ, և վասն անին Տեառն
ոչ՛ երբէք մեղան ինձ. և ոչ գարհուրեցայ ի նոցանէ, և ոչ երկեաւ սիրտ իմ. գի յուսացեալ էի
ի տէր Աստուած արարիչ ամենայնի:

234 «Այլ վասն այսօրիկ գիտեմ, գի տգի-
տութեամբ արարէք գոր ինչ արարէքն: Բայց
արդ՛ դարձարուք և ծաներուք գՏէր, գի ողոր-
մեսցի և կեցուսցէ գձեզ. և գապանեալ կենդա-
նիան բարեխօս արարէք. գի կենդանիք են և չեն
մեռեալք. և ծաներուք գԱստուած, գի նա ինքն
է Տէր ամենայնի. և ի բաց թողէք այսուհետև

Approach the throne of his grace and you will obtain mercy from him [cf. Heb. 4.16]. Throw off every stain of evil lawlessness. Wash your souls with living water [cf. Heb. 10.22], and you will become worthy to clothe your souls in robes of glorious light [cf. Rom. 13.12].

233. "But as for saint Rhipsimē, you yourselves know how the Lord preserved her and saved her from your hands, from impious pollution. And you yourself know the measure of the strength and firmness of your own bones, how you became weakened in front of a single girl. For the power of the Lord of all, Christ, preserved her. And as for me, you know that for fifteen years I have been in the dark and incredibly deep pit, dwelling amidst snakes[1] — yet for fear of the Lord they never harmed me, nor was I terrified of them nor was my heart dismayed. For I hoped in the Lord God the creator of all [cf. Ps. 26.3].

234. "But this I know, that it was in ignorance that you did what you did [cf. Eph. 4.18]. Nevertheless, turn now and recognize the Lord [cf. Heb. 8.11], that he may have mercy on you and give you life. Call upon those whom you killed, but who are alive,[1] as intercessors;[2] for they are alive and are not dead. Recognize God, for he is Lord of all. Abandon henceforth

զպղծութեան պաշտամունդ, զքարեղէն և գփայ-
տեղէն, զարձաթեղէն և գոսկեղէն պղնձածոյլ
պատկերացդ, զի սուտ են և անտի։

235 «Եւ ո՞չ զայդ իսկ ասացի ձեզ վաղագոյն վասն մոլորութեանդ ձերոյ, թէ մառախուղ
ստուերացն խաւարին թանձրութեան նստեալ է
ի վերայ ձերոյ աչաց սրտին, ոչ կարացեալ հայել իմանալ, աճել գմտաւ, և զՆերարիչն ճա-
նաչել։ Արդ՝ թէ ի ձէնջ ես ուզղութիւն ինչ
տեսանէի՝ առ ատուածութիւնն պաշտամամբ
մերձենալ՝ ոչ դաղարէի գցայդ և գգերեկ աղա-
չել վասն ձեր, զի մի՛ կորիցէք։ Այլ վասն բազում մարդասիրութեան Արարչին, որ անքնին
և անպատում է առ արարածս իւր. որ երկայն-
մտութեամբ ներէ թողու անսայ խնայէ. վասն
բազում գթութեան իւրոյ։

236 «Որ յաւուրզն առաջնոց թոյլ ետ գնալ
մարդկան ըստ կամաց իւրեանց, որպէս և ասեն
իսկ. «Քարձի թողի գնոսա՝ երթալ գհետ կամաց
սրտից իւրեանց։ Եւ գնացին նոքա ըստ կամս
անձանց իւրեանց»։ Այլ այժմիկ սկսեալ է կոչել
գձեզ յիւր փառսն և յանեղծութիւն, լինել ձեզ
ժառանգաւոր յաւէժ կենդանութեանն որ ոչն
անցանէ։

237 «Վասն որոյ իսկ գիւր վկայսն սիրելիս
առաքեաց առ ձեզ. որք ի վկայեն իւրեանց վկա-
յեցին գմիասնական տէրութիւնն Երրորդական՝

the foul worship of images of stone and wood, silver and gold and bronze, which are false and vain.

235.   "Did I not tell you earlier[1] about your error that a fog of thick and murky darkness has settled over the eyes of your heart [cf. Is. 60.2; Ez. 34.12], so that you are unable to see, comprehend, consider or recognize the creator. Now if I were to see in you some inclination to approach the divinity piously, I would not cease to pray night and day on your behalf that you perish not. For the great benevolence of the creator towards his creatures is inscrutable and ineffable; he is long suffering in forgiving, pardoning, nourishing and caring because of his great mercy.

236.   "From the first days he allowed men to walk according to their own wishes, as (scripture) says: 'I have permitted them to follow the wishes of their own hearts; and they went according to their own desires' [Ps. 80.13]. But now he has begun to call you to his own glory and incorruptibility [cf. II Tim. 1.10], for you to become heirs of the eternal life that passes not away. [cf. Tit. 3.7].

237.   "For that reason he sent his beloved martyrs to you; who in their martyrdom bore witness to the consubstantial majesty of the Trinity,

ընդ ամենայն ի վերայ ամենայնի զԱստուած,
որ նա ինքն է յաւիտեանս յաւիտենից. արքայութիւն նորա արքայութիւն յաւիտենից, և տէ-
րութեան նորա վախճան ոչ գոյ. Եւ զմահՆ իւրեանց եդին կնիք հաւատարիմ հաստատական՝
իւրեանց ճշմարտութեան հաւատոց. որոց անա-
լասիկ և ճառք ի միջի ձերում պատմին. որք
կենդանի են առ Աստուած և բարեխոս տօնողացն,
որ մաղթեմք բարեխոս ունել զնոսա առ Աստուած։
Քանզի վասն Աստուծոյ մեռան՝ կարող են գմեղելութիւն բաղմաց կենդանացուցանել։

238 «Վասն այսորիկ նոքօք հաշտեցարուք
առ Աստուած, ի ձեռն մահուան Որդւոյն Աստուծոյ. վասն զի Որդին Աստուծոյ մեռաւ, զի
գմեղելութիւն արաբածոց կենդանացուսցէ. իսկ
սոքա մեռան, զի վկայք լիցին Աստուածութեան նորա։ Եւ զի ոչ եթէ առանց իւրոյ մա-
հուաՆն կենդանութիւն տալ մեզ ոչ կարէր, այլ
զի մեծացուսցէ զբարաբձա իւրով յանարգու-
թիւն իջանելովն. զի գանարգս բարձրացուսցէ
իւրովն իբրև գմեզ լինելովն։

239 «Իսկ ոչ եթէ առանց սոցա վկայու-
թեան չլինէր արդեօք հաւատարիմ, այլ զի մե-
ծացին սոքա որ սիրեցին զնա։ Եւ գմեր շունչս
պանեալ ի մարմնի մերում. զի Թէպէտ և հասին
մեզ նեղութիւնք մարմնոյ վշտաց և աննարին
ցաւոց, աւելի տանջեալ քան գամենայն մար-

God with all and above all, who exists for all eternity. His kingdom is an eternal kingdom, and of his rule there is no end [cf. Ps. 47.15; 144.13]. They made their death a faithful and firm seal of the truth of their faith [cf. Rom. 4.11], the account of which is now being related in your midst.[1] They are alive with God and intercede for those who commemorate them;[2] we pray[3] to have their intercession with God.[4] Because they died for God they can turn the death of many into life.

238. "Therefore through them be reconciled to God by means of the death of the Son of God [cf. Rom. 5.10]. For the Son of God died to vivify the mortality of creatures [cf. Rom. 8.11]; whereas they died to become witnesses to his Godhead. Not indeed[1] that he was unable to give life without dying himself, but in order to magnify the creatures by his own descent to humility, and to elevate the humble by his becoming like us [cf. Heb. 2.17].

239. "Not indeed[1] that he could not be believed without their testimony, but that those who loved him might magnify him. And he preserved our breath in our body, although there came upon us afflictions of bodily sufferings and terrible pains. We were tormented more than any other men.

դիկ. գիՓրդ Ճնար էր միոբեայ տոկալ մարդկա
յին բնութեանս մարմնոյ այսմ աՃագին վտանգի
չարչարանացն։ Կամ թէ կեցցէ արդեօք մարդ
լոկ միոբեայ ժամանակի յանՃնարբին ի խոր վի
րապի անդ յայնմիկ, յորում թաղեայն կայի եօ
ի մէջ օձիցն իբրև ի շՓղշի, և եօային գմարմ
նովք իմովք, պատեալ կային շուրջ գինե և
կայտոային գանդամովք իմովք. սակայն մեծա
սքանչ ողորմութիւն Տեառն պաՃեաց գիս կեն
դանի։ Եւ որում ոչ ես էի արժանի՝ գբանս մշա
կութեան բժշկութեան օգտի ողող և մարմնոց
մշակեմք աւասիկ ի միՓի ձերում. բժիշկ ողող
և մարմնոց ձերոց պատրաստեցաք՝ գձեր օգուան
ձեգ մատուցանել·

240 «ՅԱստուծոյ ի բարերարութենէ անտի
սկացուք գպատգամս երկնաւորս ձեգ Համբել. գի
եթէ լուիՓիք բանին իրաւանց, քարոզութեան
Աւետարանին, Հրամանաց Արարչին ամենայնի՝
վրկեայք սրբեայք լինիՓիք ի փոքր պատուՀա
սէդ, և ի յաւիտենական կեանան վայելեսՓիք.
բանին աստուածութեան լուիՓիք, և գբարութիւն
երկնից արքայութեանն յանձինս ձեր ընկալՓիք։

241 «Միայն թէ յակամայ ողիտութենէ
մեղացդ, ի քարապաշտ ի փայտապաշտութենէդ
սրբեալ լիՓիք, և գանձառ բարբին Աստուծոյ
յանձինս ձեր ընդունել մարթասՓիք. ապա և
սուրբ վկայքն Աստուծոյ, գոր դուքն չարչարե

How was it possible for human bodily nature to endure for one day the fearful severity of those tortures? Or how could a man live for a single day in that terribly deep pit in which I was buried amidst piles of snakes that swarmed around my body and wrapped themselves around me and crawled over my limbs? But the wonderful mercy of the Lord preserved me alive. And of what I was previously unworthy, behold we now serve among you words of healing labor and profit for souls and bodies. We have been made the doctor[2] of your souls and bodies to offer you help.

240. "By the benevolence of God let us begin to nourish you with heavenly words [cf. Ez. 3.2]. For if you will listen to the word of truth, the message of the gospel and the commands of the creator of all, you will be delivered and cleansed from your minor punishment and you will enjoy eternal life. Hear the divine word, and you will receive in your souls the blessing of the kingdom of heaven [cf. Heb. 12.28].

241. "Only if you are cleansed of the unwilling ignorance of your sins, from the worship of stones and wood, will you be able to receive in your souls the ineffable blessings of God. Then the holy martyrs of God, whom you tortured,

ցէք՝ վասն ձեր և նոքա բարեխօսութիւն կարեն
մատուցանել. և մեր բանքս և ձառքս և ջանս և
վատտակս ձեզ յօգուտ սերմանեցցի. բարեկեաց
շատակեաց կենօք գձեզ յերկրի վայելեցուսցէ, և
յերկինս հանդերձեալ կենացն գձեզ ժառանգորդս
արասցէ։

242 «Սապա եթէ ոչ կամիցիք լսել քարոզութեան բանին կենաց՝ ապտէն հարբալ վրի-
ժուքն չարաչար հարուածովք գձեզ ստակեցցէ,
և ի ձեռն օտար թշնամեաց գձեզ դատեցցի, և
միանդամայն իսկ գքէն վրիժուցն հանեալ՝ ի մահ
գձեզ մատնիցէ»:

243 Եւ իբրև խօսեցաւ երանելին Գրիգորիոս պայս ամենայն՝ առ հասարակ գձեռս գո-
ձիւք արկեալ՝ գպատմուճանն պատառէին. Թագաւորն և նախարարքն, և այլ բազմութիւն մարդկանն իջեալ ի գետին ընդ մոխիր Թաւալեալ՝
ասէին առ հասարակ իբրև ընդ մի բերան. «Արդ
կայցէ ինչ մեզ յոյս Թողութեան յԱստուծոյ. գի
մեք կորուսեալ էաք ի տգիտութեան մերում և
ի խաւարային ձանապարհս. արդ՝ իցէ թէ թող-
ցին մեզքս այս մեր բազումք»:

244 Եւ պատասխանի Գրիգորիոս և ասէ
«Մարդասէր է Տէր, երկայնամիտ և բազումողորմ է. գԹած առ ամենեսեան որ կարդան առ
նա, և որ ինդրեն ի նմանէ՝ Թողու նոցա»:

245 Իսկ նոքա ասէին, թէ «Ծանռ մեզ, և

will be able to offer intercession on your behalf; and our words and discourses and effort and labor will be sown as profit for you, they will let you enjoy on earth long and happy lives, and make you heirs in heaven to eternal life [cf. Tit. 3.7].

242. "But if you refuse to hear the preaching of the word of life, then he will strike and kill you with vengeful and cruel blows, and he will judge you by means of foreign enemies, and also taking revenge on you will bring you to death."

243. When blessed Gregory had said all this, they all together put their hands to their collars[1] and tore their garments [cf. I Macc. 4.39]. The king and the princes and the rest of the multitude of the populace fell to the ground and rolled in ashes and said together as with one mouth: "Now have we any hope of forgiveness from God? For we were lost in our ignorance on the path of darkness [cf. Eph. 4.18]. Can now these many sins of ours be forgiven?"

244. Gregory replied, saying: "God is benevolent, long-suffering and very merciful [cf. Ps. 85.15; 102.8; 144.8]. He is kind to all those who invoke him [cf. Ps. 144.18] and he forgives[1] those who beseech him."

245. Then they said: "Inform us and

հաստատեն գմխաս մեր, զի մարթասցուք ապա-
չել գերեսս Արարչին մերոյ դոր ոչն գիտեաք.
եթէ դարձեալ արդարն դարձցէ՝ և ընկալցէ՝ գմեզ
յապաշխարութիւն. և կայցէ՝ ես տեղի դարձի, և
չիցէ՝ արդեօք հատեալ յոյս կենաց մերոյ ի
նմանէն։ Կամ դու արդեօք ոչ յիշեացես գշա-
րիան, դոր մեք ընդ քեզ արարաք. և տայցես
մեզ գուղիդ վարդապետութիւն, և ոչ կալեալ
ընդ մեզ ոխս, և ոչ չարականիցես գմեզ, և ոչ
արկանիցես գմեզ յարդարև յուղիդ ճանապար-
հէն»:

246 Եւ առ հասարակ գոչիւն բարձեալ մարդկանն ի գոչիւն լալոյ Թագաւորաւն հանդերձ՝
ամենայն մարդիկն անկեալ Թաւալէին առաջի
նորա. գի սակաւիկ մի ոչ կարէին մեկնել ի
նմանէ, վասն աննսարին հարուածոցն բարկութեան դիւացամոլ տանջանացն։ Զի թէ լինէին
երբեք ուրեք մեկնեալ ի նմանէ՝ անդէն դիւացն
ի վերայ հասեալ գայրագնեցուցանէին, անդէն
իւրեանց առաամամբքն ուտէլ մարդկան գմարմինս իւրեանց:

247 Արդ՝ իբրև լուաւ սուրբն Գրիգորիոս
դայս ամենայն բանս դոր խոսեցան նոքա առաջի նորա, իսկ նա յարտասուս հարեալ աս գնու-
աս. «Դուք ինքնին գիտէք գայն ամենայն չարիս, դոր դուքն ընդ իս արարէք. գիւմրդ կարիցէ
մարդ տոկալ յայնչափ չարչարանաց վերայ, կամ

confirm our minds that we may be able to appeal to the face of our creator whom we did not know,[1] if he will turn and accept our repentance and if there is still opportunity for conversion; or has he not already cut off our hope of life [cf. Eph. 4.19]? Do you not remember the crimes which we did to you, and will you give us true teaching, and not hold rancor against us nor regard us with antipathy nor hinder us from the true road?"

246.   And all the populace raised a cry and the king wept too, and they all fell and rolled before him [cf. III Macc. 5.28]. For they could not bear to be separated from him even for a moment because of the terrible torments inflicted by the demons. For if they ever went away from him a little, then the demons pounced on them and made them mad, so that the people ate their own flesh with their own teeth.

247.   When saint Gregory heard all these words that they had spoken before him, he wept and said to them: "You yourselves know all the crimes which you did to me. How could a man endure so many tortures, or

գոյր ճնար տոկալ ժամ մի՝ լոկ ի տեղենէ օծի
մրոջ բացուստ ի բաց, թող թէ ի մէջ բազմութեան օծիցն լինել ամա ճգետասան, և ողջ ապրել, և տոկալ և բնակել եա ճանապաղ ի մէջ
նոցա։

248 «Նախ յայգմ իսկ տեսէք զզօրութիւն
Արարչին. գի որ գամենայն արար՝ գիարդ և կամի, յորժամ և կամի կարող է գիւրաքանչիւր
բարս փոփոխել. գի և գայն գմեղանչական գթու-
նաւոր գագանս որ յանճնարին գբի անդ՝ ընդ իս
անարժանի ընդ իւրում ծառայիս քաղցրացու-
ցանէր· Չի թէպէտ և մեք անարժանք էաք՝ սակայն վասն ձերոյ օգտի գմեզ պանեալ՝ երևեցոյց
գիւրող աքանչելեացն գօրութիւն. գի գմեզ պա-
ճեալ աձեալ, և ի ձեր մշակութեան գործն եկեալ,
և գոգունան գձեր բերեալ, Աստուծոյ մարդասի-
րութիւնն մեօք առ ձեզ կատարեցոյ։

249 «Եւ կամ էր արդեօք ճնար աղջկան
մրոջ մանկամարդոյ՝ ունել գգեմ առն սկայի,
որպէս տեսէք իսկ աշօք ձերովք. գիմբրդ էր ճնար
այգմ լինել, եթէ ոչ Աստուծոյ էր տուեալ գի-
րաւունս յաղթութեանն՝ պանել գիւր վկայան
անարատութեամբ ի ձերոց յանցուածոց յանո-
րէնութենէ։ Արդ՝ վասն մանուան այնոցիկ սբբ-
բոց երանելեացն, որոց արիւն նոցա ճեղեալ
յերկրի ձերում, որք արժանի եղեն ատուածութեան շնորճացն և պատարագեցան, վասն

be able to bear for even one hour the mere sight of a snake from afar, let alone dwell in the midst of a mass of snakes for fifteen years and survive unscathed and continue to live among them?

248. "So in this first of all you see the power of the creator. For he who made everything just as he wished, whenever he wishes he can change each thing's character. For those harmful and poisonous animals which were in the terrible pit with me, his unworthy servant, he mollified. Although we were unworthy, nonetheless he preserved us for your benefit and revealed the power of his miracles, in order that by preserving us and bringing us to the task of your education and your benefit, the benevolence of God might be fulfilled through us towards you.

249. "Was it really possible for a single young girl to resist a giant, as you saw with your own eyes? How could this have happened, unless God had given the right of victory in order to save his martyrs without spot from your iniquitous impiety? So now, on account of the death of these blessed saints, whose blood was poured on your land and who became worthy of divine grace and were sacrificed,

որոյ և ձեզ այց և ինդիր եղեալ Հայաստան աշխարհիս. վասն նոցա արդար արեանն հեղլոյ և
ձեզ քաւութիւն շնորհի աւադիկ ձերով ապաշ-
խարութեամբդ յամենապարգևէն Աստուծոյ։

250 Իսկ վասն իմ՝ արդեօք ես ո՞չ էի ի
հրամանէ Աստուծոյ ձեզ քարոզ, այլ ի կամս
մտաց իմոց. և գիտող ՞նար էր այնմ լինել։ Իսկ
արդ գո՞յր ինձ արդեօք ՞նար իշխանութեան՝ իշ-
խել բան մի ի ձէնջ թաքուցանել, թող թէ հրաման առևալ յԱստուծոյ։ Զի և ես ի խոր վիրապի անդ գամենայն օր տեսիլ տեսեալ աշօք
բացօք գգրեշտակ Աստուծոյ, գի հանապազ քա-
ջալերէր գիս և ասէր, որպէս և այժմ իսկ գնոյն
տեսիլ տեսանեմ, որ ասէ ցիս, թէ «Քաջալերեաց, պինդ կաց, գի տէր Աստուած պահեաց
գքեզ և արժանի համարեցաւ արբանեկութեան
իւրոյ. և եաս քեզ գգործս մշակութեան իւրոյ,
գի և դու ընդ այլ մշական մտեալ՝ վարձս առցես գանապական պարգևացն Քրիստոսի»։

251 «Զի և ձեր իսկ արկեալ գիս ի խոր
վիրապան, յանՆարին տեղին մահուան, և եղեալ
անտի ողջանդամ կամօքն Աստուծոյ։ Իբրև ոչ
եթէ գայս ասելով՝ անձինս պարձանս տամ, այլ
գի ոչ իսկ ՞նար է թաքուցանել գզքանչելիսն
Աստուծոյ. քանզի ոչ իսկ թաքչի, այլ պատմի։
Վասն գի գիս ապրեցոյց ի մահուանէ, որ յայս
ձեր մեռեալ համարեալ էի, որպէս և դուք իսկ

therefore[1] you have been visited and this land of Armenia has been heeded. Behold, by the all-bountiful God you are granted propitiation for the shedding of their just blood through this repentance of yours.

250. "But as for me, was I a preacher to you not by God's command, but at my own decision? How could this be? Did I really have the power to hide anything from you, especially if I had been commanded by God? For in the deep pit every day I saw a vision with eyes wide open: an angel of God continually encouraged me and said—just as I see the same vision now, saying: 'Be of good cheer, be firm,[1] for the Lord God has preserved you and considered you worthy of his service; he has entrusted you with the task of his labor, that you and the other laborers may enter and receive as reward the incorruptible gifts of Christ [cf. Matt. 20].'[2]

251. "For you indeed threw me into the deep pit, that fearful place of death, from which by the will of God I emerged safe and sound. I say this not in order to boast of myself, but because it is impossible to hide God's miracles; they are not to be hidden but related [cf. Tobit 12.7]. For he saved me from death—and in your eyes I was considered dead, as you

ճեղէն վկայէք ինձ. և դուք զի մեռեալ էիք ի
մեղս ձեր՝ անհաւադիկ մեռեալըդ ի ճեռն մեռելոյս կենդանանայք։ Վասն զի տուաւ ի ճեռս իմ
պատումել ձեզ զԳրամանս Աստուծոյ, դարձուցա-
նել զձեզ ի ստուգութիւն, ի ճշմարտութեան
ճանապարհն, և ի բաց լինել ձեզ յունայնութեան
պաշտամանց անտի, ի քարեղէն, ի փայտեղէն,
յարձաթժագործ, ի պղնձագործ պատկերաց այտի,
որ ոչ ինչ իսկ են և ոչ ումեք պիտանացու.
դառնալ առ Աստուած կենդանի, որ արար զերկինս և զերկիր և զծով և զամենայն որ է ի նոսա, և ի Բան նորա՝ յՈրդին միածին, և ի Հոգին կենդանի և կենդանարար, սրբիչ և քաւիչ
երկրպագուաց և փառաւորչաց իւրոց։

252 «Իսկ եթէ զձեզ յորդոր յօժարութեամբ
տեսանիցեմք դարձեալ առ աստուածութիւն անդր՝
ախորժ յօժարութեամբ սկիզբն արասցուք ձեզ
պատմելոյ վասն արարչութեանցն, թէ զիարդ
բարի աշխարհս ստեղծաւ ի բարերարէ անտի,
թէ զիարդ վարեցան կարգք աշխարհիս. զի ումանք
ի մարդկանէ զնածութիւն բարեացն յիւրանց կամաց կատարեցին առ Աստուած. թէ որ զչարն
գործեցին՝ աստէն պատժեցան յերկրի. թէ զիարդ եկն Որդին Աստուծոյ մարմնով յաշխարհ
անարդութեամբ. թէ զիարդ գալոց է ի վախճանի նովին մարմնով և փառօք Հօր, և վասն
լինելոց բարեացն և հանդերձեալ դատաստանին.

yourselves bear me witness. And you who were dead in your sins [cf. Eph. 2.1; Col. 2.13], behold now through this dead one are brought back to life from earth. For I was entrusted with telling you of the commands of God, bringing you back to right belief, to the path of truth, and away from the vanity of idolatry, from images of stone, wood, silver or bronze, which are nothing and of no use to anyone; to turn you towards the living God who created heaven and earth and the sea and everything that is in them, and to his word, the only-begotten Son, and to the living and vivifying Spirit, the purifer and expiator of those who worship and adore him.

252. "If we see you turning towards the divinity with prompt readiness, we shall with good-will begin to expound to you the creation; how this good world was created by the benevolent one, how the orders of this world were arranged. For some men willingly fulfilled for God his good pleasure [cf. II Thess. 1.11], whereas those who did evil were punished on the earth. How the Son of God came in the flesh to the world in humility; how he will come at the end in the same body and in the glory of the Father; and about the blessings to be and the future judgment.

և թէ առ այժմ զիարդ օրէն է մեզ զնալ պա-
տուիրանօք րստ կամացն Աստուծոյ. և թէ զիարդ ապաշխարութիւն գտանել, րնդ նմին և զթո-
դութիւն մեղաց. և թէ զիարդ զմեղուցեալսն
տգիտութեամբ՝ քաւել, և րստ կամացն Աստուծոյ փախչել ի չարէ և զբարիս գործել և խոստացելոց բարեացն հասանել. և թէ զիարդ արժան է զնալ ի ճանապարհս Աստուծոյ: Զայս
ամենայն կարգաւ մի րստ միոջէ ոճով պատմե-
ցից, անաշխատ լեզուաւ և անհանգիստ բերանով. զի և Տէր րստ իւրում մարդասիրութեանն
րնկալցի զձեր ապաշխարութիւնդ, և դուք արժանի լիջիք մտանել ի շնորհս մարդասիրութեան ի ձեռն Տեառն մերոյ Յիսուսի Քրիստոսի:

253 «Սակայն մեք ձեզ ի եկզբանցն սկիզբն
աբարեալ՝ սկացուք ցուցանել գաշխարհի գարաբ-
չութիւնն, բարեբարութեան բարեացն ի բարե-
բարէն, եթէ դուք կամիցիք սրտի մտօք ուն-
կրնդիր լինել և հաւատալ: Սակայն մեք անտուստ ի քէն սկիզբն աբասցուք պատմելոյ ձեզ
նախ վասն մեծի միոյ միայնոյ բարերարին, և
ապա՛ եղելոցս ամենեցուն ի նմանէ: Այլ գամենայն ի ձեր աշակերտելոցդ յոգուտ փութամբ
կատարել րստ հրամանի աստուածութեանն. կա-
բերագոյն համարեցաք րնդ նորա և վասն նորին դիպանագոյն և նմանագոյն բանիւք գփո-

And how for the present we must walk following the commandments according to God's will; how to find repentance and therewith the forgiveness of sins; how to expiate sins committed in ignorance, and according to the will of God to flee from evil, do good works, and attain the promised blessings; how one must walk in the paths of God. All this in its proper order I shall narrate, with unwearying tongue and tireless mouth, that the Lord in his benevolence may receive your repentance and that you may be made worthy to enter into the grace of his loving kindness through our Lord Jesus Christ.[1]

253. "We shall begin from the beginning and start by showing you the creation of the world, the gracious blessings from the benevolent one, if you desire to attend sincerely and believe. But at the very beginning we shall tell you of the one and only benevolent one, and then of all the things created by him. We shall strive to complete everything for the profit of your instruction, following the divine command. We considered it of great importance to conduct our discourse about him in suitable and appropriate terms,

խանակն թելադրել․ զի վասն աստուածութեան են բանքս․ քանզի գիտեմք, թէ նա է ճշմարիտ Աստուած․

254 «Այլ ոչ եթէ գանհաս բնութենէն կարբիցէ ոք ճառել, և որպէս էն՝ զայն կարբիցէ ոք պատմել․ զի աննհաս և անբաւ և անբաւանդակ և անքննին է, անմատոյց և անիմաց է յամենայն արարածոց, աներևոյթ ի տեսլենէ և մօտ առ ամենեսին ինամով տեսչութեամբ գթութեամբ, չնորհօք մարդասիրութեան իւրոյ․ ոչ տեսաւ երբէք ի մահկանացու մարմնաւորաց, նա և ոչ ի հոգեղինաց և ի հրեղինաց գուարթնոց։ Միայն փառաւորեալ յամենայն արարածոց․ քանզի ամենայն ինչ ի նմանէ է, բայց նա միայն ինքնութեամբ։

255 «Սակայն արք արդարք ի մարդկանէ, որ արժանի եղեն ճանաչել զբարեչութիւն նորա, և երկրպագութեամբ կամացն հնազանդեալ հրամանակատարք մշանջենականին և ատուածամերձ կենացն պատմող մարգարէք անուանեցան ի դարս առաջինս յաստուածապաշտ յազգէն եբրայեցւոց, յԱբրահամեան զաւակէն, որ աստուածապաշտութեան ընտրեալ՝ ամենայն ազգաց հայր անուանեալ․ զի ի գլուխս հաւատոց արդարութեան ամենեցուն ելեալ նստիցի յառաջճահաւատան պարծանօք, արդարև իսկ հայր անուանեալ․ յորոյ օրինակ և ծնունդքն սերեալք ի

since we are speaking about the diety. For we know that he is the true God [cf. I Jn. 5.20].

254. "Not that anyone could speak about his incomprehensible nature or expound how he is. Because he is incomprehensible, infinite, uncircumscribed, and inscrutable; he cannot be approached or understood by any created beings; he is invisible to sight, yet near to all through his care and providential mercy and benevolent grace. He has never been seen by mortal or bodily creatures, nor by the spiritual and fiery angels. He alone is glorified by all creatures, because everything is from him, save he alone in his essence.

255. "But just men who were made worthy to know his creation, and who with reverent will obeyed and fulfilled his commandments were called prophets, tellers of the eternal and divine life, in the first ages by the pious race of Hebrews, the seed of Abraham, who was chosen for his piety and called the father of all races [Gen. 17.4], so that he might sit at the head of the just faith of all, and by the boast of being the first believer was rightly named 'father.' Likewise the generations born from

նմանէ՝ ժողովուրդ առաջին և սեպհական անուա-
նեալ։

256 «Յորոց միջի և մարգարէքն իբրև լուսաւորք աստուածապայծառ պատգամօքն ծագեցին, որք Հոգւոյն չնորհագ աստուածութեանն
արժանի եղեն՝ ուսուցանել ամենեցուն գործնա
Աստուծոյ, և գկամս և գկարգս նորուն ուղղու-
թեան երկնաւոր հրամանացն ամենայն ուրուք
առաջի դնելով, որպէս նոցուն իսկ մատեանք
մարգարէութեան հաւաստեաւ պատմեն. որ յամենեցունց յոզուտ մինչ ի վախճան ընթացեալ,
լի աբարեալ գոիեզերս յօրինեալ ընթերցուա-
ծովքն յանղիման կացուցանել գարուեստն մարգարէական աստուածեղէն բանից. որպէս գի
հնար լիցի ամենայն հնազանդելոցն բանից նո-
ցա՝ գԱստուած ինքնին գլխովին յանղիման տեսանել բատ տեսչութեանն։

257 Արդ՝ ի մէջ սբբոցն աստուածապաշտ
գնդաց մարգարէից ոմն յարուցեալ մեծ մար-
գարէ, որոյ անունն Մովսէս կարդացեալ, արժանի եղեալ աստուածութեան չնորհագն. որոյ
սկիգբն աբաբեալ ուսուցանելոյ յամենատեղ
յակզենագործ ժամանակէն՝ աշխարհախամար աշ-
խարհապատում մարգարէութեամբ՝ ամենեցուն
աւանդեաց գճչմարիտ գիտութիւն։ Բատ նմին
օրինակի և մեր անտի սկիգբն աբաբեալ՝ ամե-
նուսոյց չնորհօք Հոգւոյն բան ի գործ արաս-

him were called the first and special people [cf. Ex. 19.5; Titus 2.14].[1]

256. "Among them the prophets arose like luminaries [cf. Phil. 2.15] with God's shining words; they were made worthy of the Spirit's divine grace to teach everyone the laws of God; everywhere they set out his will and his right order of heavenly commandments, just as their prophetic books truly narrate. Until their death they served the profit of everyone. They filled the world with ordained readings, showing forth the tenor of their prophetic and divine words, that all believers in their words might be able to see God, in his providence, face to face [cf. I Cor. 13.12].

257. "Now among the saintly and pious bands of prophets there arose one great prophet called Moses. He was made worthy of divine grace, and began teaching about the time of the first creation; by his prophecy and description of the world[1] he handed down to everyone true knowledge. Similarly, we shall begin by the omniscient grace of the Spirit to undertake

ցուք վարդապետել ձեզ, փոյթ յանձին կալեալ
վասն երկուց աշխարհաց հաստատելոց ի բարե–
րարէն Աստուծոյ, վասն սկզբան և կատարածի,
վասն անցաւորիս և վասն յաւիտենական մշտըն–
ջենաւորին։ Մեզ տացին բանք ի բերան, մեզ՝
ցուցանել զօգուտն, և ձեզ՝ լսել, ընդունել և
հաւատալ, և քակել ի սատանայական գործոց
չարութենէ, և աստուածամուխ կենացն լինել
ժառանգորդ։

258 «Արդ՝ սկացուք շնորհօքն Քրիստոսի
ձեզ պատմել մի ըստ միոջէ մանրապատում նշա–
նակօք, և դուք ունկնդիր եղեալ սրտի մտոք
լուիջիք»։

your instruction, taking note of the two worlds created by benevolent God, of the beginning and the end, of this transitory one and the eternal everlasting one. May words be placed in our mouth for us to indicate what is profitable. It is for you to listen, to receive and to believe, to break away from your satanic and evil deeds and to become heirs of divine life.

258.   "So let us begin by the grace of Christ to relate to you in order with detailed indications. And do you attend and sincerely pay heed."[1]

[B. The Teaching of Saint Gregory
(§259-715)]

ԴԱՐՁ ՓՐԿՈՒԹԵԱՆ ԱՇԽԱՐՀԻՍ ՀԱՅԱՍՏԱՆ

ԸՆԴ ՉԵՌՆ ԱՌՆ ՄՐԲՈՅ ՆԱՀԱՏԱԿԻ

716   Արդ՝ եկայք, եղբարք, զօգուտն
վասն հասարակաց շինութեան փութացուցուք.
զի և ի ձէնջ պատուհասքդ վերասցին, և լիցի ի
խռովութենէդ հասելոյ վաղվաղակի խաղաղութիւն, և ի գերեալ մոլորութեանցդ՝ դարձ փրր-
կութեան։ Այլ ես դամենայն պատդամա Աստուածութեանն կարգեցի և եդի ի լսելիս ձեր
առ հասարակ, ոչ թաքուցեալ զօգուտն. ի սկզ-
բանցն մինչև ի վախճան՝ դամենայն պատմե-
ցաք ձեզ։

717   «Արդ՝ եկայք ամփոփեսցուք զգանձն
Աստուածութեան, զի յայնմանէ պարգևեսցի ձեզ
բժշկութիւն ամենեցուն։ Մատուցդւք զգրոա
ի հանգիստ, և շինեսցուք վկայարանս ի վերայ
դղցա, տաճարս աղօթից միաբանութեան, հա-
նապազորդ խնդրել յԱստուծոյ նախ՝ զհաշտու-
թիւն և զխաղաղութիւն աշխարհի և զողորմութիւն հալատովք, յուսով և սիրով, և ընդ նմին
զկեանս և զարքայութիւն Աստուծոյ։

THE CONVERSION TO SALVATION OF THIS LAND OF ARMENIA THROUGH THE HOLY MARTYR

[C. Gregory's final exhortation; the Armenians beg for healing]

716. "So come, brethren, let us concern ourselves with our common profit and advantage, that your punishments may be removed from you, that peace may straightway replace the trouble that has fallen upon you, and that (you may gain) conversion to salvation from the errors to which you were prisoners. I have set out in order for your ears all the sayings of the Godhead, hiding nothing profitable. From the beginning to the very end I have told you everything.

717. "So come, let us grasp the treasure of the Godhead, that therefrom you may all be given healing. Let us put these (martyrs) to rest and build chapels[1] over them, temples of united prayer, to seek continually from God, first, reconciliation and peace for the world and mercy with faith, hope and love, and also life and the kingdom of God;

718 «Զի և դուք ազատեսջիք ի ծառայու-
թեանց անձնակամութեան գործոցն խաւարի, և
գփառս լուսեղէնս Աստուածութեանն ըմբռնես-
ջիք, ապոթիւք և բարեխօսութեամբ սոցա առ
Աստուած. զի և սոքա հանդուսցեն դանձինս ձեր
ի տանջանաց պատուհասիցդ եկելոց, և սրքօք
հաշտեսջիք ընդ Աստուծոյ։ Զի Աստուածութիւնն, որ ընակեալն է ի սոսա՝ գթացցի ի ձեզ
ձերովն ապաշխարութեամբ, խստովանութեամբ,
խոնարհութեամբ, հնազանդութեանն հաւատոց,
և կրօնաւորեալ ձեզ պահովք, անկել ի սիրտս և
առնուլ ի միտ՝ սփռել զկամացն խորհուրդս, և
արժանի լինել լուացման մկրտութեանն սրբութեան, և սրբոցդ մասին ժառանգութեան՝ լուսոյ վիճակին հասանել և պարծանաց խայլն, «որ
կորուսելոցն յիմարութիւն է, և ձեզ որ գտայքդ՝
իմաստութիւն և զօրութիւն և փրկութիւն Աստուծոյ»։

719 «Զորս Որդեգրութեան արժանիս արասցէ Աստուածութեանն, Յն2ել գմեզս ձեր և թողուլ զպարտիս ձեր, և ընդունել գմանն պսակի
սրբոցս որ առ ձեզս են։ Զի և դուք լի2իք փա-
ռաւորիջք Աստուածութեան, դասուց փառաւոր-
չացն հաղորդեալք ի կցորդութիւն օրհնութեամբ
Հոգւոյն սրբոյ, և արժանի լի2իք դուք գխոր-
հուրդն Աստուածութեանն առնուլ։ Զի լուա-
ցեալ իցէք յաղտոյն ատանայի, և նա ձերոց

718.   "that by their prayer and intercession to God
you may be freed from willing servitude to deeds of
darkness and gain the glorious light of the Godhead;
that they may give your souls rest from the torments
that have come upon you as punishment, and through
them you may be reconciled with God. For the Godhead who dwells in them will have pity on you through
their repentance, confession, humility and obedient
faith. Thus through abstemious fasting you may im-
plant in your hearts and grasp in your minds (the fear
of God),[1] cast off the thoughts of your own minds,
become worthy of the bath of holy baptism and attain
the portion of the inheritance[2] of those saints, the
grace of light and the glory of the cross, 'which to
the lost is foolishness, but to you who have been
found is God's wisdom and power and salvation' [cf.
I Cor. 1.18, 23-24].

719.   "He will make you worthy of divine adoption,
wash away your sins and forgive your debts, and grant
you a share of the crown of these saints who are
among you; that you may become praisers of the
Godhead, sharing in the ranks of praisers by the blessing of the holy Spirit, and that you may become worthy of receiving the mystery of the Godhead; that you
may be cleansed from the stain of Satan

ուրցն գարշապարաց կոխան լիցի։ Եւ դուք
մատալք և հաղորդեալք իցէք ի հարսանիս Աստուածութեան սիրոյն, ուտել գմիս ճշմարիտ
գառին Որդւոյն Աստուծոյ, և ըմպել գարիւն
նորա։ Եւ կցորդ իցէք չարչարանացն Աստուծոյ,
և հաղորդ փառացն, և լինիչիք ի մի ոգի և ի
նա կցորդիցէք մարմնով և արեամբ նորա։

720 «Եւ վկայքս այս լինիցին ձեզ ոզոր-
մութեամբ նորա բերդ ամուր և աշտարակ հզոր
ամրութեան և վերակացուք բարեխսութեամբ,
հեղմամբ արեանն քաջացեալք, նախատակու-
թեամբն իւրեանց գձեզ առեալ առ Աստուած
մատուցանիցեն. որ շանեալք գձեզ՝ գիւրեանց
նախատակութեանն մարտին ցուցին ձեզ գյաղ-
թող գործութիւնն։

721 «Եւ գի այսօր ընդ երեկս է՝ երթայք
ի հանգիստ քնոյ, խաղաղութեամբ ննջեցէք. և
ի վաղուէ հետէ փոյթ լիցի ձեզ շինել գյարկս
հանգատոցաց։ Զի և սոքա փոխարէն ընդ հոգե-
ղէն յարկացն գոր սոցայն շինիցէք աստ՝ պատ-
րաստեցեն ձեզ յարկս լուսեղէնս յարքայութեանն երկնից. որում ակն ունիմք հասանել
բարեխսութեամբ սրբոցս, ի նոյն ժողով միաբանութեան յարքայութեանն Քրիստոսի։ Զի նորա են փառք և գործութիւն և պատիւ յաւիտեանս
յաւիտենից. Ամէն»։

722 Եւ զայս ասացեալ՝ արձակեաց

and he be trodden under your feet; that you may enter and share in the wedding feast of the divine love, eat the flesh of the true lamb, the Son of God, and drink his blood [cf. Jn. 6.53]; and that you may become partakers in the torments of God, and share his glory [cf. Rom. 8.17], and become one spirit and sharers with him through his body and blood [cf. I Cor. 12.13].

720. "And these martyrs through his mercy will be for you a strong fortress and mighty tower [cf. Ps. 60.4], your advocates[1] by intercession, your strengtheners by the shedding of their blood, and by their martyrdom they will bring you near to God. They will bring you profit and show you the victorious power of their heroic struggle.

721. "And because it is now evening, go and rest and sleep in peace. In the morning you must make haste to build sanctuaries, that they, in place of the earthly habitations which you built for them here, may prepare for you habitations of light in the kingdom of heaven. And by the intercession of these saints we hope to attain the same united gathering in the kingdom of Christ. For his are glory and power and honor for ever and ever. Amen" [cf. I Tim. 6.16; I Pet. 5.11].

722. Having said all this, he dismissed

գամբոխն. բայց թագաւորն և մեծամեծքն ոչ երբեք մեկնէին ի նմանէ, զի հարուածեալք էին և անաբեկեալք. և գգայգ և գգերեկ կայէն առ նմա, և օթեվանք նոցա առ նմա լինէին ի մէջ այգլոյն, առ դուրս ննջանին. գգեցեալ քուրձ և նստեալ ի վերայ մոխրոյ, և պանեալ լինէին պանա աւուրա վաթսուն և վեց։ Եւ այսպէս երանելին Գրիգորիոս անհանգիստ և անդադար գգայգ և գգերեկ ոչ դադարէր երբեք աւուրս վաթսուն և հինգ, խօսել, խրատել և ուսուցանել և հաստատել։ Իբրև իմաստուն բժիշկ գտանել Ջանայր դղեղն օգտութեան. զի նոքա մատուցեն առ նա դանձինս իբրև գշիւանդացեալս, և նա իբրև գնարտարապետ բժշկեացէ գանձինս նոցա Աւետարանաւն Քրիստոսի։

723 Համօրէն տեղեկացուցեալ խելամտեցուցանէր. ոչ եթէ ծայրաքաղ ինչ արարեալ օգաբանս կամ սրավարս խօսեցաւ, այլ յատակապատում արարեալ ուսուցանէր ամենեցուն. ի սկզբանց անտի ակիգբն արարեալ, յաշխարհահամար յաշխարհապատում արաքչութենէ անտի, մինչև ի քուն սրբոյն պատգամախօսացն Աստուծոյ, ամէնեցուն իւրաքանչիւր գործոց առաքինութեան և հոգեպատում պատգամացն ընդելյա և ծանօթս կացուցանէր։

724 Եւ գարանգն ատռուածասիրաց ըստ քրիստոսալանդ հրաշանգելոյն իճչմարտութեան,

the crowd. But the king and the nobles never parted from him because they were in torments and fear. Day and night they stayed with him, dwelling by the door of the vat-store in the middle of the vineyard. They were dressed in hair-shirts, and sat on ashes, and fasted for sixty-six days. And in this way for sixty-five days blessed Gregory tirelessly and unceasingly, day and night, never ceased from reasoning, advising, teaching, and confirming them. Like a wise doctor[1] he tried to find the appropriate remedy that they might entrust themselves to him as patients, and he like a skilled physician might heal their souls with the gospel of Christ.

723.   He informed and enlightened them about everything, abbreviating nothing and speaking neither superficially[1] nor hastily. But he taught them all most clearly, beginning from the beginning, from the creation of the world, up to the holy speakers of God's words; he made them all acquainted with and aware of the virtuous deeds of each one and their inspired sayings.

724.   He informed them by individual name of each one of the men who loved God, of those instructed in the truth handed down by Christ,

պայր իւրաքանչիւր աստուածամուխ կենօք և
վաստակասէր հոգևոր վարուք իւրովք, հանդերձ
վկայութեամբ գմի ոք ի նոցանէ առանձինն յա-
կանէ յանուանէ ծանուցանէր. և նոցին յԱստուծոյ ասացելովքն՝ կարգեալս և յարմարեալս ըն-
ծայեցուցանէր դամենայն ասացեալ դպատգաման
Հոգւոյն սրբոյ, և ըստ նմին դմեկնութիւն Նորուն հանդերձեալ դրեաց նորին դորութեամբն:

725 Իսկ նոքա ժողովեալք կուտեալք հասեալք անթիւ մարդկանն, դմիմեամբք դոու-
թեալ՝ խնճոյս կացուցանէին՝ ունկնդրութեան
վարդապետութեանն մատուցանել դլսելիս. քաղ-
մութիւնք անհուսք անչափութեամբք, անհնարին շատութեամբ ժողովեալք ի հոչակէն, տեսանել և լսել դանպայման աքանչելիս Աստուածութեանն: Ժողովեալք յիւրաքանչիւր գաւառաց
արբ և կանայք և մանկտի, աՀապեկեալք յանէն
դորութեանց արարչութեանն, լինէին Հնազան-
դեալք և ունէին դՀալատս: Ճեպէին առ ի տեսիլ ցուցական աքանչելեացն, մտերմութեամբ
Հասեալք լինէին օդտակար խրատուն կենսաբեր
քարոդութեանն քանին կենաց աւետեաց Աւետարանին: Զամենայն յանձ առեալ՝ Թագաւորն
և իշխանքն փութային առնել դինչ և Հրամա.
յիցէ:

726   Արդ՝ ի ընուլ վաշտաներորդի վե-
ցերորդի աւուրն, ընդ այդուն առաւօտանալն,

of each one's godly life and spiritual labor and witness and their sayings (inspired) by God. And he expounded all the words of the holy Spirit in proper order and explained their interpretation by the power of the same (Spirit).

725. They were gathered together in a numberless assemblage of men, jostling each other and sitting as at a banquet, to give their attention to the teaching. The crowds were infinite, gathered in vast numbers from afar in order to see and hear the amazing miracles of the Godhead. Men, women and children had gathered from each one's province, awed at the power of the creator, and they submitted and believed. They hastened to see the incontestible miracles,[1] they willingly attended to the profitable advice of the life-giving preaching of the word of life [cf. Phil. 2.16], the gospel. The king and the nobles accepted everything and hastened to do whatever he might command.

726. When the sixty-sixth day came round,[1] at the dawn of morning,

մատուցեալ իշխանքն Թագաւորաւն և նախարա֊
րօքն և խառնիճաղանճ ամբոխիւն հանդերձ, նա
և կանանւոյն ժողովեալ մատաղ մանկտովք ան֊
մեղօք, երամ երամ և դասադասեալք անկանէին
առաջի սրբոյն Գրիգորի, աղաչէին և խնդրէին
գեժշկութիւն գտանել հարուածոցն պատուհասին
հասելոյ. քանզի հարեալք էին բարկութեան գա֊
ւազանաւն յարդար դատաստանէն։

727 Մանաւանդ Թագաւորն, զի էր նա փո֊
խեալ ի կերպարանս աղէկայոյզ խոզաց. քանզի
Թաւացեալ էին առ հասարակ ամենայն մար֊
մինքն, և ընդ անդամս ոսկերացն բուսեալ էր
խոզանատաև իբրև գմեծամեծ վարազաց վայ֊
րենեաց. և եղնգունք ծայրից մատանց ոտիցն և
ձեռացն կճղակացեալք էին իբրև զգետնաբիր և
գարմատակեր կնճացն։ Նա և պատկեր երեւացն
դիմացն շրջեալ էր ի պատկեր և ի կնճիթ գո֊
ճանացն յեղեգան բնակելոց. իբրև յիւրոց ի գա֊
գանամիտ բարուցն բնութենէ և ի վարուց՝ ի
Թագաւորութեանն շռոյ սատակութենէ անկեալ,
շրջեալ ի տեսիլ նմանութեան անասուն խոտա֊
կեր գազանաց. և շրջէր ի մէջ գազանացն ի
Ներքս յեղեգանն, կորուսեալ ի միջոյ մարդ֊
կանէ։

728 Իսկ իբրև եկն եհաս եղեալ ի բանդէ
վիրապին խոստովանողն Քրիստոսի Գրիգորիոս,
հաաանէր ի տեղի վկայելոյն՝ իբրև ի տեսչու֊

the nobles and king and princes and the common
people, with the crowd of women and young children,
approached and fell down in flocks before saint Gregory, beseeching and begging for healing from the torments which had fallen on them as punishment, because they had been struck in a just judgment by the
rod of (God's) anger [cf. Is. 10.5].

727. Especially the king, because he had been
changed into the form of a wallowing pig. For his
whole body had become hairy, and on his limbs bris-
tles had grown like those of great wild boars. And
the nails of his hands and feet had hardened like the
claws of beasts that dig the earth or eat roots. Similarly the appearance of his face had turned into the
likeness of the hard snout of an animal living among
reeds. Because of the beast-like nature of his way of
life he had fallen from the honor of his throne, and he
roamed about in the likeness of pasturing beasts [cf.
Ps. 48.13] among the animals in the reeds, lost to the
society of men.

728. When Gregory, the confessor of Christ, had
come forth from the dungeon-pit and reached the
place of the martyrs, as if by the providence

թենէն Աստուծոյ ի մի վայր ամենեքեան ժո-
ղովեալ՝ այսամտեալք ամենեքին, ի տեղին հասեալք յայտնեցան։ Եւ թագաւորն խոզացեալ՝
մեծամեծ ճչեր, կանչեր, խանչեր բունբունելով,
վրվիրացեալ, դիզացեալ, կնճթակերպ երեսօք՚ն,
լեալ ի նմանութիւն չորքոտանւոյ, ընթացեալ
յեղեգնաքնակ երամէ գազանացն ի միջոյ՝ հասանէր յայն տեղի։

729 Իսկ երանելին Գրիգորիոս յաղօթս կա-
ցեալ՝ խնդրեր յամենապարգեւէն Աստուծոյ առ
մի նուագ՝ ոչ զկերպարանացն հարուածելոց
առողջութիւն, այլ գմտացն ունկնդրութիւն վարդապետութեանն, զգաստանալ, առնուլ ի միտ
դասացեալսն Աստուծոյ պատգամացն։ Եւ լեալ
բժշկութիւն այսչափ միայն—քաշ լեւ եւ ի միտ
առնուլ եւ համարձակ խոսել։ Եւ մինչեւ ի վախճան եւ ի վեց օրն զաւուրս վարդապետութեանն՝
ի նոյն կայր կերպարանս, ճորճապատեալ, պա-
տատեալ, ի մէջ բազմամբոխ աշխարհաժողով
հրապարակացն կուտակելոց մարդկանն.

730 Իբրև սկսան Թաւալել անկանել առաջի
նորա եւ խնդրել բժշկութիւն,—քանզի Թագաւորն
պատեալ էր կերպարանօքն ի մարդկային բնութենէ ճազաղծանակ տեսլեամբն, բայց միայն ի
բանիմաստ խոսարանացն եւ ի լելոյն.—իսկ նա
յետ ազաճանացն տուեալ պատասխանի աստ
ցնոսա, եթէ «Եւ ես ընդ ձեզ իբրև զմի ի ձէնչ

of God all those possessed by demons gathered together in that same place. And the king, in swinish
form, cried out in a loud voice, he called out, grunted
and slobbered and foamed at the mouth in his snout-
like face, and in the likeness of a four-footed beast
ran from the boars' reedy pasture to the same spot.

729.   But blessed Gregory prayed for a brief while,
begging from the all-bountiful God not healing for
the various torments but attention to his teaching,
that they might come to their senses and comprehend
the message of God's words. And they had just enough
healing to be able to hear, comprehend and speak
freely. And all through the sixty-six days of instruction
(the king) remained in the same form, though wrapped
in garments, in the midst of the great crowd of the
assembled populace.

730.   When they began to wallow and fall before
him and to ask for healing—because the king had lost
his natural human form for that ridiculous appearance, except for the ability to speak and hear[1]—then
after their supplications he replied and said to them:
"I too like one of you

խնդրեցից գձեր օզուան, և դուք սրտի մտօք
խնդրեցէք գձեր բժշկութիւնն, քանզի մարդասէր Աստուածութիւնն ողորմեցոյ ձեզ։ Բայց
փութացարո՛ւք շիսեցէք գվկայարանան, գի հան-
գուցցուք գվկայաս Աստուծոյ, գի և սրքա գձեզ
հանգուցցեն ի տանջանաց պատուհասից, և ապ-
րեսջիք յահագին և ի դառն պատրաստեալ հանդերձեալ խոստացեալ դատաստանացն, և արժանի լիջիք արքայութեանն Քրիստոսի»։ Իսկ նոցա
խնդրեալ, գի փութով հրամայեցէ, որպէս և
կամիցի գիՆչ և կամիցի առնել։ Իսկ նորա տեսիլ
պատմեալ նոցա՛ ասէ.—

731   Արդ՛ եկա՛յք պատմեցուք ձեզ,
եղբարք, գցուցական սիրոյն արբշչութեան առ
ձեզ, որ ինձ երեկեցաւ անաւորութիւն տեսլեանն։
Աստուածութեանն խոնարհեալ առ սուրբ վկայս
իւր, և գառա յանհամեմման բարձրութիւն,
յանպատուման վերացուցեալ, յանգուցականու-
թիւն արքայութեան երկնից։ Արդ՛ գլխելոցն
ընդ ձեզ գկեցուցաքեր տուչութիւնն գոր շնոր-
հելոց է՛ յայանեաց ինձ, և երեկեալ ինձ տեսիլ
ատուածակերպ աքանչելի անպատում, գործոյ
փոքր ի շատե առի գհանգամանան։

732 Արդ՛ ի հասարակել գիշերիս այս-
միկ, գի խոնչեալ դուք ի քուն լեալ էիք
ի ծանրութենէ աշխատութեան ի տքնութենէ
այոի, և ես դեռ ի գարթման հարեալ էի և մտա-

will seek your advantage. And do you sincerely request healing, because the benevolent deity will have
mercy upon you. But hasten and build chapels in order
to give repose to the martyrs of God, that they in turn
may give you respite from the torments of your punishment, and that you may be saved from the terrible
and bitter judgments that have been promised and
prepared for the future, and that you may become
worthy of the kingdom of Christ." Then they begged
him quickly to command as he might wish and whatever he might wish to be done. But he related to them
a vision as follows.

[Chapter 8. Gregory's vision]

731. "So come, we shall tell you, brethren, of the
Creator's love shown towards you, which was revealed
to me as an awesome vision. The Godhead condes-
cended to his holy martyrs and raised them up to the
incomparable, ineffable and inaccessible height of the
kingdom of heaven. Now he revealed to me the vivifying providence that he intends to bestow on you,
and there appeared to me a divine, wonderful, and
ineffable vision, the details of which I grasped in brief.

732. "Now, in the middle of that night when you
were tired and sleeping from the severity of the labor
and vigil, I was still awake and

խորհ կայի վասն յանկարծահաս դիպելոյ անքնին աքանչելեացս ողորմութեան Աստուածութեանն այց առնելոյ ձեզ, արկանելոյ զձեզ ի
բովս խրատու հանձարագիտութեան ատուա-
ծագէտ վարդապետութեանն։ Զմտաւ ածէի և
գսէր վկայիցն առ իւրեանց սիրեցեալ արարչու-
թիւնն, և գվտոխարէն դարձուածան անպատուման
պատրաստեալս նոցա, թէ որպիսիք իցեն։

733 Յանկարծակի եղև ձայն ատակութեան,
բումբիւն որոտման, աՀաւոր թնդիւն, իբրև գձայն
եռանդան կուտակելոյ ծովու ալեաց խռովու-
թեան։ Եւ բացաւ խորանաշէն յարկն Հատա-
տութեան երկնից. և իջեալ այր մի ի կերպարանս
լուսոյ. կոչեաց գանունն իմ և ասէ. Գրիգորիէ.
և իմ նայեցեալ տեսի գկերպարանս նորա, և
գարհուրեալ դողացեալ յերկիր կործանեցայ։ Եւ
ասէ ցիս. Նայեաց դու ի վեր, և տես գսքան-
չելիս գոր ցուցանեմ քեզ։

734 Եւ իմ նայեցեալ՝ տեսի բացեալ գհաս-
տատութիւն երկնից, և գջուրսն որ ի վերայ
նորա՝ րստ Հաստատութեանն պատառելոյ, գի
րստ նմանութեան ձորոց իբրև գկատարս լերանց՝
յայս կոյս յայն կոյս բաժանեալ դիգեալ կային
անբաւութիւնք անկշռելութեան ական տեսանե-
լոյ։ Եւ լոյսն հոսեալ վերուստ ի վայր մինչև
յերկիր հասանէր. և ընդ լուսոյն՝ գօրք անչափք
լուսեղէնք երկիթևանք ի տեսիլ մարդկան, և

was contemplating the unexpected and inscrutable miracles of God's mercy in visiting you and casting you into the furnace[1] of instruction of the wise, divine teaching. I also considered the martyrs' love for their beloved creator, and what would be the ineffable rewards prepared for them.

733. "Suddenly there was a great sound, the thunder of lightning, a fearful noise like the sound of the roaring tumult of the waves of the piling sea. And the cube-shaped vault of the firmament of heaven[1] was opened, and a man descended in the form of light. He called my name and said: 'Gregory.' And I looked up and saw his form, and terrorstruck I fell to the ground. Then he said to me: 'Look up and see the wonders that I shall show you.'

734. "And I looked up and saw the firmament of heaven opened, and the waters above it[1] divided like the firmament, for like valleys and mountain-tops they were divided and their infinite expanses were piled up on either side beyond sight. And the light flowed from above down to the earth, and with the light numberless hosts of shining two-winged creatures in human appearance and

Թէքն իբրև գհուր։ Եւ ըստ նմանութեան մանրամաղ փոշւոյ հիւղէի, որ ի ժամանակս արեգակնակէզ գարնանւոյն ըստ պատուհանացն կամ
լւյսանցւյց երդւյն ի շողսն խաղասցէ բազմութիւն մանրամաղ փոշւոյն, նոյնպէս և գործն
ընդ լւսոյն լցին գառ ի ստորևս ամէնայն, և
առաջն ցուկեալ յատիջանէին լւսոյն, և գործն
ընդ նմին։

735 Եւ մի անաւոր տեսիլ մարդւյ բարձր
և անհեղ, որ գառաջն ունէր և գեջան ի վերուստ
մինչև ի խոնարհ առաջապան յատաջեալ, և ի
ձեռինն իւրում ուռն մի մեծ ոսկի. և այն ամենային գհետ խաղացեալ գայր։ Եւ ինքն սպացեալ
խոյացեալ գայր՝ ըստ նմանութեան արագաթև
արծուււ. և եկն էջ եհաս մինչև մօտ ի յատակս
երկրիս, ի շինամէջ քաղաքին, և բաղխեաց
գԹանձրութիւն լայնատարած գետնոյն, և մեծ
և անչափ դղնդիւնքն հնչեցին ի սանդարամետս
անդնդոց. և ամենային երկիր յերևելիս, յական
տեսանելեաց բալեւյ, հարթ հաւասար դաշտա-
ձև յատակեցաւ։

736 Եւ տեսանէի ի մէջ քաղաքիս, մօտ յա-
պարանան արքունի, խարսխանձ ճախարականձ
խարխս ոսկի, մեծութեամբ իբրև գմեծ մի
բլուր, և ի վերայ նորա սիւն մի հրեղէն բարձր
մինչև յոյժ, և ի վերայ նորա Թակաղաղ մի
ամպեայ, և խաչն լւսոյ ի վերայ նորա։

with wings like fire. And in the likeness of minute
specks of dust which in the sunny springtime play in
their myriads in the rays passing through windows or
sky-lights,[2] so too these hosts filled everything below
with their light, and as the light streamed forward
so did the hosts with it.

735. "And (there was) an awesome vision of a man,
tall and fearful, who governed the front and the rear
guards and, descending from above, advanced as
leader.[1] And in his hand was a great hammer of gold,
and they all followed him. He himself flew swiftly in
the likeness of a fleet-winged eagle. And he descended
and came down near to the ground of the earth in the
middle of the city. And he struck the wide expanse of
the solid ground, and great and immeasurable rumb-
lings sounded in the depths of hell.[2] And the whole
earth as far as the eye could see was struck as level
as a plain.

736. "And I saw in the middle of the city, near the
royal palace, a circular base[1] of gold, as great as a
hill, and on it an exceedingly tall column of fire, and
on top of that a capital of cloud, and on top of that
again a cross of light.

737 Եւ նայեցայ, և տեսանեմ այլ խարիսխս երիս. մի՛ ի տեղւոջն ուր վկայեաց սուրբն Գայիանէ երկուք ընկերօքն. և մի՛ ի տեղւոջն ուր վկայեաց սուրբն Հռիփսիմէ երեսուն և երկու ընկերօքն, և մի՛ ի տեղւոջ ննջանին։ Եւ այս խարիսխք՝ կարմիրք էին ի գոյն արեան, և սիւնք ամպեղէնք, և խոյակք հրեղէնք. և ի վերայ սեանցն երից խաչք լուսեղէնք ըստ նմանութեան տեառնանման խաչին. և այս սեանց խաչքն հալասարբք էին այնր լուսեղէն սեանն Թակաղապ, գի նա բարձր էր քան գնոսա։ Եւ ի չորեցունց սեանցն ի վերայ խաչիցն կամարք գարմանատեսք ի միմեանս կապեցան. և ի վերայ այնորիկ տեսի գմբեթաձև խորանարդ ամպեղէն շինուած աստուածակերտ գարմանալի։ Եւ ի ներքոյ խորանին և վերայ կամարացն տեսի գուրբ վկայաս գայտասիկ դերեսուն և գեօթն, իբրև ի լուսաւոր կերպարանս սպիտակութեան հանդերձանօք, գոր ոչ բաւեմ պատմել։

738 Եւ ի կատար շինուածոյն տեսանէի աթոռ գարմանալի աստուածակերտ ս.քանչելի հրեղէն, և գխաչն տերունական ի վերայ նորա. գորով փարեալ լոյան համատարած՝ խաւնեցաւ ընդ ճառագայթս խաչին, և մածեալ ի նոյն միացաւ. և սիւն գործեաց լոյան շողացեալ, և ծագեաց ի մէջ ներքին սեանցն խարսխաց։

739 Եւ բղխեաց աղբիւր յորդաբուղխ, և

737. "And I looked up and saw three other bases: one in the place where saint Gaianē was martyred with her two companions, and one in the place where saint Rhipsimē was martyred with her thirty-two[1] companions, and one in the place of the wine-press. And these bases were red, the color of blood,[2] and the columns were of cloud and the capitals of fire. And on top of the three columns were crosses of light in the likeness of the Lord's cross. And the crosses of these columns were level with the capital of the column of light, for that one was higher than they. And from the four columns, above the crosses, marvelous vaults fitted into each other. And above this I saw a canopy of cloud, wonderfully and divinely constructed in the form of a dome. Under the canopy[3] but above the vaults I saw these thirty-seven[4] holy martyrs in shining light, with white garments, which I am not capable of describing.

738. "At the summit of this edifice I saw a wonderful and divine throne of fire with the Lord's cross above it.[1] Around it spread light in every direction, mingled with the rays of the cross and joined to the same. And the column made of light shone out among the bases of the lower columns.

739. "And there gushed forth an abundant spring,

հոսեցաւ ծաւալեցաւ ընդ դաշտս ամենայն, և
եղից առ հասարակ՝ որչափ ակն բաւեաց։ Եւ
եղև ծով լի և կապուտակագոյն, և երկնագոյն
երևեցան դաշտք առ հասարակ։ Եւ տեսի բազմութիւն հրեղէն սեղանոց անչափ բազմու-
թեամբ. և սիւն մի մի առ սեղան, և խաչ մի
մի ի վերայ նորա. և իբրև գաստեղս բազմու-
թեամբ՝ այնպիսի երևեաք և անչափ փայլեաք։

740 Եւ տեսի հօտս անթիւս այձեաց ի գոյն
սևութեան, որք անցեաք ընդ Ջուրն՝ յօդիս դարձան. և զգոյնս իւրեանց ի կերպարանս սպիտակութեան շրչեցին, և լուսակիզն սարն փայլեր
առ հասարակ, մինչև ճառագայթք հատանէին ի
նոցանէս։ Եւ մինչ դեռ նայէի ես՝ յանկարծակի
ծնան հօտքն և բազմացան, և ծնունդքն լցին
զվայրն. և ծնեալ գառինքն ամենայն լուսակիզն էին։ Իսկ յանկարծ այլ ծնունդք յաճախե-
ցին բազմացան, և կէսքն անկեալ ելին յայնկոյս
Չրոյն։ Եւ գառինքն գայլք եղեն թուխք, և յար-
ձակեցան ելին ի մէջ հօտիցն, և սկսան կոտորել, և եղեն արեան ճապաղիք։ Եւ մինչ դեռ
նայէի՛ և տեսի, և բուսան թևք հօտիցն, և եղեն
Թևաւորք, և վերացան խառնեցան ի գօրս լուսե-
ղէնս։ Եւ յարեաւ հեղեղ հրեղէն, և արկեալ տա-
րաւ զգայլսն։

741 Եւ ես նայեցեալ գարմացեալ կայի։ Եւ
այլըն, որ յառաջնումն կարդաց դանուն իմ և

flowing over all the plains and filling them completely as far as the eye could see. There was made a vast bluish sea, and the plains appeared altogether the color of heaven. And I saw a numberless multitude of fiery altars, and a column on each altar, and a cross on each column. And they shone out in infinite number like the stars.

740. "And I saw numberless herds of goats, black in color, who having passed through the water turned into sheep, and their color became white and their fleeces sparkled like shining wool as rays flashed out from them. While I was still looking, suddenly the flocks gave birth and multiplied and their offspring filled the land. And the lambs that were born were covered in shining wool. Then suddenly still more offspring multiplied, and half of them crossed to the other side of the water. And these lambs became brown wolves and attacked the flocks and began to slaughter them, and there was shedding of blood. While I was looking, I saw that the flocks grew wings and flew up and joined the shining hosts. And there arose a torrent of fire which bore away the wolves.

741. "Beholding this I was amazed. And the man, who had earlier called my name and

ցուցանէր ինձ՝ ասէ ցիս, թէ «Այր դու, զի՞ կաս
գարմացեալ, և ո՞չ ի միտ առնուս զմեծամեծս
Աստուծոյ»: Եւ ես ասեմ. «Ո՞րպէս, Տէր»: Եւ
ասէ ցիս. «Տեսիլ ցուցաւ քեզ այս՝ զի ի միտ առցես: Զի բացեալ են աղդիկ երկինք՝ գիտեա՛
զի բացեալ են դրունք մարդասիրութեանն Քրիստոսի առ իւր արարածս: Եւ ձայն բարբառոյ
որոտմանն, գիտեա՛ զի իջանէ անձրև ողորմութեանն և գթութեանն Աստուծոյ: Բացեալ են
աւանիկ դրունք երկնից, բացան և ջուրքն որ ի
վերայ նորա, զի մի՛ արգել լիցի այսմ աշխարհի
մարդկան՝ ելանել ի վեր: Զի սուրբք վկայքս այս
որ աստ վկայեցին՝ հիւսիսական կողմանցս ճանապարհ գործեցին. զի ինքեանք եւին և այլոց
շաւիղս ուղղեցին:

742 Աւասիկ լյոս զի ելից զվայրս՝ այս քա-
րոզութիւն Աւետարանին է, որ և զկողմ́ն հիւսիսոյ լնու: Եւ գործք լուսեղէնք ցանկացեալ փա-
փագեցին իջանել ի հող անոյշ ծաղկածև վար-
դագոյն արեան վկայիցն, նա այսուհետև խառ-
նելոց են ընդ մարդկան ի բնակութիւն բազմու-
թիւնք հրեշտակաց:

743 Իսկ այրս անաւոր և շքեղաւոր, որ գա-
ռաջան ունի գլուսոյն և գուռնն ոսկի ի ձեռին
իւրում, և բաղխեաց գաանդարամետոան՝ այս տես-
չութիւնն Աստուծոյ է, «որ հայի յերկիր, և տայ
դողալ. մերձի ի լերինս, և ծխին»: Այն ահ Աս-

showed me (this), said to me: 'O man, why do you stand in amazement without pondering the miracles of God?' And I said: 'How, Lord?' And he said to me: 'This vision has been revealed to you, that you might pay heed to it. For behold the heavens have been opened [cf. Ez. 1.1]: know that the gates of Christ's love [cf. Ps. 77.23; Tit. 3.4] for his creatures have been opened. As for the sound of the voice of thunder, know that the rain of God's mercy and pity [cf. Lk. 1.78] is descending. Behold the gates of heaven have been opened and the waters above have been opened,[1] that there be no impediment for men of this world to rise up. For the holy martyrs who were martyred here have made a road for these Northern regions, since they have gone up and made paths for others.[2]

742. "Behold this light which filled the land is the preaching of the gospel [cf. Jn. 1.4], which also fills the Northern region. And the hosts of light greatly desired to descend to the sweet odor [cf. II Cor. 2.15], like that of a rose-colored flower, of the martyrs' blood; from henceforth multitudes of angels will mingle and live with mankind.

743. "And the fearsome and splendid man, who in the vanguard held the golden hammer in his hand and struck the depths of hell,[1] he is the providence of God,[2] 'who looks on the earth and makes it shake; he approaches the hills, and they smoke' [Ps. 103.32]. This fear

տուածութեանն հարթեաց կործանեաց ընկեց գմոլորութիւնս յերկրէ։ Այն զի հնչեաց երկիր՝ գձայն ծառայութեանն հնազանդութեան բարբառեցաւ։

744 Որոյ սեանն խարիսխն ոսկի է, և նոբուն սիւնն հրեղէն, և Թակաղադն ամպեայ, և խաչն լուսեղէն ի վերայ նորա. ոսկի խարիսխն՝ վէմն հաստատութեան անշարժութեան է. և սիւնն հրեղէն՝ կաթողիկէ եկեղեցի է, որ ժողովք գամենայն ժողովուրդս ի մի միաբանութիւն հալատոց ի ներքոյ թևոց իւրոց։ Ել Թակաղադն ամպեայ՝ որ ընդունելոց է գարդարան, յորժամ թուիցեն ի տեառնագալատեանն ընդ առաջ նմա վերանալ։

745 Իսկ խաչն լուսաւոր ի նմա՝ է ինքն մեծ քահանայապետութիւնն ի մէջ ժողովրդոցն, օրինակ Քրիստոսի պատկերին մարմնացելոյ քահանայապետութեանն օծութեան Աստուածորդւոյն։ Ել տեղին այն լիցի տաճար Աստուծոյ, և տուն աղօթից խնդրուածոց ամենայն հալատացելոց, և աթոռ քահանայապետութեանն։

746 Ել խարիսխքն երեք, որ կարմիրքն էին ի գոյն արեան՝ վասն չարչարանացն եկելոց նեղութեանց մահու համբերութեանն. գի գմանի իւրեանց աբարին խարիսխ ճշմարտութեան հալատոց, հեղմամբ արեան իւրեանց։ Ել սիւնքն՝ ամպեղէնք յայն սակս երեքեան, վասն գի ամին

of the Godhead has flattened[3] and destroyed and overthrown error from the earth. And the echoing earth was the voice of servitude and obedience.

744. "As for the golden base of the pillar, and its fiery column[1] and capital of cloud and the shining cross above it—the base of gold is the immovable rock of establishment [cf. Matt. 7.25]; the fiery column is the Catholic church[2] which gathers all peoples to one unity of faith under her wings [cf. Eph. 4.13]; and the capital of cloud is to receive the just when they will fly up before the Lord at his coming [cf. I Thess. 4.16].

745. "Now the shining cross on it is the great high-priest [cf. Heb. 3.14] himself among the peoples, the type[1] of Christ's image, the incarnate high priesthood of the anointed Son of God. And that place will be a temple of God and a house of prayer [cf. Matt. 21.13] for the requests of all the faithful, and a throne of the high priesthood.

746. "And the three bases which were red, the color of blood,[1] represent the torments and afflictions which came upon (the martyrs) and their endurance unto death. For they made their death the basis [cf. Heb. 6.19][2] of the true faith by the shedding of their blood. And the columns appeared of cloud for this reason, because the cloud

ունի գԹեԹևութիւն արագութեան ի յարութեանն
յերկինս վերանալոյ։ Եւ Թակագադն՝ հրեղէն, զի
ընակութիւն նոցա լինելոց է ի հուր Աստուածութեանն լուսոյն։

747 Եւ խաչքն ունին գշարչարանս վկայիցն, որ նմանեցին Տեառն չարչարանացն, և
մեռան փոխանակ նորա. զի Աստուծով կեցին և
ընդ Քրիստոսի խաչեցան, և կենդանի է Քրիստոս յոսկերս նոցա՝ ցուցանել ամենեցուն զկեն-
դանութիւն նոցա. յայտնի առնել գհոռ անու-
շութեան գիտութեան իւրոյ ի նոցանէ և հոչակել զառաքինութիւնս նոցա ընդ տիեզերս։ Զի
սպանին նոքա գմարմինս երկրաւորս, և կախե-
ցին գվերունական խաչէն. եղեն Տեառն իւրեանց չարչարակից, նոյնպէս և փառաց և գորութեանն լինելոց են հաղորդք։

748 Այլ առաջին խաչն որ ցուցաւ քեզ՝
ունի գպարծանս քահանայութեան պատուին,
պանծացեալ ի խաչն Քրիստոսի։ Իսկ երեք ես,
որ ունէին գտեղի վկայարանացն հանգստի սըր-
բոցն՝ զի ի տեղւոջ հեղման արեանն իւրեանց
շինեցին վկայարանք հանգստի ոսկերաց իւր-
եանց։ Իսկ զի բարձր է սիւնն առաջին՝ զի մեծ
և բարձր է պատիւ կաԹողիկէ եկեղեցւոյ քան
գամենայն բարձրութիւնս սրբոցն։ Իսկ կամարքն
որ ի սեանց անտի ի միմեանս կապէին՝ այս
ինքն է հաւասարութիւն միաբանութեան կաԹո-

has lightness to rise swiftly up to heaven at the resurrection.[3] And the capital was fiery because their habitation will be in the fire of the divine light.

747. "And the crosses represent the sufferings of the
martyrs, who imitated the sufferings of the Lord and
died for him. For they lived in God and were crucified with Christ, and Christ lives in their bones[1] in
order to show everyone their life, to reveal by them
the sweet odor[2] of his knowledge, and to spread
abroad their virtue throughout the world. For they
killed their earthly bodies and hung from the Lord's
cross; they became fellow-sufferers with their Lord,
and likewise will share in his glory and power [cf.
Rom. 8.17].

748. "Now the first cross that was revealed to you
represents the boast of the honor of priesthood, which
glories in the cross of Christ. But the other three represented the places for the chapels of repose of the
saints, because in the place where their blood was
shed will be built chapels of repose for their bones.
Now the first column was high, because the honor of
the Catholic church is greater and higher than all the
heights of the saints. And the arches that were linked
to each other from the columns are the equality and
unity of the Catholic

դիկէ եկեղեցւոյ։ Իսկ խորանն ի վերայ՝ ունի
գօրինակ վերնոյ քաղաքին, գժողովարանն միաբանութեան արքայութեանն երկնից։

749 Եւ զի երկեէին քեզ վկայքն՝ գիտեա զի
մահս ժամանակեան է, ասէ, և կենդանութիւն
նոցա յաւիտենական, փառաւորեալ ի փառս
Աստուածորդւոյն. վասն այսորիկ և գօրինակ
խաչի նորա տպաւորեալ յանձինս նոցա։

750 Եւ ի վերայ կատարոյ շինուածոյն գոր
տեսանես, նոյն ինքն աթոռ ամենագօր բնութեան Աստուածութեանն, բարձրութեան ինք-
նութեանն. զի նա ինքն գլուխ է եկեղեցւոյ
սրբոյ և կատարիչ ամենայն բարութեանց, և ի
նա ամենայն շինուածն պատշաճի, և անէ գա-
ճումն Աստուծոյ, յոր ամենայն մարմին յօդիւք
և խաղալեօք և անդամօք հաստատեալ և կազ-
մեալ։

751 Եւ լոյսն զի փարի գխաչիւն՝ այս ինքն
Հոգի Աստուածութեանն որ գՈրդին փառաւոր
առնէ։ Եւ զի խառնեցաւ ընդ ճառագայթս նու-
րա՝ այս ինքն զի յՈրդւոյն առնու և պատմէ
սիրելեաց իւրոց։ Եւ զի միացաւ ի նոյն՝ զի
մի է բնութիւն Աստուածութեանն։ Եւ զի ծագեաց լոյսն ի մէջ սեանցն չորեցունց, և բղխե-
ցոյց գաղբիւրն յորդաբուղխ՝ զի ի կաթողիկէ
եկեղեցւոյն շնորհք Հոգւոյն ի մէջ վկայելոցն
և ի մէջ քահանայութեանն բղխելոց է աղբիւր

church. And the canopy above represents the type[1] of the celestial city [cf. Gal. 4.26], the united gathering-place of the kingdom of heaven.

749. "And because the martyrs appeared to you, know,' he said, 'that their death is temporary and their life eternal and glorious in the glory of the Son of God. Therefore they figured in themselves the pattern[1] of his cross.

750. "And what you see above the top of the building is the throne of the almighty nature of the Godhead, of his essential height. For he is the head of the holy church [cf. Col. 1.18] and the worker of all blessings.[1] And in him is held together the whole edifice, and it increases the glory of God [cf. Col. 2.19], in whom is firmly established the whole body with limbs and joints [cf. Eph. 2.21-22; 4.16].

751. "And the light which surrounded the cross is the Spirit of God who glorifies the Son. And it mingled with its[1] rays, because it receives from the Son and tells (of him) to his beloved [cf. Jn. 16.14]. And it was united to the same, because the nature of the Godhead is one. And the light shone from the midst of the four columns and caused an abundant torrent to flow forth, because the grace of the Spirit will flow from the Catholic church amid the martyrs and the priesthood as the fountain

մկրտութեան, լուանալ գաղտ ոգլոյն մարմնովքն հանդերձ։ Եւ այն զի յորդեաց եղից զքացում վայրս՝ զի լինելոց է փրկութիւն մկրտութեամբ բազում ժողովրդոց։ Եւ զի երկնագոյն երկե֊ ցան դաշտք ամենայն՝ այս ինքն է՝ զի երկիրս իբրև զերկինս լինելոց է, խառնուրդք հրեշտա֊ կաց և մարդկան։

752 Եւ հրեղէն սեղանոգն բագմութիւնք որ քեզգ երկին՝ ճշմարտիւ իսկ լինելոց են սե֊ դանք Աստուծոյ, որ դքալութիւն բաշխեն ամե֊ նեցուն։ Եւ հրեղէն յայն սակս երևեցաւ, զի պաշտոն Հոգւոյն եղիցի փառօք։ Եւ սիւնք մի մի առ սեղան՝ պաշտոն աղօթից քահանայու֊ թեան։ Եւ խաչք ի վերայ նոցա, այս ինքն զի սուրբ անուՆն Քրիստոսի փառաւոր լեցի ընդ ամենայն տեղիս։ Եւ զի բազում էին իբրև գաս֊ տեդս՝ զի պաշտամունք սրբութեանն իբրև գաս֊ տեդս բազմասցին։

753 Եւ հոտք բագմութեան այժեացն սևու֊ թեան, որք յիջանել ի Յուրբան յոդիս դարձեալ սպիտակութեան՝ աւադիկ աշն Աստուածութեան շնորհացն ի ձեռն քահանայապետութեան հասա֊ նելուց է. յորոյ ձեռն բղխեսցէ աղբիւր մկըր֊ տութեան. ի թողութիւն քաւութեան բագում մեղաւորաց։ Եւ որ լուսակիդն ասր նոցա փայ֊ լեալ պայծառացեալ էր՝ այս ինքն՝ մկրտեալքն լոյս գգենլոց են, և արքայութեանն խոստացե֊

of baptism, to wash away the stain of the soul with the body. And it spread out and filled many places because it will become salvation for many peoples through baptism. And the fact that all the plains appeared the color of heaven means that this earth will become like heaven—the common abode of angels and men.[2]

752. "And the multitudes of fiery altars which appeared to you, will truly be the altars of God which will distribute expiation to all. And they appeared fiery for this reason, because the worship of the Spirit will take place gloriously. And the columns by each altar (represent) the worship of the prayers of the priesthood.[1] And the crosses above them signify that the holy name of Christ will be glorified in every place. And they were as many as the stars because the services of holiness will multiply like the stars.

753. "And the herds of many black goats who in going down to the waters turned into sheep, behold (this means that) the right hand of God's grace will come through the high priesthood,[1] through which the fountain of baptism will flow for the forgiveness and expiation of many sinners. And their white wool which shone and sparkled signifies that the baptised will be clothed in light and become worthy of the promised kingdom.

լոց արժանաւոր լինելոց։ Եւ զի ծնան հօրքն և
բազմացան և լցին գվայրան՝ այս ինքն է՝ զբազում ժամանակս անեցուցանէ զբարողութիւնն,
և ծնանին նոր ծնունդք նորոգութեան, և բազ-
մացուցանէ զմկրտութիւնն։

754 Եւ զի կէսքն անկեալ ելեալ էին հօրքն
ընդ Յուբան, ի նոյն կողմն ուստի անցեալն էին՝
այս ինքն է՝ ի յետին ժամանակս անօրինելոց
են, անկեալք ի ճշմարտութենէն. ընկենլոց են
յետս դդրոշմ ուխտին սրբութեան Աստուածութեանն, և բազումք թողուն գլխան սրբու-
թեան։ Եւ ի դառանցն լինելոց են գայլք, որ
կոտորելոց են զոսլբբ դաոինս. այս ինքն որ
գնան ի ճշմարտութենէ անտի և յուխտէ քահա-
նայիցն՝ լինելոց են գայլք, և հանեն ճապաղիս
արեան գառանցն, այս ինքն ուխտին և քահանայութեանն, և խոռովուլթիւն ժողովրդոցն։ Իսկ
որ համբերենն միամտութեամբ ի գառանցն, ի
ժողովրդոցն կամ ի քահանայիցն՝ թխս առնու-
ցուն և յարքայութիւնն Քրիստոսի վերանան։
Իսկ որ գմիտս գայլոցն կամ զգործծ յափշտա-
կութեան նոցա ունիցին՝ ի հուրն անշէջ մատ-
նեսցին։

755 Եւ դու, ասէ ցիս այրն, պինտ կաց,
քաջ լեր, զգօյշ լեր. զի գործ ի ձեռն եկեալ
հասեալ է քեզ. զի քեզ բարութիւն դիւրաւ լինելոց է, զի և դու ընդ ճշմարիտ մշակս վարձ

And the fact that the flocks gave birth and multiplied and filled the land signifies that the preaching will be increased for a long time, and new, renewed offspring will be born and baptism will be increased.

754. "And the fact that half of the flocks went through the waters and (turned back) to the same side from which they had passed[1] means that in times to come there will be impious ones who depart from the truth; they will fall behind the standard of the holy covenant of the Godhead, and many will abandon the holy covenant. And from lambs they will become wolves who will slaughter the holy lambs—that is, those who depart from the truth and the priestly covenant will become wolves and will cause the shedding of the blood of the lambs, that is of the covenant and of the priesthood, and (will cause) confusion for the people. But those lambs which endure faithfully, either from among the people or the priests, will receive wings and rise to the kingdom of Christ. But those who will have the intentions of wolves or commit their rapacious deeds will be handed over to unquenchable fire.

755. "And you," said the man to me, "stand firm, be strong, be attentive. For a task has been put upon you; you will easily receive blessing, for with the true laborers you will receive reward

առնես յանպատում պարգևացն Քրիստոսի․ Արդ՝
զգո՛յշ լեր աւանդիդ, որ քեզդ հաւատացաւ ի
տեառնէ Յիսուսէ Քրիստոսէ. չինեաչիր զտա-
ճար անուանն Աստուծոյ ի տեղւոջն որ ցուցաւ
քեզ, ուր սիւնն հրեղէն ունէր գոսկի խարիսխն,
և զվկայարանս սրբոցն ի տեղիսն՝ ուր գեսան
ինքեանք ի կենդանութիւն Աստուածութեան
յուսոյն։ Զի բժշկեսցին հարուածեալքդ, և քարոզութեանն յաՉողուած յառաջագէմ լիցի հա-
նապարգորդութեամբ օր ըստ օրէ, հասանել
ամենեցուն ի չափ կատարման հասակի հաւա-
տոյն Քրիստոսի»։ Եւ գայս ասացեալ՝ շարժունն
եղեալ, և ընդ առաւօտանալն ծածկեցաւ տե-
սիլն։

756   «Արդ՝ ամենարարն, ամենաստեղծն,
ամենահաստիչն, ամենիմաստն, ամենատեքն, ամե-
նակալն, ամենագիւտն, ամենաբժիչկն խրատեաց
գձեզ, գի Աստուածութեանն իւրոյ գձեզ մեր-
ձաւորս արասցէ։ Վասն այսորիկ ցուցեալ ձեզ
մեօք զկենաց ճանապարհս և գգրկութեան հանգամանս, գթողութիւն միանդամայն աձել հասուցանել ի վերայ. վասն այսորիկ գոտեսիլ հան-
դերձելոցն երևեցոյց ինձ պատմել ձեզ, առ ժա-
մանակիս գիւր կաման առ ձեզ կատարելով։ Արդ՝
և դուք գասացեալն ըստ հրամանացն փութա-
յսրունք կատարել։ Եւ արդ՝ եկա՛յք չինեացունք
գվկայարանն, փոսել գվկայս ի հանգիստ. գի

from the ineffable gifts of Christ. Now, be attentive to the tradition entrusted you by the Lord Jesus Christ. Construct the temple of God's name in the place which has been shown you, where the fiery column had its base of gold, and (build) the holy martyrs' chapels in the places where they were sacrificed to life in divine hope; that the tormented may be healed and the gospel be preached ever more successfully day after day, to bring everyone to the measure of the perfect stature of Christ's faith" [cf. Eph. 4.13]. When he had said this there was an earthquake, and as day dawned the vision was obscured.

756. "Now the creator of all, the maker and fashioner of all, God the all-wise, the almighty and omnipotent Lord of all, the supreme healer has instructed you in order to make you familiar with his divinity. Therefore he has shown you through us the path to life and the way to salvation whereby you may obtain forgiveness. For this reason he revealed to me the vision of the future, for me to inform you and fulfill among you his will at this time. So now come, hasten to fulfill his words according to his commands. Come, let us build the chapels and put the martyrs to rest,

և սոքա փոխեցեն գձեզ ի նորոգութիւն»։

757 Եւ դայս ասացեալ՝ հրամայեաց գի
գնիւթ շինուածոյն վաղվաղակի պատրաստե-
ցեն։ Եւ ամենայն բազմութեան մարդկանն լուեալ դայն՝ իւրաքանչիւր ընթացան պատրաստել
գնիւթան։ Եւ կուտէին ի հրամայեալ տեղին
ոմն վէմ, ոմն քար, ոմն ադիւս, ոմն գմայր փայտն,
պատրաստէին խնդալից փութով և մեծաւ եր-
կիւղիւ։

758 Եւ ինքն սուրբն Գրիգորիոս ղլար ճար-
տարութեան շինողացն ի ձեռն առեալ՝ գերանե-
լեացն վկայարան հանգատարանացն գձիմունան
յորինէր։ Եւ մէն մի իւրաքանչիւր ամենայն
բազմութեանն սատարութիւն ի ձեռն առեալ,
բստ գեղեցկադէր յարմարելոյ հիմնարկին ի կատարումն շինուածոյն կանգնեցին։ Ամենայն ոք
ձեռն ի գործ արկեալ, և կանանւոյն անգամ սա-
տարեալ բստ իւրեանց տկարութեան կանացի ու-
ժոյն, և այսպէս առ հատարակ գործէին զգործն
հաւատովք և մեծաւ երկիւղիւ, զի մի ոք ամե-
նեկին անմասն եղեալ ի փրկութենէ շնորհացն, ի
բժշկութենէն գրկեցի։

759 Եւ կանգնեալ երիս վկայարանս, մի՛ ի
հիւսխոյ յարևելից կողմանէ քաղաքին, ուր վկայեաց սանակ.անն Հռիփսիմէ երեսուն և երկու
ընկերօք։ Եւ գմիւսն շինեցին ի հարաւակողմ
կուսէ անտի, ուր վկայեացն Գայիանէ նորուն

that they in turn may bring us to renewal."

[Chapter 9. Chapels are built and the nuns buried;
        the king and people are cured]

757. Having said this he ordered them quickly to
prepare the material for the building. When the whole
crowd of the populace heard this, each ran to prepare
the materials. In the appointed places some piled up
rocks, others stones, others bricks, others cedar wood;
they made their preparations in joy, and in haste and
in great fear.

758. Saint Gregory himself took up the architect's
line[1] and set out the foundations for the saints' chapels
of repose. Each one in the whole crowd lent his help,
and following the well-laid-out foundations they built
up the completed edifice. Everyone put his hand to
the task, women also helping according to their
weaker feminine strength.[2] And thus they all worked
together in faith and great fear, lest anyone fail to
obtain his share in the grace of salvation or be deprived of healing.

759. So they raised three chapels: one on the Northeastern side of the city where the young Rhipsimē
had been martyred with thirty-two[1] companions. They
built the second to the South where Gaianē, her guardian, had been martyred

մնուցիչն երկու ընկերօքն։ Եւ զմիսն իւ մօտ
ի ճնձանն ի մէջ այգւոյն, ուր էին վանք նոցա։
Շինեցին կազմեցին գտեղիսն, և գարդարեցին
ոսկի և արծաթի կանթեղօք լուցելովք, և լապ-
տերօք վառելովք, և աշտանակօք բորբոքելովք։

760   Եւ հրամայեաց մէն մի իւրաքանչիւր արկղագործ, տախտակամած, մայրափայ-
տեայ, բևեռապինդ, հաստահեղոյս, երկաթագամ
տապան գործել։ Եւ ամենայն ըստ աասցելոյ
պատուիրանին արարեալ, հանդերձեալ կազմեալ
պատրաստեցին։ ըստ եղեալ հրամանին տուեյոյ
բերին գարկեղան արարեալ հանգատի սրբոցն առ
դուրս ճնձանին, առաջի սրբոյն Գրիգորի։ Իսկ
նա առեալ՝ ինքն միայն ի ներքս մտանէր, և ոչ
թողոյր գայլ ոք ամենևին ի ներքս մտանել.
ասէ. «Ոչ է պարտ ձեզ հուպ լինել և մերձենալ
առ նոսա, որ չեդ էք բժշկեալ, որ չեդ էք սրբ-
բեալ մկրտութեամբ»։ Այլ ինքն միայն առանձ-
նացեալ, գմի մի իւրաքանչիւր ի սրբոցն առեալ
յիւրաքանչիւր արկեղ դնէր՝ իւրաքանչիւր հան-
դերձով և իւրեանց կազմութեամբ պնդէր, և
կնքէր քրիստոսական կնքովն։

761 Իսկ Թագաւորն և արքայագունքն ամենայն և մեծամեծքն և նախարարքն և ազատքն
և գօրքն ամենայն՝ իւրաքանչիւր բերէին իւղա
անուշունս և խունկս ազնիւս, և զգունագոյն
նարոտս պատանաց, գմետաքսաւէտ չա ոսկեթել

with two[2] companions. And the third they built close to the vat-store in the vineyard, where their lodging had been.[3] They constructed and arranged these places, and adorned them with burning lamps of gold and silver and kindled lanterns and lighted candelabras.[4]

760. And he ordered a casket to be made for each one of them, box-shaped, of cedar planks firmly jointed together with iron nails. They all followed his orders and prepared as he had said. At his command they brought the caskets made for the repose of the saints[1] to the door of the vat-store in front of saint Gregory. He took them and entered alone, allowing no one else at all to go inside. "It is not right for you to come near or approach them, for you have not been healed or purified by baptism." But he withdrew alone and placed each of the saints in one of the caskets; he wrapped each one in her clothing and sealed them with the seal of Christ.[2]

761. But the king and all the royal court and the magnates and princes and nobles and the entire army, all brought sweet oils and precious incense and decorated bands of various colors, woven with silken and golden threads.

կերպասուց։ Եւ կին թագաւորին եւ օրիորդք
թագաւորագունք եւ կանայք պատուականացն եւ
մեծամեծացն դստերք՝ բերէին ձիրանիս եւ գու-
կեհունն դիպակն եւ գերկնագոյնն, եւ գսպիտակ
իբրեւ գձիւն հանդերձանս սրբոյն։ Նոյնպէս եւ
գոսկին եւ գարծաթն եւ գկաւեան փութով կուտէին առ դուլսա հնձանին։

762 Արդ՝ եղեալ տեսանէր սուրբն Գրիգորիոս, գի շեղձ շեղձ կուտեալ էին առ դուրսա
հնձանին։ Իսկ նա ոչ առնոյր յանձն գնոցա ինչ
առ նոսա մատուցանել. ասէ. «Ո՛չ վաղ իսկ
ասացի, եթէ ոչ է պատշաճ գձեր ինչ, մինչ շեղ
էք սրբեալ միկրտութեամբ՝ առ նոսա մատուցանել. այլ յօժարութիւնդ ձեր բարիոք է վասն
ձերոյ փրկութեան։ Այլ այս ամենայն յարբու-
նական գանձուն պանեալ կայցէ, մինչեւ ձեզ հովիւ եւ վարդապետ ի տուչութենէ բարերարու-
թեան Աստուծոյ պարգեսցի, եւ երկեսցէն ձեզ
առաջնորդք, քանանայապետք, տեսուչք եպիսկոպոսք եւ երիցունք եկեղեցական կարգի լուսաւորութեան սիրոյն Աստուծոյ. եւ այդ ամենայն
երթիցէ ի սպաս պաշտամման փառաւորբնկալ
սեղանոյն Աստուծոյ ի ձեռն քանանայապետին
կացելոյ։ Այլ այժմ եկայք գոսա յիւրաքանչիւր
հանգիստա մատուցուք»։

763   Իսկ թագաւորն Տրդատ յայնժամ
գեռ եւ էր յամենայն կերպարանս խողի, բայց

And the queen and the royal princesses and the honorable women and nobles' daughters brought for the saints purple robes and brocades of gold and blue and garments as white as snow. Similarly they hastened to pile up at the door of the vat-store gold and silver and linen.

762. When saint Gregory came out he saw these piled up by the door of the vat-store. But he did not allow them to offer anything of theirs to the saints, saying: "Did I not tell you earlier that it is unfitting for you to offer them anything of yours until you have been purified by baptism? Nonetheless your good will is advantageous for your salvation. But let all this remain stored in the royal treasury until you be granted a shepherd and teacher by the benevolent providence of God, and you be provided with leaders, high priests,[1] overseeing bishops and priests of the ecclesiastical order[2] for your illumination in the love of God. Then all this will go for the service of the worship at the glorious altar of God through the established high priest. But now come, let us put these to each one's repose."

763. Now king Trdat was still in the form of a pig, save

միայն ի մարդկապէսն խոսելոյ. և կճղակք ձեռացն և ոտիցն իբրև զխոզի, և դէմք երեսացն
կնճթացեալ, և ժանիք մեծամեծք իբրև զմեծա-
մեծ վարազաց, և խողանասանն Թաւացեալ զամենայն մարմնովն։ Այլ կայր պատեալ զերեսան
գլխովն հանդերձ՝ արկեալ զիւրեաւ քուրձ, և կայր
երկոյթ տեսեամբք ի մէջ ժողովրդոցն։ Արդ՝ մատուցեալ ապաշէր գուրբն Գրիգորիոս, զի գո-
նեա ձեռացն և ոտիցն ճնար լինիցի բժշկու-
Թեան, զի ի գործ շինուածոց սրբոցն արժանի
արասցէ գէթ սակաւիկ ինչ մասնաւորել զնա։

764 Իսկ երանելին Գրիգորիոս ձունբ կրրկ-
նեալ ամենատեան բարերարի մարդասիրին Աստուծոյ, երթեալ արկանէր գուրբբնկալ արկե-
դօքն երանելի մարմնոցն քրիստոսական վկայից՝
մատուցանել պաղատանս. համբարձեալ զբա-
գուկան հանապազատարած յերկինս՝ ամենայն
ժողովելոցն և Թագաւորին բժշկուԹիւն հայցեր։
Ապա դարձաւ առ Թագաւորն, շնորհելովն Քրիստոսի գտաանն նորա և գզենան բժշկէր. զի Թա-
վեցան կճղակք ոտիցն և ձեռացն. որպէս զի առ
մի նուազ հաղորդեալ լիցի ի գործ սրբոցն՝ իւրոց ձեռացն վաստակելով։

765 Իսկ նորա հարցեալ զԳրիգորիոս, Թէ
զինչ հրամայեացէ նմա. և նա տայր դշավի ար-
կեղացն սբրոց, զի հատեալ գտեղիան իւրաքանչիւր բնակուԹեան՝ յօրինեցէ ի ներքսա ի մար-

only that he could speak in human fashion. The claws of his hands and feet were those of a pig, his face was like a snout, he had great teeth like a boar, and he was hairy all over his body. He stood covering his face and head, wrapped in a hair shirt[1]—an obvious sight in the midst of the people. Then he came forward and begged saint Gregory that at least his hands and feet might be healed so that he might be worthy to participate at least a little in the construction of the saints' chapels.

764.   Then blessed Gregory knelt to the Lord of all, the kind and benevolent God, throwing himself by the caskets which contained the blessed bodies of Christ's martyrs, and offered supplications, raising his arms to heaven and begging healing for all the people and the king.[1] Then he turned to the king and by the grace of Christ cured his feet and hands: the claws of his feet and hands fell off, so that he could play a small part in the holy work, laboring with his own hands.

765.   Then he asked Gregory what he would order him to do. And he gave him the measure of the holy caskets that he might dig places for each one to lie in, and arrange these inside

տիրոսական յարկին հանգստեան։ Իսկ նորա ա-
ղաչեալ զԳիրգորիոս՝ զի հրամայեսցէ, մի՛ վասն
կնոջ իւրոյ Աշխենայ տիկնոջ, եւ մի՛ վասն քեռն
իւրոյ հաբագատի որում անուն էր Խոսրովիդուխտ, զի իշխեսցեն եւ նոքա հաւասարել գոր-
ծոյն։ Եւ նորա տուեալ հրաման, եւ նոցա երթեալ ընդ նմա օգնել գործոյն։ Եւ առեալ զշափ
արկեղացն՝ փոսել փորել գաեղիս հանգստի սըր-
բոցն ի ներքս ի տաճարս հանգստարանացն։

766   Արդ՝ առեալ Թագաւորին փայ-
տատ եւ բահ՝ հատանէր գլիրս հանգստոցաց սըր-
բոցն իւրաքանչիւր ըստ չափու արկեղացն։ Սոյնպէս եւ ինքեանք երկոքին, Աշխէն տիկին եւ քոյր
Թագաւորին Խոսրովիդուխտ, ըստ բրել բրողին
ի հանդերձ իւրեանց ընկալեալ գհող՝ արտաքս
պեղէին։ Եւ այսպէս կարգի կարգի յառաջակողմն
պատրաստեցին գլիրս սրբոյն Հռիփսիմեայ. եւ
գկնի նորա գերեսուն եւ գերկուցն ի տեղւոջն
յայնմիկ, ուր հեղան արիւնք վկայականք երա-
նութեան նոցա, ի տեղւոջ հանգստեան պատ-
րաստելոյ սուրբ եւ փառաւոր սեղանոյն Քրիս-
տոսի։ Սոյնպէս եւ ի վկայարանին՝ որ ի հարա-
ւակոյս քաղաքին էր՝ պատրաստեաց եւ գայն տեղին երանելւոյն Գայիանեայ եւ երկուց ընկե-
րացն։ Ինքնին Թագաւորն Տրդատ քերն Խոս-
րովիդուխտով հանդերձ եւ Աշխէն տիկնաւ գլիրս
սրբոյն իւրաքանչիւր բնակութեան յօրինէին

the resting place of the martyrs. Then he begged Gregory to command, first concerning his wife Ashkhēn and secondly for his sister Khosrovidukht, that they too might be able to join in the work. And he gave a command, and they went with him to help in the task. And he took the measure of the caskets in order to dig out places for the repose of the saints inside the funerary chapels.

766.   Then the king took an axe and spade and dug out places for the repose of the saints according to the measure of the caskets. Similarly the other two, the queen Ashkhēn and the king's sister Khosrovidukht, as he dug gathered the earth into their clothes and removed it. And in this way they prepared in order first the spot for saint Rhipsimē, and then that for the thirty-two[1] in the place where their blessed martyrs' blood had been shed, in the place of repose prepared for the holy and glorious altar of Christ. Similarly also at the chapel which was to the South of the city he prepared the spot for the blessed Gaianē and her two[2] companions. King Trdat himself and his sister Khosrovidukht and queen Ashkhēn arranged the resting-places for each of the saints

իւրեանց ձեռօքն.

767 Եւ եկն թագաւորն, խնդրեաց հրաժեշտ
ի սրբոյն Գրիգորէ եօթնօրեայ ճանապարհ կալեալ ի վեր ի բարձր լեառն ի Մասիս։ Եւ անտի ի գլխոյ լեռնէն առեալ վէմս արաստոյ,
անտաշս, անփորկս, յաղթս, ծանունս, երկայնս,
ստուարս և մեծամեծս, որ գմի մի ոչ ումեք
լինէր հնար, թէ և դիպելոյ բազմութեան ի
մարդկանէ՝ գայն շարժել. արդ՝ առեալ սկայազօրն
հայկաբար գուժ արձանան՝ ի վերայ իւրոց թի-
կանցն գայն դնէր և լատանձնեալ բերէր ի վկայարանս տանջարացն։ Մէն չորս արձանս սեամս
կանգնէր՝ իբրև փոխարէն անմիտ մարտին, գոր
ընդ սրբոյն պատերազմեալ յիւրում սենեկին.
ուր ամենապաճ շնորհացն յաղթեալ՝ գայնչափ
գարմանալիան գործեաց։ Եւ սա պսակ յաղթու-
թեան՝ գիւրոյ ձեռացն գործութեան գվաստակն
ամենեցուն ցուցանէր.

768 Աբարեալ շինեալ կազմեալ գսուրբ
վկայարանան երեսին՝ հանդերձեցին գարդարեցին և օրհնօք յարդարեցին. և ապա առեալ գիւրաքանչիւր յիւրաքանչիւր տեղի վկայութեանն
մատուցանէին։ Զսուրբն Գայիանէ ի կողմն հարաւոյ, իւրոյ մարտիրոսութեանն երկու ընկերօքն դնէր ի վկայարանի տաճարին։ Սոյնպէս և
գերանելին Հռիփսիմէ երեսուն և երկու ընկերօքն ի կողմն արևելից ի շինածի տաճարին

with their own hands.

767.   Then the king came and asked leave from saint Gregory to make a seven-day journey to the great and lofty[1] mountain Masis.[2] From the summit of the mountain he took solid stones, unworked, unhewn,[3] immense, solid, wide, enormous and huge, which no single person could ever move, not even a great number of men.[4] But he with giant strength like Hayk's[5] picked up eight blocks and carried them on his own back to the chapels. On his own he set up four blocks as a threshold, in compensation as it were for the thoughtless struggle which he had waged with the saint in his own chamber, where conquering by the Savior's grace she had done such marvels. He now showed everyone as a crown of victory the labor of his own hands.[6]

768.   Having constructed all three chapels, they adorned them and suitably decorated them. Then they brought each one to her place of martyrdom. Saint Gaianē he placed in the chapel to the South with the two companions of her martyrdom. Similarly the blessed Rhipsimē with the thirty-two[1] companions they placed in the chapel constructed to the East.

դնէին։ Եւ գմիաւորն, որ ի հնձանին սպանաւ՝ սորա տաճարն ի կողմանէ քաղաքին ի հիւսիսոյ կուսէ։ Եւ գամենայն սուրբան ի միասին գումարեալ, զխաչական վկայսն Քրիստոսի՝ յերբաքանչիւր հանգիստա մարտիրոսական բնակութեան շինուածոցն փոխեցին։ Բատ երնելոյ հրամանին տեսեանն յառաջագոյն Գրիգորի՝ այսպէս և կատարեցաւ։

769 Եւ ի ներբսագոյն խորանացն, ի վերայ հանգտաբանացն կենդանադիր գերեզմանացն ի տեղիս սեդանոցն, յերեսին վկայարանան մէն մի կանգնեցաց գուլրբ նշան տէրունական խաչին. «Զի միայն, ասէ, առաշի այդր ամենակեցոյց նշանիդ երկիր պագանիցէք տեառն Աստուծոյ արարչին ձերոյ։ Անա․սիւնք հաստատուն կանգնեցեան ձերում խարխուլ շինուածոյն։ Այս այն սիւնք են, ասէ, որ ունիք գետեն ձանրութեան ձերոյ շինուածոյն փրկութեան. անա երեք սիւնք. և չոբբորդ սիւն կենդանութեան՝ որ գձեգ առ Աստուած վերացուցէ։ Եկայք գնկատեալ տեղին տէրունական տանն և մեզ հրամայեան ի մէջ առեալ ի պատիւ փակեցուք»։

770 Եւ Թագաւորաւն և ամենայն ժողովրդովքն հանդերձ երթեալ հասանէր անդէն ի տեղին ցուցեալ հրեղէն սեանն ոսկիակալ խարբսխին, և անդէն բարձր քաղաքորմով փակեալ գտեղին ի պատիւ, և դրամբք և դռնափակօք

And the single[2] (martyr) who had been killed in the vat-store had her chapel to the North of the city. Having brought all the saints together, they transferred the crusading martyrs of Christ each to the chapel of repose built for her. According to the command of the vision which had earlier appeared to Gregory, so was it accomplished.

769.   And in the center of the canopies,[1] over the resting-place of the life-enclosing tombs on the sites of the altars, he set up in each of the three chapels the holy sign of the Lord's cross. "Only in front of this all-saving sign," he said, "should you worship the Lord God your creator. Behold firm pillars have been set up in your insubstantial edifice. These are the pillars which bear the heavy weight of the edifice of your salvation. Behold three pillars: the fourth is the pillar of life which will raise you to God.[2] Come let us honorably enclose the place that has been indicated and commanded us for the Lord's house."

770.   So with the king and all the people he went to the place where the fiery column with the golden base had been revealed,[1] and there they honorably enclosed the spot with a high wall and secured it with doors and bolts.

ամբացուցեալ, և կանգնեալ և անդ գնչան փեր֊
կական խաչին. զի առ հասարակ հասեալ ամե֊
նային որ յայն տեղի՝ ամենագոր արարչին Աս֊
տուծոյ երկրպագեալ ծունր կրկնեցեն։

771 Եւ այսպէս լուսաւորեալ գսիրտս և գ֊
դիս ժողովրդոցն քարոզութեամբ, ապիՆ Աս֊
տուածութեանն յաղեալ համեմեալ․ Թողեալ
գպաշտօն ունայնութեան անուեաց ձեռագործ
կռոցն արարելոց, և ի պաշտօն դարձեալ մար֊
դասիրին Աստուծոյ։

772 Եւ յայնմ հետէ և անդր կանխէին
անձնակամ կամօք ի պահս և յաղօթս, և յեր֊
կիւղ և ի սէր. և յունկնդրութիւն Աստուծոյ
վարդապետութեանն փութային։

773 Արդ՝ իբրև ժողովեալք միահա֊
մուռ ի պաշտօնարան տեղւոյն յարկի տանն Աս֊
տուծոյ կային՝ խօսել սկսաւ երանելին Գրիգո֊
րիոս և ասէ. «Դիք ծունր ամենեքեան, զի ա֊
րասցէ Տէր բժշկութիւն հարուածոցդ»։ Եւ եղեալ
ծունր ամենեցուն առ Աստուած, և երանելւոյն
Գրիգորի մեծաւ աղօթիւք և պաղատանօք խնն֊
դրեալ ուժգին ճգնութեամբ և արտասուօք վասն
թագաւորին բժշկութեան։ Եւ Թագաւորն մինչ
դեռ կայր ի տեսլի կերպարանաց խոզի ընդ ժո֊
ղովրդեանն՝ յանկարծակի հարեալ ղղողման, և
գխոզրին խողի արտաքոյ մարմնոյն իւրոյ ի բաց
ընկենոյր, ժանդատեսիլ ժանեօքն և կնճթադեմ

There they set up the sign of the saving cross, that everyone might come to that spot in order to bow the knee² and worship God, the almighty creator.

771.   In this way he illuminated the hearts and souls of the people by his preaching, seasoning them with divine salt. They abandoned the vain worship of useless idols made by hand and turned to worship the benevolent God.

772.   After this they willingly set themselves to fasting and prayer, and devoted themselves to fear and love and attention to God's teaching.

773.   Now, when they had all gathered together in the place of worship of the house of God, blessed Gregory began to speak, saying: "Bend the knee, everyone, that the Lord may effect the healing of your torments." They all bent the knee to God, and blessed Gregory with fervent prayers and supplications tearfully implored healing for the king. And the king, while he was standing among the people with the appearance of a pig, suddenly trembled and threw off from his body the pig-like skin with its tusk-like teeth and snout-like face,

երեսօքն հանդերձ. խոզանացեալ մազովն թաւու֊
թեամբ գխորխացեալ կաշին ի բաց ընկենոյր։
Եւ դչմք երեսագն դարձան յիւր իսկ կերպարան֊
սըն, և մարմինն փափկացեալ մատաղացեալ լի֊
նէր իբրև գաւօրեայ մանկան ծնելոյ, և ողջան֊
դամ մարմնովքն ամենևին բժշկեցաւ։

774 Սոյնպէս և ամենայն մարդիկն, որ էին
բագմութիւնք կուտեալք՝ յիւրաքանչիւր ախտից
թօթափեալք. ումանք բորոտք, և ումանք անդա֊
մալոյծք և գոսացեալք, և Չրգողեալք որովայ֊
նիւք, և դիւահարք, և գռնճացեալք, և պատա֊
գրոսք։ Եւ այսպէս բացեալ չնորհագն մարդա֊
սիրին Քրիստոսի գիւր ամենակար բժշկարանն՝
բժշկել գամենեսին ի ձեռն Գրիգորի, ախտա֊
ցեալքն թօթափեին յիւրաքանչիւր հիւանդու֊
թեանց։ Սոյնպէս և բացեալ լինէր ալքիւր գիտու֊
թեանն Քրիստոսի, գլսելիս ամենեցուն ընուլ ձշ֊
մարտապատումվարդապետութեամբն Աստուծոյ։

775 «Անդ էր այնուհետև սրտալիր ուրա֊
խութիւն, և ակնավայել տեսիլ հայեցելոցն։
Քանգի երկիր, որ և համբաւուցն անգամ օտար
էր կողմանցն այնոցիկ, յորում ամենայն աս֊
տուածագործ սքանչելութիւնքն գործեցան՝ առ
ժամայն վաղվաղակի իրացն եղելոյ խելամուտ
լինէր. ոչ միայն առ ժամանական պաշտելոցն,
այլ և յառաջակարգ յաւիտեանցն և յապա եկե֊
լոցն, և սկզբանն և կատարածի, և ամենայն աս֊

and he cast off the skin with its pig-like hair. His face returned to its own form and his body became soft and young like that of a newly born infant; he was completely healed in all his limbs.[1]

774. In similar fashion all the people who were gathered in great numbers were cured of each one's affliction: some had been lepers, some paralytic, crippled, hydropic, possesed, suffering from worms or gout. Thus Christ in his mercy opened his all-powerful healing grace, and healed all through Gregory; those afflicted were cured of each disease. So also was the source of knowledge of Christ opened and it filled the ears of all with the true teaching of God.[1]

775. Then was there heartfelt rejoicing and a joyful visage on the onlookers. For the land, which until then had been ignorant of reports of those regions where all the divine miracles had been worked, now suddenly was informed of what had occurred—not only of what had recently been done, but also of the earlier messages and what later came about, of the beginning and the end, and of all

տուածատուր աւանդութեանցն։

776 Իսկ իբրև դշապի առեալ դիրացն հաս
տատութեան՝ համարձակագոյն և առաւելագոյն
դաշակերտութիւն նորագիւտ վարդապետու
թեանն խմբէին ուսուցանել, թեթև և պատրաս
տական քարոզութեանն անզէտ մարդկանն յո
րինել։ Որոց և ինքեանք իսկ ի կողմանց կող
մանց և ի գաւառաց գաւառաց Հայաստան աշ
խարհին՝ յորդեալք և դրդեալք հասանէին ի բա
ցեալ աղբիւրն չնորհաց գիտութեանն Քրիստո
սի։ Թանգի յԱյրարատեան գաւառին, ի Թագա
ւորանիստ կայեանսն, բղխեցին Հայոց տանն
Թորգոմայ չնորհք քարոզութեան Աւետարանին
պատուիրանացն Աստուծոյ»։

777 Առնոյր այնուհետև խորհուրդ հա
ւանութեան ընդ Թագաւորին և ընդ իշխանսն,
նախարարօքն և գօրօքն հանդերձ՝ վասն խաղա
ղութեան հասարակաց, քակել, կործանել, բառ
նալ զգայթակղութիւնսն ի միջոյ, ի բաց կո
լուսանել. զի մի՛ ումեք լիցի խէթ և խութ այ
նուհետև ընդ ուս անկանել և խափան առնել՝
ելանել յազատութիւնն վերին։ Այլ զի քաջալե
րեալք ամենեքեան հասանիցեն ի բարեացն կա
տարումն, ի նշանակեալ նպատակն երանելուին
Պաւղոսի, թէ «Միաբան հասցուք ի չափ հասա
կին Քրիստոսի», որոյ ագատութիւնն յերկինս
է. ակն ունել փրկչին մեծին Աստուծոյ, և պար

the divine traditions.

776.   When they had been informed of the exactness
of these things they were all the more willing and
anxious to learn and study the new doctrine, and as
ignorant men to be instructed and edified in this
preaching. They came from every part and region of
Armenia; in great numbers they excitedly arrived at
the opened source of the grace of knowledge of Christ.
For in the province of Ayrarat, at the royal residence,
there flowed forth for the Armenian house of Tʻorgom[1] the grace of the preaching of the gospel of God's
commandments.[2]

[Chapter 10.   The pagan shrines are overthrown]

777.   He then took counsel with the king and the
nobles, the princes and the army, concerning a common peace: they agreed to overthrow, destroy and
extiripate the scandals, to suppress them entirely lest
there be thenceforth an obstacle to anyone or a
stumbling block, preventing him from attaining celestial freedom; and that all might be strengthened and
attain perfect blessing, the goal indicated by blessed
Paul: "That in unity[1] we may attain the measure of
the stature of Christ [Eph. 4.13]," whose freedom is
in heaven, (whence) we look for the great Savior, God
[cf. Phil. 3.20],

ծանք ի խաչն, և գովութիւն ի փառս Աստուծոյ։

778 Իսկ անդէն վաղվաղակի թագաւորն ինքնիշխան հրամանաւ, և ամենեցուն հաւանութեամբ, գործ ի ձեռն տայր երանելւոյն Գրի-
գորի, զի գյառաջագոյն գհայրենական ճնամեացն
նախնեացն և զիւր կարծեալ աստուածն չաս-
տուածս անուանեալ՝ անյիշատակ առնել, ջնջել
ի միջոյ, Ապա ինքն իսկ Թագաւորն խաղայր
գնայր ամենայն գորօքն հանդերձ ի Վաղարշապատ քաղաքէ՝ երթալ յԱրտաշատ քաղաք, աւե-
րել անդ գբագինսն Անահատական դիցն, և որ
յերագամոյն տեղիսն անուանեալ կայր։ Նախ
դիպեալ ի ճանապարհի երագացոյց երագարան
պաշտամ(ան) Տրի դից, դպրի գիտութեան քրմաց,
անուանեալ Դիւան գրչի Որմզդի, ուսման ճար-
տարութեան մեհեան. Նախ ի նա ձեռն արկեալ՝
քակեալ այրեալ աւերեալ քանդեցին։

779 Ուր և երևեալ կերպարանեալ դիւացն
ի նմանութիւն առն և ձիոյ բազմութեան, կազմութեան գնդի և հետևակագորու, մկնդաւորք և
ուռնաւորք, առաջի ընթացեալք ի կերպարանս
մարդկան նմանութեան, նիզակօք և նշանօք, ի
դէն և ի գարդ վառեալք, մեծաւ գոչմամբ գա-
ղաղակ հարեալ՝ փախստեայք յԱնահատական մեհեանն անկանէին, ուստի ընդ հատալսն մարտ
եղեալ կռուէին. Նետս անոյժս քարավէժս թան-
ձրատարափս ի վերուստ ի շինուածոցն ի խո-

and our boast is in the cross and our joy in the glory of God.

778. Then straightway the king by sovereign edict, with the agreement of all, entrusted blessed Gregory with the task of obliterating and extirpating the former ancestral deities of his forefathers, falsely called gods.[1] Then the king in person hastened with all his army from the city of Vaḷarshapat and came to the city of Artashat in order to destroy the altars of the deity Anahit[2] there, and those which were at the place called Erazamoyn.[3] On the road he first came across the shrine of the god Tir,[4] the interpreter of dreams,[5] the scribe of pagan learning, who was called the secretary[6] of Ormizd,[7] a temple of learned instruction. (Here) first they set to work, and destroyed, burnt, ruined and razed it.

779. And here the demons took visible form[1] in the shape of a multitude of cavalry and a force of infantry, bearing lances and javelins, rushing forward like men armed with spears and standards. With a great shout they raised a cry and fled, rushing into the temple of Anahit whence they attacked those who had arrived. From the building they showered down on the men below harmless arrows and a dense rain of missiles,

նարՀ զմարդկան ցնդէին. զորս և սակաւ մի
զարհուրեցուցեալ, գնորանաւատ մարդիկն։ Իսկ
սուրբն Գրիգոր իբրև տեսեալ գայն՝ զնշան տէրունական խաչին առնոյր և դիմէր ի դուռն մե-
Հենին. և ամենայն շինուածք մեՀենին ի Հիմանց դղրդեալ տապալեցան. և լուցեալ յան-
կարծօրէն փայտակերան ՀրդեՀեցաւ ի տերունական նշանին զօրութենէ, և ծուխն ծառա-
ցեալ մինչև յամպս Հասանէր։

780 Եւ ամենայն դևքն ի փախուստ դար-
ձեալ՝ առաջի մարդկանն երևեցան, գոձիս զգը-
խով արկեալ, և գՃակատ Հարեալ, և գՃիչ բար-
ձեալ՝ մեծագոչ լալեօք ասէին, թէ «Վա՜յ մեզ,
վա՜յ մեզ, վա՜յ մեզ, զի յամենայն երկրէ փախստական արար զմեզ Յիսուս որդին Մարեմու,
դատերն մարդկան. և ասի հս ի ձեռն կապե-
լոյս և մեռելոյս եՀաս մեզ փախստական լինել։
Արդ՝ յ՞ոդիմեալ փախիցուք, զի փառք նորա լցին
զտիեզերս։ Այլ երթամք մեք ի բնակիչս լերինն
Կաւկասու, ի կողմանս Հիւսիսոյ. թերևս անդ
Հնար լիցի և ապրել մարթասցուք։ Զի առանց
Հանգստեան գօղ կոչեալ՝ անջատ զմեզ ի բնա-
կութենէ մարդկան՝ կատարէլ զգանկութիւն կամաց մերոց նոքօք»։

781 Եւ զայս ասացեալ առաջի ամենեցուն.
զի մարդիկն որ լուան՝ առաւել հս Հաստատեցան ի Հաւատս ամենեքին. իսկ սկզբունդ դի-

but they scarcely frightened the men with newly-found faith. But saint Gregory, when he saw this, made the sign of the Lord's cross[2] and ran to the door of the temple. Then the whole edifice of the temple shook from its foundations and collapsed. Suddenly catching fire the wooden construction[3] burned by the power of the Lord's sign, and the smoke rose up to the clouds.

780. Then all the demons turned in flight before the people, tearing their clothes at the collar and striking their foreheads [cf. I Macc. 5.14]. Raising a scream they loudly wept, saying: "Woe to us, woe to us, woe to us. For Jesus the Son of Mary, daughter of men, has made us flee from the whole land. And here too through this imprisoned and dead man he has forced us to flee. But whither shall we flee, for his glory has filled the universe [cf. Is. 6.3]? We shall go to the inhabitants of the Caucasus mountains, to the Northern regions; perhaps there we shall be able to survive. For (he has made us) ceaselessly beat the air and has separated us from the habitation of men, (preventing) us from accomplishing our desires through them."[1]

781. This they said in front of all, but the men who heard were all even more confirmed in the faith. Then the black swarm

լացն աներևոյթք եղեալ, չքոտեալք ի տեղւոյն
իբրև գձուխ պակասեցան։ Իսկ մարդկանն հասելոց անդէն քանդեալ գչիմունս նմացեալս աւե-
րէին, և զգանձն մթերեալս՝ աղքատաց, տա-
ռապելոց և չքաւորաց մասն հանէին։ Եւ զգաս-
տակերասն և գպասաւորսն քրմօքն հանդերձ և
նոցին գեանովքն և սահմանօքն ի ծառայութիւն
նուիրեցին եկեղեցլոյ սպասաւորութեան։

782 Եւ առ հասարակ ամենեցուն սերմանեալ գասուածապաշտութեան գբանն, և գամենեսեան ի Տեառնն հանապարհի կացուցանէր՝
գիտուն լինել պատուիրանաց արարչութեանն։
Եւ յամենայն քաղաքս Հայոց և ի գեօղս և յաւանս և յագարակս երևեցուցանէր գտեղիս տան
Աստուծոյ։ Բայց ոչ առնէր յայտ գչիմմարկու-
թեանն գհետ, և ոչ սեղան ուրեք ուղղեալ յանուն Աստուծոյ, գի չունէր գպատիւ քահանայութեան. այլ լոկ պարսպէր քաղաքորմով գտեղիսն, և կանգնէր գնշան տերունական խաչին։
Նոյնպէս և յելս և ի մուտս հանապարհաց և ի
փողոցս և ի հրապարակս և ի հանապարհակիցս
պահ և ապաւէն գերկրպագեան յամենեցունց
գնոյն նշան կանգնէր։

783 «Աւնոյր այնուհետև գԱրշակունեաց
տոհմի որեարն ի վարժս վարդապետութեան
պարապեցուցեալ. որոց առաջնոյն Տրդատ անուն,
որ և Թագաւորն իսկ էր, ամենայն տամբ իւ-

of demons disappeared and were lost from that place like smoke. But the people who had come razed the remaining foundations, and distributed the accumulated treasures to the poor, the suffering and the needy. And they devoted to the church's service the (temple's) property and servants with the pagan priests and their lands and territories.[1]

782.   He sowed the word of true piety among them all and set everyone on the Lord's path, informing them of the Creator's commands. In all the cities of Armenia, and the villages and hamlets and estates he indicated sites for the house of God. But he did not draw the foundation or erect an altar anywhere to the name of God, because he did not possess the rank of priesthood. But he simply encircled the places with a wall and set up the sign of the Lord's cross. He similarly set up the same sign worshipped by all as a guard and refuge at the ends and beginnings of roads, in the streets, and at squares and intersections.[1]

783.   Then he took the men of the Arsacid family and instructed them in the (Christian) doctrine. Of these the foremost was Trdat, who was the king, with all his household.

բով։ Նոյնպէս և գամենայն ոգի Ջանայր յերիւ֊
րել հասուցանել ի գիտութիւն ճշմարտութեան»։
«Եւ յորժամ այնպէս լի առնէր ընդ ամենայն
տեղիս գաւըբ Աւետարանն Տեառն, և ամենեւ֊
ցուն զգուշացուցեալ անմեղութեամբ գձանա֊
պարհս կենաց վարելոյ՝ ապա ամենեցուն գայն
դնէր ի մտի, զի «տեառն Աստուծոյ իւրեանց
միայն երկիր պագցեն, և նմա միայն ապաս
տարցին։»

784   Եւ ապա յանձն արարեալ գնոսա
ամենապահ շնորհացն Աստուծոյ, և ինքն առեալ
գԹագաւորն՝ խաղայր գնացեալ երթայր, գի և
յայլ կողմանս ամենայն սահմանացն Հայաստան
աշխարհին սերմանեսցեն գբանն կենաց։ Եւ եր֊
թայր հասանէր ի Դարանաղեաց գաւառն, գի և
անդ գանուանելոցն գոտւո աստուածոցն գբա֊
գինսան կործանեսցեն, որ էր ի գեօղն Թորդան,
մեհեան անուանեալ սպիտակափառ դիցն Բար֊
շամինայ։ նախ դնա կործանէին, և գպատկեր
նորին փշրէին. և գգանձն ամենայն, գոսկւոյն
և գարծաթոյն , աւար հարկանէին և գայն աղ֊
քատաց բաժանեալ բաշխէին։ Եւ գգեօղն ամե֊
նայն դաստակերտօքն հանդերձ և սահմանօքն
յանուն եկեղեցւոյն նուիրէին, և գամենափրկիչ
նշանին օրինակ և անդ կանգնէին։

785 «Իսկ երանելւոյն վաղվաղակի գաւե֊
տարանական արուեստն ի մէջ առեալ, ձեռն

Similarly he attempted to direct and establish every soul in the knowledge of the truth. And when he had thus filled every place with the Lord's gospel and had warned everyone to walk the paths of life in innocence, then he persuaded them all to worship only the Lord their God and to serve him alone [cf. Matt. 4.10; Lk. 4.8].[1]

784. Then he entrusted them to the all-protecting grace of God, while he himself, taking the king, hastened to the other regions of the whole territory of Armenia that they might there sow the word of life. He came to the province of Daranaḷik' in order to destroy the altars of those falsely called gods, where in the village of T'ordan[1] there was a famous temple of the glorious god Barshamin.[2] First they destroyed this and smashed his image; they plundered all the treasures, both of gold and silver, and distributed them to the poor. And the whole village with its properties and territories they devoted to the name of the church. And here too they set up a copy of the all-saving sign.[3]

785. Then the saint straightway introduced his evangelical skill;

արկեալ զգալառան, հանդերձ միամիտ սատա-
րութեամբ թագաւորին՝ գերէր գամենեսեան ի
հայրենեացն ալանդելոց ի սատանայապաշտ դի-
ւական ի սպասաւորութենէն ի ճնագանդութիւն
ծառայութեան Քրիստոսի մատուցանէր։ Եւ յորժամ ի նոսա զբանն կենաց սերմանեալ, և գամենեսեան յաստուածպաշտութիւն կրթեալ, որ
և յայոնի իսկ քնակցաց գալառին նշանք մեծամեծք երևեալ, կերպակերպ նմանութեամբք դիւացն փախստական լինելով անկանէին ի կոդ-
մանս» Ախղտեաց. և իբրև զնոսա եւ հատատէր՝
ապա երթեալ հասանէր յամուր տեղին անուանեալ Անի, ի Թագաւորաբնակ կայեանսն հան-
գատոցաց գերեզմանաց Թագաւորացն Հայոց։ Եւ
անդ կործանեցին զբագինն Զևս դիցն Արամազդայ, հօրն անուանեալ դիցն ամենայնի։ Եւ
անդ կանգնեալ գուերունական նշանն, և գալանն
ամրականաւն հանդերձ ի ծառայութիւն եկեղեցւոյն նուիրէին։

786 Եւ ապա յետ այսորիկ անդէն ի սահ-
մանակից գալառն Եկեղեաց ելանէր։ Եւ անդ
երևեալ դիւացն ի մեծ և ի բուն մեհենացն
Հայոց Թագաւորացն, ի տեղիս պաշտամանցն,
յԱնահական մեհենին, յերեզն աւանի. ուր ի
նմանութիւն վահանաւոր գորու ժողովեալ դիւացն մարանչէին, և մեծագոչ բարբառով գե-
րինա ճնչեցուցանէին։ Որբ փախստականք եղեալք,

he took over the province, and with the devoted assistance of the king brought all from their traditional customs and from the service of Satan and of demons to obedient servitude to Christ. While he was sowing the word of life among them and instructing them all in true piety, there appeared to the inhabitants of the province tremendous miracles: taking various forms the demons fled to the regions of[1] Khaḷtik'.[2] When he had further confirmed these people, then he went to the fortified site of renowned Ani,[3] the site of the royal burial ground of the Armenian kings. There they destroyed the altar of the god Zeus-Aramazd, called father of all the gods.[4] And there they set up the Lord's sign, and the town with its fortress they devoted to the service of the church.

786.   After this he came to the neighboring province of Ekeḷeats'.[1] Here the demons appeared in the places of worship of the most important shrines of the Armenian kings, in the temple of Anahit in the town of Erēz.[2] The demons gathered together and gave battle in the form of an army carrying shields;[3] with a tremendous shout they made the mountains echo. They were put to flight,

և ընդ փախչեին նոցա կործանեալ բարձրաբերձ
պարիսպքն հարթեցան։ Եւ որբք դիմեալ հասեալ
էին զգաստացեալ գորօքն, սուրբն Գրիգոր թագաւորաւն հանդերձ, փշրէին դրոսկի պատկերն
Անահտական կանացի դիցն. և ամենեին գտեղին
քանդեալ վատնէին, և դոսկին և դարձաքն աւար
առեալ։ Եւ անտի ընդ դետն Գայլ յայնկոյս ան-
ցանէին, և քանդէին գնանէական մեհեանն դըս-
տերն Արամազդայ ի Թիւն յաւանի։ Եւ զգանձս
երկիցոսն մեհենացն աւարեալ ժողովեալ՝ ի
նուէր սպասոց սուրբ եկեղեցւոյն Աստուծոյ
թողուին տեղեօքն հանդերձ։

787   Եւ այսպէս ի բազում տեղեաց
բանային զգայթակղեցուցիչան անմոունչա, գճու-
լեալն, կոփեալան կոփեալան, քանդակեալան, ան-
պիտանն, անօգուտն, վատսակարսն, արաբեալն
անմոութեամբ ցնորելոց մարդկան, դարձեալ
արթի մոօք ի հալատան հատատեալք։ «Արքայն
մեծասատ իշխանութեամբ տայր հրաման՝ սա-
տանայակուր և դիւամոլ ազգացն կողմանցն այնո-
ցիկ՝ թափել և դերձանել յունայնավար հնացելոցն
մնոտապգործ պաշտամանցն, և հնագանդ լինել
ամենահեշտ լծոյ ծառայութեանն Քրիստոսի»։

788 «Եւ յորժամ անդ ես դայս արաբեալ
հաւասարութեամբ ամենեցուն՝ առ հասարակ
լցեալ դպիտոյս քարողութեանն»՝ ոչ ինչ ապաստան լինէր յաճ և ի սատ թագաւորին՝ հաւա-

but as they fled the high walls collapsed and were flattened. Those who had arrived, saint Gregory, the king and the pious army, broke into pieces the golden image of the female deity Anahit, and they completely destroyed and pillaged the place, seizing the gold and silver. From there they crossed over the river Gayl[4] and destroyed the temple of Nanē, the daughter of Aramazd,[5] in the town of T'il.[6] They collected the plundered treasure of both temples and devoted it with the lands to the servants of the holy church of God.

787.   In this way from many places they removed the silent, cast, hammered, beaten, sculpted, useless, profitless, and harmful scandals that were constructed by the witlessness of stupid men;[1] and they were sincerely converted and confirmed in the faith. The king with his royal power gave a command to the people of those regions, who were possessed by Satan and the demons, to reject and free themselves from these useless, outworn and vain cults and to become obedient to the sweet yoke [cf. Matt. 11.30] of servitude to Christ.

788.   While he was so acting there with the support of all, he fulfilled all things necessary for preaching the gospel.[1] He did not at all rely on the awe and authority of the king

նեցուցանելոյ գամենեսին, և ոչ լոկ բանիւք մի‐
այն, այլ և նշանօք և արուեստիւք և ազգի ազ‐
գի բժշկութեամբք փառաւոր լինէր սուրբն անունն
Քրիստոսի։ Այս ամենայն գործեցաւ կամօք մար‐
դասիրին Աստուծոյ ի ձեռն Գրիգորի։ Եւ յամե‐
նայն տեղիս հասեալ ինքնին թագաւորն լինէր
քարոզ, խոստովանելով գիւր գամբարշտութիւնն.
և պատմէր գամենայն արաբեալն Աստուծոյ
գաբանչելիան որ անցին ընդ նա, և գողորմու‐
թիւն բժշկութեանն, և գայն ցուցանէր բարձ‐
րաձայն աղաղակաւ, յայտ յանդիման առաջի
ամենեցուն։

789 Ապա փութացեալ հասանէր ի գաւառն
Դերջան, զի և անդ յառաջացի ընուլ գառաբե‐
լական քարոզութեանն գառուեստ մշակութեանն
երկովք, և գերծուցանել գնոսա ի գարշելի «գիւ‐
ցական սատանայակեր բարուցն ճիւաղութենէ,
գխոժժողուժ կողմանան աշակերտելով, գխոշ‐
րագոյն և գխեցքեկագոյն բարս հեթանոսու‐
թեան շրջել ի գգաստութիւն ատուածուսոյց
իմաստութեանն. և ձանօթս աւետարանական
աւետեացն, յարդարեալս ընդելս կացուցա‐
նէր»։

790 Գայր հասանէր ի Մրհական մեհեանն
անուանեալ որդւոյն Արամագգայ, ի գիւղն գոր
Բագայառիճն կոչեն ըստ պարթևարէն լեզուին։
Եւ գայն ի հիմանց քրեալ խլէին, և գգանձան

in order to persuade everyone; nor merely by words but also by signs and miracles and various kinds of healings the holy name of Christ was made glorious. All this was done by the will of benevolent God through Gregory. The king himself came to every place and acted as a preacher, confessing his own impieties and telling of all the miracles done by God to him, and of the mercy of his healing. These things he revealed with a loud voice and clearly in the presence of all.[2]

789. Then he hastened to the province of Derjan[1] in order to spread there also the message of the apostolic preaching by works of labor, and to free them from the beastliness of their abominable and demon-possessed way of life. He instructed those barbarous regions in order to change their gross and rough heathen habits to the sobriety of the divinely taught wisdom, and to inform them of the gospel's message and make them familiar with it.[2]

790. He came to the temple of Mihr,[1] called the son of Aramazd, to the village called Bagayariĉh[2] in the Parthian tongue. This he destroyed down to its foundations;

մթերեալս աւար հարկանէին և ազգատաց բաշ-
խէին, և գտեղիսն նուիրէին եկեղեցւոյ. և զընա-
կիչս աշխարհին հաստատէր ի գիտութիւն ճշշ-
մարտութեան: Եւ յայնմհետէ փոյթ ի վերայ
ունէր «դարընթերակաց արքունիան հանդերձ
մեծամեծ աւապանունիւ և ամենայն ագատա-
գունդ բանակաւն ատուածեղէն իմաստութեամբն վարդապետել»:

791 Իսկ Թագաւորն Տրդատիոս հանդերձ միաբանութեամբ կնաւ իւրով Աշխէն տիկնաւ, և քերբ իւրով Խոսրովիդխտով, հրաման
ետ ի ժողով կոչել միաբանութեամբ ամենայն
գործաց իւրոց: Եւ վաղվաղակի հասանէին ի ժա-
մադիրն յամենայն կողմանց ըստ հրամանին՝
յԱյրարատ գաւառն ի Վաղարշապատ քաղաք:
Քանզի և Թագաւորն չու արարեալ անդր հասանէր: Եւ կուտեցան առ հասարակ գործն ամենայն, և մեծամեծք և կուսակալք, գաւառակալք,
պատուաւորք, պատուականք, գորավարք, պետք
և իշխանք, նախարարք և ապատք, դատաւորք և
գործագլուխք, և հասեալ կային առաջի Թագաւորին:

792 Խորհուրդ ի մէջ առնոյր Թագաւորն
ընդ ամենեսին, փութալ հասանել՝ բարեաց գործոց ժառանգաւոր լինել: «Եկայք, ասէ, ճեպես-
ցուք դայս առաջնորդ կենաց մերոց տուեալ մեզ
յԱստուծոյ զԳրիգորդ հովիւ կացուցանել, դի

he plundered its accumulated treasures and distributed them among the poor, and he devoted the lands to the church. The inhabitants of the land he confirmed in the knowledge of the truth. Then he took pains to instruct in the divine wisdom the accompanying courtiers with the great magnates and all the noble army.[3]

[Chapter 11. Gregory is consecrated at Caesarea]

791. Then king Tiridates, with his wife, queen Ashkhên, and his sister Khosrovidukht, ordered a gathering to be summoned of all his army. And straightway from every region, following his command, they came to the rendezvous at the city of Vaḷarshapat in the province of Ayrarat; the king also journeyed thither. The whole army came together, and the magnates and prefects, provincial governors, dignitaries and notables, leaders and nobles, princes and freemen, judges and officers,[1] and they mustered before the king.

792. The king held a council with them all, urging them to become heirs to good works: "Come," he said, "let us hurry to make as our pastor[1] Gregory, this guide of our lives given us by God, so that

լուսաւորեցէ զմեզ մկրտութեամբ և նորոգեց-
ցէ օրէնսուսոյց խորհրդովն աբարշին մերոյ Աստուծոյ»:

793 Իսկ Գրիգոր ոչ առնոյր զայս յանձն,
առնուլ զմեծ պատիւ քահանայապետութեանն.
ասէ. «Ոչ կարեմ հանդարտել բաւել վասն ան-
չափակալ բարձրութեանն գործել. զի անպատում
է այս պատիւ քրիստոսատուր փառացն առաջնորդութեան, միշնորդ կալ ընդ Աստուած և ընդ
մարդիկ. այլ գարժանին խնդրեալ գացեն»:

794 Իսկ անդէն տեսիլ սքանչելի յԱստուծոյ երևեալ թագաւորին՝ տեսանէր գրեշտակ
Աստուծոյ, զի խօսէր ընդ նմա և ասէր, թէ
«Պարտ է ձեզ գԳրիգորդ վիճակեցուցանել առանց
յապաղելոյ ի քահանայապետութիւն, զի լուսաւորեցէ զձեզ մկրտութեամբ»: Նոյնպէս երե-
ւեալ և Գրիգորի տեսիլ հրեշտակի Աստուծոյ,
զի մի իշխեսցէ ինչ պնդել յամառել վասն այնր,
«զի ի Քրիստոսէ է այդ հրամայեալ, ասէ, քեզ»:
Իսկ նա հաւանեալ վաղվաղակի բարբառեալ ասէր,
թէ «Կամք Աստուծոյ կատարեսցին»:

795   Յայնժամ Թագաւորն վաղվաղակի փութով և երկիւղիւ և մեծաւ խնդութեամբ
հոգացեալ, գումարեաց զզխսալուրս նախարարացն և զկուսակալս աշխարհացն. առաջին՝ իշխանն Անգեղ տան, երկրորդ՝ իշխանն Աղձնեաց,
որ է բդեաշխն մեծ. երրորդ՝ իշխանն մարդպե-

he can illuminate us with baptism and as a teacher
of the law [cf. Acts 5.34][2] renew us by the sacrament
of God our creator."

793.   But Gregory would not agree to accept the
honor of the high priesthood, saying: "I am unable to
undertake this because of its immeasurable height.
For this honor of the glory given by Christ of being
guide and intermediary between God and men is ineffable [cf. I Tim. 2.5]. But let them seek and find one
who is worthy."

794.   However, there then appeared a wonderful vision from God to the king; he saw the angel of God
speaking to him and saying: "You must without delay
have Gregory ordained to the high priesthood, so that
he may illuminate you by baptism." Similarly the vision of God's angel appeared to Gregory to prevent
him from persisting in this matter: "For this," he said,
"has been commanded you by Christ." Then he was
convinced,[1] and straightway said: "May God's will be
accomplished [cf. Acts 21.14]."

795.   Then the king immediately, in haste and fear
and great joy, gathered the leading princes and governors of the land.[1] The first was the prince of the house
of Angl;[2] the second the prince of Aḷdznikʻ,[3] who was
the great *bdeashkh*;[4] the third the prince

տութեան իշխանութեանն, չորրորդ՝ իշխանն Թա-
գակապ իշխանութեան ասպետութեանն, հինգ-
երորդ՝ իշխանն սպարապետութեան, գորավաք
Հայոց աշխարհին. վեցերորդ՝ իշխանն Կորդով-
տաց աշխարհին, եօթներորդ՝ իշխանն ծոփաց
աշխարհին. ութերորդ՝ իշխանն Գուգարացւոց
աշխարհին, որ միւս անուանեալ բդեաշխն. ին-
ներորդ՝ իշխանն Ռշտունեաց աշխարհին. տաս-
ներորդ՝ իշխանն Մոկաց աշխարհին. մետասան-
երորդ՝ իշխանն Սիւնեաց աշխարհին. երկոտա-
սաներորդ՝ իշխանն Ծաւդէից աշխարհին. երեք-
տասաներորդ՝ իշխանն Ուտիացւոց աշխարհին.
չորեքտասաներորդ՝ իշխանն չահապ Զարաւանդ
և Հեր գաւառի. հնգետասաներորդ՝ իշխանն
մաղխազութեան տանն. վեշտասաներորդ՝ իշխանն Արծրունեաց։

796 Այս իշխանք են ընտիրք, կուսակալք,
կողմնակալք, հազարաւորք, բիւրաւորք ի մէջ Հայաստան աշխարհի տանն Թորգոմայ, գորս գումարեաց Թագաւորն Տրդատ և առաքեաց գնոսա
ի կողմանս Կապուտկացւոց, ի քաղաքն Կեսարացւոց, գոր ըստ հայերէն լեզուին Մաժաք կոչեն. գի տարեալ գԳիրգորն՝ քահանայապետ կա-
ցուսցեն իւրեանց աշխարհին. և հանդերձեցան
դէտ ակն ունել ճանապարհացն։ Եւ հրամայեաց
հրովարտակ գրել օրինակ գայս. —

of the princedom of *Mardpet-dom*;[5] the fourth the
prince of the crowning-rank, the *aspet*;[6] the fifth the
prince *sparapet*,[7] the general of the Armenian land;
the sixth the prince of the land of Korduk';[8] the seventh the prince of the land of Tsop'k';[9] the eighth the
prince of the land of Gugark',[10] called *the other bdeashkh*;[11] the ninth the prince of the land of the Rshtunik';[12] the tenth the prince of the land of Mokk';[13]
the eleventh the prince of the land of Siwnik';[14] the
twelfth the prince of the land of Tsawdēk';[15] the thirteenth the prince of the land of Uti;[16] the fourteenth
the prince prefect of the province of Zaravand and
Her;[17] the fifteenth the prince of the house of the
Maḷkhaz-dom;[18] the sixteenth the prince of the Artsrunik'.[19]

796.   These were the chosen princes, the prefects,
governors, generals and marshals in Armenia, the
house of T'orgom,[1] whom king Trdat gathered together and sent to the region of Cappadocia, to the
city of Caesarea, called in the Armenian tongue *Mazhak*,[2] in order to bring Gregory to be ordained high
priest for their country. So they made their preparations for the journey.[3] And (the king) commanded an
edict to be written as follows:

ՊԱՏՃԷՆ ՀՐՈՎԱՐՏԱԿԻՆ

797 «Ի վաղնջուց հետէ կորուսեալք, տգի
տութեամբ մեղացն պաշարեալք, մառախլա
պատք, միգապատք, ափշեալք, ոչ կարացեալ
հայել իմանալ նկատել, զարեգակն արդարու
թեան տեսանել. վասն այսորիկ խաւարեալք էաք,
ի մութ թաթաւեաք։ Իսկ յորժամ քաղցրութիւն
և մարդասիրութիւն արարչին մերոյ Աստուծոյ
երևեցաւ՝ խրատել և լուսաւորել զմեզ զարա
րածս իւր՝ ծագեաց զնշոյլ կենդանի լուսոյն
իւրոյ ի սիրտս մեր, և կենդանացոյց զմեռելու
թիւնս մեր, զիւր գուրբ զսիրելի գվկայս իւր
յայս կողմանս առաքելով։

798 «Որք եկեալ՝ մերում անմտութեանս
գիւրեանց քաջութեան նահատակութեան առա
քինութեան գնանդէսն ցուցին։ Իբրև զի Տէրն
գիտէր իսկ զնոցա քաջութիւնն թէ որպիսիք են.
այլ զի և մեզ անմտացս ուսուցցէ գիմաստու
թիւն, թէ որչափ սիրով սիրեցին սոքա զՏէրն
իւրեանց, վասն այսորիկ ընդ մարտին նոցա
առաքինութեանն՝ տէր Աստուած սքանցգործ այն
չափ արար զիւր աքանչելիս և մեզ սատիկ պա
տիժա պատուհասից՝ մինչև թագաւորիս մերում
լինել խող, և ընդ վայրագասուն գազանս արա
ծել։ Ապա ողորմեալ մեզ բարեխոսութեամբ ա
ղօթից վկայելոցս, ի ձեռն այլր վկայեցելոյդ Գրի

COPY OF THE EDICT

797. "From earliest times we were lost, enveloped in the ignorance of sin, wrapped in mist and fog [cf. Ez. 34.12], rendered stupid [cf. Mk. 8.17], unable to see, understand, or discern the sun of righteousness [cf. Mal. 4.2]; therefore we were blinded and immersed in darkness [cf. Is. 59.9]. But when the sweetness and benevolence of God our creator appeared [cf. Tit. 3.4] to admonish and illuminate us his creatures, he shot the rays of his living light [cf. Wis. 7.26] into our hearts and vivified our mortality by sending his holy and beloved martyrs to these regions.

798. "They came here and revealed to our foolishness their fortitude, bravery and virtue. The Lord indeed already knew how great was their fortitude, but in order to teach us foolish ones wisdom —with how great a love they loved their Lord—therefore through their virtuous struggle the Lord God wrought such amazing miracles and inflicted such severe punishments on us, so that our king even became a pig and pastured with the wild beasts. But then he had mercy on us at the intercession of these martyrs' prayers, and through the martyred Gregory

գործի կամ են ես եան գմեզ բ ժ շ կ ե աց։

799 «Քանգի և դա առաւել ես վկայ գտաւ, առաւել քան գառաւել նա հ ա տ ակ ե ա լ, վ ա ս ն այ-սորիկ յԱստուծոյ մեզ տուեալ առաջնորդ։ Եւ ի ձեռն դորա գ ն ա խ ն ա կ ա ն կ ա ր գ ս ս ո վ ո ր ո ւ թ ե ա ն ո ւ ն ա յ ն ո ւ թ ե ա ն, կ ր ա պ ա շ տ ո ւ թ ե ա ն հ ա յ ր ե ն ե ա ց ն, խ լ ե ա ց ե բ ա ր ձ ի մ ի ջ ո յ. և ո ւ ս ո յ ց ա մ ե ն ե ց ո ւ ն մ ե զ գ ի ւ ր գ վ կ ա յ ո ւ թ ի ւ ն ս ն և գ հ ր ա մ ա ն ս, բ ա տ ի ւ ր ո ց կ ա մ ա ց ն գ ն ա լ. մ ի ն չ և տ ա լ մ ե զ հ ր ա մ ա ն յ ա յ տ յ ա ն դ ի մ ա ն` գ գ ո յ ն ի ն ք ն գ Գ ր ի գ ո ր դ մ ե զ հ ո-վ ի ւ և տ ե ս ո ւ չ և վ ա ր դ ա պ ե տ ձ շ մ ա ր տ ա պ ա տ ո ւ մ կ ա ց ո ւ ց ա ն ե լ։

800 «Վասն այսորիկ և մեր ապատան ե-դ ե ա լ յ ո ղ ն ա կ ա ն ո ւ թ ի ւ ն ը ն դ ո ւ ն ե լ ո ւ թ ե ա ն ա ղ օ թ ի ց ձ ե ր ո ց և ս ր բ ո ւ թ ե ա ն դ, Զ ե ն ո դ ի ո ս ա ր բ ե պ ի ս կ ո-պ ո ս Կ ե ս ա ր ո ւ և ա մ ե ն ա յ ն ո ւ խ տ ք ա ն ա ն ա յ ո ւ-թ ե ա ն դ ս ր բ ո յ ե կ ե ղ ե ց ւ ո յ, ո ր ա յ դ ր է ք, մ ե ք յ ո-գ ո ր մ ո ւ թ ե ն է Տ ե ա ռ ն ա ղ օ թ ի ւ ք ձ ե ր ո վ ք ա ռ ց ո ւ ք ո ղ ջ ո յ ն, Տ ր դ ա տ ի ո ս թ ա գ ա ւ ո ր, ա մ ե ն ա յ ն գ ո ր ծ ք ե ր կ ր ի ս Հ ա յ ո ց մ ե ծ ա ց, և Ա շ խ ե ն տ ի կ ի ն, և օ ր ի-ո ր դ մ ե ծ Խ ո ս ր ո վ ի դ ո ւ խ տ։ Վ ա ս ն ա յ ս ո ր ի կ ա ռ ա-ք ե ց ա ք մ ե ք ա ռ ձ ե զ ա ր ս գ լ խ ա ւ ո ր ս` ի շ խ ա ն ս պ ա տ ո ւ ա կ ա ն ս դ ա շ խ ա ր հ ի ս մ ե ր ո յ մ ե ծ ի, գ ի պ ա տ-մ ե ս ց ե ն ձ ե զ գ ա մ ե ն ա յ ն ս ք ա ն չ ե լ ի ս Ա ս տ ո ւ ծ ո յ, ո ր ա ս տ յ ա յ ս մ ա շ խ ա ր հ ի ս գ ո ր ծ ե ց ա ւ ը ն դ մ ե զ։

801 «Եւ տ ո ւ ա ք մ ե ք ա ձ ե լ ա ռ ձ ե զ գ ո ւ ր բ խ ո ս տ ո վ ա ն ո ղ դ Ք ր ի ս տ ո ս ի գ Գ ր ի գ ո ր ի ո ս. և դ ա յ ս

healed us all.

799.   "Now because he was even more a martyr and an even greater champion,[1] therefore he has been given us by God as a leader. Through him (God) has destroyed and abolished our former vain habits of worshiping ancestral idols, and he has taught us all his testimonies and commandments for us to follow his will. He has even given us a clear command to appoint this same Gregory as our shepherd and overseer[2] and truthful teacher.

800.   "Therefore, trusting in the support of your acceptable and holy prayers, O Leontius[1] Archbishop of Caesarea and all the priestly clergy of your holy church there, by God's mercy and through your prayers we send you greetings—I king Tiridates with all the army of Greater Armenia, and queen Ashkhēn and princess Khosrovidukht. Therefore we have sent to you the principal men, the honorable nobles of our great country, to inform you of all God's miracles which have been done amongst us in this land.

801.   "And we have had sent to you the holy confessor of Christ, Gregory. And

հրովարտակ մեր առ ձեզ գրեցաք, զի ըստ տու-
չութեան ալանդութեան հոգևոր աստուածատուր շնորհին Քրիստոսի՝ մեզ զԳրիգորդ տեսուչ
և վարդապետ առաջնորդութեան աստուածա-
գնաց ճանապարհացն, և հովիւ և քժիշկ կացուս-
ջիք, որպէս և մեզ յԱստուծոյ հրամայեցաւ։ Եւ
աղօթս արասջիք, զի զմեզ արժանիս արասցէ
Աստուած իւրոյ ողորմութեանն, առողջութեամբ
գնալ ի ճանապարհս նորա, և ձեր սէրն և ողջոյն եկեալ հանգիցէ առ մեզ»։ Եւ պատճէն հրո-
վարտակին դայս օրինակ գրեցաւ։

    802   Եւ կազմեցան պատրաստեցան,
առին ընդ իւրեանս պատարագս՝ ոսկի և արծաթ, ձիս և ջորիս և հանդերձս գունակ գու-
նակս ի զարդ և ի սպաս պատուական տեղեացն
սրբոց տանցն Աստուծոյ՝ ուր առաքեալքն էին,
և ամենայն եկեղեցեացն առնէին պատրաստութիւն պատարագաց՝ ընդ որ էին անցանելոց։

    803 Եւ հանէին զԳրիգոր յոսկիապատ կառ-
սըն արքունականս՝ սպիտակաձիգ ջորւոչն։ Եւ
ամենայն իշխանքն գումարեալք ընդ նմա կա-
ռոք և երիվարոք, զօրոք, նշանակոք, իւրաքանչիւր գնդաւ խաղացին գնացին յԱյրարատեան
գաւառն, ի Վաղարշապատ քաղաքէ. և հասեալ
ի սահմանս Յունաց՝ բազում պատիս կազմութեան հիւրամեծարութեան գտանէին ի քաղաքաց քաղաքաց։ Եւ բազում խնդութիւնս և կայ-

we have written this edict[1] to you that you may ordain
for us Gregory as overseer and teacher and leader in
God's paths and shepherd and doctor, according to
the providential tradition of the spiritual and divine
grace of Christ, just as has been commanded us by
God. And so pray that God may make us worthy of
his mercy and that we may walk rightously in his
paths, and that your love and greeting may give us
peace."[2] In such terms was the copy of the edict
written.

802.   So they made their preparations and took with
them gifts—gold and silver, horses and mules, garments of various colors for the decoration and service
of the honorable places of the holy houses of God
where they were being sent. And for all the churches
by which they would pass they took prepared gifts.

803.   They put Gregory in the royal carriage that was
decorated in gold and drawn by white mules. All the
nobles gathered around him with carriages and horses,
with their forces, standards and each one's following.
They quickly left the province of Ayrarat and the city
of Valarshapat, and arrived in Greek territory. In
every city they were received with great honor and
elaborate hospitality. They (the Greeks) made much
rejoicing

տիրա ընծու(ժեան, խնձոյս ուրախու(ժեան կացուցանէին, իբրև լսէին զԱստուծոյ արարեալ
զքանչելիսն, և գՀատելոց դարձ փրկու(ժեան և
գձանապարհս օգտակարս:

804 Այսպէս պատուեալ ըստ ճանապար-
Հացն՝ մինչև գային Հասանէին ի քաղաքն Կեսարացւոց. և անդ տեսանէին գուրբ կաթողիկոսն Ղեոնղիոս, և գամենայն եկեղեցական գուն-
դրս գունդս սրբոցն կղերիկոսացն և գղաս դաս
Հրեշտակակրօն պաշտօնէից: Տուեալ ողջոյն և
պատմեալ նոցա՝ որ ինչ մրանգամ եղեալ էր
յԱստուծոյ, և մատուցին գթուղթ թագաւորին
առաջի սրբոյ քանանայապետին. և նորա մեծաւ
խնղութեամբ ընկալեալ և ամենայն քաղաքաց-
եացն մեծաւ ուրախու(ժեամբ: Եւ ամենեքեան
առնէին տօն ընծու(ժեան, և գուրբն Գրիգոր
պատուեալ ըստ արժանի առաքինու(ժեանցն ճրգ-
նու(ժեանցն վկայօրէն մարտին՝ կանթեղօք և
սաղմոսիւք և երգովք Հոգեւորօք փառաւորէին:
«Եւ իշխանաց քաղաքին ցուցեալ բագում մեծարանս Հասելոցն և ընկալեալ Հոգաբարձու-
(ժեամբ ըստ Քրիստոսի անուանելոյն կարգի»:
Եւ այսպէս մեծապատիւ յամենեցունց մեծարեալ ըստ արժանաւորու(ժեանն երանու(ժեան
վկայական անուան սացելոյ:

805 Եւ եղեալ ժողով բազմու(ժեան եպիսկոպոսաց ի քաղաքն Կեսարացւոց, գի ճեռնա-

and merriment and feasting [cf. III Macc. 6.22] when
they heard of the miracles worked by God, and of
their visitors' conversion to salvation and their journey for support.[1]

804.   They were honored in this way on their journey
until they arrived at the city of Caesarea; there they
saw the holy Catholicos[1] Leontius and all the assembled company of the church, the holy clerics and the
rows of angelic ministers. Greeting them, they informed them of what had been done by God, and they
presented the king's letter to the holy high-priest. He
received it with great happiness and all the citizens
rejoiced. They all celebrated a joyful festival and
honored saint Gregory for his meritorious virtue and
endurance in his martyr-like struggle, giving thanks
with candles and psalms and spiritual songs [cf. Col.
3:16]. And the nobles of the city showed great honor
to the visitors and received them with great solicitude
according to the Christian custom.[2] In this way he
was greatly honored by everyone according to the
merit of the blessed name of martyr that he had
gained.

805.   And there took place a council[1] of many[2] bishops in the city of Caesarea so that they might ordain

դրեացէն գաւըրն Գրիգորիոս և աւանդեալ ի
նա զպատիւ խոնարհութեան քանանայութեանն
Քրիստոսի, և զբարձրութիւն եպիսկոպոսութեան
փառաւորութեանն Աստուծոյ, զպատիւն և զփառ-
սըն մեծ։ Սրբով Աւետարանաւն եդին ի վերայ
նորա ձեռս ժողովք եպիսկոպոսացն, որոց գըլ-
խաւորն Ղևոնդիոս, զի աւցէ նա իշխանութիւն
յերկինա և յերկրի, առնուլ զփականա արքայութեանն երկնից, կապել և լուձանել յերկրի։

806 Մեծաւ պատուով և թղթով և ժողովով
զաւըրն Գրիգորիոս անդուստ յուղարկեցին իշ-
խանօքն հանդերձ։ Եառուն ողջոյն, և յուղի անկեալ անտի ի շնորհա տեառն մերոյ Յիսուսի
Քրիստոսի՝ գային հասանէին ի քաղաքն Սեբաս-
տացւոց, և անդ յեցան յերեկոյս աւուրա ոչ
սակաւ։ Եւ անդ գտանէր բազմութիւն եղբարց,
գորա հաւանեցուցանէր ընդ իւր գալ, զի վիճա-
կեցուսցէ զնոսա ի քանանայութիւն յիւրում
աշխարհին, և բազում գունդա գունդա յաձախ-
եալ առնոյր ընդ իւր, «և մեծարանօք մեծարեալ յեպիսկոպոսաց աշխարհին և յիշխանաց և ի
ժողովրդոց»։

807 Իսկ ընդ որ անցանէին՝ կուտէին ժո-
ղովուրդք ի վերայ ժողովրդոց՝ տեսանել զաւըր
եպիսկոպոսն Գրիգորիոս, զի օրհնեսցին ի նմանէ. և ասէին ցմիմեանս. «Եկայք տեսցուք
զաւըր եպիսկոպոսն Գրիգորիոս. զի այա այն

saint Gregory; and they handed on to him the honor
of the humility of Christ's priesthood, and the high-
ness of the episcopacy of God's glory—great honor
and glory.[3] Holding the holy gospel the assembled
bishops, of whom the chief was Leontius, placed their
hands on him that he might receive authority in heav-
en and on earth to receive the keys of the kingdom of
heaven, to bind and loose on earth [cf. Matt. 16.19].

806.   With great honor and a letter and an escort
they sent off saint Gregory with the nobles. They ex-
changed greetings, and in the grace of our Lord Jesus
Christ they went on their way. They arrived in the city
of Sebaste, and there they lodged not a few days. He
found there a good number of brethren whom he persuaded to accompany him so that he[1] might elevate
them to the priesthood in his own country; and a very
large number he took with him. And he was greatly
honored by the bishops of the land and the nobles
and the people.[2]

807.   Then wherever they passed, great crowds assembled to see the holy bishop[1] Gregory and to be
blessed by him. They said to each other: "Come, let
us see the holy bishop Gregory. For he is that

այր է, ասէին, որ վասն Քրիստոսի համբեր
չարչարանաց, վկայ հաւատարիմ գտեալ, գխո-
տովանողական անուն ժառանգեաց»։

808 «Եւ յետ այսորիկ առնոյր ընդ իւր
զբազմութիւն հաւանելոցն՝ նախարարակոյտ գո-
լուն հանդերձ. հրաժարեալ այնուհետեւ չնորհա-
տուր պարգեւօքն եւ ամենայն իւրայովքն յանձն
եղեալ չնորհացն Աստուծոյ՝ ճանապարհորդ լինէր. եւ այսպէս զբազում օթեվանօք անցեալ՝
առողջութեամբ, յաջողութեամբ եւ հոգելից ուրախութեամբ եկեալ հասանէին ի Հայաստան
աշխարհն»։

809   Եւ իբրե եկն եհաս ի սահմանս
Հայոց՝ լուաւ Գրիգորիոս, թէ Վահէվանեան մեհեանն մնացեալ է յերկրին Տարօնոյ, մեհեանն
մեծագանձ, լի ոսկւով եւ արծաթով, եւ բազում
նուէրք մեծամեծ թագաւորաց ձօնեալ անդ. ու-
թերորդ պաշտօն հոչակաւոր, անուանեալն Վի-
շապաքաղն Վահագնի, յաշտից տեղիք թագաւորացն Հայոց Մեծաց, ի մնարս լերինն Քար-
քեայ, ի վերայ գետոյն Եփրատայ, որ հանդեպ
հայի մեծի լերինն Տաւրոսի, որ եւ անուանեալ
ըստ յանձախաշատ պաշտամա ն տեղեացն՝ Յաշ-
տիշատ։ Զի յայնժամ դեռ եւս չէն կային երեք
բագինք ի նմա. առաջին՝ մեհեանն Վահէվանեան, երկրորդ՝ Ոսկեմօր Ոսկեծին դից, եւ բա-
դինն իսկ յայս անունն անուանեալ Ոսկեհատ Ոս-

man," they said, "who for Christ's sake endured torments; being found a faithful martyr, he has inherited the title of Confessor."[2]

808.   Then he took with him the great number of (monks) whom he had persuaded (to accompany him) and the princes and soldiers. Then taking leave with liberal gifts and trusting in the grace of God, with his escort he took to the road. And thus, after passing the many stages in health, success and spiritual joy, they arrived in Armenia.[1]

[Chapter 12.   Gregory builds the first churches
                in Armenia; the king and the
                people are baptised]

809.   When he arrived at the borders of Armenia, Gregory heard that there remained in the land of Tarawn[1] the temple of Vahagn[2] —a very wealthy temple, full of gold and silver [cf. I Macc. 6.1-2], to which many offerings had been presented by the greatest kings. It was the eighth famous shrine[3] and was devoted to the cult of Vahagn, called the *Dragon-handler,*[4] a place of sacrifice for the kings of Greater Armenia, on the summit of the mountain Karkē[5] on the river Euphrates, which looks across to the great Taurus range; it was called Yashtishat[6] from the frequent cultic sacrifices of the site. For at that time there still stood three altars in it; the first was the temple of Vahagn;[7] the second that of the Golden-mother,[8] the Golden-born goddess, and the altar was called after her golden-built

կեմօր դից. և երրորդ՝ մեհեանն անուանեալ Աստղկան դից, Սենեակ Վահագնի կարդացեալ, որ է ըստ յունականին Ափրոդիտէ։ Արդ՝ դիմեաց զալ սուրբն Գրիգորիոս, զի քանդեսցէ և զայն ես, զի տակաւին իսկ տղէտ մարդիկ խառնակութեան գործէին յայս բագինս մնացեալ։

810 Եւ իբրև դարձեալ գայր նա ի կողմանցն Յունաց՝ բարձեալ բերէր ընդ իւր նշխարս ինչ յոսկերաց մեծի մարգարէին երանեալ մկրտչին Յովհաննու և գուռբը վկային Քրիստոսի զԱթանագինէի։ Եւ իբրև եկին հասին յանդիման մեհենացն, մօտ ի գեանն Եփրատ՝ կամէր հանել գնաս ի վեր, ի բարձրաւանդակ տեղի մեհենացն, կործանել զբագինսն, և շինել զվկայարանս նոցա։

811 Իբրև եկին մօտ եղեն ի գեանն Եփրատ իբրև ձիոյ արշաւանօք երկուք, և դեռ ընդ փոքր ձորակ մի անցանել կամէին, ընդ ջուր մի սակաւ՝ գտեղի առին սպիտակ ջորիք կառացն, ուր կային գանձքն աստուածայինն, նշխարք սրբոցն. ոչ կարացին հանել ըստ ձորակն։ Եւ յայտնեալ առ Գրիգոր հրեշտակ Տեառն՝ ասէ. «Հաճեցաւ Տէր գենակել սրբոցդ Աստուծոյ ի տեղւոջդ»։ Ուր և անդէն բագմութեան գօրացն, մէն սակաւ ստտապեալ՝շինեցին զվկայարանն, և գուրբան ի հանգիստ փոխեցին։

812   Եւ մինչ դեռ դշինուած մատ-

of the Golden-mother goddess; the third was the temple named for the goddess Astḷik,[9] called the spouse of Vahagn,[10] who is in Greek Aphrodite. For this site Gregory set out in order to destroy it also, since ignorant men still made profane sacrifices at these surviving altars.

810. When he returned from Greek territory he brought with him some relics from the bones of the great prophet, blessed John the baptist, and of the holy martyr of Christ, Athenogenes.[1] When they arrived opposite these temples, near the river Euphrates, he wished to take them (the relics) up to the highest place of the temples in order to destroy the altars and build chapels for them.

811. When they had approached the Euphrates to about two horse-courses[1] and were still intending to pass a small valley with a little water in it, the white mules of the carriage which carried the divine treasures, the saints' relics, halted; they were unable to drive them beyond the valley. And the angel of the Lord appeared to Gregory, saying: "It has pleased the Lord that these saints of God should dwell in this spot."[2] So there the whole multitude of the army set to work and built the chapel and transferred the saints to rest.

812. While they were constructing the chapel

բանն կազմէին՝ հրաման ետ Գրիգոր գօրականին
և իշխանացն որ ընդ իւրն էին, զի եղցեն և
մրձօք տապալեցցեն զշինուածս բագնացն։ Որք
ելեալ շատ ջանացան, և ոչ կարացին զդուրս
բագնացն գտանել՝ թէ ի ներքս մացեն, զի ձած-
կեցին դեքն ի նոցանէն։ և ի կողմանէ արտա-
քուստ ջանացան, և ոչ գձեաց անդ երկաթ
գործլոյն։ ապա փութացան հասին իշխանքն և
պատմեցին նմա դամենայն։

813 Իսկ նա առնոյր զնշան տերունական
խաչին, և ելեալ ի ձորակէն եկաց յանդիման
բարձրաբերձ տեղեացն շինուածոցն և ասէ.
«Հրեշտակ քո, Տէր, հալածեցցէ զնոսա»։ Եւ ընդ
բանիցն հողմ ուժգին բղխեաց ի խաչանիշ փայ-
տէն, գոր ունէր ի ձեռին իւրում սուրբ եպիս-
կոպոսն։ Եւ երթայր հողմն ուռուցեալ լերինն
հաւասար, և չոգաւ հարթեաց, տապալեաց, ըն-
կէց դամենային շինուածան բագնացն։ Եւ այնչափ
կորոյս, զի յետ այնորիկ ոչ ինչ օք յայնմ տեղ-
լոջ նշմարանա կարէր գտանել, ոչ քարի և ոչ
փայտի, ոչ ոսկւոյ և ոչ արձաթոյ, և ոչ բնաւ
երևէր, թէ լեալ ինչ իցէ անդ։ Եւ անթիւք կո-
տորեցան մարդիկ պաշտամանն քրմութեան որ ի
տեղւոջ անդ էին, և աննետ եղեն ոսկերք նոցա.
և որք տեսինն՝ անթիւ մարդիկ հալատացին։ Եւ
ասէ սուրբն Գրիգոր. «Արդ տեսէք, թէ որպէս
ՁնՁեցան դայթակղութիւնքն ձեր, զի և չէին իսկ

Gregory ordered the soldiers and nobles who were with him to come forth and destroy with their hammers the edifices of the altars. They came forth and made great efforts, yet they were unable to find the gates of the temples in order to enter, because the demons had hidden them from them. They tried from the outside, but their iron tools made no impression. Then the nobles hastened back and told him everything.

813.   So he took the sign of the Lord's cross, and leaving the valley came up to the high place of the buildings and said: "Let your angel, Lord, drive them away." At his words a mighty wind blew from the wooden cross which the holy bishop was holding in his hand. The wind, like a hurricane, rose up as high as the mountain and struck, destroyed and overthrew all the constructions of the altars.[1] It destroyed them so thoroughly that afterwards no one was able to find traces in that spot, neither of stone nor wood, neither of gold nor silver; and it did not appear at all that there had ever been anything there. And numberless men who were associated with the cult and pagan priesthood in that place were slaughtered and no trace left of their bones. And the countless men who saw this believed. And saint Gregory said: "See now how your stumbling blocks have been erased, for they were

ինչ. այլ ձառայեցէք յայսմհետէ տեառն Աստուծոյ որ արար զերկինս և զերկիր»:

814 Եւ յետ այսորիկ ելանէր նա ի տեղիս
մեհենացն, և ժողովեալ դարձուցանէր գմարդիկ
աշխարհին յաստուածապաշտութիւն: Եւ եղ անդ
գշիմունս եկեղեցւոյն, և ուղղեաց սեղան փառացն Քրիստոսի. զի նախ անդ արար սկիզբն
շինելոյ եկեղեցեաց: Եւ ուղղեալ սեղան յանուն
սուրբ Երրորդութեանն, և կազմեալ աւազան
մկրտութեան, նախ գայնոսիկ լուսաւորեաց մկր-
տութեամբն՝ որ ընդ իւրն էին մեծամեծ նախարարքն, որ ընդ նմայն երթեալ էին ի քաղաքն Կեսարացւոց, և ապա զզաւառականան,
զԳնակիչս երկրին: Ալուրս քան երեկոթս աւ-
նէր, և մկրտէր անդ աւելի քան զինն և տասն
բիւր մարդկան, և կանգնէր սեղան ի վկայարանի սրբոցն Հանգստի գոր շինեացն, և մատուցանէր զպատարագն փրկութեան, և բաշխէր
անդ գմարմին և զարիւն կենարարին Քրիստոսի:

815 Եւ հրամայեաց կատարել անդ ամ յամէ, ի նմին տեղւոջ ժողովեալ ամենեցուն, գյի-
շատակ սրբոցն, որ օր եօթն էր ամսոյն սահմի,
գի խնդութեամբ ժողովեալ՝ գոր տօնին խմբես-
ցեն. գի նախ անտի սկիզբն արար շինելոյ գե-
կեղեցիս: Եւ կացուցանէր քահանայս ի տեղիս
տեղիս. և ելից գվայրան եկեղեցւովք շինելովք
և քահանայիւք:

nothing.[2] But serve henceforth the Lord God who made heaven and earth."

814.   After this he went forth to the place of the temples, and gathering the inhabitants of the land he converted them to true piety. He set there foundations for the church and erected an altar for the glory of Christ: for it was there that he first made a beginning of building churches.[1] He erected an altar to the name of the holy Trinity and arranged a baptismal font. First he illuminated with baptism[2] those great princes who were with him and had traveled with him to the city of Caesarea, and then the people of the province, the inhabitants of the land.[3] He lodged (there) for twenty days and baptized more than one hundred and ninety thousand persons.[4] He erected an altar in the chapel of repose of the saints which he had built, and he offered the saving liturgy, and distributed there the life-giving body and blood of Christ.

815.   And he ordered that year by year everyone should come together at that same spot and celebrate the commemoration of the martyrs, which was the seventh day of the month Sahmi,[1] that gathering joyfully they should assemble on that feast day. For there he first began building churches. And he established priests in every place and filled the land with church buildings and priests.[2]

816 Եւ ինքն չու արարեալ անտի՝ մեծա
պանծ պարծանօք գործութեան խաչին Քրիստոսի
և բարձ նշխարս անտի կէս մի ի սրբոցն, զի
և յայլ տեղիս հաստատեցէ գլիշատակս նոցա։
Եւ ընդ ամենայն տեղիս և ընդ ամենայն գա
լառս շրջէր․ յաւանս և յագարակս շինէր եկե
ղեցիս, և առնէր մկրտութիւն և կացուցանէր
քահանայս։

817 Լուաւ ապա և մեծ թագաւորն
Տրդատ, եթէ Գրիգոր եկեալ հասեալ է յերկիրս
Հայոց։ Առ զզօրս իւր և զԱշխէն տիկին և զգոյրն
իւր զԽոսրովիդուխտ, և չու արարեալ յԱյրա
րատեան գաւառէն, ի Վաղարշապատ քաղաքէ,
ընդ առաջ Գրիգորի, գայր հասանէր ի քաղա
քագեօղն Բագաւան, որ անուանեալ կոչի ի
պարթևարէն լեզուէն՝ Դիցաւան. և անդ սպաս
եալ մնայր նմա ամսօրեայ ժամանակս։ Իսկ նա
շրջէր, զի լցցէ զկողմանս կողմանս եկեղեցեօք
և քահանայիւք և պաշտօնէիւք և ամենայն աստ
ուածագործ սպասաւորութեանն կարգօք, և լու
սաւորեցէ զքապումս մկրտութեամբ։

818 Ապա գայր հասանէր յանուանեալ Դի
ցաւանն ամենայն մեծամեծօքն և գօրօքն և աշ
խարհակոյա ամբոխիւն, որք էին ժողովեալ ի
կողմանց կողմանց, և գնային շրջէին գնետ նո
րա և գատնէին բժշկութիւն և ընուին պղետս
իրաքանշիւր ի նմանէ։ Եւ նա ամենատիւ

816.   He himself set out from there with the sublime splendor of the power of the cross of Christ, and he took a part of the saints' relics in order to establish their commemorations in other places. He journeyed through every place and every province. In the towns and estates he built churches, conducted baptism and established priests.[1]

817.   Then the great king Trdat heard that Gregory had arrived in Armenia. He took his army and his wife Ashkhēn and sister Khosrovidukht and set out from the province of Ayrarat, from the city of Valarshapat, to meet Gregory. He arrived in the town of Bagavan, called in the Parthian language Ditsavan,[1] and there he remained for a month waiting for him. But he (Gregory) moved around in order to fill every region with churches, priests, ministers, and all the ranks of divine service, and to illuminate many by baptism.

818.   Then he arrived in the (town) called Ditsavan with all the magnates and the army and the mass of the common people, who had gathered from every region and were following him around and obtaining from him healing and the fulfilment of each one's needs. And he, through his teaching that spread to all,

վարդապետութեամբն ամենեցուն սերմանէր
գբանն կենաց, և «հանդերձ ամենային սպասաւորօք Աւետարանին որ ընդ իւրն էին, դոր չէ
օք բաւական ըստ իւրաքանչիւր անուանցն նշանակել, քարոզէր զԱւետարանն։ Որովք յանձն
եղեալ երանելի եպիսկոպոսն շնորհացն Աստու-
ծոյ՝ գայր հասանէր առ ստորոտով նպատական
լերինն»։

819 «Ընդ առաջ եւլանէր նմա Թագաւորն
ամենային գործօքն հանդերձ, առ աւին Եփրատ գետոյն, որ և ընդ պատահէին իսկ լի առնէր գամենեսեան ողջունիւ Աւետարանին Քրիստոսի, և
բագում ընդունելութեամբ և ուրախութեամբ յաւանն
դառնային»։ Եւ անդ մատուցեալ Թագաւորին
իշխանքն եկեալք գբերեալ պատասխանին ողջու-
նաբեր Թղթոյն, գի գրեալ էր գպատճէնն օրինակ գայս.—

820 «Գանեալքդ՝ և խրատեալքդ, հարու-
ծեալքդ՝ և ողոքեալքդ, տանջեալքդ՝ և նուա-
ճեալքդ, կորուսեալքդ՝ և գտեալքդ, մոլորեալքդ՝
և դարձուցեալքդ, յակն առեալքդ՝ և սիրեցեալքդ
Տեառն, Տրդատէս Թագաւոր Հայոց մեծաց և
Աշխէն տիկին և օրիորդ մեծ Խոսրովիդուխտ, և
ամենային հրապարակք բազմամբոխ ժողովրդոց

sowed in everyone the word of life; and with all the
servants of the gospel who were with him, whom no
one could name individually, he preached the gospel.
With these the blessed bishop, trusting in God's grace,
came to the base of the mountain[1] Npat.[2]

819.   The king with all his army went out to greet
him on the bank of the river Euphrates, and at their
meeting he filled them all with the salutation of
Christ's gospel; with great rejoicing and joy they returned to the town.[1] And there the nobles presented
to the king the reply they had brought to his letter of
greeting, which was written in the following terms.

COPY OF THE REPLY TO THE LETTER

820.   "To you who have been beaten and admon-
ished, tormented and calmed, tortured and subdued,
lost and found [cf. Lk. 15.4], gone astray and converted, noticed and beloved by the Lord,[1] to Tiridates king of Greater Armenia and queen Ashkhēn
and princess Khosrovidukht and all the populace

որ իցեն Հայոց Մեծաց. Զկնդես արքեպիսկո-
պոս մետրոպոլիտ մեգադէ Կեսարու և ամենայն
ուխտ սրբոյ եկեղեցլոյ քահանայութեան, եպիսկոպոսաց, երիցանց, սարկաւագաց և ժողովրբր-
դոց. ի Տէր խնդալ.

821 «Վասն կենսատու փրկութեանդ հաւե-
լոյ ձեզ յԱստուծոյ, որպէս մեզ պատմեցաւ,
անպայման ուրախութեամբ գոհացաք զանդեղ-
ջական փառացն Քրիստոս, և վասն սրբոց վկայ-
իցդ Աստուծոյ որ ի ձերում միջի, յաշխարհիդ
ձերում փառաւորեցան. Զի և դուք նայեցեալք
յելս գնացից նոցա և նմանողք լեալ հաւատոց
նոցա՝ փառաւորեսչիք, նոցա պսակօքն պսակե-
լով պսակեսչիք։

822 «Զի արարիչն ամենեցուն և ամենայն
աշխարհաց, որ ընդ ամենեցուն հաճեալ գի առ-
ցեն գործեգրութիւն, իւրով հաճոյական կամօքն
խրատէ զամենեսին, որով մինքարեցէ ի անա-
վատատ աշխատութենէն, յիւրումն արքայութեանն հանգուցէ զբեռնաւորսն զաշխատականն,
«գի լուծ նորա քաղցր է և բեռն իւր փոքրոգի»։
առ իւր Թեարկէ, վարդապետէ, գի իւրում հան-
գրատեանն արժանիս արասցէ զամենեսին։

823 «Եւ վասն գի ոչ կանխեալ գիտացեալ
ձեր գարժանն՝ վասն այսորիկ ած գանարժան
գալագանն ի վերայ ձեր, և իբրև ի քնոյ ընդոստուցեալ, գի գիտասչիք զգգատութիւնն,

of Greater Armenia—Leontius Archbishop and Metropolitan[2] of great Caesarea and all the priestly clergy of the holy church, bishops, priests, deacons and people, greetings in the Lord.

821. "For the life-giving salvation bestowed on you by God, as has been narrated to us, with unbounded joy we have thanked the immutable glory of Christ, as also for the holy martyrs of God who were glorified among you, in your country. And may you, reflecting on the outcome of their labor and imitating their faith [cf. Heb. 13.7], also be glorified and crowned with their crowns.

822. "For the creator of everything and of all worlds, who wishes that all may receive adoption [cf. Eph. 1.5], by the pleasure of his own will advises everyone that he will give consolation from the toil of vain works, and in his kingdom give rest to those with burdens and those who have labored. 'For his yoke is sweet and his load is light.' [Matt. 11.28-30]. (These) he takes under his protection and instructs, in order that he may make everyone worthy of his rest.

823. "And because you did not previously realize what was worthy, therefore he brought this unworthy scourge upon you and awoke you as if from sleep that you might know the sobriety

որ արժանն է։ Եւ դի ոչ իմացայք դուք կմարդ֊
կանն ի մարդկապէսն՝ գիտուն արար գձեզ ի
չմարդկապէսն։ Եւ գոր յանգիտութեանն արհա֊
մարհեցէք՝ հաստատեաց գձեզ յանշարժ գիտու֊
թիւնն. դի վեՖն իսկ որ ի շինողացդ անարգեալ՝
եղե նա ձեզ գլուխ անկեան։

824 Զի գոր ուրացութեամբն բարկացու֊
ցէք արասուօք հաշտեցուսՖիք։ Զի գոր կա֊
փուցեալ պաչս ձեր, համարէիք խաւար՝ ծա֊
գեաց եբաց և լուսաւորեաց գտեսանելիս ձեր,
մերկեաց ի ձեՖ֊ֆ գգեցեալ գխաւարն հեֆանո֊
սութեան, և գձառագայֆարձակ գգեցոյց գպատ֊
մունՖանն։ Իսկ գոր համարեալ անմտութիւն, կո֊
լուսանել պանձայիք՝ նոյն ինքն ձեզ իմաստնա֊
ցուցիչ տուաւ, և նոյն ինքն ձեզ գտիչ պար֊
գևեցաւ։

825 «Արդ՝ մեք իբրև տեսաք գայսպիսի այր
հրաշալի և լուաք գմեծամեծ սքանչելիան որ ի
ձեռն սորա առ ձեզ կատարեցան՝ ընկղմեցաք ի
խորութիւն սիրոյ Աստուծոյ իբրև ի Ֆուրս սաս֊
տիկս ալեաց բագմութեան, անհատական գովու֊
թեամբ, և ի վերայ այսորիկ՝ անդադար բերա֊
նով և աննանգիստ բարբառով գտէր մեր գֆի֊
սուս Քրիստոս, գբարերարն գաքանչելագործն
գպարգևապաշին օրՖնեցաք, և առ Աստուած հայրն
ամենայնի գոՖութիւնս մատուցաք, չնորհելով
Գրիգորի գանապական պարգևս սուրբ Հոգւոյն,

which was fitting. And because you did not understand what was human by human means, he made you
aware by non-human means. And the man whom in
your ignorance you despised has confirmed you in
immovable knowledge. For the rock which was dis-
honored by the builders became for you the chief
cornerstone [cf. Matt. 21.42; Acts 4.11; I Pet. 2.7].

824. "For him whom you angered by your denial,
with tears you will placate. He to whom you closed
your eyes and considered as darkness [cf. Matt. 13.15]
has shone forth and opened and illuminated your vision; he has stripped off from you the pagan darkness
that enveloped you and put on you raiments of shining
light. He whom you presumed in your boastful [cf. Lk.
18.9] ignorance to destroy, the same has been given
you as teacher of wisdom and has been bestowed upon
you as mentor.[1]

825. "Now when we saw this man who is so marvelous, and when we heard of the mighty wonders
which were accomplished through him among you, we
were submerged in the depths of God's love as in the
vast waters of the numberless waves; and with con-
stant joy for this reason, and with unceasing mouth
and unresting voice we blessed our Lord Jesus Christ,
the benevolent, the worker of miracles and dispenser
of gifts. And we offered thanksgiving to God the Father of all, by giving Gregory the incorruptible gifts
of the holy Spirit,

որով և դուք արժանի լիջիք շնորհին ողջունի
արքայութեանն երկնից։ Եւ զմեզ, հեռի մարմնով, մերձ համարեալ հոգլով՝ յիշեցէք ի ձեր
ի նորաթեք յաղօթսդ, ի ձերում պարգևեալ փրր-
կութեանդ, մանաւանդ յորժամ գլիշատակ արր-
բոցդ խմբիցէք ձերով ուրախութեամբդ։

826 «Եւ հաստատեալ կացցէ վկայութիւն
ի մէջ երկոցունց կողմանց, զի պարգևապա-
շխութիւն նորոգ քահանայապետութեանդ ձերոյդ
նահանգիդ առ ի մէնջ՝ կացցէ անշարժ յեկեղեց-
լոյս Կեսարու, ուստի և հանդերձեցաւ ձեզ
պատրաստեալ՝ փրկութեան ձեռնադրութիւն։
Որով անապական պարգէք խորհրդոյն ձեզ բաշ-
խիցին վկայացեալ աջովդ, շնորհօք նորոգու-
թեանդ մկրտութեան և փրկական խաչին, և
կենդանարար մարմնոյն և քաւիչ արեանն Քրիստոսի, և երանութեամբ բաղմացելոց քահանա-
յութեանց. որով և դուք լիջիք վերացեալք խառնեալք, աղօթաբուղխք մշանջենաւորք, ի գօրս
քրիստոսակեցոյց գնդին։ Ողջ լերովք ի Քրիստոս, և հանապաղ վայելեսջիք ի փրկութեանն
Տեառն»։

827   Եւ ուրախ եղեն ընդ մխիթարութիւն թղթոյն. և զի եկեալ հասեալ էին ուղե-
գնացքն լուսաւորութեամբ, և երևեալ աստուա-
ծաշնորհ պարգևօք, առաւել գհոգեոր սիրոյն
գանձուկան սփռէին՝ և ես քան գես ի հաւատան

whereby you too might become worthy of the felici-
tous grace of the kingdom of heaven. Now do you remember us, far off in the body but near in the spirit,
in your neophyte prayers, in the salvation granted
you, and especially when you gather in your joy to
commemorate your saints.[1]

826. "And may the testimony between our two regions remain firm, that the gift of your new high
priestly rank from us may remain immovably in our
church of Caesarea, whence has been prepared for
you the ordination of salvation.[1] Thus the incorruptible gifts of the sacrament will be distributed to you
by the right hand of the martyred one,[2] through the
grace of the renewal of baptism and of the saving cross
and of the life-giving body and expiatory blood of
Christ, and through the blessing of the increasing
priesthood. Thus you will be raised and, making con-
stant prayer, will be joined to the hosts of Christ's
company. Be well in Christ, and may you continually
enjoy the salvation of the Lord."

827. They were happy at the consolation of the letter; and because the travelers had returned illuminated and with visible gifts of divine grace, they spread
all the more their fervor of divine love[1] and were
established ever more firmly in the faith

հաստատեցան մեծաւ և ցնծալից բերկրութեամբ։

828 Իսկ նա անդէն «և անդ ընդելական
սովորութեամբն ի գործ արկեալ գանդաղար
վարդապետութիւնն հաւասարութեամբ բարե-
պաշտ» աբքային Տրդատայ՝ «զիւր արուեստն
առաջի դներ. խրատէր յորդորելով. որով առաւելագոյն հնազանդէին նմա բստ հրամանացն
Աստուծոյ, թագաւորն և գօրքն ամէնային հանդերձ աշխարհախումբ բագմութեամբն, որոց
յանձն առեալ ամէնեցուն զինդրելին կատարել»,
և զհրամայեալն ի գործ արկանել։

829 Եւ նորա տուեալ հրաման աբքայա-
գունդ բանակացն՝ ամսօրեայ ժամանակաւ ի
պանս և յաղօթս յամենալ։ «Եւ իւրում անձինն՝
գոռորականն առաջի դներ, իւրայովքն անդուստ
ամէլովքն հաւասարօքն, զպանս և զաղօթս,
զոքնութիւնս, զպաղատանս արտօսրաբերս,
զխստամբերութիւնս, զհոդս աշխարհահեծս, յուշ
առնելով զասացեալն հոգեպատում մարգարէին,
թէ «Յորժամ հեծեծեսցես՝ յայնժամ կեցցես»։

830 «Այսպէս բազում աշխատութեամբ
տարեալ՝ վասն համաշխարհին բարեաց ինչ օձան
գտանելոյ. որում և պարգեւեր իսկ վիճակ յամե-
նաշնորհն Աստուծոյ, հայրական չափուն ծնանել
ծնունդ նորոգ և սքանչելի, պարգեւաբաշխ սուրբ
աշովն իւրով»։ դամենայն ի Չրոյ և ի Հոգլոյ
յարգանդէ՝ մկրտութեամբ միւսանգամ վերստին

with great and joyous happiness.

828.   Then he according to his usual habit set himself to unceasing instruction, and with the assistance of the pious[1] king Trdat set forth his skill and continuously gave admonition. Thus ever more people came to obey him according to God's commands, the king and all the army with the mass of the common people, all undertaking to fulfill his request[2] and execute his orders.

829.   And he commanded the royal camp to spend a month in fasting and prayer. With his companions that he had brought thence he imposed on himself his customary fasting and prayer, vigils, tearful supplications, austerities, world-lamenting[1] cares, having regard for the words of the inspired prophet: "When you will lament, then you will live" [Is. 30.15].

830.   In this way he exerted much effort to find blessing and grace for the whole land. To him the gift was granted by all-gracious God to produce a new and wonderful birth in fatherly fashion,[1] by his holy and liberal right hand;[2] to give birth once again to everyone by baptism from water and the womb of the Spirit [cf. Jn. 3.5],

ծնանել, առնել կատարել, սրբել, դրոշմել մի
ժողովուրդ Տեառն:

831 Եւ եղ անդ հրամունս, և շինեաց եկե-
ղեցի․ և զնշխարան գոր ունէր յոսկերաց սրբոցն՝
ի տեղունական տանն բնակեցուցանէր: Սոյնպէս
և ընդ ամենայն կողմանս գաւառացն դնէր հի-
մունս եկեղեցեաց, և ուղղէր սեղանս, և կացուցանէր քահանայս: Եւ ամենայն երկիրն դարձեալ սրտիւք իւրեանց կանխէին ի պատս և ի
պաշտօն և յերկիւղն Աստուծոյ:

832   Իսկ ի լնուլ կիսոյն եղելոյ պա-
հոցն կատարելոյ, առեալ երանելւոյն Գրիգորի
զաշխարհաբանակ զօրացն, և զինքենին զթագա-
լորն, և զկին նորա Աշխէն, և գմեծ օրիորդն
Խոսրովիդուխտ, և զմեծամեծան ամենայն, և
ամենայն մարդկաւ բանակին հանդերձ՝ ընդ այգն
ի լուսանալ առաւօտուն յափն Եփրատ գետոյն
մատուցանէր, և անդէն մկրտէր առ հասարակ
զամենեսեան յանուն Հօր և Որդւոյ և Հոգւոյն
սրբոյ:

833 Եւ իբրև իջանէին մարդիկն ամենայն
և Թագալորն ի մկրտութիւն անդր, ի Ճուրսն
Եփրատ գետոյն՝ նշան աբանչելի երևեալ յԱս-
տուծոյ․ զի գետող առեալ Ճուրք գետոյն՝ անդրէն
դարձան ընդ կրուկն: Եւ լոյս սատիկ երևեալ
ի նմանութիւն սեան լուսաւորի՝ և եկաց ի վերայ Ճուրց գետոյն, և ի վերայ նորա նմանու-

to perfect, purify and seal one people of the Lord.

831.   There he set foundations and built a church; and the relics which he had of the saints' bones he deposited in the Lord's house. In this way throughout all parts of the provinces he set foundations for churches and erected altars and established priests. The whole land was converted, and with all their hearts they were assiduous in fasting and in the service and fear of God.

832.   Then at the final completion of the fast, blessed Gregory took the mass of the army and the king himself and his wife Ashkhēn and the princess Khosrovidukht and all the magnates with all the people of the camp, and in the morning at dawn he brought them to the banks of the river Euphrates, and there he baptized them all together in the name of the Father and of the Son and of the Holy Spirit [cf. Matt. 28.19].

833.   And when all the people and the king went down to baptism in the water of the river Euphrates, a wonderful sign was revealed by God: the waters of the river stopped and then turned back again.[1] And a bright light appeared[2] in the likeness of a shining pillar, and it stood over the waters of the river; and above it was the likeness

թիւն տերունական խաչին. եւ այնչափ ծագեաց
լոյսն, մինչեւ արգելոյր գճառագայթս արեգա֊
կանն եւ նուագեցուցանէր։ Եւ իւրն օծութեան,
զոր արկանէր Գրիգորիոս ի վերայ մարդկանն՝
շրջան առեալ ի մէջ գետոյն շուրջ գմարդկան
խաղայր։ Եւ ամենեքեան գարմացեալք բարձրա֊
ցուցանէին գործնութիւն ի փառս Աստուծոյ։ Եւ
ընդ երեկս աւուրն նշանն աներեւոյթ լինէր, եւ
նոքա ի վեր յաւանն դառնային։ Եւ որք մկր֊
տեցանն յաւուր յայնմիկ՝ աւելի քան գննգետա֊
սան բիւր մարդկան յարքունական գօրացն։

834 Եւ անտի եղեալ մեծաւ ցնծութեամբ
եւ ապտակագգեստ հանդերձիւք, սաղմոսիւք եւ
օրհնութեամբք, կանթեղօք վառելովք, եւ մոմե֊
ղինօք լուցելովք, եւ ջահիւք բորբոքելովք, մե֊
ծաւ լրջմտութեամբ եւ բագում գուարթութեամբ
լուսաւորեալք եւ հրեշտակացեալք. եւ առեալ գա֊
նունն որդեգրութեանն Աստուծոյ, եւ մտեալ ի
ժառանգութիւն սրբոյ Աւետարանին, եւ ի վի֊
ճակ սրբոցն խառնեալք, ծաղկեալք ի նոտ անոյշ
ի Քրիստոս, եւ եղեալք ի վեր ի տերունական
տունն դառնային։ Եւ անդ մատուցանէր գործ֊
նութեան պատարագն, հաղորդէր գամենեսեան
ի խորհուրդն գոհութեան. բաշխէր ամենեցուն
գսուրբ մարմինն եւ գպատուական արիւնն ամե֊
նափրկչին Քրիստոսի, գկենդանարարն եւ գկե֊
ցուցիչն ամենայն մարդկան, եւ գարաբիչն եւ

of the Lord's cross. And the light shone out so brightly
that it obscured and weakened the rays of the sun.
And the oil of annointing[3] which Gregory poured
over the people, floated around them in the river.
Everyone was amazed and raised blessings to God's
glory. In the evening the sign disappeared, and they
returned to the town. And those who were baptized
on that day were more than one hundred and fifty
thousand persons from the royal army.[4]

834.   They went forth in great joy, in white garments,
with psalms and blessings [cf. Eph. 5.19] and lighted
lamps and burning candles and blazing torches,[1] with
great rejoicing and happiness, illuminated and become
like the angels. They had received the title of God's
adoption [cf. Rom. 8.15, etc.], had entered the heritage of the holy gospel [cf. Eph. 1.18], and being
joined to the rank of the saints [cf. Acts 26.18] were
flowering with sweet odor in Christ [cf. Eph. 5.2; Phil.
4.18]. So they went forth and returned to the Lord's
house. There he offered the blessed sacrifice and com-
municated them all with the blessed sacrament, dis-
tributing to all the holy body and precious blood of
Christ the Savior of all, who vivifies and gives life to
all men, the creator and

գաշխարհագործն ամենայն արարածոց, զաստ-
ուածատուր չնորհան առ ամենեսեան առատա-
պէս մատակարարէր։

835 Եւ դադարեաց անդ յետ այսորիկ աւուրս եօթն վասն հոգեոր մխիթարու-
թեան։ Եւ յայնմ աւուրս եօթանս որ մկրտե-
ցան յարքունական բանակէ անտի՝ ընդ այր և
ընդ կին և ընդ մանուկ աւելի քան գչորեքա-
րիւր քիւր։

836 Եւ գյիշատակս վկայիցն բերելոց ժա-
մադրեաց ի տօն մեծ հոչակել, սնոտեացն պաշտաման ի ժամանակի՝ դիցն Ամանորոյ ամենա-
բեր նոր պաղոգ տօնին, Հիւրընկալ դիցն Վա-
նատրի, գոր յառաջագոյն իսկ ի նմին տեղւոջ
պաշտէին յուրախութեան նաւասարդ աւուր։ Չի
ժողովեալ ի յիշատակ մեծի երանելւոյն Յովհաննու և սրբոյ վկային Աստուծոյ Աթանագի-
նէի՝ աւուր խմբեալ ի նմին յաւանին տօնես-
ցեն։

837 «Յորում և երանելւոյն Գրիգորի գվար-
դապետութիւնն իւր ի գործ արկեալ, և ժողովելոցն առ ընդունել քաղցրացուցեալ», «և ծո-
վացուցեալ գվարդապետութեանն գխորութիւն,
և լցեալ գեղեալ ամենայն հոգեոր բարութեամբք»։
«Յետ այսորիկ հասեալ նմա քովանդակ ի վերայ ամենայն երկրին սահմանացն Հայոց Մեծաց
աշխարհին», շինելով եկեղեցիս յամենայն աշ-

fashioner of all creatures;[2] and he liberally adminis-
tered to all the divinely-given grace.

835.   After this he remained there seven days for spiritual consolation. And in those seven days from the
royal camp there were baptized—men, women and
children—more than four million.

836.   And he fixed the date for celebrating the commemoration of the martyrs that he had brought as a
major festival, at the time of the worship of the former vain (gods): the god Amanor the bringer of the
new fruits (and) the god *Hiwrĕnkal* Vanatur,[1] which
they previously used to celebrate in that same place
on the festival of the New Year's Day.[2] (He commanded) that gathering for the commemoration of the
great and blessed John and the holy martyr of God,
Athenogenes, they should celebrate their festival on
that day in the same town.[3]

[Chapter 13.   Gregory's missionary activities;
                his sons are brought to Armenia]

837.   Then blessed Gregory undertook to give his
instruction, and he softened the crowds to accept it;[1]
and pursuing ever more profound teaching he filled
everyone with spiritual blessings.[2] After that he journeyed over all districts of Greater Armenia,[3] building
churches in all

խարհս, ի գաւառս, ի կողմանս, ի քաղաքս, յա֊
ւանս, ի շէնս, ի գեօղս և յաղարակս։ Սոյնպէս
և Թագաւորն յամենայն իշխանութեան իւրում
առ հասարակ՝ գրեաց չորս չորս հոգս երդոյ
յամենայն ագարակ տեղիս, իսկ յաւանան եօթն
եօթն հոգս երդոյ՝ ի ծառայութիւն սպասաւո֊
րութեան քանանայութեանն, նուէր պտղոյ Տեա֊
ռն մատուցանէր։

838 Եւ կացուցանէր քանանայս յամենայն
տեղիս, և հրաման տուեալ, զի պաշտեսցեն դպէր
Աստուած միայն, զարարիչն երկնի և երկրի. և
բազմացուցանէր զպաշտօնեայս սեղանոյն Տեառն
ընդ ամենայն տեղիս, և կացուցանէր քանանայս
առ սեղան սեղան յամենայն եկեղեցիսն։ Սոյն֊
պէս և գեղիսկոպոսն վիճակեցուցանէր ի գլխա֊
ւորութիւն ժողովրդոցն Տեառն, և հրաման տայր
նոցա՝ հաւատարիմ առաջնորդութեամբ վերա֊
կացու լինել լուսաւորապէս հօտին Քրիստոսի։

839 Նոյնպէս հաւանեցուցանէր զԹա֊
գաւորն. «զի ի գաւառաց գաւառաց և կողմանց
կողմանց ի տեղիս տեղիս ժողովեսցեն բազմու֊
թիւն մանկտւոյ, առ ի նիւթ վարդապետու֊
թեան, զգազանամիտ գվայրենագոյն գճիւաղա֊
բարոյ գաշխարհաբնակսն. զորս առեալ արկանէր
ի բովս վարդապետութեան, և հոգևոր սիրոյն
եռանդմամբ պաղոն և գմանգն գշարաւահոտ
ղիւացն և գնոտիագործ պաշտամանցն ի բաց

lands, provinces, quarters, cities, towns, inhabited regions, villages and estates. Similarly the king throughout his whole realm decreed that four fields in every estate and seven fields[4] in each town should be dedicated to the use of the servants of the priesthood for them to offer the fruits thereof to the Lord.

838. And he established priests in every place and commanded that they worship the Lord God only, the creator of heaven and earth. And he increased the ministers of the Lord's altar in every place, and established priests for each altar in every church.[1] Similarly he elevated bishops to primacy over the peoples of the Lord, and commanded them to be faithful in their leadership and to illuminate and oversee the flock of Christ [cf. Tit. 1.9].

839. Similarly he persuaded the king that from every province and region they should bring to various places numbers of children in order to instruct them. So these barbarous, savage and wild natives he took and cast into the furnace of instruction,[1] and by the heat of his spiritual love burnt away the impurity and rust of the putrid demons and vain cults.

քերէր։ Եւ այնչափ անձատր ի հայրենեացն բնակացն իւրեանց՝ մինչև ասել նոցա, թէ «Մոռացայ գժողովուրդ և գառւն հօր իմոյ»։

840 «Եւ ի տեղեաց տեղեաց սահմանացն Հայոց՝ տայր հրաման Թագաւորն Տրդատ՝ իւրոյ իշխանութեանն յաշխարհաց և ի գաւառաց բազմութիւն մատաղ մանկաղոյ ածել յարուեստ դպրութեան, և կարգել ի վերայ հաւատարիմ վարդապետաս. առաւել գազգս պղծագործ քրմացն և գմանկունս նոցա ի նոյն ժողովել, գումարել յարժանաւոր տեղիս դաստ դասս, և դարման ռոճկաց կարգել»։ Եւ գնոսա յերկուս բաժանեալ, գոմանս յԱսորի դպրութիւն կարգեալ, և գոմանս ի Հելլէն»։ «Որով անդէն յական թօթափել վայրենամիտքն և դատարկասունքն և անասնաբարոյ աշխարհաբնակէն վաղվաղակի մարգարէագէտք և առաքելածանօթք և աւետարանաժառանգք լինէին, և ամենայն աւանդելոցն Աստուծոյ ոչ իւիք անտեղեակք»։

841 «Հասանէր և յառաջի դաստակերտան իւր, յորոստակն Այրարատեան գաւառին ի Վաղարշապատ քաղաք», ուստի նախ գառաջինն ատուածատատ հրամանացն լինէր ակիզբն. ուր նախ նշմարեցին ևնշանակեալ կանգնեաց գնշան խաչին սրբոյ, ուր և սուրբ վկային Աստուծոյ գետեղեցան. և ինոցա վկայարանն կանգնեաց սեդանս Աստուծոյ ի հանգիստ սրբոցն. և գնկա-

And he so detached them from their ancestral customs
that they could say: "I have forgotten your people and
the house of my father" [Ps. 44.11].[2]

840.   And from every place within the borders of
Armenia and from the lands and provinces of his
realm king Trdat commanded many young children
to be introduced to the art of writing[1] and faithful
teachers to be put in charge. Especially the families
of the impure pagan priests and their children[2] were
to be brought together in groups in suitable places,
and an adequate stipend paid them.[3] These he divided
into two groups, some being set to Syriac and others
to Greek.[4] Thus in the twinkling of an eye these savage and idle and oafish peasants suddenly became acquainted with the prophets and familiar with the apostles and heirs to the gospel and fully informed about
all the traditions of God.[5]

841.   He[1] (Gregory) then arrived in his former dwelling,[2] the capital[3] of the province of Ayrarat, in the
city of Valarshapat where a beginning of the divine
commands had first been made; where he had first
observed (the vision) and set up the indicated sign of
the holy cross; where the holy martyrs of God were
buried and he had set up in their chapels altars to God,
in these saints' resting-places;

տեալ տեղին տանն Աստուծոյ շինեաց, զզուցեալն նմա ի տեղեանն, դյառաջագոյն դրոշմեալն իւր, և կանգնեաց անդ դեկեղեցին Քրիստոսի։ Սոյնպէս և ի տեղիս մեւենացն զոր կործանեաց յառա֊ ջագոյն․ սոյնպէս և յԱրտաշատ քաղաքի և յա֊ մենայն տեղիս։ յաշխարհս և ի գաւառ առ հա֊ սարակ, սոյն օրինակ գործեաց և բազմացոյց դեկեղեցիս, և կացոյց քահանայս․ և քրիստո֊ սեան դրոշմաւն գամենեսին առ հասարակ ըն֊ ծայեցուցանէր՝ լինել ամենեցուն Հոգւովն սրբով։

842 Եւ այսպէս ընդ ամենայն երկիրն Հա֊ յոց, ի ծագաց մինչև ի ծագս, ձգտէր տարա֊ ծանէր գմշակութիւն քարոզութեանն և աւետա֊ րանութեանն․ ի Սատաղացւոց քաղաքէն մինչև առ աշխարհաւն Խաղտեաց, մինչև առ Կաղար֊ Ջօք, մինչ ի սպառ ի սահմանս Մասքթաց, մին֊ չև ի դրունս Աղանաց, մինչ ի սահմանս Կաս֊ պից, ի Փայտակարան քաղաք արքայութեանն Հայոց․ և յԱմդացւոց քաղաքէն մինչև առ Մըծ֊ բին քաղաքաւ, քերէր առ սահմանօքն Ասորւոց առ նոր Շիրական երկրաւն, և առ Կորդուօք մին֊ չև յամուր աշխարհն Մարաց։ մինչև առ տամբն Մահքր—Տան իշխանին, մինչև յԱտրպատական ձգտէր տարածանէր գաւետարանութիւնն իւր։

843 «Զամենայն ժամանակս կենաց իւրոց, գամառն և գձմեռն, գցիւ և գգիշեր, անվեհեր առանց յապաղելոյ իւրով իսկ աւետարանական

and he had built the indicated place for the house of
God, which had been shown him in the vision and had
been earlier prefigured to him, and where he had
erected the church of Christ. And just as in the places
of the temples which he had earlier destroyed, so in
the city of Artashat and everywhere, in all lands and
provinces, in such fashion he acted, multiplying
churches, establishing priests, imposing on everyone
the sign of Christ,[4] so that all became (filled) with
the holy Spirit.

842. Thus throughout the whole land of Armenia,
from end to end, he extended the labor of preaching
the gospel. From the city of Satala to the land of
Khaltik',[1] to Kalarjik',[2] to the very borders[3] of the
Massagetae, to the gate of the Alans,[4] to the borders
of the Kaspk',[5] to P'aytakaran,[6] the city of the Armenian kingdom; from the city of Amida to the city
of Nisibis he passed along the borders of Syria, the
land of Nor-Shirakan[7] and Korduk',[8] to the secure[9]
land of the Medes, to the house of the prince of
Mahk'r-tun,[10] to Azerbaijan[11]—he spread his gospel-
preaching.[12]

843. All the time of his life, summer and winter, day
and night, intrepidly and without hesitation in his
course of preaching

և ողջունապատում գնացիւքն, առաջի թագաւո֊
րաց և իշխանաց և ամենայն հեթանոսաց՝ ան֊
ընդդիմակաց ի հակառակորդաց գամենափրկչին
անունն Յիսուսի կրեաց, և գամենայն ոգի աս֊
տուածազգեստս և ոգեղէնս վառեաց»։

844 «Եւ բազում բանդականաց և կալանա֊
ւորաց և տագնապելոց ի բռնաւորաց փրկու֊
թիւն արարեալ, կորզելով գնոսա անաւոր գո֊
րութեամբ փառացն Քրիստոսի. և բազում մուր֊
հակս անիրաւագիրս անիրաւութեան պատա֊
ռեաց։ Եւ բազում սգաւորաց կարձամտելոց մխի֊
թարական վարդապետութեամբն գանկալութիւն
յուսոյն րստ յայտնութեան փառաց մեծին Աս֊
տուծոյ և ամենափրկչին Յիսուսի Քրիստոսի
նուաճեաց. և գամենայն միանգամայն յաս֊
տուածապաշտութեան պայմանն փոխեաց»։

845 «Եւ դարձեալ բազում և աննա֊
մար գունդս գունս վանականաց ի չէնս և յան֊
չէնս, դաշտականս շինակեցացս, և լեռնականս
անձեւամ ուտս և արգելականս հաստատէր»։ Եւ
գոմանս յորդւոց քրմացն առեալ իւր՝ գառա֊
ջեաւատունս ձեռնասունս առնէր. փոյթ ուսման
ի վերայ ունէր՝ ընդ հոգևոր խնամով և երկիւ֊
ղիւ անուցանել։ Որ յաստիճան եպիսկոպոսու֊
թեան լինէին արժանի կալոյ, առեալ ձեռնա֊
դրութիւն ի նմանէ. որոց առաջնոյն՝ Աղբիանոս
անուն, որ ապա կողմանցն Եփրատական գե֊

the good word, before the king and princes and all the heathen without let or hindrance he bore the name of Jesus the Savior of all, and he furnished every soul with divine vesture and spiritual arms.[1]

844. He afforded salvation to many prisoners and captives and people oppressed by tyrants, freeing them by the awesome power of Christ's glory. And he tore up many unjust and illegal rescripts.[1] And to many in mourning or disheartened, through his consoling teaching he gave the expectation of hope in the appearance of the glory of the great God and the Savior of all, Jesus Christ. And he turned everyone to the state of true piety.[2]

845. Furthermore he established many and innumerable groups of monks in both inhabited and uninhabited areas, in the populous plains and the caves and retreats of the mountains.[1] He took some of the pagan priests' children and brought them up in his own sight and under his own care, giving them instruction and raising them with spiritual care and fear. Those who were worthy of attaining the rank of bishop received ordination from him: of these the first was called Albianos,[2] who was then made overseer of the area of the Euphrates river;

տոյն լինէր վերակացու. երկրորդին՝ Եւտադիոս,
որ ի կողմանս վայրացն Բասենոյ կացեալ լինէր
հովիւ. երրորդն՝ Բասոս. չորրորդն՝ Մովսէս.
հինգերորդն՝ Եւսեբիոս. վեցերորդն՝ Յովհաննէս.
եօթներորդն՝ Ագապէս. ութերորդն՝ Արտիթէս.
իններորդն՝ Արսուկէս. տասներորդն՝ Անտիոքէս.
մետասաներորդն՝ Տիրիկէս. երկոտասաներորդն՝
Կիւրակոս։ Այսք՝ որ յորդւոց քրմացն ընտրեց-
ցան լինել եպիսկոպոսք կողմանց կողմանց, անե-
ցուցանել դքարոզութիւնն։ Եւ գայլոցն անուանա
թէ և կամիցի ոք՝ ոչ կարասցէ շարել։

846 Եւ զԱղբիանոս պայր ճշմարիտ և աս-
տուածասէր՝ վերակացու Թողոյր արքունական
դրան թանակին։ Եւ ինքն «ընդ ժամանակս ժամանակս յանապատ լերինս ելանէր, ուր և ինքեան իւրով անձամբն իսկ օրինակ ցուցանէր։
Աւետալ գումանս ումանս յաշակերտացն յիւրաքանչիւր մենաստանաց՝ երթեալ, լեռնակեաց,
մենակեաց, սորամուտ, ծակախիթ եղեալ, և դա-
ռօրեակն խոտաբուտ ճարակոք վճարեալ։ Եւ այսպէս վշտակեաց տկարութեան գանձին տուեալ,
մանաւանդ որոց հայեցեալ էս ի մխիթարութիւն առաքելական բանիցն, թէ «Յորժամ վասն
Քրիստոսի տկարանամ՝ յայնժամ զօրացեալ լի-
նիմ»։ Եւ թէ՝ «Նաւ եսս լիցի պարծել տկարու-
թեամբ, զի ընակեսցէ յիս զօրութիւնն Քրիստոսի»։

the second was Euthalius, who became shepherd of
the wild regions of Basean;[3] the third was Bassus, the
fourth Moses, the fifth Eusebius, the sixth John, the
seventh Agapus, the eighth Artithes, the ninth Ar-
sukēs, the tenth Antiochus, the eleventh Tirikēs, the
twelfth Kyrakos.[4] These are they who were chosen
from among the pagan priests' children to become
bishops of various areas and to increase the preaching
of the gospel. And the names of the others, even if
one wished one would be unable to list.

846.   Albianos, an honest and God-loving man, he
left as overseer of the royal court. He himself at frequent intervals went out to deserted mountains where
he made himself an example. He took various of the
pupils from each monastery and went to live in the
mountains in solitude; in grottoes and caverns they
made herbs their daily food. Thus they gave themselves over to austere mortifications, especially because they looked to the consolation of the apostolic
sayings: "When I am weak for Christ, then am I
strong" [II Cor. 12.10], and: "It would be better to
boast in (my) weakness, that the power of Christ may
dwell in me" [II Cor. 12.9].[1]

847 «Անդ էր ապա չարբենալ գինեով, այլ առաւելուլ հոգւով, և պատրաստել գսիրաս երգովք հոգեւորք ի փառս և ի գովութիւն Աստուծոյ։ Անդ կրթութիւն քաղցրութսոյց ընթերցուածոց հոգեպատում գրոց։ Անդ քաշալերութիւն յորդորական լուսաւոր վարդապետութեան, առ ի յառաջադէմ ընտրութիւն պատկանամբար քրիստոսադիր կեանն։ Անդ եռալ հոգւով աստուածապաշտ ծառայութեամբ։ Անդ աղոթք ադերսալիք և պաղատանք փարբելիք և խնդրուածք հաշտեցուցիչք վասն ամենեցուն կենաց առ մարդասէրն Աստուած»։

848 «Եւ նովին հոգեկրօն արուեստիւն հանեալ աւուրս բազումս յանապատ տեղիս», յակունս Եփրատական գետոյն, յայրս և ի քարաձերպս երկըերն բնակեալ լինէր, և ի կատարս լեռանց, գործնակ առեալ գմեծի մարգապէին եղիայի, և կամ գերանեալ գմկրտչին առաքինլոյն Յովհաննու․ բարեաց գործող նախանձաւոր եղեալ՝ գնոյն կեանս վարուցն քաջութեան աստուածամուխ կենացն անձին մատուցանէր։

849 Եւ թէ երբեք երբեք իջանել լինէր, շրջել գորացուցանել գաշակերտեական ճըշմարտութեան հոգւով, «իրաց իրաց պիտոյից օգտակարաց ամենայն եկեղեցեացն հասեալ յօգնականութիւն՝ չնորհօքն Աստուծոյ առանց յապաղելոյ, առանց իրիք դպաղելոյ, հանապագ իջա

847.   Then there was there no being drunk with wine
but growth in the spirit and a preparation of their
hearts with spiritual songs to the glory and praise of
God [cf. Eph. 5.18-20]. There was pursued the study
of the sweet readings of the inspired scriptures. There
encouragement was continuous in illuminating teaching with a view to progressive election to the goal of
the crown bestowed by Christ [cf. Phil. 3.14]. Then
there was spiritual fervor in divine service [cf. Rom.
12.11]. There arose to benevolent God prayers of
supplication and desirous petitions and conciliatory
requests on behalf of life for all.[1]

848.   With these same spiritual practices he passed
many days in desert places,[1] at the source of the Euphrates river, dwelling in grottoes and caverns in the
ground[2] and on the summits of mountains, taking as
example the great Elijah or the blessed baptist, the
virtous John. Zealous for good works[3] he led the same
life of fortitude and devotion to God.

849.   And when from time to time he descended, he
went around strengthening his pupils with the spirit
of truth. He provided assistance in needful matters to
all the churches by the grace of God without delay
or other distraction. He continually

ներ ի Թրկունս դիպաց դիպաց պատանելոց, և
վճարէր գործութեամբն Աստուծոյ։ Եւ յորդորա-
գոյնս և պարաբարագոյնս և անփակ բերանով
դվւակա վարդապետութեանն ի սիրոս լողացն
սերմանեալ ծաւալեցուցանէր. և դայս արարեալ
գամենային ժամանակս իւր՝ վասն անձին և վասն
աշխարհի»։

850 «Քանդի սովոր իսկ են ճշմարիտ վար-
դապետք՝ գանձանց առաքինութիւն կանոն աշակերտելոցն դնել. մանաւանդ յուշ առնելով գոհ-
րունական գմիոյն գմիայնոյն գիմաստնոյն Աստուծոյ. քանդի աստ. «Սկսաւ Յիսուս առնել և
ուսուցանել»։ Որպ բագում անգամ առեալ գա-
շակերտան ուրոյն, և աննիագական անճամբն
օրինակ կարոտելոցն լինէր, յորժամ ի Թաբորա-
կան լերինն գաւետեացն գերանութիւն տայր, և
կամ յորժամ ի նմին լերինն գկանոնական ա-
ղօթան առնէր, մինչ դեռ աշակերտքն ի Տիբե-
րական ծովուն նաւէին։ Եւ դարձեալ՝ յալուրս
բազարչակերացն յօրինական տօնին գգիշերոյն
աղօթս երիցա անգամ ի Ձիթաստանեաց լերինն
առանձինն մատուցանէր։ Ուստի և յայտ իսկ է
և առանց վենէրելոյ, եթէ ոչ վասն անձին ամե-
նատէրն, այլ համաշխարհի յուսումն դայն գոր-
ծէր, որ է օրինակ ամենային հնագանդելոց. վասն
որոյ և ասէըն իսկ, թէ «Արթուն կացէք յաղօթս կացէք, դի մի մտանիցէք ի փորձութին»։

gave support in all occurrences, acting by the power of God. With unceasing mouth he spread the abundant and fertile rivers of his teaching in the hearts of his listeners. This he did all his days, for himself and for the country.[1]

850.   For true teachers are accustomed to set their own virtue as a canon to their pupils, taking especial note of the (saying) concerning the Lord,[1] the one and only wise God; for (scripture) says: "Jesus began to do and to teach" [Acts 1.1]. He often took his pupils aside and in his perfect person served as example to those who lacked (perfection)—(as) when on Mount Tabor he gave his blessed message [cf. Matt. 5.1-11; Lk. 6.20-49], or when on the same mountain he made the canonical prayer while the disciples were sailing on Lake Tiberias [cf. Jn. 6.15].[2] Again, in the days of unleavened bread on the legal festival he made the evening prayer three times on the Mount of Olives alone [cf. Matt. 26.39-44]. So it is undoubtedly obvious that the Lord of all did this not for himself but to teach the whole world as an example to all the obedient. Therefore he said: "Be awake and pray, lest you enter into temptation" [Matt. 26.41; Mk. 14.38; Lk. 22.46].[3]

851 «Իսկ արդ՝ եթէ թեթևագոյն արուեստից պակասագոյն ի գիտութենէ են ազգք երկրածնաց, որչափ այնմ արուեստի ոք համարիցի անգիտանալ, որ ընդ աստուածախօսան կատարի, որում երանելին Պաւղոս ամենեցուն անգիտանալ ասէ. վասն որոյ և զամենակեցոյց Հոգին ի Թիկունս հասանել անմռունչ հեծութեամբ բարեխօս գիտէ»:

852 «Իսկ արդ՝ յորժամ լսիցեմք, եթէ «Սկաւ Յիսուս առնել և ուսուցանել»՝ ապաքէն առնել՝ զի ուսուցէ, և ոչ եթէ զի պարգևեցի, իմանալի է. և բարեխօսեն նորա վասն սրբոց, և բարեխօսել Հոգւոյն սրբոյ՝ առ ի վարդապետելոյ մեզ, զի ընդ միմեանց բարեխօսիցեմք. և ոչ եթէ առ բարձրագոյն ոք Միածնին կամ Հոգւոյն սրբոյ բարեխօսելն գիտելի է. քանզի միապատիւ է աստուածականն, և ոչ բազմաբար. Իսկ երանելի առաքելոցն ընկալեալ ի վարդապետութենէ ճշմարտութեանն՝ նախ կարօտական անձանցն օգուտ մատակարարէին, և ապա օրինակ աշակերտելոցն բարձեալ տանէին. երբեմն առանձինն, և երբեմն ժողովովք գումարելովք՝ զփառսն Քրիստոսի առաւելովքն բարձրացուցանէին»:

853 «Քանզի առաւել օգտակար իսկ է յամենայն աշխարհակիր գեսսանաց առանձինն սահմանել, և միայն աստուածապաշտութեան պա-

851. Now if earth-born races lack the knowledge of the lightest skills, how much would one be considered ignorant of that skill which is only fulfilled among those who speak with God, of which blessed Paul says all are ignorant [cf. I Cor. 14.36-8]? Therefore he knows that the all-vivifying Spirit comes to (our) support as intercessor through (our) inarticulate groaning [cf. Rom. 8.26].[1]

852. Now when we hear that "Jesus began to do and to teach" [Acts 1.1], then "to do" must be understood that (he so acted) in order to teach and not that he might be rewarded. And his intercession was for the saints, while the intercession of the holy Spirit is to instruct us that we intercede for each other; and the intercession of the Only-begotten or of the holy Spirit is not to be understood as (being directed) to some higher person, because the divine is one in honor and not multiple. But the holy apostles received from the teaching of the truth, and first they provided profit for their own weak[1] selves, and then they provided an example to the disciples; sometimes alone and sometimes gathered in groups they exalted the glory of Christ.[2]

853. For it is more profitable to separate oneself from all worldly distractions and concern oneself solely with the service of God.

բապել։ Զոր և մարդարէքն յառաշագոյն գործէին, որք ի լերինս և յանապատ, յայրս և ի
փապարս վիմաց պատուածեղէն կրօնիցն դձա-
ռայութիւն հարկանէին։ Նոյնպէս և ամենայն
հարքն որ յաջորդեցան, յառաքելական կանո-
նացն կրեալ՝ ինքեանք անձամբ թերէին օրինակ
վերշնոցս։ Ուստի և երանելիս այս բարձեալ
տանէր դաւանդելոցն պատիւ, և ամենայն մա-
տուցելոց առ նա գնոյն պատուիրեալ գուշակէր։
Եւ այնպէս յառաշ, ամենայն ատուածեղէն
գանձուցն վայելչութեամբք լցեալ պարարտա-
ցուցեալ ամեթութեամբք գամենեսեան՝ խադա-
ցեալ գայր ի բազում ժամանակս, և նովին ի
նոյն կանխեալ և ի նմին հանապագորդեալ»։

854   «Յայսմ ժամանակի երանելի
ցանկալի և անպայման իքանչելի լինէր երկիրս
Հայոց. որպէս զՄովսէս, որ յանկարծ ուրեմն
օրէնուսոյց հեբրայական թանակին լինէր, ամենայն մարգարէական դասուն, և կամ իբրև գյա-
ռաշագդէն Պաղոս բովանդակ առաքելական
գնդաւն, հանդերձ աշխարհակեցոյց աւետարանաւն Քրիստոսի՝ սոյնպէս և սա եկեալ հասեալ
երևեալ՝ հայաքարքառ հայերէնախոս գտաւ»։

855 Արդ՝ բառ գաւառագ գաւառագ երթեալ ընութէր անձին իւրում կայս հանգստեան
յանապատ տեղիան և անդ բնակէր, և յանապա-
տացն լուսաւորէր գամենեսեան։

This the prophets did in the past, who in the mountains and deserts, in grottoes and caves in the rock [cf. Heb. 11.38] pursued the service of divine religion. Likewise all the fathers who succeeded them, guided by the apostolic canons, themselves bore the example of their predecessors. So this blessed saint also bore the honor of these traditions and enjoined the same honor to all who approached him. Proceeding thus he filled, comforted and fortified everyone in the enjoyment of all the divine treasure. And on many occasions he was prompt (in performing such tasks) and continued to persevere therein.[1]

854.   At that time our land of Armenia was blessed, envied and truly admired. Like Moses, who suddenly became a teacher of the law to the Hebrew camp with all the ranks of the prophets, or like the outstanding[1] Paul with the entire group of the apostles, with the gospel of Christ that brings life to the world, so too did he come and appear and speak Armenian to the Armenians.[2]

855.   Then he went through every province and chose for himself a spot for repose in desert places and there he dwelt, illuminating everyone from the desert.

856 Եւ բազմացոյց կացոյց տեսուչս եպիս֊
կոպոսս յամենայն գաւառս Հայոց իշխանութեան
իւրոյ. եւ որ յատրճան եպիսկոպոսութեան ձեռ֊
նադրեցան ի նմանէ՝ աւելի քան դշորեքարիւր
եպիսկոպոս, որք կացին տեսուչք տեղեաց տեղ֊
եաց։ Իսկ կարգք երիցանց կամ սարկաւագաց
կամ անագնուաց, եւ որ այլ ևս ի պաշտօն
Տեառն կացին՝ անթիւք էին ի բազմութեանէ։

857 Իսկ Թագաւորն Տրդատ՝ ուստ գայս
դնէր ընդ ամենայն մարդոյ, որ միանդամ ընդ
նորա տէրութեամբն էին, ընդ մեծի եւ ընդ
փոքու, զի ամենեցունց հաստատութիւն այն
կայցէ առ նա, զի անխորշ եւ անխէթ ատուա֊
ծաշրամ ան պատուիրանացն հնազանդեսցին ա֊
ռանց երկմտութեան, եւ աբախչութեանն հաւա֊
տալ յամենայն սրտէ։ Եւ ամենեցուն հաւանեալ
այսմ՝ փութային կատարել վազվազակի գշրա֊
մանան։

858 Իսկ Թագաւորն շատ ապաչեաց դԳրի֊
գոր վան հանապագործ առ նմա կալոյ, զի ընդ
ինքեան շրշեցուցանէ. որում ոչ հաւանեալ չառ֊
նոյր յանձն, այլ յանապատ տեղիս հանջեալ բնա֊
կութեամբ, պանովք կոխեալ դինքն, զի մի տա֊
ցէ հպարտութեանն բարձրանալ կոխել դինքն.
այլ կէտ եդեալ ինքեան՝դամենայն աւուրս կենաց
իւրոյ գբառասուն քառասուն օր պանովք ձգտել
մինչեւ յօր քրիստոսակոչ հանգստեանն իւրոյ վախ֊

856.   He increased the number of overseeing bishops in all the Armenian provinces under his jurisdiction.[1] Those who were ordained to the rank of bishop by him were more than four hundred bishops, who were established as overseers for every region. But the ranks of priests or deacons or readers[2] and the others who were in the Lord's service were innumerable in their multitude.

857.   And king Trdat made this covenant with all the people who were under his rule, both great and small, that all might have this firm pact with him: to obey ardently and frankly the divine commandments without doubting,[1] and to believe in the Creator with all their heart. They all agreed to this and straightway hastened to fulfill the commands.

858.   The king greatly implored Gregory to remain with him continuously and to travel around with him, but he did not agree; he rather preferred to live in desert places, suppressing himself by fasts to prevent pride from rising up and trampling him down. He had made a rule for himself that all the days of his life he would extend his fasts over forty days until the day of his death when summoned by Christ to rest.[1]

ճանիս։

859 Իսկ իբրև կարի կարօտեալ թագաւորն
աշխարհաւն հանդերձ գնմանէն, զի ի մէջ նոցա
բնակեցէ, և քանքատէին կարօտեալք ի կայս
նորա՝ յայնմ ժամանակի լուան յոմանց ի տե-
դեկաց, որ գիտակ արարին զթագաւորն վասն
սրբոյն Գրիգորի, զի յայնժամ յառաջ ես, մինչ
դեռ ի մանկութեան աստին էր գինուորու-
թեամբ՝ ամուսնացեալ և երկուս որդիս ստա-
ցեալ. որոց առաջնոյն անուն ճանաչէր Վրթա-
նէս, որ յաշխարհակեաց կեանս էր. որ ապա և
նա յաստիճան պաշտաման կաց երիցութեան. և
երկրորդին՝ Արիստակէս, որ ի մանկութենէ ըստ
աստուածագործ ծառայութեան մնեալ էր. «որ
ի միայնակեաց լեռնակեաց ի կրօնս մտեալ էր,
և բագում և ազգի ազգի վշտակեցութիւն ըստ
Աւետարանին կրեալ ամենայն կրթութեամբ, և
ամենայն իրաց հոգեւորաց դանձն տուեալ—միայ-
նաւորութեան, լեռնակեցութեան, քաղցի և ծա-
րաւոյ և բանջարաճաշակ կենաց, արգելանաց
անլուսից, խարագնադգեստ և գետնատարած ան-
կողնոց. և բագում անդամ գնեշտական հան-
գիստն գիշերաց, գճարկ քնոյ, յոռնաւոր տքնու-
թեան ի թօթափել ական վճարէր. և դայ արաբեալ ոչ սակաւ ժամանակս։ Եւ գտեալ ես գու-
մանս՝ լինքն յարեցուցեալ և աշակերտեալ սմին
աւետարանական սպառաւորութեան։ Եւ այսպես

859.   Now while the king and his country were sorely
wishing him to dwell amongst them and lamenting his
absence, then they heard from some informed persons
who told the king that in time past, when Gregory
was still in the flower of his youth and of military age,
he had been married and had had two sons.[1] The first
of these was called Vrt'anēs, who led a secular life,[2]
though later he too was raised to the priesthood; and
the second was Aristakēs, who from his childhood had
been brought up in the service of God. He had entered
the religious life of hermits in the mountains, and had
undertaken many and various austerities according to
the gospel with all diligence, and had given himself
entirely to spiritual affairs—to solitude, dwelling in
the mountains, hunger and thirst and living off vegetables, being shut up without light, wearing a hair shirt,
using the ground as a bed, often spending the sweet
repose of night—the need of sleep—in wakeful vigils
on his feet. This he did for no little time. And finding
other (disciples) he associated them with himself and
instructed them in this same service of the gospel.
Thus

ամենայն փորձութեանց ի վերայ հասելոց կա-
մայական քաջութեամբ տարեալ, և նովիմբ լուսաւորեալ և պայծառացեալ, և ձանօթական և
հանոյ եղեալ առաջի Աստուծոյ և ամենայն
մարդկան»։

860 Արդ՝ իբրև լուաւ զայս ամենայն թագաւորն Տրդատ՝ վաղվաղակի փութով և անզգա-
դապէս արձակէր արս երիս աւագս փառաւորս
պատուականս հրովարտակօք հանդերձ, զի զերկոսին որդիսն Գրիգորի վաղ առ նա հասուցեն։
Եւ որք առաքեցանն յարքայէ զնոցանէն, զի
ածցեն զնոսա՝ այսոքիկ են. առաջնոյն անուն
Արտաւազդ, որ սպարապետն էր ամենայն գո-
րածն Հայոց Մեծաց. և երկրորդին Տանատ
անուն, իշխան Աշոցաց գաւառին. երրորդին՝
Դատ անուն, կարապետ արքայի։

861 Արդ՝ եկին հասին նոքա յաշխարհս Կապուտկացւոց և դտին զՎրթանէս ի
Կեսարացւոց քաղաքին, և զսուրբն Արիստակէս
ընակեալ յանապատի, յիւրում մենաւորատա-
նին. ապա ոչ հաւանէր նա իջանել յանապատէ
անտի. մինչև եղև ժողով բագմութեան քրիստոնէից, որք հաւանեցուցին զնա զնալ անտի. զի
«Լաւ է, ասեն, քեզ գործ մշակութեանն Աս-
տուծոյ՝ քան զայդ մենաւորութիւն ընակութեան յանապատի այդր»։ Զորս այնունետև և
յուղարկեցին զնոսա անտի։ Իսկ նոքա եկին հա-

he willingly and bravely endured all trials which came upon him, and thereby was illuminated and became renowned, and he was known and pleasing before God and all men.[3]

860. Now when king Trdat heard all this, he straightway in haste and without delay sent three noble, famous and honorable men with letters to bring the two sons of Gregory quickly to him. And those who were sent by the king to bring them were these: the first was called Artavazd,[1] who was the commander in chief[2] of all the army of Greater Armenia; the second was called Tachat,[3] prince of the province of Ashots'k';[4] the third was called Dat, the royal herald.[5]

861. So they arrived in the country of Cappadocia and found Vrt'anēs in the city of Caesarea, and the saintly Aristakēs dwelling in the desert in his own hermitage. But he did not agree to come down from the desert until a gathering of many Christians was held, who persuaded him to leave there. "The task of God's labor," they said, "is better for you than this solitary living in the desert." So then they sent them off. They returned

ոքն յերկիրն Հայոց, և յանդիման ունէին գա-
ձեալսն, զերկոսին որդիսն Գրիգորի, առաջի
թագաւորին. զորս առեալ թագաւորին՝ ինքնին
նոքօք հանդերձ ի խնդիր եղանէր սրբոյն Գրի-
գորի՝ ուր և գացցէ։ Եւ եկեալ գտանէին ի Դարանաղեաց գաւառին, ի լեռինն որ կոչի Մա-
նեայ Այրք, յանապատին։

862 Ապա ապաշեաց երանելի թագաւորն
Տրդատ զաւրբն Գրիգորիոս, զի փոխանակ
այնր, զի ոչ հաւանեցաւ նա կալ և շրջել ընդ
նմա, և սիրեաց զմենաւորութեան կեանս՝ ձեռ-
նադրեցէ և տացէ նմա եպիսկոպոս զաւրբ որդին իւր, զոր եւս աճել ինքն՝ զԱրիստակէս։ Զոր
ձեռնադրեաց յեպիսկոպոսութիւն փոխանակ իւր.
որպէս բստ գրեցելոյն ի դեզ, թէ «Փոխանակ
հարց եղիցին որդիք՝ կալ իշխան ի վերայ երկրի»։ Որ առաւել եւս քան գհայրն վերագոյն երե-
ւեցուցանէր զիւր վարդապետութիւնն առ հար-
բրն. և յետ նորա կալաւ գտեղի հայրենեացն և
անդէն նստաւ յաթոռ կաթողիկոսութեան Հայոց Մեծաց։ Ապա և ինքն իսկ մեծն Գրիգորիոս
«եղանէր զտեղօքն կարգելովք և զգաւառքն
աշակերտելովք յաշխարհին Հայոց՝ զուարթացու-
ցանել, զօրացուցանել, նորոգել և հաստատել
զամենեսեան»։

863 Եւ աստուածատէր թագաւորն Տրդատիոս բարեպաշտութեամբ սպասաւորեալ, ըստ

to Armenia and presented to the king the two sons of
Gregory whom they had brought. The king received
them, and in person went out with them to seek saint
Gregory, wherever he might find him. And they came
and found him in the province of Daranalik',[1] on the
mountain called the Caves of Manē,[2] in the wilderness.

862.   Then the blessed king Trdat begged saint Gregory that since he had not agreed to remain and go
around with him and because he loved the solitary
life, he would in return ordain and give him as bishop
his saintly son Aristakēs, whom he had had brought.
He ordained him to the episcopacy in his place,[1] according to the appropriate saying: "The sons will take
the place of the fathers, to be ruler over the land"
[Ps. 44.17].[2] He was even more successful in his teaching than his father during the latter's lifetime, and after
him he held his father's position and sat on the throne
of the Catholicos[3] of Greater Armenia. Then the great
Gregory himself went out around the places he had set
in order and the provinces where he had taught in
Armenia to comfort, strengthen, renew and confirm[4]
everyone.

863.   And the God-loving king Trdat served piously

աշակերտական հաւատոց ի Քրիստոս՝ երկիւղած
գտանէր, որ և տեղեկացեալ և վարժեալ աստ-
ուածակեաց հրամանօքն, և ցանկալի եղեալ օրի-
նապահ ընկալելուվքն, և բարեաց օրինակ ամենայն աշխարհի։ «Եւ անդէն ի նմին ուշ եղեալ
փութով ընթերթուածոց աստուածեղէն գրոց»:
Զի յունական աշխարհական դպրութեանն, երկրաւոր իմաստութեանն, յառաջադոյն էր տեղ-
եակ, առաւել փիլիսոփայական մաց հանճարա-
գիտութեան հմուտ էր, զի ուսեալ էր գայն:

864 Արդ՝ ընկալեալ և զշնորհս երկնաւոր
պարգևացն, «որով առժամայն լուսաւորեալ և
թեակորդ թեամուխ եղեալ աստուածատուր հրամանացն ի հանգամանս, և ամենայն պատրաս-
տութեամբ գանձն յարդարեալ», «և ըստ աւետարանական չափոցն ի ծառայութիւն Աստուծոյ մարդասիրին դարձեալ։ Մերկացեալ այնուհետև զհեթանոսակիր ցանկութիւնսն, և առեալ
զնշան պարծանաց խաչին յանձն իւր, և երթեալ
զկնի ամենակեցոյց խաչելոյն՝ հաճել զհրամա-
նացն պայման, զկնի խաչակիր գնդին Քրիստոսի
աշակերտելոյն հետևեալ»։ Եւ անգին իւրում
եղեալ սանման պանծ և ոքնութեամբ «աղօթս
մշանջենամուունչա և բագկատարած պաղատանս
առ Աստուած, և արտասուս հանապազաբուղխս»
վասն աշխարհին իւրոյ։ Նոյնպէս և վասն իւր
խնդրէր, զի մի լիշեսցին մեղքն որ յառաջին

the apostolic faith in Christ. He was God-fearing, and was informed and instructed in the divine commandments, he was loved[1] for his acceptance and respect for the law, and was an example of goodness to the whole land; he also was very diligent in the reading of the divine scriptures.[2] For he was very expert in Greek secular literature and earthly wisdom, and he was especially versed in the science of philosophical reasoning, for he had studied it.

864.   So he received the grace of the heavenly gifts whereby he was then illuminated, and he was completely devoted to the requirements of the divine commandments, and in great willingness accommodated himself (to them), and according to the rule of the gospel turned to the service of the benevolent God. Thenceforth he stripped off pagan vices and accepted the sign of the cross of boasting, following the crucified Savior of all, fulfilling the demands of the commandments and following the crusading band of Christ's disciples.[1] He imposed upon himself fasts and vigils and unceasing prayers and supplications to God with arms outstretched, and ever-flowing tears[2] for his country. Similarly he asked on his own behalf that his sins, committed in his earlier

տղիտութեանն, յայնժամ գոր ի հեթանոսու֊
թեանն անդ գործէր։

ë65 «Եւ բազում և ամենայն ուժով նպաս֊
տաւորութիւն ընծայեցուցեալ աւետարանագործ
վարդապետութեանն, և հնազանդութեամբ հպա֊
տակութիւն ցուցեալ և ծառայեալ ըստ Աւետա֊
րանին վայելչութեամբ»։ և այսպէս խրատեալ
և զգատացեալ կրօնաւորական վարուք, ամե֊
նայն ուղղութեամբ յամենայն գործս բարու֊
թեանց առաւել եւ պայծառացուցանէր զվար֊
դապետութեանն ստաբութիւն։

866 Իսկ մեծ արքեպիսկոպոսն երանելին
Գրիգորիոս, սուրբ որդւոյն իւրով Արիստակէ֊
սաւ և ամենայն երևելի օգնականօքն, զամե֊
նայն աշակերտովքն շրջէր, և հաստատէր զնոսա՝
կալ ի պատուիրանին ճշմարտութեան։

867 Ընդ ժամանական ընդ այնոսիկ
Թագաւորեաց Կոստանդիանոս որդի Կոստան֊
դեայ արքայի յերկրին Սպանիացւոց և Գաղիա֊
ցւոց. և հաւատաց նա յԱստուած, յարարիչն
երկնի և երկրի, և ի ծնունդն ի Բանն նորա,
յՈրդին Միածին, և ի Հոգին սուրբ Աստուա֊
ծութեան նորա։ Եւ կուտեաց գումարեաց առ
ինքն զբազմութիւն զօրաց իւրոց առ ափն Ով֊
կիանոս անագին ծովուն. և ուխտէր գայս բան
ընդ ամենեսին, զի առ հասարակ ամենայն ոք
ճշմարտութեանն հաւատասցէ. «միով աստուա֊

ignorance when he was a pagan, might not be remembered.

865. With great solicitude he assisted the work of the teaching of the gospel, showing willing help and happily serving according to the gospel.[1] And thus, leading a reformed and sober and religious life, in all rectitude and in every good work he rendered glorious the task of teaching [cf. II Tim. 3.16-17].

866. The great archbishop,[1] the blessed Gregory, with his son Aristakēs and all his illustrious helpers went around among his pupils and strengthened them to stand firm in the commandment of truth.

[Chapter 14. Gregory and Trdat visit Constantine; the Council of Nicaea; Gregory's last years]

867. At that time Constantine,[1] son of Constantius the king, became emperor in Spain and Gaul. And he believed in God, in the creator of heaven and earth, and in his offspring, the Word, the only-begotten Son, and the holy Spirit of his Godhead. He gathered to himself a multitude of his forces by the shore of the fearsome Ocean sea,[2] and he made this covenant with them all, that they should all in unison believe in the truth, and with a single

ծաբարբառ պատգամօք՝ մի ազգ կատարեալ փառաւորիչ միոյ Աստուծոյ լինել»։

868 Եւ յԱստուած խրախուսեալ՝ դիմէր ի վերայ հեթանոսական թագաւորացն, և անդէն ստակէր առ հասարակ գամենեսեան, գորս կործանէր գորւթեամբ ասատւածեան խաչին, գպիղծ և գանօրէն Թագաւորսն, գԴիոկղետիանոս և գՄարկիանոս և գՄաքսիմիանոս և գԼիկիանոս և գՄաքսենտիոս, և գամենայն գաւակ պղծալից Թագաւորացն հեթանոսաց Ջնջէր ի միջոյ։

869 Շինէր և գաւերեալ եկեղեցիսն, և կանդնէր գտեղանսն կործանեալս ի տան Տեառն. շինէր և գառաքինարանսն վկայից, և բագմացուցանէր գփառաւորւթիւն յիշատակաց երանելեացն մարտիրոսաց, և յաճախէր գպատիւ քահանայիցն Աստուծոյ, միանգամայն առնել խաղաղւթիւն երկրաւորաց, բառնալ գգայթակղւթիւնս ի միջոյ. գի մի ոք մի իւիք սայթաքիցէ յասատւածագնաց ճանապարհէն։ Աւերէր գպղծ ծալից մեհեանս դիւացն, և գնոսա առ հասարակ միանգամայն իսկ իւրեանց պաշտօնէիւքն ի փախուստ դարձուցեալ պակասեցուցանէր։ Պատիւս և պարգես այնոցիկ շնորհէր, որք յասատւածապաշտւթեան ճշմարտւթեան կացեալ էին, և ոչ երբեք գնասատատւթիւնն Թողեալ։ Վասն այսորիկ յաղթւթիւն տուաւ նմա ի վերայ ամենայնի, վասն գի առ նա գնչան յաղ-

divine voice they should be a perfect race glorifying the one God.[3]

868.   And trusting in God he marched against the heathen kings, and there suppressed them all, destroying them by the power of the divine cross, the foul and impious kings Diocletian and Marcianos[1] and Maximianos and Licinius and Maxentius; and all the offspring of these foul heathen kings he exterminated.[2]

869.   He rebuilt the destroyed churches and restored the overthrown altars in the house of the Lord. He built chapels for the martyrs, and multiplied the glory of the commemorations of the blessed martyrs, and increased the honor of the priests of God, at once bestowing peace on the inhabitants of the earth and removing scandals, that no one in any way might slip from the path that leads to God. He destroyed the impure temples of the demons and obliterated them altogether, turning their ministers to flight. Honors and gifts he bestowed on those who kept to true piety and never abandoned its security. Therefore victory was given him over everyone, because he took for himself the sign

Թուխեան խաչին յանձն իւր։

870 Եւ գՀրաման ստատկութեան պատուի֊
րանին ճշմարտութեան, կալ յայսմիկ ի Հաստա֊
տութեան Հալատոցն գոր առ ի Տեառնէ՝ Հրո֊
վարտակօք իւրովք ընդ տիեզերս տարածանէր,
սպառնացեալ յաղթող զօրութեամբն՝ լուսոյն
Հալատող որ առ ի Տէր ունել գբարեպաշտու֊
թիւնն. և այսուիկ Հալածէր զգորս խալարին, և
ի վերայ ամենայնի վերնոյն զօրութեամբ գեր
ի վերոյ լինէր։ Իսկ որք այսմ Հալանեալք՝ գի
երկրպագուք լիցին ճշմարտութեանն՝ դնոստ բա֊
րեկամեալ մերձեալ պատուեալ՝ առ ինքն մա֊
տուցանէր։ Եւ այսու օրինակաւ Հգոր երևեալ՝
ի վերայ մարդկանն Հաստատէր գԹագաւորու֊
թիւնն իւր, աստուածակարգ Թագաւորութիւն
գիւր Թագաւորութիւնն անուանեալ, մինչ այն֊
չափ Հգորացեալ ի վերայ ամենայն մարդկան՝
իրաւացի լինէր պայծառացեալ։

871 Եւ այսպէս յաղթող երևեալ գինքն Հա֊
ստատէր՝ մինչև գամենայն աւուրս կենաց իւրոց
Հրեշտակ յերկնից երևեալ, գոր Հանապագ նմա
սպասաւոր կացեալ՝ ընդ առաւօտս առաւօտս
գբրիստոսեան նշան Թագի նորին առեալ՝ ի նո֊
րին գլուխն դնէր. և այսպէս տեսեալ գերկնա֊
ւոր գՀրեշտակն յիւրում սպասաւորութեան երա֊
նելին և ցանկալին ամենայն Թագաւորաց Կոս֊
տանդիանոս։ Որ և գիւր Թագաւորութեանն ծի֊

of the victorious cross.

870. And the firm order of the commandment of truth—to stand firmly in the faith [cf. I Tim. 2-15] which comes from the Lord—he spread throughout the world by his edicts, terrifying (everyone) by his victorious power to cleave to the true piety of the light of faith in the Lord. Thus he pursued the hosts of darkness and overcame them all by his power from above. Those who agreed to become worshipers of the truth he honored and treated as his friends. In this fashion he became powerful and strengthened his rule over mankind, calling his kingdom a divinely-established kingdom. He became so powerful over all men that truly he was glorified.

871. Thus he so consolidated his victorious position that all the days of his life an angel[1] appeared from heaven continuously serving him every day: every morning he took the crown (marked) with Christ's sign[2] and put it on his head. So the blessed and most wonderful of all kings, Constantine, saw the heavenly angel in his service. And he,

բանիս Քրիստոսի աւանդէր, աստուածատէրն և
յազթողն ի վերայ ամենեցուն, որ հաստատէր
զԹագաւորուԹիւնն հալատովք, և յամենայն եկեղեցիսն հաստատէր գնալատան ճշմարտուԹեան:

872   Յայնմ ժամանակի լու եղև այս
յերկիրն Հայոց Մեծաց, ի դուռն Թագաւորու-
Թեանն Արշակունեաց, առ Տրդատ արքայ Հայոց
Մեծաց: Որ իբրև լուաւ գայս՝ բազում փառա-
լորուԹիւն ամենատեառնն մատուցանէր. խռն-
դուԹեամբ և մեծաւ ուրախուԹեամբ գոհանայր
գայսմանէ, որ ընդ ամենայն երկիր գիւր սուրբ
անունն փառաւոր առնէր:

873 Ապա իբրև լուաւ գայս ամենայն մեծ
արքայն Հայոց Տրդատ՝ խորհուրդ առնոյր վասն
ճանապարհացն այնոցիկ. հանդերձէր կազմէր առնոյր ընդ իւր գմեծ արքեպիսկոպոսն գԳրիգորիոս
և գնորբին որդին գԱրիստակէս եպիսկոպոս և գմիւս
եպիսկոպոսն գԱղբիանոս: Եւ ի գինուորական
կողմանէն՝ գչորեսին գանԳերէցան իւրոյ տաճարին,
որ բդեաշխքն կոչին. գառաջին սահմանակալն ի
Նոր Շիրական կողմանէն, և գերկրորդ սահմանակալն յԱսորեստանեայց կողմանէն, և գեռրորդն՝
յԱրուաստան կողմանէն, գչորրորդն՝ ի ՄասքԹաց
կողմանէն. գմեծ իշխանն Անգեղ տան, և գԹա-
գագիր ասպետն, և գապարապետն մեծ, և գիշխանն Մոկաց, և գիշխանն Սիւնեաց, և գիշխանն
Ռշտունեաց, և գիշխանն ՄաղխագուԹեան տանն,

the pious and all-victorious, who established his kingdom in faith and confirmed the true faith in all churches, offered the purple of his royalty to Christ.

872.   At that time this news reached Greater Armenia, the royal court of the Arsacids, and Trdat king of Greater Armenia. When he heard this he rendered great glory to the Lord of all. With joy and rejoicing he thanked him who had made his holy name glorious throughout all the land.

873.   Then when the great king of Armenia, Trdat, heard this he held council to consider this journey. He made preparations and took with him the great archbishop Gregory and his son bishop Aristakēs and the other bishop, Albianos;[1] and from the armed forces the four most senior ranking of his court, who are called *bdeashkh*:[2] the first the border-guard from the district of Nor Shirakan,[3] the second the border-guard from Assyria, the third from the district of Aruastan,[4] the fourth from the district of the Massagetae;[5] the great prince of the house of Angl,[6] and the *aspet*[7] who crowned (the kings), and the great High-Constable,[8] and the prince of Mokk',[9] the prince of Siwnik',[10] the prince of the Rshtunik',[11] the prince of the house of the *Malkhazdom*,[12] the

և դշաճապն Շաճապիվանի, և գիշխանն սպաս-
կապետութեանն։ Եւ այլ բազում մեծամեծօք, և
եօթանասուն ճազարաւ ընտիր գօրու ճանդերձ՝
խաղայր գնայր յԱյրարատ գաւառէ ի Վաղարշապատ քաղաքէ՝ անցանել ի սաճմանս Յունաց։

874 «Զանց առնէր գբազում օթեւանօք մեծաւ ուրախութեամբ»։ Եւ բազում պատիւս
պատրաստութեան նպատակութեան, ըստ քաղաքաց քաղաքաց դիպելոց և իշխանաց իշխանաց
պատանէլոց, գտանէին մեծարանս ընդունելու-
թեան։ Ընդ ցամաք և ընդ ծով փութացեալ աճապարէին, մինչ երթային ճասանէին յաշխարհն
Իտալիացւոց, յերկիրն Դաղմատացւոց, ի թա-
գաւորական քաղաքն Հռովմայեցւոց։

875 «Զորմէ իսկոյն պատմեալ յարքունական պաղատանն. գոր իբրև լուաւ աստուածակարգ թագաւորն պատուական աշխուռյն Կոստանդիանոս, և ճայրապետն մեծ, արքեպիսկոպոսն աշխարճամուտ դրանն, որում անուն կոչէր Եւսեբիոս՝ մեծաւ սիրով պատիւ արարեալ՝
ընդ առաջ ելանէին, և տուեալ մինեանց գնան-
գիտապատիւ ողջոյնն ուրախ լինէին։ Եւ եղեալ
ժամանակս ինչ անդէն ի տիեզերական քաղաքին»՝ ապա գարմացեալ աստուածատէր կայսրն
Կոստանդիանոս, ճարցանելով գարքայն Տրդատ,
թէ «ԶիմՁրդ կամ ՚ճրպէս եղեն առ քեզ Աստուծոյ սքանչելիքն»։

prefect of Shahapivan[13] and the master of the court.[14] And with many other magnates and with seventy thousand chosen troops he hastened from the province of Ayrarat, from the city of Vaḷarshapat to pass into Greek territory.[15]

874. In great joy they passed many stages,[1] and met with honorable receptions and solicitous honors from every city they came to and from every noble they met. By land and by sea they hastened on their way until they arrived in the empire of the Italians, in the land of the Dalmatians,[2] in the royal capital of Rome.

875. Straightway news of this was reported to the royal palace.[1] When the emperor Constantine, established by God and honorable holder of the throne, and the great Patriarch,[2] archbishop of the imperial court who was called Eusebius,[3] heard this, with great love they honored them and went out to meet them. Greeting each other mutually they rejoiced. And when they had been some while in the universal city,[4] then the pious emperor Constantine was amazed, and he asked king Trdat: "How and in what manner did these miracles of God occur among you?"

876 Իսկ նա կաց պատմեաց առաջի կայսերն զամենայն արարեալն Աստուծոյ առ նա
զբարերարութիւնն։ Եւ զանճառին զպատու-
ճան, զլինել ի կերպարանս անասնոյ, ոչ ամօթ
համարեցաւ պատմել նմա։ Եւ զդամբերութիւն
նահատակեալ վկայից քաջութեան, և որ գործ
գործեցան և որպէս բնութիւն զօրութեան նո-
ցա։ Կամ զոր անդէն իսկ յանդիման ցուցանէր
կայսերն զտարբեալն ընդ իւր զԳրիգոր, եթէ
«Այս այն այր է, ասէ, յոյր ձեռն ձանեաք մեք
զմարդասիրութիւնն Աստուծոյ, և զնորին ժուժկալութիւն համբերութեանն նշանաւոր գործա-
նագործութեանցն։ Վասն որոյ զարմացեալ կայսրն Կոստանդիանոս, խոնարհեցուցեալ զանձն՝
անկանէր առաջի Գրիգորի, զի օրհնեսցի ի նմանէ. և բազում վայելուչ մեծարանօք պատիւ
արարեալ նմա, իբրև խոստովանողի Քրիստոսի,
ըստ արժանաւորութեան նորա։

877 Սոյնպէս և արքային Տրդատայ, իբրև
եղբօր սիրելւոյ, սէր ցուցեալ ուրախութեամբ
մեծաւ, մանաւանդ վասն աստուածածանօթու-
թեան նորա՝ առաւել դաշինս կռէր ընդ նմա,
միշնորդ կալեալ զհաւատսն որ ի տէր Քրիստոսն էր, զի անշուշտ միմ ի բուն զհաւատա-
րիմ սէրն ի մէջ Թագաւորութեանցն պանեսց-
ցեն. զի ես քան զես առաւելագոյն զարքայն
Հայոց հաստատեցէ յերբորդութեան հալատն.

876. Then he stood before the emperor and told him of all the blessings performed by God for him; nor was he ashamed to narrate the fearful punishment of his being in the form of an animal. And he told about the heroic endurance of the brave martyrs, and what deeds were done, and what was their strength. Then he introduced to the emperor Gregory, whom he had brought with him, saying: "This is the man through whom we came to know God's benevolence [cf. Tit. 3.4] and the long-suffering endurance of his wondrous miracles." At this the emperor Constantine was amazed, and humbled himself and fell before Gregory to be blessed by him. And with many splendid honors he exalted him as a confessor of Christ according to his merits.

877. Similarly with great happiness he showed love for king Trdat as for a dear brother, especially because of his recognition of God. And furthermore he made an alliance[1] with him, holding their faith in the Lord Christ as an intermediary so that they might constantly and for ever keep faithful love between their kingdoms, and that he might confirm the Armenian king ever more and more in faith in the Trinity.

Իսկ Տրդատիոս պատմէր և վասն վկայիցն Աստուծոյ, թէ որպէս կամ զինչ օրինակ վկայեցին։

878 Ապա և կայսրն Կոստանդիանոս սկսաւ պատմել նմա վասն ագնուական վարուց նոցա, զոր յառաջագոյն գիտէր՝ մինչդեռ էին անդէն յիւրեանց աշխարհին, թէ որպէս հաճոյ վարուքն էին և կամ որպէս ագնուականք ի մարմնաւոր կոդմանէ տոհմակցաց իւրեանց։ Եւ զգործան գործութեան յաղթութեանն՝ յԱստուծոյ նմա տուելոյ՝ պատմէր, առ ամենայն թշնամիսն ճշմարտութեանն յաղթող երևեալ։ Ասէ. «Գիտեմ, եղբայր, զի Աստուած յամենայն երկրէ երկեցուցանէ զիւր ողորմութիւն գործութեանն. զի ամենայն արարածք նորա ձանիցեն դնա և լինիցին նորա փառաւորիչք ճշմարտութեամբ, «քանզի այնպիսի երկրպագուս իւր խնդրէ»։

879 Ապա յետ այսորիկ «մեծարեալ լինէին դարմանօք և մեծապատիւ շքեղութեան կարգօք յարքունեացն և յեկեղեցեացն և ի պատուական իշխանաց քաղաքին. և մեծամեծ պատարագօք և երևելի պարգևօք պատուեալ սիրով»։

880 «Եւ ապա հրաժարեալ ի ձիրանափառ օգոստականացն և ի սրբոյ կաթողիկոսէն, ընկալեալ ողջոյն յեկեղեցւոյն և յերեւելի իշխանաց քաղաքին, և ամենայն իրօք. յաջողեալք՝ ելանէին յուղիապատ կառս արքունատուրս, և մեծաւ

Then Tiridates told about the martyrs of God and how and in what way they had been martyred.[2]

878.   Then the emperor Constantine began to tell him about their honorable life. For he had previously known, while they were still in their own land, how pleasing their life had been and how they were of noble descent.[1] And he told of the powerful and victorious deeds given him by God so that he became victorious over all the enemies of the truth. He said: "Know, brother, that God reveals in every land his powerful mercy so that all his creatures may know him and become his praisers in truth, 'because he seeks such worshippers [Jn. 4.23].' "

879.   Then after this they were honored with great solicitude and splendid pomp by the court and the ecclesiastical officials and the honorable princes of the city.[1] And with great offerings and notable presents they were lovingly honored.[2]

880.   Then they took their leave from the purpled Augusti and the holy Catholicos,[1] being greeted by the church and the notable princes of the city, and triumphant in every way they mounted the imperial carriage decorated in gold, and with great

շքով և բազում վայելչութեամբ ունէին գձանապարհս արքունականս»։

881 «Եւ ամենայն քաղաքաց պատանելոց
պայծառագոյն երևէին, և մեծամեծս բատ արժանաւորութեան արքայութեանն պատուեալ ան-
դստին, մինչև գային հասանէին» յերկիրն Հայոց, յԱյրարատեան գաւառ, ի Վաղարշապատ
քաղաք, ի հանգստակայս սրբոցն։

882 Եւ բերէին գպարգևան տուեալս ան-
դստին, գոսկին և գարծաթն և գպատուական կա-
րասին, ի նուէր սպատու եկեղեցւոյն Աստուծոյ,
և ի տունս նուիրաց սրբոց վկայիցն դնէին։ նաև
գտուեալ գոսկի սպաս կայսերն ի նոյն հանգիստ
սրբոցն դնէին։ Եւ առաւել գիւրեանց եկեղեց-
ցեան շինեալ հաստատէին։

883 Եւ մեծն Գրիգոր առ շրջել ընդ աշա-
կերտեալան յառաջագոյն, և հաստատէր գնոսա
ի ճշմարիտ վարդապետութեանն։

884 Ապա յետ այսորիկ հրաման ետ
մեծ կայսրն, օգոստականն Կոստանդիանոս՝ ժողովել ամենայն եպիսկոպոսաց ի քաղաքն Նի-
կիացւոց։ Յայնժամ մեծ արքայն Տրդատ և սուրբ
կաթողիկոսն Գրիգորիոս հանդերձեցին և արձա-
կեցին գԱրիստակէս, որ երթեալ հասանէր ի մեծ
ժողովն Նիկիայ ընդ եպիսկոպոսան ամենայն. ուր
ամենայն տիեզերաց կարգեցաւ ընդունելութեան
աւանդութեանն հաւատք և կարգք լուսաւորու-

éclat and much splendor they set out on their royal journey.[2]

881.   And in all the cities they passed they were splendidly treated and greatly honored according to their royal dignity until they arrived[1] in Armenia, in the province of Ayrarat at the city of Vaḷarshapat and the martyr's resting-places.

882.   And they brought the gifts they had been given as an offering for the service of the church of God, gold and silver and precious furniture; these they placed in the chapels of the holy martyrs. Likewise they placed in the same (chapels) of repose of the saints the gold vessels of the emperor that they had been given. And they embellished even more elaborately their churches.[1]

883.   And the great Gregory began to travel around among his previous disciples; and he confirmed them in the true doctrine.

884.   Then after this the great emperor, the Augustus Constantine, commanded that all the bishops should assemble in the city of Nicaea.[1] Then the great king Trdat and the holy Catholicos[2] Gregory made preparations and dispatched Aristakēs.[3] He arrived at the great Council of Nicaea with all the bishops. There were defined the acceptable traditional faith for the whole world, and the illuminating ordinances,

Թեան, կանոնք պայմանաւորք, աստուածատուր
գործութիւն հանոյիցն Աստուծոյ անչափ բարձ-
րութեանցն։ Ուր և մեծ կայսրն Կոստանդիանոս
մտեալ խոստովան լինէր գհաւատան և օրհնութեամբ պատկեալ ի ժողովոյն՝ դանուն յերկրի
Թողոյր և գարդարութիւն յերկկինս հատատէր։

885 Իսկ երանելին Արիստակէս «գայր պայ-
ծառ ծագեալ հաւատովքն և հատատուն ա-
ստուածահանոյ Նիկիական կանոնօքն երևել ի
Հայաստան երկրին. և առջի դնէր թագաւորին.
և կաթողիկոսին սրբոյ՝ գբերեալ աւանդու-
թիւնսն»։ Որով սրբոյն Գրիգորի ի նոյն լուսաւոր կանոնսան յաւելեալ, առաւել ևս գիւր վի-
ճակն, գՀայաստան երկիրն, պայծառացուցեալ,
հանդերձ միաբանութեամբ աբքային Տրդատայ՝
գամենայն աւուրս կենաց՝իւրոց լուսաւորէր։

886 «Ապա յետ այնպիսի գործոց դարձեալ
առաւել բարձրագոյն վարդապետութեամբ սկե-
սեալ երանելւոյն Գրիգորի ճառս յաճախագոյնս
դժուարապատումս, առակս խորիմացս դիւրա-
լուրս բազմադիմիս չնորհագիրս, յարդարեալս ի
գործութենէ և ի հիւթոյ գրոց մարգարէականաց,
լի ամենայն ճաշակօք կարգեալս և յօրինեալս
աւետարանական հաւատողն ճշմարտութեան։
Յորս բազում նմանութիւնս և օրինակ յանցա-
ւորաց աստի, առաւել վասն յարութենական յուսոյն առ ի հանդերձեալան յերիւրեալ, զի հեշտա-

the regular canons, the divine power of the will of God the all-highest. There the great emperor Constantine entered and confessed the faith and was crowned with blessing by the council, leaving on earth renown and assuring justification in heaven.[4]

885. The blessed Aristakēs returned with the glorious faith and the confirmed and pleasing-to-God Nicene canons to make them known in Armenia. And he presented to the king and the holy Catholicos the traditions he had brought. Then saint Gregory made additions to these illuminating canons, making still more glorious his own see of Armenia,[1] which with the assistance of king Trdat he illuminated all the days of his life.

886. Then after such deeds, with even more profound teaching blessed Gregory began to compose many discourses, difficult of language, profound parables, easy to listen to, many-faceted, composed by grace, composed from the power and matter of the prophetic writings, full of all subtleties, and arranged and ordered in the truth of the evangelical faith. In these he set out many similes and examples from the transitory world, especially concerning the hope of the resurrection for the future life, that

ընկալք և դիւրահատոյցք տխմարագունից և մարմնական իրօք ջբաղելոցն լինիցին, առ ի սթափել գուարթացուցանել և հատանհիմ առ խոստացեալ աւետիսն քաջալերել»:

887 «Զաւետարանական ընթացան և գվերացուցութիւն եկեղեցւոյ սրբոյ՝ շնորհօքն Աստուծոյ առանց պակասութեան տանէր. և առաւել փութայր գուն եղեալ՝ գամենայն ոք յորդորելով առ ի բարեացն քաջալերութիւն»:

888 «Զցայդ և գցերեկ պանօք և աղօթիւք և ուժգին խնդրուածովք, և բարձրագոյն բարբառովք գասատուածաղիր պատուիրանացն գիրամանան յուշ առնելով գգուշացուցանէր ամենայն մարդոյ: «Զաւր քուն աչաց, և ոչ նինջ արտևանաց, և ոչ հանգիստ իրանացն», մինչև հասանել ի հանգիստ Տեառն»:

889 «Եւ այսպէս հանդերձ թագաւորան և ամենայն աշակերտելովքն գամենայն ժամանակս իւրեանց ընթերցուածոց գրոց ծախէին գոիւ և գգիշեր. և նովին ծաղկեալք և շահաւետեալք, և օրինակ բարեաց ուսումնասէր աղընթերակացան լինէին»:

890 «Մանաւանդ գի ունէին ես պատուիրանս գգուշացուցիչս յատուածակարգ պատգամաւորացն, որոց առաջինն հրամայէ, թէ «Յոյս Տեառն խորհեցիս ի տուէ և ի գիշերի». և երկրորդն գհամագունական պատուիրէ, թէ

they might be intelligible and easily understood by the ignorant and those occupied with worldly affairs, in order to awaken and arouse and urge them on firmly to the promised good news.[1]

887.   By the grace of God he fulfilled his preaching journeys and the oversight of the holy church without any failure. And he made all the greater effort to urge everyone on to good works.[1]

888.   Day and night, with fasting and prayers and ardent requests and strong[1] words he commended the divine commandments to everyone. "He gave no sleep to his eyes, no respite to his eyebrows, no rest to his limbs" [Ps. 131.4] until he attained the rest of the Lord.[2]

889.   And thus with the king and all his pupils they spent all their time, day and night, in the reading of the scriptures. Adorned and profited thereby, they were an example of good works to their studious companions.[1]

890.   For in particular they had the commandments of the divinely-appointed messengers admonishing them, of which the first orders: "Contemplate the law of the Lord day and night" [Ps. 1.2] and the second commands the same:

«Մին դիր ընթերցուածոց մեթիմարութեան վարդապետութեան. մի անպոյթ առներ դշնորհացդ
որ ի քեզ են. յայդ խորհեաց և ի դոյն կան-
խեսջիր, զի քո յառաջադիմութիւնդ յայտնի լիցի ամենեցուն. զգոյշ լինիջիր անձինդ և վար-
դապետութեանդ, և ի դմին յամեսջիր. զայդ եթէ
առնիցես՝ և զանձն ապրեցուսցես և զայնոսիկ
որ քեզն լսիցեն»:

891 Արդ՝ այսու օրինակաւ գամենայն ա-
ւուրս կենաց իւրոց առաքելական առաքելա-
գործ վարեալ, գետտ երթեալ հրամանացն ընկա-
լելոց մինչև ի վախճան կատարածին գայ առնէր ամ յամէ, և Թադեալ ի սէրն Քրիստոսի
լուսաւորէր:

———

892 Իսկ մեք որպէս ընկալաք գչրամանս
քոյոց Թագաւորութեանդ, քաջդ արանց Տրդատ,
գրեալ գայս ամենայն՝ որպէս օրէն է ժամա-
նակապիր մատենից՝ ըստ այնմ ձևոյ դրոշմեցաք,
ըստ օրինակի յունական ճարտարութեանն արկեալ ի շար գամենայն:

893 «Բայց նայեցաք իբրև ի ցուցող հա-
յելի յասաուածադիր բարձրութիւն տունչութեան
հրամանացն, որ առ երանելին Մովսէս եկեալ
վասն ամենայն իրացն եղելոց և ասաուածեղէն
պատգամացն ասանդելոց՝ մատենագրել ի պա-
հեստ յաւիտեանցն որ գալոցն են»:

"Attend to the readings of the teaching of consolation. Do not neglect the grace which is in you. Think on this and be prompt in the same, that your progress may be clear to all. Take care for yourself and your teaching, and persevere in the same. If you do this you will save yourself and those who hear you" [I Tim. 4.13-16].[1]

891. So in this fashion he spent all the days of his life in acts like those of the Apostles, following the commands he had received year by year until his death.[1] And immersed in Christ's love he shone forth.[2]

[EPILOGUE]

892. Now as we have received the command of your majesty, bravest of men Trdat, to write down all this as is suitable for a writer of chronicles, in this way we composed our work, setting everything in order according to the form of Greek literary skill.[1]

893. But we looked, as in a mirror [cf. I Cor. 13.12], at the divinely imposed and most elevated commandments given to the blessed Moses, in order to write of everything that occurred and of the divine sayings handed down, and to preserve them for the ages to come [cf. Deut. 31.19-24].[1]

894 «Նոյնպիսիք և այլոց մարգարէիցն հրամայեալ. «Ա՛ռ, ասէ, քարտէզ նոր մեծ և գրեա՛ ի նմա գրչաւ դպրի ճարտարի», և այլուր՝ թէ «Գրեա՛ գաեսիլդ ի տախտակի և ի գիր հաստատեա՛, զի որ ընթեռնուն՝ համարձակ ընթեռնուցու»։

895 «Իսկ Դաւիթ յայտնագոյն ևս վասն ամենայն ազգաց դվիճակ ատուածատուր օրինացն նշանակէ ասելովս, թէ «Գրեսցի այս յազգ այլ», և թէ՛ «Տէր պատմեսցէ գրովք ժողովրրդոց»։

896 «Զոր եկեալ կատարեաց ամենափրրկիչն Քրիստոս շնորհատուր հրամանաւն, թէ «Ելէք ընդ ամենայն ազգս», և թէ՛ «Քարոզեսցի Աւետարանս ի նեՐքոյ երկնից»։ ուստի և երանելւոյս այսորիկ համարձակութիւն առեալ յուսալից փութով երեկելի և արդիւնակատար ըստ Աւետարանին գիրՐ մշակութիւնն ցուցանէր։

897 «Եւ արդ՝ քանզի ըստ օրինակի գրելոցս առ ի մէն՛ջ՝ ի կատարումն դարձուցաք, ոչ եթէ ի հին համբաւուց տեղեկացեալ և մատենագրեալ զայս կարգեցաք, այլ որոց մեզէն իսկ ականատեսք եղեալ կերպարանացն և աղՐնթերաԿաց հոգերաԿան գործոցն և լՐոդ շնորհապատում վարդապետութեանն, և նոցին արբանեակք ըստ աւետարանական հրամանացն։ Ոչ սուտապատում ճարտարախոս եղեալ առ ի մե-

894.   Such commandments were also given to other prophets: "Take a new and large sheet and write on it with the pen of an experienced scribe" [Is. 8.1] and elsewhere: "Write this vision on a tablet and establish it in writing, that he who reads may read freely" [Hab. 2.2; cf. Is. 30.8].[1]

895.   But David very clearly indicates that the lot of the divinely-given laws applies to all races: "Let this be written for another race" [Ps. 101.19] and: "The Lord will narrate in writing to the peoples" [Ps. 86.6].[1]

896.   Christ, the savior of all, came and completed this with his gracious command: "Go to all races" [Matt. 28.19] and: "Let this gospel be preached under heaven" [Matt. 24.14; 26.13; Mk. 14.9]. So this blessed one freely, with hopeful concern and profitably, demonstrated his efforts according to the gospel.[1]

897.   So, to bring to completion our narrative in the proper fashion, we have not set all this in writing by deriving it from old tales but from the spiritual deeds that we ourselves saw with our own eyes and were present at, and from the graceful teaching that we heard and of which we were servants [cf. Lk. 1.2] according to the precepts of the gospel. We did not make skillful yet false stories from

բոց բանից, այլ գյանձախագոյնան թողեալ և ի
նշանաւոր գիտակաց քաղելով՝ գհամառօտան կարգեցաք. որք ոչ մեզ միայն, ո'վ Թագաւոր, այլ
յորժամ քո առաջի գմատեանդ ընթեռնուցուն՝
յայյանի է»:

898 «Թանգի չէաք իսկ հանդուրժող գամենայն արաբեալս սրբոցն գտակաւ գիւրաքան-
չիւրան նշանակել, այլ ի դիւրագոյն և ի հեշ-
տագոյն յառաքելականն անդր գանձինս պատ-
րապարեցաք, որոյ անցեալ գբագմախուռն արգա-
սեօք սրբոցն առ ի մանրակրկիտ առնելոյ՝ գկա-
բենորագոյնան և գոգտակարագոյնան պատմեացս»:

899 «Ուստի և մեր առեալ հանգոյն ասա-
ցաք. ոչ ի պատիւ ընտրեյոց Աստուծոյ, որք
ամէնապարծ և կենդանատուր խաչին ծանու-
ցեալք յարգեցան, այլ յօրինակ քաջալերիչ հո-
գեւոր ծննդոց իւրեանց, և որք նոքօք աշակեր-
լոց իցեն յազգս ազգաց», ըստ բանի հոգելորա-
կան երգչին, որ ասէ. «Զի գոր ինչ միանգամ
պատուիրեաց հարցն մերոց՝ ցուցանել գայս որդլոց իւրեանց, գի ծանիցէ ազգ այլ. որդիք որ
ծնանին՝ յարիցեն և պատմեսցեն որդլոց իւրեանց, գի դիցեն առ Աստուած գյոյս իւրեանց,
և մի մոռասցին գգործս Աստուծոյ, և գպատուի-
րանս նորա խնդրելով խնդրեսցեն, գի մի եղիցին իբրև գհարս իւրեանց»:

900 Զի նոքա առ արարչութիւն անդր այս-

our own words, but leaving aside the details and gathering from famous and knowledgeable (men), we have set down the main points in brief. Which not merely to us, O king, but whenever this book is read before you, will be apparent.[1]

898.   For we were not able to indicate precisely every detail of all that was done by the saints, but we have taken refuge in the easy and delightful and apostolic practice (of Luke),[1] who passing over the many and various deeds of the saints omitted the details and narrated (only) the most important and most profitable points.[2]

899.   Hence in similar fashion we have made our narrative, not for the honor of God's elect who through his glorious and vivifying cross have become famous and honored, but for an inspiring example to their spiritual offspring and those who in every race will be instructed by them,[1] according to the word of the spiritual singer who says: "Whatever he commanded our fathers to indicate to their sons that another race might know. The sons who are born will rise up and tell their own sons, that they may place their hope in God and not forget God's deeds, and may seek his commandments, lest they become like their fathers" [Ps. 77.5-8].

900.   So that they, speaking such words to the Creator,

պիսի բարբառ արձակեալ ասացեն. «Տէր Աստուած մեր դու ես. և նա ասացէ ցնոսա. Ժողովուրդ իմ էք դուք»:

—————

1 Այս են հաւատք ճշմարիտ. հաւատամք՝
որպէս և մկրտեցաք, և փառաւորեմք՝ որպէս և
տեսաք զլոյս աւագանին:

2 Հաւատամք յանուն Հօր և Որդւոյ և Հոգւոյն սրբոյ, որպէս ասաց Քրկիչն յԱւետարա-
նին առ աշակերտան, թէ «Գնացէք այսուհետև
աշակերտեցէք զամենայն հեթանոս, մկրտեցէք
զնոսա յանուն Հօր և Որդւոյ և Հոգւոյն սրբոյ»:

3 Հաւատամք ի Հայր՝ Աստուած կատարեալ, և յՈրդի՝ Աստուած բովանդակ, և ի Հոգի սուրբ՝ Աստուած բաւական. մի ատուա-
ծութիւն սրբոյ Երրորդութեանն, մի էութիւն,
մի կամք, երեք անձինք կատարեալք:

4 Հաւատամք ի մի Աստուած Հայր, անէր
և աբաբիչ ամենայնի. և ի միածին Որդին, որ ի
Հօրէ և առ Հօր և ընդ Հօր. և ի Հոգին սուրբ,
որ ի Նորին էութենէ, և նովաւ արար զամենայն արարածս:

5 Որ է մի տեսութիւն, մի գործութիւն, մի
իշխանութիւն, մի մեծութիւն, մի գիտութիւն,
մի խորհուրդ, մի պետութիւն, մի անսկզբնա-

may say: "You are our Lord God" [Jer. 3.22]. And he will say to them: "You are my people" [Jer. 7.23; 11.4; cf. Hos. 2.24].[1]

[APPENDIX]

1.   This is the true faith.[1] We believe as we have been baptized, and we glorify as we have seen the light of the font.

2.   We believe in the name of the Father and of the Son and of the holy Spirit, as the Savior said in the gospel to the disciples: "Go henceforth and make disciples of all the heathen; baptize them in the name of the Father and of the Son and of the holy Spirit." [Matt. 28.19]

3.   We believe in the Father, perfect God; and in the Son, complete God; and in the holy Spirit, powerful God—one divinity of the holy Trinity, one essence, one will, three perfect persons.

4.   We believe in one God the Father, Lord and Creator of all; and in the only-begotten Son, who is from the Father and in the presence of the Father and with the Father; and in the holy Spirit, who is from the essence of the same, and with him created all creatures.

5.   Who is one lordship, one power, one authority, one greatness, one knowledge, one council, one leadership, one hypostasis without beginning.

կան գործութիւն։

6 Երեք կատարեալ անձինք, և մի կատա֊
րեալ կամք. անպատում, անքնին միութիւն եր֊
րորդութեանն. մի իսկութիւն, մի բնութիւն, մի
ասողութիւն Հօր և Որդւոյ և Հոգւոյն սրբոյ։

7 Երեք անձինք, մի գործութիւն ասողած֊
ութեանն. Հայր յանձնէ, Որդի ի Հօրէ, Հոգին
սուրբ ի նոցունց ի նոսին. իսկութեամբ, էու֊
թեամբ, ասողածութեամբ՝ հարթ հաւասար
հաստարակ, ի խորութիւնս, ի բարձրութիւնս, ի
լայնութիւնս, յերկայնութիւնս։

8 Որ աներևակի գործութեամբքն թափան֊
ցանց լուսով իւրով եղանէ. մերձ է առ ամենե֊
սին և հեռի յամենեցունց. անտեսական ի նկա֊
տողաց և անքնին ի քննողաց, և անըմբռնելի է
յամենեցունց բնութիւն նորա. մի է էութիւն
բնութեանն, և լի է երկինք և երկիր փառօք
նորա։

9 Այս է մեծութիւն միութեան սրբոյ եր֊
րորդութեանն. բայց դի պայման գովութեան
այլ և այլ է, և այն չէ ծածկեալ յիմաստնոց.
այն դի՝ Հայր չծնեալ և ծնող է, և Որդին չծը֊
նող և ծնունդ է, և Հոգին սուրբ ոչ ծնող և ոչ
ծնունդ, այլ ելող։

10 Եւ խոստովանիմք գՀայր՝ անսկիզբն,
աներևոյթ, անհասական, անճառ, անքակ, ան֊
քաժին, ամենակալ արարիչ երևելեաց և ան֊

6. Three perfect persons, and one perfect will, ineffable, an inscrutable unity of the Trinity, one being, one nature, one divinity of the Father and of the Son and of the holy Spirit.

7. Three persons, one hypostasis of the Godhead; the Father from himself, the Son from the Father, the holy Spirit from the same and in them; in being, essence, divinity, equal, alike, together, in depth, in height, in width, in length.

8. In his invisible powers he proceeds with penetrating light. He is near to all and far from all. He is invisible to those who look, and inscrutable to those who examine, and his nature is ungraspable by all. One is the essence of his nature, and the heavens and earth are full of his glory.

9. This is the greatness of the unity of the holy Trinity. But because the mode of praise differs, he is not hidden from the wise; for the Father is not born but begets, and the Son does not beget but is begotten, and the holy Spirit neither begets nor is begotten but proceeds.

10. And we confess the Father without beginning, invisible, incomprehensible, ineffable, inseparable, indivisible, omnipotent creator of things visible and

երևոյթից, նախակարծ յառաջիմաց քան զամենայն արաբեայս և հաստատեայս:

11 Եւ զԲանն Աստուած Որդի՝ ծնունդ ի
Հօրէ յառաջ քան զյաւիտեանս, առանց սկզբան
ժամանակի. անճառ, առանց բաժանելոյ, ան-
քակ՝ առանց մեկնելոյ. առանց չարչարանաց.
առանց միջնորդի. և նոյն ծնունդ՝ ի կուսէն
մարմնով ծնեալ ի վախճանի:

12 Առաքեցաւ Աստուած յԱստուծոյ Որդի,
առ մարմին ի կուսէն, և եղև մարդ կատարեալ.
բովանդակեցաւ ճշմարտութեամբ ի մարմին և
ճշմարիտ իսկ մարդ եղև:

13 Խոնարհեցաւ և խառնեաց զաստուածու-
թիւնն ընդ մարդկութիւնս և զանմեռն ընդ մե-
ռոտս, զի զմարդկութիւնս անքակ արասցէ յան-
մահութենէ աստուածութեան իւրոյ:

14 Զի որպէս կամեցաւ, զինչ կամեցաւ՝ և
եղև. և որպէս կամեցաւ՝ և արար. քանզի չիք
ինչ աննարաւորութիւն ի նմա. և յամենայնի
զօրաւոր է, և որ ինչ կամի, ոչ դանցանէ. և
զմեր հոդեղէն բնութիւնս զգեցաւ և խառնեաց
յանխառն աստուածութիւն իւր և յանապակա-
նութիւնն

15 Վասն մեր էարբ զպատժակն մահու և եւս
մեզ զպատժակն անմահութեան, և զմեռելութիւն
արարածոցս կենդանացոյց մահուամբն իւրով,
յորժամ յարեաւ մարմնովի և նստաւ ընդ աջմէ

invisible, foreseeing and providing for all things created and established.

11.   And the Word, God the Son, born of the Father before ages, without beginning in time, ineffable, without division, unsundered, without separation, without suffering, without intermediary; and the same born from the virgin in the flesh at the end.

12.   God the Word was sent by God; he took flesh from the virgin and became a perfect man. He truly became complete in the flesh and became a true man.

13.   He was humbled and joined his divinity to our humanity, and the immortal with this mortal, in order to make our humanity inseparable from the immortality of his divinity.

14.   For as he wished, what he wished also occurred; and as he wished, so he did. For there is nothing impossible with him. In everything he is powerful, and whatever he wishes he does not pass over. He put on our earthly nature and joined it to his unmingled divinity and incorruptibility.

15.   For our sake he drank the cup of death and gave to us the cup of immortality. And he gave life to the mortality of us creatures by his death, when he rose in the flesh and sat at the right hand

ծնողին իւրոյ և խառնեաց յաստուածութիւն
իւր Մ'իածինն։

16 Եւ դարձեալ գալոց է փառօք՝ դատել
զկենդանիս և զմեռեալս։ Եւ Հայր կենդանացոյց
զամենեսեան որք ի նայն հաւատացին։

17 Հաւատամք և ի սուրբ Հոգին աստուածեղէն, հոգի սուրբ, Աստուած կատարեալ, ա-
ռանց առնելոյ. բղխումն մշանշենաւոր առ ի
Հօրէ. որ խօսեցաւ յօրէնս և ի մարգարէսն և
յառաքեալսն, և էջ ի Յորդանան գետ։

18 Այսուհետև հոգի պետութեան, հոգի
ազատութեան, հոգի բերանոյ Աստուծոյ, նորուն
էութեան Հօր և Որդւոյ. ոչ արարած, ոչ ծա-
ռայ. ոչ հրամանատու, այլ հրամանատու. քանզի մի գործ է Հօր և Որդւոյ և Հոգւոյն. որպէս
ասաց իսկ Քրիստոս փրկիչն աշխարհաց, թէ
«Ես և Հայր», և «Հոգին ճշմարտութեան, որ ի
Հօրէ ելանէ»։ Ելանէ, և ոչ բաժանի. բղխէ, և ոչ
սպառի։

19 Այս են երեքանձնականք միութիւն
սուրբ Երրորդութեան. և մեք զայս ճշմարիտ
հաւատս ունիմք ի սուրբ Գրոց և յօրինաց եկե-
ղեցւոյ՝ առաջնորդ ճանապարհի առ Աստուած և
ի սուրբ Գիրս վարդապետութեան։

20 Հաւատամք և խոստովանիմք զհամաշ-
խարհական սուրբ կաթուղիկէ եկեղեցի, և ակն
ունիմք յարութեան մարմնոց ի մեռելոց և զկե-

of his begettor, and the Only-begotten joined it to his divinity.

16.   He will come again in glory to judge the living and the dead. And the Father gave life to all who believed in the same.

17.   We also believe in the divine holy Spirit, holy spirit, perfect God, without being created, an eternal flowing forth from the Father; who spoke in the law and the prophets and the apostles, and descended to the river Jordan.

18.   Consequently spirit of leadership, spirit of freedom, spirit of God's mouth, of the same essence as the Father and the Son; not created, not a servant, not a commandment-doer but a commandment-giver. For one is the work of the Father and of the Son and of the holy Spirit, as Christ the Savior of the world said: "I and the Father" [Jn. 10.30 etc.] and: "The spirit of truth who proceeds from the Father" [Jn. 15.26]. He proceeds and is not divided; he flows forth and is not exhausted.

19.   This is the unity of the three persons of the Trinity. And we hold this true faith from the holy scriptures and the law of the church, the guide for the road to God and for the teaching in the holy scriptures.

20.   We believe and confess the universal holy Catholic church, and we look for the resurrection of the flesh from the dead and

Նացն յաւիտենականաց, և փառաւորեմք առ հասարակ ի միասին զաուրբ Երրորդութիւնն այժմ և անվախճան յաւիտեանսն. ամէն և եղիցի եղեն:

eternal life, and we glorify in unison and together the holy Trinity, now and for endless ages. Amen, and may it so be.

NOTES TO THE INTRODUCTION

1. The most comprehensive bibliographical information about Agathangelos is to be found in the article "Agat'angelos" in H. A. Anasyan, *Haykakan Matenagitut'yun,* Part I (Erevan, 1959), cols. 151-213. Anasyan gives details of the printed editions of the Armenian text, of the manuscripts and fragments; a précis of the contents (taken from the précis of the Tiflis edition of 1909); a list of both ancient versions and modern translations; and a bibliography of secondary works in Armenian and Western languages.

2. G. Galēmk'erean, *Agat'angelosi krknagir bnagirĕ, Huschard-zan* (Vienna, 1911), pp. 67-160, gives the full text; for the manuscript see also Y. Tashean, *Ts'uts'ak hayerēn dzeragrats'* (Vienna, 1891), no. 56. The second writing is the *Commentary on the Revelation of John* by Andrew of Caesarea.

3. See P. M. Muradyan, "Agat'angelosi Patmut'yan hnagoyn patařikner," *Lraber* (1971), no. 12 (348), 37-48.

4. G. Tēr-Mkrtch'ean and St. Kanayeants', *Agat'angelay Patmut'iwn Hayots'* (Tiflis, 1909). The text was reprinted unchanged in *Agat'angelay Patmut'iwn Hayots', Lukasean Matenadaran,* no. 15 (Tiflis, 1914).

5. "Agathangelus," neu herausgegeben von Paul de Lagarde, *Abhandlungen der historisch-philologischen Classe der königlichen Gesellschaft der Wissenschaften zu Göttingen,* 35 Band, 1 Heft (Göttingen, 1888; published 1889).

6. G. Lafontaine, "La Version grecque ancienne du livre arménien d'Agathange," *Publications de l'Institut Orientaliste de Louvain* 7(1973).

7. Details in G. Garitte, *Documents pour l'étude du livre d'Agathange (Studi e Testi* 127) (Vatican City, 1946), pp. 5-6, Lafontaine, pp. 103ff.

8. Full text in A. Ter-Levondyan, *Agat'angelosi arabakan nor khmbagrut'yunĕ* (Erevan, 1968).

9. Details, with Latin translation, in Garitte, *Documents,* pp. 13-16. See also P. M. Muradyan, "Agat'angelosi 'Patmut'yan' mi hatvatsi hin vratseren t'argmanut'yunĕ," *P.H.* (1972), pt. 1 (56), pp. 63-76. The Armenian of Agathangelos also lies behind most of a Georgian treatise attributed to Hippolytus; see G. Garitte, "Le traité géorgien 'sur la foi' attribué à Hippolyte," *Le Muséon* 78 (1965): 119-172.

10. Published with commentary in Garitte, *Documents.*

11. See G. Garitte, "La vie grecque inédite de saint Grégoire d'Arménie (ms. 4 d'Ochrida), *Analecta Bollandiana* 83 (1965): 233-290.

12. For *Sinai* 455 see A. N. Ter-Levondyan, "Agat'angelosi arab-akan khmbagrutyan norahayt amboljakan bnagirĕ," *P.H.* (1973), pt. 1 (60), pp. 209-228. The text of *Sinai* 460 was published by N. Marr, *Zapiski Vostochnago Otdelenya Imperatorskago Russkago Arkheologicheskago Obschestva,* vol. 16 (1905), pp. 63-211; Latin translation and commentary in Garitte, *Documents.*

13. Text and commentary in M. Van Esbroek, "Un nouveau témoin du livre d'Agathange," *R.E.A.,* n.s. vol. 8 (1971): 13-167.

14. *Ag* has one paragraph with a résumé of §1-6; *Ar* omits the prologue and begins at §18. *Vg* and *Va* begin with the confronta-tion between Gregory and Trdat (§48); *Vo* is truncated and begins at the end of §36. *Vk* has an entirely different introduction: it gives a brief résumé of the conversion of king Sanatruk and the martyr-dom of Addai (*Vk* 1-4), see below, p. xxvii.

15. The prologue is found in $\underline{a\ b\ c\ d}$ (beginning at §7 "lucid histories") and in *A B G D E Z Ē,* but these last seven MSS lack §2 "to their friends" . . . §15 "after these times have passed." α and β begin at §48.

16. See the references in the notes to §1 and 6.

17. See below, p. lxxxix.

18. Lazar, *Patmut'iwn Hayots'* (Tiflis, 1904), p. 1; for the refer-ence in his *Letter* to a different book called *History of the Martyr Gregory,* see below, p. xcv.

19. See further below, p. lxxxiii, and cf. H. Delehaye, *Les passions des martyres et les genres littéraires,* 2d ed. (Brussels, 1966), pp. 182-183. In a more general context see W. Speyer, *Die literarische Fälschung im heidnischen und Christlichen Altertum* (*Handbuch der Altertumswissenschaft* I 2) (München, 1971).

20. On this episode see Garitte, *Documents*, pp. 272-279, and N. Akinean, "Artashir Papakani vēpĕ," *H.A.* 61 (1947), cols. 567-581. The brief references in Moses Khorenats'i (II 70) to Artaban's death, and in Moses Daskhurants'i (II 1) to Artashir in the *History of Agathangelos* do not prove that the Pahlavi romance had found its way into the *Aa* tradition.

21. On the tendentious motivation of the editor of *Vk* see Van Esbroek, "Nouveau témoin," pp. 162-167. Cf. also Moses Khoren-ats'i, II 34.

21a. For the epic character of these martial exploits see M. Abelyan, *Erker* I (Erevan 1966), pp. 194-195 and esp. pp. 258-259.

22. See below, p. xxxvi.

23. However, Melik'-Ohanjanyan makes much of this phrase and supposes that the ancestry provided Gregory in later writers was designed to cover up his foreign origin. He also concludes that in view of the political situation in the fifth century it had become important to provide a *national* foundation for the church; see his *Agat'angelosi,* pp. 64ff.

24. It is noteworthy that *Vg* and *Va* describe the journey of Gregory to Caesarea for consecration in greater detail than the *A* recension; cf. Garitte, *Documents*, pp. 315-317.

25. Cf. also *Vk* 8.

26. Cf. Faustos, III 12, 14; IV 3.

27. Hence the references in Faustos to Thaddaeus have sometimes been taken as interpolations; see L. S. Kogean, *Hayots' Ekelets'in* (Beirut, 1961), p.31. But Van Esbroeck, "Le roi Sanatrouk et l'apôtre Thaddée," *R.E.A.,* n.s., vol. 9 (1972), p. 269 ff., shows that Thaddaeus was probably known to Faustos.

28. Armenian text in *Labubneay, "T'ult'Abgaru"*(Venice, 1868). Carrière did not accept the traditional date of the Armenian translation; see his *La légende d'Abgar* (Paris, 1895), pp. 372-374. For a recent discussion of the Syrian tradition, see J. B. Segal, *Edessa, 'The Blessed City'* (Oxford, 1970), pp. 62-81.

29. *Vk* 1-4.

30. Elishē, pp. 71-72.

31. On the connection with Rome see below, note 131.

32. This tradition, unknown to any other Armenian writer, was taken up by Zonaras; see M.L. Chaumont, *Recherches sur l'histoire d'Arménie* (Paris, 1969), p. 54. But Akinean interprets "uncles" as "relatives," *Elishē* III, p. 68.

33. We must note here the suspicious circumstance that so many of these names tally so well with the role played by their holder. Burdar means "carrier, bringer" (H. Hübschmann, *Armenische Grammatik* [Leipzig, 1897], p. 33), while Mariam and David as the wife and ancestor of the hero suggest an obvious allusion to Jesus Christ. K. M. Melik'-Ōhanjanyan (*Agat'angelosi*, P. H. 27 [1964], pp. 53-82) stresses that this ancestry, found in Moses Khorenats'i and Zenob, is an obvious forgery and a pious fiction, and he draws parallels with the ancestry of Moses and Jesus. The name Anak

means "evil" (F. Justi, *Iranisches Namenbuch* [Marburg, 1895], p. 15), and is also a curiously appropriate name—as indeed is Agathangelos. Nicomachus is unknown to the *B.H.G.*

34. See Garitte, *Documents*, p. 309.

35. *Vg* 93-97. This episode comes later in the narrative, but is discussed here because of its relevance for Gregory's early years.

36. On Julitta see Garitte, *Documents*, p. 216; she was martyred at Caesarea in the time of Diocletian.

37. Garitte, *Documents*, pp. 309-310. On Moses' elaborations see further below, p. xciv ff.

38. See below, pp. lxxviii-lxxxix.

39. These names were taken (apparently at random) from Eusebius' *Chronicle,* a source on which Moses Khorenats'i greatly relied.

39a. Cf. Toumanoff, *Arsacids,* p. 270, note 193.

40. But the implication is that this emperor was Diocletian, cf. §152.

41. The following three paragraphs follow the conclusions of C. Toumanoff, *The Third-century Armenian Arsacids, R.E.A., N.S.,* vol. 6 (1969), pp. 233-281.

42. Moses Khorenats'i, II 77; Agathangelos, §36.

43. On this province see Hübschmann, *A.O.N.,* p. 286

44. Strabo, *Geography,* XI 14, 16.

45. §49. But Agathangelos did not have any real idea of the cult offered to Anahit; the "thick branches" have biblical parallels. See esp. §49, n.1.

46. §786 and 809. On Anahit's cult, see M.-L. Chaumont, "Le culte de la déesse Anahita dans la religion des monarques d'Iran et d'Arménie au le siècle de notre ère," *Journal asiatique* 253 (1965): pp. 167-181.

47. §779.

48. Faustos, V 25: *at'or Anahtay.* All the manuscripts read *Nahatay,* but on the form see Hübschmann, *Grammatik,* p. 18.

49. Moses Khorenats'i, II 12, 14.

50. *Ibid.,* II 59.

51. A. Carrière, *Les huit sanctuaires de l'Arménie payenne* (Paris, 1899), esp. pp. 26-27.

52. §53, 68, 127.

53. §53, 809.

54. §785. On Anahit see further H. Gelzer, "Zur armenischen Götterlehre," *Berichte der Königlichen sächischen Gesellschaft der Wissenschaften* 48 (1896): 111-117; K. V. Melik'-P'ashayan, *Anahit Dits'uhu Pashtamunk'ĕ* (Erevan, 1963), esp. ch. 2.

55. See Hübschmann, *Grammatik,* pp. 24-25, 62-63.

56. §53, 68, 127.

57. §785, 786, 790.

58. Cf. Lagarde, *Agathangelus,* p. 139.

59. Eznik, §145-200; Ełishē, pp. 24, 25, 31.

60. Cf. the remarks of Vrt'anēs in the early seventh century; see Der Nersessian, *Images,* p. 63. But John Awdznets'i distinguishes between the Persian Ormizd and the Armenian Aramazd, *Opera,* p. 85, as does Ananias Shirakats'i, *Matenagrut'iwn,* p. 376. Cf. the variants Aramazd-Ormizd of the shrine at Garizim, §836, note 1.

61. τοῖς ἑπτὰ ἱεροῖς. The Armenian *bagin,* here translated "altar," also means "temple"; it is derived from Iranian *Bâga,* see A. Meillet, "Sur les termes religieux iraniens en arménien," *R.E.A.,* 1 (1920-21): 233; Widengren, *Die Religionen Irans* (Stuttgart, 1965), p. 191. *Mehean,* here translated "temple," is derived from **mihriyan* (μιθρεῖον), see Meillet, *ibid.,* Widengren, *ibid.,* p. 186.

62. E.g., Faustos, III 3.

63. As Chaumont suggests, *Histoire,* p. 72.

64. §809.

65. This may be rendered schematically as follows:

§778	Artashat	Anahit
	(Erazamoyn)	Tir
784	T'ordan	Barshamin
785	Ani	Aramazd
786	Erēz	Anahit
	T'il	Nanē
790	Bagayařich	Mihr
809	Ashtishat	Vahagn
		Anahit
		Astłik

Adontz' theory of a connection between the seven altars or shrines and the Iranian mythical *Heftanbokht* is superfluous: cf., N. Adontz, "Grégoire l'Illuminateur et Anak le Parthe," *R.E.A.* 8 (1928): 233-243, esp. p. 243.

66. E.g., §67, 73. Cf. the more elaborate treatment in the *Teaching,* §284, and especially §522-526.

67. S. Wikander, *Feuerpriester in Kleinasien und Iran* (Lund, 1946), p. 93. Cf. the twigs used in the ritual at Palmyra, J. B. Segal, *Edessa* (Oxford, 1970), p. 47.

68. See §49, note 1. On the importance of the Maccabees see below, pp. lxxxiii-lxxxiv.

69. Agathangelos, §22; Eḷishē, p. 12. See further §22, note 1.

70. A classic exposition is found in Athanasius, *Contra Gentes,* 18. For Armenian evidence, cf. Eznik §158 and Moses Khorenats'i' I, 14.

71. Cf. the last sentence in §780.

72. See G. W. H. Lampe, *Patristic Greek Lexicon* (Oxford,1961-68), s.v. δαιμών D 3a, and θεός J 2b; and in general, A. Michel, s.v. "Idolatrie," in *Dictionnaire de Théologie Catholique,* vol. 7 (Paris, 1930), cols. 602-669.

73. For a general discussion of the Iranian, Greek and Syrian influences in Armenian paganism, see Gelzer, *Götterlehre.*

74. §75-98.

75. On the parallels in Agathangelos with other hagiographical works, see below, p. lxxxv.

76. See pp. lxxxv-lxxxvii.

77. See Delehaye, *Passions,* p. 175.

78. However, if one accepts the chronology of Moses Khorenats'i, II 82, then Gregory's imprisonment would have lasted from 287/8 to 302/3, and the martyrdom of the nuns would then correspond to Diocletian's own persecution, as described in his letter to Trdat, §154. But Moses' account is historically unacceptable, see above, p.

79. See P. Peters, "S. Grégoire l'Illuminateur," *A.B.* 60 (1942): 106; Toumanoff, *Arsacids,* p. 271, regards the martyrdoms as part of Trdat's pro-Roman policy between 303 and 313.

80. See §137, note 1.

81. In *Vk,* 78, they separate, forty going to Dvin and the others to Ayvavan.

82. *Vg,* 40: "To the emperor, Caesar, king of the Romans, Diocletian, Tiridates king of Greater Armenia. Having been nourished and educated from early youth among you, being (now) within (my) hereditary kingdom, and hailing the gods who preserve our power as well as those above me, I abhor the so-called Christians. More-

over, I have tortured and given over to a most bitter death a friend of mine, Gregory, a Cappadocian who had learned the teachings of the Christians, by throwing him into a pit where dragons live who eat up those cast down. And now, lord emperor, I shall perform your commands with zeal and willingness. Be well."

83. As Chaumont claims, *Histoire,* p. 140; cf. Garitte, *Documents,* p. 293.

84. Peeters, "Grégoire," p. 108. (The last year in which the last day of Hori would correspond with the first of September is 587; the earliest year in which the first of Hori would correspond with the last day of September is 348.)

85. On these dates see the extended discussion in Peeters, "Grégoire," pp. 107ff.

86. Cf. Daniel, ch. 4.

87. The length of Gregory's imprisonment is variously given as 13 or 15 years; see §122, note 4.

88. On this date see above, p. xxv.

89. On this see below, pp. lxiv-lxvi and chapter 11.

90. See chapter 9.

91. See R. W. Thomson, *The Teaching of Saint Gregory: An Early Armenian Catechism* (Cambridge, Mass., 1970; published 1971.

92. See Garitte, "Le traité," pp. 119-172.

93. See G. Garitte, "Un petit florilège grec diphysite traduit de l'armenien," *Analecta Biblica* 12 (1959): 102-112.

94. On this vision see the discussion in A. Khatchatrian, *L'Architecture arménienne du IV ͤ au VI ͤ siècle* (Paris, 1971), pp. 73-86.

95. For example, the vision of Sahak which Lazar specifically says was parallel to that of Gregory, p. 28: *ēst awrinaki margarēakan tesleann or ts'uts'aw surb nahatakin Grigori.* But the vision is undoubtedly an interpolation; for a discussion of its date see Adontz, "L'age et l'origine de l'empereur Basile I," *Etudes,* pp. 96-104 and Garitte, "La vision de S. Sahak en grec," *Le Muséon* 71 (1958), pp. 255-278.

96. See the discussion in Garitte, *Documents*, pp. 338-350.

97. Cf. M. E. Stone, "The Apocryphal Literature in the Armenian Tradition," *Proceedings of the Israel Academy of Sciences and Humanities,* vol. 4 (1969), pp. 59-78.

98. See below, p. lxxxiv.

99. Cf. A. Meillet, "Remarques sur le texte de l'historien arménien Agathange," J. A., 10th series, vol. 16 (1910), p. 475.

100. See the details below, pp. lxxxviii-lxxxix.

101. §859ff.

102. On the story of Gregory's wife cf. above, pp. xxx-xxxiii.

102a. On the traditions concerning the fate of the pagan priests, see §781, note 1.

103. See note 65 above.

104. Cf. F. Justi, *Iranisches Namenbuch,* p. 325.

105. On names in *Tir-* see W. B. Henning, "A Note on Tir," B.S.O.A.S. 24 (1961): 191; E. Benveniste, *Titres et noms propres en iranien ancien* (Paris, 1966), p. 116. Cf. also Hübschmann, *Grammatik,* p. 89. One may also note that the fourth Armenian month is called *Trē.*

106. See. Ł. Alishan, *Hin Hawatk‘* (Venice, 1910), p. 311. But he gives no references, and the name Hermes appears in the Armenian vulgate.

107. Cf. note 51 above.

108. On the legends surrounding Gregory's burial see Van Esbroeck, *Témoignages littéraires sur les sépultures de S. Grégoire l'Illuminateur, A.B.,* vol. 89 (1971), pp. 387-418.

109. On Barshamin see further Gelzer, *Götterlehre,* pp. 119-123. Cf. Moses Khorenats‘i I 13 for the deification of Barsham.

110. Cf. R. N. Frye, *The Heritage of Persia* (Cleveland and New York, 1963), pp. 149-150, 191-192.

111. see further Gelzer, *Götterlehre,* pp. 123-124.

112. Cf. H. Acharyan, *Hayots‘ Andznanunneri Bararan,* vol. 3 (Erevan, 1946), pp. 331-336, and Hübschmann, *Grammatik,* pp. 53-54. Cf. also the seventh Armenian month *mehekani* and the term *mehean* (on which see note 61 above).

113. Ełishē, pp. 32, 35. For the cult of Mithra in Armenia in ancient times, see Strabo, XI 14.9.

114. Łazar, pp. 45-46.

115. Ełishē, p. 165; on the title *anderdzapet,* see Hübschmann, *Grammatik,* p. 99; Leroy, "Les composés arméniens en-*pet*," *Annuaire de l'Institut de Philologie et d'histoire orientales et slaves,* vol. 15 (1958-60), p. 120.

116. Ełishē, p. 185: *i Mihr astuats erdueal im.*

117. Moses Khorenats‘i, III 17: *erdueal i Mihr mets astuats;* Sebeos, p. 58.

118. Cf. Garitte, *Documents,* p. 210.

119. Moses Khorenats'i, II 14: the site is spelled *Bagayarinj* in the text with a variant *Bagarinj.* On the variants in other writers see Hübschmann, *Grammatik,* p. 113.

120. Cf. Garitte, *Documents,* p. 210. But Hephaistos was not the customary identification for Mithra in the west; see E. Wüst, "Mithras," *P.W.* vol. 30, especially cols. 2145-2146 (*Synkretismus*).

121. See §809.

122. On Anahit see above, pp. 16-17.

123. Cf. Hübschmann, *Grammatik,* pp. 75-77; Gelzer, *Götterlehre,* pp. 104-108. For the identification with Hercules, see Faustos III 14; cf. Wikander, *Feuerpriester,* p. 171. On the adjectival form *Vahēvanean,* see §809, note 2.

124. See C. Toumanoff, *Studies in Christian Caucasian History,* Georgetown University Press, 1963, p. 215.

125. See G. Dumézil, *Vahagn, Revue de l'histoire des religions,* vol. 117 (1938), pp. 152-170.

126. See Hübschmann, *Grammatik,* p. 421; Gelzer, *Götterlehre,* pp.122-123.

127. Moses Khorenats'i, II 14: *zAp'roditay zpatkern ibrew Erakleay tarp'awori.* But *Aa* reads: *meheann annuaneal Astḷkan dits', seneak Vahagni kardats'eal.* Cf. also Moses, I 6.

128. See Moses Khorenats'i, II 50.

129. Thomas Artsruni, p. 99; for the statue of Astḷik see *ibid.,* p.98. But this part of his *History* is almost entirely legendary.

130. *Movsesi Khorenats'woy, Matenagrut'iwnk'* (Venice, 1865), p.301.

131. *Vk,* 239; but it was the same Leontius who consecrated Gregory. The only comparable reference to Rome in early Armenian literature is in Eḷishē, see above, p. xxx. But Eḷishē may have had in mind the supposed visit of Gregory and Trdat to Rome in order to see Constantine (on which see chapter 12).

132. In *Aa* this is mentioned later, §820-826.

133. For precise details of these differences between the *A* and *V* recensions see Garitte, *Documents,* pp. 314-317.

134. See Garitte, *Documents,* p. 222.

135. See Garitte, *Documents,* pp. 229-30.

136. On this council and its probable connection with Gregory see P. Ananian, "La data e le circostanze della consecrazione di S. Gregorio Illuminatore," *Le Muséon* 84 (1961): 43-73 and 317-360.

For the text of the canons of this council (in an Armenian version)
see J. Lebon, "Sur un concile de Césarée," *Le Muséon* 51 (1938):
89-132.

137. See above, p. xxxv.

138. Or thirteen in some passages; see above, p. lii and §122,
note 4.

139. See the details below, pp. lxxxviii-lxxxix.

140. See above, pp. lxii-lxiv.

141. Faustos, III 3, 19.

142. The site of a famous battle when the patriarch Nersēs stood
with arms raised like Moses, praying for victory over the Persians;
Faustos, V 4. (The Persians were defeated.)

143. On these common hagiographical themes, see the notes to
§833.

144. On this festival, see the discussion in §836, note 1.

145. For precise details of these differences between the *A* and *V*
recensions see Garitte, *Documents,* pp. 317-323.

146. Cf. above pp. xxxiii.

147. Cf. Garitte, *Documents,* p. 139. Constantine's feast day was
May 22, following the usage at Jerusalem; see A. Renoux, "Le
Codex arménien Jérusalem 121," Pt. 2 *(Patrologia Orientalis,* vol.
36, fasc. 2; Turnhout, 1971), p. 199 [337].

148. Cf. H. Gelzer, H. Hilgenfeld and O. Cuntz, *Patrum Nicaenorum Nomina* (Leipzig, 1898), p. lxii.

149. This visit may be a reflection of the visit to Rome of Tiridates
I in order to receive his crown from Nero; on which see F. Cumont,
"L'Iniziazione di Nerone da parte di Tiridate d'Armenia," *Rivista di
Filologia* 61 (1933): 145-154. Faustos, III 21, refers to the pact
between Trdat and Constantine on the occasion of a later Armenian embassy to Constantinople; on this see W. Enssling, "Zu dem
vermuteten Perserfeldzug des rex Hannibalianus," *Klio* 29 (1936):
102-110.

150. See Van Esbroeck, "Un nouveau témoin," p. 19; on the
legends surrounding Gregory's burial see also Van Esbroeck, "Témoignages littéraires," pp. 387-418.

151. Not directly relevant, but interesting in this regard, is the
much later dispute between rival Catholicoi for the possession of
the relic of Gregory's right hand; cf. M. Ormanian, *Azgapatum,* vol.
2 (Beirut, 1960), cols. 2110, 2189ff.; F. Tournebize, *Histoire politique et religieuse de l'Arménie* (Paris, 1910), p. 225; M. Van

Esbroeck, "Chronique arménienne," *A.B.* 80 (1962): 445; Aṙak'el, ch. 30.

152. Note that *Buzandats'i* does not mean "of Byzantium" (for Byzantium in Armenian is *Biwzandion*), but "of Buzanda," i.e. Podandus in the Taurus. Faustos therefore came from Lesser Armenia, not the East Roman capital.

153. Cf. V. Langlois, *Collection des historiens anciens et modernes, de l'Arménie,* vol. I (Paris, 1867), pp. 204-205. See also note 15A.

154. See the *Introduction* to the Venice 1832 edition, p. 6. The editors of the Venice 1889 edition are non-committed; but the editors of the Venice 1933 edition assume a Greek origin. However, Peeters was inclined to postulate a Syriac original; see P. Peeters, "Le début de la persecution de Sapor d'après Fauste de Byzance," *R.E.A.* 1 (1920-21): p. 21, note 5, and also "L'Intervention politique de Constance II dans la Grande Arménie en 338," *Bulletin de l'Academie royale de Belgique, Classe des lettres,* vol. 17 (1931): 17. (Both of these articles are reprinted in *Recherches d'histoire et de philologie orientales,* vol. I [Subsidia Hagiographica 27; Brussels, 1951].) Cf. also M. Van Esbroeck, "Le roi Sanatrouk et l'apôtre Thaddée," *R.E.A.* N.S., vol. 9 (1972), p. 269.

155. Cf. Faustos, IV 4, 7, 9.

156. See Norayr Biwzandats'i, *Koriwn Vardapet ew norin T'argmanut'iwnk'* (Tiflis, 1900).

157. Faustos, III 1, 12, 14; IV, 3. But see note 27 above.

158. See above, note 28.

159. Moses Khorenats'i, II 34; Zenob, p. 10. On the whole question of apostolic foundations, see F. Dvornik, *The Idea of Apostolicity in Byzantium and the Legend of the Apostle Andrew* (Dumbarton Oaks Studies 4; Cambridge, Mass., 1958).

160. Faustos, III 19; IV 4, 14.

161. Faustos, III 1: *ayn amenayn* (i.e., the account from the time of Thaddaeus to the death of Trdat) *i dzeṙn aylots'n grets'an.*

162. Faustos, III 2.

163. Faustos, III 14.

164. Faustos, III 3, 14.

165. Faustos, III 3, 19; IV 14.

166. Faustos, III 14, at *Hats'eats' drakht* ("garden of ash-trees," cf. Hübschmann, *A.O.N.,* p. 444).

167. Faustos mentions Gregory's retreat, *Oskik',* VI 16, and his place of burial, *T'ordan,* III 2.

168. Faustos, III 6.

169. That is, in the longer and original recension. The short recension, which shows the influence of Moses Khorenats'i, refers to the extinction of the line of Saint Gregory, p. 61. On Koriun see further note 242 below.

170. Admittedly, these writers are not describing the events of the early fourth century. But it is surprising that neither Koriun nor Elishē, who are particularly concerned with the role of the Armenian church, even mention its founder.

171. Lazar, ch. 2.

172. *Girk'T'lt'ots'* (Tiflis, 1901), p. 51.

173. *Girk'T'lt'ots',* p. 78.

174. K. Tēr Mkrtch'ean, *Knik' Hawatoy* (Ejmiatsin, 1914): From *Agathangelos:* pp. 146-155, 248-249, 258, 263, 300-302, 303-304. From *Yachakhapatum:* pp. 18-22. The Yachakhapatum contains 23 homilies; on their attribution to Masht'ots, see A. N. Srabyan, " 'Yachakhapatum' chaṙeri helinaki harts'ē," *Telekagir* (1962), no. 5, 25-38. But they are definitely not by Masht'ots' and belong to a later period; see H. Achaṙyan, *Hayots' Grēre* (Erevan, 1968), pp. 339-346, with references to earlier literature.

175. Moses Khorenats'i, II 80.

176. An interesting example of confusion between Gregory the Illuminator and various other Gregories was made in a letter sent by George, bishop of the Arabs, to a hermit in 714. See the text and discussion in Garitte, *Documents,* pp. 407-426.

177. As is clear from §814 and 817, though at §824 and elsewhere the metaphorical sense of banishing ignorance is found. For "illumination" as baptism see Lampe, *Lexicon,* s.v. φωτίζω B viii. Melik'-Ōhanjanyan's attempts to draw Iranian parallels are based on false premises, *Agat'angelosi,* pp. 79ff.

178. Lazar, pp. 90, 192.

179. Lazar, p. 139.

180. See especially §762, 796, 866.

181. See Lampe, *Lexicon,* s.v. ἀρχιερεύς E.

182. §804, 862.

183. Faustos, III 17: *(z)hayrapetut'eann (z)kat'olikosut'iwn.*

184. Admittedly, "patriarch" was used in a vaguer sense in the early church than in the fifth century; see Lampe, *Lexicon,* s.v. πατριάρχης C. The jurisdiction claimed by the metropolitans of Caesarea over the Armenian church was limited to the consecra-

tion of the new patriarchs after their election by the Armenian clergy and nobility. When King Pap appointed Yusik as patriarch without this ceremony, the metropolitan of Caesarea summoned a council which deprived Yusik of his authority; Faustos, V 29: *lutsin zishkhanut'iwnn kat'oḷikosut'eann.*

185. Koriun, p. 15.

186. See L. Leloir, *(Versions) Orientales de la Bible, II, Versions arméniennes, Dictionnaire de la Bible, Supplément,* vol. 6 (Paris, 1960), cols. 810-818.

187. See G. Zarp'analean, *Matenadaran Haykakan T'argmanut Nakhneats'* (Venice, 1889). For those Armenian versions published by the Mekhitarists see J. Muyldermans, *L'apport des éditions arméniennes de Venise à la patristique, Bazmavēp* (Venice, 1949), 386-398, and M. Djanachian, *Les Arménistes et les Mekhitaristes, Armeniaca* (Venice, 1969), pp. 383-445.

188. For an index of biblical quotations and allusions see below, pp. 516 ff. But undoubtedly there are many more biblical allusions, not immediately obvious, which have not been identified and which would swell that list.

189. *Aa* §180.

190. §124; III Kings 17.

191. §212; Daniel 4.

192. §218; John 11.43

193. §219; Job 30.30

194. §222; Acts 10.26

195. §758; Ezechiel 40.

196. See A. Khatchatrian, *L'Architecture arménienne du IVe au VIe siècle* (Paris, 1971), pp. 73-86.

197. On the influence of Cyril of Jerusalem's theology, see Thomson, *Teaching,* pp. 32-34; on the influence of the liturgical practice of Jerusalem, see A. Renoux, *Le Codex arménien Jérusalem 121,* I (*Patrologia orientalis,* vol. 25, fasc. 1; Turnhout, 1969), pp. 19-32, and the various previous studies by Renoux listed in his bibliography, *idem,* vol. II (1971), p. 11 [149].

198. Cf. Toumanoff, *Studies,* pp. 201-202; Moses Khorenats'i, II 3.

199. Faustos, III 11; Eḷishē, p. 105.

200. On the Armenian version of Maccabees see Tsovakan (= Norayr Poḷarean), "Koriwn ew Makabayets'wots' hay t'argmani-ch'ē," *Sion* (1935), 181-187 (with a detailed comparison of the vo-

cabulary of Maccabees I-III and Koriun), and H. S. Kogean, *Maka-bayets'wots' B. grk'in hayerēn t'argmanut'iwnē* (Vienna, 1923).

201. For the references to Maccabees see the text and notes for the appropriate paragraph in the translation, and also the Index of biblical quotations at p. 519 ff.

202. §762; I Macc. 4.46.

203. Especially §92-93.

204. On all these stock themes see Delehaye, *Passions,* ch. 3, *Les passions épiques.*

205. §176; cf. *P.G.* 115, col. 169.

206. §102; *Acts of Sharbil,* p. 54.

207. §109, 115; *Martyrdom of Shmona and Guria,* §35.

208. §119; *Acts of Sharbil,* p. 54

209. See Koriun, pp. 14, 30. On the general question of Syrian-Armenian relations, see E. Ter Minassiantz, *Die armenische Kirche in ihre Beziehungen zu den syrischen* (Leipzig, 1904), and the more recent study (devoted to the third to fifth centuries) of H. G. Melk'onyan, *Hay-asorakan haraberut'yunneri patmut'yunits'* (Erevan, 1970).

210. See the *Introduction* to R. W. Thomson, *The Teaching of Saint Gregory* (Cambridge, 1971).

211. Cf. Lampe, *Lexicon,* s.v. νυμφιός and 'Αβρααμ.

212. Cyril of Jerusalem, *Catecheses,* 18.10.

213. Proclus, *Orationes,* 6.11.

214. See M. Tallon, "Livre des Lettres," *Mélanges de l'Université Saint Joseph,* vol. 32 (1955), ch. 2.

215. The threefold parallel between Eve and Mary, the punishment of Adam and the death of Christ, and the tree of knowledge and the wood of the cross, is also found in John Chrysostom, *Homilia in sanctum pascha* 2 (P.G. 52, esp. col. 768). Chrysostom goes on to elaborate on the theme of the cross. On Armenian parallels to the idea of Christ as a dead image, see §81, note 1.

216. See Lampe, *Lexicon,* s.v. ἄγκιστρον.

217. See J. Daniélou, *The Theology of Jewish Christianity* (Chicago, 1964), p. 277.

218. §489; see the discussion *ad loc.* in Thomson, *Teaching.*

219. §585.

220. Cf. Daniélou, *Theology,* ch. 9.

221. §22; Ełishē, p. 12.

222. §141; Ełishē, p. 6.

223. §203; Eḷishē, p. 26.

224. I believe Eḷishē's History to be later than Ḷazar's, of which it is an elaboration. For a detailed study see N. Akinean, *Eḷishē Vardapet,* 3 vols. (Vienna, 1932-60).

225. §750; Faustos, V 24.

226. §830; Faustos III 12.

227. §856; Faustos V 21.

228. §858; Faustos III 2.

229. §867; Faustos IV 6.

230. §884; Faustos V 44.

231. Norayr Biwzandats'i, using these and other similar verbal parallels as a basis, thought that the same translator (i.e., Koriun) was responsible for the Armenian versions of Agathangelos and Faustos, see his *Koriwn Vardapet ew norin t'argmanut'iwnk'* (Tiflis, 1900). But one should note that many of the correspondences adduced between the text of Agathangelos and other writers or translated texts are but single words, and direct dependence on the part of Agathangelos is difficult to prove. See the review by P. Peeters of N. Akinean, *Niwt'er hay vkayabanut'ean usumnasirut'- ean hamar* (Vienna 1914) in *R.E.A.* vol. 1 (1920-21), 383-387. Cf. also the later study by N. Akinean, *Vkayabanut'iwn srboyn Kiwrḷi (Kiwrakosi) ew mōr nora Annayi Agat'angeḷosi aḷbiwrnerēn, H.A.* (1948), esp. cols. 139-143.

232. A table is given in the Tiflis edition of 1909, Appendix pp. 14-15.

233. §774; Koriun, p. 19.

234. §785-790; 827-830; 837; 839; 843-854; 862. For the parallels in Koriun, see the notes to these paragraphs.

235. §804, 806; Koriun, pp. 14, 15.

236. §808; Koriun, pp. 15-16.

237. §819; Koriun, p. 17.

238. §840; Koriun, p. 28.

239. §846; 859; 863-865; 888-890. For the parallels in Koriun, see the notes to these paragraphs.

240. §874-881; Koriun, p. 25.

241. §886; Koriun, p. 32.

242. Cf. P. Peeters, "Pour l'histoire des origines de l'alphabet ar- ménien," *R.E.A.,* vol. 9 (1929), 203-237 (reprinted in *Recherches d'histoire et de philologie orientales I,* Subsidia hagiographica 27; Brussels, 1951). But the chronology of Koriun is confused, which

has enabled N. Akinean in his critical edition to take wide liberties with the ordering of the various sections: N. Akinean, *Patmut'iwn Varuts' S. Masht'ots' Vardapeti, Mkhit'ar Tōnagirk'*
(Vienna, 1949), pp. 171-320.

243. See above p. xli and note 84.

244. For a summary of these events see J. Mécérian, "Bilan des
relations arméno-iraniennes au 5ᵉ siécle ap. J.C.," *Mélanges de
l'Université Saint Joseph* 30 (1953): 67-98.

245. For Armenian accounts of these events, see the Histories of
Lazar and Eḷishē.

246. See above, p. lvii.

247. In his vision, especially §740, 753-754.

248. Cf. Toumanoff, *Studies,* pp. 201-202; 209-211.

249. See Garitte, "Vie grecque indédite," esp. pp. 246, 249.

250. See *P.H.* (1973) pt. 1, esp. pp. 214-215.

251. For a review of the arguments on the date of Moses Khorenats'i, see C. Toumanoff, "On the Date of the Pseudo-Moses of
Chorene," *Handes Amsorya* 75 (1961), cols. 467-476, and *Studies,*
pp. 330-334.

252. Lazar, p. 203. A similar work may have been intended by
Sebēos, p. 197, where he refers to the *gir srboyn Grigori.* Although
this is often interpreted as the *History* of Agathangelos (e.g., N.
Akinean, "Artashir," *H.A.* 61 [1947], col. 578), the context implies
a document giving the Armenian church's attitude to the first four
ecumenical councils. This does not suggest an Armenian recension
of Agathangelos which might lie behind the *Vk* tradition.

253. But the references to Thaddaeus may be later interpolations. See note 27 above.

254. For the influence of Syria, see H. G. Melk'onyan, *Hay-
asorakan haraberut'yunneri patmut'yunits'* (Erevan, 1970), which
has a review of earlier literature.

255. On this see M. Tallon, "Livre des lettres."

256. For these see G. Garitte, *Narratio de Rebus Armeniae* (Louvain, 1952).

257. See R. W. Thomson, "An Armenian List of Heresies," *Journal of Theological Studies,* 16 (1965), esp. pp. 359-361.

NOTES TO THE TRANSLATION

§1   1. For Armenian parallels to such nautical images, compare Ełishē, p. 5, 1.10ff; Koriun, p. 2, 1.8ff; Łazar, p. 6, 1.18, p. 7, 1.5ff.; Moses III 62. They are commonplace in classical antiquity and in patristic authors such as Gregory Nazianzenus. For Syriac evidence see R. Murray, *Symbols of Church and Kingdom* (Cambridge, 1975), pp. 250-252.

2. There is a close parallel to this theme of merchants forgetting their labors once their treasure has been gained in Łazar, p. 6, 1.11ff.

§2   1. *To their friends* . . . §15 *after these times have passed*: omitted in *A B G D E Z Ē.*

§6   1. *Sea of wisdom:* cf. Koriun, p. 2, 1.10, p. 26, 1.27. The metaphor was common in Plato (cf. P. Louis, *Les métaphores de Platon* [Paris, 1945], pp. 50-51), and there are parallels in patristic literature (see Lampe, *Lexicon,* s.v. πέλαγος).

2. The merchant as a figure for the sophist is frequent in Plato (Louis, p. 75, 207). Patristic writers generally oppose the merchant (κάπηλος) and the philosopher, but metaphors using ἐμπορία in a spiritual sense are not uncommon (see Lampe, *Lexicon,* s.v.). For Syriac evidence see Murray, *Symbols,* pp. 174-175.

§7   1. *Poor stores of our intelligence: (z)ałk'atimast khanut's mer.*
2. *Literary trade: vacharakanut'iwn banits'.*
3. Cf. the famous dictum in Moses Khorenats'i: "there is no history without chronology *(zhamanakagrutiwn),*" II 82.

§8   1. For Armenian royal dress, see C. Toumanoff, *Studies,* pp. 134-135.

§10   1. For the Sea of sin cf. §16. The figure is common in the *Teaching* (§556, 568, 636).
2. *Heavenly navigator: erknawor nawapetin.* Cf. Zeus in Homer, *Iliad* VII 69. For the theme in patristic writers see Lampe, *Lexicon,* s.v. κυβερνᾶν and κυβερνήτης.

§12   1. On "Agathangelos," see *Introduction,* pp. xxiv-xxvi.
2. The Arsacids were a branch of the Parthian royal family and were confirmed as rulers of Armenia by Nero in A.D. 66. On

the founding of this dynasty see Toumanoff, *Studies,* p. 76; Chaumont, *Histoire,* p. 4 ff.

§13   1. From literary historical sources: *i dzernaŕkut'enē nshanagir zhamanakagrats'n.* Although the implication is that "Agathangelos" was using *written* sources, this is contradicted in §14. But the Prologue is hardly to be taken literally.

2. *Equal to his father's: hawramoyn,* which renders in I Macc. 6.17; II Macc. 10.10.

3. The double tyranny in Artashat probably means both Gregory's imprisonment in that city (§122) and his destruction of the pagan temples there (§778). Artashat (in Greek, Artaxata) was founded by Artashes I as his capital in the early second century B.C. (see H. A. Manandian, *The Trade and Cities of Armenia* (Lisbon, 1965), pp. 44 ff., and Hübschmann, *Grammatik,* p. 28).

4. *Heir: merdzawor,* close, related.

§14   1. *We have not composed... gospel:* this is taken almost verbatim from Koriun, p. 42, 1.15-20, where he describes his close relationship to Masht'ots'. On the theme of the eyewitness, see *Introduction,* p. xxvi.

2. *Teaching:* this is the long catechism (§259-715 of the *History*) which has been omitted from this study. See *Introduction,* pp. liii-lv.

3. On the various ecclesiastical titles given to Gregory, see *Introduction,* pp. lxvi-lxix.

§15   1. Is this a confused reminiscence of the theme of the chariot in the *Phaedrus*? For a Christian adaptation of the image of horse-racing, see R. R. Ruether, *Gregory of Nazianzus, Rhetor and Philosopher* (Oxford, 1969), pp. 90-91.

2. *So that... sea:* this is taken almost verbatim from Koriun, p. 2, 1.8-10.

§16   1. The significance of T'orgom is that he was the father of Hayk, the eponymous ancestor of the Armenians; see Moses Khorenats'i, I 5, 9. According to Gen. 10.3 T'orgom, Ashkenaz and Ribat were all sons of Gomer. Through T'orgom, son of Gomer, son of Japheth, the Armenians could claim descent from Noah—a theme known to Greek writers, cf. Syncellus, *Chronographia,* 49c; Hippolytus, *Chronik,* p. 12. Cf. also Kekelidzé, *Chro-*

nique d'Hippolyte. Moses Khorenats'i, I 5, makes Tiras [who in
I Chron. 1.5 is a brother of Gomer] the son of Gomer, thus adding
an extra generation. Ashkenaz was also claimed as an ancestor of
the Armenian race; see Koriun, p. 1, 1.1.

It is worth noting here that the Armenians did not identify
the mountain where Noah landed with the modern Mt. Ararat. According to Moses Khorenats'i, the province of Ayrarat was only
later settled by Hayk (I, 10) and Armenian writers as late as the
twelfth century are unaware of the precise mountain on which the
ark came to rest, though they consider it to have been in south-
western Armenia. E.g., Thomas Artsruni, p. 45: Noah landed in
the mountains of Korduk'. On the general question see Peeters, *La
légende de saint Jacques,* p. 318-336; V. Inglisian, *Armenien in der
Bibel* (Vienna, 1935), pp. 21 ff; J. Markwart, *Südarmenien und die
Tigrisquellen* (Vienna, 1930), pp. 231-232.

2. *Prosperity, peace, plenty:* according to Trdat's edict (§128),
these same blessings are given by the pagan gods if they are properly
appeased. Cf. also Moses' description of Tigran I (I 24).

3. *Sea of sin:* cf. §10 n.l.

§17   1. On the generally hagiographic character of Agathangelos'
attitude to the history he purports to be telling, see M. Avdalbegyan, *Hay Geḷarvestakan Ardzaki Skzbnvorumĕ* (Erevan, 1971), pp.
200 ff.

2. *Noblest of men: k'aj arants',* ὁ σεβαστός in Acts 25.21, 25;
used of Khosrov in Moses III 48. For Iranian evidence see H. W.
Bailey, *Zoroastrian Problems in the Ninth-century Books,* rev. ed.
(Oxford 1971), p. xvii.

3. Between the *Prologue* and the beginning of the *History*
proper, *Ag* (and later Metaphrastic Greek texts) inserts an episode
extraneous to the life of Gregory, an account of the revolt of Artashir. See *Introduction,* pp. xxvi-xxvii.

§18   1. On Artashir's coup d'état see A. Christensen, *L'Iran sous
les Sassanides* (Paris, 1936), pp. 81 ff; Frye, *Heritage,* pp. 198-199;
Chaumont, *Histoire,* pp. 22-23.

2. Stahr is near Persepolis ; see Hübschmann, *Grammatik,*
p. 75.

3. On the relation of the Armenian Arsacids to the Parthians
see Chaumont, *Histoire,* pp. 25 ff.

4. Khosrov's attempt to help Artavan against Artashir is also

described (though in different terms) by Moses Khorenats'i, II 71 ff. For a discussion of these events in a wider context see Chaumont, *Histoire,* ch. 2: *Chute de la dynastie arsacide en Arménie et invasion perse,* Toumanoff, *Arsacids,* p. 251.

§19   1. *Albanians: Aluank',* in Greek Ἀλβανοί; cf. Strabo, *Geography,* XI 4.

2. *Georgians: Virk',* in Greek Ἴβηροι; cf. Strabo, *Geography,* XI 3.

3. *Gates of the Alans: Drunk' Alanats':* the Darialan, the main pass through the Caucasus on the Aragvi river (the route of the later Georgian Military Highway).

4. *Stronghold of the Chor: Choray pahak:* the Chor is the pass near Darband on the Caspian Sea.

5. *Huns: Honk':* they are equated with the Kushans in §20 and by Eḷishē (p. 11, 1.23: *Honats'. . . zor K'ushans anuanen*). The term "Huns" is an imprecise one (see the pertinent remarks of Frye, *Heritage,* p. 216, and O. J. Maenschen Helfen, *The World of the Huns* [California, 1973], p. 6 and esp. 458); here it is the anachronism of a fifth-century writer.

6. *Asorestan:* not the ancient Assyria but Mesopotamia in Sassanian times; classical Syria was known as the land of the *Asorik'.* Cf. Hübschmann, *Grammatik,* p. 22.

7. *Their: Ag* reads "his brother's." This assertion is not directly supported elsewhere, but on the very close relation of the Arsacid kings and the Parthian royal family see Chaumont, *Histoire,* p. 25 (Procopius does not specify that this Khosrov was a brother of the Parthian king, *De Aedificiis,* III 1, as Chaumont claims).

8. *Lp'ink':* Λιφίννιοι in *Ag,* the *Lubieni* of Pliny, *H.N.,* VI 10.

9. *Chilpk':* Σιλβανοί in *Ag;* their lands were at the foot of the Caucasus on the way from Albania to the pass of Chor. Cf. Moses Daskhurants'i, II 39, where *Chor = Choḷ;* on this variant see Hübschmann, *Grammatik,* p. 218.

10. *Kaspk':* Κασπῖται in *Ag;* the inhabitants of the Caspian shore below Darband. Strabo, *Geography,* XI 4, 5, says that they gave their name to the Caspian Sea but had disappeared by his time.

§20   1. Meillet, *Remarques,* p. 465, notes that the first *t'epēt'ew* of this paragraph makes no sense; it must be an accidental repetition of the "although" of the next sentence.

2. On the Kushans see *International Conference on the History, Archaeology and Culture of Central Asia in the Kushan Period (Dushanbe 1968): An annotated bibliography* (Moscow, 1968). *Ag* omits all reference to the Kushans; the Armenian text from "contingents" to "yet" is probably a later interpolation based on the confusion in F.B. V 7 and 37 which makes the Kushans Arsacids.

§21   1. Vałarshapat rose to prominence in the early second century A.D. in the reign of the Arsacid Vałarsh. It was declared the capital of Armenia in 163 by the Romans and then renamed καινὴ πόλις   (New City, the *Nor K'alak'* of §150 below). See Manadian, *Cities,* pp. 83ff.; H. Hübschmann, *Altarmenischen Ortsnamen* (Strassbourg, 1904), p. 469. For the traditional Armenian account of the founding of Valarshapat see Moses Khorenats'i, II 65.

§22   1. *Seven altars . . . idols: Ag* reads more simply "to the seven temples." On the question of these seven shrines see *Introduction,* p. xl.

2. *He honoured . . . family:* omitted in *Ag.*

3. *Gold crowns and silver altars:* omitted in *Ag.* For crowns see also §49.

4. There are close parallels to this form of sacrifice, notably the white oxen, rams and crowns, in the description of Yazdgerd's thanksgiving for his success against the Huns, Ełishē, p. 12. Cf. also E. Benveniste, "La terminologie iranienne du sacrifice," J. A., vol. 252 (1964), esp. p. 48.

§23   1. *Tachiks:* Σαρακηνοί in *Ag;* the Arabs of Mesopotamia. For the etymology of *Tachik* (from the name of the Arab tribe Tay) see Hübschmann, *Grammatik,* p. 86.

2. For "eleven" in the printed text of *Aa* read "ten," with most Armenian MSS, *Ag* and Moses Khorenats'i, II 67, who gives a résumé of Agathangelos' own words.

§24   1. Agathangelos often presents us with long lists of titles. *Ag* reads merely "kings and governors [τοπάρχας] and generals." The list in *Aa* is another instance of the piling up of synonyms (or near synonyms) so dear to Agathangelos and no emphasis should be placed on them. Unlike the more precise lists of noble families (e.g., §795, 873) this list has no historical value.

§25 1. *Anak:* Ag adds: "from the kin [ἐκ τῆς συγγενείας] of Khosrov the king." Vk calls Anak "the brother" of Khosrov. See *Introduction,* p. xxviii.

§26 1. *Native:* reading *zbnut'iwn* with *a b d* and *Ag* rather than *zbnakut'iwn(n)* with the other Armenian MSS. *Ag* omits "your own Pahlav," cf. §32 n.l.

§28 1. *Khaḷkhaḷ:* Eḷishē describes this town as the winter quarters of the Albanian kings (p. 75, 1.17). On the province of Uti and Khaḷkhaḷ see Hübschmann, *AON,* pp. 270 ff. On the variants to the account in *Aa* see *Introduction,* pp. xxvii-xxviii.

§32 1. *Which was called Pahlav:* omitted in *Ag.*

§33 1. On the river Metsamawr (the great swamp) see Hübschmann, *AON,* p. 452. It is incorrectly rendered in *Ag* as "deep river" (ποταμοῦ βάθεος), cf. §206, note 2. On the later changes of course of the Metsamawr, which joined the Araxes at Artashat, see A. Soukry, *Géographie de Moise de Chorène* (Venice, 1881), p. 34.

2. On this river see L. Inchichean, *Storagrut'iwn hin Hayastaneayts'* (Venice, 1822), p. 487; cf. Faustos, III 12. *Ag* omits the name.

§34 1. *Two:* according to Moses Khorenats'i, II 74, only one son of Anak's survived, i.e., Gregory; cf. *Introduction,* p. xxix. Zenob, p. 21, calls Gregory's brother "Suren"; cf. Moses II 27.

2. *Someone: Ag* reads "one of his closest kin": τις τῶν ἐγγυτάτων.

3. *Only two . . . fled:* this sentence is omitted in the Armenian manuscripts *A* and *Z*; in its place they insert the account of Gregory's upbringing found in Zenob, pp. 22-23: *Isk Burdar . . . hawrn iwroy.*

§35 1. *Firetemples: atrushants'n,* on which see Hübschmann, *Grammatik,* p. 110; also Wikander, *Feuerpriester,* p. 219 and Benveniste, *Terminologie,* p. 57. *Ag* translates as "temples of the demons," τοῖς ἱεροῖς τῶν δαιμόνων.

§36 1. *An infant:* The Laurèntianus MS mistranslates the indefinite *mi* as the negative particle (οὐ), a striking proof that it is a translation of the Armenian and not vice-versa.

2. Moses Khorenats'i, II 76, says that Artavazd Mandakuni took Trdat to the Byzantine court (where Mandakuni is a tenden-

tious alteration of Mamikonean).

3. *The Pit: Soyzn,* translated in *Ag* as "place of abyss," τόπος χάσματος. (The Armenian manuscripts all have [meaningless] corruptions except *b,* which reads *Soyzn.*) Moses Khorenats'i, II 77, says that Artashir renewed the border established by Artashēs by fixing stones in the ground, but that the emperor Probus was responsible for the ditches. On the Iranian occupation of Armenia see Chaumont, *Histoire,* pp. 57ff.

4. *He deported . . . land:* omitted in *Ag.* Nor does Moses Khorenats'i mention it.

§37   1. *h* adds "in Rome." From here to §46 the Greek form *Trdatēs* or *Trdatios* is found instead of the Armenian *Trdat;* cf. A. von Gutschmid, "Agathangelos," *Zeitschrift der deutschen morgenländischen Gesellschaft* 31 (1877): pp. 44 ff.

2. *Likianēs:* in *Aa* and *Ag* he is entitled count (*koms,* κόμης). He is mentioned in retrospect by *Vg* as "Roman general and consul" ('Ρωμαίων στρατηγὸς καὶ ὕπατος) and by *Va* as "patrician," i.e., Licinius the colleague of Constantine; cf. Toumanoff, *Arsacids,* p. 270. *Aa* and *Ag* include Licinius among the impious kings overthrown by Constantine (§868).

3. *He was brought up by his tutors:* The Armenian makes this phrase active: *merdzaworeal zna snoyts' dayekawk',* which literally would mean "he (i.e., an unnamed person), having adopted him, raised him with tutors." But Agathangelos (*Aa* and *Ag*) has no reference to Burdar: cf. *Introduction,* p. xxxi.

§38   1. The story has jumped to a time when Gregory and Trdat were adult. The persecution may be that of Aurelian or Probus, but this paragraph has little connection with the development of the story. The name of the Greek emperor is not mentioned in *Aa* (though Moses Khorenats'i associates Trdat's military exploits with Probus, II 79). Later in *Aa* (§152) it is implied, though not expressly stated, that Diocletian restored Trdat to Armenia.

§39   1. Moses Khorenats'i and other late Armenian writers place this episode in the reign of Probus (A.D. 276-282); see Chaumont, *Histoire,* pp. 95 ff.

2. *Champion: akhoyean,* ἀντίπαλος in *Ag;* cf. Faustos, V 43; Sebēos, pp. 106-107.

§40   1. *They:* all the MSS of *Aa* except *a* and *d* make the verb singular.

2. *Because . . . opposing army;* omitted in *Ag.*2.

§41 1. *To the nobles . . . command: ar ishkhans ew qawrs zwrut-'ean iwroy: Ag* reads "to the generals of his command." The text in *Aa* is corrupt, for *zawrs* does not mean "generals" but "troops" or "army." Meillet, *Remarques,* p. 465, regards *ar ishkhans* as an addition and reads *zawravars* (generals) for *zawrs,* but this emendation lacks MS authority. *a b d* omit *zawrut'ean.*

§42 1. *Forage: khar, darman kerakroy.* Meillet regards the second phrase as a gloss to the hapax *khar, Remarques,* p. 465. But all MSS read as the text.

2. *Many donkeys:* the text in *Aa* (and *Ag*) is corrupt. My translation follows most MSS of the Armenian and *Ag* (Lafontaine) against the printed text (and Laurentianus).

§43 1. On the possibility of these stories about Trdat being selections from larger series of epic tales about heroes *(diuts'azn),* see Y. Tashean, *Agat'angelos ar̄ Georgay asori episkoposin ew usumnas-irut'iwn Agat'angeḷeay grots'* (Vienna, 1891), p. 132, and Gutsch-mid, *Agathangelos,* p. 58. Cf. the expression *i bans kargi arakats'* (among the proverbial sayings), §123.

§46 1. On the problems surrounding the date of Trdat's restoration to the Armenian throne see *Introduction,* pp. xxxv-xxxvii.

§47 1. This implies that Trdat reunited all of Armenia. After the defeat of Narseh in 297? See *Introduction,* p. xxxvi.

§48 1. *They: Ag* reads "the king and the army."

2. *Ekeleats:* Akilisene, see Hübschmann, *AON,* p. 286.

3. *Erēz:* the modern Erzinjan, see Hübschmann, *AON,* p. 425.

4. *Temple of Anahit:* Strabo, *Geography,* XI 14. 16, describes the ritual prostitution at this famous temple, and Procopius, *Bell. Pers.* I 17, gives an account of its mythical origin. According to Moses Khorenats'i, II 14, Tigran II set up statues of Greek deities in various parts of Armenia, including one of Artemis here. But see *Introduction,* p. xxxix. On this site see also Wikander, *Feurpriester,* p. 93, and Widengren, *Religionen,* p. 179.

5. *Gayl:* the river Lycus (as rendered by *Ag*). This is not the river that flows into the Black Sea, but a tributary of the Euphrates; see Hübschmann, *AON,* pp. 415-416.

§49 1. On the worship offered to Anahit see Wikander, *Feuer-priester,* p. 93; he compares the branches to the *barsmunk'* (twigs) used in Zurvanite worship of which Eznik frequently speaks (Eznik, §145, etc.). See also note 67 above. But there are biblical parallels to the "thick branches" *(t'aw osts)* in references to the feast of tabernacles, e.g., Neh. 8.15, II Macc. 10.7. In II Macc. 14.4 there is a precise reference to "thick branches" used for the honor of the temple *(i patiw mehenin)* and also to crowns of gold. It is unlikely that Agathangelos had any real idea of the cult offered to Anahit at Erëz. Rather, steeped in biblical lore (cf. *Introduction,* p. xli), here too he is drawing upon his knowledge of the bible.

§50   1. *Stranger and foreigner: ayr mi awtarakan ew anashkharhik.* Melik'-Ōhanjanyan, *Agat'angelosi,* pp. 64 ff., makes much of this phrase: later tradition was forced to invent elaborate genealogies to cover up Gregory's foreign origin. But the expression is not unreasonable at this stage of the narrative, before Gregory's real identity has been revealed and while he is naturally taken to be a native of Cappadocia. For the term *anashkharik,* cf. I Macc. 3.41; III Macc. 7.3.

§51   1. *To reward: kets'uts'anel,* lit. "to save, give life to"; *Ag* reads ἀποδοῦναι τὴν χάριν.

§52   1. This last sentence is phrased quite differently in *Ag.* The text of *Aa* is difficult: "and everything else" is in the nominative, though a more coherent rendering would take it in the genitive, "creator . . . of earth . . . and of everything else . . ." or in the dative, which would give my English translation. But there is no MS support for such a change.

§53   1. *Anahit:* Artemis in *Ag;* see *Introduction,* pp. xxxviii-xxxix.
      2. *Aramazd:* Zeus in *Ag;* see *Introduction,* pp. xxxix-xl.
§54   1. *Ag* paraphrases this with a quotation from Heb. 11.6.

§56   1. For the theme of Abraham's banquet see §149 note 2.

§58   1. This paragraph is somewhat abbreviated in *Ag.*

§59   1. For Agathangelos' theories about the origin of idolatry, see *Introduction,* pp. xli-xlii.

§60   1. *Establisher: hastich'* renders   κτίστης   in I Pet. 4.19, where it is applied to God the creator.
      2. *Disposer: kazmich';* the verbal form *kazmel* is frequent in the bible as a rendering for   κατασκευάζω,   καταρτίζω   or κοσμέω,   all terms that are often associated in patristic writers with creation.

3. *God the creator . . . creatures:* *Ag* reads "God. For he brought from non-existence everything with his only-begotten Son and the holy Spirit."

4. *Rose:* the text of *Aa* has *ekeats'* (came to life), but read *ekats'* (stood up, arose) with *Ag* and *a A B Z* in the Armenian; cf. Meillet, *Remarques,* p. 467.

5. *Model: awrinak,* for which see Thomson, *Teaching,* p. 16.

§61 1. Similar wording in Luke 13.16 of the girl loosed from the bonds of Satan.

§62 1. There is no verb in *Aa.* Meillet, *Remarques,* p. 473, supposes that *anhnarin t'shnamans* (terrible insults, accusative plural) may be a mistaken correction from a genitive found in *Ag.* (But all the Armenian MSS read as the text.) If this correction is justified, would it have been originally a genitive of exclamation? "How terrible are the insults that you have made to the gods and even to us kings (i.e., me)!" But the genitive case for exclamations is a Greek and not an Armenian construction. However, for a similar problematic genitive, see *Teaching,* §706 n. 4.

§64 1. *Flesh:* *a* reads "of all the dead," a reflection of I Cor. 15.52.
    2. *Men: A B Z* read "our" (breath).
    3. *Clothed in the same flesh:* cf. *Teaching* §368-369. But *Ag* has altered this: "that he may renew the souls of men which have put on incorruption in the same body ($\tau \grave{a}s$ $\psi v \chi \grave{a}s$ $\tau \hat{\omega} v$ $\dot{a} v \theta \rho \acute{\omega} \pi \omega v$, $\dot{\epsilon} v \delta \epsilon \delta v \mu \acute{\epsilon} v \underline{a s}$ $\dot{\epsilon} v$ $\tau \hat{\omega}$ $a \dot{v} \tau \hat{\omega}$ $\sigma \acute{\omega} \mu a \tau \iota$ $\dot{a} \phi \theta a \rho \sigma \acute{\iota} a v$). There is no variant in *Aa* to *zgets'eal,* which being in the nominative (or acc. sing.) can only refer to the subject of the sentence, not to *shunch's* (breath, pl.) or to men (*mardkan,* gen. sing.).

§65 1. *And called and invited:* omitted in *Ag.* "Invited" is very common in the *Teaching,* cf. §484 nl.
    2. On the second coming cf. *Teaching,* §471.
    3. On the theme of men becoming angels cf. *Teaching,* §414 and nl.

§68 1. On Anahit see *Introduction,* pp. xxxviii-xxxix.
    2. On Aramazd see *Introduction,* pp. xxxix-xl.

§70. 1. Cf. §66 above.

§72 1. *Hanging:* reading *kakhets'er* with α *β b d g* and *Ag* and §69 against *kapets'er* of the printed text (which is due to the following *kapanawk';* cf. Meillet, *Remarques,* pp. 467-468).

2. The witnesses to *Aa* differ between a singular *(α b c g)* and a plural (the other MSS.) verb. Originally the reference was to the Lord Jesus Christ, creator, as in *Ag* (ἐλπίζω εἰς τὸν κύριόν μου Ἰησοῦν Χριστὸν τὸν πάντων δημιουργόν, ὅτι . . .). *Aa* then expanded the text to include a reference to the Trinity, but the revisor did not rework the whole passage successfully.

3. *In the seventh age to come: Ag* alters this to read "when the seven weeks of years are fulfilled," a reference to Dan. 9.25. On the notion of seven ages *(dar)*, which plays an important role in Agathangelos, see *Teaching,* §668 n2.

§75 1. On the general character of these public prayers in martyrdoms see Delehaye, *Passions,* pp. 195-197. There is a good example of such a prayer recited from a hanging position in the *Martyrdom of Shmona and Guria,* §37.

2. *I am grateful . . . (gohanam);* M. Avdalbegyan, *Hay gełarvestakan Ardzaki Skzbnvorumĕ* (Erevan 1971), p. 214 nl9, draws a parallel with the *Martyrdom of Mark,* M. Awgerean, *Liakatar Vark',* VII, p. 229, but more significant are the parallels with liturgical expressions; see Y. Gat'rchean, *Srbazan Pataragamatoyts'k' Hayots'* (Vienna 1897), p. 106. Cf. also Lazar, pp. 90-91.

3. Cf. *Teaching,* §277. The first part of this sentence is not conditional, being in the aorist and not the imperfect.

4. On the relationship of the Trinity, cf. *Teaching,* §259. In *Ag* "Not that . . . being" is altered: "Not that the tree was so called of life and death, but you wished thus to demonstrate your will and that of your only-begotten Son, for he is the offspring of your divinity, and the will of your holy Spirit, for he proceeds from you and fills the ends of the earth."

§76 1. For the idyllic life that man might have enjoyed see Athanasius, *contra Gentes* 2, *de Incarnatione* 3, 11. The theme is taken up in the *Teaching,* §270.

2. *Awrinak* (τύπος in *Ag*); on this term see Thomson, *Teaching,* p. 16.

3. On man becoming like the angels cf. *Teaching,* §414 nl.

§77 1. On the jealousy of the devil cf. *Teaching,* §278.

2. *Aa* follows the Armenian Vulgate, which differs here from the Septuagint.

§78 1. On the role of the prophets cf. *Teaching,* §337ff.

§79   1. For the comparison between Eve and the Virgin (a variant on I Cor. 15.21) made by patristic writers, see the many references in Lampe, *Lexicon,* s.v.   παρθένος,   IV C. See also *Introduction,* pp. lxxxvi.

   Will enter: here *Ag* has an aorist tense. All witnesses to *Aa* read as the text.

§80   1. Cf. *Teaching,* §381.

   2. *Image of men:* the same expression is used by Proclus of Constantinople, *Oratio,* VI 11. Cf. *Introduction,* p. lxxxvi. Proclus was highly regarded in Armenia, notably for his *Tome* which was important in bringing the Armenians to accept the decrees of the Council of Ephesus. For a study of this *Tome,* see M. Tallon, *Livre des Lettres,* ch. 2.

§81   1. *Dead image:* this figure was later taken up by the iconophiles in defence of images. This particular passage from Agathangelos is quoted in the *Apology* attributed to Vrt'anēs, *locum tenens* of the Armenian patriarchate from 604 to 607; see S. Der Nersessian, *Une aplogie des images au septième siècle, Byzantion* 17 (1944-45), 57-87, esp. 61 and note 15, where she notes that the Patriarch of Constantinople, Nicephorus, also quoted from this passage. On this passage cf. *Introduction,* p. lxxxvi.

   2. *Hook: kart'* as Matt. 17.26 (v. 27 in the Greek). For the frequent references to Christ's humanity as a hook, snare or bait aimed at the devil, see Lampe, *Lexicon,* s.v. ἄγκιστρον·

   3. *Food: kerakur* (βρῶμα in *Ag*) is a reference to the Eucharist. Cf. §84 below. The theme of the eucharistic body as a hook or bait is elaborated in Ełishē, *Matenagrutiwnk'* (Venice, 1859), p. 338.

   4. Cf. Luke 5.10, where the Armenian Vulgate and the Peshitta add "for life" after "you will catch men."

§82   1. On this important theme, see *Teaching,* §489.

§83   1. A reference to John 3.14; 8.28; 12.32, etc. For the patristic exegesis of this theme, see Lampe, *Lexicon,* sv. ὑψόω·

§84   1. Cf. §81 n3.

   2. On the theme of the invitation to the wedding banquet, see *Teaching,* §508, 510, 672.

   3. *And their cities . . . anger:* omitted in *Ag.*

§85   1. On this theme in patristic literature, see Lampe, *Lexicon,* s.v. ξύλον, B 6.

2. In *Aa* it is the images that have human form; *Ag* alters this to read: "the image in human form instead of the impure image" (αὐτὴ ἡ ἀνθρωπόμορφος εἰκὼν ἀντὶ τῆς βδελυρᾶς εἰκόνος).

3. On this theme, see Lampe, *Lexicon,* s.v. αἷμα, E 2.

§89   1. *Fire-worship: mokhrapashtut'iwn,* literally "ash-worship." It refers to the care bestowed on the ashes of the holy fire, cf. Eḷishē, p. 53. On this term see Wikander, *Feuerpriester,* p. 89; and Beneviste, *Terminologie,* p. 54. *Ag* renders this expression by "vain worship" (ματαίῳ σεβάσματι). Ḷazar calls the fire temples "houses of ashes" (*tun mokhranots'in),* p. 39.

§90   1. *Ag* adds "and your only-begotten Son and your holy Spirit."
2. Cf. *Teaching,* §648.

§91   1. Cf. *Teaching,* §267.
2. Example: *awrinak,* on which see Thomson, *Teaching,* p. 16.

3. The Son as sun; cf. *Teaching,* §566. For further references in patristic literature, see Lampe, *Lexicon,* s.v. ἥλιος, B 4.

§92   1. For the moon as an image of resurrection cf. Cyril Jer., *Catecheses,* XVIII 10. There are several parallels with this homily in §91-92.

2. The completion of the parables and types is an important theme in the *Teaching;* see §372, 423.

3. These last two paragraphs are taken almost verbatim from the liturgy, see Gat'rchean, *Pataragamatoyts'k',* p. 108.

§93   1. For further liturgical parallels to this paragraph see Gat - rchean, *Pataragamatoyts'k',* p. 90.

§95   1. Cf. Thomson, *Teaching,* p. 14.
2. Cf. Thomson, *Teaching,* p. 19 and §364.
3. Cf. *Teaching,* §407, 589.

§96   1. *Joined: Khaṙnets'er;* on this technical expression see Thomson, *Teaching,* p. 19.
2. Cf. *Teaching,* §598.

§97   1. Cf. §84 n2 above.

§98   1. *In . . . kingdom: Ag* reads "eternally in your kingdom."
2. *Essence, being, individuality:* on these terms see Thomson,

Teaching, pp. 11-12. *Ag* renders essence *(ēut'iwn)* by ἀειδιότης (= ἀϊδιότης), being *(iskut'iwn)* by ἀναρχότης, and individuality *(ink'nut'iwn)* by ἀκαταληψία. This last probably reflects the corruption *yank'nut'eand* (sic! not *yank'nnut'eand*) found in **β** *a b d g.*

3. Cf. *Teaching,* §407, 452 n2.

§99 1. *Scribes of the tribunal: atenakal dpirk'n nshanagrats'n,* which *Ag* renders οἱ ὑνομνηματογράφοι διὰ σημείων. On such scribes see R. Aigrain, *L'hagiographie* (Paris, 1953), pp. 132ff. There are close parallels in the *Martyrdom of Shmona and Guria,* §39, and the *Martyrdom of Habbib,* §39. But this passage is to be taken no more seriously than Agathangelos' own claim to have been an eyewitness. Cf. also §176.

§102 1. For a parallel to this type of torture cf. *Acts of Sharbil,* p. 54.

2. The insensibility of martyrs to their pain is a stock theme in hagiography; see Delehaye, *Passions,* pp. 207ff.

§103 1. For parallels to this type of torture, cf. Delehaye, *Passions,* p. 204.

§107 1. *Sack: Parks:* the witnesses to the Armenian text all make "sack" plural, but *Ag* has the singular. The latter must be correct as the following sentences indicate. Cf. Meillet, *Remarques,* pp. 465-466.

§109 1. *Cords of wineskins: (i) hrapoyrs tkats'; hrapoyrk'* is used in Faustos, IV 55, of the way in which queen P'arandzem was bound and exposed to insults. For a parallel to this torture, cf. the *Martyrdom of Shmona and Guria,* §35.

§110. 1. *My: imoy* in the text, but it should be *imum* to agree with "God." It is omitted by **β** *a b d A B G D.*

2. *And the Son . . . wisdom:* although this phrase is also in *Ag* it must be an addition to the original Armenian, for "Lord God" is in the dative (after the verb "to worship"), whereas "Son" and "Spirit" are in the accusative case. There is a similar revision in §72. Cf. Meillet, *Remarques,* p. 473.

§111 1. On torture by scraping, cf. *Acts of the 45 Martyrs of Nicopolis,* §16 (*P.G.* 115, 337); *Martyrdom of Shmona and Guria,* §19; *Acts of Sharbil,* p. 51; *Martyrdom of Habbib,* §8.

2. *God:* the Armenian reads *or* ("who," or "which"). But the relative pronoun cannot refer to "covenant," its logical antecedent, but must refer to God. *Ag* also makes the relative masculine after a feminine antecedent.

§112   1. *Thistles: tatask, τρίβολος* in *Ag* (as also in Matt. 7.16 etc.). These were used as caltrops to lame horses.

2. This phrase begins with *minch'zi,* which makes little sense and is probably a corruption from the preceding *minch'ew* (until). *Ag* omits "until . . . torn" and reads "until no place remained whole in his body." On the text of this paragraph, see Meillet, *Remarques,* p. 462.

§113   1. *Ag* reads "the king" for the Armenian "him."

2. *Stay:* reading *kas* with **α β** *b d A B G Z* and *Ag* for the *keas* of the printed text. Cf. Meillet, *Remarques,* p. 467.

3. *Such:* as *Ag,* omitted in *Aa.*

§115   1. For a parallel to this torture, cf. *Martyrdom of Shmona and Guria,* §35.

§116   1. *Fourth:* third **α β** *a b d h n w z* and *Ag.*

§117   1. *These same souls . . . body:* this passage was considered self-contradictory by Meillet, *Remarques,* p. 463. "Soul" is singular in *A B G D* and "bodies" is plural in **β** a d; *Ag* reads as the printed text of *Aa.* But "souls" is natural here since the reference is to many people, while each soul has one body. Similarly in §529 of the *Teaching,* when also referring to the general resurrection, Agathangelos speaks of the same bodies (pl.) rising from the tomb with the same soul (sing.).

§119   1. On parallels to this torture by molten lead, cf. *Acts of Sharbil,* p. 54, and in general Delehaye, *Passions,* p. 202.

§121   1. *The tortures:* omitted in *Aa* but added in *Ag.*

2. *Whose name . . . Constable:* omitted by **β** *a d A B G Z* and *Ag;* the addition of the name is a later gloss based on Moses Khorenats'i, II 78, 82. On the office of High Constable *(sparapet)* see Toumanoff, *Studies,* p. 209, and N. Adontz/N.G. Garsoian, *Armenia in the Period of Justinian* (Lisbon, 1970), p. 510 n29a for full references.

3. *Guilty man: vrizhapartin,* lit. "of one meriting vengeance."

§122   1. *Acropolis: dgheak berdin,* λόφος τοῦ κάστρου in *Ag.*
       2. On *Artashat* cf. §13 n1.
       3. *Bottommost pit: virap nerk'in,* τὸ κατώτατον χάος
in *Ag.* The place of imprisonment thus became known as the
Virap or *khor* (deep) *virap.*
       4. *Thirteen:* fourteen in *Ag.* There is some variation in the
History concerning the length of Gregory's imprisonment: 13 years
in §122, 124, 132; but 15 years in §215, 233. Cf. *Introduction,* p. lii.

§123   1. *Asorestan:* 'Ασσυρία in *Ag;* cf. §19 n6 above.
       2. There is a somewhat similar exaggerated boast in Faustos,
IV 54: Vasak boasts of standing with his feet on two mountains
which sank when he pressed down—these were the kings of Persia
and of Byzantium. On the possibility of these stories coming from
epic tales now lost, see the references in §43 n1.
       3. *Syria: Asorwots':* Most MSS of *Ag* do not distinguish
between Syria and Asorestan, with 'Ασσυρία for Συρία.
Cf. §19 n6.
       4. *Commander: aṙajnord,* a vague term meaning "leader."
(It is often used by Agathangelos in an ecclesiastical sense to refer
to the primate of Armenia, e.g. §762, 792, 799.)
       5. On the wars of Trdat after his restoration, cf. Moses
Khorenats'i, II 82, 87. There may be here some reminiscence of the
war with Narseh; cf. Chaumont, *Histoire,* p. 118.

§124   1. *Thirteen:* fourteen in *Ag;* cf. §122 n4.
       2. *Vg and Va,* though in general offering a much abbreviated
account, add that Gregory was also provided with water.
       3. *Nourished: kerakreal.* This term and *nkanak* for "loaf" are
used in III Kings 17.2, 13; we are thus directly reminded of Elijah
and the widow. *(Vg* has "woman" for "widow.") However, *Vk*
explicitly compares this episode to the feeding of Daniel in the pit.
But there are no parallels in the vocabulary of *Aa* with the Armenian text of Dan. 14. 32 ff.

§127   1. These are Zeus, Artemis and Heracles in *Ag.* On these
deities, see *Introduction,* p. xxviii-xxx, lxiii, and notes *ad loc.*
       2. *May . . . :* Ag omits the rest of the text of this edict from
here to the end of §131, merely saying "etcetera."
       3. *Province: dastakert;* for a justification of this rendering
see G. Kh. Sarapyan, *O dvukh znacheniyakh termina dastakert b
rannykh armjanskikh istochnikakh, Ellinisticheskij blizhnij Vostok,*

Vizantija i Iran (Moscow, 1967), pp. 97-101; cf. also *idem,* "Das-takertnĕre ev agaraknĕre V dari haykakan aḷbyurnerum," *P.H.* (1962), pt. 3, pp. 77-94.

4. *Glory: p'aŕk',* the Iranian *farrah,* for which see Bailey, *Zoroastrian Problems,* ch. 1 and 2. A parallel may be seen in Eḷishē, p. 145,[17] where the Christian saints are surrounded by a luminous aura, described by a Persian as "the luminous *p'aŕavorut'iun* of the gods." Cf. also the *p'aŕk'* of the Aryans in Ḷazar, p. 149[30], and the *p'aŕk'* of Shapuh's immortal ancestors in Moses Khorenats'i, III 42.

5. The second part of this paragraph is most obscurely worded; for a slightly different translation see Chaumont, *Histoire,* p. 137 nl.

§129. 1. An example of such edicts promulgated in the Roman empire at the beginning of the fourth century A.D. is that of Maximin, reported by Eusebius, *H.e.* IX 7. This has particular interest since Eusebius then goes on to describe Maximin's campaign against the Armenian Christians. On this see the recent comments by Toumanoff, *Arsacids,* p. 271 n.201. It is interesting to note that Justinian's *Novella* 133 also stresses that religious conformity is necessary to ensure prosperity.

§131 1. *Princes and magnates:* reading *ew* after "princes" with *a b d A B G Z;* the printed text reads "Great princes."

§132 1. Fourteen in *Ag;* cf. §122 n4.

§133 1. The implication would be that this persecution dates from the last year of Gregory's imprisonment (311 ? cf. *Introduction,* p. lii), though in §137 we return to the reign of Diocletian (abdicated 305). But strict chronology can hardly be expected in a hagiographical work of this kind.

§134 1. On the form of greeting, cf. Eḷishē, p. 9, 1.16-17; and also III Macc. 3.8; II Macc. 11.28.

§135 1. *Be they . . . thousands:* omitted in *Ag.*

2. For an example of this literary genre of edicts against Christians, cf. the *Martyrdom of the 45 Martyrs of Nicopolis (P.G.* 115.324) which begins with an edict attributed to Licinius.

§137 1. Such searches for an imperial bride were not uncommon in Byzantium, cf. F. Dvornik, *Les légendes de Constantin et de Méthode vues de Byzance* (Prague, 1933), pp. 19-22; and C. Diehl,

Impératrices de Byzance (Paris, 1959), pp. 13 ff. But the biblical parallel in Esther ch. 2 is probably more apposite.

§138 1. *Were worthy:* "did not cease" *Ag.*

2. *Ag* adds: "and there were many others (fem.) with them." On Rhipsimē's noble ancestry, see also §167, 878; for the etymology of Rhipsimē, see §175. Outside the *History* of Agathangelos, Rhipsimē and Gaianē are rarely mentioned in the earliest Armenian authors, though Faustos, III 14, gives a passing reference to their burial place in the province of Ayrarat, and Sebēos, ch. 25, mentions the chapel of Rhipsimē built by the Catholicos Sahak and the church built by Komitas in 618 on that site.

§140 1. *Unbridled passion: molegnakan ts'ankut'eamb,* cf. Moses Khorenats'i, I 15, where he speaks of Semiramis' *ts'ankakan molegnut'iwn.*

§141 1. *Mask: vahanak eresats',* a headpiece of armor. This whole paragraph is closely paralleled in Eḷishē, p. 6, where the king who is filled with poisonous darts in Yazdgerd II.

§142 1. *Corpses: meṙelotwots',* which is also used by extension for idols. *Ag* expands slightly to make this meaning clearer: "the images of dead men" (τὰς τῶν νεκρῶν στήλας).

§146 1. On this (false) etymology of Israel, which refers to Gen. 32.28, see the references in Lampe, *Lexicon,* s.v. Ἰσραηλ.

§149 1. *To a distant land:* omitted in *Ag.*

2. *Abraham's banquet: i bazmakans Abrahamu,* literally "among Abraham's company *or* guests." *Ag* reads: ἀνακλίσεως τοῦ   πατριάρχου   Ἀβραάμ. In the Armenian bible *bazmakan* often renders (συν) ανακειμένος. Cf. the messianic banquet in the *Teaching,* §508, 510. The reference to Abraham is presumably a combination of the two concepts of the future banquet or wedding feast (cf. the "divine bridegroom" in the preceding line) and of Abraham's bosom as a figure for the rest of the departed (on which see Lampe, *Lexicon,* s.v. Ἀβρααμ). Cf. §56.

§150 1. *On Nor K'alak',* see §21 above.

2. *Vat-stores: i hndzanayarks,* the buildings housing the wine presses. *Ag* has simply "in the wine-presses" εἰς   τὰς   ληνούς, an expression with a long history of symbolic meaning, especially as a figure for the church; see Lampe, *Lexicon,* s.v. ληνός.

3. *Skill . . . pearls: Ag* abbreviates to   εἰδυῖα ὑελουργεῖν.
On glass-making in Armenia at this period, see B.N. Arakʻelyan,
G.A. Tiratsʻyan, Zh. D. Khachʻatryan, *Hin Hayastani Apakin* (Ere-
van, 1969).

§151 1. *Edict: hrovartak,* an expression with a wide range of
meanings from "an order sent to tributary kings" (e.g., Eḷishē, p. 9,
1.13) to "a synodical letter." *Ag* reads simply: ἐπιστολή. Cf. §801
n1.

§152 1. Chaumont, *Histoire,* p. 139 n4, notes that the title in *Vg* is
less flattering than that of *Aa* and *Ag,* omitting the term "colleague"
(atʻoŕakitsʻ).

§153 1. For parallels to such edicts concerning the Christians see
Delehaye, *Passions,* pp. 175-176.

§154 1. *And they teach . . . gods:* a repetition of the last phrase in
§153. omitted in *a b d A B D Z.*

2. *During their lifetime: kendanwoyn.* Meillet, *Remarques,*
p. 466, proposed the emendation *kendanwotsʻ* (to make this word
agree with "women"). But *kendanwoyn* is frequently found as an
indeclinable adverb meaning "alive," see *Nor Baŕgirkʻ Haykazean
Lezvi* (Venice, 1836-37), s.v. *kendanwoyn.* Similar scorn is poured
on celibacy in the edict of Mihr Nerseh, Eḷishē, p. 27.

§156 1. For "worship" *ABDZ* read "help," for which cf. §127.

2. A reply from Trdat to Diocletian is found in *Vg* §40, see
Garitte, *Documents,* p. 293. For the text, see *Introduction,* p. xlviii.
n82; the text with translation is also given in Chaumont, *Histoire,*
p. 140.

§159 1. The oil is presumably for the torches rather than the
candlesticks. Agathangelos' style is frequently overloaded with
mixed metaphors, some of which are more successful than others.
For oil as a figure of faith, see Lampe, *Lexicon,* s.v. ἔλαιον.

§160 1. Christ's nature is his divinity, see *Teaching,* §369 n1 and
further references there.

2. *To share his own nature:* a theme also elaborated in the
Teaching, cf. §385 n1. But *Ag* alters this phrase to read: εἰς
τὴν ἰδίαν υἱοθεσίαν (to his own adoption), which is based on Gal.
4.5 and Eph. 1.5.

§162 1. *Two:* three in *a d A B D Z* and *Ag.*

2. *Wonderful: zanazan,* literally: distinctive.

§163　1. This bombastic paragraph is somewhat simplified in *Ag.*

§167　1. On Rhipsimē's noble ancestry, see §878 n1.

§168　1. On this stance for prayer, see Lampe, *Lexicon,* s.v. σταυρός.

§169　1. *Lord God . . . dry land:* cf. *Teaching,* §259-260.

　　　2. *Eighth generation:* i.e. of patriarchs; see *Teaching,* §295 n1.

　　　3. *Cross-like wood:* The ark was frequently used as a figure for the church (cf. Lampe, *Lexicon,*s.v.　κιβωτός).　Here the comparison is between the ark which saved Noah and the cross which saved mankind, the two being linked by their common material—wood. There is a very close parallel in Justin, *Dial.* 138, 2 (on which see the comments in Daniélou, *Theology,* p. 277). See further *Introduction,* pp. lxxxvi-lxxviii.

§170　1. *Over us. This: i veray mer, zor.* The text in *Aa* is difficult. *Ag* changes the relative pronoun *zor* and begins a new sentence "Now this." *A* and *Z* omit "over . . . you." *I veray mer* could also mean "on our behalf."

§171　1. *The alloted number: t'iw vichakats',* τὸν ἀριθμὸν τοῦ κλήρου in *Ag. Vichak* in the bible frequently means "inheritance" and in the plural "allotment," cf. I Pet 5.3. This passage is based on Col. 1.12 and the common biblical motif of κληρονομία.

§172　1. *Your images:* i.e., men, cf. *Teaching,* §263ff.

　　　2. Cf. the biblical quotation in §170. *Ag* omits "While if . . . will."

§173　1. *To marry her: zi tarts'in zna knut'ean,* an expression used for the father of the bride.

§175　1. *Northern regions:* a common expression in Agathangelos for Armenia, cf. §741, 742 (and also Koriun, p. 24, 1.12, Moses I 10, 17, esp. III 68). In fact Vaḷarshapat, on lat. 40° is farther south than Rome, lat. 42°, from where Agathangelos claims to come. Geographic or climatic considerations apart, the expression may perhaps be explained by the notion reflected in Moses Khorenats'i that Armenia was settled from the south; cf. Moses I 10 ff. But it may well be that "Northern" is a reflection of the classical division of Asia into northern and southern regions on either side of the Taurus; see Strabo, *Geography,* XI 1.1-4. The biblical notion of Ararat being in the North (of Assyria) may also have played a part here.

2. Agathangelos derives "Rhipsimē" from the Greek verb ῥίπτω, "to throw"; cf. *Ag:* Ῥιψίμη . . . ἀληθῶς ἐξερρίφης. This Greek verb can be used of casting away or exposing children (cf. *Ad Diognetum* 5.6, where this practice is repudiated). There is no suggestion in Agathangelos that Rhipsimē was a foundling (on her ancestry, see §878), but Gaianē does say "you left and abandoned the honor and splendor of your fathers . . . (§167)." N. Akinean bases a theory of Rhipsimē's origin as a slave girl on the unattested meaning of ῥίπτω as "to imprison"; cf. *K'ristonēut'ean Mutk'ē Hayastan ew Vrastan* (Vienna, 1949), p. 340. This would make Rhipsimē a double of Nunē, the apostle of Georgia. But *Rhipsimē* is not a passive participle derived from ῥίπτω which would correspond with the Armenian *ēnkets'eal;* this folk-etymology must be abandoned. Both names, Rhipsimē and Gaianē, are of unknown origin.

§176　1. This turmoil is reminiscent of the tempest which followed the martyrdom of Mark, destroying buildings and killing many people, *P.G.,* vol. 115, col. 169.

2. *Secretaries: nshanagirk',* see §99 n1.

3. *Because . . . king:* omitted in *Ag.*

§180　1. *Songs and dancing:* parallel phrasing in Moses Khorenats'i, I 6.

§181　1. *Had returned: dardzeal er. A B Z* read *ehas* (reached) and *Ag* παρέλαβεν, which has overtones of receiving by inheritance.

2. For the exploits of Trdat in Greek lands, see §42-45 and especially §202 and notes. On his exploits in Armenia, see §123.

§183　1. Omitting the *ē* of the printed text after "today," with *a d A B D Z.*

§185　1. *Rich man:* + in hell *Ag.*

2. *Us:* + if we endure, *Ag,* cf. II Tim. 2.10.

3. Cf. §175.

4. *Us: Ag* reads σε (you, sing.), but the Armenian has a plural adjective *arzhanis* (worthy) and no pronoun, so *arzhanis* must refer to the last plural pronoun—"us," not "you."

5. *Dwell: (lits'uk') bnakich'k',* but *Ag* reads　　γενώμεθα

ναοὶ   θεΐκου   φωτός   (that we may become temples of divine light), which is presumably based on the various references to "temple" in I and II Corinthians.

§186   1. *His power: Ag* reads "him."

2. *Who glorifies the humbled: anargamets'ar,* cf. Lk. 1.52. But this term is not biblical; it is also found in Koriun, p. 6, 1.5. *Ag* reads "(Lord) of the humble."

3. *We shall endure: hamberests'uk';* this is not the Armenian vulgate text. *Ag* reads   θανατούμεθα   (we die). In *Aa* there is confusion between Ps. 43.23 (also quoted, correctly, in §207) and Ps. 24.5.

§187   1. *Was wounded: viraworts'aw.* But *A B D Z* and *Ag* read: "was handed over" (*varets'aw,*   παρεδόθη).

§188   1. *Handmaid: aḷakhin,* reminiscent of Lk. 1.38.

2. *Him face to face: Ag* reads "his face."

§189   1. *Latin: barbaṙ Hṙomayets'wots'* (the dialect of the Romans), cf. §12, *hṙomayerēn.* Armenian rarely uses the term "Latin" before the 13th century. [In the N.T. (Lk. 23.38, Jn. 19.20) the curious rendering *dalmaṫēren* (in the Dalmatian language) for Latin is found. Cf. §874 n2.[

§192   1. *Sungate: Areg duṙn. Areg* is the genitive of *arew,* sun; cf. E. Benveniste, *Arménien* Aregakh *"soleil" et la formation nominale en* -akn, *R.E.A., N.S.,* vol. 2 (1965), 5-19, esp. 9. *Ag* reads simply: "the gate," but in §206 renders the "South gate" by   τῆς   ἡλιακῆς   πύλης   (the sun-gate).

§194   1. *Our:* as *b A B D Z* and *Ag,* rather than the "your" of the printed text.

§195   1. *The hearts of the sons of men: Ag* reads   κατὰ   μόνας   τὰς   καρδίας   τῶν   ἀνθρώπων   (individually the hearts of men).

2. *To be joined to the company:* a common expression in the *Teaching;* cf. Thomson, *Teaching,* p. 19.

§196.   1. *That cast us low: a* and *Ag* make the verb 2nd singular.

2. *Your inheritance:* τὰς   δούλας   σου   (your maid-servants) *Ag.*

§197   1. *Torturers: dahchawk'n,* "soldiers" in *Ag,* the usual expression in Ḷazar and Eḷishē for the Persian jailers.

2. *Offered her tongue:* the wording is identical with II Macc.

474 *NOTES*

7.10 (martyrdom of the third brother). For parallels in Christian martyrdoms, see Delehaye, *Passions,* p. 203, and further references in Lampe, *Lexicon,* s.v. γλωσσοκοπέω and γλωσσοτομέω.

§199 1. There was a total of 37 martyrs (§209), but sometimes the single nun in the vat-store (§201) is omitted in the numbering. So Rhipsimē has 33 fellowmartyrs in §210, but only 32 in §737.

§200 1. *Iniquities:* + "for we are the sheep of your glorious name" *Ag.*

§201 1. *There was one:* + ἀσθενοῦσαν (ill) *Ag.*

2. *Who loved you:* omitted in *Ag.*

§202 1. *Paid no regard . . . ashamed: Ag* reads: "was greatly put to shame."

2. *Greek Olympics:* This is elaborated in Moses Khorenats'i, II 79, where Trdat is said to have outshone Clitostratus and Cerasus—names taken by Moses from Eusebius' *Chronicle.*

3. Battles among the Tachiks (Σαρακήνοι in *Ag*): on this term see §23 n1. On Trdat's prowess in war cf. Moses Khorenats'i, II 79, 82, 85.

4. *Gravely wounded:* + "fleeing the battle so as not to be taken" *Ag,* which the Armenian redactor may well have omitted deliberately as a reflection on his hero. In Moses Khorenats'i, II 79, it is Trdat's horse that is wounded, not Trdat himself. See *Introduction,* p. xxxv. For the historical occasion, cf. Toumanoff, *Arsacids,* p. 270 n. 193.

5. *To his back: i t'ikuns i veray mkanants'n.* The first two words are a gloss to the rare *mkanats',* cf. Meillet, *Remarques,* p. 466.

§203 1. *They deprive them of:* they despise *Ag.* The Armenian expression has a parallel in Ełishē, p. 26: Christianity deprives one of the pleasures of the world (edict of Mihrnerseh).

2. *Our Parthian . . . Azerbaijan:* "the regions of the Parthians, Assyria and Persia" *Ag.* On Tachikistan and Asorestan, see §19 n6 and §23 n1; on the form *Atrpatakan,* see Hübschmann, *Grammatik,* p. 23. *Ag* here renders Azerbaijan by Persia, but cf. §842 n11 where Atrapatakan is glossed as πυροχωρία. In the text of *Aa* for "homeland" (*bnut'iwn*) *A B D Z* and *a* corr read "habitat" (*bkanut'iwn*).

§205 1. *Since she had dared:* + φησίν (he said) *Ag. Ag* makes the rest of the sentence into a speech by Trdat.

2. *And her advice . . . beauty:* omitted in *Ag.*

§206   1. *South gate:* τῆς ἡλιακῆς πύλης   (sun gate) *Ag;* cf. §192 n1.

2. *Mets'amawr bridge: Ag* reads: the bridge τοῦ βαθυτάτου καλουμένου   ποταμοῦ   (of the river called "very deep"); cf. §33 n1.

§207   1. *I: a d* and *Ag* make this section plural throughout.

§208   1. *Breasts:* + "even up to their hair" *Ag.*

2. On the tradition of a final beheading after innumerable tortures see Delehaye, *Legends,* p. 97.

§209   1. *And had arrived . . . Armenia:* omitted in *Ag.*

§210   1. 26th Hori: 26 September in *Ag, Vg, Vo.* This simple equivalence was a common way of rough reckoning and does not necessarily prove that the translation was made when the two dates coincided, i.e., between 464 and 468; see Peeters, *Grégoire,* p. 108 and note 84 above. *Vo* (§37) gives the date as 26th October, but *Ar* follows *Ag* (26th Eylul = Sept.). In the latter *synaxarion* of Ter Israel the date is given as 5th October, which reflects the fixed Armenian calendar of John the Deacon, established in the twelfth century (cf. V. Grumel, *La Chronologie* [Paris, 1958], p. 179). In *Vg* (§50) *all* the nuns die on the same day, 26th September. In §815 a different date for the feast to commemorate the martyrs is instituted, the 7th Sahmi (in *Ag* 7th October)

2. *Ag* omits the number 33.

§211   1. *He had his soldiers . . . set:* "and when the foot soldiers had prepared the nets" *Ag.*

2. *P'arakan Shemak:* cf. Hübschmann, *AON,* s.v. *P'ara-kank',* p. 477. Sebēos, *The Primary History,* p. 10, mentions the place as a famous hunting resort. *P'arakan,* "pack of hounds," see G.V. Abgaryan, *Sebeosi Patmut' yunē ev Ananuni Areltsvatsē* (Erevan 1965), p. 116 note 192.

§212   1. The description of the malady of Trdat is based on the Armenian text of Daniel, 4.12-13 (=LXX 4.15-16), 22 and 25. There are several parallels in hagiographical literature; cf. Delehaye, *Passions,* pp. 217-218. On the theme of eating one's own flesh cf. Delehaye, *ibid.,* p. 197: St. Christopher prays that the persecuting emperor may be so punished.

2. *In senseless abandon . . . grass:* omitted in *Ag.*

3. *Wallowed: kotselov,* literally "beating himself," as Mk. 5.5, an expression frequently used of mourners and madmen. *Ag* reads simply "went about."

§214   1. Moses Khorenats‘i, II 82, paints an idealised portrait of Khosrovidukht "who did not have an open mouth like other women."

§215   1. *15 years:* on the length of Gregory's imprisonment see §122 n4.

§216   1. *Again, five times:* "a second and third time" *Ag.*
2. *Angel's:* "of the vision," *Ag.*

§217   1. *Awtay:* Moses Khorenats‘i, II 77, 82, gives further details about Awtay, who was from the Amatuni family and had been the guardian *(snuts‘oḷ)* of Khosrovidukht. The text in *b* has been expanded to include these details from Moses.

§218   1. *Somewhere down there:* "still among the living" *Ag.*

§223   1. For other examples in hagiography of the incorruptibility of saints' bodies, see W. Deonna, " Εὐωδία , Croyances antiques et modernes: l'odeur suave des dieux et des élus," *Genava* 7 (1939): 167-263, esp. 199.

§226   1. For Agathangelos' ideas on creation see *Teaching,* §259, and Thomson, *Teaching,* p. 14, for the technical vocabulary.

§229   1. In §226-228 the audience was addressed in the plural; in §229-230 the verbs are in the singular. This speech is directed at Trdat, as *Ag* makes clear in §233 by adding "O king" to "you yourself" (sing. not pl. as in *Aa*).

§231   1. *Portion of the inheritance: i masn zharhangut‘ean,* an expression found also in §718 and in Faustos, V 24. It is a conflate of Col. 1.12 with Heb. 11.8; Eph. 1.18; Acts 20.32.

§233   1. *Snakes:* + "and scorpions" *Ag,* by assimilation with Lk. 10.19.

§234   1. *But who are alive:* + "in God" *Ag;* cf. Acts 17.28 etc.
2. On the intercession of the martyrs, see *Teaching,* §564 and n1.

§235   1. *Earlier:* i.e. in §71ff., where Gregory inveighs against idolatry.

§237 1. *Account . . . midst:* omitted in *Ag.*

2. *Those who commemorate them: tawnoḷats'n.* But **β** *a b d A B D* read *stats'awḷats'*, "those who possess," a term with overtones of being a patron; cf. *Ag:* τοῖς δυναμένοις κτήσασθαι αὐτούς.

3. *We pray:* or *maḷt'emk,* but *mart en* (who are able) in **β** *a d.*

4. *We pray . . . God:* omitted in *Ag.*

§238 1. Before "not indeed" *Ag* adds: "for he suffered." The theme of this paragraph is very reminiscent of Athanasius, *De Incarnatione,* 54.

§239 1. Before "not indeed" *Ag* adds: "again these ones (αὗται) died."

2. *Doctor:* for parallels to this metaphor as applied to martyrs, see *Teaching,* §285 n1.

§243 1. *Put their hands to their collars:* this expression, frequently found in the Armenian text of I Maccabees, is omitted in *Ag.* Cf. Eḷishē, pp. 58⁸, 78²²: *zawdzis pataṙeal* (rending the collar).

§244 1. *He forgives: Ag* reads   μισθαποδότης   γίνεται =Heb. 11. 6.

§245 1. *Whom we did not know:* omitted in *Ag.*

§249 1. *Therefore: vasn oroy. Ag* reads δι' αὐτῶν "through whom" (i.e. the martyrs), but see variants *ad loc.* The Armenian is singular and either refers to "the death" or is to be taken as a neuter.

§250 1. *Be of good cheer, be firm:* omitted in *Ag.*

2. *The incorruptible gifts of Christ:* omitted in   *a b d.* [*Vardzs,* here translated "as reward" can then be rendered "(your) reward."]

§252 1. **β** ends here. §252-258 summarise the main themes of the *Teaching.*

§255 1. Cf. *Teaching,* §580.

§257 1. *Description of the world:* cf. *Teaching,* §311, where Moses' knowledge of the physical world and of creation is also mentioned.

§258 1. For the *Teaching,* which follows see *Introduction,* pp. liii-lv.

§717 1. *Chapels: vkayarans,* more precisely "martyria."

§718   1. *The fear of God:* an addition in *Ag*.

2. *Portion of the inheritance:* a conflate of several biblical quotations; see §231 nl.

§720   1. *Advocates: verakats'uk'* (ἐπιστάται in *Ag*). Although this term basically means "one who is set over" (and hence renders προϊστάμενος in the N.T.), there are numerous examples of its meaning "defender, advocate"; cf. *Nor Baṙgirk'*, s.v. *verakats'u*.

§722   1. For the simile of the doctor, see §239 n2.

§723   1. *Superficially: awdabans (khawsets'aw)*, an expression reminiscent of I Cor. 14.9. *Ag* reads ἀεροβατῶν ἐν τοῖς λόγοις (puffed-up in his words).

§725   1. *To see the incontestible miracles: i tesil ts'uts'akan sk'anch'eleats'n* (*Ag* reads "for they saw the miracles"). *Ts'uts'akan* is really a demonstrative adjective: perhaps "the miracles illustrative (of God's providence?)."

§726   1. *Ag* reads "when the sixty days were completed."

§730   1. *Because the king . . . and hear:* omitted in *Ag*.

§732   1. *Furnace:* This metaphor has a long and detailed elaboration in the *Teaching*, §632-639.

§733   1. *Cube-shaped vault of heaven:* cf. *Teaching*, §259 n5.

§734   1. *Waters above the firmament:* cf. *Teaching*, §260 and §741 below. On the imagery, see Khatchatrian, *L'architecture*, p. 76.

2. *Sky-light: erdik,* the hole in the roof of Armenian houses; see the important comments on the *erdik* in Khatchatrian, *L'architecture*, pp. 46 and 63 ff. For patristic parallels to the image of light flooding through windows, see *ibid.*, p. 76.

§735   1. The procession of the hosts of heaven led by a divine hero has many parallels in pagan cosmic imagery; see the discussion in Khatchatrian, *L'architecture*, pp. 74 ff. This hero was identified in later Armenian tradition with Christ, hence the name *Ejmiatsin* ("the Only-begotten descended") came to be applied to the cathedral, but only after the twelfth century; cf. Khatchatrian, p. 85. However, from earliest times an angelic origin was ascribed to the cathedral: cf. Łazar, p. 32: *zhreshtakats'oyts' himnarkut'iwn srboy tann Astuts'oy, mets'i ekeḷets'woyn*. In §743 below the hero is

called "providence" and *Va* (61) calls him "potestas Omnipotentis."
Vk (258) refers to Gregory's building a church at the spot "where
the light of life descended."

2. *Depths of hell: i sandaramets andundots'; on sandaramet,*
see §743 nl.

§736 1. The base is the site of the cathedral to be built at Vałarshapat; the three bases in §737 refer to the martyria of Rhipsimē,
Gaianē and the unnamed martyr of the vat-store. This last site
came to be called *sholakat'* (effusion of light), though originally
this was the title given to the cathedral; cf. Khatchatrian, p. 85.

§737 1. *Thirty-two:* 33 in *β a d* and *Ag.*

2. *The color of blood:* omitted in *Ag.*

3. *Canopy: khoran.* The structure here described is at once
a tent, a cosmic image and a Christian symbol. The columns are
triumphant or commemorative stelae, while the whole is the image
of a church. See the extended discussion in Khatchatrian, *L'architecture,* pp. 77 ff.

4. *Thirty-seven:* 30 in *Ag.*

§738 1. The throne and cross perhaps reflect the decoration in
the dome of the Armenian martyria which formed the basis for
this part of Gregory's vision. Below the cross come the winged
angels in the drum, and then the martyrs in the arches. For a
discussion of this iconographic scheme see Khatchatrian, *L'architecture,* pp. 81 ff., with references to previous literature. The position of the martyrs in §737 is not quite clear: *i veray kamarats'n*
could mean "on the vaults" or "above the vaults," i.e. in the drum
(?). The angels played a significant part in the composition; it was in
their honor that the Catholicos Nerses III (642-662) built the famous
church of Zuart'nots' (of the vigilant ones = angels) near Vałarshapat on the model of Gregory's vision. Cf. Sebēos, ch. 33.

§741 1. *Opened:* "divided" *Ag.*

2. For the theme of the way being prepared for others to
follow, cf. Lampe, *Lexicon,* s.v. ἄνοδος.

§743 1. *The depths of hell: (z)sandarametsn* (cf. §735 n2), which
in Ez. 31.16 renders γῆ, but in Phil. 2.11 καταχθόνων. (*Ag* reads:
τὸ πάχος τῆς γῆς, the denseness of the earth). For *sandaramet,*
see Hübschmann, *Grammatik,* pp. 73-74, s.v. *Spandaramet* (Genie
der Erde); Meillet, *Termes religieux,* pp. 234-235; and H. W. Bailey,

Saka śśandramata, Festschrift für Wilhelm Eilers (Wiesbaden, 1967), pp. 136-143.

2. *Providence of God:* The ms. *A* adds explicitly "the same who is our Lord Jesus Christ." See §735 n1 above.

3. *Flattened: hart 'eats',* reminiscent of Is. 43.2.

§744   1. On the theme of the triumphal column, see Khatchatrian, *L'architecture,* p. 77.

2. *Catholic church: kat' olikē ekelets'i.* The cathedral itself was called *kat'olike,* in a different sense; cf. Khatchatrian, *L'architecture,* p. 85

§745   1. On the important motif of types in Agathangelos, see Thomson, *Teaching,* pp. 15ff. The emphasis on the cathedral is brought out by the terms "throne" (*at 'or* = cathedra) and "high priesthood"; Gregory is frequently called "high priest" in Agathangelos and other early Armenian writers: see *Introduction,* p. lxxviii.

§746   1. *Color of blood:* omitted in *Ag.*

2. *Basis: Khariskh,* as Heb. 6.19. *Ag* does not render this allusion, reading βάσις instead of ἄγκυρα.

3. *Ag* brings out the parallel with the resurrection more clearly. ἐπειδὴ ἡ νεφέλη ἔχει τὴν κουφότητα καὶ τὴν ὀξύτητα, τύπον ἔχει τῆς ἀναστάσεως καὶ τῆς ἀναλήψεως εἰς οὐρανόν (since the cloud has lightness and swiftness, it represents a type of the resurrection and ascension to heaven).

§747   1. Christ lives in the bones of the martyrs: cf. *Teaching,* §564 and n1.

2. *The sweet odor:* On the various symbolic meanings applied to this biblical phrase, see Lampe, *Lexicon,* s.v. εὐωδία, and the reference in §223 n1.

§748   1. *Type: awrinak,* on which see Thomson, *Teaching,* p. 15ff. On the architectural symbolism of the celestial city, see Khatchatrian, *L'architecture,* pp. 76ff.

§749   1. For the martyrs' pattern, see *Teaching,* §583.

§750   1. *Worker of all blessings: katarich' amenayn barut'eants',* not a biblical expression, but it is also found in Faustos, V 24.

§751   1. *Its:* i.e., of the cross which itself is shining; cf. §744.

2. *The common abode of angels and men:* The theme of man becoming similar to the angels is prominent in the *Teaching,* cf. §414, 640, 674.

§752   1. The theme of the columns representing the worship of the church is based on I Tim. 3.15; cf. also Lampe, *Lexicon*, s.v. στῦλος.

§753   1. For the equation of the office of bishop (=high priest, see *Introduction*, p. lxxviii) with the right hand, see Lampe, *Lexicon*, s.v. δεξιός   B 1. It is worth noting that the supposed relic of Gregory's own right hand became particularly important in the later Armenian church, and its possession (or the desire to possess it) caused many disputes; cf. *Introduction*, n151.

§754   1. The Armenian of this clause is not very clear, but Ḷazar in commenting on this passage (p. 42, 1.6ff) indicates that these sheep turn back on their steps. Ḷazar understands this passage to refer to back-sliding on the part of some Armenians in the struggle against Persia in A.D. 450. (On this see also A. Khatchatrian, "Données historiques sur la fondation d'Edjmiatsin à la lumière des fouilles récentes," *H.A.* (1962), col 100-109, esp. 104 ff.) It is noteworthy also that Agathangelos refers explicitly to the "covenant" *(ukht)* which, though it could have a general meaning, is most likely a reminiscence of the solemn covenant of the Armenian church which figures so prominently in the *History* of Eḷishē.
    Va offers a briefer explanation of the image of the wolves and lambs in which Marr saw allusions to the Christological disputes which affected Armenia in the sixth and following centuries; text in Garitte §60: "lupi, hi sunt duces qui revertuntur et secum detrahunt alios et eos ducunt ad arbitrium suum." But Garitte wisely cautions against reading too much into such a vague statement, *Documents*, pp. 342ff. See *Introduction*, pp. lvi-lvii.

§758   1. *Architect's line:* this passage is reminiscent of Job 38.5 and esp. Ez. 40.3.
    2. *Women . . . strength:* omitted in *Ag.*

§759   1. *Thirty-two:* 33 in *Ag,* as in §766.
    2. *Two:* 3 in *Ag,* as in §766.
    3. The precise orientation of the chapels differs in Agathangelos: Rhipsimē's is to the northeast or east (cf. §768); Gaianē's is always to the south; the third is to the north (as in §768) or northeast (as in §150). On the later history of these chapels, see Khatchatrian, *L'architecture*, pp. 32-33, 37.
    4. Cf. §834 n1.

§760   1. *Made for the repose of the saints:* omitted in *Ag; A B* omit "for the repose of the saints."

2. *Seal of Christ:* i.e., the sign of the cross.

§762 1. The first high priest is Gregory himself after his consecration. (On the use of this expression by early Armenian authors, see *Introduction,* p. lxxviii.) For the delay until Armenia receives a shepherd, see *Introduction,* p. lxxxiv.

2. Agathangelos, as so often in giving lists, is vague in his terminology; *Ag* is more explicit, reading for "leaders . . . ecclesiastical order": ἱερεῖς καὶ ἐπίσκοποι καὶ πᾶσα ἐκκλησιαστικὴ ἀκολουθία (priests and bishops and the entire ecclesiastical order). *b A B* read: (and) "ecclesiastical orders."

§763 1. *Hair shirt: burdz* (=sackcloth), the garment of mourning. The description of Trdat is reminiscent of that of Nebuchadnezzar in Daniel 4.30.

§764 1. *King: Ag* adds "and everyone's crying and wailing and weeping filled the air."

§766 1. *Thirty-two:* 33 in *β a d* and *Ag;* cf. §759.
2. *Two:* 3 in *Ag;* cf. §750.

§767 1. *Great and lofty:* reading *i mets i bardzr* (with *Ag*) as suggested by Meillet, *Remarques,* p. 469.

2. Masis is Mt. Ararat, the site of the settlement of Hayk, the Armenians' eponymous ancestor; see Moses Khorenats'i, I 10-11. [For Moses' etymology of Masis, see I 12.] See further §16 n1.

3. It is interesting to note that in I Maccabees 4.47 the stones for the temple were unhewn "according to the law." See further, *Introduction,* p. lxxiv.

4. The description of these stones is reminiscent of the massive blocks used in fifth-century architecture; cf. Khatchatrian, *L'architecture,* p. 20.

5. *Like Hayk's:* omitted in *Ag.* On the legends about Hayk see M. Abeḷyan, *Erker* I (Erevan, 1966), pp. 38-53.

6. Where conquering . . . hands: ἀντεισφέρων τῶν πόνων *Ag* (with overtones of compensation).

§768 1. *Thirty-two:* 33 in *β a d* and *Ag;* cf. §766.
2. *Single:* ἀσθενῆ (sickly) *Ag;* cf. §201 n1.

§769 1. *In the center of the canopies: i nerk'sagoyn khoranats'n,* a reminiscence of the same phrase used in Koriun (p. 41) of Masht'ots'' tomb. *Khoran* is a baldacchino, the symbol both of the house of God and of the universe; see §737 n3 and the discussion in

Khatchatrian, *L'architecture,* pp. 77ff.

    2. On the pillars, cf. §752 n1.

§770   1. This is the site of the cathedral. On the history of this edifice see Khatchatrian, *L'architecture,* ch. II, and A.A. Sahinyan, *Ejmiatsni mayr tachari skzbnakan tesk'ĕ, P.H.* (1966) pt. 3, pp. 71-93, and *idem, Recherches scientifiques sous les voûtes de la cathédrale d'Etchmiadzine, R.E.A. N.S.,* vol. 3 (1966), 39-71.

    2. On the importance of the veneration of the cross in Jerusalem and its adoption in the Caucasus, see the comments in A. Baumstark, *Liturgie comparée,* 3rd ed. (Chevtogne, 1953), p. 47. Agathangelos stresses the number of crosses erected in Armenia; see §782.

§773   1. *In all his limbs: oljandam marmnovk'n.* The second word is probably a gloss; see Meillet, *Remarques,* pp. 465-466.

§774   1. *So also was the source* . . . end of §766: this entire passage is taken from Koriun's description of Armenia's blessings following the invention of the Armenian script by Masht'ots', p. 19. Agathangelos has merely omitted all reference to the preaching being done in the Armenian tongue.

§776   1. *T'orgom:* see above §16 n1.

    2. See §774 n1 above.

§777   1. *In unity:* "all" *Ag* (though neither *Aa* nor *Ag* follow the biblical text exactly).

§778   1. *Falsely called gods:* +"and their altars" *Ag.*

    2. On the temple of Anahit at Artashat, see *Introduction,* p. xxxviii.

    3. *Erazamoyn:* (oracle) of dreams (*Ag* [ἐν] τόποις ὀνειρομούσοις). This site is not mentioned by other Armenian writers.

    4. The oracle of Tir is not otherwise known; for this deity see *Introduction,* p. lxi. The rendering of *Ag* of the passage, "The shrine of the god Tir . . . instruction," is somewhat different; see Gelzer, *Gotterlehre,* p. 110. The form *Tiur,* found in the Venice 1835 and Tiflis 1883 editions, has no manuscript authority. But both *Tir* and *Tiur* would give the attested gen. *Tri.*

    5. *Interpreter of dreams: erazats'oyts', erazahan,* on the second term, cf. M.X.II. 48, Gen. 41.8, 24, Deut. 13.1, 3, 5.

    6. *Secretary: divan grich'.* The term *divan* means "chancellery" and *grich'* means "scribe." *Ag reads:* χαρτουλαρίου.

7. On the form Ormizd, see *Introduction,* p. xxxix.

§779 1. The demons take visible form as in §786, though Chaumont, *Histoire,* p. 144, sees here a figure of the dispossessed pagan priests. But see the following note.

2. For the efficacy of the cross in putting demons to flight, cf. Athanasius, *contra Gentes* 1: πᾶσα δὲ δαιμόνων φαντασία τῷ σημείῳ τούτῳ ἀπελαύνεται. Chaumont's theory (see n1 above) seems even less plausible when we compare what follows with Koriun, p. 11, where he describes the flight of the demons from Golt'n on the arrival there of Masht'ots'.

3. *Wooden construction: p'aytakertn* (literally "made of wood"); cf. Faustos, IV 55, where the wooden and stone buildings in a city are distinguished. The term can also mean "wooden *roof"*; see Khatchatrian, *L'architecture,* pp. 89-90.

§780 1. This last sentence is very obscure in the Armenian; my translation follows the rendering in *Ag.* For the idea of demons leading men astray, cf. §59.

§781 1. The phrase "servants with the pagan priests may be a reflection of the Greek term ἱερόδουλοι; see A. G. Perikhanian, *Khramovye ob'edinenija Maloi Azii i Armenii* (Moscow, 1959), pp. 130ff. Cf. also M.X. II 48 for temple slaves *(tsaṙays).* Here and in §840 *Aa* mentions the conversion of the pagan priests, but in §813 speaks of the massacre of the priests of Vahagn at Astishat. In the *V* recension the priests are forcibly converted; cf. note 102a above. Moses Khorenats'i contradicts Agathangelos by claiming (II 8) that the priests of Vahagn were converted, thus providing an etymology for the Vahuni family. The confiscation of the temple properties is frequently stressed by Agathangelos, cf. §785, 790. The wealth of the early Armenian church—or rather of the patriarchal family, the Pahlavuni—may be judged from the properties in its possession as enumerated by Faustos; see H. Gelzer, "Die Anfänge der armenischen Kirche," *Berichte der Königlichen sächsischen Gesellschaft der Wissenschaften* 47 (1895): 149 ff.

§782 1. On the importance of the cross in Armenia, cf. §770 n2. On early Armenian crosses, see also Der Nersessian, *Images,* pp. 74ff. On the emphasis on the delay until Gregory was consecrated, see *Introduction,* p. lxxxiv.

§783 1. This paragraph is a pastiche of verbatim quotations from

Koriun, p. 20 (where Sahak instructs the Mamikonean nobility and mentions their leading members by name) and p. 24 (where Masht'ots' travels around Armenia with his disciples).

§784 1. On Daranałik' and T'ordan, see Hübschmann, *AON*, pp. 283-284. Gregory himself was later buried in T'ordan (Faustos, III 2), though Agathangelos seems unaware of this tradition, cf. §891. See further Van Esbroeck, *Témoignages*.

2. On Barshamin and his sanctuary, see *Introduction*, p. lxi.

3. *All saving* (sign): *amenap'rkich'*. No other reference to the use of this term in Armenian as applied to the cross is given in the *Nor Bařgirk'*, s.v. *khach'*.

§785 1. *Then the saint . . . regions of:* this first part of the paragraph is taken directly from Koriun, p. 11, where he describes the missionary work of Masht'ots' in Gołt'n and the flight of the demons.

2. Khałtik' (Χάλτοι in *Ag*) is west of Erzerum, see Hübschmann, *AON*, pp. 200 and 432.

3. Ani is Kamakha in the province of Daranałik' (see Hübschmann, *AON*, pp. 283-284) and is not to be confused with the later Armenian capital on the river Akhurean. For the royal cemetery at Ani, see G. Kh. Sargsyan, *Hellenistikan Darashrjani Hayastanĕ ev Movses Khorenats'in* (Erevan, 1966), p. 62; cf. F. B. III 11, IV 24. It remained a royal burial site after the conversion to Christianity according to Moses Khorenats'i III 10, 27. The text of *Aa* here is not that of any one MS: *yamur . . . kayeansn* was corrupted before the translation into Greek: *yanuaneal yAni* may well be a gloss; see Meillet, *Remarques,* p. 474.

4. On Zeus-Aramazd see *Introduction,* p. xxxix.

§786 1. *Ekełeats':* see Hübschmann, *AON*, p. 286.

2. For the shrine of Anahit at Erez see *Introduction,* p. xxxviii. This is the same shrine where Trdat had ordered Gregory to sacrifice in the first year of his reign, cf. §48.

3. For demons like an army, cf. §779.

4. *Gayl:* the river Lycus, a tributary of the Euphrates. See §48 n5.

5. *Nanē:* on this goddess, see *Introduction,* pp. lxi-lxii.

6. *T'il:* see Hübschmann, *AON*, p. 286.

§787 1. This description of idols is reminiscent of that in the *Teaching,* §522.

§788 1. The second sentence of §787 and the first of §788 are
taken verbatim from Koriun, pp. 28-29; but there the king and the
people are Arsval and the Caucasian Albanians.

2. The Christian virtues of king Trdat are especially extolled
in Moses Khorenats'i, II 92.

§789 1. *Derjan:* see Hübschmann, *AON,* p. 287.

2. *From the beastliness . . . with it:* All this is taken from
Koriun, p. 17, but there these unflattering epithets are applied to the
regions of the Mark' (Medes). Similar scorn for the barbarous
inhabitants of the Caucasus is shown in Moses Khorenats'i, III 54.

§790 1. On Mihr see *Introduction,* p. lxii.

2. On the form of this name see Hübschmann, *Grammatik,*
p. 113, *AON,* p. 379; and also J. Markwart, "La province de Parskahayk'," *R.E.A.,* N.S., vol. 3 (1966), p. 283; and E. Benveniste,
"Les nominatifs arméniens en-i," *R.E.A.* 10 (1930): pp. 81-84, esp.
82. On the site, see Hübschmann, *AON,* pp. 284, 287 and T'. Kh.
Hakobyan, *Urvagtser Hayastani Patmakan Ashkharhagrut'yan*
(Erevan, 1960), p. 222.

3. The last sentence is taken from Koriun, p. 20, where he
refers to the preaching of Masht'ots' and Sahak; cf. §783 n1.

§791 1. The list of dignitaries is another example of Agathangelos'
love for the piling up of virtual synonyms. These ranks do not all
correspond to precise offices or positions, nor are they in a regular
order of descent. Not surprisingly *Ag* abbreviates somewhat:
μεγιστᾶνες καὶ φύλαρχοι καὶ τόπαρχαι καὶ οἱ ἐν ἀξιώματι ἔντιμοι
στρατοπεδάρχαι καὶ οἱ ἐπ' ἐξουσιῶν ἄρχοντες, σατράπαι τε καὶ
ἐλεύθεροι. *Vg* and *Va* are much briefer still.

§792 1. *Pastor: hoviw* (= ποιμήν in the N.T.), which in patristic
use is applied especially to bishops.

2. *As a teacher of the law: awrēnsusoyts'* (omitted in *Ag*). In
Acts 5.34 this term is applied to Gamaliel, and in Koriun, p. 19, 1.2,
to Moses. There may be overtones here also (as in §762) of the wait
for a prophet; see *Introduction,* p. lxxxiv. A similar term is used of
the Armenian Catholicos in the (fake) letter of Photius to Zacharia;
Pravoslavnij Palestinskij Sbornik XI (1892), p. 179, 1. 12: *surb
veraditol ew awrēnsats'oyts' Araratean ashkharhid.* Cf. also Lazar,
p. 45[38] for its application to Magi.

§794 1. Such disclaimers of unworthiness were *de rigueur* in hagiographical writings. For another example of hesitation overcome by an angel appearing in a vision, cf. the ordination of Gregory the Wonderworker, Augerean, *Vark'*, IX, p. 10.

§795 1. There are many examples of such lists of noble families in early Armenian writers. See below §873 and also Faustos III 12, IV 4, 11; Łazar, p. 45; Ełishē, p. 43; Life of Nersēs, pp. 32-39. On the present list, see M.-L. Chaumont, "L'ordre des preséances à la cour des Arsacides d'Arménie," *JA* 254 (1966): 471-497; she shows that this list is closer to the situation of early fourth-century Armenia than that in §873, and that it has parallels with the *Notitiae* of the first two Sassanian monarchs. Cf. also J. Markwart, *Die Genealogie der Bagratiden, Caucasica,* fasc. 6, pt. 2 (1930), pp. 32-33. For a general discussion of the Armenian lists, see Adontz/Garsoian, *Armenia,* pp. 230 ff. and Toumanoff, *Studies,* pp. 159 ff., where he compares the names and titles in all the versions of Agathangelos; his study absolves us from the need to note here the variants between *Aa* and *Ag, Vg* and *Va* (*Vo* omits this list, and *Vk* merely refers to "the sixteen kings of Armenia"!).

2. *Angeł-tun:* see Hübschmann, *AON*, pp. 303-304.

3. *Ałdznik':* Arzanene, see Hübschmann, *AON*, pp. 248-251.

4. *Bdeashkh:* on this office, see Toumanoff, *Studies,* pp. 155-158, and on the "great bdeashkh," *ibid.,* p. 131.

5. *Mardpet-dom:* i.e. the Grand Chamberlain, see Toumanoff, *Studies,* pp. 131 and 169.

6. *Aspet:* the commander of the cavalry; but see Toumanoff, *Studies,* pp. 325-326.

7. *Sparapet:* the High Constable, see Toumanoff, *Studies,* pp. 325-326.

8. *Korduk':* Corduene, see Hübschmann, *AON*, pp. 333-334. The form *Kordovtats'* in *Aa* is derived from the Greek form Κορδοβίτων ; cf. Garitte, *Documents,* p. 220.

9. *Tsop'k':* Sophene, see Hübschmann, *AON*, pp. 294-297.

10. *Gugark':* Gogarene, see Hübschmann, *AON*, pp. 275-276.

11. *The other bdeashkh:* on this title, see Toumanoff, *Studies,* p. 131.

12. *Rshtunik';* a princely family in Vaspurakan, see Hübschmann, *AON*, p. 339.

13. *Mokk':* Moxoene, see Hübschmann, *AON*, pp. 331-333.

14. *Siwnik':* see Hübschmann, *AON*, pp. 263-265.

15. *Tsawdek':* Zabdicene, see Hübschmann, *AON,* pp. 321-322.

16. *Uti:* Otene, see Hübschmann, *AON*, pp. 271-272.

17. *Zaravand and Her:* see Hübschmann, *AON*, pp. 259-261.

18. *Maḷkhaz-dom:* on this title, see Toumanoff, *Studies,* pp. 208-209.

19. *Artsrunik':* a princely family in Vaspurakan.

§796   1. *T'orgom:* see §16 n1.

2. *Mazhak:* On Mazaca, cf. Strabo, *Geography,* XII 2, 7ff. It is noteworthy that Agathangelos gives what he calls the "Armenian (hayerēn)" equivalent for the name which goes back to Seleucid times; Faustos only uses the Greek form Caesarea (in general use after the first century A.D.), which was also standard in Armenia. Moses Khorenats'i, I 14, gives a fanciful Armenian etymology for Mazhak, deriving it from an ancient hero called Mshak.

3. On the version in *Vk* where Gregory is sent to Rome for consecration, see *Introduction,* p. lxv.

§799   1. The title "martyr" was applied in the early church not only to those who died for their faith but also to those who survived tortures; see Lampe, *Lexicon,* s.v. μάρτυς III. The title "champion" (*nahatakeal,* a verbal form from *nahatak* which is frequent in Maccabees as a rendering of ἀθλητής) was widely applied to martyrs and ascetics; see Lampe, *Lexicon,* s.v. ἀθλητής. Gregory is also called "contessor," §807.

2. *Overseer: tesuch',* a calque on ἐπίσκοπος.

§800   1. Leontius attended the Council of Nicaea (A.D. 325) and was bishop of Caesarea by 314 (see Gelzer, *Anfänge,* p. 166), the possible date of Gregory's consecration. See further Garitte, *Documents,* p. 222. Here Leontius is called "archbishop," in §804 "catholicos" and §820 "metropolitan."

§801   1. *Edict: hrovartak,* cf. §151 nl. *Ag* renders this by προσηγορία, a common patristic term for "salutation, greeting."

2. The textual tradition of this paragraph is quite floating, see Meillet, *Remarques,* p. 469.

§803   1. *Journey for support: (z)chanaparhs awgtakars,* a curious phrase since *awgtakar* means "supporting, useful" whereas the context seems to require "seeking support," cf. *Ag:* τὰς ἐν ὠφελείᾳ πορείας αὐτῶν, where ἐν is changed in most

MSS to ἐπ'.

§804   1. *Catholicos:* In §862 the same title is applied to the chief bishop of Armenia; see further *Introduction,* p. lxxix. The noun was used for archbishops and the adjective for the principal church of a diocese of province; see Lampe, *Lexicon,* s.v.   καθολικός.   As usual Agathangelos fluctuates in his nomenclature, calling Leontius "high priest, chief of bishops," §805, as well as "archbishop, metropolitan," §820.

    2. *And the nobles . . . custom:* this is taken directly from Koriun, p. 14, where he describes the reception given Masht'ots' in Edessa and Amida.

§805   1. *Council:* on the date of this council, see *Introduction,* pp. lxv-lxvi.

    2. *Many:* omitted in *Ag.* The precise number 20 is found in *Vg* (§133) but in no other version. *Vo* reads   πλῆθος   (§123). See further *Introduction,* p. lxvi.

    3. *Great honor and glory:* omitted in *Ag.*

§806   1. *He: Ag* adds "the most holy archbishop."

    2. This last sentence has parallels with Koriun's description of the reception accorded Masht'ots' in Samosata (p. 15), but the borrowing is not so explicit as usual. The wording of *Ag* does not follow the Armenian very closely in this paragraph.

§807   1. *Bishop:* "archbishop" in *Ag,* a frequent change in this version. On the various titles given to Gregory in different Armenian authors, see *Introduction* pp. lxxvii-lxxviii.

    2. *Confessor:* on this title, see Lampe, *Lexicon,* s.v. ὁμολο-γητής. On similar titles given to Gregory, see §799 n1 above.

§808   1. This paragraph is taken almost verbatim from the description in Koriun, pp. 15-16, of Masht'ots' return to Armenia after the invention of an Armenian script.

§809   1. *Tarawn:* a province west of Lake Van; cf. Hübschmann, *AON,* pp. 325-327.

    2. *Temple of Vahagn: Vahēvanean meheann.* Hübschmann, *Grammatik,* p. 77 n1, regards the form *Vahēvanean* as an adjective derived from Vahagn; but for Benveniste, *Vahēvan* is a different deity; see E. Benveniste, *Terminologie,* p. 50. However, there is no other reference to Vahēvan in Armenian literature, and from the context clearly the cult of Vahagn is intended, not that of a fourth

deity. On Vahagn, see *Introduction,* p. lxiii. The form *Vahēvanean* is found only in β ; all other witnesses to *Aa* read Vahēvahean (Vahevahean in *a*). Cf. the Vahēvuni princely house which played an important role in Armenian paganism, Toumanoff, *Studies,* p. 215. L. Pʻ. Shahinyan, "Movses Khorenatsʻu Patmutʻean mej hishatakvol Vahēi masin," *P.B.H.,* 1973, no. 4, pp. 172-78, derives the form *Vahēvahean* from Vahē- whom he takes to be a sun-god parallel to Mithra. His interpretation is based on the equation of Vahē in Moses Khorenatsʻi I 31 with Mithraustes, the Armenian general at Gaugamela.

    3. *Eighth shrine:* i.e., the eighth that Gregory destroyed; see *Introduction,* p. .xl.

    4. *Dragon-handler: Vishapakʻaḷ.* Abeḷyan, *Erker* I, pp. 88-90, notes that this term does not mean *"vishap*-strangler" or "-slayer," which would render the terms Vrtragna, Vrtrhan (cf. p. lxiii above), but rather "(one who) picks up *vishaps* (from the ground)." On the *vishap,* which figures so prominently in Armenian folklore, see E. Benveniste, *L'origine du vishap arménien, R.E.A.,* vol. 7 (1927), pp. 7-9.

    5. *Karkē:* see Hübschmann, *AON,* p. 401.

    6. *Yashtishat:* a popular form for Ashtishat, falsely derived from *Yasht* (sacrifice) and *shat* (much); see Hübschmann, *Grammatik,* p. 212. (The true etymology is given by Markward, *Parskahaykʻ,* p. 283: "Joy of Astarte.") On the site, see Hübschmann, *AON,* pp. 400-401; Toumanoff, *Studies,* p. 215; Adontz/Garsoian, *Armenia,* p. 243.

    7. *Temple of Vahagn: Meheann Vahēvahean;* see n2 above.

    8. *Golden-mother:* i.e. Anahit, cf. *Introduction,* p. xxxix.

    9. *Astḷik:* Aphrodite, cf. Garitte, *Documents,* p. 206. Moses Khorenatsʻi, II 12, 14, claims that Artashēs brought Aphrodite's statue to Armenia and that Tigran erected it at Ashtishat. But Moses was copying Agathangelos; see *Introduction,* p. xxxix.

    10. *Vahagn:* Heracles for *Ag* and Moses Khorenatsʻi; cf. *Introduction,* p. lxiii.

§810 1. Athenogenes was martyred at Sebaste in the reign of Diocletian; according to Basil he was burnt, according to Metaphrastes he was beheaded. For secondary literature, see Garitte, *Documents,* p. 195. For the festivals of these two saints at Ashtishat and Bagavan, see §815 and 836.

§811   1. *Two horse courses: three stadia* in *Ag. Arshavan* is equivalent to *asparēz* (see Acharyan, *Aŕmatakan Baŕaran,* s.v. *arshavan*)
which is the length of a course in a stadium.

2. Cf. Moses Khorenats'i II 14 for (fake) omens indicating
the desired residence of pagan gods; *bnakel* is common to both
texts.

§813   1. For the motif of such miraculous destructions of temples,
see Delehaye, *Passions,* pp. 215-216.

2. *They were nothing:* a common expression for idols in
martyrologies, cf. *Acts of Sharbil, passim.* For the massacre of the
priests, see §781 note 1 above.

§814   1. Faustos, III 3, 14, also stresses that the church at Ashtishat
was the first in Armenia.

2. On "illumination," cf. *Introduction,* p. lxxviii.

3. *To the city of Caesarea . . . land:* omitted in *Vg.*

4. *190,000:* the figure is omitted in *Vg, Vo* and *Va.* In *Vk*
the separate baptisms of *Aa* §814 and 833 are run together.

§815   1. The 7th of Sahmi becomes 7 October in *Ag,* a correspon-
dence that occurred from 464-468. But this simple equivalence
was a common way of rough reckoning. See §210 n1. (In the
Synaxarion of Ter Israel this commemoration is celebrated on 16
October.) Note that this festival was celebrated in Bagavan on New
Year's day, *Navasard* (§836).

2. *And priests:* as β a d. b A B read "and establishing
priests."

§816   1. This paragraph interrupts the coherence of the story. But
the whole of the latter part of the *History* of Agathangelos is
incoherent; the repetitions and doublets show that the account of
Gregory's missionary activity was based on several similar traditions which were not properly reconciled.

§817   1. *Bagavan-Ditsavan,* a correct etymology, *bag* being Iranian for "god," and *dits'* the Armenian genitive for the noun with the
same meaning; *avan* is "town" in both Armenian and Iranian. Cf.
Hübschmann, *Grammatik,* p. 113. Moses Khorenats'i proposes a
different (and false) etymology from *bagin* "altar." On the site see
Hübschmann, *AON* p. 411. Cf. also Sebēos, ch. 33, where he
describes the church built by Nersēs III on the road by which Trdat
went out to meet Gregory—the famous church of Zuart'nots' ("of
the angels").

§818   1. *And with all . . . mountain:* this is taken directly from Koriun's account of Masht'ots' setting out for Goļt'n, p. 21, 1.1-4.

2. *Npat:* just south of Bagavan, near the source of the Aratsani; cf. Hübschmann, *AON,* p. 457. It was the site of a famous battle where the Catholicos Nersēs I prayed with arms raised like Moses, Faustos, V 4.

§819   1. *The king . . . town:* this is a close parallel to the account in Koriun, p. 17, 1.12 ff., which describes the king greeting Masht'ots' on his return to Armenia with the new script. But the borrowing is not so close verbally as that in §818.

§820   1. The dual parallelisms are reminiscent of II Cor. 6.9-10.

2. On Leontius' titles, see §800 n1.

§824   1. *Mentor: gtich',* literally "finder," an expression based on the parables in Luke 15. *Ag* renders "Teacher of wisdom . . . mentor" by σοφία καὶ γραμματεὺς τῆς ζωῆς (wisdom and scribe of life), perhaps reading *grich'* for *gtich'.*

§825   1. There are many variants in the Armenian text of §822-825, but these are of little significance for the meaning.

§826   1. The version of this letter in *Vg* and *Va* does not emphasize the position of Caesarea with regard to Armenia. On this close connection and the initial dependence of the Armenian patriarchs, see the discussion and bibliographies in Garitte, *Narratio,* pp. 56-57, 101. Cf. also Faustos, V 29, where he describes the anger of the bishop of Caesarea when the Armenian king unilaterally appointed Yusik as patriarch. Cf. above, n 184.

2. *By the right hand of the martyred one:* omitted in *Ag.* On the significance of the right hand *(aj),* see §753 n1.

§827   1. *They spread . . . divine love:* a verbal borrowing from Koriun, p. 27, 1.24, which refers to Masht'ots'' sojourn at Nor K'aļak' before he set out for Albania.

§828   1. *According . . . pious:* from Koriun, p. 21, 1.5-7, which refers to Masht'ots'' preaching in Goļt'n with the support of the local prince.

2. *Set forth . . . request:* from Koriun, p. 22, 1.22-p. 23, 1.1, which refers to Masht'ots'' preaching in Georgia.

§829   1. *World-lamenting: ashkharhahets (ashkharhahog* in Koriun). The editors of *Aa* compare the German expression "Weltschmerz."

§830 1. The simile of "fatherly begetting" is also found in Faustos, III 12, applied to Yusik, Gregory's grandson.

2. §829 *With . . .* §830 *Hand:* from Koriun, p. 14, 1.13-23, which refers to Masht'ots'' troubles before the final invention of the Armenian script.

§833 1. Cf. the parallel in the *Life of Gregory the Wonderworker* by Gregory of Nyssa, *P.G.,* vol. 46, vol. 933: at the former's baptism the Jordan was turned back from its impetuous course. There is an Armenian parallel in the later story concerning Peter Getadardz in Aristakēs Lastivertts'i, pp. 31-32.

2. The appearance of a light at someone's baptism is a common hagiographic theme, cf. the *Life of Gregory Nazianzenus* in the Armenian version, Awgerean, *Vark'*, I, p. 291 (but this is not found in the later Greek life published in *P.G.* vol. 35). See also Moses Khorenats'i II 89.

3. For the use of oil in the baptismal rite see Lampe, *Lexicon,* s.v. ἔλαιον and μύρον.

4. The account of this baptism is quite different in *Vg* and *Va,* see *Introduction,* pp. lxviii-lxix.

§834 1. *With psalms . . . torches:* this is very close to the descriptions of Masht'ots'' funeral procession (Koriun, p. 41) and of Nersēs' funeral (Faustos, V 24). Cf. also §759 above and Faustos, III 11 and V 31.

2. *Who vivifies . . . creatures:* this is omitted in *β a d.* The phrase is very awkward in the Armenian, as the words *zkendanararn, zkets'ats'uch'n, zararich'n, zashkharagortsn* grammatically refer to the body and blood, though clearly the last two must refer to Christ.

§836 1. The reference to the harvest festival is unique (for the account in Moses Khorenats'i depends on Agathangelos) and poses certain problems. The Armenian implies that there are two gods: Amanor and Vanatur, the former being the bearer of the new fruits, the latter being the god of hospitality (*vanatur* = giving asylum). Vanatur's epithet *hiwrēnkal* (hospitable) is explained by Moses Khorenats'i, II 66; he claims that Vaḷarsh instituted the new year's festival at Bagavan, where the last Tigran had erected an altar over his brother's tomb; at this altar travelers could participate in the sacrifices and spend the night as guests. The only parallel in early Armenian is the rendering of Διὸς Ξενίου in II Maccabees 6.2:

hiwrasēr Ormzdakan dits'n vanatri. (But referring to the same temple in Garizim, the Armenian version of Eusebius *Chronicle* [Aucher, II, p. 240] reads: *Aramazday awtarasirin.*) Yet there is no parallel to Amanor ("day of the [new] time"; see Acharyan, *Armatakan Bařaran, s.v. amanak*). Gelzer was prompted to suppose that the term "god" (a plural noun in Armenian) should be read with the adjective "vain," and that *Amanor* should be translated as "new Year season"; *Götterlehre,* pp. 132-133. *β*a d do have a somewhat simpler text: ". . . major festival, of the vain worship of the god Amanor . . . ." But the implication remains that Amanor and Vanatur were separate deities. Clearly by the mid-fifth century the recollection of the old harvest festival was rather hazy in the ecclesiastical circles which produced "Agathangelos."

2. *New Year's Day:* Navasard, on which see Hübschmann, *Grammatik,* p. 202. The commemoration of John and Athenogenes at Ashtishat was on a different date, see §815.

3. *Town: Ag* explicitly adds "Bagavan."

§837   1. *Then . . . it:* this is taken from Koriun, p. 26, 1.12-14, where he refers to Masht'ots'' after his return from Constantinople.

2. *And pursuing . . . blessings:* this is from Koriun, p. 26, 1.27-p. 27, 1.2, which refers to Masht'ots'' refuting heretics.

3. *He journeyed . . . Armenia:* this is from Koriun, p. 21, 1.20-21, which refers to Masht'ots'' activity in Siunik.

4. *Field: hoḷ erdoy,* glossed in E. Ciakciak, *Dizionario Armeno-Italiano* (Venice, 1837), as the amount of land sufficient to support one family. Faustos, V 31, refers to this grant: King Pap confiscated to the court five out of the seven *hoḷ* which Trdat in the time of Gregory had given to the church's service.

§838   1. *And he increased . . . church:* omitted in *β*a d.

§839   1. *Furnace of instruction:* cf. *Teaching,* §638-639.

2. This paragraph is based on Koriun, p. 23, 1.5-13, which refers to Masht'ots'' work in Georgia.

§840   1. *And from every . . . writing:* this is taken from Koriun, p. 28, 1.9-11, which refers to Masht'ots'' work in Albania.

2. Cf. §781 where the pagan priests are made to serve the church (as opposed to their slaughter in §813).

3. *Were to be . . . them:* a continuation of the quotation from Koriun; see n1 above.

4. *These . . . Greek:* this is from Koriun, p. 14, 1.10-12, which refers to Masht'ots" own pupils. For "Greek" *Aa* has *Hellēn* as opposed to the usual *Yoyn. Hellēn* is common in Koriun, but in this particular passage Koriun has *Yunakan.*

5. *Thus . . . God:* a continuation of the quotation from Koriun, p. 28, 1.18-23.

§841   1. *He: Ag* reads "the archbishop"; cf. §806 n1.

2. *His former dwelling:* taken from Koriun, p. 21, 1.4-5.

3. *Capital: r̃otastak,* a principal city or metropolis; cf. Acharyan, *Armatakan Bar̃aran,* s.v. *r̃otastak. Ag* omits the term.

4. *Sign of Christ:* i.e. baptism.

§842   1. *Khaltik':* Chaldia, see Hübschmann, *AON,* p. 200.

2. *Kalarjik':* Klarjeti, or Cholarzene, see Hübschmann, *AON,* p. 356.

3. *To the very borders: i spar̃ i sahmans.* For *spar̃ β a b d* read *sar̃* and all the other witnesses *sar̃i;* the editors of *Aa* suggest that this could be a proper name. *Ag* reads "borders." On the Massagetae see below §873 n5.

4. *Gates of the Alans:* cf. §19 n3.

5. *Kaspk':* see §19 n10.

6. *P'aytakaran:* see Hübschmann, *AON,* pp. 267-270.

7. *Nor Shirakan:* see Hübschmann, *AON,* pp. 319-320.

8. *Korduk':* see §795 n6.

9. *Secure: amur,* fortified; this expression is often found in Armenian writers to describe Media.

10. *Mahk'r-tun:* see Hübschmann, *AON,* p. 320.

11. *Azerbaijan: Ag* adds ἥτις καλεῖται πυροχωρία κατὰ τὴν περσικὴν γλῶτταν (which is called 'land of fire' in Persian); cf. §203 n2.

12. Note that these confines are the same as those mentioned in Faustos, IV 50, V 8-19, as the border areas of Armenia. On this paragraph see the discussion in Toumanoff, *Studies,* pp. 458-460 (n98).

§843   1. This paragraph is taken verbatim from Koriun, p. 33, 1.2-9, which describes Masht'ots"; missionary activity in the Caucasus. There are also very close parallels in Faustos' description of the virtues of the Catholicos Nersēs, IV 4.

§844   1. *Rescripts: murhaks* (γραμμάτια *Ag*), on which see Hübschmann, *Grammatik,* p. 197.

2. This paragraph is a continuation of the borrowing from Koriun, p. 33, 1.9-19, with parallels in Faustos, IV 4.

§845   1. *Furthermore . . . mountains:* a continuation of the borrowing from Koriun, p. 33, 1.20-23.

2. The form *Aḷbianos* is found in the printed text here and in §846 and 873, but *a b d A B* read *Albios* or a variant thereof. See the comments of Garitte, *Documents,* pp. 197-198.

3. *Basean:* see Hübschmann, *AON*, pp. 362-363.

4. *Ag* omits the last two names. On this list of bishops, see the references to each in Garitte, *Documents,* pp. 196 ff.; on the list as a whole, see J. Markwart, *Die Entstehung der armenischen Bistumer, Orientalia Christiana,* vol. 27 (1932), pp. 150 ff., and especially Adontz/Garsoian, *Armenia,* pp. 266 ff. Some of the bishops are also mentioned in Faustos: Moses at VI 13, John at VI 8-10, Artithes at VI 7, Tirikes at VI 13, Kyrakos at VI 11. But Faustos knows nothing of their supposed pagan background, nor were they ordained by Gregory as they lived much later in the fourth century.

§846   1. *He himself . . . "in me.":* this continues the verbatim borrowing from Koriun interrupted by the list of bishops in the preceding paragraph (Koriun, p. 33, 1.23-p. 34, 1.7). There is an exact parallel to this way of life in Faustos, VI 15.

§847   1. This paragraph is a continuation of the borrowing from Koriun, p. 34, 1.8-18.

§848   1. *With these . . . places:* a continuation of the borrowing from Koriun, p. 34, 1.18-19.

2. *Grottoes . . . ground:* a verbatim parallel in Faustos, VI 16, describes the ascetic practices of Gind.

3. *Zealous for good works:* a verbatim parallel is found in Koriun, p. 7, 1.20-21, applied to Masht'ots'.

§849   1. *He provided . . . country:* this continues the borrowing from Koriun, p. 34, 1.20-p. 35, 1.2; there is also a close parallel in Faustos, VI 15.

§850   1. *Concerning the Lord: (z)terunakann,* which would more naturally mean "the (saying) *of* the Lord," as rendered in *Ag:* τὸ δεσποτικὸν ῥητόν.

2. *While . . . Tiberias:* omitted in *Ag*.

3. This paragraph is entirely from Koriun, p. 35, 1.2-21.

§851   1. This paragraph continues the verbatim borrowing from Koriun, p. 35, 1.22-p. 36, 1.2; it is much abbreviated in *Ag*.

§852   1. *Weak: karawtakan,* omitted in *β a d* (but it is in Koriun, see next note).

2. This paragraph is from Koriun, p. 36, 1.2-15; the first half of the paragraph is quite different in *Ag*.

§853   1. This paragraph is from Koriun, p. 36, 1.15-p. 37, 1.3; but in Koriun the last sentence is in the plural and refers to Mashʻotsʻ and his pupils.

§854   1. *Outstanding: yarhajadēm,* rendered in *Ag* by παρρησιαστικώτατος.

2. This paragraph is also from Koriun, but from an earlier section describing the benefits to Armenia of the newly invented script (p. 18, 1.27-p. 19, 1.7). Again the last phrase is in the plural in Koriun, where it refers to Mashtʻotsʻ and Sahak.

§856   1. The first sentence has verbal parallels in Faustos, V 21, which refers to the activity of the Catholicos Nersēs I.

2. *Readers: anagnovs,* ἀναγνώστων in *Ag*. Apart from this instance, H. Acharyan, *Armatakan Bararan* (Erevan 1926-35), only notes the occurrence of this form in writers of the twelfth and later centuries. The usual Armenian term for "reader" is *ĕntʻertsʻoḷ*.

§857   1. *Without doubting:* cf. *Teaching,* §626. *Ag* omits this phrase.

§858   1. *Until . . . rest:* the identical phrase is used in Faustos, III 2, of Gregory's death.

§859   1. For the story of Gregory's marriage and the variants in the versions see the discussion in Garitte, *Documents,* pp. 323 ff. Cf. also *Introduction,* pp. xxxi-xxxiii.

2. *Secular life: yashkharakeatsʻ keans,* ἐν τῷ βίῳ διαπρέπων *Ag*. The same expression is also found in Faustos, IV 3, applied to Nersēs' early life.

3. *He had entered . . . men:* this is taken from Koriun's description of Mashtʻotsʻ after he left the secular world, p. 10, 1.10-26.

§860   1. Moses Khorenatsʻi, II 76, tendentiously calls this Artavazd Mandakuni, not Mamikonean; cf. next note.

2. *Commander in chief: sparapet,* στρατοπεδάρχης in *Ag*. On this office, see Hübschmann, *Grammatik,* p. 240; Tou-

manoff, *Studies,* p. 97 n144; and Adontz/Garsoian, *Armenia,* p. 510 n29a. In the fifth century this position was hereditary in the Mamikonean family, in which Artavazd was a particularly common name; cf. H. Achaṙyan, *Hayots' Andznanunneri Baṙaran* (Erevan, 1942-62), s.v. *Artavazd.*

3. On Tachat, see Toumanoff, *Studies,* p. 191 n199.

4. *Ashots'k':* see Hübschmann, *AON,* p. 365.

5. *Herald: karapet* (προμηνυτής in *Ag*), which is the usual Armenian term for John πρόδρομος (the Baptist); on its etymology, see Hübschmann, *Grammatik,* p. 166, and M. Leroy, *Les composés arméniens en-pet, Annuaire de l'institut de philologie et d'histoire orientales et slaves,* vol. 15 (1958-60), p. 111.

§861 1. *Daranaḷik':* see Hübschmann, *AON,* p. 283.

2. *The Caves of Manē: Maneay Ayrk';* see Hübschmann, *AON,* p. 450. Moses Khorenats'i, II 91, claims that Manē was a companion of Rhipsimē's; according to *Vk* (291) Manē escaped martyrdom with the other nuns and was later buried by Gregory when he retired to that mountain.

§862 1. *He ordained ... place: Ag* reads merely "which indeed he did."

2. This quotation from Ps. 44 does not follow the Armenian vulgate at all closely; *Ag* follows the Septuagint.

3. *Catholicos:* on this title, see *Introduction,* p. lxxix.

4. *Went out ... confirm:* from Koriun, p. 24, 1.1-3, which refers to Masht'ots' after his return from Georgia.

863 1. *Loved: ts'ankali,* "desirable," a frequent epithet for Masht'ots' in Koriun.

2. *He also ... scriptures:* from Koriun, p. 9, 1.25-26, applied to Masht'ots.

§864 1. *Whereby ... disciples:* a continuation of the borrowing from Koriun, p. 9, 1.26-p. 10, 1.10.

2. *Unceasing prayers ... tears:* from Koriun, p. 11, 1.17-19. In *Ag* the passage has been assimilated with Rom. 8.26.

§865 1. *With great ... gospel:* from Koriun, p. 22, 1.8-11, which refers to Masht'ots' in Siwnik'.

§866 1. *Archbishop:* on this title, see *Introduction,* p. lxxviii.

§867 1. On the variants between *Aa* and the versions for this description of the visit to Constantine, see Garitte, *Documents,* pp. 327ff., and *Introduction,* pp. lxxii-lxxiii.

2. *Fearsome Ocean sea:* the identical expression is used in Faustos, IV 6, for the site of Nersēs' exile.

3. *And with a single ... God:* from Koriun, p. 23, 1.15-17, which refers to Masht'ots' in Georgia.

§868   1. *Marcianos:* Gutschmid, *Agathangelos,* p. 41, suggests that this may be an error for Martinianos, the co-Caesar of Licinius. "Martinianos" is indeed found in the Tiflis edition of 1883, but it has no manuscript authority. The name is omitted in *a d A B.*

2. There is a vast literature on Constantine; see the important monograph by N. H. Baynes, "Constantine the Great and the Christian Church," *Proceedings of the British Academy* 15 (1929): 341-442. For a brief recent account, see A. H. M. Jones, *Constantine and the Conversion of Europe* (New York, 1962), especially ch. 5 and 8 for Constantine's rise to sole power. For the picture of Constantine in Agathangelos, cf. Eusebius, *H.E.* IX 9.

§871   1. *An angel:* plural in *Ag.* A similar story in found in Faustos, III 10: Jacob of Nisibis saw at the Council of Nicaea that Constantine wore a hair shirt under his purple robes and was served by a guardian angel. This was unknown to the other bishops. And Constantine in turn saw Jacob's guardian angel and raised his seat *(at'or)* above most of the others.

2. *Crown marked with Christ's sign: (z)K'ristosean nshan t'agi,* τὸ σημειόχριστον διάδημα *Ag.* This Greek adjective is also used in *Ag* 152 for baptism: σημειοχρίστους πάντας πεποιηκώς, where *Aa* has *K'ristosean droshm* (§841).

§873   1. *And the other bishop Albianos:* on the name, see §845 n2.

2. *Who are called bdeashkh:* omitted in *Ag.* On the meaning and etymology of this title see Toumanoff, pp. 155 ff. Cf. §795.

3. *Nor Shirakan:* see §842 n7.

4. *Aruastan:* see Hübschmann, *AON,* p. 319.

5. *Massagetae: Ag* adds "Huns." On the *Mask't'k',* see Toumanoff, *Studies,* p. 459 (n98) and for the Huns, cf. §19 n5.

6. *Angl:* see §795 n2.

7. *Aspet:* see §795 n6.

8. *High Constable:* see §795 n7.

9. *Mokk':* see §795 n13.

10. *Siwnik':* see §795 n14.

11. *Rshtunik':* see §795 n12.

12. *Prince of the house of Maḷkhazdom:* ἀπογράφοντα ἄρχοντα in *Ag.* On this curious translation, see Toumanoff, *Studies,* p. 162 n40, and on the title, *ibid.,* pp. 208-209.

13. *Shahapivan:* see Hübschmann, *AON,* p. 457.

14. *Master of the court: (z)ishkhann spaskapetut'eann;* on this term see Benveniste, *Composés,* p. 633.

15. On this list as a whole, see the detailed discussion in Toumanoff, *Studies,* pp. 161ff., and further bibliographical references in §795 n1.

§874 1. *In great joy ... stages:* from Koriun, p. 16, 1.3-4, which refers to Masht'ots'' return to Armenia after the invention of the script.

2. *In the land of the Dalmatians:* omitted in *a d* and *Ag.* Meillet considers this to be a later addition, *Remarques,* p. 471. *Dalmaterēn* is twice used in the N.T. for "Latin" (Lk. 23.38; Jn. 19.10) and the biblical parallel may lie behind this curious geography. Dalmatia is mentioned in the *Teaching* (§689) as one of the lands to which the apostles went, while Italy is not included in that list.

§875 1. *Straightway ... palace:* from Koriun, p. 25, 1.5, which refers to Masht'ots'' visit to Constantinople.

2. *Patriarch:* omitted in *a d* and *Ag.* The title "patriarch" for the bishop of Constantinople reflects a post-Chalcedonian date, but early Armenian usage is vague. E.g., Faustos, IV 4, calls Eusebius of Caesarea in Cappadocia "Catholicos of Catholicoi."

3. *Archbishop ... Eusebius:* ὁ ἀρχιεπίσκοπος, εἰσπορευ-όμενος ἐν τῷ αὐτοῦ παλατίῳ πάντοτε, ὁ καλούμενος Εὐσέβιος *Ag.* Y. Tashean, *Agat'angeḷos aṙ Georgay asori episkoposin ew usumnasirut' iwn Agat'angeḷay grots'* (Vienna, p. 64, derives εἰσπορευόμενος from a mistranslation of *ashkharh-a-mut,* here translated as "imperial," cf. Ciakciak, *Dizionario,* s.v. *ashkharhamut.* But *Ag* reflects the historical reality more closely than *Aa,* for Eusebius of Nicomedia only became bishop of Constantinople after Constantine's death, though he had earlier exercised great influence at court. Eusebius was not, of course, bishop of Rome; so *b* ᶜᵒʳʳ *D G E Ĕ* and the editions of Venice 1835 and Constantinople 1710 and 1824 read "Silvester."

The latter was bishop of Rome from 314-335 and in later legend is supposed to have baptized Constantine at the Lateran.

4. *Universal city:* + "so that they might rest from the length of the journey" *Ag.*

§877 1. *Alliance:* Faustos, III 21, also refers to this alliance in similar terms. Cf. Ełishē, p. 72, for the pact between Tiridates and the (unnamed) Roman emperor.

2. *Then Tiridates ... martyred:* omitted in *Ag.*

§878 1. *They were of noble descent: aznuakank' i marmnawor koghmanē tohmakts'ats' iwreants'. Ag* makes them related to Constantine: συγγενίδες αὐτοῦ ὑπάρχουσι (!). On the noble ancestry of Rhipsimē and her companions, cf. §138, 167. This pedigree is elaborated in the eulogy of the martyrs attributed to Moses Khorenats'i (ed. of 1865, pp. 297ff.), where the author claims to have found the details in the book of David of Rome. On this see Gutschmid, *Agathangelos,* p. 36.

§879 1. *They were honored ... city:* from Koriun, p. 25, 1.11-13, which refers to the return of Masht'ots' from Constantinople.

2. *And with ... honored:* from Koriun, p. 25, 1.20-21.

§880 1. *Catholicos:* archbishop in *Ag,* cf. §806 n1, 841, n1.

2. The entire paragraph is from Koriun, p. 25, 1.24-p.26, 1.1.

§881 1. *And in all ... arrived:* from Koriun, p. 26, 1.2-4.

§882 1. The last sentence is obscure (καὶ πλέον τῆς ἰδίας ἐκκλησίας ἐκόσμησαν in *Ag*); it seems to imply that the gifts offered to the Armenians were more than sufficient for the martyrs' chapels.

§884 1. On the council of Nicaea in other early Armenian writers, cf. Faustos, III 10, and Moses Khorenats'i, II 89-91.

2. *Catholicos:* on this title as given to Gregory, see *Introduction,* p. lxxix.

3. *Aristakes:* + "the bishop," *Ag.*

4. *Leaving ... heaven:* a very close parallel is found in Faustos, V 44, on the occasion of the death of Manuel Mamikonean the *sparapet.*

§885 1. *The blessed ... Armenia:* this is based on Koriun's description (p. 31) of the return of Eznik and Łewond from Constantinople with the canons of Nicaea and Ephesus and with patristic writings and "accurate" *(hastatun)* copies of the scriptures. Here the same adjective *hastatun,* translated as "confirmed," is used of the canons. Moses Khorenats'i, III 61, in his usual fashion, has expanded this episode. *Ag* omits all reference to the additions made by Gregory to the canons.

§886   1. This paragraph is taken directly from Koriun's description of Masht'ots' own compositions, p. 32, 1.14-27. On the various theories concerning the identification of these discourses, see Thomson, *Teaching,* p. 37. It is likely that the homilies known as the *Yachakhapatum* and attributed to Gregory were in the mind of Koriun (or the later redactor).

§887   1. This paragraph is taken from Koriun, p. 39, 1.5-9. The identical words are also used in Faustos, III 6, of Grigoris, son of Vrt'anēs.

§888   1. *Day . . . strong:* this phrase is also found in Faustos, III 6, applied to Grigoris.
        2. This paragraph continues the borrowing from Koriun, p. 39, 1.9-13 and 16-18.

§889   1. This paragraph is also from Koriun, but from an earlier section describing the activity of Masht'ots'' pupils, p. 31, 1.27-p. 32, 1.4.

§890   1. This paragraph is a continuation of the borrowing from Koriun, p. 32, 1.4-13.

§891   1. Agathangelos does not know of Gregory's burial place — T'ordan in the province of Daranalik' — which is first mentioned in Faustos, III 2. On the whole question of Gregory's tomb, see Van Esbroeck, *Témoignages littéraires.*
        2. *β* ends here.

§892   1. Cf. *Prologue,* esp. §12. This Epilogue is based on Koriun's own ending to his biography of Masht'ots'.

§893   1. This paragraph is taken from Koriun, p. 18, 1.6-11, which refers to the first works written in the newly invented Armenian script.

§894   1. A continuation of the borrowing from Koriun, p. 18, 1.13-17.

§895   1. A continuation of the borrowing from Koriun, p. 18, 1.17-21.

§896   1. A continuation of the borrowing from Koriun, p. 18, 1.21-28.

§897   1. This paragraph is from the epilogue to Koriun, p. 42, 1.13-25; Agathangelos has added the references to king Trdat.

§898   1. The reference to Luke is made explicit in *Ag:* ὡς καὶ ὁ πανάγιος Λούκας.

2. This paragraph is a continuation of the borrowing from Koriun, p. 42, 1.25-p. 43, 1.4.

§899   1. *Hence ... them:* a continuation of the borrowing from Koriun, p. 43, 1.5-9.

§900   1. *Ag* adds: "to him (be) glory for ever, Amen."

Appendix

1. Although this creed is printed after the text of Agathangelos' *History,* it is found only in *c* (but a different hand) and *A B G Z.* In its terminology it is generally dependent on the *Teaching:*

§3-6: cf. *Teaching,* §362, 383
§7:   cf. *Teaching,* §665
§8:   cf. *Teaching,* §356
§9:   cf. *Teaching,* §707
§10: cf. *Teaching,* §355
§11: cf. *Teaching,* §366
§12: cf. *Teaching,* §368
§13: cf. *Teaching,* §369
§14: cf. *Teaching,* §363
§15: cf. *Teaching,* §385
§18: cf. *Teaching,* §260; 707
§19: cf. *Teaching,* §389; 699-700.

SOURCES

Abbreviations

A.B. — *Analecta Bollandiana* (Brussels)

B.H.G. — *Bibliotheca Hagiographica Graeca,* 3rd ed., ed. F. Halkin (Brussels, 1957)

B.S.O.A.S. — *Bulletin of the School of Oriental and African Studies* (London)

G.C.S. — *Griechischen Christlichen Schriftsteller (Berlin)*

H.A. — *Handēs Amsoreay* (Vienna)

J.A. — *Journal asiatique* (Paris)

P.G. — J.-P. Migne, *Patrologia Graeca* (Paris)

P.H. — *Patmabanasirakan Handēs (Erevan)*

P.W. — *Paulys Real-Encyclopädie der classischen Altertumswissenschaft begonnen von G. Wissowa* (Stuttgart)

R.E.A. — *Revue des Etudes arméniennes* (Paris)

Texts of Agathangelos

Aa = G. Tēr-Mkrtch'ean and St. Kanayeants', *Agat'angelay Patmut'iwn Hayots'.* Tiflis, 1909.

Ag = G. Lafontaine, *La version grecque ancienne du livre arménien d'Agathange* (Publications de l'Institut orientaliste de Louvain 7), Louvain, 1973.

Aar = A. Ter-Ḷevondyan, *Agat'angelosi arabakan khmbagrut'yan norahayt bnagirě, P.H.* (1973), p. 1 (60), pp. 209-228.

Ar = A. Ter-Ḷevondyan, *Agat'angelosi arabakan nor khmbagrut'yuně.* Erevan, 1968.

Vg = Escorial, gr. X.III 6, published in Garitte, *Documents.*

Va = Sinai, ar. 460, translated in Garitte, *Documents.*

Vo = Ochrid, ms. 4, partially published in Garitte, *Vie grecque inédite.*

Vk = Saint Mark, Jerusalem, karshuni 38, published in Van Esbroeck, *Nouveau témoin.*

504

Manuscripts of the Armenian Agathangelos (Aa)

Only those manuscripts quoted in the notes are listed here. For full details see the *Introduction* to the edition of Tiflis 1909. In addition to the old number the present number of the MS in the Matenadaran collection is given. See Ō. Eganyan, A. Zeyt'unyan, P'. Ant'abyan, *Ts'uts'ak Dzeragrats' Masht'ots'i Anvan Matenadarani,* 2 vols. Erevan, 1965, 1970.

E = *Ejmiatsni himnakan havak'atsu*
G = *"Gevorkyan" havak'atsu*
K = *Karenyants' ts'uts'ak*
M = *Matenadaran*

α	G 130, late 12th cent.	M 3782
β	E 1753, A.D. 1220	M 1912
a	E 1655, A.D. 1293	M 1479
b	E 1656, A.D. 1261	M 1481
c	E 1658, 17th cent. (copy of *a*)	M 1881
d	E 1659, 16th cent.	M 1859
g	E 943, A.D. 1201	M 1525
h	E 940, A.D. 1456	M 993
n	G 672, 14/15th cent.	M 3797
w	E 938, A.D. 1401/2	M 1524
z	E 1754, 16/17th cent.	M 1730
A	K 1615, A.D. 1569	M 1920
B	G 611, A.D. 1672	M 2639
G	E 1668, A.D. 1661-1676	M 1863
D	E 1661, A.D. 1676-8	M 1482
E	G 613, A.D. 1692	M 3306
Z	E 1660, A.D. 1705	M 1458
Ĕ	G 612, A.D. 1714	M 3305
Ē	G 614, 18th cent.	M 3516

Armenian Texts

Ananias Shirakats'i. *Matenagrut'yunĕ.* Ed. A. G. Abrahamyan. Erevan, 1944.
Aṙak'el Davrizhets'i. *Patmut'iwn.* Vaḷarshapat, 1896.

Aristakēs Lastivertts'i. *Patmut'iwn.* Ed. K. N. Yuzbashyan. Erevan, 1963.

Cyril of Jerusalem. *Koch'umn Ĕntsayut'ean.* Vienna, 1832.

Eḷishē. *Vasn Vardanay ew Hayots' Paterazmin.* Ed. E. Tēr-Minasean. Erevan, 1957. *Matenagrut'iwnk'.* Venice, 1832.

Eusebius. *Chronicon.* Ed. J. B. Aucher. Venice, 1838 (2 vols.).

Eznik. *De Deo.* Ed. L. Mariès and Ch. Mercier *(Patrologia orientalis,* vol. 28, fasc. 3, 4). Paris, 1959.

Faustos Buzandats'i. *Patmut'iwn Hayots'.* 4th ed. Venice, 1933.

Girk' T'ḷt'ots'. Tiflis, 1901.

Hippolytus. *Chronik.* Ed. A. Bauer (GCS 46). Berlin, 1955.

Johannis Ozniensis. *Opera.* Venice, 1834.

Knik' Hawatoy. Ed. K. Tēr-Mkrtch'ean. Ejmiatsin, 1914.

Koriun. *Patmut'iwn varuts' ew mahuan srboyn Mesropay Vardapeti (Ḷukasean Matenadaran* 13). Tiflis, 1913.

Labubna. *T'uḷt' Abgaru.* Venice, 1868.

Ḷazar. *Patmut'iwn Hayots'.* Ed. G. Tēr-Mkrtch'ean and St. Malkhasean. Tiflis, 1904.

Life of Nerses = *Patmut'iwn srboyn Nersisi Part'ewi.* Sop'erk' Haykakank' 6. Venice, 1853.

Moses Daskhurants'i = Moses Kaḷankatuats'i. *Patmut'iwn Aluanits' Ashkharhi.* (Ḷukasean Matenadaran 8). Tiflis, 1912.

Moses Khorenats'i. *Géographie.* Ed. A Soukry. Venice, 1881.

———. *Matenagrut'iwnk.* Venice, 1865.

———. *Patmut'iwn Hayots'.* Ed. M. Abeḷean and S. Yarut'iwnean. Tiflis, 1913.

Sebēos. *Patmut'iwn i Herakln.* (Ḷukasean Matenadaran 7). Tiflis, 1913.

Ter Israel. *Le synaxaire arménien.* Ed. G. Bayan *(Patrologia orientalis,* V 3, VI 2, XV 3, XVI 1, XVIII 1, XIX 1, XXI 1-6). Paris, 1909-1930.

Thomas Artsruni. *Patmut'iwn Tann Artsruneats'.* (Ḷukasean Matenadaran 15). Tiflis, 1917.

Yachakhapatum Chaṙk'. Venice, 1954.

Zenob Asori. *Patmut'iwn Tarōnoy.* 2d ed. Venice, 1889.

Greek Texts

Acts of the Forty-five martyrs of Nicopolis. P.G., vol. 115.

Ad Diognetum. In *Apostolic Fathers* II. Loeb Classical Library edition.

Athanasius. *Contra Gentes* and *De Incarnatione.* Ed. R. W. Thomson, Oxford Early Christian Texts. Oxford, 1971.

Cyril of Jerusalem. *Catecheses.* Vol. I. Ed. G. C. Reischl, Munich, 1848; vol. II ed. J. Rupp, Munich, 1860.

Eusebius. *Historia ecclesiastica,* Loeb Classical Library edition.

Gregory of Nyssa. *Life of Gregory the Wonderworker. P.G.,* vol. 46.

John Chrysostom. *Homilia in sanctum pascha. P.G.,* vol. 52.

Martyrdom of Mark. P.G., vol. 115.

Proclus (of Constantinople). *Orationes. P.G.,* vol. 65.

Procopius. *De Aedificiis,* Loeb edition.

— — —. *De Bello Persico,* Loeb edition.

Strabo. *Geography,* Loeb edition.

(George) Syncellus. *Chronographia.* Bonn, 1829.

Syriac Texts

Acts of Sharbil. Ed. W. Cureton, *Ancient Syriac Documents.* London, 1864.

Martyrdom of Habbib. Ed. F. C. Burkitt, *Euphemia and the Goth.* London, 1913.

Martyrdom of Shmona and Guria. Ed. F. C. Burkitt, *Euphemia and the Goth.* London, 1913 [The Armenian version published in *Ararat* 1896 (August) was not available to me; cf. E. von Dobschütz, *Die Akten der Edessenischen Bekenner,* Texte und Untersuchungen (3rd series) vol. 37, no. 2, Leipzig, 1911.]

Secondary Literature

Spellings in brackets are those of Library of Congress cards.

Abelyan, M. [Abeghian]. *Erker* I. Erevan, 1966.

Abgaryan, G. V. *Sebeosi Patmut'yunĕ ev Ananuni Aṙeltsvatsĕ.* Erevan, 1965.

Acharyan, H. [Acharhian]. *Armatakan Baṙaran.* 7 vols. Erevan, 1926-35.

― ― ―. *Hayots' Andznanunneri Baṙaran.* 5 vols. Erevan, 1942-62.

― ― ―. *Hayots' Grerĕ.* Erevan, 1968.

Adontz, N. G. [Adonts]. *Etudes arméno-byzantines.* Lisbon, 1965.

― ― ―. "Grégoire l'Illuminateur et Anak le Parthe," *R.E.A.,* vol. 8 (1928), pp. 233-243.

― ― ―. *Armenia in the Period of Justinian.* Translated with partial revisions by Nina G. Garsoian. Lisbon, 1970.

Aigrain, R. *L'hagiographie.* Paris, 1953.

Akinean, N. [Akinian]. "Artashir Babakani vēpĕ yunaren Agat'-angelosi mej ew S. Grigori noragiwt yunarēn vark'ĕ," *H.A.* 61 (1947), cols. 567-581.

― ― ―. *Elishē vardapet,* 3 vols. Vienna, 1932, 1936, 1960.

― ― ―. *K'ristonēut'ean Mutk'ĕ Hayastan ew Vrastan.* Vienna, 1949.

― ― ―. *Niwt'er Hay Vkayabanut'ean usumnasirut'ean hamar.* Vienna, 1914.

― ― ―. "Patmut'iwn Varuts' S. Masht'ots' Vardapeti," *Mkhit'ar Tōnagirk'.* Vienna, 1949. Pp. 171-320.

― ― ―. "Vkayabanut'iwn srboyn Kiwrli (Kiwrakosi) ew Mōr nora Annayi Agat'angelosi albiwrnerēn," *H.A.* (1948), cols. 139-143.

Alishan, L. *Hin Hawatk' kam het'anosakan Krōnk' Hayots'.* Venice, 1910.

Ananian, P. "La data e le circostanze della consecrazione di S. Gregorio Illuminatore," *Le Muséon,* vol. 84 (1961), pp. 43-73, 319-360.

Anasyan, H. A. *Haykakan Matenagitut' yun.* Vol. 1. Erevan, 1959.

Arak'elyan, B. N. [Arhak'elyan], Tirats'yan, G. A., Khach'atryan, Zh. D. *Hin Hayastani Apakin.* Erevan, 1969.

Avdalbegyan, M. *Hay Gelarvestakan Ardzaki Skzbnvorumĕ.* Erevan, 1971.

Awgerean, M. [Awgerian]. *Liakatar Vark' ew Vkayabanut'iwnk' Srbots',* 12 vols. Venice, 1810-15.

Bailey, H. W. "Saka *śśandrāmata,*" *Festschrift für Wilhelm Eilers.* Wiesbaden, 1967. Pp. 136-143.

———. *Zoroastrian Problems in the Ninth-century Books,* rev. ed. Oxford, 1971.

Baumstark, A. *Liturgie comparée,* 3rd ed. Revised by Dom Bernard Botte. Chevtogne, 1953.

Baynes, N. H. "Constantine the Great and the Christian Church," *Proceedings of the British Academy,* vol. 15 (1929), pp. 341-442; also published separately in 1930.

Benveniste, E. "Armenian Aregakn 'soleil' et la formation nominale en -akn," *R.E.A.,* N.S., vol. 2 (1965), pp. 5-19.

———. "Remarques sur les composés armeniens en -pet," *H.A.* (1961), cols. 631-640.

———. "Les nominatifs arméniens en -i," *R.E.A.,* vol. 10 (1930), pp. 81-84.

———. "L'origine du vishap arménien," *R.E.A.,* vol. 7 (1927), pp. 7-9.

———. "La terminologie iranienne du sacrifice," *J.A.,* vol. 252 (1964), pp. 45-58.

———. *Titres et noms propres en iranien ancien.* Paris, 1966.

Biwzandats'i, Norayr. *Koriwn Vardapet ew norin T'argmanut'iwnk'.* Tiflis, 1900.

Carrière, A. *La légende d'Abgar dans l'Histoire d'Arménie de Moise de Khoren.* Paris, 1895.

———. *Les huit sanctuaires de l'Arménie payenne.* Paris, 1899.

Chaumont, M.-L. *Recherches sur l'histoire d'Arménie.* Paris, 1969.

———. "Le culte de la déesse Anahita dans la religion des monarques d'Iran et d'Armenie au 1e siècle de notre ère," *J.A.,* vol. 253 (1965), pp. 167-181.

———. "L'ordre des preséances à la cour des Arsacides d'Arménie," *J.A.,* vol. 254 (1966), pp. 471-497.

Christensen, A. *L'Iran sous les Sassanides (Annales du Musée Guimet* 48). Paris, 1936.

Ciakciak, E. *Dizionario Armeno-Italiano,* 2 vols. Venice, 1837.

Cumont, F. "L'iniziazione di Nerone da parte di Tiridate d'Armenia," *Rivista di Filologia,* vol. 61 (1933), pp. 145-154.

Daniélou, J. *The Theology of Jewish Christianity.* Chicago, 1964.

Delehaye, H. *Les légendes hagiographiques* (*Subsidia hagiographica* 18). Brussels, 1927.

———. *Les passions des martyres et les genres littéraires,* 2nd ed. (*Subsidia hagiographica* 13B). Brussels, 1966.

Deonna, W. "Εὐωδία, Croyances antiques et modernes: l'odeur suave des dieux et des élus," *Genava,* vol. 17 (1939), pp. 167-263.

Der Nersessian, S. "Une apologie des images au septiéme siècle," *Byzantion,* vol. 17 (1944-45), pp. 57-87. Reprinted in *Etudes byzantines et arméniennes,* Louvain, 1973, pp. 379-403.

Diehl, C. *Impératrices de Byzance.* Paris, 1959.

Djanachian, M. "Les Armenistes et les Mekhitaristes," *Armeniaca* (Venice, 1969), pp. 383-445.

Dumézil, G. "Vahagn," *Revue de l'histoire des religions,* vol. 117 (1938), pp. 152-170.

Dvornik, F. *Les légendes de Constantin et de Methode vues de Byzance.* Prague, 1933.

———. *The Idea of Apostolicity in Byzantium and the Legend of the Apostle Andrew* (*Dumbarton Oaks Studies* 4). Cambridge, Mass., 1958.

Enselin, W. "Zu dem vermuteten Perserfeldzug des rex Hannibalianus," *Klio,* vol. 29 (1936), pp. 102-110.

Eremyan, A. "Hayastani V-VII dd. gmbetavor kaṙuyts'neri nakhagtsman masin," *Lraber* (1974), no. 10, pp. 56-82.

Frye, R. N. *The Heritage of Persia.* Cleveland and New York, 1963.

Galēmk'earean, "Agat'angeḷosi krknagir bnagirě," *Huschardzan* (Vienna, 1911), pp. 67-160.

Garitte, G. *Documents pour l'étude du livre d'Agathange* (*Studi e Testi* 127). Vatican City, 1946.

———. "Le traité géorgien 'sur la foi' attribué à Hippolyte," *Le Muséon,* vol. 78 (1965), pp. 119-172.

———. *La Narratio de Rebus Armeniae* (*Corpus Scriptorum Christianorum Orientalium, Subsidia* 4). Louvain, 1952.

———. "Un petit florilège grec diphysite traduit de l'arménien," *Analecta Biblica,* vol. 12 (1959), pp. 102-112.

———. "La Vie grecque inédite de saint Grégoire d'Arménie," *Analecta Bollandiana,* vol. 83 (1965), pp. 233-290.

Gat'rchean, Y. V. *Srbazan Pataragamatoyts'k' Hayots' (Die Liturgien bei den Armeniern).* Vienna, 1897.

Gelzer, H. "Die Anfänge der armenischen Kirche," *Berichte der königlichen sächischen Gesellschaft der Wissenschaften,* vol. 47 (1895), pp. 109-174.

— — —. "Zur armenischen Götterlehre," *Berichte der königlichen sächischen Gesellschaft der Wissenschaften,* vol. 48 (1896), pp. 99-148.

— — —. Hilgenfeld, H., Cuntz, O. *Patrum Nicaenorum Nomina.* Leipzig, 1898.

Grumel, V. *La Chronologie (Bibliothèque byzantine; Traité d'études byzantines* 1). Paris 1958.

Gutschmid, A. von. "Agathangelos," *Zeitschrift der deutschen morgenländischen Gesellschaft,* vol. 31 (1877), pp. 1-60. Reprinted in *Kleine Schriften,* ed. F. Rühl, vol. 3 (Leipzig, 1892), pp. 339-420.

Hakobyan, T. Kh. [Yakobean]. *Urvagtser Hayastani Patmakan Ashkharhagrut'yan* Erevan, 1960.

Henning, W. B. "A Note on Tir," *B.S.O.A.S.,* vol. 24 (1961), p. 191.

Hubschmann, H. *Die altarmenischen Ortsnamen.* Strassburg, 1904. Reprinted Amsterdam, 1969.

— — —. *Armenische Grammatik, Erster Teil: Armenische Etymologie.* Leipzig, 1897. Reprinted Hildesheim, 1962.

Inchichean, L. [Inchichian]. *Storagrut'iwn hin Hayastaneayts'.* Venice, 1822.

Inglisian, V. *Armenien in der Bibel.* Vienna, 1935.

International Conference on the History, Archaeology and Culture of Central Asia in the Kushan Period (Dushanbe, 1968). *An Annotated Bibliography.* Moscow, 1968.

Jones, A. H. M. *Constantine and the Conversion of Europe.* New rev. ed. New York, 1962.

Justi, F. *Iranisches Namenbuch.* Marburg, 1895. Reprinted Hildesheim, 1963.

Karst, J. *Die Chronik des Eusebius aus dem armenischen übersetzt (Griechischen Christlichen Schriftsteller* 20). Leipzig, 1911.

Kekelidzé, K. "Chronique d'Hippolyte et l'historien géorgien Leonti Mroveli," *Bedi Kartlisa,* nos. 45-6 (1964), pp. 88-94.

Khatchatrian, A. "Données historiques sur la fondation d'Edjmiatsin à la lumière des fouilles récentes," *H.A.* (1962), cols. 100-109.

— — —. *L'architecture arménienne du IVe au VI ^e siècle (Bibliothèque des Cahiers Archéologiques* 7). Paris, 1971.

Kogean, H.S. [Kogian]. *Hayots' Ekełets'in.* Beirut, 1961.

— — —. *Makabayets'wots' B. grk'in hayerēn t'argmanut'iwnĕ.*

Vienna, 1923.

Lagarde, P. de. *Agathangelus, Abhandlungen der Königlichen Gesellschaft der Wissenschaften zu Göttingen,* 35 (1888), pp. 1-88.

Lampe, G. W. *A Patristic Greek Lexicon,* 5 parts. Oxford, 1961-68.

Langlois, V. *Collection des historiens anciens et modernes de l'Arménie,* 2 vols. Paris, 1867, 1869.

Lebon, J. "Sur un concile de Césarée," *Le Muséon,* vol. 51 (1938), pp. 89-132.

Leloir, L. "(Versions) Orientales de la Bible II, Versions arméniennes," *Dictionnaire de la Bible, Supplément,* vol. 6, cols. 810-818. Paris, 1960.

Leroy, M. "Les composés arméniens en -pet," *Annuaire de l'Institut de philologie et d'histoire orientales et slaves,* vol. 15 (1958-60), pp. 109-128.

Louis, P. *Les métaphores de Platon.* Paris, 1945.

Maenchen-Helfen, O. J. *The World of the Huns.* California, 1973.

Manandian, H. A. *The Trade and Cities of Armenia in Relation to Ancient World Trade.* Translated by Nina G. Garsoian. Lisbon, 1965.

Markwart, J. *Die Entstehung der armenischen Bistümer.* Ed. J. Messina, *Orientalia Christiana,* vol. 27 (1932), pp. 141-236.

———. "Die Genealogie der Bagratiden," *Caucasica,* fasc. 6, pt. 2 (1930), pp. 10-77.

———. "La province de Parskahayk'," *R.E.A.,* N.S., vol. 3 (1966), pp. 252-314.

———. *Südarmenien und die Tigrisquellen. Vienna, 1930.*

Mécérian, J. "Bilan des relations arméno-iraniennes au 5 [e] siècle ap. J. C.," *Mélanges de l'Université Saint Joseph,* vol. 30 (1953), pp. 67-98.

Meillet, A. "De l'influence parthe sur la langue arménienne," *R.E.A.,* vol. 1 (1920-21), pp. 9-14.

———. "Remarques sur le texte de l'historien arménien Agathange," *J.A.* 10th series, vol. 16 (1910), pp. 457-481.

———. "Sur les termes religieux iraniens en arménien," *R.E.A.,* vol. 1 (1920-21), pp. 233-236.

Melik'-Ōhanjanyan, K. M. "Agat'angeḷosi banahyusakan aḷbiwrneri harts'i shurjě," *P.H.,* no. 27 (1964), pp. 53-82.

Melik'-P'ashyan, K. V. *Anahit Dits'uhu Pashtamunk'ě*. Erevan, 1963.

Melk'onyan, H. G. *Hay-asorakan haraberut'yunneri patmut'yunits'*. Erevan, 1970.

Michel, A. Article, "Idolatrie," *Dictionnaire de Théologie Catholique,* vol. 7, cols. 602-669. Paris, 1930.

Muradyan, P. M. "Agat'angelosi Patmut'yan hnagoyn patařikner," *Lraber* (1971), no. 12, pp. 37-48.

— — —. "Agat'angelosi Patmut'yan mi hatvatsi hin vratseren t'argmanut'yuně," *P.H.* (1972), pt. 1, pp. 63-66.

Murray, R. *Symbols of Church and Kingdom.* Cambridge, 1975.

Muyldermans, J. "L'apport des éditions arméniennes de Venise à la patristique," *Bazmavēp* (1949), pp. 386-398.

Nor Baŕgirk' Haykazean Lezwi. Ed. G. Awetik'ean [Awetik'ian], Kh. Siwrmēlean, M. Awgerean, 2 vols. Venice, 1836-37.

Ormanian, M. *Azgapatum,* 3 vols. 2nd ed. Beirut, 1959-61.

Peeters, P. "S. Grégoire l'Illuminateur dans le calendrier lapidaire de Naples," *A.B.,* vol. 60 (1942), pp. 91-130.

— — —. "La légende de saint Jacques de Nisibe," *A.B.,* vol. 38 (1920), pp. 285-373.

— — —. "Le début de la persecution de Sapor d'apres Fauste de Byzance,"*R.E.A.,* vol. 1 (1920-21), pp. 15-33.

— — —. "L'intervention politique de Constance II dans la Grande Arménie en 338," *Bulletin de l'Académie royale de Belgique, Classe des Lettres,* vol. 17 (1931), pp. 10-47.

— — —. "Pour l'histoire des origines de l'alphabet arménien," *R.E.A.,* vol. 9 (1929), pp. 203-237.

— — —. *Recherches d'histoire et de philologie orientales (Subsidia hagiographica* 27). Brussels, 1951.

Perikhanian, A. G. *Khramovye ob'edinenija Maloi azii i Armenii.* Moscow, 1959.

Renoux, A. *Le Codex arménien Jérusalem 121,* 2 vols. *(Patrologia orientalis,* vol. 35, fasc. 1; vol. 36, fasc. 2). Turnhout, 1969, 1971.

Ruether, R. R. *Gregory of Nazianzenus, Rhetor and Philosopher.* Oxford, 1969.

Sahinyan, A. "Ejmiatsni mayr tachari skzbakan tesk'ě," *P.H.* (1966), pt. 3, pp. 71-93.

— — —. "Recherches scientifiques sous les voûtes de la cathédrale d'Etchmiadzine," *R.E.A.,* N.S., vol. 3 (1966), pp. 39-71.

Sargisean, B. V. [Sargisian]. *Agat'angelos ew iwr bazmadarean Galtnik'n.* Venice, 1890.

Sargsyan, G. Kh. "Dastakertnerĕ ev agaraknerĕ V dari haykakan albyurnerum" *P.H.* (1962), pt. 3, pp. 77-94.

— — —. *Hellenistakan Darashrjani Hayastanĕ ev Movses Khorenats'in.* Erevan, 1966.

— — —. "O dvikh znacheniyakh termina dastakert b rannykh armyanskikh istochnikakh," *Ellinisticheskij blizhniy Vostok, Vizantija i Iran,* Moscow, 1967, pp. 97-101. Cf. *R.E.A.,* vol. 5 (1968), pp. 43-50.

Segal, J. B. *Edessa, 'The Blessed City.'* Oxford, 1970.

Shahinyan, L. P'. "Movses Khorenats'u 'Patmut'ean' mej hishatakvol Vahēi masin," *P.B.H.* (1973), no. 4, pp. 172-178.

Speyer, W. *Die literarische Fälschung im heidnischen und christlichen Altertum (Handbuch der Altertumswissenschaft* I 2). München, 1971.

Srabyan, A. N. " 'Yachakhapatum' chaṙeri helinaki harts'ĕ," *Telekagir* (1962), no. 5, pp. 25-38.

Stone, M. E. "The Apocryphal Literature in the Armenian Tradition," *Proceedings of the Israel Academy of Sciences and Humanities,* vol. 4 (1969), pp. 59-78.

Tallon, M. "Livre des lettres, I [er] groupe," *Mélanges de l'Université Saint Joseph,* vol. 32 (1955), fasc. 1.

Tashean, Y [Tashian]. *Agat'angelos aṙ Georgay asori episkoposin ew usumnasirut'iwn Agat'angeleay grots'.* Vienna, 1891.

— — —. *Ts'uts'ak hayerēn dzeragrats'.* Vienna, 1891.

Ter Minassiantz, E. *Die armenische Kirche in ihre Beziehungen zu den syrischen.* Leipzig, 1904.

Thomson, R. W. "An Armenian List of Heresies," *Journal of Theological Studies,* N.S., 16 (1965), pp. 348-367.

— — —. *The Teaching of Saint Gregory: An Early Armenian Catechism.* Cambridge, Mass., 1970 (published 1971).

Toumanoff, C. "The Third-century Armenian Arsacids; A Chronological and Genealogical Commentary," *R.E.A.,* N.S., vol. 6 (1969), pp. 233-281.

— — —. "Caucasia and Byzantium," *Traditio,* vol. 27 (1971), pp. 111-158.

———. "On the Date of the Pseudo-Moses of Chorene," *H.A.* 75 (1961), cols. 467-476.

———. *Studies in Christian Caucasian History.* Georgetown University Press, 1963.

Tournebize, F. *Histoire politique et religieuse de l'Arménie.* Paris, 1910.

Tsovakan (pseudonym for Norayr Polarean). "Koriwn ew Makabayets'wots' hay t'argmanich'ĕ," *Sion* (1936), pp. 181-187.

Van Esbroeck, M. "Chronique arménienne," *A.B.,* vol. 80 (1962), pp. 423-445.

———. "Un nouveau témoin du livre d'Agathange," *R.E.A.,* N.S., vol. 8 (1971), pp. 13-167.

———. "Le roi Sanatrouk et l'apôtre Thaddée," *R.E.A.,* N.S., vol. 9 (1972), pp. 241-283.

———. "Témoignages littéraires sur les sépultures de S. Grégoire l'Illuminateur," *A.B.,* vol. 89 (1971), pp. 387-418.

Widengren, G. *Die Religionen Irans.* Stuttgart, 1965.

Wikander, S. *Feuerpriester in Kleinasien und Iran.* Lund, 1946.

Wust, E. Article "Mithras," *P.W.,* vol. 30, Stuttgart, 1932.

Zarphanalean, G. *Matenadaran Haykakan T'argmanut'eants' Nakhneats'.* Venice, 1889.'

INDEXES

Biblical Quotations and Allusions

The references are to the paragraph numbers of the translation. Direct quotations are marked with an asterisk. Note that the numbering of the verses and chapters of the various biblical books follows that of the *Armenian* vulgate.

GENERAL INDEX

Names which introduce scriptural quotations or are mentioned within them are omitted.

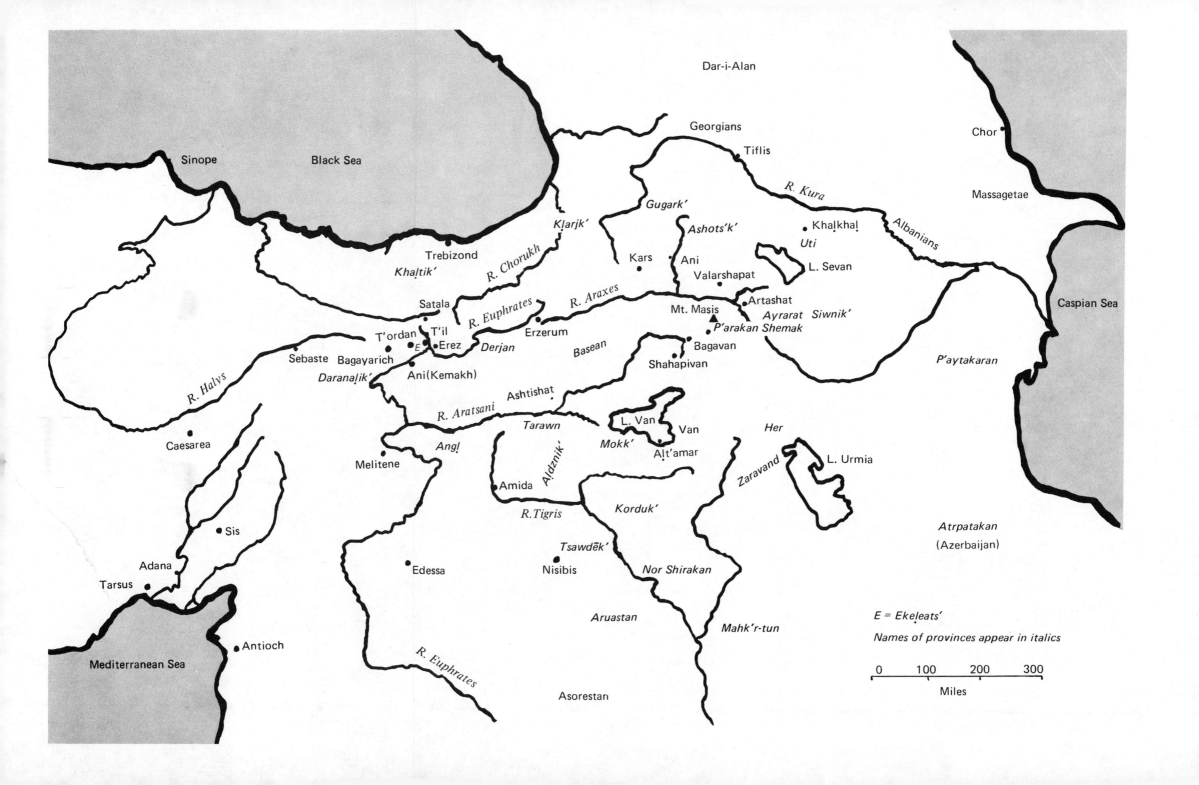

Dar-i-Alan

Black Sea

Sinope

Georgians

Tiflis

R. Kura

Chor

Massagetae

Caspian Sea

Klarjk'

Gugark'

Ashots'k'

Khalkhal

Uti

Trebizond

R. Chorukh

Kars

Ani

Valarshapat

L. Sevan

Khaltik'

Satala

R. Euphrates

R. Araxes

Mt. Masis

Artashat

Ayrarat

Siwnik'

T'ordan

T'il

Erez

E

Erzerum

Derjan

Basean

P'arakan Shemak

Bagavan

P'aytakaran

Sebaste

Bagayarich

Shahapivan

Daranalik'

Ani(Kemakh)

Ashtishat

R. Halys

R. Aratsani

Tarawn

L. Van

Van

Her

Caesarea

Angl

Mokk'

Alt'amar

Zaravand

L. Urmia

Melitene

Aldznik'

Amida

R. Tigris

Korduk'

Atrpatakan

Sis

(Azerbaijan)

Tsawdēk'

Adana

Edessa

Nisibis

Nor Shirakan

Tarsus

Aruastan

Mahk'r-tun

Antioch

R. Euphrates

Mediterranean Sea

Asorestan

E = Ekeleats'

Names of provinces appear in italics

0   100   200   300

Miles